THE WPA GUIDE TO
PHILADELPHIA

THE WPA GUIDE TO
PHILADELPHIA

Compiled by the Federal Writers' Project of the
Works Progress Administration for the Commonwealth
of Pennsylvania

With a new Preface by E. Digby Baltzell
and an Introduction by Richard J. Webster

Published in cooperation with the Pennsylvania
Historical and Museum Commission

upp

University of Pennsylvania Press
Philadelphia

Originally published as *Philadelphia: A Guide to the Nation's Birthplace* in 1937 by the William Penn Association. Copyright 1937 by the Pennsylvania Historical Commission

Original photographs made available courtesy of the Pennsylvania State Archives, Harrisburg

Library of Congress Cataloging-in-Publication Data

Philadelphia, a guide to the nation's birthplace.
    The WPA guide to Philadelphia / compiled and written by the Federal Writers' Project of the Works Progress Administration for the Commonwealth of Pennsylvania; with a new preface by E. Digby Baltzell; and an introduction by Richard J. Webster.
        p.   cm.
    Reprint. Originally published: Philadelphia, a guide to the nation's birthplace. 1st ed. [Philadelphia]: William Penn Association of Philadelphia. 1937. (American guide series)
    Bibliography: p.
    Includes index.
    ISBN 0-8122-1270-3 (pbk.)
    1. Philadelphia (Pa.)–Description–Guide-books.   I. Federal Writers' Project (Pa.) , II. Title.   III. Series: American guide series.
F158.18.P46 1988
917.48'110443–dc19   88-10662
                                                                                CIP

THE WPA GUIDE TO PHILADELPHIA

Preface to the 1988 Edition   vii
    E. Digby Baltzell
Introduction to the 1988 Edition   ix
    Richard J. Webster
Further Reading About Philadelphia   xix
Philadelphia: A Guide to the Nation's Birthplace
    facsimile   xxi

PREFACE TO THE 1988 EDITION
E. Digby Baltzell

T HIS gigantic and absolutely absorbing book was first published in 1937 when I was a sophomore at the University of Pennsylvania. It is not only a fine guide to the city in that year; it is also an exhaustive social, economic, political, and cultural history of the city. I shall limit myself to a few comparisons between Philadelphia today and half a century ago. The first major difference was that the city in 1937 was in the midst of a Great Depression, while today it is affluent and booming. A few contrasts in prices, for example: tuition at Penn was $200 per term in 1937; most of the students were commuters who could purchase a subway or trolley fare for 8 cents, or two tokens for 15 cents; good hotel rooms ranged from $2 upwards; first rate businessman's lunches could be had for less than one dollar; the main airport for the city was at Crescent Boulevard, Camden (taxi fare from the Bellevue Hotel was $1.50).

As with today, Philadelphia was a sporting city, but on a much smaller scale: although Municipal Stadium (John F. Kennedy Stadium after 1964) was one of the largest in the world (120,757 watched the Dempsey-Tunney fight in 1926) it was mostly the site of the annual Army-Navy classic; Franklin Field (80,000) drew the biggest crowds in the fall; one of the first professional football teams in the nation, the Frankford Yellow Jackets, played in a stadium with a seating capacity of 5,000; winter sports were held at the Arena (capacity 6,000 to 10,000) in West Philadelphia. Finally, we had two major league baseball teams in those days: the Phillies played in Baker Bowl (18,500) at Huntington and North Broad Streets and the Athletics at Shibe Park (29,000) at Broad and Lehigh.

Philadelphia was a pioneer city in motion pictures: in 1860, Dr. Coleman Sellers made the first photographs of motion and patented a machine for showing them in 1861. The first motion pictures from flexible films were cast upon a screen at the Franklin Institute, in 1894, and the first in a Philadelphia theatre, at Keith's Bijou, in 1896. In 1937, center city had eleven large and ornate, first-run theatres, the Aldine, Arcadia, Boyd, Earle, Erlanger, Fox, Karlton, Stanley, Stanton, and Trans-Lux. In addition the Europa showed the best European films and the Mastbaum, the largest house in the city, had for years displayed first-run films of exceptional merit.

In addition to the Depression, a major difference between the city today and in 1937 was that then we were one of the leading manufacturing cities in the world while today we are mainly a service city. Philadelphia's first important industry, the manufacture of textiles, was still the most important in 1937; its mills, the majority in Kensington and Frankford, produced five percent of the nation's output. The city led the nation in carpet manufacture. Most of this is gone today. In 1937, every man walking the streets of center city, cheering at sporting events and so forth, wore a hat; the Philadelphia-made Stetson was synonymous with men's headgear throughout the nation; the Stetson plant in North Philadelphia employed 5,460 men and women in a building with a floor area of 25 acres. Today most men no longer wear felt hats downtown and the Stetson factory is no more. And so with hundreds of plants large and small such as the Disston Saws, the leather and sugar refining industries, and the famous J. G. Brill (world's largest maker of city transit equipment) and Budd companies.

This great manufacturing city was the home of a highly skilled labor force, home-loving and thrifty. As of 1937, every visitor to the city was immediately impressed by Billy Penn, atop City Hall, and the four red letters PSFS atop the new Philadelphia Savings Fund Society skyscraper, just behind City Hall as one approached the city along the Parkway from the Museum (still being built in 1937).

What a book about our fine city half a century ago!

E. DIGBY BALTZELL

Philadelphia, February 1988

viii

INTRODUCTION TO THE 1988 EDITION
Richard J. Webster

I F you are unfamiliar with this volume, you may be skeptical of its value, and silently ask why a knowledgeable press would reprint a fifty-year-old city guide. The answer is simple; no other guide portrays Philadelphia as sensitively and thoroughly as this one.[1] In short, it is a valuable historical document laden with contemporary relevance and usefulness.

The Philadelphia guide was a product of the Federal Writers' Project, one of the many activities funded by the Works Progress Administration, which, in turn, was established by the Emergency Relief Appropriation Act in April 1935. As Paul Comly French, Pennsylvania State Director of the Federal Writers' Project, points out in the 1937 preface, the project's immediate and practical purpose was "to provide work for unemployed newspapermen and magazine writers." Gradually, however, these enterprises developed a loftier, more "ambitious objective of presenting to the American people a portrait of America," according to Harry Hopkins, Administrator of the WPA, in his standard statement at the front of these guides.

This portrait, unlike the picture painted in so many contemporary guides, included the warts as well as the beauty marks. Social conditions were described and political opinions were stated, often with a rich rhetoric that set a uniquely depression-era mood. After describing the Old World flavor of South Philadelphia's ethnic neighborhoods, for example, the writers remind us that "slum areas splotch the scene like open sores . . . and society pays the usual price for its apathy in a high mortality, disease, and crime rate." Although some of the social commentary may cause us to wince, we must remember that its authors were victims of the Great Depression; their lives were kept afloat by a program that critics roundly condemned as un-American. In spite of their suspect status and uncertain tenure, these men and women produced a volume that remains superior to anything generated by the private sector in the past half century.

Federal Writers' Project officials directed a scholarly program of redefining American civilization.[2] Fundamental to that effort was the relatively new concept of culture. To them culture was not the nineteenth-century idea of the cultivated arts and belles-lettres but the anthropological concept of a group within a defined time and space sharing unstated goals and values. Project officials operated on the assumption that the United States has an indigenous folk culture whose uniqueness is its pluralism. With this intellectual underpinning, they were able to define America in cultural and political terms that set the country apart from Europe. No longer feeling compelled to compete with Europe in those areas where the young United States traditionally had fallen short, they could emphasize arts and crafts that generated both local and national pride. In addition, in a world where totalitarianism was gaining strength, in part through suppression of differences, they could seek a stronger sense of national community by celebrating cultural pluralism. In short, they saw unity in diversity. To a great degree these guidebooks became the declaration of American cultural independence that Emerson had called for a century earlier.

Although the essays form the guides' intellectual core, the books were aimed at the tourist. The tourist the editors conceived was not the pleasure-seeker expecting guaranteed fun in the sun but the traveler, the person who wanted to explore and discover. Consequently tours are central to the guidebooks' appeal. Here the emphasis was not on hotels, restaurants, and local boosterism, but on history, geography, and the anthropological present, the stuff of ordinary life that set a community apart from its neighbors. In this regard the guides reflect much of the New Deal ethos, both in their inclusion of common people and work places and in their appeal to the traveler and the nascent tourist industry. After all, the Federal Writers' Project, like all New Deal relief programs, justified its existence through its contribution to the nation's economic recovery.

The city described in the Philadelphia guide remains recognizable; it has not aged over the past fifty years so much as it has been transformed. Some of its historical buildings, such as the Pennsylvania Academy of the Fine Arts, have been cleaned and refurbished and look better today than they did in 1937; others, such as Grumblethorpe and Philosophical Hall, have been taken back in time through restorations and look more authentically old; still others, ranging from Independence Hall to the PSFS Building, have been well maintained and appear little changed on the outside.

Nevertheless, there have been substantial changes, which become apparent when you venture into the city's old industrial sectors, such as Kensington or Southwest Philadelphia. Once booming industrial centers, they are now crumbling collections of vacant or underutilized factories with well-worn or abandoned rowhouses sometimes literally standing in factories' shadows. Philadelphia, once one of the nation's great industrial cities, now has a service economy. In 1937 nearly 293,000 people worked in the city's industries; by 1987, when there are more retail than manufacturing employees in the city, that figure has dropped to approximately 99,000 industrial workers.[3] Such local concerns as the Stetson Hat Company, the Disston Saw Works, and the Baldwin Locomotive Works enjoyed national reputations and markets in 1937, and receive extensive commentary in this guide. Today they are only memories of an industrial past. Stetson shut down in 1971 and many of its buildings fell to demolition contractors and fire in 1979 and 1980; Disston gradually shifted its operations elsewhere during the late 1950s; and Baldwin, which left the city for nearby Eddystone between 1924 and 1928, closed shop in 1972. The Bromley & Sons Lehigh Mills in Kensington were representative of many of these massive manufacturing complexes. Touted by the 1937 guide as "one of the largest centers for the manufacture of rugs, lace, and lace curtains in the country," Bromley's factories filled an entire city block. By the 1970s, however, a number of small concerns occupied the buildings, leaving them poorly maintained and vulnerable to fire, which struck in 1979 with a spectacular nine-alarm blaze. Surviving mills stand today as decaying monuments of a time when factory labor meant hard and dangerous work with meager compensation, unpaid furloughs, and violent strikes, and factory ownership could bring affluence, power, and leisure—or bankruptcy.

More constructive changes include the two major highways that slice along the edges of Penn's expansive grid plan to give new access to the city. The Schuylkill Expressway opened in 1952 and wends along the Schuylkill River between the Pennsylvania Turnpike and the Walt Whitman Bridge. Although an engineering nightmare popularly ridiculed as the "Surekill Crawlway," the expressway's construction did little damage to the city's fabric. It carves into Fairmont Park at one point, upsetting purists, but West River Drive prevents it from encroaching on the river's banks. The same cannot be said for I-95, which runs along the eastern side of the Delaware River. Constructed during the late 1960s, I-95 cut a destructive swath through river communities from Girard Point to Kensington. Like monstrous concrete scar tissue, it stretches today along the waterfront where once stood many fine, modest eighteenth- and early-nineteenth-century buildings. Most unfortunately, it severs the city from the Delaware River, Philadelphia's natural and historic eastern boundary. The expressway and I-95, however, are in many respects modern expressions of a Philadelphia pattern. As the Pennsylvania Railroad once arrogantly strode along its infamous "Chinese Wall" to the gates of City Hall, spewing noise, pollution, and the promise of prosperity and convenience, so do the thousands of private automobiles on I-95. It is the democracy of transportation.

Like so many cities after World War II, Philadelphia has endured urban renewal. Its first significant project was Penn Center, which rose like a phoenix from the dust of Broad Street Station and its elevated tracks, the Chinese Wall noted above. Less a roadway than a roadblock, the Chinese Wall stymied commercial development north and west of City Hall. It served as a grim backdrop for small parking lots and marginal retailers and a public urinal for vagrants. Its demolition in 1953 stands as one of the best arguments for urban renewal. Nevertheless, when construction on the fourteen-acre site began in 1956, local bankers were less than sanguine, as the first simple, cheaply built office slabs indicate. Over the past thirty years, however, confidence has grown, the architecture has improved, and other projects have come to fruition. Market Street East is still in the process of becoming, but to date it has produced two major shopping centers (Gallery I and II), a distinctive neo-Art Deco office tower (One Reading Center), and the commuter tunnel, which connects the former Pennsylvania and Reading commuter rail lines.

Such projects have encouraged the erection of many individual buildings, which collectively have modernized the city's streetscape. Some, such as Mitchell/Giurgola's 1962 Philadelphia Life Insurance Company Building on North Broad Street, relate to their neighbors in scale and proportion so well that they barely stand out by themselves. Others dominate their environments. The most dominant of the lot is One Liberty Place, which rises 921 feet above Seventeenth and Chestnut Streets and more than 400 feet above City Hall. When developer Willard G. Rouse 3rd unveiled his plans in the spring of 1984, he unleashed an open-ended controversy. It initially focused on the gentlemen's agreement that nothing should exceed the height of the statue of William Penn atop City Hall, but it soon included aesthetic, economic, humane, and symbolic concerns as well. For a few months Philadelphians wrestled with their feelings for the past, their hopes for the future, and the symbolic meaning of their City Hall. Rouse stifled the debate by imposing a construction deadline, which helped him win has case before City Council and the mayor, but allowed city officials to dodge the nagging dilemma of a booming commercial downtown and ailing residential neighborhoods. Completed in late 1987 from the designs of Chicago architect Helmut Jahn, One Liberty Place has radically transformed the city's skyline, shifting its focal point westward and visually overwhelming City Hall. "Rouse's rogue" commands national architectural attention, and is Philadelphia's first tall building to receive such acclaim since the PSFS Building in 1932. One Liberty Place is exciting, romantic, and full of paradoxes. Resembling New York's Chrysler Building, its blunt but elegant form, while rooted in the past, forges new directions for the city's commercial future.

Another major transformation, unique to Philadelphia, stemmed from the postwar decision to turn the Independence Hall neighborhood into a national historical park. The commonwealth joined the enterprise by planning a large mall on the north side of the historic landmark. This state-federal cooperation destroyed scores of nineteenth-century commercial buildings and wrought a fundamental reconfiguration of an approximately seven-block expanse. During the 1960s and '70s, large-scale federal and commercial buildings rose along the mall's borders. Only the Bourse survived, to be extensively renovated as a shopping and office complex. The result was the transformation of not only the Independence Hall neighborhood but also Independence Hall itself. The former statehouse, large by Georgian standards, is now dwarfed by its gargantuan neighbors and the yawning expanse of dead open space to its front. The motivating force behind these changes, however, was less a concern for architectural scale or historical accuracy than an unarticulated mythic goal, to pay homage to a national shrine. In 1976 the icon within the shrine, the Liberty Bell, was removed to new quarters, a climate-controlled glass jewel box on the mall, making it all the easier to be revered.

Federal investment in history around Independence Hall encouraged private investment in nearby Society Hill. Seedy at best in 1937, the neighborhood continued its decline after World War II until 1950, when the Redevelopment Authority, the City Planning Commission, the Philadelphia Historical Commission, and the Old Philadelphia Development Corporation began to work cooperatively—and successfully—to resuscitate Society Hill. It is now one of the city's most prestigious and pricey addresses. Two crucial catalysts in the change were the removal of the city's produce center from Dock Street to a new food distribution center in South Philadelphia and the construction of I.M. Pei's Society Hill Towers and their adjacent townhouses. The former removed a source of traffic congestion and olfactory offenses; the latter established a graceful focal point and a significant investment in contemporary residences. Both actions helped to make Society Hill *au courant.*

With Society Hill a proven success, real estate entrepreneurs and aspiring individuals in the 1970s covetously cast their sights on nearby neighborhoods that shared Society Hill's economic and residential potential. Southwark, Old City, and Northern Liberties received the most attention. Because of its brick nineteenth-century rowhouses, Southwark enjoyed a sound, but less-than-spectacular renaissance in spite of the devastation wreaked by I-95 on its eastern boundary. The market in Northern Liberties has moved more slowly, partly it seems because of its mixture of residential and commercial and old and new buildings.

Old City, on the other hand, presented an unusual challenge. An industrial and commercial area in the nineteenth century, Old City evolved during the early twentieth century into a down-at-the-heels wholesale district for small businesses. Yet it was blessed with many historic sites, ranging from the extremely popular (but historically undocumented) Betsy Ross House to the mid-nineteenth-century Bank Row. Perhaps most significantly, Old City had been spared urban renewal, when in the 1970s a number of factors coincided to transform the area. Wholesalers' preference for horizontal storage facilities outside the city emptied lofts at the same time that artists, architects, young professionals, and enterprising restauranteurs were looking for inexpensive working and living space. Old City's designation as a National Register Historic District in 1972 enhanced its reputation, and, after the Tax Act of 1976, enabled commercial property owners to benefit from generous investment tax credits if they rehabilitated their historic buildings according to federal guidelines. Investors, who fifteen or twenty years ago would have demolished these old commercial buildings for new construction, have instead refurbished them as offices, apartments, and condominiums. Profitable preservation has revitalized Old City.

Fundamental to Old City's success story and to the preservation of many of Philadelphia's important old buildings has been the federal tax code. Beginning with the Tax Act of 1976, investors who rehabilitate historically certified income-producing buildings receive federal tax credits. As of December 1986 those tax credits in Philadelphia added up to an investment of $970 million in 763 projects, approximately half of the construction during that decade. These projects range from the obscure (such as the renovation of the Harrington Machine Shop at Seventeenth and Callowhill Streets into condominiums) to the prominent (such as the restoration of Reading Terminal). Two of the city's greatest projects are Frankford Arsenal in Bridesburg and Lit Brothers in center city. Vacated in stages between 1976 and 1978, the sprawling 86-acre arsenal complex is gradually and quietly being put back to work as offices, laboratories, and small manufactories. Lit Brothers department store, on the other hand, was a $100 million undertaking that survived two dates with the wrecking ball in the early 1980s to draw headlines in the fall of 1987 when it reopened as Mellon Independence Center. Large or small, such renovations are central to the city's economic health and architectural integrity. With many old buildings and little open space, Philadelphia's future rests less with new construction than with rebuilding what it already has.

New construction, however, has been almost synonymous with the Northeast. The 1937 guide treats the Northeast as an extension of North Philadelphia, although neither section is cited by those names. Geographically the guide remains correct, but in the past fifty years social and economic changes have eradicated historical ties and rendered geographical relationships irrelevant. In 1937 middle-class dwellings and social institutions lined Roosevelt Boulevard, but beyond it lay acres and acres of undeveloped land. After World War II those acres sprouted hundreds of new rowhouses and semi-detached residences, many on the crescents and cul-de-sacs that were so fashionable at the time. The Northeast became Philadelphia's internal suburb, populated almost exclusively by whites abandoning run-down nineteenth-century housing closer to center city. Black migrants from the south filled what white natives fled. The pattern, however, is not permanent; it broke down in the Temple Stadium area, where during the 1970s blacks moved into previously white-owned postwar houses.

Suburban development outside the city's borders has been even more extensive, in part because there have been fewer limits on space. In retracing the 1937 "jaunts to the environs," travelers today find nearly all of the cited landmarks, but roadways are lined with the shopping malls, industrial parks, and the standard support services endemic to America's highways. Because suburbs are socially defined as much as geographically determined, they have been moving inexorably outward from Philadelphia until they now encompass county seats like Doylestown, Norristown, and West Chester. These suburbs are characterized not only by tract developments and automobile dependence but also by relative affluence. Although some of the older suburbs are beginning to develop urban-like social and economic problems, the prosperity gap between the city and its suburbs continues to grow.

Reasons for this prosperity gap are manifold, ranging from the city's wage tax to the American Dream of a detached house and a front lawn. Both a cause and effect of the gap, however, rest in the city's changed population. In the past fifty years Philadelphia's population has declined by nearly 15 percent, and continues to drop at the rate of 8100 people a year. At the same time the number of minorities has increased. The

Hispanic population has grown from statistically insignificant numbers in 1930 to 3.8 percent of the city's inhabitants in 1980; during the same period the percentage of Orientals has increased ten times, from 0.08 percent to 0.8 percent. Equally significant is the increase of blacks in the city in the past fifty years, from 11 percent to nearly 38 percent. This increase has had a noticeable effect on city schools and politics, helping to account for a black school superintendent (Dr. Constance Clayton) and a black mayor (Honorable W. Wilson Goode).

The city's changed composition, however, has not completely altered its political reputation as a "corrupt but contented" place. In the 1980s alone, for example, the federal Abscam operation netted two city congressmen, the president of City Council, and two other Council members. Other federal investigations led to convictions of over thirty policemen, including a deputy commissioner and two chief inspectors, and indictments against five city judges. Nevertheless, many political scientists would argue that Philadelphia's government today possesses more integrity and professionalism than ever before.

Yet the federal convictions, like the attention given to the recently refurbished Penn statue atop City Hall or the lighted silhouettes of Boathouse Row and Benjamin Franklin Bridge or South Philadelphia's neighborhood loyalties, suggest that a certain Philadelphia character persists in the face of change. As noted at the beginning of this essay, few books communicate this character as well as the 1937 guide. While some of the guide's tours today illustrate how much the city has changed in the past half century, others are remarkable for showing the durability of the city's built and natural environments. Some of the great industrial sites described in the guide are now gone, of course, but the story it tells is true, making this volume both a solid historical work and a rich guide to the Philadelphia area. Few fifty-year-old books can muster such a tribute.

NOTES

1. In any work as extensive as this one, however, there are some errors. Some of them are corrected here. William Strickland, for example, not Benjamin Henry Latrobe, was the architect of the Second Bank of the United States (p. 404). The Morris House on South Eighth Street was the home of Luke Morris, not Robert Morris (p. 415). The Art Club, at Broad and Chancellor Streets, was not initially a private residence; it was built as a clubhouse from the designs of Frank Miles Day, and unfortunately was demolished for a parking lot in 1975–76 (p. 444). The Weidner Memorial Library at Broad Street and Girard Avenue was decorated by George Herzog; it was designed by Willis G. Hale. The house, which had been used as offices since 1946, burned in 1980 (p. 463). The

Universalist Church of the Messiah, at Broad Street and Montgomery Avenue, was designed by two men, not three: Hazlehurst and Huckel. It has since been replaced by a Temple University classroom building (p. 464).

2. Jerrold Hirsch thoroughly discusses the politics and methodology of the Federal Writers' Project state guidebooks in the new introduction to the Tennessee Guide (Knoxville: University of Tennessee Press, 1986), pp. xi–lv.

3. I am indebted to John A. Haak, city planner with the Philadelphia City Planning Commission, for these figures. They were drawn from *Industrial Development in Philadelphia* (Philadelphia: Chamber of Commerce of Philadelphia, 1943), *Shifts in the Location of Pennsylvania Industry, 1920–1955* (Harrisburg: Pennsylvania Department of Internal Affairs, 1956), and the Pennsylvania Office of Employment Security.

FURTHER READING ABOUT PHILADELPHIA

Baltzell, Edward Digby. *Philadelphia Gentlemen: The Making of a National Upper Class.* Glencoe, Ill.: Free Press, 1958. Repr. Philadelphia: University of Pennsylvania Press, 1979.

Baltzell, Edward Digby. *Puritan Boston and Quaker Philadelphia: Two Protestant Ethics and the Spirit of Class Authority and Leadership.* New York: Free Press, 1979. Repr. Boston: Beacon Press, 1982.

Burke, Bobbye, Otto Sperr, Hugh J. McCauley, and Trina Vaux. *Historic Rittenhouse: A Philadelphia Neighborhood.* Philadelphia: University of Pennsylvania Press, 1985.

Cutler, William G., III, and Howard Gillette, Jr. *The Divided Metropolis: Social and Spatial Dimensions of Philadelphia, 1800–1975.* Westport, Conn.: Greenwood Press, 1980.

Davis, Allen F., and Mark H. Haller, eds. *The Peoples of Philadelphia: A History of Ethnic Groups and Lower-Class Life, 1790–1940.* Philadelphia: Temple University Press, 1973.

Drawing Toward Building: Philadelphia Architectural Graphics, 1732–1984. Philadelphia: Pennsylvania Academy of Fine Arts. University of Pennsylvania Press, 1986.

Dunn, Richard S., and Mary Maples Dunn, eds. *The World of William Penn.* Philadelphia: University of Pennsylvania Press, 1986.

Eisenhart, Luther P., ed. *Historic Philadelphia: From the Founding until the Early Nineteenth Century, Twenty-Seven Papers Dealing with Its Peoples and Its Buildings.* Transactions of the American Philosophical Society vol. 43, pt. 1. Philadelphia: American Philosophical Society, 1953.

Finkel, Kenneth, ed. *Nineteenth Century Photography in Philadelphia: 250 Historic Prints from the Library Company of Philadelphia.* New York: Dover Publications; Philadelphia: Library Company of Philadelphia, 1980.

Garvan, Beatrice B. *Federal Philadelphia 1785–1825: The Athens of The Western World.* Philadelphia: Museum of Art, 1987. Distributed by University of Pennsylvania Press.

Golab, Caroline. *Immigrant Destinations.* Philadelphia: Temple University Press, 1977.

Hershberg, Theodore, ed. *Philadelphia: Work, Space, Family and Group Experience in the Nineteenth Century: Essays Toward an Interdisciplinary History of the City.* New York: Oxford University Press, 1981.

Looney, Robert F., compiler. *Old Philadelphia in Early Photographs, 1839–1914: Two Hundred and Fifteen Prints from the Collection of the Free Library of Philadelphia.* New York: Dover Publications, 1976.

Miller, Frederic M., Morris J. Vogel, and Allen F. Davis. *Still Philadelphia: A Photographic History, 1890–1940.* Philadelphia: Temple University Press, 1983.

Scranton, Philip, and Walter Licht. *Work Sights: Industrial Philadelphia, 1890–1950.* Philadelphia: Temple University Press, 1986.

Sewall, Darrel, ed. *Philadelphia: Three Centuries of American Art.* Philadelphia: Philadelphia Museum of Art, 1976.

Tatum, George B. *Penn's Great Town: 250 Years of Philadelphia Architecture Illustrated in Prints and Drawings.* Philadelphia: Philadelphia Art Alliance and the College of Fellows of the American Institute of Architects. University of Pennsylvania Press, 1961.

———. *Philadelphia Georgian: The City House of Samuel Powel and Some of Its Eighteenth Century Neighbors.* Middletown, Conn.: Wesleyan University Press, 1976.

Teitelman, S. Robert. *Birch's Views of Philadelphia: A Reduced Facsimile of "The City of Philadelphia . . . As it Appeared in the year 1800": with Photographs of the Sites in 1960 and 1982.* Philadelphia: The Free Library of Philadelphia, 1982; University of Pennsylvania Press, 1983.

Warner, Sam Bass. *The Private City: Philadelphia in Three Periods of Its Growth.* Philadelphia: University of Pennsylvania Press, 1968. Revised paperback edition. 1987.

Webster, Richard J. *Philadelphia Preserved: A Catalog of the Historic American Buildings Survey.* Rev. ed. Philadelphia: Temple University Press, 1981.

Wiegley, Russel F., et al. *Philadelphia: A Three Hundred Year History.* New York: W. W. Norton & Co., 1982.

Wolf, Edwin, II. *Philadelphia, Portrait of an American City: Bicentennial History.* Harrisburg, Pa.: Stackpole Books, 1975.

THE AMERICAN GUIDE SERIES

The Philadelphia Guide is one of the publications in the American Guide Series, written by members of the Federal Writers' Project of the Works Progress Administration. Designed primarily to give useful employment to needy unemployed writers and research workers, this project has gradually developed the ambitious objective of presenting to the American people a portrait of America — its history, folklore, scenery, cultural backgrounds, social and economic trends, and racial factors. In one respect, at any rate, this undertaking is unique ; it represents a farflung effort at cooperative research and writing, drawing upon all the varied abilities of its personnel. All the workers contribute according to their talents ; the field worker collects data in the field, the research worker burrows in libraries, the art and literary critics cover material relevant to their own specialties, architects describe notable historical buildings and monuments ; and the final editing of copy as it flows in from all corners of a state is done by the more experienced authors in the central offices. The ultimate product, whatever its faults or merits, represents a blend of the work of the entire personnel, aided by consultants, members of university faculties, specialists, officers of learned societies, oldest residents, who have volunteered their services everywhere most generously.

A great many books and brochures are being written for this series. As they appear in increasing numbers we hope the American public will come to appreciate more fully not only the unusual scope of this undertaking, but also the devotion shown by the workers, from the humblest field worker to the most accomplished editors engaged in the final rewrite. The Federal Writers' Project, directed by Henry G. Alsberg, is in the Division of Women's and Professional Projects under Ellen S. Woodward, Assistant Administrator.

Administrator
Works Progress Administration

FOREWORD

A spirit of achievement abounds in Philadelphia, marking the renaissance of Philadelphia's renown as a center of business, culture and enterprise.

Philadelphia is a rich city. Not only is it wealthy in memories of those stirring times when a great political philosophy was born in Independence Hall, but it is laden with things which are richly American, such as the warm sincerity and hospitality of its people.

I like to think of Philadelphia as a typical Pennsylvania city, shipping the stores of anthracite coal to every part of the world, marketing the products of the rich Pennsylvania farmlands, planning its future greatness with the other communities throughout the Commonwealth.

A book can tell only a part of Philadelphia's story. The whole story can be known by seeing and enjoying these things which Philadelphia holds for visitors and Philadelphians alike.

Hans Wilson

Mayor of Philadelphia

PREFACE

THE *Philadelphia Guide*, one of the American Guide series of regional, state, city, county and sectional Guides being compiled by the Federal Writers' Projects, Works Progress Administration, marks the completion of the first major publication by the Pennsylvania staff. Representing almost two years' work by the Philadelphia Project and the State staff, it presents the traditions and history of the old city and the swiftly changing contemporary scene. It should prove interesting and instructive to Philadelphians, recalling as it does the quaintness and peace of the Quaker town, which served as the nucleus for the modern industrial city. It is believed visitors will find it valuable.

The first material was assembled in November 1935, when the Federal Writers' Project was started in Pennsylvania. During the following months a staff of editors, reporters, copy desk men, artists, map makers, research workers, and typists compiled, assembled, and edited the material. Historic lore uncovered by reporters was checked for authenticity by recognized authorities. Among the consultants were religious leaders, industrialists, educators, geologists, musicians, actors, painters, architects, scientists, librarians, physicians, labor leaders, social service workers, and bankers, who have given freely of their knowledge to ensure the accuracy of the *Philadelphia Guide*. During this period, of course, work on numerous other books and pamphlets was being carried forward.

The project, part of the WPA program, was planned to provide work for unemployed newspapermen and magazine writers in a sphere where their talents and abilities could find expression in channels of value to the Nation.

The first phase has been passed. It remains for those who read the *Guide* to decide whether the second objective has been attained.

The gradual change in personnel and duties which has necessarily occurred during the long months the *Guide* was in the course of preparation makes it impossible to give the entire staff, individually, the credit which each worker so richly deserves. Since the inception of the task, more than two hundred and forty men and women have at various times been engaged in some phase of the work of compiling, writing, checking, editing, and illustrating this modern Baedeker of the Quaker City, meanwhile carrying on their work on other publications of the American Guide Series. Death has taken the pen from the hands of some ; opportunity in private industry has called others. But throughout this kaleidoscopic change in the staff there has persisted a fine *esprit d'corps* of which the *Philadelphia Guide* is the first tangible memorial.

We offer the *Guide* with a feeling of satisfaction and confidence ; satisfaction, that we have contributed something worthy to the city ; and confidence, that it will prove of real value to those who use it.

Paul Comly French
Pennsylvania State Director
Federal Writers' Project

Philadelphia
December 1, 1937

TABLE OF CONTENTS

| | | Page |
THE AMERICAN GUIDE SERIES xxi
  by Harry L. Hopkins, Administrator
    Works Progress Administration
FOREWORD xxiii
  by S. Davis Wilson
    Mayor of Philadelphia
PREFACE xxv
  by Paul Comly French, State Director
    Federal Writers' Project
ACKNOWLEDGMENTS xxix
GENERAL INFORMATION xxxv
  Information Facilities   Climate
  Travel   Sports
  Accommodations   Theatres
  Shopping   Night Clubs
CALENDAR OF ANNUAL EVENTS xlii
POINTS OF SPECIAL INTEREST xliv

THE CITY AND ITS BACKGROUND

PORTRAIT OF PHILADELPHIA 3
NATURE'S HANDIWORK 11
THE FIRST INHABITANTS 16
THE SAGA OF A CITY
  Prologue 20
  Penn and the Holy Experiment 23
  Early Settlement 31
  The Revolutionary Period 45
  A Century of Growth 60
  The Modern Metropolis 77
OLD WAYS AND OLD TALES 88
THE IMPRINT OF NATIONS 98
GOVERNMENTAL MACHINERY 109
PHILADELPHIA'S ECONOMIC CHARACTER
  Hub of Commerce and Industry 112
  Cradle of American Finance 125
  Public Utilities 137
  Transportation 142
  Labor and Labor Problems 147
THE CITY'S CULTURAL ASPECTS
  Religions 159
  Education 173
  Literature 184
  Growth of the Press 202
  Stage and Screen 213
  Music 234
  Painting and Sculpture 243
  Colonial Mansion to Skyscraper
    Architecture, The City of Yesterday and Today 256
    Old Plans and New, The City of Tomorrow 279
  Science 284
  Medicine 293
  Social Service 304

POINTS OF SPECIAL INTEREST

INDEPENDENCE SQUARE GROUP 319
CARPENTERS' HALL 339
BETSY ROSS HOUSE AND THE LEGEND OF THE FLAG 342
THE POWEL HOUSE 345
THE ACADEMY OF MUSIC 348
LOGAN SQUARE LIBRARY 350
FRANKLIN INSTITUTE AND THE FELS PLANETARIUM 353
PENNSYLVANIA MUSEUM OF ART 360
GIRARD COLLEGE 370
UNITED STATES MINT 375

ROADS AND RAMBLES IN AND AROUND THE CITY

(Maps with all tours)

HEART OF THE CITY 379
WHERE THE FATHERS WALKED
    1. North of old "High Street" (City Tour 1) 385
    2. From City Hall to "Society Hall" (City Tour 2) 399
TO THE SCHUYLKILL'S BANK (City Tour 3) 431
"LONGEST STRAIGHT STREET"
    1. South Broad Street—Through the Melting Pot (City Tour 4) .. 441
    2. North Broad Street—Where Houses Stand in Regiments
        (City Tour 5) 450
HISTORIC GERMANTOWN (City Tour 6) 475
WEST PHILADELPHIA
    1. City of Apartments (City Tour 7) 493
    2. Toward the Suburbs (City Tour 8) 505
THROUGH INDUSTRIAL PHILADELPHIA (City Tour 9) 513
ALONG THE WATER FRONT (City Tour 10) 533
FAIRMOUNT PARK
    1. East Park (City Tour 11) 547
    2. West Park (City Tour 12) 561
THE TREE-LINED PARKWAY (City Tour 13) 575
AROUND PENN'S CAMPUS (City Tour 14) 587
SIX WOODLAND HIKES
    Hills and Dales of the Wissahickon
    1. The Lower Valley (City Tour 15) 601
    2. Along Sparkling Cresheim Creek (City Tour 16) 607
    3. Around Valley Green (City Tour 17) 615
    Woodland Shadows of the Pennypack
    1. By the "Ol' Swimming Hole" (City Tour 18) 620
    2. Rendezvous for Izaak Waltons (City Tour 19) 621
    By Placid Cobbs Creek (City Tour 20) 625
JAUNTS TO THE ENVIRONS
    To Brandywine Battlefield (Environs Tour 1) 629
    To Bryn Athyn Cathedral (Environs Tour 2) 651
    To New Hope and Washington Crossing (Environs Tour 3) 657
    Valley Forge (Environs Tour 4) 673
CHRONOLOGY 686
BIBLIOGRAPHY 690
INDEX 692

xxviii

ACKNOWLEDGMENTS

Among the consultants, who gave generously of their time and knowledge are men and women prominent in many fields of activity in the City. While it would be impossible to give credit individually to all of those who assisted us, yet we are anxious for them to know that their advice and suggestions aided materially in the preparation of the *Guide*.

There are some, however, to whom we are especially grateful. Included among these are Henry B. Allen, Director, Franklin Institute; Dr. Jacob Billikopf, Chairman of the former Philadelphia Regional Labor Relations Board; Reverend Frederick W. Blatz, St. Peter's Church; L. Wharton Bickley, Building Superintendent, Federal Reserve Bank; Dr. Samuel Bradbury, Medical Director, Pennsylvania Hospital; Lieut. Com. William W. Behrens, U. S. N.; Julian P. Boyd, Historical Society of Pennsylvania; Carl Boyer, Director, Wagner Free Institute of Science; Charles M. B. Cadwalader, President, Academy of Natural Sciences; Paul P. Cret, Architect; Horace T. Carpenter, Curator, Independence Hall; Frank A. Cook, Building Manager, Philadelphia Saving Fund Society; Mabel Corry, Secretary, New Century Club; Charles N. Christman, Director, Philadelphia Commercial Museum; Karl de Schweinitz, Secretary, Pennsylvania Department of Public Assistance; John C. Donecker, Secretary, Girard College; E. H. Dressel, Superintendent, U. S. Mint; Ross B. Davis, Chief Engineer, Bureau of Fire.

George H. Fairchild, Historical Society of Pennsylvania; Samuel Fleisher, Graphic Sketch Club; Harry H. Givens, Periodical Department, Historical Society of Pennsylvania; Samuel G. Gordon, Academy of Natural Sciences; Dorothy Grafly, Art Critic; Richard Gimbel of the Poe House; Carl F. Haussman, Rector, Zion German Lutheran Church; WillB Hadley, City Treasurer; Norman F. Hall, Chamber of Commerce; William Heim, Metropolitan Opera House; J. St. George Joyce, Director of Public Relations, Temple University; Fiske Kimball, Director, Pennsylvania Museum of Art; Howard A. Keiser, Superintendent, Academy of Music; Dorothy Kohl, Executive Director, Philadelphia Art Alliance; Elizabeth Kunkel, Secretary to the Director of Cedar Grove Mansion, Letitia Street House, Memorial Hall and Rodin Museum; George I. Lovatt, Architect; Reverend Clarence Long of Old Pine Street Church; Percy E. Lawler, Manager, Rosenbach Galleries; Albert Mordell, Author; J. Hampton Moore, former Mayor of Philadelphia; Henry T. Murdock, Dramatic Editor, Evening Public Ledger; Henri Marceau, Assistant Director, Pennsylvania Museum of Art; Edith P. MacKendrick, Assist. Treas., Monthly Meeting of Friends; Reverend W. R. McKean, Minister in charge of Christ Church; Dr. Louis Nusbaum, Board of Education.

Reverend Dr. E. A. E. Palmquist, Executive Secretary, Philadelphia Federation of Churches; Dr. Francis W. Pennell, Academy of Natural Sciences; Franklin H. Price, Librarian, Logan Square Library; Richard Peters, Jr., Secretary, Historical Society of Pennsylvania; David Philips, Public Relations Manager, P. R. T.; William J. Patterson, Librarian, Masonic Temple Library; Ormond Rambo, Jr., American Swedish Historical Museum; Reverend John Craig Roak, of Gloria Dei Church; Dr. C. Dudley Saul, Physician; Judge Frank Smith; Dr. Frank G. Speck, Professor of Anthropology, University of Pennsylvania; Dr. Witmer Stone, Academy of Natural Sciences; R. C. Sutton, Chief Administrative Assistant, Fort Mifflin; Herbert J. Tily, President, Strawbridge and Clothier; Dr. Francis H. Tees, Minister of St. George's Church; William Henry Welsh, Dir. of School Extension, Board of Education; Frances A. Wister, President, Philadelphia Society for Preservation of Landmarks; Louis W. Wilgarde, Secretary to Mayor Wilson; Harold A. West, Librarian, Mercantile Library; Thomas Washington, Rear Admiral, U. S. N.; and John E. Zimmermann, President, U. G. I.

The editors of the *Philadelphia Guide* are indebted to Mr. William M. Campbell, delineator ; the Philadelphia Chapter, A.I.A. copyright holders ; and the J. L. Smith Co., publishers ; for permission to reproduce as an end piece the map *Philadelphia from the map made by John Reed in 1774.*

xxix

ILLUSTRATIONS AND MAPS

Penn in Armor	Courtesy of the Historical Society of Pennsylvania	Frontis- piece
Liberty Bell	Ritter	2
Delaware River Bridge	Drawing by Schmidt	7
Christ Church Tower	Drawing by Palmer	10
Scene in Fairmount Park	Ritter	15
Penn's Ship "Welcome"	Drawing by Schmidt	20
Workmans Place	Ritter	27
Friend's Meeting House	Ritter	43
Portrait of Benjamin Franklin by Joseph Wright	Courtesy of the Academy of Fine Arts	44
State House	From old prints	47
1776 and 1876	Courtesy of the Historical Society of Pennsylvania	
Declaration Table in Independence Hall	Ritter	50
Betsy Ross House Today	Ritter	53
Before Its Restoration	Carter	53
Shippen-Wistar House	Ritter	57
James Wilson's Grave at Christ Church	Ritter	59
Musical Fund Hall	Drawing by Schmidt	65
Monument to Negro Soldiers	Ritter	67
Smith Memorial	Ritter	76
Dewey's "Olympia," Philadelphia Navy Yard	Ritter	82
Tacony-Palmyra Bridge	Drawing by Schmidt	85
Slum Scene	Ritter	86
New Year "Shooter"	Drawing by Palmer	91
Fire Plaques	Kalmar	93
Old Market	Ritter	99
Curb Market at Ninth Street and Washington Avenue	Egan	105
City Hall Tower	Ritter	110
Hosiery Worker	Drawing by Palmer	113
Breaking up the Final	Courtesy of John P. Mudd The Midvale Company	116
Old Ships and New	Egan	122
Statue of Robert Morris at the Old Custom House	Ritter	130
Girard Bank	Ritter	135
Old Schuylkill Navigation Canal Lock in Fairmount Park	Ritter	144
Melted Steel	Courtesy of John P. Mudd The Midvale Company	152
St. Paul's Protestant Episcopal Church	Ritter	165
Stenton House	Barnum	165
Gateway of Old Christ Church	Ritter	171
Board of Education Administration Building	Egan	174
Penn Charter School	Egan	174
The Poe House	Kalmar	187
Poe House Interior	Kalmar	187
Thomas Paine	Drawing by Schmidt	189
Front Page News in The Pennsylvania Evening Post	Reproduction copy	206
Transmitting Station of WCAU	Courtesy of WCAU	211
Walnut Street Theatre	Egan	218
First Chestnut Street Theatre	Drawing by Schmidt	218
Hedgerow Theatre	Ritter	231
Memorial Arch at Valley Forge	Drawing by Palmer	233
Academy of Music	Ritter	235

Rodin's "The Kiss"	Ritter	252
Mosaic, "The Dream Garden" after	Courtesy of Curtis	
Maxfield Parrish	Publishing Company	255
Four Towers		
City Hall and Independence Hall	Ritter	260
Old Stock Exchange and Philadelphia		
Saving Fund Society	Ritter	261
The Chew Mansion	Highton	269
Doorway of Mt. Pleasant	Courtesy of the Pennsyl-	
	vania Museum of Art	269
Home of Robert Morris	Egan	273
Swimming Pool at the Carl Mackley House	Courtesy of Museum of	
	Modern Art, New York	275
Carl Mackley House	Ritter	275
Founder's Hall, Girard College	Egan	276
Federal Reserve Bank Building	Ritter	276
Natural Habitat Exhibits		
Academy of Natural Sciences	Ritter	291
Fitch's Steamboat "Perseverance" Drawing by	Palmer	292
Laboratory	Courtsey of	
	Sharp & Dohme	296
An Operation at Hahnemann	Courtesy of Hahnemann	
	Medical College	302
Preston Retreat	Kalmar	309
City Skyline from the Art Museum	Egan	316

Points of Special Interest

Old Gate at Independence Square Drawing by	Schmidt	318
Statue of Barry and Independence Hall	Highton	322
Congress Hall	Ritter	330
Old City Hall	Ritter	330
American Philosophical Society	Ritter	332
Interior of Independence Hall	Ritter	335
Benjamin Franklin's Chair	Ritter	338
Carpenters' Hall	Ritter	340
The Powel House	Ritter	347
Franklin Institute by Night	Egan	354
League Island Navy Yard Crane Drawing by	Palmer	354
Zeiss Projector in the Fels Planetarium	Ritter	361
East Wing of Art Museum	Egan	364
Art Museum and the Old Water Works	Kalmar	369
Founder's Hall at Girard College	Egan	372
Stephen Girard Sarcophagus at Girard		
College	Egan	372
United States Mint Drawing by	Palmer	374
City Hall and Skyline	Ritter	378

City Tours

St. George's Methodist Church	Kalmar	389
Elfreth's Alley	Ritter	391
Benjamin Franklin's Grave	Ritter	391
Christ Church Doorway	Ritter	397
Drinker House Drawing by	Schmidt	405
St. Peter's Church	Ritter	409
St. Joseph's Roman Catholic Church	Ritter	409
Philadelphia Contributionship	Ritter	413
Mikveh Israel Cemetery Drawing by	Schmidt	417
William Penn Statue, Pennsylvania		
Hospital	Highton	419
Camac Street	Ritter	423
Clinton Street	Ritter	423
Sailing Boat Drawing by	Giordano	429
Doorway of St. Mark's Church	Ritter	434
Armory of First Troop, Philadelphia		
City Cavalry	Barnum	434

Rittenhouse Square	Ritter	437
Ridgway Library	Ritter	446
American Swedish Historical Museum	Ritter	449
Academy of Fine Arts	Ritter	454
Observatory at Central High School	Kalmar	460
Rodeph Shalom Synagogue	Egan	460
Dome of Lu Lu Temple	Egan	462
Mitten Hall, Temple University	Egan	465
Rear of Temple University Dormitories	Barnum	465
Main Altar, Church of the Holy Child	Courtesy of William Rittase	472
Germantown Academy	Highton	482
The Wyck House	Barnum	484
Germantown Mennonite Church	Barnum	484
The Billmeyer House	Barnum	488
Convention Hall	Kalmar	494
Detail of Bartram House	Ritter	496
Bartram House	Ritter	499
Interior of Bartram House	Highton	499
U. S. Naval Home	Kalmar	502
Thirtieth Street Station, P.R.R.	Drawing by Palmer	507
Wynnestay	Kalmar	509
Seminary of St. Charles Borromeo	Ritter	511
St. Joseph's College	Ritter	511
Stetson Hat Company	Courtesy of John B. Stetson Co.	516
Curtis Publishing Company	Courtesy of Curtis Pub. Co.	516
Plant of J. G. Brill Co.	Kalmar	522
Delaware River Bridge	Egan	536
Sail Ship	Drawing by Palmer	538
Delaware Avenue at Noon	Ritter	539
Old Swedes' Church	Ritter	541
Old Swedes' Church Graveyard	Ritter	541
Old Sailing Vessels	Egan	544
Indian Medicine Man	Ritter	550
Exterior of Mt. Pleasant	Ritter	553
Interior of Mt. Pleasant	Courtesy of the Pennsylvania Museum of Art	553
Schuylkill River from West River Drive	Ritter	556
Boathouse Row	Ritter	558
Old Solitude	Himes	563
Interior of Letitia Street House	Highton	565
Sweet Briar	Highton	567
Letitia Street House	Ritter	569
Interior of Cedar Grove Mansion	Courtesy of Pennsylvania Museum of Art	569
Horticultural Hall	Kalmar	573
Cathedral of SS. Peter and Paul	Himes	577
Entrance Gate of Rodin Museum	Highton	577
Facade of Rodin Museum	Egan	582
Train	Drawing by Palmer	585
Irvine Auditorium	Ritter	591
Entrance to U. of P. Quadrangle	Ritter	591
Franklin Field	Drawing by Palmer	593
Dormitories at Pennsylvania	Ritter	595
Statue of Benjamin Franklin	Ritter	598
Rittenhouse Mill	Carter	606
Devil's Pool	Barnum	611
Indian Statue	Barnum	613
Old Covered Bridge	Barnum	616
Livezey House	Carter	616
Concrete Bridge over Pennypack Creek	Egan	620
Pennypack Baptist Church	Egan	623
Cobbs Creek Park Trail	Ritter	626

Environs Tours

Swarthmore College	Ritter	633
Glen Riddle Homes	Ritter	635
Concord Meetinghouse	Ritter	635
Octagonal Schoolhouse	Ritter	642
Sproul Observatory	Ritter	642
Fort Mifflin	Ritter	647
Fort Mifflin—Basking in an Olden Glory	Ritter	647
The Swedenborgian Cathedral	Egan	652
Swedenborgian Cathedral, A Vaulted Portico	Egan	655
Robbins House	Ritter	659
Old Forge Inn	Ritter	659
Friends Meetinghouse at Horsham	Ritter	662
Keith House at Graeme Park	Ritter	662
Canal at New Hope	Ritter	668
Gulph Mills	Ritter	675
Sign at King of Prussia Inn	Ritter	675
Valley Forge Chapel Interior	Himes	677
Washington Memorial National Carillon	Himes	680
Cabin at Valley Forge	Ritter	682

MAPS

HEART OF PHILADELPHIA	Introductory Tour	xxx
WHERE THE CITY FATHERS WALKED		
1. North of old "High Street"	City Tour 1	384
2. From City Hall to Society Hill	City Tour 2	398
TO THE SCHUYLKILL'S BANK	City Tour 3	430
"LONGEST STRAIGHT STREET"		
1. South Broad Street and Through the Melting Pot	City Tour 4	442
2. North Broad Street Where Houses Stand in Regiments	City Tour 5	451
ROOSEVELT BOULEVARD	City Tour 5A	470
HISTORIC GERMANTOWN	City Tour 6	476
WEST PHILADELPHIA		
1. City of Apartments	City Tour 7	492
2. Towards the Suburbs	City Tour 8	506
THROUGH INDUSTRIAL PHILADELPHIA	City Tour 9	514
ALONG THE WATER FRONT	City Tour 10	534
FAIRMOUNT PARK		
1. East Park	City Tour 11	548
2. West Park	City Tour 12	560
THE TREE-LINED PARKWAY	City Tour 13	574
AROUND PENN'S CAMPUS	City Tour 14	586
SIX WOODLAND HIKES		
Hills and Dales of the Wissahickon		
1. The Lower Valley	City Tour 15	600
2. Along Sparkling Cresheim Creek	City Tour 16	608
3. Around Valley Green	City Tour 17	614
Woodland Shadows of the Pennypack		
1. By the "Ol' Swimming Hole"	City Tour 18	618
2. Rendezvous for Izaak Waltons	City Tour 19	622
By Placid Cobbs Creek	City Tour 20	624
FOUR TOURS TO THE CITY'S ENVIRONS		
Along the Brandywine	Environs Tour 1	628
Swarthmore College Campus	Environs Tour 1A	630
To Bryn Athyn's Cathedral	Environs Tour 2	650
New Hope, Artists' Colonial Rendezvous	Environs Tour 3	656
Valley Forge	Environs Tour 4	672
TRANSPORTATION IN THE CITY		Pocket
FAIRMOUNT PARK PICTORIAL (Reverse)		
HIGHWAY BY-PASSES AROUND PHILADELPHIA		Pocket

HEART OF THE CITY

SEVENTEENTH STREET

LATHAM APARTMENTS

K Y W WCAU BROADCASTING STATIONS

RACQUET CLUB

SIXTEENTH STREET

STATE LIQUOR STORE

FIFTEENTH STREET

MITTEN BUILDING

BELLEVUE STRATFORD HOTEL

ART CLUB

MANUFACTURERS CLUB UNION LEAGUE

STATE LIQUOR STORE

SUBWAY STATIONS

⑤

BROAD ST. STATION PENNA. RAILROAD

⑥

REYBURN PLAZA

⑦ BAND STAND

CENTRAL Y M C A

U. G. I.

SUBWAY STATIONS

① CITY HALL

BROAD STREET

BROAD APTS.

RITZ CARLTON HOTEL

LIQUOR STORE

④

③

W F I L

MASONIC TEMPLE

⑧

LAFAYETTE HOTEL

JUNIPER STREET

POOR RICHARD CLUB

PHILADELPHIA CLUB

WANAMAKER'S DEPARTMENT STORE

②

①B

①A

CITY HALL ANNEX

BULLETIN BUILDING

⑨

HOTEL VENDIG

BUS STATION

THIRTEENTH STREET

ST. JAMES HOTEL

PRINCETON CLUB

ADELPHIA HOTEL

W D A S BROADCASTING STATION

SUBWAY STATIONS

BUS STATION

BUS STATION

BUS STATION

STATE LIQUOR

LOCUST

WALNUT

SANSOM

CHESTNUT

MARKET

FILBERT

ARCH

CHERRY

TWELFTH STREET

CHAMBER OF COMMERCE

SNELLENBURG'S DEPARTMENT STORE

READING TERMINAL

TERMINAL MARKET

ELEVENTH STREET

SUBWAY STATIONS

FRANK & SEDERS DEPARTMENT STORE

JEFFERSON HOSPITAL

TENTH STREET

AMERICAN GUIDE PENNSYLVANIA

McALPIN HOTEL

N

FEDERAL COURTS BUILDING

NINTH STREET

BENJAMIN FRANKLIN HOTEL

GIMBEL BROTHERS DEPARTMENT STORE

LEARY'S BOOK STORE

STRAWBRIDGE & CLOTHIER DEPARTMENT STORE

W I P

EIGHTH STREET

SUBWAY STATIONS

LII BROTHERS

1. City Hall
1a. City Hall Annex
1b. Market Street Nat Bank Bldg.
2. Wanamaker Store
3. Lincoln-Liberty Bld
4. Girard Trust Co. B
5. Mitten Bank
6. Broad Street Statio
7. Reyburn Plaza
8. Masonic Temple
9. Bulletin Building

Legend numbers refe points of interest descr in chapter, Heart of City, page 379.

GENERAL INFORMATION

The Philadelphia which greeted travelers
in former days is revealed in the excerpts
from old Bacdeker Guides.

Information Facilities in Philadelphia

Information Service. General information concerning Philadelphia may be obtained at railroad and bus stations ; street railway, air line, and steamship offices ; department stores ; newspaper offices ; and various civic agencies. (See Transportation section.)

Travelers' Aid Society, 307 S. Juniper St., maintains information desks at principal railroad stations.

Philadelphia Rapid Transit Company (P. R. T.), 224 S. Broad St., supplies information concerning trolleys, busses, subways, and elevated railways.

American Airlines, Inc., Eastern Airlines, Inc., and United Air Lines, ticket office, 1339 Walnut St.; Pan-American Airway System, 1620 Walnut St.; Transcontinental & Western Air Lines, Inc., 1417 Chestnut St.

The two major automobile clubs—the A. A. A., at 23 S. 23d St., and the Keystone, at Broad and Vine Sts.—furnish road maps and special service to member and keep on file folders descriptive of places of special interest to visitors. They outline motor routes, indicating detours and roads under construction.

The Chamber of Commerce, 12th and Walnut Sts., and the Board of Trade, Bourse Bldg., 5th St. near Chestnut, supply data concerning commercial Philadelphia.

The leading daily newspapers are: *Record* (morning); *Inquirer* (morning); *Evening Bulletin*; *Evening Public Ledger*; *Daily News* (evening). All except the *Bulletin* and *Daily News* conduct resort and travel bureaus.

Publications. The following will be found useful: *Boyd's Official Philadelphia Street and Trolley Guide* and the *Bulletin Almanac and Year Book,* both available at newsstands and stationery stores; *Glimpses of Philadelphia,* Chamber of Commerce, 12th and Walnut Sts.; *Hotel Greeters Guide of Philadelphia* and *This Week in Philadelphia,* both available at most of the large hotels; *Philadelphia Guide Book,* Horn and Hardart "Automat" restaurants; *The P.R.T. Traveler, P.R.T. Traveler's Lecture List,* and *P.R.T. Route Map,* Philadelphia Rapid Transit Co., N.W. corner Broad and Locust Sts.; and *Unique Tours,* Automobile Club of Philadelphia, 23 S. 23d St.

Transportation

Railroad Stations. Pennsylvania R.R.—Thirtieth St. Station, 30th and Market Sts.; Broad St. Station, Broad and Market Sts.; Suburban Station, 16th St. and Pennsylvania Boulevard; North Philadelphia Station, Broad St. and Glenwood Ave.

Baltimore & Ohio—24th and Chestnut Sts.

Pennsylvania-Reading Seashore Lines—Market St. Ferry.

Reading Company—Terminal, 12th and Market Sts.; North Broad St. Station, Broad and Huntingdon Sts.

> *Baedeker's (1893):* . . . *Tramways run from all* . . . *suburban stations* . . . *or ferries to the chief centres of the city and Hotel Omnibuses (25c) meet the principal trains.*

Highways. Six US highways lead into Philadelphia.
(See Philadelphia and vicinity map for highways and by-passes) Two bridges connect Philadelphia with New Jersey: Delaware River Bridge from Camden (toll 20 cents) ; Tacony-Palmyra Bridge (toll 30 cents).

Bus Stations. Greyhound Lines—terminal, Broad Street Station.
Reading Transportation Co.—terminal, 12th and Market Sts.
Doylestown and Easton Coach Co.—terminals, Broad Street Station, Reading Terminal, 12th and Filbert Sts., and Broad St. and Erie Ave.
Island Beach Stages—terminal, 1233 Filbert St.
Martz Trailways—terminal, 13th and Filbert Sts.
Public Service Interstate Transportation Co.—terminal, 13th and Filbert Sts.
Trenton-Philadelphia Coach Co.—terminals, 13th and Filbert Sts., Broad St. and Erie Ave., 5th St. and Roosevelt Blvd.
Short Line—terminal, 1311 Arch St.
Safeways Trails System—terminal, 13th and Filbert Sts.
Red Star—terminal, 13th and Filbert Sts.
Pan-American Bus Lines—terminal, 1233 Filbert St.
In addition there are fleets of busses, with terminals on Filbert St. between 12th and 13th Sts., that cover metropolitan Philadelphia, Pennsylvania, and adjacent States. Broad Street (east side), is the converging place for most busses from New Jersey points.

Suburban electric railway lines with their terminus at 69th St. provide access to the city via 69th St. Terminal.
The High-Speed Line (fare 10 cents), between Philadelphia and Camden, across the Delaware River Bridge, connects with subway lines at 8th and Market Sts., Philadelphia, and with seashore trains in Camden.

Airports. Central Airport, Crescent Blvd., Camden, 5 mi. S. E. of city for American Airlines, Inc., Eastern Airlines, Inc., Pan-American Airways System, and United Airlines. Ticket office, 1339 Walnut St. ; Transcontinental and Western Airlines, Inc., 1417 Chestnut St. (regular limousine service from 1417 Chestnut St. and Bellevue-Stratford Hotel, 75 cents; taxi fare from City Hall, $1.50; bus fare, 20 cents).
Planes entering Central Airport are served from the Eastern Airlines, T.W.A., American Airlines, and United States Airmail Service.

Ferries across Delaware River. Pennsylvania ferries dock at the Market St. wharf (fare 5 cents, 10 tokens for 30 cents; automobiles, 20 cents, strip of 10 tickets, $1.50). Reading ferries dock at the Chestnut St. wharf and South St. wharf (fare 4 cents, 10 tickets for 25 cents ; automobiles, 25 cents).

Passenger Steamship Piers. Wilson Line, Delaware Ave. and Chestnut St.; to Pennsgrove, N. J., Chester, Pa., and Wilmington, Del. This line also offers moonlight excursions on the river.
Ericsson Line, Inc., Delaware Ave. and South St.; to Baltimore, by way of the Delaware & Chesapeake Canal.

Local Street cars and busses. The Philadelphia Rapid Transit Company (trolley and subway fare, 8 cents; 2 tokens, 15 cents; bus fare, 10 cents) operates trolleys, subway lines, and busses to virtually every part of the city.

> *Baedeker's (1893): . . . Electric, Cable or Horse cars traverse*
> *all the principal Sts., (fare 5c, transfer tickets 8c) . . . Omni-*
> *buses ply up and down Broad St. and in Diamond Street. . . .*

Passengers may obtain free transfer tickets, when fare is paid by cash or token, enabling them to connect with other trolleys or subway lines. These are accepted on most of the routes. To connect with certain other routes an "exchange ticket" is sold for three cents, at the time fare is paid. Conductors will explain when a free transfer will do and when an exchange is necessary, if informed of the destination desired.

Taxis. Adequate service to all parts of city and suburbs (rates 20 cents for first ¼ mile, 5 cents each additional ¼ mile).

> *Baedeker's (1893) : . . . Hansoms (1-2 persons) 1½ M., 25c . . . Four wheelers, 1-2 pers. 50c., 75c . . . One trunk or valise free, each extra article of luggage 6c . . .*

Sight-seeing Busses. Tours of the historical, business, and residential sections, Fairmount Park, and Valley Forge are offered daily by two companies: the Royal Blue Line Company of Philadelphia, Benjamin Franklin Hotel, Ninth and Chestnut Sts.; the Gray Line, Keith's Theatre Bldg., 1116 Chestnut St. (rates, city tour, 3 hours $2.00; 1½ hours, $1.00; Valley Forge tour, $3.00).

Chartered bus transportation is obtainable through the Mertz White Way Lines, Inc., 3210 Spring Garden St.; the P.R.T. Co., Broad and Locust Sts.; and the two sight-seeing bus companies listed above.

Accommodations

Hotels. These run the gamut from 25-cent "flop-houses" to the palatial central city hotels. Room rates in the better hotels range from $2 up. (See Central City map.)

> *Baedeker's (1893) : . . . Aldine, 1910 Chestnut St., a good family hotel, $3½-5 . . . Green's, 8th and Chestnut Sts., R. from $1, for men . . .*

Restaurants. Every type, from lunch wagons and automats to famous sea food houses and pretentious dining rooms. There are a number of foreign restaurants, including Italian, French, Jewish, Russian, Swedish, German, Rumanian, and Chinese.

> *Baedeker's (1893) . . . Bellevue Hotel (somewhat expensive) . . . Reisser, 5th St. above Chestnut, for men, with a "Rathskeller" downstairs . . . Dennett's Lunch Room, 529 Chestnut St., 13 S. 9th St., and 1313 Market St. (Low prices.)*

Liquor Stores. As the sale of liquors and wines in Pennsylvania is a State monopoly, spirituous beverages in Philadelphia are dispensed through State liquor stores operated by the Pennsylvania Liquor Control Board. Beverages are sold in sealed containers, which must not be opened on the premises. Liquor is sold by the drink only in taprooms and restaurants licensed for the purpose. Beer, ale, and porter cannot be obtained in liquor stores, but are offered for sale in thousands of taprooms throughout the city.

State liquor stores, conveniently placed in every section of the city, are open from 10 to 9 daily, except Sundays and legal holidays. However, two central stores are open until 11 p. m.—one at 1334 Walnut St., the other at 734 Market St.

Street Numbering

The numbered streets run north and south. A system which allots one hundred numbers to each block is used for designating all addresses. In general, the north and south streets are numbered each way from Market St.—odd numbers on the east side, even numbers on the west.

In the central section of the city, the east-west streets are numbered westward from Delaware Ave., on the eastern water front. Farther north, where the city stretches eastward, Front St. is the dividing line from which the numbers start in either direction. On all east and west streets, odd numbers are on the north side, and even numbers on the south.

Germantown, Manayunk, Kensington, and other outlying sections have their own numbering arrangements, dating back to the time when they were separate towns.

Shopping Information

The shopping center of Philadelphia a half century ago was at 8th and Market Sts. Today most of the leading stores are on Chestnut St. from 10th to 19th, on Walnut St. from 10th to 17th, and on Market St. from 7th to Broad. Most of the city's largest department stores are in the last-named section.

On Market St. from 6th to 16th, and on cross streets between Arch and Walnut, may be found a great number of smaller shops which deal mainly in lower-priced merchandise.

The important retail jewelry establishments are on Chestnut St., east of Broad. The wholesale jewelry trade is centered on Sansom St. between 7th and 8th, and the jewelers' "curb market" operates in this vicinity.

Exclusive dress and fur shops are on Chestnut and Walnut Sts. between 10th and 17th, as well as on cross streets between these thoroughfares. Stores carrying select men's goods are also on Chestnut St. between 10th and 19th, and on Walnut St. east of Broad.

Some of the downtown stores have branches in sections outside the congested areas. These sections include West Philadelphia, Germantown, Kensington, and Frankford, and such suburbs as Upper Darby (69th St.), Ardmore, and Jenkintown.

The Dock St. Market is the largest wholesale produce center in Philadelphia. Prominent among the retail produce centers is the Reading Terminal Market, 12th St. between Filbert and Arch. On South and Bainbridge Sts., from 2d to 10th Sts., *schleppers*, or barkers, buttonhole the passerby in front of many stores.

On 9th St., between Christian and Wharton, is the city's colorful Italian market. Here pushcarts, filled with fish, meats, and vegetables, line the curbs on both sides of the street. The typical Jewish market is on 4th St. between South and Catharine. Here, in addition to foodstuffs, a large assortment of dry goods and wearing apparel of the cheaper grade is offered for sale. Along Marshall St. between Poplar St. and Girard Ave. is another Jewish market.

The oldest market in the city is the Second St. or "Headhouse" Market, at 2d and Pine Sts. The first section of the market house was built in 1745, the "Headhouse" in 1800. Here is carried on a flourishing trade in meats and general produce.

Climate and Clothing

Summer temperatures in Philadelphia occasionally rise above 100, but the summer mean is well below that figure. The high humidity, however, often renders the atmosphere oppressive. Garments suggested for the warm season are those of pongee, silk, linen, cotton, Palm Beach cloth, and other lightweight fabrics.

In winter, as a rule, there are fewer than 100 days with a temperature below freezing. Here again, however, the high humidity accentuates the discomfort. Zero temperatures are seldom experienced. During part of the season it is possible to get along in comfort with a light overcoat. It is advisable to be equipped with all

the accessories for winter wear, including raincoats and overshoes, since much of
the precipitation occurs in the form of rain or sleet, rather than snow. Blizzards
are rare—only once or twice in a lifetime does the average Philadelphian see
his city snowbound.

Amusements and Sports

Philadelphia is well supplied with facilities for every type of sport and amusement, both indoor and outdoor. The city's great breathing spot, Fairmount Park,
furnishes exceptional opportunities for recreation. In addition there are, in the
city and vicinity, numerous baseball fields, among them the two major-league
parks, football and other athletic stadia, golf links, tennis courts, bathing beaches,
swimming pools, a famous regatta course, gymnasiums, concert halls, auditoriums,
theatres, and night clubs.

Public Parks. Numbering nearly 150 and set here and there in the various sections of the city, these help fill the recreational needs of both children and
adults. Except for the extensive areas covered by Fairmount and the other large
parks, each occupies one or two city blocks.

The central city parks are: Rittenhouse Square, 19th and Walnut Sts.; Logan
Circle, 19th St. and the Parkway; the Parkway proper; Independence Square, 6th
and Chestnut Sts.; Washington Square, 6th and Walnut Sts.; and Franklin
Square, 6th and Race Sts.

Amusement Parks. Woodside Park, Ford Road and Monument Ave., in Fairmount Park (open June, July, and August), is the only amusement park within
the city limits. Fireworks displays are a regular Friday evening feature.

Willow Grove Park, Easton and Old York Roads, Willow Grove, (open, June,
July and August), has served as a popular amusement park for Philadelphians
for more than 40 years.

Lakeview Park, 8400 Pine Road, Fox Chase, and Penn Valley Park, Trevose,
are on the outskirts of the city.

Stadia and Other Athletic Fields. Municipal Stadium, Broad St. and Pattison
Ave. (seating capacity, 102,000), owned by the city, is one of the largest stadia
in the world. Among the sports presented here are football, baseball, track,
boxing, wrestling, midget, auto racing, bicycle racing, and soccer.

Major league baseball fields: National League, Broad and Huntingdon Sts.
(seating capacity, 18,500); American League, 21st St. and Lehigh Ave., (seating
capacity, 29,000). The latter is generally known as Shibe Park.

Franklin Field, 34th and Spruce Sts. (seating capacity, 80,000), is the outdoor
stadium of the University of Pennsylvania.

Temple University Stadium, Vernon Road and Michener St. (seating capacity,
40,000).

German-American Field, 8th St. and Tabor Road (seating capacity, 1,500), is
equipped for soccer, tennis, and trapshooting.

Yellowjackets' Field, Frankford Ave. and Devereaux St. (seating capacity,
5,000), is the scene of motorcycle and midget auto races and football games.

Indoor sports events are presented at the Arena, 4500 Market St. (seating
capacity, 6,000 to 10,000). Boxing, wrestling, and tennis matches and ice-hockey
and basketball games are presented here. At times it is turned into a public ice-
skating rink. Adjoining is an outdoor stadium (seating capacity, 9,500) in which
boxing and wrestling matches are held in warm weather.

The University of Pennsylvania Palestra, 33d and Chancellor Sts. (seating
capacity, 10,000), is equipped for basketball.

Golf Links and Tennis Courts: (See map for complete list.)

Municipal and semipublic golf courses within city limits : Karakung and

Cobbs Creek, 72d St. and Lansdowne Ave.; Holmesburg, 9500 Frankford Ave.; Juniata, M and Cayuga Sts.; and League Island, League Island Park.

In suburban sections: Baederwood at Noble; Beverly Hills at Beverly Hills; Glenside at Glenside ; Hi-Top at Drexel Hill ; Langhorne at Langhorne ; Mary Lyon and Sharpless at Swarthmore; Pennsylvania at Llanerch; Valley Forge at King of Prussia; and Wissahickon at Ft. Washington. In all of these the "pay as you play" plan is in force.

Numerous private golf courses and country clubs lie within a 25-mile radius of the center of Philadelphia. Most of these are available only to members and their guests.

Municipal and public tennis courts within city limits: Allen's Lane, 283 Rochelle Ave.; Baederwood, Old York Road, north of Hart Lane; Chamounix, Return Drive east of Ford Road; Cobbs Creek, 63d and Walnut Sts.; English Building, 52d St. and Parkside Ave.; Fisher's Park, 5th and Spencer Sts.; Garden Court, 47th and Pine Sts.; Hunting Park, 9th St. and Hunting Park Ave.; Kingsessing Recreation Center, 49th St. and Chester Ave.; League Island Park, Broad St. and Pattison Ave.; Passon, B St. and Olney Ave.; Spruce Tennis Club, 49th and Spruce Sts.; Walnut Park Plaza, 62d and Walnut Sts.; and Woodford, 33d and Dauphin Sts.

Private tennis courts are connected with colleges, country clubs, and athletic organizations, such as the Penn Athletic Club, Drexel University, Y.M.C.A., Philadelphia Country Club, Racquet Club, etc. Their use is limited to members and their guests.

Swimming Pools and Bathing Beaches. Most of the public recreation grounds have outdoor swimming pools, and virtually every sport and social club, as well as every branch of the Y.M.C.A. and Y.W.C.A., has its pool. Most of the latter are indoors. Other swimming pools to which the general public is admitted are in hotels, apartment houses, athletic fields, etc.

The city's two public bathing beaches are Pleasant Hill Park, Torresdale, on the Delaware River, and League Island Park, near the junction of the Delaware and Schuylkill Rivers. These facilities, open to all, are well policed and carefully guarded.

Concert Halls and Auditoriums. Academy of Music, Broad and Locust Sts. (seating capacity, 2,729), and the Academy of Music Foyer, in the same building, are used for musical productions and for lectures, debates, and addresses. This building is the home of the Philadelphia Orchestra and the Philadelphia Forum.

Municipal Auditorium, better known as Convention Hall, 34th St. and Vintage Ave. (seating capacity, 13,500).

Witherspoon Auditorium, Juniper and Walnut Sts. (seating capacity, 1,000).

Among the auditoriums on the University of Pennsylvania campus is Irvine Auditorium, 34th and Spruce Sts. (seating capacity, 2,127).

All the leading hotels have ballrooms which are used for amateur theatricals as well as for dancing.

Robin Hood Dell, in the heart of Fairmount Park, (seating capacity, 6,000), is an open-air amphitheatre, where both symphony and opera are presented on summer evenings.

Theatres. Philadelphia supports four legitimate theatres, although the bookings are not continuous: Forrest Theatre, Walnut and Quince Sts. (seating capacity, 2,000) ; the Erlanger Theatre, 21st and Market Sts. (seating capacity, 2,000) ; the Locust Theatre, Broad and Locust Sts. (seating capacity, 1,580) ; and the Chestnut Street Opera House, Chestnut St. between 10th and 11th (seating capacity, 1,646).

Several of Philadelphia's theatres have become landmarks. Among them are

xl

the Walnut Street Theatre, 9th and Walnut Sts. (seating capacity, 1,512), which presents Yiddish plays; the Metropolitan Opera House, Broad and Poplar Sts., (seating capacity, 3,482), which lends itself to various forms of entertainment from motion pictures to opera ; and the Academy of Music, mentioned above.

Burlesque : Bijou, 8th and Race Sts. (seating capacity, 1,400) ; Trocadero, 10th and Arch Sts. (seating capacity, 1,100) ; and Shubert, Broad St. below Locust (seating capacity, 1,700).

Negro productions: Nixon Grand, Broad St. and Montgomery Ave. (seating capacity, 3,200).

Amateur and semi-professional : Plays and Players, 1714 Delancey St. ; Alden Park Little Theatre, Chelten and Wissahickon Aves.; Students' Little Theatre, 2032 Chancellor St. ; the Germantown Theatre Guild, 4821 Germantown Ave.

Motion Pictures: There are approximately 200 motion picture houses. The largest of those in central city are the Aldine, 19th and Chestnut Sts. (seating capacity, 1,400) ; the Boyd, Chestnut St. west of 19th, (seating capacity, 2,500) ; the Fox, 16th and Market Sts. (seating capacity, 2,467) ; the Stanley, 19th and Market Sts. (seating capacity, 3,100).

Night Clubs: Philadelphia has numerous night clubs and cabarets, ranging from those having a cover charge to the less luxurious with neither cover nor minimum charge. Some of the best of the night clubs are operated in hotels and restaurants of established reputation, mostly in the central city section.

Broadcasting Stations

WCAU (1170 kw)—1622 Chestnut Street. (An affiliate of the Columbia Broadcasting System)

KYW (1020 kw)—1622 Chestnut Street.

WFIL (560 kw)—Widener Building (KYW and WFIL are affiliated with the National Broadcasting Co., Inc.)

WIP Broadcasting Station (610 kw)—35 So. 9th St. (An affiliate of the Mutual Broadcasting System)

WDAS Broadcasting Station, Inc. (1370 kw)—1211 Chestnut St.

WHAT Broadcasting Station (1310 kw)—Ledger Building

WPEN Studios (920 kw)—22d and Walnut Sts.

WTEL Studios (1310 kw)—3701 N. Broad St.

All may be visited by tourists.

ANNUAL EVENTS

Dates in many of the following events of general interest vary annually. Events lacking definite dates are either listed in the week in which they usually occur or are marked "n.f.d." (no fixed date) and take place during the month under which they are listed.

January

1	Mummers Parade, northward on Broad St.
1	Welsh Eisteddfod, auspices of First Presbyterian Church.
17	Poor Richard Celebration; Christ Church Services; Wreath on Franklin's grave; Banquet at Bellevue-Stratford Hotel.
30	Franklin D. Roosevelt's Birthday Ball, Convention Hall. (While President).
n.f.d.	Saddle Horse Association Indoor Show, 103d Cavalry Armory.

February

3d wk	National Home Show, Commercial Museum.
n.f.d.	Presentation of Bok Award for greatest service to city, Academy of Music.
n.f.d.	Chinese New Year Celebration—date depending on lunar condition—Race St. between 9th & 10th.

March

2d wk	Exhibition of works by blind, Gimbel Brothers Store.
last wk	Flower Show, Commercial Museum.
n.f.d.	Charity Horse Show, 103d Cavalry Armory.
n.f.d.	Motorboat and Sportsmen's Show, Commercial Museum.

April

last wk	Penn Relay Carnival, Franklin Field. (Last Friday and Saturday).
Easter	Sunrise Services, Reyburn Plaza, Franklin Field, and Temple Stadium.

May

30	Launching of ship of flowers on the Delaware in memory of deceased naval veterans, Race St. Pier.
1st wk	Boys Week, ending Saturday with parade on the Parkway to Independence Hall via Chestnut St.
2d wk	Dewey Day Celebration at Navy Yard.
2d wk	Folklore Festival, Academy of Music.
2d wk	Philadelphia on Parade, Convention Hall.
3d wk	Flower Mart, Rittenhouse Square.
3d wk	Germantown May Market, Vernon Park.
n.f.d.	Hobby League, Annual Show and Exhibition, Franklin Institute. (Usually held early in May, but some years in latter part of April).

xlii

June

14	Flag Day Celebration, Betsy Ross House.
1st wk	Field Mass for Police and Firemen, Logan Circle.
1st wk	Clothes Line Art Exhibit, Rittenhouse Square.
1st wk	Wissahickon Day, Riders and Drivers Meet, Wissahickon Farms.
2d wk	Historical Pageant and Fete at Old Swedes' (Gloria Dei) Church.
last wk	Opening of Robin Hood Dell concert season, Fairmount Park.

July

4	Celebration in Independence Square.
4	People's Regatta on the Schuylkill River.
4	Clan-na-Gael Athletic Games, Northeast High School Field.

September

6	Lafayette Day, observed at Independence Hall.
1st wk	Constatter Volkfest Verein. (German Celebration held Labor Day and following Tuesday), Philadelphia Rifle Club.

October

12	Columbus Day Celebration at monument in Fairmount Park.
27	Navy Day, open house at Navy Yard.
1st wk	Electrical and Radio Show, Convention Hall.
2d wk	Opening of Philadelphia Orchestra concert season, Academy of Music.
n.f.d.	Food Fair and Better Homes Exposition at Commercial Museum.
n.f.d.	Opening of Philadelphia Forum season, Academy of Music.

November

1-2	Kennel Club dog show, Convention Hall.
2d wk	Automobile show, Convention Hall.
last wk	Thanksgiving Day Gimbel Toyland Parade (morning). Penn-Cornell Football Game (afternoon).
last wk	Army-Navy Football Game, Municipal Stadium. (Schedule for Philadelphia from 1936 to 1938. Takes place Saturday following Thanksgiving Day.

December

24	Christmas Ball, Bellevue-Stratford Hotel.
24	Christmas Eve carol singing, Reyburn Plaza.
31	Sounding of Liberty Bell, Independence Hall.
n.f.d.	Assembly Ball, Bellevue-Stratford Hotel. (Held 1st or 2d Friday).
n.f.d.	Charity Ball, Bellevue-Stratford Hotel. (Some years held late in Nov.).

POINTS OF SPECIAL INTEREST

Its position as a center of many of the cultural fields enables Philadelphia to offer, from its wealth of sight-seeing treasures, an array of places of special interest to the visitor. Reference to the index will guide the reader to more complete information on the places included in the following lists :

HISTORIC BUILDINGS
>   Carpenters' Hall, Chestnut St., east of 4th.
>   Christ Church, 2d St., north of Market.
>   Independence Hall, Independence Square, 6th and Chestnut Sts.
>   Old Swedes' Church, Swanson St., south of Christian.
>   William Penn (Letitia Street) House, Fairmount Park, west of
>   Girard Ave. Bridge.
>   Betsy Ross House, 239 Arch St.

HISTORICAL COLLECTIONS
>   American Philosophical Society, 5th and Chestnut Sts.
>   Historical Society of Pennsylvania, 13th and Locust Sts.
>   Independence Hall, Independence Square, 6th and Chestnut Sts.
>   Library Company of Philadelphia, Juniper and Locust Sts.

PERMANENT ART COLLECTIONS
>   Free Library of Philadelphia, 19th St. and the Parkway.
>   Graphic Sketch Club, 711-19 Catharine St.
>   La France Art Museum, 4420 Paul St., Frankford.
>   Memorial Hall, Parkside Ave. at 43d St.
>   Pennsylvania Academy of the Fine Arts, Broad and Cherry Sts.
>   Pennsylvania Museum of Art, 25th St. and the Parkway.
>   Rodin Museum, 22d St. and the Parkway.

SCIENTIFIC COLLECTIONS
>   Academy of Natural Sciences, 19th St. and the Parkway.
>   Franklin Institute Museum and Fels Planetarium, 20th St. and
>   the Parkway.
>   Wagner Free Institute of Science Museum, 17th St. and Montgomery Ave.
>   Wistar Institute of Anatomy and Biology, 36th St. and Woodland
>   Ave.

xliv

LITERARY

Edgar Allan Poe House, 530 N. 7th St.
Free Library of Philadelphia, 19th St. and the Parkway
Historical Society of Pennsylvania, 13th and Locust Sts.
Leary's Book Store, 9 S. 9th St.
Library of University of Pennsylvania, 34th St., north of Spruce.
Mercantile Library of Philadelphia, 14 S. 10th St.
Sullivan Memorial Library, Park Ave. and Berks St.

BOTANICAL

Awbury Arboretum, Washington Lane and Chew St.
Bartram's Gardens, 54th St. and Eastwick Ave.
Botanical Gardens of University of Pennsylvania, South St., west
of Schuylkill River.
Fairmount Park.
Herbarium of Academy of Natural Sciences, 19th St. and the
Parkway.
Horticultural Hall, Fairmount Park at 44th St. and Parkside Ave.
Morris Arboretum, Meadowbrook Lane and Stenton Ave.
Woodward Estate, Mermaid Lane and McCallum St.

RELIGIOUS

Cathedral of SS. Peter and Paul, 18th St. and the Parkway.
Church of the Brethren, 6613 Germantown Ave.
Friends Arch Street Meeting House (Orthodox), 4th and Arch
Sts.
Old Pine Street Presbyterian Church, 4th and Pine Sts.
Rodeph Shalom Synagogue, Broad and Mount Vernon Sts.

St. George's Methodist Episcopal Church, 4th St., above Race.
St. Joseph's R. C. Church, Willing's Alley (between 3d and 4th
Sts., south of Walnut).
Race Street Meeting House (Hicksite), S. W. Cor. 15th and Race
Sts.
First Church of Christ (Scientist), 4012 Walnut St.
Holy Trinity Episcopal Church, S. W. Cor. 19th and Walnut Sts.
Grace Baptist Temple, S. E. Cor. Broad and Berks Sts.
Swedenborgian Church (Church of the New Jerusalem), N. E.
Cor. 22nd and Chestnut Sts.

MUSIC

Academy of Music, Broad and Locust Sts.
Curtis Institute of Music, 18th and Locust Sts.
Robin Hood Dell, Fairmount Park, west of Ridge Ave. and Huntingdon St.
Settlement Music School, 416 Queen St.

ART CLUBS

Art Alliance, 251 S. 18th St.
Art Club of Philadelphia, 220 S. Broad St.
Philadelphia Sketch Club, 235 S. Camac St.
Plastic Club, 247 S. Camac St.
Print Club, 1614 Latimer St.
Graphic Sketch Club, 719 Catharine St.

COMMERCIAL ART GALLERIES

Boyer Galleries, Broad St. Suburban Station Building, 16th St.
and Pennsylvania Blvd.
Gimbel Galleries, Gimbel Store, 9th and Chestnut Sts.
Modern Galleries, 1720 Chestnut St.
Newman Galleries, 1625 Walnut St.
Rosenbach Galleries, 1320 Walnut St.

BURIAL GROUNDS

Christ Church Burial Ground, 5th and Arch Sts. (Grave of Benja-
min Franklin).
Portuguese Hebrew Burial Grounds, Spruce Street, east of Ninth.
(Grave of Rebecca Gratz).

STATUES AND MEMORIALS

Benjamin Franklin Statue, 9th and Chestnut Sts.
Catholic Total Abstinence Union Fountain, Fairmount Park near
52d St. and Parkside Ave.
Christopher Columbus Statute, Belmont and Parkside Aves.
Cowboy Monument (Frederic Remington), East River Drive
above Girard Ave. Bridge.
Equestrian Statue of Gen. U. S. Grant, East River Drive, Fair-
mount Park.
Equestrian Statues of Generals McClellan, Reynolds, and Meade,
north plaza of City Hall.
Joan of Arc Statue, Fairmount Park near 31st St. and Girard
Ave.
Lincoln Monument, Lemon Hill, Fairmount Park.
Robert Morris Statue, Chestnut St., between 4th and 5th Sts.
Smith Memorial, Fairmount Park near 42d St. and Parkside Ave.
Washington Monument, 25th St. and the Parkway.
Washington Statue, Chestnut St. between 5th and 6th Sts.
William Penn Statue, atop City Hall.

Seal of Philadelphia
"Let Brotherly Love Continue"

The
CITY
and its
BACKGROUND

Liberty Bell
"Ring out for Liberty"

PORTRAIT OF PHILADELPHIA

P HILADELPHIA through the countless changes of the past two hundred and fifty years has retained something of the rhythm and color of its pioneer days and some of the spirit and intentions of its founder. While it lacks a certain sophistication common in the larger American cities, yet beneath its surface calm throbs a pulse of activity peculiarly Philadephian. Despite its air of provincialism, the City of Penn claims justly a record of solid accomplishments not only in the arts and sciences, but in industry and commerce.

Actually, Philadelphia is neither "slow" nor quiet. Against the bronze statue of William Penn atop City Hall beat the sound waves of a million-tongued titan ; alien accents and the stridency of the Machine mingling with the gentler tones of an older day. (Gone is the "Greene Countrie Towne" established among the tall pines two and one-half centuries ago; the alchemy of progress has transmuted it into a great industrial city, and the ferment of commerce has altered its face.) Its voice is the voice of a city of contrasts— a city of wealth and poverty, of turmoil and tranquillity, of stern laws often mitigated by mild enforcement ; a city proud of its world-molding past and sometimes slow to heed the promptings of modern thought.

Its Colonial primacy, which the Republic's growth has long since annulled, has set it apart, in some respects, from its American sisters. But, like many other centers of conservatism, Philadelphia during the 1930's has given evidence of a better understanding of the place it should occupy in the national scene.

Although it wears with somber dignity the halo of great age, it was only yesterday that its colonization ceased, and time began to amalgamate the many nationalities composing its citizenry. Thus it bears the stamp in greater or less degree of a polyglot humanity —the sedate Quaker; the Swede, touched by mysticism; the thrifty and methodical German; the imperturbable Englishman; the Celt, excitable, idealistic; the energetic and vivid Jew; the underprivileged Negro ; the mercurial Italian ; and the fatalistic Slav.

Except for its tree-shaded squares and parks, Penn could not have envisioned the present municipality, with its 129 square miles en-

3

compassing a far-flung checkerboard of streets—thoroughfares crowded with raucous traffic and flanked by solid rows of buildings. With one exception, Penn's open squares are preserved in the city's heart just as he laid them out.

A spirit of reserve has become proverbially characteristic of the city and its people. Philadelphia is hesitant in proclaiming the efficiency of its soundly welded commercial and industrial mechanism. Sanctuary of artist and scientist though it is, it makes no vulgar display of the refinements of cultural and scientific preeminence which clothe it with traditions reminiscent of Old World capitals.

Nucleus of a "holy experiment" in colonization, it was dearly loved by the early settlers, and that love endures among its people today. Though ranking among the great cities of America, there survives beneath its urbanity more than a trace of provincialism. Like most American centers of population, its growth has been the result of consolidation. Made up of a number of communities, it is essentially a city of *faubourgs* combined with Penn's original town under a dual city and county government. Today, despite mass transportation, mass schooling, and mass thought, these sections retain many of the mannerisms, local loyalties, and physical idiosyncrasies inherited from the Quaker, Swede, and German communities of early days. Districts such as Frankford, Kensington, Nicetown, Roxborough, Manayunk, Germantown, and West Philadelphia—independent in local government until the Act of Consolidation of 1854— have their own newspapers, community interests, shopping centers, and Main Streets.

The staid manner of the early Quakers has left its impress on the city's character and has perhaps been responsible for the long preservation of such anachronistic statutes as the Sunday Blue Laws of 1794. Some of these laws were repealed in 1935. Although the Quaker element in general has abandoned its traditional sedateness for more modern modes and manners, there are many Friends who still observe quaint amenities of the past in the intimacy of their homes, *thee*-ing and *thou*-ing one another as in the days of Penn.

Philadelphia's broad expanse rests upon lands generally flat or rolling, except where the Wissahickon and Fairmount hills or the Chestnut Hill and the Manayunk elevations break the terrain. To the stranger it may seem peculiar that, in a city with so much room, the houses crouch side by side in rows; and that in congested areas where space is scarce there are notably few skyscrapers. The reason for the prevailing "row house" may have its root in the provincialism of the city, but skyscrapers are few for a reason obviously economic—there is no great demand for them.

Until comparatively recent years the city's low horizon was broken only by the looming tower of City Hall. This building is still the

4

city's highest, but now its eminence is challenged by newer giants nearby—in particular, the ultra-modern Philadelphia Saving Fund Society building, two blocks eastward. Nearby to the northwestward, where in former years sprawled an ugly *mélange* of dilapidated dwellings, rise stately temples of art and science which overlook the landscaped Parkway and lend grace and dignity to the central city.

Also pleasing to the eye are such remote portions of the city as Germantown, Chestnut Hill, Overbrook, and Oak Lane. These are residential sections where imposing homes, spacious lawns, and a multiplicity of trees provide the dominant scene. Even the row houses here have individuality. The traditional red brick often gives way to stucco and field stone, and variations in design break the monotony of constant repetition.

In its multiplex building design, Philadelphia presents another facet of its paradoxical make-up. Within and around it is preserved a heritage of fine Colonial architecture in brick and stone, perhaps unsurpassed by that of any other city in the Nation. To the first structures, built by the Swedes, have been added buildings by Welshmen, Englishmen, and later craftsmen of various nationalities.

A short walk in older sections of Penn's "Towne" reveals a wealth of historic buildings — public, ecclesiastical, and domestic — and quaint back streets and courts. The many well-designed doorways, dormer windows, iron handrails, foot scrapers, and fire plaques make a stroll through these streets an interesting adventure. Interspersed with pre-Revolutionary structures are public buildings of the early Republic and the grotesque architecture of the late nineteenth century. The twentieth century, too, has thrust its bulk and ultra-modernism upon the city, without effacing the Philadelphia of yesteryear. Though the shadow of skyscrapers may fall across such hallowed shrines as Independence Hall and Christ Church, the heavy hand of commerce leaves them unscathed.

But Philadelphia has its "tenderloin" and its slums. The former finds its fullest expression in the region bordering Eighth Street north of Arch, where for several blocks it basks in the tawdry glory of brash neon signs and burlesque posters. Cheap restaurants and hot-dog stands fill the air with odors that mingle with the reek of alcohol. the stench of uncollected garbage, and the smell of humanity unwashed. Here, in this section of flophouses, shooting galleries, missions, and bawdy houses, live and circulate the least prepossessing of Philadelphia's citizenry.

Even more odious are the city's slums. Two areas especially poisonous have their eastern extremities along the Delaware River: one bounded, approximately, on the south by Race Street, on the west by Fifth, and on the north by Girard Avenue; the other embraced in the area between Christian Street on the south and Lombard

5

on the north, with its western limit near Eighth Street. These are neighborhoods of the bandbox house and the vermin-infested hovel. Here man's need for shelter has been exploited to the utmost. It is only fair to add that preliminary steps have been taken to eliminate not only these slum sections, but also others scattered in various parts of the city.

Viewed from an airplane, central Philadelphia presents an orderly pattern of squares laid within the angles formed by two coordinate axes: Broad Street and Market Street. The former, reputedly the longest straight intracity thoroughfare in the world, forms the north-to-south axis; the latter, the east-to-west. Diagonal avenues, many following across the city the course of Colonial highways, occasionally modify the geometrical rigidity of these squares.

If the plane approaches from the west, Fairmount Park's wooded hills and glens appear as a small wilderness entrapped, but unravaged, by the encircling tentacles of municipal and suburban development. From the southernmost limit of its green depths, the broad, tree-lined Parkway sweeps majestically toward City Hall, which stands directly upon what would be the intersection of Broad and Market Streets.

The mammoth Thirtieth Street Station of the Pennsylvania Railroad and the new Post Office building can be picked out readily from above, standing as they do on the west bank of the Schuylkill River — a stream silvery in Penn's time, but now blackened and polluted by the waste of factories. The railroad tracks leap across the river to parallel Market Street, flanking the northern side of the Market Street axis with a gigantic welt of masonry and steel. This elevated right-of-way, or "Chinese Wall" as it is locally termed, has long been considered a civic nuisance.

Not far south of the wall stand ancient dwellings, once the homes of Philadelphia's old families. The old families have long since departed, and many of the homes have become rooming houses or taprooms. Nearby are the luxurious apartment hotels of Rittenhouse Square and the age-mellowed dwellings of Delancey Street — last strongholds of that old aristocracy most of whose members have retreated to the suburbs, leaving a diminishing rear guard to stem the tide of change.

A point directly over City Hall offers the best view of the blocks of squares spreading in every direction — big blocks, for Penn intended that each householder should have sufficient space for a garden plot. There are few such plots now; all available footage has been given over to solid ranks of houses, one row backed up against another in shameless intimacy.

Farther eastward, beyond the Philadelphia Saving Fund Society skyscraper, the skyline undulates to the water front, where the city ends abruptly in a region of piers, wharves, and warehouses. Here, on the Delaware River's west bank and stretching for miles to north and south, lies the only large fresh-water port on the Atlantic seaboard — a port which, though 88 miles from the Delaware capes, ranks among the world's greatest shipping terminals in point of cargo tonnage as well as in wharfage facilities.

Stretching across the river is one of the world's largest suspension bridges — the Delaware River Bridge, linking Philadelphia with Camden, N. J. Beneath its span move tug and barge in endless procession ; in its shadow huge freighters are constantly loading and unloading cargoes consigned to or brought from every corner of the globe.

Southward lies a virtual honeycomb of homes. Block after block of houses extend to the brink of the Delaware River, to within a mile and a half of the Philadelphia Navy Yard and to the gigantic oil refineries that have added to Philadelphia's economic worth at the expense of its fragrance.

Immediately south of the business district is the second largest Negro section, a patchwork made up of bits of Memphis, Birmingham, and New Orleans transplanted to Philadelphia. Here are the laborers and the children of laborers, imported principally by the politico-contractor firms.

Philadelphia's "Little Italy" stretches south from the Negro section to the oil-suffused flats of the Delaware near the Navy Yard. This district, thoroughly alive, teems with humanity; reflecting struggle, emotion, and Latin intrigue. Provalone cheeses dangle in store windows, sloe-eyed sons of Sicily and Calabria loiter on corners, and the musty odor of red wine predominates.

Delaware River Bridge

7

South of Oregon Avenue and a bit west, the marshes that fringe the Delaware are dotted with huge silvery tanks. Here and there cabins and the frame shacks of produce farmers appear, but the rustic cry of the rooster is lost in the mournful blasts of foghorns as oil tankers move into their slips in the Delaware or the lower Schuylkill.

Considering facets which, even though intangible, are important in a summation of the city's character, Philadelphia is figuratively two cities. One is the sprawling municipality of two million persons living and working compactly within the corporate limits. The other is the "city" of a half million which does its work within Philadelphia, but lives its private life on the exclusive Main Line or in other suburbs. Each morning by train, motorcar, bus and trolley the half million descend upon the city to assume their duties in its offices and mills and factories, until evening speeds them homeward.

Among these half-million commuters are most of those who hold social and commercial hegemony over Philadelphia — members of old families who regard themselves as the real Philadelphians. They are the holders of the city's vested trusts, members of its exclusive Assembly ; and of such organizations as the Racquet Club and the Union League — the latter a political stronghold, where tenets of the Republican party have been entrenched since the Civil War. They govern the city's banks and its insurance companies, and establish the financial policies of its industries.

Endowed with inherited wealth and traditional conservatism, most of them are reluctant to change. Under their guidance, until recently, the average citizen remained quiescent; with few exceptions labor troubles were of little consequence, despite the city's heritage in unionism, and radical economic philosophies made no appreciable headway. Much of this apathy may have been due to the fact that Philadelphia, prior to the Wall Street panic of 1929, had an average of owner-occupied homes reaching 50 per cent or higher. It is significant that when many of those homes were forfeited by foreclosures, chiefly because of the collapse of building and loan associations, the yeast of change began to ferment. In the political and economical mutations of the current decade, moreover, there permeated through every strata of society the realization that the right of the worker to a job is an essential factor in the economic well-being of the nation.

Locally known as the "City of Homes" and the "Workshop of the World," Philadelphia is both of these within certain limitations. The former designation has lost much of its appropriateness since the social cataclysm of the early 1930's, when thousands of homeowners, bereft of their property, had to rent apartments or portions of single dwellings. With the easing of the economic tension, some of these again began to acquire homes for themselves, but the majority have

8

demonstrated their ability to live contentedly in apartments or rented dwellings.

The city's reputation as a world's workshop has continued up to the present materially undamaged. Philadelphia has fulfilled the economic destiny prescribed for it by its geographical position close to nature's storehouses of ores and fuel, and linked to them by ample facilities for rail and water transportation. Within its boundaries are contained thousands of factories engaged in scores of different industries. While its industrial activities are centered in no particular section, the northeast region, embracing Kensington, Frankford, and Tacony, has the most diversified manufactures and the greatest number of plants in operation. This is the country's leading district for textiles and the home of the largest saw-making plant in existence. Other famous Philadelphia-made products are radio reception units, hats, streetcars, automobile bodies, cigars, and carpets. The value of its industrial output is approximately a billion dollars annually.

Since the days of Benjamin Franklin, David Rittenhouse, James Logan, and Benjamin West, Philadelphia has maintained a high position in the world of culture and learning. Although such a skyscraper institution as Temple University is symptomatic of the intrusion of modern influences upon the city's ancient dignity, this college has become as much a part of educational Philadelphia as has a much older institution, the famed University of Pennsylvania. The city of Penn may cherish the old, but it does not shun the new. Thus there are century-old banks, hospitals, colleges, manufactories, clubs, hotels, and libraries standing side by side with those of recent origin. Forces ancient and modern, along with those transitional influences which link the new and the old in Philadelphia, impart to the city an atmosphere distinctly its own, and place their indelible imprint upon the living mosaic of its people.

Thousands of its residents have never seen the Liberty Bell ; many thousands have never attended a concert of the world-famous Philadelphia Orchestra. Naturally, only a small percentage of the city's population is represented in the student bodies of its art academies, music schools, and other institutions of specialized or general instruction. But these cultural and historic institutions, whether or not they are of traditional prominence in their various realms, give to the Philadelphian a complacent pride which outsiders often misinterpret as deliberate snobbery.

The city can be seen in its most rollicking aspect on New Year's Day, when King Momus and his court rule Broad Street, filling the wide thoroughfare with joyous nonsense. It can be seen in its quietest hours from two to five every morning, when even downtown streets are virtually deserted. After seven and up to nine in the morning, and from five until seven in the evening the central area is a bedlam

9

of clanging trolleys, rumbling busses, snarling motorcars, and hurrying throngs.

Commuters and shoppers from outlying districts and suburbs entrain at Reading Terminal or the Pennsylvania Railroad stations, or take subway or elevated line leading west to 69th Street, north to Olney, northeast to Frankford, or east across the Delaware River Bridge to Camden. Out the broad Parkway from City Hall flows a river of automobiles, halting at regular intervals before the commanding glare of intersection lights.

By 7:30 there is a lull in the central city as the sphere of activity shifts to the home. Though in any large community the suspension of traffic at this hour is noticeable, in Philadelphia the dinner hour quietude is as definite a demarcation between the day's work and the evening's recreation as twilight is between sunshine and darkness.

To many Philadelphians the evening's entertainment may include a "show" at one of the few remaining theaters, a film at one of the numerous movie palaces, or perhaps an athletic contest at one of the sports centers. Others may attend a concert or a lecture at the Academy of Music, while another element inevitably gravitates toward taproom or night club. But the greater number of Philadelphians will remain at their hearths. From countless rows of houses, standing in block-long anonymity against the blackness of night, will come in imperishable steadfastness the soft, warm lights of home, and the gentle tumult of children being marshaled for bed. On the morrow the city will arise to cope anew with its current problems; it will turn an inquiring face to the future, even while looking back in memory to the misted glory of its yesterdays.

Christ Church Tower
"Whose bells rang on market day"

10

NATURE'S HANDIWORK

Topography

P HILADELPHIA and its suburbs comprise an area unusual in the variety of its landscape. The region lies in parts of three distinct physiographic provinces — tracts of country in which geographic and topographic features derive from definitely different geological conditions. These three provinces, which form the borderlands of the Philadelphia area, are known scientifically as the Atlantic Coastal Plain, the Piedmont Plateau, and the Triassic Lowland.

Philadelphia County, coextensive with the city, forms an area of 129.714 square miles. The entire Philadelphia district, geologically, comprises 915.285 square miles, extending approximately 34.50 miles from north to south and 26.53 miles from east to west.

The county itself is bounded on the south by Bow Creek, Back Channel, Delaware County line, and the Delaware River ; on the east by the Delaware River and Poquessing Creek ; on the north by Poquessing Creek, the Montgomery County line, the Philadelphia, Newtown & New York Railroad (a branch of the Reading Co.), Cheltenham Avenue, Cresheim Avenue, Stenton Avenue, and Northwestern Avenue ; on the west by the Schuylkill River, City Line Avenue, and Cobbs Creek.

The Coastal Plain, within which the southeastern corner of the county lies, consists of a raised section of sea deposits, covered in part by subsequent erosion products brought down largely by the Delaware and Schuylkill Rivers from higher land nearby, and in part by "glacial outwashes," glacial clay, and sands washed down from the region north of Easton.

The process by which the Coastal Plain originated causes the Philadelphia area to be flat, with a gentle rise eastward from the Schuylkill, and a gradual decline southward to the Delaware. The formations in this area are composed of sands, clays, and gravels, with subterranean watercourses here and there which form quicksands.

The Piedmont Plateau, a higher elevation, underlies the major part of the Philadelphia area. The rock formations of this area, very ancient geologically, appear along the East River Drive in Fairmount Park, along Wissahickon Creek, and in the Germantown and Chestnut Hill sections.

11

The rock structure of the Triassic Lowland is scientifically the least revealing within the Philadelphia area. It lies to the north of Whitemarsh Valley, and includes the wide region of flat and rolling country extending northeast and west from Fort Washington, Norristown, and the Trenton cutoff of the Pennsylvania Railroad, running as far as the Reading Hills and even extending into Lancaster County. The Triassic Lowland includes a great part of Bucks, Montgomery, Lancaster, Chester, and Delaware Counties.

Rivers : Two major streams, the Delaware and Schuylkill Rivers, form a junction at the southernmost extremity of Philadelphia. The former skirts the city on the east ; the latter takes a southerly course through the city before flowing into the larger stream.

The Delaware River, from its source to the point where it flows into Delaware Bay, is 410 miles long, and drains an area of 12,012 square miles. It is navigable by ocean steamers as far as Trenton, the tidal limit, 130 miles from the Delaware capes. For approximately 35 miles the Delaware flows through the Philadelphia area. The stream is subject to seasonal fluctuations in volume.

The Schuylkill, approximately 100 miles long, has a drainage area of 1,915 square miles. With headwaters in the anthracite belt of Schuylkill County, it flows across the Triassic Lowland and the Piedmont Plateau. Its chief tributaries are the Perkiomen and Wissahickon Creeks.

The divide separating the basins of the Delaware and Schuylkill Rivers in the southwest is marked in general by the route of the western division of the Pennsylvania Railroad. In this southern region, the Delaware watershed is drained by Cobbs, Darby, Crum, Ridley, and Chester Creeks, which empty into the Delaware River ; and the Brandywine, Red Clay, and White Clay Creeks, which empty into the Christiana River, a tributary of the Delaware. On the divide between the Schuylkill and Delaware basins on the northeast are Germantown and Chestnut Hill. In this section the watershed is drained by Pennypack, Tacony, Poquessing, Neshaminy, Mill, Common, Durham, Brock, and Pidcock Creeks.

Flora

PHILADELPHIA'S flora differs little from that of other large cities in the East. However, the city's progress in the field of experimental horticulture is noteworthy. This experimentation was begun by pioneer settlers in the district. Members of the Penn family, in fact, brought to the New World saplings of cherished trees, shoots of cultivated plants, and many types of shrubs and flowers.

By far the greatest of early horticulturists was John Bartram. Not satisfied to confine his researches to his home area, Bartram roved from Canada to Florida, obtaining an inclusive collection of American plants for the botanical gardens of Colonial Philadelphia, and for shipment to England. Many of the trees he planted before the Revolutionary War still stand.

The horticultural halls and greenhouses of Philadelphia contain a myriad of trees, plants and shrubs, and the naturalist finds the flora of Fairmount Park most interesting. Trees comparatively rare may be found throughout the city's park system. These include the transplanted balsam fir, red spruce, Chinese juniper, and Chinese elm, and the native shagbark hickory and sweet gum. Poisonous plants found in the section are poison ivy and poison sumach.

Among the more common American trees growing in the Philadelphia district are the red or soft maple, a tree that graces the banks of streams or marshes ; the flowering dogwood ; the white ash ; the black oak ; the white oak ; and the beech.

Common locally are the black locust, the wood of which is valuable for shipbuilding and lathe work ; the American plum, a small tree productive of delicious fruit ; the wild cherry ; the black or sour gum ; the black ash ; the green ash ; the hackberry, and the red mulberry.

Other trees familiar in the area include the sycamore or buttonwood ; the black walnut ; the butternut ; the mockernut hickory ; the shellbark hickory ; the red birch ; the sweet or black birch ; the hop-hornbeam or ironwood ; the linden, and the sugar or hard maple.

In the glades and woods of the area are found the blue-water beech ; the large-toothed poplar ; the hemlock spruce, and the red cedar.

Members of Philadelphia's arboreal family more rarely encountered in or near the city include the tulip tree ; the papaw, a small tree found in the rich bottom lands ; the horse chestnut, originally a native of southern Asia but long since naturalized as a shade tree ; the box elder, or ash-leaved maple, a tree that occasionally beautifies the banks of streams and lakes in the area, and the white pine.

According to tree census figures for 1937, Philadelphia contains more trees than any other city in the world. Reports of the Fairmount Park Commission show that there are 157,773 trees on the city streets, and approximately 500,000 in Fairmount Park, and a million in the various other parks throughout the city.

Some curious kinds of plants may be found in certain sections of Philadelphia. Some are indigenous, others have been transplanted from foreign countries and various parts of the United States. The common dodder's or love vine has small white flowers ; a parasite, it feeds on the herbs and shrubs to which it clings. The ghost plant, usually found under pine or oak trees, takes its nourishment from the roots of other plants. The compass plant, a foreign species, re-

13

ceives its name from the fact that some of the leaves point north, others south, enabling the lost traveler to reestablish his position. The mad dog skullcap, found in shaded, wet places, was once considered a cure for rabid dogs ; this plant belongs to the mint family, and has blue flowers and a smooth stem.

The indigenous skunk cabbage, known to the early Swedish settlers in the Philadelphia section as "bear weed," is among the first harbingers of spring. It has a thick rootstalk and a cluster of large veiny leaves. It is a perennial herb, with an unpleasant odor. Brightening sandy spots of suburban Philadelphia is the butterfly weed, so named because of its gaily colored flowers. The flowers are brilliant orange and borne in dense clusters.

Fauna

DURING the migratory season, many transient birds visit southeastern Pennsylvania. Among the winter birds are the song, tree, and English sparrows; starling, winter wren, slate-colored snowbird, white-throated cardinal, tufted titmouse, red and white-winged crossbills, pine finch and gold finch, herring gull, titlark, brown creeper, and golden-crowned kinglet. Birds of prey include the redtailed, sharp-shinned and sparrow hawks ; the snowy owl, and the long-eared, short-eared and saw-whet owls.

With the arrival of spring, Philadelphia's bird kingdom is well established. Crows fill the moist, warm air with raucous cries, snowbirds and tree sparrows linger in the fields, the fox-colored sparrow appears, cedar birds perch on the branches of red cedars, and the melody of song sparrows vies with the hammered tattoo of the woodpeckers. Other visitors are the robin, bluebird, house wren, dove, red-winged blackbird, and purple grackle. The crow, quail, horned owl, downy woodpecker, screech owl, barn owl, and cedar bird are found here through the year.

The European starling, now common to many Atlantic coastal cities, where it nests in the niches of public buildings, first appeared in Philadelphia in 1904. According to ornithologists, the starling now outnumbers even the English sparrow in the city and suburbs.

The starling has "taken over" many of Philadelphia's central city commercial buildings and many public buildings on the Parkway. In the autumn countless flocks nightly perch in the eaves of the Art Museum and the Public Library, to the annoyance of custodians. Attempts to discourage this pest by firing roman candles at their roosting places have resulted in only temporary relief.

With so much of the wildwood atmosphere still preserved, Philadelphia has its share of bats, squirrels, chipmunks, rabbits, weasels, and the smaller rodents, such as the meadow mouse and the white-footed deer mouse. The raccoon and opossum are now rarely found, but are still encountered in the deeper rural sections of this district.

Scene in Fairmount Park
"Sylvan glades and purling streams"

THE FIRST INHABITANTS

THE first men known to occupy what is now Philadelphia were Indians of the Lenni-Lenape tribes. The Lenni-Lenape, whom the English later named the Delawares, were one of the more important nations inhabiting the eastern regions when Europeans first arrived. They belonged to the great Algonkian linguistic stock and, according to their own legends, had migrated eastward from the country beyond the Mississippi.

The Lenni-Lenape nation was divided into three main tribal groups — the Munsee, Unami, and Unalachtigo. Philadelphia history is concerned chiefly with the Unami (or "Turtle") tribe of Lenape, though the Susquehannocks and Shawnees (the former of Iroquoian stock, the latter of Central Algonkian) figured in the city's early history.

Penn's land treaties were negotiated with the Unami, who occupied both sides of the Delaware from the mouth of the Lehigh River to what is now New Castle, Del. Their main village or capital, Shackamaxon, (Ind., *place of eels)* is generally supposed to have been the scene of the famous treaty conference held by William Penn on the west bank of the Delaware in the autumn of 1682. The village site, now part of Philadelphia, is known as Penn Treaty Park, and one of the streets in the vicinity bears the name "Shackamaxon."

Many other sections of the city retain names given them by the Indians. Some of the more picturesque are Manayunk, "where we go to drink"; Wissahickon, "yellow stream" or "catfish stream"; Passyunk, "in the valley"; and Wingohocking, "a favorite spot for planting." Others are Kingsessing, "bog meadow" or "the place where there is a meadow"; Pennypack, "still water"; Tacony, "wood or uninhabited place"; Tioga, "at the forks"; Tulpehocken, "the land of turtles"; and Wissinoming, or Wissinaming, "where we were frightened" or "a place where grapes grow." The area embraced in Philadelphia was called Coaquannock, or "grove of tall pines."

The Unamis had large heads and faces, and their noses were sharply hooked. Mainly a sedentary and agricultural people, they lived on maize, fish, and game. Men of the tribe dressed in breech clout, leggings, and moccasins, with skin mantle or blanket thrown over one shoulder. Their heads were shaved or clipped, except for a scalp lock generously pomaded with bear's grease and bedecked with ornaments. The women garbed themselves in leather shirt or bodice,

16

with skirt of the same material. They wore their hair plaited, the long tails falling over their shoulders.

Before the advent of Dutch and Swede upon the Philadelphia scene, the Indians lived in lodges of birch bark. The more sturdy log hut of later date probably was copied from the whites, although Iroquoian peoples lived in log dwellings prior to white contact.

Not long before Penn arrived in the New World, a group of Shawnees had migrated northward into Pennsylvania, some of them locating for a time on the flats below Philadelphia. The Susquehannocks from Maryland, known as "Black Minquas" to the Swedes, had preceded them and were well known to the early settlers.

After a brief sojourn in the vicinity, the Shawnees moved northward to the Wyoming Valley, and thence to western Pennsylvania and Ohio. The Susquehannocks, waging bitter warfare with the Iroquois Confederacy, were driven from their Pennsylvania strongholds early in the period of white colonization.

Probably no more intimate picture of the Indian living in and near Philadelphia can be given than that of William Penn to the Free Society of Traders in his letter of 1683. Penn wrote :

For their persons, they are generally tall, straight, well built, and of singular Proportion. They tread strong and clever, and mostly walk with a lofty Chin. Of complexion Black, but by design, as the Gipsies in England. They grease themselves with Bear's fat clarified ; and using no defence against sun or weather, their skins must needs be swarthy. Their eye is little and black, not unlike a straight-look't Jew. The thick Lip and flat Nose, so frequent with the East Indians and Blacks, are not common to them ; for I have seen as comely European-like faces among them, of both sexes, as on your side of the Sea. And truly an Italian Complexion hath not much more of the White ; and the Noses of several of them have as much of the Roman. Their Language is lofty, yet narrow ; but like the Hebrew in signification, full. Like short-hand in writing, one word serveth in the place of three, and the rest are supplied by the Understanding of the Hearer ; Imperfect in their Tenses, wanting in their Moods, Participles, Adverbs, Conjunctions and Interjections. I have made it my business to understand it that I might not want an Interpreter on any occasion, and I must say that I know not of a language spoken in Europe that hath words of more sweetness or greatness, in Accent and Emphasis than theirs ; For instance, Octokekon, Rancocas, Oricton, Shak, Marian, Poquesian, all of which are names of places, and have grandeur in them — Sepassen, Passijon, the names of places; Tamane, Secane, Menanse and Secatareus, are the names of persons.

If an European comes to see them, or calls for Lodgings at their House or Wigwam, they give him the best place, and first cut. If they come to visit us they salute us with an *Itah!* which is as much as to say, "Good be to you !" and set them down, which is mostly on the ground, close to their heels, their legs upright ; it may be they speak not a word, but observe all passages. If you give them anything to

17

eat or drink, be it little or much, if it is given with kindness they are well pleased ; else they will go away sullen, but say nothing.

In sickness, impatient to be cured ; and for it give anything, especially for their children to whom they are extremely natural. They drink at those times a tisan, or Decoction of some Roots in Spring Water ; and if they eat any flesh it must be of the Female of any Creature. If they dye, they bury them with their Apparel, be they Men or Women, and the nearest of Kin fling in something precious with them as a token of Love. Their Mourning is blacking of their faces, which they continue for a year. Some of the young women are said to take undue liberty before Marriage for a portion ; but when married chaste.

Their Government is by Kings, which they call *Sachama*, and those by succession, but always of the Mother's side. For instance, children of him who is now King will not succeed, but his Brother by the Mother, or the Children of his Sister, whose Sons (and after them the Children of her Daughters) will reign ; for Woman inherits. The Reason they render for this way of Descent is, that their issue may not be spurious. The Justice they have is Pecuniary. In case of any Wrong or evil Fact, be it Murther itself, they atone by Feasts and Presents of their wampun, which is proportioned to the quality of the Offence, or Person injured or of the Sex they are of.

For their Original, I am ready to believe them of the Jewish Races.

Penn's entire approach to the native was the outgrowth of a combination of characteristics that today seem contradictory. He held an unquestioning belief in the right of the white men, whom he considered God's chosen people, to populate the new land, in the right of Christians to dispossess the aborigines. But his abiding sense of humanity softened to gentleness the stern measures to which such a belief would appear naturally to lead. Although a shrewd real estate man, promoting his interests even to the extent of circularizing Europe, he dealt generously with the Indians. The result indicated the promptings of his heart, which softened his views on the subject of white invasions and confirmed his belief that peaceful expansion of the Colony depended on the courteous and kind treatment of the natives.

It is doubtful if even the best intentions could have saved the Indians from a fate that hinged, not so much on the wishes of individual men, as on the inexorable forces working upon European society. Penn treated the Indians with more consideration than any other Colonial Governor. His successors acted in a quite different spirit. It was not long after Penn was in his grave, that the Proprietors tricked the Indians out of a large slice of land by means of the notorious Walking Purchase.

The Walking Purchase of 1737 was resorted to in settling a controversy due to a loosely drawn deed covering a tract extending from a point a short distance above Trenton, west to Wrightstown in Bucks County, northwest and paralleling the Delaware River as far as a

18

man could walk in a day and a half, and then east to the Delaware, following a line not defined in the deed.

Thomas Penn finally prevailed upon the Indians to agree to the terms of the document, and preparations were made for the walk. Instead of the leisurely method of walking, which the natives expected, the whites advertised for fast walkers, marked trees to insure a straight line of travel, and made every effort to procure the greatest amount of land. Three walkers were hired, two of whom fell out, but the third reached a point more than 60 miles from the start. The deceit was continued by drawing the line at an angle, rather than straight, thus claiming the best lands of the Minisink region.

With the development of Philadelphia, Indians retreated to the outskirts, and finally to remoter regions, being pushed northward and westward as the frontiers spread out. Not long after the Walking Purchase, the last Delaware council fire died out upon the Wissahickon's hills, leaving Philadelphia to the white man and the white man's ways. Today about 150 Indians live in the city. They are not subjected to discrimination, and on the whole are entirely adjusted socially. The descendants of the Delawares and their historic allies are now domiciled in Oklahoma, numbering about 1,200 ; in Ontario about 400; with some scattered in Kansas and Wisconsin. Research in this important field, long neglected, has been carried on since 1928 through the University of Pennsylvania Research Fund.

Two small plots of ground were set aside in 1755 by John Penn, William Penn's grandson, as camping sites for Indian delegations visiting the city. One plot, formerly part of the Penn lawn, is off Second Street, behind the Keystone Telephone Building, between Walnut and Chestnut Streets. The other is behind the Ritz Carlton Hotel. Believed to have been deeded to the Six Nations, the grants in recent years have been the source of much publicity and a certain amount of legal bickering. In 1922 five Indian chiefs from New York visited Philadelphia to ascertain the legal status of their claim upon the onetime reservations. At this time, John Caskell Hall, a descendant of William Penn, "rededicated" the Second Street tract as an Indian camping site in the presence of Pennsylvania's Governor and Philadelphia's mayor. The ceremony was considered, even by the visiting chiefs, as nothing more than a rhetorical gesture.

Philadelphia is unimportant archeologically. Although most of the city stands upon a very ancient land mass, possibly rich in paleontological and archeological remains, no evidence that man existed in the area prior to the coming of the Indian has been found. The nearest approach to a paleontological discovery was a section of a petrified tree dug up in 1931 by workmen excavating for the Eighth Street Subway. Even that find has not yet proved to be of scientific value, since neither its age nor its origin has been determined.

19

HISTORY

And thou, Philadelphia, the virgin settlement named before thou
wert born, what love, what care, what service and what travail has
there been to bring thee forth, and to preserve thee from such as
would abuse and defile thee.

WILLIAM PENN

PROLOGUE

A TINY ship, with weather-beaten sails billowing above her cluttered deck, limped into Delaware Bay on the afternoon of October 24, 1682, and beat slowly upriver against a northerly wind. She was the 300-ton *Welcome*, bound from Deal, England, to New Castle, Delaware, with Capt. Robert Greenway in command and William Penn as one

Penn's Ship "Welcome"

of her 70 passengers.
High-sterned, and perilously low at the stem, the vessel was
crowded with men, women, and children. Cows, pigs, and sheep took
up much of her deck space ; her alleyways were glutted with masses
of baggage, household utensils, and boxes of provisions. Her 'tween-
decks exuded the miasma of contagion ; and from everywhere came
the stench of crowded humans and penned-up livestock.

For eight weeks the *Welcome*, pushing her slender bow through
the North Atlantic seas, had battled gales and the scourge of smallpox. On September 1, she had raised anchor and stood down the
English Channel with 100 passengers, among them one who had come
aboard at Deal bearing the deadly germs. Within a few weeks nearly
half the crew and passengers were down with the plague. The
bodies of 30 victims had been committed to the sea before land was
sighted.

Under such discouraging circumstances did William Penn first look
upon American soil, and to the travaïl of storm and death there was

20

now to be added the opposition of wind and tide. Though within the capes, the *Welcome* had to struggle against headwinds for three days before reaching New Castle.

On the morning of the 28th (the *Welcome* actually had arrived the evening before) Penn landed in New Castle, there to be greeted by his cousin, Capt. William Markham, resplendent in naval uniform, and by a gathering of Dutch, Welsh and English settlers. Tall, handsome, and still of slender figure, Penn made an impressive appearance on that autumn Saturday as he formally took possession of the Delaware territory by receiving the "turf, twig and water" symbols of ownership, and renewed the commissions of incumbent magistrates.

Impatient to see his Province of Pennsylvania, he proceeded that afternoon to Upland (now Chester) — settled by the Swedes about 40 years before — and landed at the mouth of Chester Creek, named by the Indians *Mee-chop-penack-han*, or "the stream where large potatoes grow." Here he was entertained over the weekend at Essex House, home of Robert Wade, a Friend whom Penn had known in London.

Sometime during the first week in November, Penn and a party of friends rowed up river to the tongue of land formed by the converging Schuylkill and Delaware Rivers, where the town of Philadelphia was being laid out. They continued past the Schuylkill's mouth, proceeding up the Delaware to where Dock Creek led into a large green clearing on the west bank of the river. The place was called *Coaquannock* by the Indians because of its tall pines. In the vicinity such small Swedish settlements as Wicaco and Tacony had been established.

Some of the land desired by Penn was owned by these early Swedes, and still more belonged to the original owners — the Indians, particularly the Unamis of the Lenni-Lenape nation. Adjustments were made later with the Swedes ; but since Penn's agents already had acquired considerable acreage from the Indians, the clearing on the Delaware was even now taking on the semblance of a real estate development.

Under the supervision of Capt. Thomas Holme, the surveyor general whom Penn had sent to America with the advance guard of settlers, trees were being felled and cut into logs, plots were being leveled, streets graded, houses built, and the city was being laid out in accordance with Penn's plan.

During the next few weeks Penn was busy. He visited New York to pay his respects to representatives of the Duke of York (from whom he had received the Lower Counties), made frequent trips to Philadelphia to observe the growth of his "greene countrie towne," and in Chester worked on the plan of government for his Province. Meanwhile he kept in contact with his agents in London, circularizing

21

Europe with pamphlets — in English, German, and other languages — which pictured the beauties of America and outlined the advantages to be gained by coming to the new land.

As a result of this promotion campaign, immigrants poured into Pennsylvania during the ensuing years. Among them were so many Germans that James Logan, Penn's secretary, expressed a fear that it would become a German colony. One of the features attracting Europeans was Penn's Great Law and Frame of Government, which made provisions for free education, promotion of the arts and sciences, religious toleration, freely elected representatives, and trial by jury in open court.

Many of the earliest settlers in Philadelphia found existence far from comfortable. Great numbers of them had to live for a time in dug-outs gouged from the Delaware's banks. There was no let-up in building ; during the first year after Penn's arrival more than 100 dwellings of brick, logs, and wide clapboards were constructed, among them homes with balconies as well as porches. Brick houses were few at first, but the number increased rapidly as soon as bricks could be manufactured locally, making importation of that material unnecessary.

Within a year of Penn's landing the growing town boasted 600 houses. The Blue Anchor Inn, built in 1682 on the bank at the mouth of Dock Creek, and serving as Philadelphia's tavern, trade headquarters, and community center, was no longer the most substantial building in town. Some of the homes were becoming almost pretentious, wharves were growing in size and number along the Delaware, and surrounding farms by the hundreds were being cleared and tilled. Penn, with pardonable pride, was able to write to his friends in England : "I have led the greatest colony into America that ever man did upon a private credit. I will show a province in seven years equal to her neighbors of forty years' planting."

Thus was founded the City of Brotherly Love — not only a haven for the persecuted, but also a sound business venture promoted by one who had a clearer understanding of human nature than most men of his time. This latter trait was especially made manifest in his dealings with the Indians. "Be grave," he had importuned his commissioners before coming himself to America, "they (the Indians) like not to be smiled upon."

PENN AND THE HOLY EXPERIMENT

BORN October 14, 1644, the son of Admiral Sir William Penn, Pennsylvania's founder received his early education at a small free school at Chigwell, near Wanstead, England. A brooding lad, with a leaning toward spiritual thoughts, his behavior frequently exasperated his energetic sire. On October 26, 1660, after being tutored at home, young Penn was sent to Christ Church College, Oxford. Here he associated with members of a growing sect known as Friends, or Quakers, and became a convert. In this environment he heard Quaker leaders discussing plans for a colony across the sea. Members of the established Anglican Church already had such a settlement in Virginia ; the Puritans had a refuge in New England ; and the Quakers now dreamed of escaping persecution by establishing a colony in America.

At first intimation of his son's interest in the Quaker faith, Sir William became greatly perturbed. Then, when young Penn was expelled for refusing to wear a surplice in chapel, he ordered his son home and attempted to break the boy's will by physical discipline. In reference to the incident, Pennsylvania's founder later spoke bitterly of the "Usage I underwent when I returned to my father ; whipping, beating, and turning out of doors in 1662."

But punishment proved useless, so young Penn was sent on a tour of France. At Saumur he spent a year and a half studying in the Huguenot College under Moses Amyraut. Upon his return to England he studied law for a while, then accompanied his father to sea with the British fleet. Naval life did not appeal to him, however, and in 1666 (the year of the great London fire) he was sent to Ireland to manage his father's Shannigary estate. Once again Penn came under Quaker influence, and this time he was committed irrevocably to the faith.

In 1668, at the age of 24, he began to preach and write, producing the pamphlet *The Sandy Foundation Shaken,* which offended the Anglican clergy. That same year he was confined in the Tower of London for nine months because of his religious activities. A few years later he was a prisoner in Newgate. "My prison shall be my grave before I will budge a jot," he declared stubbornly. After his release he continued to campaign, winning a wide reputation as a Quaker leader and as author of *No Cross, No Crown* and *Innocency*

23

With Her Open Face. His father at last in 1670 was forced to reconcile himself to the son's work, but that reconciliation did not come until the elder Penn lay upon his deathbed.

On April 4, 1672, Penn married Gulielma Maria Springett. There followed an idyllic interlude, marred only by repeated persecution of the Quakers. In 1680 more than 10,000 were thrown into prison, 243 dying in loathsome cells. On others exorbitant fines were imposed, or their estates confiscated. By this time Penn's wife had given birth to seven children, three of whom, including twins, died in infancy.

In 1681, as payment for a debt of £16,000 owed by Charles II to his father "for money advanced and services rendered," Penn received the grant of a vast territory in the New World. Thus his role in history entered a newer, brighter, and more glorious period.

In signing the patent, the King stipulated that "two beaver skins be delivered at our castle of Windsor on the first day of January in every year, and also the fifth part of all gold and silver ore found."

The patent was signed March 4, 1681, and on April 2 Charles issued a public proclamation to the inhabitants of the Province, enjoining them to yield obedience to Penn and his deputies. At the same time Penn addressed a message to the colonists, expressing the hope that he would be able to join them without delay, and urging them to pay their dues to his deputy governor, Captain Markham, who left for America that summer.

On April 25, 1682, he completed his famous "Frame of Government." He called the document *The Frame of Government of the Province of Pennsylvania in America, together with certain laws agreed upon in England by the Governor and divers Freemen of the aforesaid Province to be further explained by the First Provincial Council that shall be held if they see fit.* In the constitution he declared the divine right of government was twofold, to "terrify evildoers and to cherish those that do well." He also pointed out that "any government is free to the people under it, whatever be the frame, where the laws rule and the people are a party to those laws."

Meanwhile the Free Society of Traders was incorporated, with a capital stock of £10,000 for the purpose of developing the Province. Penn sold the society 20,000 acres in a single tract. The company did not prosper, but the generous terms under which the land was offered resulted in many purchases in London, Bristol, and even in Dutch and German cities.

On May 5, 1682, Penn's Code of Laws was passed in England to be altered or amended in Pennsylvania. In this historic document, 40 statements were promulgated which, in large measure, became the fundamental law of the Province. Among the provisions were that elections should be voluntary ; taxes were to be levied by law for purposes specified ; complaints were to be received upon oath or affirmation ; trials were to be by a jury of twelve men, peers of good character and of the neighborhood. If the crime carried the death penalty, the sheriff was to summon a grand inquest of twenty-four men ; fees were to be moderate ; each county was to have a prison that would serve also as a workhouse for felons, vagrants, and idle persons ; and public officers and legislators were to take oath to speak the truth and profess belief in Jesus Christ.

Penn was now ready to turn his back upon England and start a new chapter in the wilderness of America. So, winding up the last of his affairs, he boarded the *Welcome* at Deal on September 1, 1682, and set sail for Pennsylvania. For three quarters of a century Europe had looked with covetous eyes upon that virgin wilderness, and for about 40 years there had been attempts to colonize it. Now it was to become the scene of action of one of history's most colorful characters — the testing ground for his "holy experiment."

The Years of Discovery

A MAJESTIC river skirted one boundary of the wilderness commonwealth in which Penn was to make his great experiment. Important to the Indians before the arrival of the whites, the Delaware River later played an important part in the development of town and Province, city and State.

The first European known to have viewed the stream was Henry Hudson, who on August 28, 1609, sailed his *Half Moon* up the bay while seeking a northwest passage to China. The second recorded voyage to Delaware Bay was made in July 1610, by Capt. Samuel Argall, English navigator. Argall named the bay Delaware, in honor of Thomas West—Lord de La Warr—who but recently had arrived in Jamestown as Governor of Virginia.

In 1614 the Dutch States General passed an ordinance claiming exclusive trade privileges to all America. That same year Capt. Cornelis Jacobson Mey, representing the United New Netherland Company, explored Delaware Bay, giving to the east cape the name of Cape Mey (May), and to the west cape the name of Cornelis, which he afterwards changed to Hindlopen — later corrupted to Henlopen. When Mey returned to Europe, Capt. Cornelis Hendricksen, an associate of Mey, determined to explore the Zuydt, or South (now Delaware) River more fully. He went as far north as the mouth of the Schuylkill, and in his report to the States General declared he had discovered a bay and three rivers.

In 1621 the States General chartered the Dutch West India Company with sovereign powers, giving it a trade monopoly and rights to colonize on the coast of Africa from the Tropic of Cancer to the Cape of Good Hope, and on the American coast from the Straits of

25

Magellan to Newfoundland. The territory claimed by the company in North America was called the Province of New Netherland. Thus culminated a long-drawn fight by the Amsterdam merchant, William Usselincx, for a powerful colonizing, navigation, and trading organization. The company did not prove successful. Usselincx was later appointed Swedish agent in Holland.

The company sent its first ship to America in March 1623, under command of Captain Mey. The latter erected Fort Nassau on the New Jersey side of the Delaware at Timber (now Sassackon) Creek, opposite what is now League Island. Here trade with the Indians was carried on for a time, the site being alternately abandoned and reoccupied by the Dutch until 1651, when they moved to Fort Casimir at New Castle, Del. This was the first European attempt at permanent settlement on the Delaware.

Some time after the formation of the Dutch West India Company, the disappointed Usselincx persuaded Gustavus Adolphus, King of Sweden, to grant him a commission to form a Swedish West India Company. Letters patent were issued July 2, 1626, and the project was recommended to the people of Sweden and Germany, Gustavus himself pledging the Royal Treasury up to 450,000 riksdalers. The Diet confirmed the measure in 1627, but the German war delayed organization. Gustavus was killed in battle, in 1632, and the plan was dropped temporarily. Chancellor Axel Oxenstierna, regent and guardian for the little Queen Christina, soon renewed the patent of the company, with Usselincx as director. Pamphlets and circulars outlining the project were distributed throughout Europe. Several wealthy Dutchmen became interested in the enterprise, and by 1637 actual preparations were under way to found a Swedish colony on the Delaware.

Meanwhile, in America, the Dutch West India Company had permitted a landed aristocracy to develop. Wealthy Dutchmen, acquiring large grants from the company, set themselves up as patroons or feudal chiefs of extensive territories. Among those interested in colonizing the Delaware was David Pietersen (or Pieterszoon) De Vries. The site of Philadelphia, however, lay untouched by white colonization, in fact, unseen until on January 10, 1633, De Vries sailed his ship up the river beyond the Schuylkill's mouth, anchoring off what is now Camden, N. J. The Indians were then at war with one another, and De Vries, afraid to trust them, did not go ashore, but dropped down the river to Chester Creek, where his vessel was ice-bound for two weeks. He then sailed down the Delaware and went on to Virginia. Returning to the river in March, he captured a few whales, but because of their small yield in oil he decided to return to Holland.

That same year Arent Corssen, commissary at Fort Nassau, was commissioned by the Dutch governor at New Amsterdam to buy from

Workman's Place
"A Bit of Stockholm"

the Indians a tract of land on the Schuylkill. Upon this land, about a half mile north of the present Penrose Ferry Bridge, Fort Beversrede later was erected. In the meantime, difficulties sprang up between the patroons of New Netherland and the Dutch West India Company. It finally was agreed that the company would purchase the property and rights of the patroons, and on November 27, 1634, all the claims to the land on both sides of the Delaware passed to the West India Company.

The influence of the Swedes on the Delaware was now to be felt. The New Sweden Company, a hybrid organization financed equally by Dutch and Swedes, founded its first colony in 1638, on the present site of Wilmington, Del. The first governor, Peter Minuit, had been the Dutch governor at New Amsterdam for six years, until replaced by Wouter Van Twiller. As governor of New Sweden, Minuit erected Fort Christiana and purchased from the Indians all the land on the west bank of the Delaware as far north as the Schuylkill. Pursuing a policy of fair dealing with the Indians, Minuit gained their good will and succeeded in obtaining almost all the fur trade.

Settlement of the Swedes upon the Delaware was sharply resented by the Dutch at New Amsterdam, who declared the Zuydt River of New Netherland had long been in their possession. Minuit was succeeded in 1640 by Peter Hollandaer (or Hollander), who purchased the land extending from the Schuylkill north to Falls of the Delaware, at what is now Trenton.

Then came John Printz, a huge man of 400 pounds. Printz was to become the greatest of New Sweden's governors. After a career in five universities and meritorious service in the Baltic wars, he had been knighted and sent to America. In 1643 he built New Gotheberg (or Gottenburg) — a log fort, and a cluster of rude shelters for the immigrants — on Tinicum Island, now part of Tinicum Township, Delaware County. For himself he erected a fine brick house called "Printz Hall," which stood as a landmark for a century and a half. The fort was soon destroyed by an accidental fire.

Printz, known among the Indians as the "Big Tub," ruled Tinicum for ten years. He liked neither the Indians nor the Dutch, and his hatred of the latter was intensified when in 1645 the New Amsterdam governor sent Andreas Hudde to erect Fort Beversrede. Despite his grievances, Printz developed a brisk trade in pelts and tobacco, and made plans for the building of mills and forts. He married off his daughter, Armegat, to the valiant Johan Papegoja, vice governor of the Swedes on the Delaware. This was the first marriage ceremony between white persons within the present limits of Pennsylvania. Printz then returned to Sweden, leaving affairs in the hands of his new son-in-law. Papegoja was soon relieved by John Classon Rysingh.

At last the friction between Dutch and Swedes resulted in open violence. A new governor, "Headstrong" Peter Stuyvesant, had come to New Amsterdam. Passionate, honest, and blunt, Stuyvesant stumped through the affairs of the New World on his wooden leg, hating the Swedes with characteristic intensity. He removed the Fort Nassau garrison to Fort Casimir, and when told of the fall of his new fort, he gave way to a mighty rage. In the autumn of 1655, with an expedition of seven vessels and 600 men, he entered the Delaware, lowered the Swedish flag everywhere and hoisted the Dutch in its place, reestablishing the mastery of Holland throughout the lower valley.

Rysingh returned to Sweden and died in poverty. The leading Swedish settlers followed him home, while others surrendered their fur trade and moved upstream ahead of the conquering Dutch. Thus the wavelets of Swedish migration beat upon the shores of the Delaware, to leave the church, Gloria Dei, as a monument to their courage and their faith.

But there was never any extensive settlement by either Swedes or Dutch. In the entire section of Tacony, as the Swedes called what is now Philadelphia, court records in 1677 showed 65 males between the ages of 16 and 60. The Dutch as well as the Swedes were destined to lose their hold in this part of the New World, and at last evil days fell upon "Old Wooden Leg" Stuyvesant. Geographically, the English had him bottled up and were pressing their advantage. "Alas," he wrote in despair to the West India Company, "the English are ten to one in number to us, and are able to deprive us of the country when they please."

English Encroachment

AS early as 1634, two Englishmen, Thomas Young and Robert Evelyn, journeyed as far north on the Delaware as the present site of Philadelphia. They built a small fort at the mouth of the Schuylkill River, but remained there only five days. The next year, by order of the Governor of Virginia, an expedition under Capt. George Holmes attempted to seize Fort Nassau on the New Jersey side. The attempt was frustrated by the Dutch, who captured Holmes and sent him to New Amsterdam in chains. In 1641, sixty Puritans from New Haven went up the Delaware with the intention of settling permanently at the Schuylkill's mouth. (All Delaware River wayfarers recognized the value of that particular spot, the embryonic Philadelphia). The Puritans erected a blockhouse, but before long it was burned to the ground by raiders in the Dutch service, and the Connecticut colonizers were sent to New Amsterdam.

At last, after the long years of claims and counter-claims, of voyages of exploration and attempts at colonization, came the Treaty of Breda in 1667, whereby England gained possession of the territory now contained in the States of Pennsylvania, New Jersey, Delaware, and New York. Vital changes in affairs of the New World were linked intimately with developments in the Old. On March 20, 1664, Charles II presented to his brother James, Duke of York and Albany, the lands between the Connecticut and Delaware Rivers. James gave to Sir George Carteret and John, Lord Berkeley, courtiers and favorites, possession of the territory between the Hudson and the Delaware. Carteret had held the Island of Jersey for the Cavaliers against the might of Cromwell, and so the new province, at first named *Nova Caesarea*, was then called *New Jersey*.

The fortunes of Col. Richard Nicolls, a follower of the Duke of York, also entered a period of brightness under the favor of the royal brothers. Nicolls dispossessed Stuyvesant in 1664 but he treated the Dutch and Swedes on the Delaware with consideration. He established the Duke of York's system of laws, which provided for trial by jury, religious freedom, and equality of taxation.

After Nicolls, Col. Francis Lovelace governed on the Delaware (1667-1673), and then the Dutch gained ascendancy in 1673, following the fortunes of a fresh war overseas. They maintained this position for only a year, during which time Peter Alrichs was deputy governor of the Colonies on the west side of the Delaware. With the Treaty of Westminster, in 1674, the English again were masters on this side of the Atlantic.

Four years later, in 1678, the English ship *Shield* sailed up the Delaware, passing the Indian place, Coaquannock, which lay under a thin mantle of snow on the river's western bank. The site of Philadelphia was then an almost unbroken wilderness, save for a few scattered clearings and an occasional log cabin sending its wreaths of smoke upward through the trees.

The *Shield*, bound up-river for the new settlement of Burlington (N. J.), tacked close in to shore — so close that some of the rigging scraped against branches of trees lining the water's edge. One of the crew gazed in awe at the broad flat forests stretching away from the placid Delaware, then turned to a shipmate and exclaimed : "Here is a fine place for a town !"

EARLY SETTLEMENT

O N April 23, 1682, Captain Holme set sail from London on the *Amity*, having been commissioned by William Penn as surveyor general of Pennsylvania. Holme arrived on the site of Philadelphia late in June, and immediately began the task of laying out the city on the elevated ground between the Delaware and Schuylkill Rivers.

The starting point of the city rose from tide level to an altitude of no more than 50 feet, its forest-covered surface drained by a half dozen creeks. Most of the area, except for early Swedish clearings along rivers and creeks, was primitive wilderness ; Indian encampments had encroached very little upon the tall pines.

Several plots had already been surveyed before the arrival of Holme, and a small number of buildings had been erected, principally along Dock Creek. Choice sections of water-front land were obtained from the Swedes, who were given other tracts in exchange, and during midsummer a large area in what is now Bucks County was purchased from the Indians.

The acreage obtained from the Swedes included frontage on both rivers. In plan at least, the city was extended westward to the Schuylkill River and from Vine Street to South — two miles east to west, and one mile north to south. In the shadow of the Coaquannock woods Philadelphia thus slowly began to rise, while in England William Penn was busily engaged in preaching the gospel of emigration and making last-minute preparations for departure.

Among his many schemes for development of the city and Province, Penn set great store on the Free Society of Traders, a land and commercial company chartered in London. Its president was Nicholas Moore, a London doctor, who came to Philadelphia shortly after Penn's arrival and later became speaker of the assembly and chief justice. The treasurer was James Claypoole, an able and energetic man who also made his home in the New World.

One of the plans of the society was to erect an autonomous "Manor of Frank, which should hold its court-baron, court-leet and view of frankpledge." For this purpose to the society was granted a tract of 20,000 acres about 20 miles northwest of the city. By June 1682, the total stock subscribed to the company had reached £10,000, but the undertaking later collapsed for a reason still undetermined. Possibly

31

the society had made plans on too vast a scale. At any rate, manorial reservations and courts were not adaptable to democratic society.

In order to attract wealthy individuals, Penn offered parcels of 5,000 acres for £100, with 50 acres additional for every indentured servant brought to Pennsylvania. An opportunity was given entire families to purchase tracts of 500 acres, to be paid for in annual installments over a period of years. Moreover, Philadelphia was to be built up "after the proportion of 10 acres for each 500 acres purchased, if the place would allow it." (Instead of becoming a colony of landed gentry, Philadelphia became a center for tradesmen, laborers, and seekers after homesteads.)

Penn had been expected in Philadelphia for a long time before he arrived. The reason for his delay was that he was busy on his Frame of Government constitution. He consulted many persons, notably Algernon Sidney, who wished England to become a republic and who finally gave his life for his liberal principles. Sidney did not approve some of Penn's ideas, although both were Whigs, and each was in his own way eager to help mankind. Penn made as many. as 20 drafts of his constitution, each a considerable advance over the first, which would have created a landed aristocracy.

Under Penn's rule there was to be a governor, a provincial council, and an assembly. The council was to be composed of 72 freemen, who were to serve for three years, one-third being replaced each year. The governor was to have three votes in the council, but no power of veto. The council alone had the right to originate bills. The governor and council together constituted the executive power, and by division into committees were to manage the affairs of the Province. The assembly was to consist, for the first year, of all the freemen of the Province, and after that of 200 persons to be elected each year.

It soon became evident that changes were necessary. Under the existing arrangement, the governor was impotent, and therefore the right of veto was granted him in 1696. Penn also modernized the method of impeachment, and was the first person to lay down the principle that any law which violated the constitution should be void. The final draft was completed April 25, 1682.

When Penn and his contingent of settlers finally arrived, they found the season well advanced and the problem of shelter for their first winter in the new land a grave one. Of the situation Pastorius wrote: "The caves of that time were only holes digged in the ground, covered with earth, a matter of 5 or 6 feet deep, 10 or 12 feet wide and about 20 feet long. Whereof neither the sides or the floors have been planked. Herein we lived more contentedly than many nowadays in their painted and wainscoted palaces, as I, without the least hyperbole, may call them in comparison of the aforesaid subterraneous catacombs or dens."

32

Building construction was carried on with renewed vigor in the spring. For himself Penn had ordered a house commanding a view of the Delaware, but it was not until March 10, 1683, that he took up residence in Philadelphia. By this time the Province had been divided into Philadelphia, Chester and Bucks counties, and both the Great Law and the Frame of Government had been adopted by the assembly, which had its first session in Chester, December 4, 1682.

During 1683 a number of settlers made their way into the wilderness. More than 20 vessels loaded with immigrants arrived in Philadelphia before the end of the year. Penn's great plan apparently was moving toward the success for which he had prayed and labored. His gratification at the progress of his Province found expression in many letters. "Colonies," he wrote, "are the seeds of the Nation." He called the Delaware a "glorious river," and declared that the Schuylkill being "boatable 100 miles above the falls — and opening the way to the heart of the Province, is likely to attract settlers' in that direction."

In sending back to England a copy of the city plan, he wrote:

> This I will say for the good Providence of God, that of all the many places I have seen in the world, I remember not one better seated, so that it seems to me to have been appointed for a town, whether we regard the rivers or the conveniency of the coves, docks, springs, the loftiness and soundness of the land and the air held by the people of these parts to be very good. It is advanced within less than a year to about fourscore houses and cottages, such as they are, where merchants and handicrafts are following their vocations as fast as they can, while the countrymen are close at their farms.

Thomas Paschall, a pewterer, may be taken as a typical colonist. He came from Bristol, and with his family of seven children settled on a 500-acre tract between what are now Angora and Mount Moriah Cemetery. Paschallville was named for him. "Here is a place called Philadelphia where is a market kept as also at Upland," he wrote in 1683. Attending a fair at Burlington, N. J., he saw "most sorts of goods to be sold and a great resort of people. The country is full of goods." He declared that within a year 24 ships had sailed up the Delaware, which he termed "a brave, pleasant river as can be desired." The same year saw the arrival of at least 50 ships, bringing hundreds of Welsh settlers and the first of the German immigrants.

From the very beginning the Welsh seemed to prefer the Schuylkill. In a short time other Quaker colonists arrived from Wales, purchasing 5,000 acres of unsurveyed land, a part of a larger tract set aside by Penn for the exclusive use of the Welsh. Penn's charter permitted him to erect manors, and perhaps the Welsh expected to have "manorial jurisdiction." However, only for a time did they enjoy special privileges of local self-government. The tract of 40,000 acres which they ultimately obtained was often called the Welsh Barony.

33

Here were founded the townships of Merion, Radnor, and Haverford, west of the Schuylkill. Many notable Philadelphians trace their ancestry to the first settlers of the Welsh tract.

Gwynne Friends came later than the Quakers who settled on the Welsh tract. Hugh Roberts, "a man of much enthusiasm," went to Wales and stirred up the ancient Britons to a realization of the advantages of the new Province. As a result a new group arrived and purchased from Robert Turner a tract 18 miles from the heart of Philadelphia.

Not all the Welsh immigrants were Quakers, however. A large number of Welsh churchmen from Radnorshire settled at Radnor, sometimes called Welshtown, and built the famous St. David's Protestant Episcopal Church. Here the old Tory, Judge Moore, of Moore Hall, and the patriot, Gen. Anthony Wayne, worshiped and were buried.

Pastorius and the Founding of Germantown

ON JUNE 10, 1683, the ship *America*, with Capt. Joseph Wasey in command, sailed from Deal, England, with a scholarly gentleman aboard — a man who was to play an important role in the history of Philadelphia. He was Francis Daniel Pastorius, founder of Germantown and forerunner of a great wave of immigration. Pastorius and his party of nine arrived in Philadelphia on August 20, six weeks earlier than the main body of the first Germantown colonists, the so-called Mennonite weavers. These, coming from Crefeld, arrived on the *Concord*, commanded by Capt. William Jefferies, on October 6, 1683. They were not of German origin, as is commonly supposed, but were Dutch Quaker descendants of Mennonites who had taken up residence in the Rhine country after being driven from the Netherlands.

The Krisheimers (or Cresheimers) likewise had their origin in the Netherlands, afterwards migrating to Switzerland and then to Germany before coming to America. Preceding the bulk of German migration to Germantown and its environs, the Krisheimers and Crefelders did much to industrialize the Wissahickon region and develop agriculture along Cresheim Creek before the turn of the eighteenth century.

Pastorius was born at Sommerhausen on the Main, Franconia, Sept. 26, 1651, three years after the close of the Thirty Years War. His name in Low German was Scepers, but was Latinized into Pastorius.

He attended four universities and spent years in study, travel, and association with cultured persons, becoming one of the great scholars of his time. One of the Frankfort Pietists, he was an important influence in the great religious awakening that took place in the second half of the seventeenth century.

Pastorius had as a fellow-passenger on the trip from Deal, Thomas Lloyd, who was accompanied by his wife and nine children. The weather was foul, whales struck the ship, and sailors went crazy; but Pastorius and Lloyd paced the deck, conversing in Latin and discussing their hopes for the new colony.

The *America* brought over 80 persons, among them Catholics, Lutherans, Calvinists, Anabaptists, Episcopalians, and one Quaker. Pastorius at first lived in a cave dwelling, but soon built a "little house in Philadelphia 30 feet long and 15 feet wide." Further describing his home, he wrote: "Because of the scarcity of glass, the windows were of oiled paper. Over the house door I had written: '*Parva domus, sed amica bonis, procul este prophani*' (A little house, but a friend of the good; remain at a distance, ye profane)."

Six days after his arrival, Pastorius obtained from Penn a warrant for approximately 6,000 acres on the east side of the Schuylkill. The tract was divided between the German Company or Society (the so-called Frankfurters) and the Crefelders. German Town settlement was laid out with a main street 60 feet wide, and cross streets 40 feet wide. For each house a lot of three acres was provided. Pastorius doubling the acreage for his own dwelling. The little settlement grew, and in 1685, Pastorius reported that 12 families, numbering 41 persons, were living in the colony.

Germantown was incorporated as a borough in 1689, by a patent William Penn had issued in England. Pastorius acted as the borough's first bailiff. Two members of the Op de Graeff family, and Jacob Fellner, were selected to serve as magistrates. These, together with eight yeomen, formed a general court which sat once a month, making laws and levying taxes.

In August 1700, Pastorius turned over to the agents of the reorganized German Company all the property in his charge. Then he became lawgiver, schoolmaster, burgher, scrivener, and writer of prose and verse. He served as schoolmaster of the Friends School from 1698 to 1700. He was the prototype of the titular character in Whittier's *Pennsylvania Pilgrim*.

Penn's Policy of Good Will

IN LONDON on March 4, 1681, Penn had written triumphantly to Robert Turner: "This day my country was confirmed to me under the great seal of England." On April 8 he sent a letter to America, assuring the Swedes on the Delaware and all other settlers in his Province that "You shall be governed by laws of your own making, and live a free, and if you will, a sober and industrious people."

Under the Duke of York, the Swedes had obtained title to large tracts of fine land. Penn either purchased their properties or gave better lands in exchange for them. One instance of this policy is furnished in his treatment of the Svenssons or Swansons. These were Sven, Olave, and Andrew, the sons of Sven Gunnasson, all of whom, including the father, had settled at Wicaco, in the vicinity of what is now Front Street and Washington Avenue. Penn gave the Swansons good land on the Schuylkill, and they surrendered the Wicaco title.

On April 10, 1681, Penn sent his cousin, William Markham, as deputy governor, to take possession of the Province. Markham was to read the King's proclamation and the proprietor's letter to the inhabitants, call a council, settle boundary disputes, erect courts, and preserve order. Markham was bold, resolute, and devoted to the proprietor. He is believed to have landed at Boston. By June 26 he was in New York, where Lieut. Anthony Brockholls, president of the council, governing in the absence of Sir Edmund Andros, yielded his authority on the Delaware in the name of the Duke of York

At Upland (or Mecopanoca, as the Indians called it), nine men, selected by Markham, met in council on August 3. A court was set up, and government was established. Thomas Revail was chosen clerk of the court, and John Test named sheriff. The court took the place of the Kingsesse or Kingsessing Court on the West Bank of the Schuyl-kill — Philadelphia's Blockley Township. There were two Swedes in Penn's first council : Justice Otto Ernest Cock, an old Tinicum man, and Capt. Lasse Cock of Passyunk. Among the English members was Robert Wade, of Upland, first Quaker west of the Delaware. His place, Essex House, was a popular resort for Friends.

Others in the Council were the Burlington settlers : Morgan Drewet, of Marcus Hook ; William Warner, William Clayton, William Woodmanson, Friends of the Upland section ; and Thomas Fairman, surveyor, who had built a house in the projected town of Shacka-maxon on a 300-acre tract. Fairman had boats and horses, and was of great service in the founding of Philadelphia.

Philadelphia is a name taken out of ancient history (from Lydia, in Asia Minor) and means "brotherly love," a term that expresses the very essence of Penn's philosophy. Another ancient city also was said to have been in Penn's mind, not for its name, but for its plan — Babylon, with its miracles in masonry.

At any rate, Penn did astonish the world by the Babylonian big-ness of his plans. He told Markham to allocate 10,000 acres as a site for the new city. Holme's assistant, Henry Hollingsworth, is said to have left a journal, believed destroyed by the British at Elkton in 1777, in which he declared that notwithstanding the manifest advan-tages of the Philadelphia site, Penn would have located his capital at Upland if he had not feared that place was too close to the northern boundary of Lord Baltimore's grant.

According to Watson, Penn said : "Let the rivers and creeks be sounded on my side of the Delaware River, especially Upland, in order to settle a great towne." Watson also mentions the once projected site of "Old Philadelphia" near the "Bakehouse," on the south side of Poquessing Creek in Byberry, which was abandoned, it is said, because of sunken rocks known as "the hen and chickens."

"Pennsbury (in Bucks County) was rejected after survey," says Westcott, "probably because the water was insufficient." Other sites were considered, but all were rejected for Coaquannock, the grove of tall pines between the Delaware and Schuylkill Rivers.

Boundaries and Treaties

ALTHOUGH the infant colony continued to make steady progress, Penn soon became troubled by boundary disputes. In June, 1683, the year after his arrival, Maryland commissioners crossed from Chesapeake Bay to the Delaware on a grand hunt for the fortieth degree of latitude, which had been fixed by Charles I as the northern boundary of the Maryland grant.

At New Castle the Marylanders borrowed a ship sextant. To their intense joy they found, according to their calculations, that they were far below the fortieth degree. With Lord Baltimore and 40 armed men, they proceeded to Upland that autumn, telling Markham that Upland, and probably Philadelphia itself, was in Maryland territory, and the Quakers would have to vacate. The Marylanders charged Penn's London lawyers with trickery in an effort to obtain a water exit at the mouth of the Susquehanna.

Markham pointed out that Penn had no seacoast, and all he wanted was an outlet to the Atlantic. Penn, Markham informed them, had an instrument with which to lay out the bounds, but the instrument was out of order. The Marylanders laughed at this, and told Markham they already had determined the latitude at Upland by means of the borrowed sextant, and that it was 39° 47′ 5″.

Markham reminded them that whatever Charles I might have granted to Cecil Calvert, Charles II had granted to William Penn the land "from 12 miles distance northward of New Castle Towne." The Marylanders replied that "His Majesty must have long compasses." Markham refused permission for the expedition to proceed farther up the Delaware, and Lord Baltimore demanded and received the refusal in writing. As the Chesapeake party journeyed homeward, they stopped at Marcus Hook to warn the residents against paying quit-rent to Penn.

The dispute in the London courts over Penn's southern boundary lasted as long as did the proprietorships of the contending families. A compromise in 1760 fixed the line at 39° 43′ 26.3″, and in 1767 Charles Mason and Jeremiah Dixon ran the line that exists as the boundary today.

Concerning this trouble with Lord Baltimore, Penn wrote to Lord Halifax in England :

> The only interruption I meet with is from the unkindness of my neighbour proprietor, who not only refuseth compliance to the King's commands, and the grant he and the duke have gratuitously made me, but as impatient of the decision of our joynt sovereign, would anticipate that by indirect ways of his own. He taketh himself to be a prince, that, even to his fellow subject and brother proprietor, can by right determine difference by force, and we have been threatened with troops of horse.

Penn's relations with the Indians, however, were always amicable. Before his arrival in America, he had entrusted to Markham the task of making several land treaties with the red men, and also had sent letters addressed to them to be read at treaty conferences. When he came to Pennsylvania he visited the various tribes, cultivating their good will and establishing friendships that were to last throughout his lifetime.

He sat with them at feasts, watched their games, took part in their sports, and smoked (though he detested smoking) the pipe of peace with them. To white audiences Penn may often have seemed verbose, pompous, and somewhat of a bore, but the Indians received him as a man without guile, a man in whom dwelt a passion for fair play.

Among relics preserved by The Historical Society of Pennsylvania in Philadelphia is a wampum belt of white and purple shells. This commemorates the treaty "not sworn to and never broken." The Indians gave it to Penn in token of their love and friendship, to last "as long as the sun and moon shall endure." The emblem traditionally has been identified with the celebrated Elm Treaty of Shackamaxon, which treaty may have been negotiated in the autumn of 1682 or the summer of 1683, on the site marked by a gigantic elm until 1810, and now by a marble obelisk. This meeting with the Delawares, Susquehannocks, and possibly the Shawnees has been incorrectly portrayed on canvas by Benjamin West, and embroidered with fiction by careless writers. Some of the most dependable historians are prone to regard the Great Elm Treaty as a beautiful legend rather than as a historic fact, because the time and place of the meeting have been a source of so much dispute. No written record was preserved ; Penn never specifically mentioned it in any of his numerous letters ; and repeated searches disclosed no land deeds associating Shackamaxon with Penn and the Indians.

These arguments, however, do not have sufficient force to dislodge the monument of marble from the site of Shackamaxon's famous elm. And this is as it should be. In time's inexorable perspective, Penn has to some extent lost fame as a colonizer, as an administrator, and as a true leader in the cause for which, earlier in life, he braved the wrath of kings and suffered the ignominy of prison. However, no historian can annul the covenants of amity written by Penn under countless unmarked trees. Whether or not he held a treaty conference with the Indians at Shackamaxon is immaterial; he treated with them often, and in various places. The monument should be regarded not as a memorial to a single historic episode, but as a symbol of that quality in Penn which alone would give him immortality — the quality that made him the beloved Miquon of Indian council fires long after land-hungry heirs had succeeded him.

Later Years of Proprietorship

IN 1684, Penn sailed for Europe, to remain there 15 years. During this protracted sojourn in England and on the Continent, he experienced many important changes in his private and public life. Becoming involved in royal intrigue, he was arrested on several occasions and had to submit to humiliating investigations. He was ousted from the proprietorship of Pennsylvania on March 10, 1692; not until August 9, 1694, was the Province restored to him.

On February 23 of the latter year his wife died, and was buried beside four of their children. A fifth child died in 1696. In February, 1696, Penn married Hannah Callowhill, daughter of a Bristol linen dealer, a woman of character and determination. Of his second union there were six children: John, born in the slate-roofed house in Philadelphia; Thomas, Hannah, Margaret, Richard, and Dennis. He was 64 when his youngest child was born.

Eager now to return to Pennsylvania, the Founder set about winding up his affairs in England. He made a preaching tour through Ireland, stayed for a while at the Shannigarry estate, and then sailed for America with his wife and daughter, Letitia. They took passage on the *Canterbury*, which left Cowes Road, Isle of Wight, on September 9, 1699. The passage was long and tedious, and by the time they arrived in Philadelphia winter had set in. It was not a pleasant home-coming, though Penn's heart must have thrilled at sight of the busy water front, the long rows of red-brick houses, and the tidy little farms girdling his compact town.

At Chester he had found yellow fever epidemic, and in Philadelphia he was to find the assembly a difficult body of men with which to deal. This latter fact was not long in making itself apparent. Two bills presented by Penn — one to prohibit the sale of rum to Indians, the other to provide for the decent marriage of Negroes — were rejected with humiliating bluntness. The council was even more hostile. Penn soon realized he was proprietor in name only. To the Indians he was still the great sachem, the King of Men, but to the settlers in Philadelphia and the growing Province he was an over-scrupulous old man obstructing progress.

For a while the Founder lived in the slate-roofed house at Second Street and Norris Alley (now Sansom Street), afterward moving to his Pennsbury estate along the Delaware River in Bucks County. Here he lived in more or less political seclusion, though his restless nature took him abroad throughout the Province on visits to Indian villages and to outlying settlements. He maintained a six-oared barge on the river; he kept blooded horses, a well-stocked pantry and cellar. Always a lover of good victuals, he now began to take on considerable weight.

This bucolic existence was rudely interrupted in 1701 by news that the English Parliament was attempting to bring Pennsylvania under direct royal control. Though keenly desirous that Penn should hurry to England and thwart the bill, the assembly appropriated money for the purpose only after repeated and maddening delays. By that time Penn's finances were in a deplorable condition, and even the large acreage of his Pennsbury estate had dwindled.

Word of the Founder's imminent departure was treated with indifference by Philadelphians, but Indians by the score came into the little city to say farewell to their Onas. Penn appointed Col. Andrew Hamilton, the former Governor of East and West Jersey, as deputy governor of Pennsylvania, and James Logan as Colonial secretary. Then, in October, 1701, he set sail for Portsmouth, England, with his wife and family.

Penn intended to remain abroad only long enough to straighten out the affairs of the Province. However, forces which had no connection with problems of state kept him from ever returning to America. By 1705 he had obtained unquestioned autonomy for Pennsylvania, through a grant obtained from Queen Anne, despite the Crown's growing tendency to check proprietary power in the New World. His private affairs, however, became so involved in claims and counter-claims that eventually he became a voluntary inmate of a debtor's prison.

The autumn of 1708 found him living quietly with his wife and some of their children at Brentford, England. Penn was now in his middle sixties, extremely corpulent, and constantly ailing. His health declined rapidly and his mind became affected. In spite of this mental and physical decay, there persisted a stubborn spark of that energy which in middle age had driven him to wild frontiers, and now in the twilight of life guided his tottering footsteps in restless walks through the garden.

In the spring of 1712 he suffered a paralytic stroke while on a visit in London. He had a second stroke in Bristol that autumn, and a third at Ruscombe in January 1713. During 1715 he suffered several minor strokes; his memory for long periods at a time thereafter was a complete blank. He died July 30, 1718, at the age of 74, and was buried August 5 at Jordan's Cemetery near Chalfont St. Giles, Buckinghamshire.

Ben Franklin Appears

THE next score of years saw the waning of Penn's empire in Pennsylvania, and the gradual decline of Quaker dominance in the political affairs of Philadelphia. These years also witnessed civic improvement, expansion of foreign industry, and periodic epidemics of malignant diseases. While Philadelphia itself was engaged in paving streets, organizing fire companies, and developing industries, pioneers on the remote frontiers were struggling with a stubborn wilderness.

Probably the greatest public figure to make an impression upon Philadelphia's consciousness during this era was Benjamin Franklin. His influence began to be felt shortly after his arrival from Boston in the summer of 1723, but it was not until after his two-year sojourn in England that he became a really important factor in Philadelphia affairs.

Franklin had little sympathy with the pacific leanings of the Quakers, and less with their stern sectarian morality. He badgered them and ridiculed them. Though he earned the lifelong enmity of many, he managed to win over others, together with the Germans and the Irish, in his relentless campaign against British pretensions.

He entertained a lasting dislike for Thomas Penn, who took over the proprietorship of Pennsylvania after the death of his mother, Hannah. Of the Founder's son, Franklin in 1758 wrote : "I conceive a more cordial and thorough contempt for him than I ever felt for any man living, a contempt that I cannot express in words." Ten years before, Thomas Penn had written of Franklin : "Mr. Franklin's doctrine that obedience to governors is no more due them than protection to the people is not fit to be in the heads of the unthinking multitude. He is a dangerous man and I should be glad if he inhabited any other country. However, as he is a sort of tribune of the people, he must be treated with regard."

Printer, scientist, journalist, lawmaker, business man, and philosopher, Franklin was concerned with every trend and every movement affecting Philadelphia from long before the Revolutionary War until his death in 1790. At the outbreak of the French and Indian War, he went to the frontiers to superintend personally the building of forts, and through his untiring efforts among Pennsylvania farmers General Braddock was supplied with wagons for the march upon Fort Duquesne.

After the French and Indian War he was conspicuous in the controversy with the proprietary government, meanwhile receiving a membership in the Royal Society for his contributions to science.

41

For some years he represented the Colony in England, and upon his return in 1762 was considered the foremost personage in America.

Franklin hardly had become settled at home when the Paxton Massacre occurred at Lancaster. A band of enraged Scotch-Irish settlers in Lancaster County, aroused by an Indian uprising on the frontier, had slaughtered an unresisting group of Conestoga (Susquehannock) Indians who had sought refuge in the Lancaster jail. As a result of this atrocity, about 150 peaceful Indians from nearby regions fled in terror to Philadelphia. The Lancaster men, known as the Paxton Boys, from the township of that name, recruited a large force and began to march on Philadelphia, determined to slay these refugees.

Franklin quickly organized a force of 1,000 armed citizens to protect the Indians. Even the peace-loving Quakers declared their willingness to aid in the defense. There was no bloodshed, however. The Paxton Boys reached Germantown, and there Franklin and three others conferred with their leaders and persuaded them to return home.

In the autumn of 1763. John Penn, last of the proprietaries, arrived in Philadelphia to assume his duties as governor. He was followed in a few days by Mason and Dixon, who immediately undertook their boundary line survey.

Meanwhile, most Philadelphia merchants, like those of other leading ports, were engaged in a brisk smuggling business. England had attempted to obtain a monopoly of Colonial trade by means of the Navigation Act, but this measure was flagrantly evaded. Shipping men in Philadelphia were building up fortunes by trading with countries other than Britain, in violation of the law. As long as King and Parliament were occupied in warfare, no serious attempt was made to enforce the act.

Not long after the French and Indian War, however, Great Britain began to tighten her reins of government in the Colonies in order to bring them under direct control, and at the same time enjoy increased revenue by taxation. Although some members of parliament saw danger in this step, the King and landed interests did not. On this side of the Atlantic, men of vision read clearly the handwriting upon the wall, and prepared to resist usurpation.

In 1765 the Stamp Act was passed by Parliament. This measure stipulated that certain types of legal, commercial, religious, and academic papers could not be used in the Colonies unless stamped by the British Government. As soon as word reached Philadelphia that the bill had become law, a wave of indignation spread throughout the city. Merchants assembled at the courthouse to adopt non-importation resolutions; and on the day the law went into effect, law offices, newspapers, and other publishing houses closed their doors, while the populace refrained from eating imported foods or wearing imported clothes. Stamps were destroyed whenever they were found, and ship captains carrying them were burned in effigy and at times threatened with bodily harm.

King and Parliament soon came to realize they had stirred up a gigantic hornet's nest. To pass a law was one thing ; to enforce it was another. Strong opposition to the Stamp Act rose belatedly among several of the ministry, and its days thereafter were numbered.

Friends' Meeting House
"Gray-clad they came to worship"

43

Portrait of Benjamin Franklin (by Joseph Wright)
"Statesman, Scientist and Philosopher"

44

THE REVOLUTIONARY PERIOD

O N March 18, 1766, the hated Stamp Act was repealed by Parliament. The joyous tidings were brought to Philadelphia on May 20 by the brig *Minerva*, commanded by Captain Wise. Immediately there was public rejoicing. The people gave Wise an effusive reception, and huge bonfires blazed throughout the night as the town celebrated the great event. The following day toasts of allegiance were drunk to the King at a public dinner held in the State House, and on June 4 the King's birthday was loyally commemorated with a great open-air feast on the banks of the Schuylkill.

The general feeling of amity toward the mother country turned to indignation, however, when it became apparent that the Crown had no intention of abandoning the rich revenues to be derived from the Colonies. The repeal of the Stamp Act had a string attached to it in the way of an accompanying Declaratory Act, which reiterated the right of Parliament to tax the Colonies in any way it deemed fit. Those colonists who were disposed to minimize the significance of this proviso were disillusioned when the Townshend Acts, levying heavy duties on paper, glass, tea and lead, were passed by Parliament, June 29, 1767.

The reaction of the colonists to this new imposition manifested itself in a boycott of all British goods. The trenchant arguments of John Dickinson's famous *Farmer's Letters*, a series of articles, of which the first appeared on December 2, 1767, and the last on February 15, 1768, in William Goddard's *Pennsylvania Chronicle*, helped to stiffen the determination of the colonists to resist taxation without representation. Philadelphia, as the metropolis of the Colonies, fittingly assumed the lead in the movement of resistance, which grew in intensity during the following six years.

The situation became increasingly ominous when Goddard's *Chronicle* on September 27, 1773, reported that a shipload of British tea was on the way to Philadelphia. Successive amendments had modified the acts of 1767 to a tax on tea only, importation of which now had become the main issue. By permitting the financially embarrassed East India Company to ship untaxed tea to American consignees, the British government was forcing the issue, in that a three-penny Colonial tax was to be imposed upon the commodity. The Colonies retaliated by refusing to permit the landing of the tea. In

Boston citizens disguised as Indians boarded a newly arrived tea ship one night and dumped the cargo into the harbor. In Philadelphia the resistance, though less destructive, was no less determined.

News of the Boston Tea Party reached Philadelphia on December 24. On the following day word was received that the *Polly*, a ship from London, commanded by Captain Ayres and carrying a consignment of tea to Philadelphia from the East India Company, was lying off Chester. This fanned the flames of resentment into brighter glow. A committee of action was organized, and threats were openly made that any pilot who dared to bring a British tea ship to Philadelphia would be hanged. Promises to reject the consignment were obtained from the two Philadelphia tea firms involved.

Meanwhile the *Polly* continued her course up the Delaware to Gloucester, N. J., where Captain Ayres was told politely but firmly that he would not be permitted to land his cargo. After conferring with the committee, he agreed to leave the ship and go over to Philadelphia to determine more fully the popular feeling. On the next day, December 27, a large public meeting was held in the State House, and it was unanimously resolved that the tea should be rejected and returned at once to England, and that Ayres should be allowed one day in which to provision his ship for the return voyage. After making a formal protest, Ayres agreed to comply with the demands of the committee, and on December 28 boarded the *Polly* at Reedy Island, whence he set sail for London with the cargo of rejected tea.

This incident, together with the Tea Party at Boston, constituted acts of defiance which the London government could no longer afford to ignore. As a consequence, Parliament enacted a bill to close the port of Boston to all shipping. This act was put into effect in June 1774, by the arrival of royal troops under General Gage and the coming of British men-of-war to the New England port. Paul Revere had reached Philadelphia in May, bringing a letter concerning the King's threat to close the Port of Boston, and earnest requests from the Boston leaders for support.

In Philadelphia public excitement increased daily. At a meeting of leading citizens held in the City Tavern, a resolution favoring support of Boston was adopted. Letters were dispatched to the Southern Colonies to enlist their support, and the Governor was asked to convoke the assembly. On June 1 a popular demonstration against the Boston Port Bill was staged. Stores were closed, the chimes in Christ Church were muffled, and flags were hung at half-staff. Necessity for drastic action was fast becoming acute.

46

State House in 1776
"Where freedom was fledged"

State House in 1876

The First Continental Congress

A T A MEETING held June 18, 1774, at the State House, the calling of a general congress for all the Colonies was decided upon. A committee of correspondence for the city and county was formed, with John Dickinson as chairman. The counties were urged to send delegates to a preliminary state conference to be held at Carpenters' Hall on July 15.

This conference, attended by 77 delegates from 11 counties, was presided over by Thomas Willing, as chairman ; Charles Thomson served as secretary. The meeting asserted the right of the Colonies to resist the unjust measures of Parliament and requested the Provincial Assembly to appoint delegates to the forthcoming Continental Congress. Meeting July 21, the Provincial Assembly named the following as delegates to the Continental Congress : Joseph Galloway, Samuel Rhoades, Charles Humphreys, Edward Biddle, George Ross, and Thomas Mifflin.

Since the Provincial Assembly was holding sessions in the State House, the First Continental Congress was perforce obliged to convene in Carpenters' Hall. The opening session was held on September 4, 1774, with 44 delegates first assembled and within a few weeks the number increased to 52, who represented eleven of the Thirteen Colonies. Peyton Randolph of Virginia was chosen president, and Charles Thomson secretary. Other prominent delegates were John Adams, Richard Henry Lee, George Washington, John Jay, Patrick Henry, and Samuel Adams.

In keeping with the gravity of the situation, deliberations of the Congress were held behind closed doors, and continued through a period of six weeks. When the body finally adjourned on October 26, resolutions foreshadowing the movement for independence had been adopted. The most important of these were the Declaration of Rights and the Articles of Association. The latter may be regarded as the forerunner of the Articles of Confederation.

At the close of the Congress, the Provincial Assembly entertained the delegates at a banquet in the City Tavern, at which time hopes of reconciliation with the Crown were still expressed. The proceedings of the Congress, which had been submitted to the assembly for approval, were unanimously ratified December 10, 1774.

By the opening months of 1775, tension between the mother country and the Colonies had increased. The Articles of Association adopted by the Continental Congress especially aroused the ire of King George, who saw in this covenant an overt act of treason against the Crown. On April 19 the long-brewing storm broke at last when the King's troops clashed with the Minute Men at Lexington and Concord. The War for Independence had begun !

News of the hostilities in Massachusetts reached Philadelphia on April 24, and the machinery of war was immediately set in motion. Military committees were organized for the enlisting and drilling of soldiers. The Second Continental Congress convened May 10 in the State House, in a session which lasted until December 30. As the delegates arrived in town they were greeted by officers of the military companies with their bands. In addition to the delegates who had figured prominently in the first Congress, there were present John Hancock, who subsequently replaced Peyton Randolph as president of the body, and Benjamin Franklin, who had lately returned from London. Seventy-eight delegates representing the Thirteen Colonies attended the Congress, which adjourned August 1, reassembled September 5, and finally adjourned December 30. Throughout its sessions in 1775, the Congress assumed to a great extent the responsibility of government, and appointed George Washington commander-in-chief of the army of the United Colonies.

Receiving his commission on June 17, Washington left for Cambridge, Mass., to take command of the Continental Army. He was accompanied by Thomas Mifflin, Joseph Reed, and Philip John Schuyler. The light-horse troop, since known as the First City Troop, and all the officers of the city militia served as Washington's escort as far as Kingsbridge, N. Y.

Beginning with the Second Continental Congress, Philadelphia became the center of the movement for independence. There was no longer any hesitation among local patriots in regard to the course to be taken. Young and old alike were eager to offer their services to the cause of freedom. A Committee of Safety was formed, consisting of 25 members, with Franklin at its head. The committee was organized May 11, 1775, and was empowered to call out troops and provide for the defense of the Province.

Except for brief intervals of disturbance occasioned by the progress of the war, the Congress sat in Philadelphia from 1774 to 1783. Military, financial, and legislative affairs of the Colonies were administered here; Philadelphia's geographical position, midway between the North and the South, made it the logical choice as the wartime capital.

The Declaration of Independence

WHILE the Congress was in session, the question of independence assumed greater importance in public debates. Although many of the more conservative leaders held that the time was not yet ripe for so drastic a step, public opinion was veering steadily toward action. Thomas Paine, Benjamin Franklin, Thomas Jefferson, and others succeeded in convincing the majority of the people that

Declaration Table in Independence Hall
". . . we mutually pledge to each other our Lives . . ."

the time was past for any conciliation with Britain and that complete independence was the only worthwhile goal. It was this growing conviction which led delegates in the Second Continental Congress to sign the death warrant of British authority in the Thirteen Colonies.

On June 7, 1776, Richard Henry Lee, acting on instructions from the Virginia Convention, offered to Congress the resolution that "these United Colonies are, and of right ought to be, free and independent States, and that they are absolved from all allegiance to the British Crown, and that all political connection between them and the state of Great Britain is, and ought to be, totally dissolved." The resolution was debated in the Congress for three days, and then held over until July 1 in order to allow the Colonies sufficient time in which to instruct their delegates. Meanwhile two committees were appointed by the Congress : one to prepare a declaration of independence, the other to draw up a plan of confederation for the Colonies.

The committee appointed to draw up a declaration consisted of Thomas Jefferson (who had replaced Richard Henry Lee of Virginia), John Adams, Benjamin Franklin, Robert Livingston, and Roger Sherman. As head of the committee, Jefferson prepared the draft at his lodgings in a house which stood on the southwest corner of Seventh and High (now Market) Streets.

The draft of the Declaration had been reported to the Congress by the committee, but was held over pending the vote on Lee's resolution. After nine hours of debate on July 1, there were still four Colonies not in favor of the resolution. Pennsylvania and South Carolina voted against it, Delaware was divided, and the New York delegates were unable to vote pending instructions from home. It was decided to postpone the final vote until the next day.

By the evening of July 2, however, Delaware and South Carolina had voted in the affirmative. Pennsylvania had reconsidered its action and had voted in favor of the motion by a slim margin. New York alone of all the Colonies failed to participate in the voting. Two days later, on July 4, the Declaration of Independence was formally adopted, after some alterations had been made in Jefferson's original draft. John Hancock, as presiding officer, and Charles Thomson, as secretary, signed the document. On the morning of July 8, John Nixon read it in public in the State House yard. The crowd responded with enthusiastic cheers, the militia fired their guns in salute, and the Liberty Bell in the State House clanged lustily. Bells were rung all that day and night as the city gave itself up to celebrating the birth of the Nation. The royal coat-of-arms, which had hung on the wall of the State House, was torn down and burned in a great bonfire in the State House yard. Thus ended, in an uproar of rebellious jubilation, British rule in the Colonies.

The Wartime City

DESPITE Philadelphia's preoccupation with political matters, the social and economic growth of the city had steadily increased in the decade since 1768. Civic improvements in the way of additional fire companies, newspapers, shops, and theatres continued to be made. Ships loaded with immigrants from the British Isles sailed up the Delaware. In the years just prior to the Revolution, several thousand Irish immigrants arrived in the city. Several enterprising merchants were making Philadelphia an ever more important center of commerce and finance. Improvements had been made along the Delaware for the protection of shipping.

With the war under way, civic activities moved into the background. Every effort was made to strengthen the city's defenses and to speed the enlistment of troops. The old British barracks in the vicinity of what is today Third and Green Streets had been evacuated by the royal troops in 1775, and were now used as a training camp for local recruits of the Continental Army. In July 1776, five Philadelphia battalions were sent to support Washington's forces around New York, and saw service there for several weeks. River defenses below the city were constructed, and a fleet of boats was armed to patrol the Delaware.

The general optimism that had prevailed in Philadelphia during the early months of the war began to fade as succeeding weeks brought news of defeat in the north. The theatre of war was moving nearer. Sick and wounded troops were being brought in greater numbers to the city. Smallpox and camp fever broke out among the soldiers and the civilian populace, causing many deaths. Trenches were hastily dug in Washington Square to bury the bodies.

On November 19, 1776, the city was thrown into a state of alarm by news that General Howe had driven back the Continentals in New York and had captured Fort Washington on the Hudson. A month later the British were at New Brunswick in New Jersey, and this news caused a veritable panic in Philadelphia. Fear that the city would be captured led many families to load their belongings on wagons and leave for safer places. The Congress hastily departed for Baltimore, leaving a committee in charge. All able-bodied men were ordered to muster for the militia, as martial law was declared.

Fortunately, Washington's bold tactics at Trenton and Princeton in the last weeks of 1776 relieved the situation, and for a time the city was safe from capture. During the middle months of 1777, animosity against the activities of local Tories was manifested by the arrest of about 40 pro-British citizens, many of whom, such as John Penn, Jared Ingersoll, and Benjamin Chew, were men of prominence in the city. Some Tories were jailed, others were banished.

(Above) Betsy Ross House Today
(Left) Before Its Restoration
"Here linger rich traditions of the nation's early days."

On June 14, 1777, the Congress decreed that the first American flag should have 13 stripes, alternately red and white, with a circle of 13 white stars on a field of blue. The first Fourth of July anniversary was celebrated with enthusiasm. A salute of 13 guns was fired in the afternoon, and a great dinner was given for the Congress and the leading military and civil leaders. Music was furnished by a band of captured Hessians. In the evening the Congress reviewed a parade of troops and observed a display of fireworks.

Meanwhile, Howe's army, which had been moved south to Chesapeake Bay, had landed near the head of the Elk River in Maryland and was advancing northward. The city was again in danger.

The Philadelphia Campaign

L EARNING on August 22 of Howe's advance, Washington prepared
to meet the British. His troops, concentrated north of Philadelphia, were marched into the town on August 24, prior to meeting
the enemy at the Brandywine Creek. The army made an imposing
sight as it marched through the city, with Washington riding at the
head and Lafayette at his side. The troops crossed the Schuylkill
and moved south toward Wilmington.

By constant pressure against Washington's right flank, Howe forced
the Americans to fall back. On September 11 the artillery duel across
the Brandywine at Chadd's Ford could be heard in Philadelphia.
By more skillful maneuvering, Howe had succeeded in placing his
forces between Washington's positions and Philadelphia. As the battle
progressed, fears increased in the city. After the fierce night attack
of the British at Paoli on September 20, little hope was held for
success. The Congress had fled to Lancaster on September 27, 1777,
and to York on September 30. The battle of the Brandywine was a
distinct defeat for the Americans, and enabled the British to occupy
Philadelphia.

By September 25 Howe's army had reached Germantown, and the
next day Cornwallis's division marched into Philadelphia. Local
Tories emerged from hiding to welcome the British. On October 4,
eight days after Howe's occupation of Philadelphia, Washington
launched a surprise attack on British positions around Germantown
and Mount Airy. After three hours of fierce combat, the American
attack was repulsed. Washington withdrew his men to the upper
Perkiomen, while Howe strengthened his position north of Philadelphia.

Towards the end of October 1777, Washington again advanced
nearer to the city, concentrating his troops around Whitemarsh. On
December 3 Howe moved a large body of troops out of Philadelphia,
intending to take the Americans by surprise at Whitemarsh. Warned
beforehand, Washington was prepared for the attack. After several
sharp skirmishes, Howe abandoned his offensive and marched his
men back to Philadelphia on December 8, while Washington moved
his troops across the Schuylkill and lay at Gulph Mills until December 19, when he marched to Valley Forge.

The hills at Valley Forge, overlooking all the approaches from
Philadelphia, constituted a vantage point that precluded any successful surprise attack by the British, and there Washington established
his winter quarters, remaining until evacuation of Philadelphia by
the enemy the following summer.

A tragicomic incident occurring on the Delaware River off Philadelphia during this period has gained immortality by reason of

Yankee cunning and Colonial wit. The affair took place while Washington was bivouacked at Valley Forge and the British were billeted in Philadelphia.

Some "rebels" on the Delaware north of the city conceived the idea of sending down on the ebb tide a number of kegs loaded with gunpowder and so arranged that any impact would cause them to explode. The purpose was to sink or damage British ships then lying at anchor in the river off Philadelphia.

A heavy frost came the night the kegs were put into the water upstream, and the ships in the meantime were hauled into the docks — unwittingly removed out of harm's way. One of the first kegs to come down the river, however, was observed by an inquisitive bargeman, who attempted to lift it aboard. The innocent-appearing object exploded, killing the man and several of his companions. The noise and confusion caused considerable alarm throughout the city ; British troops massed at the water front, firing at every obstacle they saw floating by.

Rumors flew thick and fast. It was asserted that the wily Continentals were drifting down the river doubled up in kegs, determined to retake Philadelphia somewhat as the ancient Greeks in the wooden horse took Troy. While squads of British soldiers on the bank were keeping up an incessant fire at the kegs, others went out on the river in vessels, bent upon checking the "invasion" at close quarters. It is related that just about the time the furor began to die down, an old marketwoman dropped a keg of cheese into the water ; and the strange "battle" was renewed with vigor.

The incident is commonly referred to as the "Battle of the Kegs," after Francis Hopkinson's doggerel of that title. The Philadelphia poet's version puts these words in the mouth of a terrified redcoat :

> "These kegs I'm told, the rebels hold,
> Packed up like pickled herring ;
> And they've come down to attack the town,
> In this new way of ferrying."

Of General Howe, Hopkinson gleefully relates :

> Now in a fright he starts upright,
> Awak'ed by such a clatter ;
> He rubbed both eyes and boldly cries ;
> "For God's sake, what's the matter?"

> At his bedside he espied
> Sir Erskine, at command, sir ;
> Upon one foot he had one boot,
> The other in his hand, sir.

> "Arise, arise!" Sir Erskine cries,
> "The rebels — more's the pity —
> Without a boat are all afloat
> And ranged before the city. . . ."

55

Save for minor skirmishes and forays, military operations around Philadelphia were suspended during the winter and spring of 1778. While the American troops were enduring cold and hunger in the snow at Valley Forge, the British were snugly billeted in Philadelphia during the long winter months. Howe's officers whiled away the time pleasantly. Balls, theatre-going, and gambling were the chief diversions. The troops were quartered in the old British barracks, in public buildings, and in private homes. The artillery was parked on Chestnut Street from Third to Sixth Streets, and in the yard of the State House. Until British transports arrived in the Delaware with provisions, conditions in the city were straitened. Food and other commodities were scarce, and there was much privation among the poor. Pillaging of private homes was a common occurrence.

The crowning social event of the British occupation was the Mischianza pageant, held May 18, 1778, as a farewell to General Howe, who was returning to England after relinquishing his command to Sir Henry Clinton. Lasting throughout the day and evening, the Mischianza was a combination of regatta, military parade and tournament, ball and banquet, attended by Tory belles and British officers.

When Howe departed for England on May 24, preparations had already been made to abandon the city. Clinton called a council of war, and by June 18 had moved his army across the Delaware to New Jersey and was marching to New York. News of the British evacuation reached Washington at Valley Forge within a few hours ; and before the last of the enemy had left, the American advance guard had entered the city and was picking up British stragglers in the streets. The general aspect of the town was one of disorder, squalor, and desolation after the nine months of British occupation. Many houses had been plundered and burned.

The Congress returned to the city on June 25 and convened in Independence Hall. Benedict Arnold, who later was to become infamous for his treacherous conduct at West Point, was appointed military commander of the city by General Washington. The following months were marked by extreme bitterness against the Tories, by treason trials, law suits, and heated controversies.

French support of the American cause changed the tide of war and led to the final capitulation of the British at Yorktown. On April 16, 1783, the conclusion of peace and Britain's acknowledgment of American independence were officially proclaimed in Philadelphia amid great public rejoicing.

With the return of peace, industry and commerce soon revived. Despite high prices, money became more abundant, and the general prosperity of the city increased. By the middle of June, 1783, 200 vessels had sailed up the Delaware River. While many fortunes had been lost by the Revolution, many others had been acquired. The

Shippen-Wistar House
"they spoke of ships and sealing wax and cabbages and kings"

old Tory families for the most part had lost their affluence and social standing, and were now supplanted by a new aristocracy composed mainly of Whigs.

The Bank of North America, first to be chartered by the Congress, was opened on January 17, 1782, on Chestnut Street near Third. Two years earlier, Robert Morris and others had founded the Bank of Pennsylvania. In 1786 the first medical dispensary in America was opened in the city by Dr. Benjamin Rush. In the following year, the archetype of present-day chambers of commerce was established as the Pennsylvania Society for the Encouragement of Manufactures and Useful Arts. Mail and stagecoach service to Reading and Pittsburgh was inaugurated.

During this period, the population of the city had grown from about 30,000 in 1778, during the British occupation, to about 42,000. New houses and shops were built to replace those destroyed during the war, and it was not long before the city had all the aspects of a thriving center of trade, with clean and neatly ordered streets and substantial homes.

57

The Constitutional Convention

WITH political activity centering on problems of internal organization, a growing need for a framework of stable government began to be felt. The earlier Articles of Confederation had proved inadequate for an integrated national government. Men of prominence were urging that a convention be called to consider a new system of unification. Finally, by a resolution of the Congress, the Constitutional Convention was called to meet on May 14, 1787, for the ostensible purpose of revising the Articles of Confederation.

Presided over by Washington, the Convention met (behind closed doors) in Independence Hall. Delegates from half of the States did not arrive in the city until ten days after the opening. Soon after the proceedings began, the sentiment increased for discarding altogether the obsolescent Articles of Confederation, and the drafting of a new constitution was urged.

This new measure engendered considerable excitement among the delegates. Heated debates continued for many weeks, feeling ran high. Franklin, now grown old and garrulous, had to be accompanied constantly by a delegate, whose duty it was to keep him from talking too freely about the secret sessions.

Supporters of the doctrine of State sovereignty violently assailed the new Constitution, the provisions and amendments of which finally were adopted by the Convention. A committee, consisting of James Madison, Alexander Hamilton, William Samuel Johnson, Rufus King, and Gouverneur Morris, was appointed to arrange and draft the document, which was ready for signing on September 17. The Convention recommended to the Congress that the new instrument be submitted to the sovereign people for ratification. This was accordingly done and the Constitution became the basic law of the United States when it was ratified by the ninth State on June 21, 1788.

In connection with the Pennsylvania State convention, called on November 21 to ratify the Constitution, considerable disorder occurred. Two of the State delegates, Jacob Miley of Dauphin County and James McCalmont of Franklin County, incurred the displeasure of the people by deliberately absenting themselves from the convention hall in order to prevent a quorum. Rioters did considerable damage to their property, and the authorities, including Benjamin Franklin, made no real effort to find and punish the guilty parties.

The following Fourth of July, ratification of the new Constitution was celebrated with fitting enthusiasm. Ships decorated to represent the ratifying States were anchored in the Delaware River from Callowhill to South Streets. General Mifflin led 5,000 soldiers and civilians in a parade through the streets. One of the features of the parade was a float with a great dome supported by 13 columns.

The new city charter, superseding the old charter of 1701, became operative in March, 1789. It inaugurated a system of popular self-government, establishing the electoral offices of mayor, aldermen, and members of a common council.

During the last decade of the century, Philadelphia was the seat of National Government. However, with the removal of the Federal Capital to Washington in 1800, and the State Capital to Lancaster in 1799, Philadelphia ceased to be the center of National and State politics.

James Wilson's Grave at Christ Church
"they sleep among the immortals"

A Century of Growth

THE first decade of the nineteenth century was marked by gradual expansion of the city, with emphasis upon municipal affairs, industry, and commerce. Hunting Park was laid out, and what is now Nicetown became a pleasure resort known as Bellevue, where sports events and picnics were held. The tongue of land between the rivers was now fairly well developed, and much of the city's activity was spreading westward beyond the Schuylkill. Traffic across the stream had been handled adequately by ferries until the Revolutionary War, when a temporary bridge on floating barges was constructed at Market Street late in August 1776. It was used by the Continental Army when enroute to the Brandywine in 1777.

This bridge was removed at the approach of the British ; replaced when the enemy evacuated the city ; and then washed away by a freshet in 1780. It was replaced by a wooden bridge completed in 1805 and covered the year following. This served for a half century, when it was reconstructed to bear the increased weight of railroad traffic. Fire destroyed it in 1875, and for several years traffic was served by a temporary bridge. Then, in 1881 the City Council passed an ordinance for the construction of a wrought-iron cantilever span. In the meantime bridges had been built at Gray's Ferry, at Callowhill Street and at Chestnut Street.

Impetus was given civic improvements as early as 1800 by the installation of water mains under the city's streets. During that year the Schuylkill Arsenal was built, and in 1809 the South Street ferry across the Delaware to connect Philadelphia with Kaighn's Point, Camden, was opened. Within the decade came the Navy Yard, the Chamber of Commerce, and the Pennsylvania Company for Insurances on Lives and Granting Annuities. Meanwhile, Stephen Girard was making his influence felt in banking circles. He purchased the building of the United States Bank, Third Street below Chestnut, and converted it into the Girard Bank, with a capital of $1,200,000.

In cultural activities the city made headway. Literary clubs, theatres, and dancing schools, flourished. The Pennsylvania Academy of Fine Arts was founded, together with the Wistar Museum and the Academy of Natural Sciences.

The War of 1812, between Great Britain and the United States, was supported enthusiastically in Philadelphia, where volunteers were

60

recruited without difficulty. Among the Philadelphians to distinguish themselves in the war were Maj. Gen. Jacob Brown, who captured Fort Erie, and Capt. Thomas Biddle, commander of artillery at Lundy's Lane. While some of the Philadelphia troops were serving on the Canadian border, others under Col. Lewis Rush served on the Delaware peninsula. In 1815, there were 21 companies on duty there under Gen. Thomas Cadwalader. When news was received of the capture of Bladensburg by the British in 1814, entrenchments were thrown up by civilian volunteers on the outskirts of the city. Militia was held in readiness at Kennett Square and at Gray's Ferry. Numerous engagements with British men-of-war were fought in Delaware Bay by Philadelphia naval officers commanding Philadelphia ships. These were the days when Decatur, Bainbridge, Stewart, Porter, James Biddle, and others won renown for themselves and the Navy.

When news of the Treaty of Ghent reached Philadelphia in 1815, the city returned to peacetime pursuits. During the next 20 years roads, canals, and railroads opened new avenues of trade with the West. The first railroad in Philadelphia was constructed in 1832 connecting the city with Germantown, six miles away. A few years later the Camden and Amboy Railroad to New York was completed, as was the Philadelphia, Wilmington and Baltimore line. The Schuylkill Canal was opened to traffic in 1825.

New banks were organized, among them the Philadelphia Savings Fund Society. Jefferson Medical College, the Philadelphia College of Pharmacy and Science, the Franklin Institute, and the Apprentices' Library were founded. In September 1822 the visit of Lafayette as "guest of the Nation" was the occasion of a gala celebration.

The third decade saw the first public school for Negroes opened (1820), the Historical Society of Pennsylvania was organized (1824), the first locomotive came from the Baldwin Locomotive plant (1831), the greatest parade thus far held in the city—to celebrate the centennial anniversary of Washington's Birthday—February 22, 1832, and the manufacture of the first illuminating gas for general consumption (by a private company in 1836). The concern was soon bought up by the city, which began operating other gas-works set up in various districts.

An epidemic of cholera marked 1832. Hundreds died before the scourge could be checked. Fifty inmates of the Arch Street Prison alone died of the disease within a few days. Religious and race riots also, prevalent throughout the country in 1834, had their repercussions in Philadelphia, where a Negro meeting-house was torn down by rioters in August of that year.

The disturbances were caused by growing agitation for the abolition of slavery, with sporadic outbreaks of violence occurring almost every year until the Civil War. In 1838 a mob destroyed Pennsylvania Hall,

61

a large edifice used for public meetings by the Pennsylvania Society for the Abolition of Slavery. Meanwhile, stations on the "Underground Railroad" for the assistance of runaway slaves were maintained in the Philadelphia area, especially after adoption of the Fugitive Slave Law.

Riots again broke out in 1840, when the Philadelphia and Trenton Railroad Company attempted to lay tracks on Front Street in Kensington, a populous section of the city. Opposition manifested itself in the tearing up of rails, burning of houses, and general rioting, in which many persons were injured.

Despite prevailing disorders during the 1840's, social reforms and civic improvement continued. These included abolition of imprisonment for debt, and granting of property rights to married women. It was during this period also that Port Richmond was incorporated, the School of Design for Women founded (1844) and Girard College for orphan boys established (1848). A year prior to the latter date, in 1847, the American Medical Association was formed.

The Native American or "Know-Nothing" movement, directed mainly against foreign-born of the Roman Catholic faith, resulted in the bloodiest riots in the city's history. Kensington, with its large Irish population, was the starting point of the disorders. The Irish resented the insulting implications of the Native Americans ; consequently, when the latter held an open-air meeting on May 3, 1844, at Second and Master Streets, the Irish broke up the gathering. Three days later, another meeting at American and Master Streets ended in a pitched battle, during which a member of the Native Americans was fatally wounded ; by the end of the day three deaths had resulted.

The next day fighting was continued with renewed fury. Six of the Native Americans were killed. At Nanny Goat Market, near American and Master Streets, the Hibernia Hose House and a number of dwellings were burned by the Native Americans in reprisal. The Catholic Church of St. Michael, Second and Jefferson Streets, was burned to the ground, as was the adjoining girls' school conducted by Catholic nuns. Although troops under Gen. George Cadwalader attempted to quell the rioters, another mob that same evening attacked the Catholic Church of St. Augustine, Fourth Street below Vine, setting fire to the church building and adjoining rectory.

On July 4 there was a recrudescence of rioting. Although the Native Americans held a big parade without any disturbance arising, a rumor reached their ears that the Catholics had concealed firearms in the Church of St. Philip de Neri, on Queen Street in Southwark. This news so intensified the feeling that, on July 5, enormous crowds gathered near the church, which was heavily guarded by troops.

Tension still ran high in the neighborhood of the church two days later. The troops were ordered to disperse the assembled crowds. Resistance was shown and the troops opened fire. Some of the rioters returned the fire. Two soldiers and seven civilians were killed, and many others were wounded. The Southwark commissioners decided that withdrawal of troops would ease the situation. The soldiers were withdrawn, and hostilities gradually ceased.

During the Mexican War, Philadelphia supplied several regiments of volunteers, who saw service in Texas and Mexico. Gens. George Cadwalader, Robert Patterson, and Persifor Smith participated in the war, as did many other Philadelphia officers who later distinguished themselves in the Civil War.

The year 1848 was marked by the first visit of Abraham Lincoln to the city, and by the Whig National Convention at which Zachary Taylor was nominated for the Presidency. In 1849 the Philadelphia County Medical Society was founded. The next year saw the beginning of Philadelphia's police force, with the appointment of two assistants to the constable. In 1851 the Spring Garden Institute and the Shakespeare Society were founded.

Consolidation of the City

WITH the growth of the city and its adjoining districts, each of which had separate municipal powers, a situation arose that necessitated the annulment of authority of the petty district governments, and their consolidation with the city. Southwark, Spring Garden, Moyamensing, Northern Liberties, Richmond, Kensington, West Philadelphia, Belmont, Germantown, Roxborough, Frankford, Manayunk, Bridesburg, Kingsessing — all of these and other districts and boroughs formed a congeries of independent and conflicting municipalities. These overlapping governments and jurisdictions gave rise to many abuses and costly inefficiencies that hampered development. The old charter restricted the city to conditions no longer consistent with the times. In 1850 the city and suburban population was more than 360,000. But the city proper, as delimited by the charter of 1789, had a population of only 121,000. Thus, while the city was steadily growing, its governmental structure was lagging behind.

Convincing proof of the evils arising from this disjointed local government was given in connection with the riots of 1844. Because of the absence of unified authority the rioters in Southwark were immune to interference from the rest of the city's governing bodies, as none of the latter had jurisdiction outside its own separate bailiwick. Under such a system a criminal could commit a felony in one district and evade arrest by crossing the street into the adjoining district. These evils accumulated to such an extent that, despite community opposition, measures were finally taken to consolidate the adjacent districts with the city.

The Act of Consolidation was passed January 30, 1854, and was

63

signed on February 2 by Governor Bigler. Boundaries of the city were extended to include the entire county, and the new City of Philadelphia took over all the property and debts of the incorporated districts. Twenty-four wards were established with a select councilman for each, and a common councilman for every 1,200 taxable inhabitants. The mayor was elected for a term of two years. Executive duties were transferred from the councils to the various city departments. The first mayor to head the consolidated city was Robert T. Conrad, Whig.

With consolidation, the city entered upon a new era of progress. Save for several financial panics and business depressions, it enjoyed an interrupted development. On July 24, 1844, Lemon Hill, comprising a tract of 45 acres, was bought by the city and later dedicated as an addition to Fairmount Park. On April 28, 1857, the city purchased the Sedgeley Park estate, and in 1866 the Lansdowne estate, adding these to the park also. In 1856 the first Republican National Convention was held at Musical Fund Hall, when John C. Fremont was nominated for the Presidency. The Academy of Music was opened in 1857. It was also in 1857 that Mayor Richard Vaux organized the fire and police systems. This same year the Schuylkill Navy was organized, and two years later the Zoological Society. In 1860 Coleman Sellers made the first photographic motion pictures.

During this period the city's developments suffered a temporary setback because of a serious economic depression. The first symptoms appeared when the Bank of Pennsylvania closed its doors in September, 1857. Within a few hours several other banks suspended specie payments. Excitement ran high, and police were called out to protect the banks from depositors clamoring for their money. Rival mass meetings were held in Independence Square either to protest against or to urge laws to suspend specie payments. George M. Wharton, John Cadwalader, and other leading citizens were opposed to legalization. The legislature, however, passed the bill.

The financial panic threw the city into such confusion that many business houses closed their doors, and thousands of unemployed soon were walking the streets. A general shut-down of mills and factories augmented the number of idle workers and increased the general unrest. A mass meeting of 10,000 workmen was held in Independence Square to demand action from State and municipal authorities toward remedying conditions. In view of the gravity of the situation and the pressure from the unemployed, Mayor Vaux instituted a program of public works and municipal improvements, although the council had favored a drastic reduction of municipal expenditures on the ground of economy. Mayor Vaux contended that the city's funds should be spent freely in order to relieve distress and allay the discontent then arising among the workers, some of whom already were shouting their slogan : "Bread or fight !" The sane liberalism of the mayor and other responsible citizens did much to relieve the suffering of the people and bring about a restoration of normal conditions.

While the depression that followed the panic of 1857 caused a general stagnation of business during the following year, railway construction in the city was continued on an increasing scale. No fewer than 14 charters were granted for the construction of railways, and workmen were kept busy tearing up streets and laying tracks. The West Philadelphia line on Market Street was put into operation. Shortly afterwards the Tenth and Eleventh Streets route was completed, as were the lines on Spruce and Pine Streets, and Chestnut and Walnut Streets. Considerable opposition was manifested for a time to the running of street cars on Sundays, but this difficulty subsequently was overcome.

John Brown's raid at Harper's Ferry caused intense and high excitement in the city. When he was hanged, December 2, 1859, local abolitionists gave vent to bitter indignation at the "murder." Feeling ran so high that Mayor Alexander Henry refused the abolitionists permission to bring Brown's body into the city. Prominent business men viewed with misgivings the predominance of anti-Southern sentiment, convinced that much of their business with the South would be seriously curtailed by such hostility. A number of young Southerners studying at local medical schools withdrew and returned home as a protest against the furor raised by the abolitionists. It was only by the strength and vigilance of the police force that serious rioting was prevented.

Musical Fund Hall
"memories of Jenny Lind
and Adelina Patti"

65

Philadelphia and the Civil War

THE abolitionist movement, the birth of the Republican party, John Brown's raid—these and other events that had occupied the attention of Philadelphians during the years preceding the Civil War slipped into the background as war clouds gathered over the Nation. By 1860 relations with the South were approaching a crisis. The threat of war, present so long that people had come to regard it as nothing more than a remote possibility, now grew serious.

The general sentiment in Philadelphia was one of conciliation, a feeling inspired mainly by the desire of financial and industrial leaders to maintain their lucrative trade with the South. Because of its proximity to the Mason-Dixon line, Philadelphia received the bulk of Southern business. There were more than 25 millionaires in the city, many of whom owed their wealth to this trade. Baldwin locomotives were used on all railroads below the Mason-Dixon line, and Southern belles showed a preference for shoes and wearing apparel made in Philadelphia. The city gave the South most of its manufactured products, and took in return such raw materials as cotton, turpentine, and lumber. In the latter part of 1860, however, there was a considerable falling off in this trade.

Despite the efforts of prominent business men to maintain a position of neutrality, public sentiment in the city began to veer definitely away from the South. This was due in large part to the Quakers, who from Colonial times had bitterly opposed slavery. With others it was a question of preserving the Union, even at the cost of armed conflict.

As the war fever increased, social distress added itself to commercial dislocation. Southerners and their sympathizers formed a considerable part of the population. Many of the city's prominent families had intermixtures of Southern blood, and with the mounting agitation these families were rent asunder. It was brother against brother, and friend against friend.

Abraham Lincoln's appearance in the city as President-elect, his raising of the Stars and Stripes on Independence Hall, February 22, 1861, and the pomp and circumstance attendant upon the event earned him his first real popularity in Philadelphia. Until then he had been considered merely a crude Illinois lawyer. So far as this city was concerned, his inauguration started a chain of events that overshadowed everything previous to it. The firing on Fort Sumter April 12, 1861, and Lincoln's call for volunteers two days later, set the city ablaze with enthusiasm.

Philadelphia became a veritable armed camp, with the arsenals working overtime to supply material and munitions. Every section of the city was filled with cantonments of soldiers. The Navy Yard seethed with the activity of equipping men-of-war for active sea service. Every member of the old military units in the city became a hero overnight. The armories were overtaxed with men and munitions. A bill appropriating $500,000 for the militia was passed by the legislature. The city council appropriated large sums for the care of soldiers' families. The city at last had determined upon one goal — defense of the Union.

Among those taking a prominent part in the drive for volunteers were Commodore Charles Stewart, hero of the War of 1812, and Maj. Gen. Robert Patterson. Although 70 years of age, Patterson entered active service and commanded troops on the Potomac above Harper's Ferry. The Scott Legion, named for Gen. Winfield Scott, and the Buena Vista Guards tasted some of the bitterest fighting of the war.

Monument to Negro Soldiers "from cotton fields to Flanders fields"

The First City Troop also played a leading part, many of its members becoming officers in the Union Army. The State Fencibles, the National Guards, Washington Grays, and other units saw active service.

During this period Philadelphia was one of the principal concentration points for New England troops. The Girard House was commandeered temporarily by the Sixth Massachusetts Regiment, which joined the Buena Vista Guards and the Scott Legion at the front. One regiment would hardly leave Philadelphia for the scene of hostilities before another arrived in the city to take its place. Late in April 1861, General Patterson led his First Division, Pennsylvania Volunteers, to Washington — the first Philadelphia unit to arrive in the Capital.

About the same time, business in Philadelphia entered a period of wartime boom. Trade with the South which had been lost was more than offset by the inrush of war orders. Baldwin's, hitting a peak of production, turned out 456 locomotives during the war. The Southwark Navy Yard, employing more than 1,700 mechanics. hummed with activity. Other shipyards worked at top speed, as did the Schuylkill and Frankford Arsenals, the textile mills, and the armament factories. Emergency arsenals and storehouses were established in various parts of the city.

Meanwhile, the steady trek to the battle front was under way. Among the first troops to reach Fort McHenry were three Philadelphia regiments under command of Gen. George Cadwalader. The units were composed of volunteers who had enlisted for three months. The First City Troop saw service under General Patterson on the Potomac and elsewhere. In all, about 5,700 short-enlistment soldiers from such organizations as the Philadelphia Grays. Cadwalader Grays, Washington Grays, Independent Grays, State Fencibles. and McMullin's Independent Rangers were under fire.

When the Confederate Congress voted an appropriation of $50,-000,000 and called for 100,000 men, President Lincoln sounded a counter call to arms — for enlistments of three years, or for duration of the war. The early Philadelphia regiments were mustered out and reorganized. The honor roll of the Union Army was to be studded with names of Philadelphia men, including nearly 400 officers who fell in action during the war. Alumni and students of the University of Pennsylvania, Central High School, and Girard College distinguished themselves on the fields of battle.

Although the city was preoccupied with war activities during the four years of conflict, events of local importance continued to fill the calendar. Religious services in the Cathedral of SS. Peter and Paul were held for the first time on April 20, 1862. League Island was purchased by the city this same year, and an epidemic of scarlet fever swept the city in 1863.

After a year and a half of war, the cause of the Union still seemed to be hanging in the balance. Prominent citizens felt that a more concerted effort was needed to strengthen the forces of the Government. It was decided to form a patriotic organization whose members would pool their resources for raising and equipping additional regiments for the Union Army. A meeting was called at the residence of Benjamin Gerhard, 226 South Fourth Street, on November 15, 1862, when measures were adopted for the formation of a Union club. The original founders were Gerhard, George Boker, Morton McMichael, Judge J. Clarke Hare, Horace Binney, Jr., and Charles Gibbons. The present title, Union League, was adopted on December 27, 1862.

The league made its headquarters at 1118 Chestnut Street, the site now occupied by Keith's Theatre. The first president was William Morris Meredith, Attorney General of the State. By February 1863, the membership had grown to more than 500. A fund was subscribed by members to form and equip regiments for the Union, and the League became a potent factor in the city's contribution to the defeat of the Confederacy. It published thousands of copies of patriotic circulars and pamphlets, and in other ways maintained the city's wartime morale. In May 1865, the league moved into its present quarters at Broad and Sansom Streets.

One of the outstanding figures of Civil War days in Philadelphia was Jay Cooke, banker. Formerly with E. W. Clark & Co., Cooke established his own banking house of Jay Cooke & Co. in January 1861. Until news of the defeat of the Union Army at Bull Run reached the city on July 22, 1861, Cooke's company had been allotted only a small part of the Government bond issues, New York and Boston bankers having received the greater part of the allotments. During the excitment that followed upon the Union defeat, Cooke on his own initiative canvassed every financial institution in the city, and in a few days had obtained pledges to a loan to the Government of $1,737,500. Cooke became subscription agent for the national loan on March 7, 1862, and in 1863 he was appointed fiscal agent for the Government by Secretary of the Treasury Chase.

Cooke organized a small army of agents to cover the country, and began a national advertising campaign remarkable for its scope and originality. It is estimated that he raised from a billion and a half to two billion dollars during the four years of war. Total profits of Jay Cooke & Co. on bond issues from July 17, 1861, to March 3, 1865 (according to official statement of Secretary of the Treasury Hugh McCulloch April 23, 1868) were $6,873,934.96. Commission on gold sales amounted to $293,782.

Defense of the City

BY 1863 Philadelphia had settled down to a routine varied only by newspaper reports of casualties and losses and gains of the Federal armies. All the glamor and excitement of the early days had been replaced by the prosaic day-to-day business of seeing the war through to the end. Factories still worked to capacity on war orders, but it was generally believed that the conflict was nearing its conclusion. The Union League and other organizations began to make preparations for a gala Fourth of July celebration.

Then came rumors that all was not well with the armies of the Union. News dispatches began to hint that the Confederate forces were advancing farther north each day. Confederate cavalry was thrusting nearer to the lower reaches of the Susquehanna River. Consternation mounted in the city at the imminence of danger. When word first arrived that Lee's army was marching through Maryland, Philadelphia was thrown into a turmoil. Business was disrupted, shops were closed, and people gathered in groups, fearing the worst.

On June 15 President Lincoln issued a new call for 100,000 militia to be enlisted for six months. Governor Curtin and Mayor Henry also issued calls for volunteers. The mayor ordered all business suspended, and urged every able-bodied man to volunteer for emergency service in preparing the city against attack. Breastworks were thrown up at strategic points in the outskirts. As fast as volunteers were forthcoming, they were equipped and sent to Harrisburg, where other Union forces were assembling.

Meade's smashing repulse of Lee at Gettysburg occurred on July 1-3, but it was not until the 7th that accurate reports of the battle reached Philadelphia. Gettysburg proved costly to the city of Penn. Thousands of its citizens fell, killed or wounded, during the three days. Although won at high cost, the victory saved Philadelphia and determined the outcome of the war.

Upon the battlefields of Bull Run, Antietam, and Ball's Bluff many Philadelphians laid down their lives. At Ball's Bluff the Philadelphia Brigade experienced its first fire, to begin a period of meritorious service that was to end in glory at Petersburg. Except for three up-State companies, the brigade was composed of local volunteers. It also saw service at Gettysburg, turning back a Confederate charge. Survivors fought with other regiments until the final victory at Appomattox. When the brigade was disbanded on June 28, 1864, its battle-flag bore 39 shot-holes.

An equally gallant combat unit was the Pennsylvania Reserves, to which Philadelphia contributed 20 companies of infantry and four batteries of artillery, numbering in all 3,000 men. Gen. George A. McCall succeeded Gen. George B. McClellan as its commander. Later,

Gen. Samuel Wylie Crawford, a surgeon in the Regular Army, led the remnants of the force down from Little Round Top into the "wheatfield" on the bloody second day at Gettysburg. Regiments of Philadelphia Negroes won honor and glory for themselves during the war, displaying great courage on the fields of battle.

The two most conspicuous military figures of Philadelphia during the war were Maj. Gen. George Brinton McClellan, commander of the Army of the Potomac from 1861 to 1862, and Maj. Gen. George Gordon Meade, who commanded the Army of the Potomac at Gettysburg and during the remainder of the war. Among the Philadelphians who figured prominently in naval activities were Rear Admirals Charles Stewart, John A. Dahlgren, David D. Porter, and George Campbell Read ; Commodores Joseph Beale, William McKean, William Truxtun, Garrett Pendergrast, and John C. Febiger ; and Commander Abner Reed.

Military hospitals were maintained in the city and suburbs for the care of the sick and wounded. Local women displayed great ability and devotion in volunteer relief work. The Christian Commission, organized by George H. Stuart, John Wanamaker, and others connected with the Philadelphia Young Men's Christian Association also did valuable relief work.

Philadelphia, during these dark days, was the scene of America's first important fair — the Council Fair of the Sanitary Commissions from New Jersey, Pennsylvania, and Delaware. It was held in Logan Square, and began June 7, 1864. President Lincoln was unable to attend the opening ceremonies, but he and Mrs. Lincoln visited the fair on June 16, together with Governor Packer of New Jersey, Governor Cannon of Delaware, and Governor Curtin of Pennsylvania.

On the morning of April 3, 1865, the Philadelphia *Inquirer* issued a bulletin announcing the fall of Richmond. Later dispatches confirmed the occupation of the Southern capital by Grant's troops. This event was the signal for spontaneous demonstrations on the part of Philadelphia's war-weary citizens. The bell in Independence Hall pealed forth the message of jubilation, as thousands formed impromptu victory processions. School children marched through the streets, waving flags and singing songs. Steam whistles shrieked throughout the city, adding their strident tones to the tumult. A cannon was placed on the top of the *Evening Bulletin* building and fired incessantly all afternoon. Business was at a standstill, and at night the city was ablaze with lights and the glare of countless bonfires. The Union was saved, and war was about to end. What more fitting cause for jubilation ! On April 10, news of Lee's surrender at Appomattox threw the city into another riot of celebration. The names of Grant and Meade were cheered, while guns thundered all through the day.

71

Gaiety and rejoicing changed to sorrow, however, when news of President Lincoln's assassination arrived on April 15. From a city bedecked with gay colors, Philadelphia was transformed overnight into a place of mourning. Office buildings, shops, and dwellings were draped with black. Requiem services were held in all churches. On Saturday, April 22, when the President's body arrived from Washington, the many bells of the city were tolled. The hearse was escorted by a vast procession to Independence Hall, and the body lay in state in the room where the Declaration had been signed.

Early the following morning the hall was opened to the public. By midnight more than 85,000 persons had viewed Lincoln's remains. Multitudes paid their last respects to the great man in prayer and fasting. The next afternoon the casket was borne to the Kensington Depot, and placed on a train to resume its journey through sorrowing throngs to its last resting place in Springfield, Ill., Lincoln's home town.

The Post-War Years

AMID the turbulence of national and local politics, returning soldiers, loyalist demonstrations, financial panics, and a mushroom growth of saloons, Philadelphia entered upon a post-war era of expansion. Rise of the saloons was probably one of the most significant features of the immediate post-war period. Owned for the most part by Germans and Irish, the saloons at first served only the finest brews, aged until wholesome and then drawn from the keg at spring-water temperature. Later, as competition became keen, iced beer was served almost as soon as brewed. In 1887, when the Brooks High License Law was passed, there were nearly 6,000 saloons in the city. A power in politics ever since the days of the first tavern, the saloon was now a force to be reckoned with in every local political struggle.

The Democrats and the Andrew Johnson Republicans set the city aflame with political controversy when they held their famous "arm-in-arm" convention on August 14, 1866. The picturesque name sprang from an incident at the gathering in which two convention delegates, one a Unionist and the other a former Confederate, marched down the aisle of the Convention Hall arm-in-arm.

Johnson's appearance in the city with Grant and Seward was the signal for a series of disorders. Although John W. Geary, Republican candidate for Governor, carried the city in the following October by a plurality of 5,000, Col. Peter Lyle, a staunch Democrat, was elected Sheriff. In November 1868, Grant's presidential plurality in the city was 5,818, notwithstanding that Daniel Fox, Democratic candidate, had been elected mayor the preceding month.

HISTORY—CENTURY OF GROWTH

With the opening of the Chestnut Street bridge on June 23, 1866, the city's westward expansion began. An increase in population from 562,529 in 1860 to 673,726 in 1870 necessitated the development of outlying districts across the Schuylkill. Factories, homes, churches, and schools sprang up. The central city section had already begun to take on the appearance of a metropolis. The main streets, such as Market, Chestnut, and Broad, were crowded with buildings and shops of substantial size.

Many large industries were making Philadelphia one of the most important centers of trade in the country. Firms such as the Cramp's Shipbuilding Company, the Baldwin Locomotive Works, and others had placed the city in the vanguard of industry and commerce. During this period, George W. Childs, who had acquired the *Public Ledger* from William M. Swain, built the new home of the newspaper at Sixth and Chestnut Streets. This building was one of the largest newspaper plants of the time.

In 1870 the Germans in Philadelphia evinced great interest in the Franco-Prussian War. A mass meeting of Negro citizens celebrated the adoption of the Fifteenth Amendment to the Constitution. In the same year the city fire department was organized, and the Philadelphia *Record* first appeared.

Numerous public disturbances occurred in 1871. Much animosity was aroused in certain sections by the enfranchisement of the Negroes. Riots broke out in the Fourth and Fifth Wards, during which two prominent Negroes, Isaiah Chase and Prof. Octavius Catto, were slain. Racial bitterness was so intense that the militia was called out to restore order.

The death of General Meade on November 6, 1872, threw the city into mourning. His funeral was held with impressive ceremony, and notables from the entire country, including President Grant, attended.

The failure of the banking houses of E. W. Clarke & Co. and Jay Cooke & Co., on September 18, 1873, precipitated a financial panic that resulted in the closing of a number of large banks in the city and throughout the country. Another local bank, the Franklin Savings Fund, in which many of the poorer citizens had placed their meagre savings, went into bankruptcy on February 6, 1874. The prevailing financial disorders and the accompanying depression of industry and commerce produced much labor unrest. Strikes occurred frequently during this period, and labor agitation for an eight-hour working day was carried on with vehemence.

The new Masonic Temple, at Broad and Filbert Streets, was dedicated in the presence of a large gathering on September 26, 1873. Three events marked July 4, 1874. These were the laying of the cornerstone of the new City Hall in Penn Square, the breaking of ground in West Fairmount Park for the Centennial Exhibition, and the opening of the Girard Avenue bridge over the Schuylkill. Built at a cost of nearly a million and a half dollars, this bridge was probably the widest in the world at the time.

The Centennial

AS the year 1875 drew to a close, preparations were made to welcome the advent of the Nation's centennial year. On New Year's Eve the city was ablaze with lights. Particularly resplendent was Carpenters' Hall, which displayed in a sign lighted by candles the words : "The Nation's Birthplace." A brilliant display of fireworks was set off at Southwark. Festivities were centered in the area from South Street to Girard Avenue, and westward to the Schuylkill.

As midnight approached, Independence Hall was surrounded by dense crowds. At 11:45 Mayor William Stokeley addressed the assemblage ; and after a prayer by the Rev. Walter Scott and a speech on the Centennial Exhibition by Benjamin Harris Brewster, the bell in Independence Hall tolled for the departing year. As the last note died away, Mayor Stokeley raised a Colonial flag aloft, while a band played *The Star Spangled Banner* and the Second Regiment fired salute after salute.

The Centennial Exhibition, commemorating 100 years of American Independence, opened on May 10, 1876, in Fairmount Park. President and Mrs. Grant, with Dom Pedro de Alcantara, Emperor of Brazil, and his wife as guests of honor, presided at the opening, which was attended by notables from all over the world and a crowd of 100,000. The dedication ceremonies were held in the space between the Main Building and Memorial Hall, two of the 180 buildings erected on the grounds. A 200-piece orchestra and a chorus of 900 voices accompanied the action of the President as he unfurled the flag. After the unfurling a 100-gun salute was fired and chimes were rung. The President and Dom Pedro started the mammoth Corliss engine in Machinery Hall, and then a reception was held for them in the Judges' Pavilion.

Thirty-eight foreign nations and 39 States and Territories were represented. Of these Massachusetts led with an appropriation of $50,000 ; New Jersey voted $10,000, and Delaware $10,000. The 250 judges of the exposition, of whom 125 were foreigners, were divided into 28 groups. All through the summer months the city was thronged with visitors. Record attendance for a single day was reached on Pennsylvania Day, September 28, when 275,000 persons passed through the turnstiles. Governor Tilden of New York attracted a crowd of 134,588 on Empire State Day; while his rival for the Presidency, Rutherford B. Hayes, drew an equally large crowd on Ohio Day, October 26. Hundreds of special events, such as the first public demonstration of the telephone, were held during the six months of the

74

exhibition. The German population dedicated a monument to Humboldt, the West Point cadets visited the fair in a body, and a number of regattas were held on the Schuylkill. On November 10, 1876, the Exhibition was officially closed by President Grant.

The year 1876 marked the beginning of a new period of architectural expression. Not only to Philadelphia, but to the Nation at large, the Exhibition had given impetus to the Ecole des Beaux Arts influence, together with other styles tending toward eclecticism in building design. The period was marked also by business expansion and labor troubles.

In July 1877 the great railroad strike that had spread over the country broke out in Philadelphia. Employees of the Reading and Pennsylvania Railroads, organized in the Brotherhood of Locomotive Engineers, struck for better wages and improved working conditions, such as full crews on all trains, and abolishment of the double train. There was little rioting, however, as major disorders were prevented by police and the National Guard.

In Pennsylvania the strike ended July 27, after freight and passenger service had for a short time been suspended. The men went back to work with an understanding that the issues would be settled by arbitration. Both sides claimed a victory.

Electric lighting came into use in stores and offices in the later seventies and early eighties. The city council opposed the use of electricity for municipal lighting, maintaining that its cost would be too great. The Brush Electric Light Company, however, offered in 1882 to light Chestnut Street for one year without charge. The offices of the *Public Ledger*, at Sixth and Chestnut Streets, and those of the *Record*, on Chestnut Street near Ninth, were equipped with electric lights in that year. Within a brief period nearly all the central city section adopted the new method of lighting. About the same time came the telephone. The Bell company established its first central office in the city at 400 Chestnut Street in 1878. In 1884 two other companies, the Baxter Overland Telephone Company and the Clay Commercial Telephone Company, opened offices on Chestnut Street. As with the telegraph, which had come into use more than 30 years earlier, the electric light and telephone soon became indispensable adjuncts to city life. During the next two decades the city, despite political bossism, enjoyed uninterrupted development.

The Bullitt Act, giving the city a new charter, was passed by the legislature in 1885. This reduced the number of city departments from 28 to eight, and placed them under the direct supervision of the mayor, who was empowered to appoint the department directors.

During the last quarter of the nineteenth century such figures as Matthew S. Quay, Boies Penrose, Alexander McClure, David and Peter Lane, William R. Leeds, and Israel Durham occupied the political limelight. Graft and corruption were rife in connection with traction franchises and the administration of the city gas works. Many large fortunes were made during this period by clever manipulators working in connivance with the political bosses. John Wanamaker, always on the side of civic virtue, attempted to overthrow the Quay machine in 1898-99, but was unsuccessful. The machine was too well organized. Would-be reformers were told bluntly by the "bosses" to stop wasting their breath.

In 1892 the first trolley car was operated on Catharine and Bainbridge Streets. The Reading Terminal at Twelfth and Market Streets was opened the following year. In 1894 Broad Street became the first thoroughfare in the city to be paved with asphalt. In 1897 the Commercial Museum was officially opened by President McKinley. The next year came the Spanish-American War, in which many Philadelphians and organizations, including the First City Troop, saw service. The first motor car to appear in the city was brought from France in 1899 by Jules Junker, a local merchant.

Smith Memorial
"We are engaged in a great civil war"

THE MODERN METROPOLIS

MANY innovations marked the transition from the old city of the nineteenth century to the high-tensioned metropolis of to-day. By 1900 the population exceeded one and a quarter millions, of which native Americans constituted 75 percent. The influx of immigrants from Europe and of Negroes from the South, together with the steadily increasing birthrate, had transformed the city proper into a hive of human beings living in congested streets. The wealthier families began their exodus to the outlying districts of the city and to the suburbs along the Main Line of the Pennsylvania Railroad.

With the advent of the automobile, the city's roughly paved streets, intended for horse-drawn vehicles, were replaced gradually by thoroughfares of asphalt.

During the first decade of the twentieth century a new crop of skyscrapers added height to Philadelphia's skyline. Among the tallest of these were the Land Title Building and the Real Estate Trust Building at Broad and Chestnut Streets ; the North American Building, Broad and Sansom Streets ; the Pennsylvania Building, Fifteenth and Chestnut Streets ; the Bellevue-Stratford Hotel, Broad and Walnut Streets ; Wanamaker's, Thirteenth and Market Streets, and the Morris Building, Chestnut Street west of Broad. Row upon row of brick dwellings were being constructed. The Market Street subway-elevated (opened in 1907) and additional trolley lines were built to link the new sections with the city center.

Events of importance during this period were the Republican National Convention in June, 1900, at which President William McKinley was renominated and Governor Theodore Roosevelt of New York designated as Vice-Presidential nominee ; the purchase by Gimbel Brothers of the Girard House, at Ninth and Chestnut Streets (May, 1900), as a site for an addition to their department store ; the first Mummers' Parade (January 1, 1901) to welcome the twentieth century ; the opening (March 1901) of a new Gray's Ferry Bridge over the Schuylkill ; the first official message sent (January 1902) over the Keystone telephone system ; and purchase (March 1902) of the site of Lit Brothers' store. Also in 1902, the Philadelphia Rapid Transit Company was chartered ; the new Central High School at Broad and Green Streets was dedicated by Theodore Roosevelt, who had succeeded to the Presidency after McKinley's assassination ; and Keith's Chestnut Street Theatre was opened.

The Poor Richard Club was organized July 23, 1907 ; and on July 1, 1907, the first contract between the city and the Philadelphia Rapid Transit Company was executed. In April 1908 Shibe Park, home of the Philadelphia American League baseball club, was opened. The same year saw the establishment of Oscar Hammerstein's Philadelphia Opera House, which opened with a presentation of Bizet's *Carmen*, and the dedication of the Y. M. C. A. Building on Arch Street. In 1909 regular passenger service over the new elevated tracks of the Philadelphia & Reading Railroad was begun from the Reading Terminal.

Motormen and conductors of the Philadelphia Rapid Transit Company declared a strike for higher wages in May 1909. Another followed in February 1910, the men receiving instructions not to return to work until their union was recognized by the company and the hourly wage-rate increased from 20 to 25 cents. During the strike, which lasted about five months before an agreement was reached, there was much rioting and disorder. Hundreds of cars were damaged, many persons were injured, and numerous arrests of strikers and union officials were made.

In the same year, the first airplane flight from New York to Philadelphia was made by Charles K. Hamilton, under the auspices of the New York *Times* and the Philadelphia *Public Ledger* ; the Historical Society of Pennsylvania opened its new building at Thirteenth and Locust Streets ; the Aquarium in Fairmount Park was completed ; and the census of 1910 showed an increase of population to 1,549,008.

During this period and up to the third decade of the century, local political affairs were controlled by dynasties of boss-rule, in which such figures as Boies Penrose, James P. McNichol, and the Vare brothers, George, Edwin, and William, were predominant. Headed by these bosses, the Republican organization enjoyed uninterrupted control of Philadelphia politics, save for a temporary setback when Rudolph Blankenburg, independent reform candidate, won the mayoralty election in 1911 against the Republican machine controlled by Penrose, in alliance with McNichol. The tie-up between the political bosses and the utilities had been scandalously close ; both had waxed rich at the expense of the citizenry. But under Blankenburg's administration many of these abuses were discontinued. In their stead, there was maintained a steady campaign of municipal development carried on in such a forthright manner that even the political machine could not criticize it.

The great fortunes founded in the previous century by such finan cial, industrial, and commercial pioneers as Cyrus H. K. Curtis, Francis and Anthony Drexel, John Wanamaker, Edward T. Stotesbury, Justin Strawbridge, Isaac Clothier, William L. Elkins, and Peter A. B. Widener had by now become consolidated, and formed an integral part of the city's growth. Newcomers were carving their fortunes in banking, real estate, motion picture theatres, oil, and other fields.

In 1913, militant women suffragists crusaded in the city to win for their sex the right to vote and participate in the direction of public affairs. Prominent in the movement was Mrs. Lucretia Blankenburg, wife of Mayor Blankenburg. President Taft and his Cabinet attended the Union League's fiftieth anniversary banquet in February of that year, and in October President Woodrow Wilson dedicated the restored Congress Hall.

Philadelphia During the World War

A SLIGHT earthquake shook the city in February 1914. A few months later, in midsummer, a far greater earthquake, nonseismic in origin, rocked the entire continent of Europe and the whole world, with repercussions of gradually heightening intensity in Philadelphia during the following four years.

The war seemed very remote from the city until the steamship *Lusitania* was sunk by a German submarine on May 7, 1915. Then public sentiment, which had been rather divided in its sympathies for the belligerents, began to swing towards the side of the Allies. Meanwhile, Philadelphia industries were obtaining lucrative contracts for munitions and war material from the Allied powers. Wages mounted as factories operated day and night to turn out their merchandise of death.

A phenomenon of the times was the sudden swarm of "jitney" busses which appeared on Broad Street and other main thoroughfares in 1915. Indifferent street-car service and the novelty of riding in automobiles, which at that time were still luxuries out of reach of many citizens, accounted for the popularity of the "jitney" (the name sprang from a slang term meaning five cents, the amount of fare charged by the new conveyances). Eventually, opposition instituted by the traction company, under Thomas E. Mitten, forced the "jitneys" out of business.

On January 22, 1917, the last contingent of Philadelphia troops which had been sent to the Mexican border the previous July in the campaign against Villa was ordered home. As if in preparation for the inevitable, many civilians were joining the National Guard units, which were conducting sham battles and drills. Army and Navy recruiting stations were opened, and the Philadelphia Navy Yard was closed to the public. Expectation that America would enter the war grew stronger.

79

Prices began to soar as commodities became more scarce and profiteering grew rampant. Potatoes sold at $3.60 per bushel. Crowds kept vigil before bulletin boards of the large newspaper offices, awaiting developments. A mass meeting was held in Independence Square, where citizens pledged themselves to uphold the national honor against German aggression. The city adhered to its pledge when Congress declared war on the Central Powers on April 6. The machinery of mobilizing the city for war was set in motion immediately. Within two months the First Liberty Loan campaign was in full swing, the Red Cross drive for funds and volunteers had started, and local draft boards were already conscripting civilians for the Army. In the first local draft quota, 161,245 Philadelphians were sent to training camps.

On April 10, 1917, a terrific explosion occurred at the Eddystone Ammunition Works, between Philadelphia and Chester. More than 100 men and women workers, many of them Philadelphians, were killed in the blast, and more than 300 maimed and injured. So terrific was the concussion that the small town of Eddystone was all but demolished, and thousands of homes in Chester and Philadelphia were shaken.

During the primary election on September 19, 1917, bitter factional strife broke out in the Fifth Ward. Patrolman George Eppley was shot and killed at Sixth and Delancey Street while protecting two citizens from imported gunmen. The murder resulted in the indictment of several public officials on conspiracy charges, though the most prominent among them were acquitted. Feeling against the gunmen implicated in the murder ran so high that a change of venue was necessary. Several of the defendants were convicted of second-degree murder and imprisoned.

The city entered upon its war work with feverish activity. Great industries, such as the Baldwin Locomotive Works and the Midvale Steel Company, were transformed into arsenals of the Army and Navy, turning out war materials. The largest ship construction plant in the world was established at Hog Island, on the southeastern fringe of the city. The first keel was laid on February 12, 1918 ; and the first ship, a cargo vessel of 7,500 tons, slid down the ways on August 5, as Mrs. Woodrow Wilson, accompanied by the President, christened it the *Quistconk*.

High wages were paid to both men and women workers in industry. This tended to some extent to offset the rising cost of living caused by the scarcity of commodities and the rationing of fuel and foodstuffs. As intensive drives for recruits and money were carried on, exhortations such as "Give Till It Hurts !" and "Your Country Needs You !" became the slogans of the time.

One of the most notorious figures in wartime Philadelphia was

80

Grover C. Bergdoll, scion of a wealthy family of brewers. Bergdoll's refusal to be drafted into the infantry created a *cause célébre* which even today remains unsettled. Prominent as a daring aviator and automobile racer, Bergdoll demanded to be assigned to the aviation corps. Placed under arrest, he escaped from the custody of Federal agents and fled to Germany.

The city had just reached the height of its production of men, money, and material for war, when news of the Armistice arrived on November 11, 1918. All activity was suspended immediately, as the entire population gave vent to unbounded joy. The months immediately following were occupied with celebrations of victory and the welcoming home of soldiers and sailors. The prevalent elation was dampened, however, by an epidemic of influenza which caused thousands of deaths in the city.

The Boom Years

A NEW city charter went into effect on January 5, 1920. By its terms the two city councils, select and common, were merged into one, and, instead of each ward having its councilman, the city was divided into councilmanic districts, each comprising several wards.

By 1922 Philadelphia had resumed its normal momentum of civic activity. The deafening obbligato of riveting-machines and roaring motor-trucks introduced the Golden Age of Prosperity. New residential communities sprang up in the outlying districts of Frankford, Olney, Logan, and elsewhere. A branch of the Market Street subway-elevated extending to Frankford Avenue and Bridge Street began operation November 5, 1922, linking the new residential sections to the central city. Tall office buildings and apartment houses appeared with each succeeding year. On Market and Chestnut Streets, palatial movie theaters were constructed to keep pace with the ever-growing population, which had increased to nearly 2,000,000.

The streets became congested with automobiles and motor-trucks. With the advent of prohibition, bootleggers, speakeasies, and gangsters sprouted like fungi. Vice, racketeering, and official corruption increased to such an extent that in January 1924, at the request of Mayor W. Freeland Kendrick, Maj. Gen. Smedley D. Butler obtained a leave of absence from the Marine Corps to accept the post of Director of Public Safety. For more than a year General Butler led an intensive drive against organized crime, whipping into greater efficiency the police department and its personnel.

Construction of the Delaware River Bridge began in 1922, and it was opened July 1, 1926. Work on the North Broad Street Subway started in August 1924. "The City Beautiful" as exemplified in the Parkway — the city's most ornate thoroughfare — became a reality,

81

Dewey's Flagship "Olympia" at the Philadelphia Navy Yard
"o'ershadowed by the Maine"

thanks to the talents of Jacques Greber and Paul Philippe Cret, its designers.

Culturally, too, the city was expanding. Under the direction of Leopold Stokowski, the Philadelphia Orchestra had developed into one of the world's outstanding symphonic organizations. The Curtis Institute, the Art Alliance, the Academy of the Fine Arts, the Free Library, the University of Pennsylvania, Temple University, and other institutions were increasing Philadelphia's prestige as a center of culture and learning.

A stimulus to civic betterment was the founding of the Philadelphia Award in 1921 by Edward W. Bok, editor of the *Ladies' Home Journal*. A trust fund of $200,000, established by Mr. Bok, provides the $10,000 award that annually goes to the man or woman living in Philadelphia or its vicinity who has performed the service, or brought to culmination the achievement considered most conducive to the advancement of the city's best interests.

The Sesqui-Centennial Exposition

PLANS for celebrating the 150th anniversary of American independence with a great international exposition were first formulated in 1920, during the first administration of Mayor J. Hampton

Moore. In April 1921 Mayor Moore requested an appropriation of $50,000 for furtherance of the plans. The public remained apathetic until the inauguration of Mayor W. Freeland Kendrick, in 1924, and his election to the presidency of the Sesqui-Centennial Exhibition Association. Sufficient funds to begin work on the undertaking were raised by public subscriptions and through appropriations by the city council. The site chosen for the exposition was a section of 1,000 acres in the southern part of the city, adjacent to the Navy Yard.

From the outset, administration of the exposition was strongly criticized because of the political graft involved. William S. Vare, construction contractor and political boss, along with his coterie of real estate speculators, had convinced the officials that the best site for the exposition was on their marshlands, upon which it was almost impossible to build. There resulted a paradoxical situation in which owners of the swamp were paid by the association not only for the right to fill it in, but also a rental for using it as a site for the exposition.

By the time this location finally was chosen, many speculators had learned the value of caution. Several artifically stimulated real estate booms had taken place in various parts of the city, after erroneous information had been given out. Those who bought up tracts near rumored sites of the fair found themselves in possession of land miles from where it eventually was held.

The exposition opened on May 31, 1926, although work on some of the buildings and exhibits was not completed until July 15. A host of visitors was attracted to Philadelphia during the six months of the exposition. Hundreds of displays, pageants, special exhibitions, and sporting events provided endless attractions and interests. (The Municipal Stadium, erected for the exposition, was the scene of the famous championship boxing match between Jack Dempsey and Gene Tunney on September 23, 1926, and the Army-Navy football game in 1936.) Almost every State in the Union and many foreign nations were represented at the exposition, either with special pavilions and exhibits or with temporary displays. Notables from many countries attended, among them Queen Marie and the Princess Ileana of Rumania, Crown Prince Gustavus Adolphus and the Princess Louise of Sweden, and President Calvin Coolidge and Mrs. Coolidge.

Innovations in architectural design and building illumination, as well as the latest inventions of applied science, were features of the exposition. Such new devices as electric refrigerators, audible motion pictures, radios, and sound amplifiers marked the progress achieved in invention during the 50 years since the Centennial Exhibition of 1876. The national air races and aviation exhibits also were outstanding features.

When the exposition closed on November 30, the city had expended a total of $9,667,896.83 on the enterprise. Owing to the vastness of the undertaking, financial difficulties were encountered, but a fairly satisfactory settlement of all expenses and liabilities was eventually made.

The fact that a once-proposed subway-elevated line to Roxborough is still in the category of "plans" is traced to the Sesqui-Centennial. A large sum of money had been set aside by the city council for use in constructing the subway-elevated line. A referendum, taken among the citizens of Roxborough, turned the money over to the exposition as an investment, although it is now generally considered as having been a gift.

The first commercial transatlantic telephone call between Philadelphia and London was made on January 29, 1927, when Josiah H. Penniman, provost of the University of Pennsylvania, spoke to Lord Dawson of Penn at the other end of the wire. The Free Library on the Parkway was opened June 2, 1927. On March 26, 1928, the Art Museum at the head of the Parkway was opened, and the new Broad Street Subway was placed in operation on September 1 of that year. On August 14, 1929, the Tacony-Palmyra Bridge was opened, and the North Philadelphia Station of the Reading Railroad Company was dedicated on September 28. The Rodin Museum on the Parkway, gift of the late Jules E. Mastbaum, was dedicated on November 29, 1929, and the Martin Maloney Memorial Clinic at the University of Pennsylvania on September 20, 1929.

Philadelphia and the Great Depression

FEW Philadelphians who awoke on a crisp autumn morning in late October, 1929, suspected that by the afternoon of that day the great American dream of unlimited and uninterrupted prosperity would be rudely dispelled by the crash of the stock market and the plunge of the entire Nation into the lowest depths of misery, privation, and despair. Not many could have foreseen that the next four years would be among the darkest in the city's history, and that hundreds of thousands of unemployed would walk the streets.

Despite rosy assurances which had been freely broadcast for more than three years that "recovery was just around the corner" and "the worst was over," banks continued to close, bankruptcies increased, financiers and business men committed suicide. bread lines in Philadelphia grew longer as unemployment increased, and the future appeared to be ever more hopeless. There seemed to be no remedy for the situation. Each day that passed saw conditions grow worse instead of better, until even the most optimistic became eventually the most rabid of pessimists.

Meanwhile, numbers of desperate workers were being converted to radicalism. In 1931, a large May Day demonstration of radical labor organizations was broken up by the police ; many arrests were made.

Probably the most impressive result of the depression in Philadelphia, politically, was the change in party sentiment from Republican to Democratic and the conviction among die-hard conservatives that the time had come for property rights and interests to give way to human rights. The election of November 1932 recorded an amazing Democratic vote, although the city had been regarded as the stronghold of entrenched Republicanism since the Civil War, and among the adherents of the new administration were those who had been pillars of the old. Meanwhile, greater numbers of desperate workers were being converted to radicalism. In 1931 a large May Day demonstration of radical labor organizations was broken up by the police and many arrests were made.

The election of November 1932 recorded an amazing Democratic vote, although the city had been regarded as the stronghold of entrenched Republicanism since the Civil War.

Upon assuming office in March 1933, President Roosevelt adopted measures to "fight the depression as we fought the war." Federal funds were appropriated for the relief of the destitute in Philadelphia, and later for the employment of the jobless. Through the efforts of the Civil Works Administration and later the Works Progress Administration, thousands of Philadelphians caught in the maelstrom of the depression were enabled to earn a livelihood for the first time since the depression. Local business was greatly stimulated through the increased purchasing power of thousands of WPA employees.

With the repeal of prohibition, State liquor stores were opened in Philadelphia in 1934, giving employment to many persons and increasing the revenue of the State. With repeal of some of the "Blue Laws" a year later, Sunday baseball games became legalized, while movie houses and other amusements were permitted to operate on the Sabbath.

Tacony-Palmyra Bridge
"a tie that binds the states"

85

Slum Scene
"the place of abandoned hope"

In spite of hard times, a number of new and imposing buildings were erected, such as the new Pennsylvania Station, Thirtieth and Market Streets ; the new Post Office, directly opposite ; the Franklin Institute, with the Fels Planetarium, on the Parkway ; the new Custom House, Second and Chestnut Streets ; the Lincoln-Liberty Building, Broad and Chestnut Streets; the Philadelphia Saving Fund Society Building, Twelfth and Market Streets ; and the Administration Building of the Board of Education, Twenty-first Street and the Parkway.

One of the highlights of 1936 in Philadelphia was the Democratic National Convention, held in the Municipal Auditorium during the week of June 23. Democratic delegations from all the States and Territories thronged the once mighty stronghold of Republicanism during the week of the convention. President Roosevelt was renominated by tumultuous acclamation ; and on Saturday evening, June 27, the President made his acceptance speech before a huge crowd in Franklin Field. Of the throng of nearly 200,000 persons, only 105,000 could be crammed into the stadium, the rest packing the streets outside.

Local Republicanism received its worst defeat on November 3, 1936, when President Roosevelt and the Democratic ticket swept the city with a plurality of more than 200,000. As the election returns began to come in that night, crowds of gleeful Democrats paraded through the musty courtyards and arcades of City Hall, north and south on Broad Street, and east and west on Market, Chestnut, and Walnut Streets. Traffic was at a standstill as one of the most spectacular and uproarious political demonstrations ever held in Philadelphia rocked the central section.

Some progress in slum clearance was made during the first six months of 1937. As a result of the collapse of two slum dwellings in late December 1936 when 7 occupants were killed, a systematic program for clearing substandard areas of the city was started. More than 1,200 dwellings and buildings unfit for habitation were condemned and demolished by order of the municipal authorities. However, no provisions were made for rehousing the tenants.

Celebration of the 150th anniversary of the Constitution of the United States was officially inaugurated May 14, 1937, with opening ceremonies in Independence Hall, during which the original draft of the Constitution was exhibited, and the Liberty Bell was rung by Mayor S. Davis Wilson, who used a gavel made of wood from old trees at Valley Forge.

OLD WAYS AND OLD TALES

MANY nationalities and religions have contributed over a period of more than 250 years to the traditions, social customs, habits of dress, entertainment, and folklore of Philadelphia — some elements of which still stand out like broken strands of silk in an old tapestry.

Although the Swedes were the earliest colonists in Philadelphia, the Quakers, who followed soon afterwards, were most instrumental in giving direction to the trend of daily life. They brought to the New World a philosophy of simplicity and conservatism. Their rather drab style of dress and staid deportment soon were to be influenced, however, by the influx of Germans, Scotch-Irish and Welsh. By 1712 the note of rigid simplicity, at least in its superficial aspect, had begun to change. Human vanity, rather than religious restraint, became the dictator of fashion.

The well-dressed Philadelphia belle of that era wore a silk petticoat, distended by hoops, and a tightly laced stomacher ornamented with gold braid. The sleeves were short and edged with wide point lace. Curls fell at her neck, and her head was protected by a light silk hood. On her feet were satin slippers. Her escort wore a silk coat, its skirts stiffened with wire and buckram. His waistcoat was long-flapped, with wide pockets, and short sleeves terminating in large, rounded cuffs. A point-lace cravat protected his throat. His shoes were square-toed, with small silver buckles ; his silk stockings reached above his knees to meet his silk breeches. On his tie-wig perched a small cocked hat trimmed with lace.

Tradesmen dressed simply. Their garb was generally of stout gray cloth, trimmed in black, with worsted stockings, and leather breeches and shoes.

Colonial days in Philadelphia witnessed rapid changes in styles and fashions. While pro-French feeling was at its height, the styles of France came into vogue. With the elaboration and brightening of fashions, the Quakers became so alarmed that at a Yearly Meeting of Friends they rigidly enforced their rules regulating dress.

Today the gray garb of the Quaker founders has disappeared almost entirely, except in some nearby rural sections. In the city, some elderly ladies still cling to a modified form of the prescribed apparel, while others dress ·in real Quaker style.

Colonial Philadelphia did not remain a citadel of conservative life for long, however. Even in pre-Revolutionary days the city became famous for its entertainment, good food, rare wines, and fine clothes. Many well-to-do Quakers were not averse to tasting these worldly pleasures.

The city became noted for its sumptuous dinners, which were in sharp contrast to the formerly frugal pioneer repast. John Adams, describing one of these feasts, said : "It was a Quaker hostess who pressed upon me at a single meal : duck, ham, chicken, beef, pig, tarts, creams, jellies, truffles, floating island, beer, porter, punch, and wine."

Tea drinking likewise marked social life, and dancing occupied the attention of the younger set. In 1740 several young men, members of families living near Christ Church, established a dancing assembly, which met every Tuesday during the winter. Concerts were given from time to time.

In 1748 a group representing the more aristocratic families founded the Philadelphia Assembly. Subscriptions sold for 40 shillings per year. The assembly's social affairs usually lasted from 6 p. m. to midnight, with card tables provided for those who did not dance. Refreshments consisted of punch and "milk bisket." The present day Assembly Ball, held annually in the second week of December, is a development of the original Philadelphia Assembly.

During the British occupation of Philadelphia in 1777-8, there was a continuous round of suppers, dances, gay theatre parties, and entertainments of all kinds. The most notable was the *Mischianza*, an elaborate pageant in which British officers and Tory civilians participated. Much of the gaiety, as far as the patriotic Philadelphians were concerned, was undoubtedly simulated.

After the war, Philadelphia returned to a comparative sobriety. Isaac Weld, a French writer, commenting on the citizenry in general, said in 1795 : "There is a coldness and reserve, as if they were suspicious of some designs against them. This chills the very heart of those who come to visit them." Other foreigners and visitors from other States likewise criticised the Philadelphia attitude toward strangers.

Sports and Amusements

WITH the diminishing of the Quaker influence, sports and amusements increased in scope and variety. From the earliest days, however, such sports as riding, swimming, fishing, and skating were countenanced even by the sedate Quaker founders. Many leaders in the life of the growing city could be seen in those days skating on the Delaware River.

Sleighing, a sport that found favor with the early Colonials, has survived. The Wissahickon Valley in winter still resounds to the jingle of sleighbells ; while in summer the creek, once the haunt of Indians and pioneer fishermen, is popular with anglers.

Horse racing in Philadelphia made its appearance in Colonial times, and soon became general on the city's streets. Finally it was stopped by law. Race Street was so named because it led directly to the race grounds. Cockfighting was popular with the more aristocratic families, while bull baiting and bear baiting were patronized by the working population.

Boxing, a sport later to hold the attention and interest of thousands of Philadelphians, at first was inhospitably received. A prize fight advertised in 1812 was stopped by constables and aldermen, but 12 years later an English pugilist was able to interest many Philadelphians in the "manly science whereby gentlemen after a few lessons will be enabled to chastise those who may offer violence and protect themselves from attacks of ruffians."

Thus, as Philadelphia acquired a more cosmopolitan population and became correspondingly more liberal in its customs, there came into popular favor many of today's amusements. Billiards, originally denounced as a means of gambling, became a favorite pastime, along with bowls, ten-pins, quoits, bullets or lawn-bowls, and shuffleboard. Even the time-honored English game of cricket had its enthusiasts, though they were not many. Baseball, the national game, made its bow in Philadelphia in 1860.

A favorite game of the younger boys, still indulged in to a certain extent, was "pecking eggs," an amusement popular at Easter time. Any youngster's challenge, "Upper ! Upper ! Who's got an egg ?" yelled at the top of his lungs, would be promptly answered by a contender. Then would ensue a session in which the boys tested the strength of their eggs by striking them together, point to point, but not before a careful examination of the opponent's ammunition, to make sure that no china or guinea egg — or perhaps an egg shell cleverly filled with plaster — had been surreptitiously introduced. Whichever egg was cracked by the impact became the property of the boy who owned the uncracked one.

Another interesting game was "plugging tops." The tops were made of lignum vitae and fitted with long and sharp steel points. The object of the game was to split the opponent's top while it was spinning on the ground by spearing it with another top.

"Shinny" or "bandy," a rudimentary form of hockey, was a sport for the hardy. "Duck on Davy" was a game in which the players attempted from a distance to knock a small stone off a larger one.

Annual Celebrations

OUT of a maze of recreational pursuits and customs, one has become a tradition not only to Philadelphians but to the entire Nation. This is the Mummers' Parade, first held on January 1, 1901, to celebrate the arrival of the new century. It has become as integral a part of Philadelphia's lighter life as the Mardi Gras has of that of New Orleans.

Mummer

The Mummers' Parade is the outgrowth of a custom imported from England in the early nineteenth century. At that time, during Christmas week and on Christmas Eve, the streets of Philadelphia were alive with brightly costumed groups of "mummers." They went from door to door, explaining in rhyme the meaning of their strange garb, and requesting donations. The ancestor of the mummers' celebration was apparently the English saturnalia celebration, under the direction of the Lord of Misrule, a fantastic personage known to the Scotch as the Abbot of Unreason.

The Mummers' tradition has been perpetuated by numerous clubs organized exclusively for the New Year's Day affair. Prizes are offered by the city and by various civic and business associations. Throughout the year the clubs work diligently upon their costumes in preparation for the clebration. Then, on New Years Day, the city's long, straight thoroughfare, Broad Street, becomes a pattern of moving color. Groups in fancy dress, with elaborate headgear and huge capes, march over miles of paved roadway.

String bands, comic divisions, and groups which burlesque current figures and events weave in gay abandon along the Mummers' right-of-way. At varying intervals in the procession are elaborately decorated floats. Along the sidewalk throng hundreds of thousands of spectators. On New Year's Day Philadelphia's spirit is truly festive.

In recent years many Mummers have been stricken with pneumonia because of exposure to the cold in their flimsy costumes. As a result, a movement was started to change the time of the celebration to spring or summer, in order to insure the comfort of spectators and participants alike. However, the tradition of holding the parade on New Year's Day was too strong. An exception was made during the Democratic National Convention in 1936, when the Mummers paraded on a hot night in June before more than 1,000,000 persons.

As the "Cradle of Liberty," Philadelphia has long cherished the

91

Fourth of July as a day of celebration. One feature is a speech by the mayor delivered at Independence Hall. There was a time when Independence Day was marked by the incessant noise of exploding firecrackers, with an attendant loss of life and limb. A present-day ordinance bars this method of celebrating, except for controlled pyrotechnic displays in parks and recreational centers. Philadelphians on Independence Day now go to the banks of the Schuylkill to watch the regatta, spend the day picnicking in the country, or motor to resorts along New Jersey's seashore.

On July 14, the "Independence Day" of the French Republic, members of the city's French societies march to the statue of Joan of Arc at the eastern end of Girard Avenue Bridge. Here a speech is delivered and a wreath placed upon the statue.

May Day in Philadelphia is greeted by the usual terpsichorean displays at various colleges. In bygone years it was claimed unofficially by fish hucksters and shad fishermen as their particular holiday. Maypoles were placed outside the taverns along the water front, and the day was given over to dancing, drinking, and feasting. Labor's traditional May Day celebration is observed in a mild manner by Philadelphia workingmen, who prefer picnics and shore trips to the standardized oratory frequently offered by old-line labor leaders. The left-wing groups, however, assemble annually on Reyburn Plaza in a demonstration of their strength and unity.

Fire Companies

PHILADELPHIA'S earliest fire insurance companies, (the first one was established in 1752) formed as protecting associations for the benefit of subscribers, offered generous rewards to encourage volunteer fire brigades. An alarm was the signal for a race between two or more brigades, the winner earning the right to save the building and collect the reward. The losers waited on the sidelines, no doubt hopeful that the flames would get beyond control, in which event they would be called into service and share in the reward. Frequently there were scrimmages between the companies on the way to a fire, while in the interval, the blaze continued unchecked.

Each insurance company, using its individual device, marked the houses under its protection with plaques placed high on an outside wall, so that the fire brigades knew by whom they would be rewarded. The unfortunate householder who had neglected to subscribe might see the apparatus race to his burning home, and then turn back when the volunteers failed to espy a plaque.

With the formation of the city's paid fire department in 1871 these "fire marks" no longer served any purpose, but many of them may still be seen on the older houses, especially in the central part of

92

the city. These plaques depict a hydrant, a hose, or some other form of early fire-fighting equipment.

Legends and Superstitions

PHILADELPHIA'S rich heritage of folklore, the legends inherited from the many races settling in the tongue of land between the Schuylkill and Delaware, today is preserved largely in historical annals. Some of the quaint beliefs, superstitions, and mythology of the early and later settlers are still retained, but the majority have passed like the Indian legends that preceded them.

To understand the legendary background of Philadelphia, a glance at the racial and religious ancestry of the city is necessary. The Quakers generally were free from superstitions, yet a few odd beliefs that arrived with the rather somber followers of Penn are still cherished by their descendants. Although Philadelphia's Quaker popula-

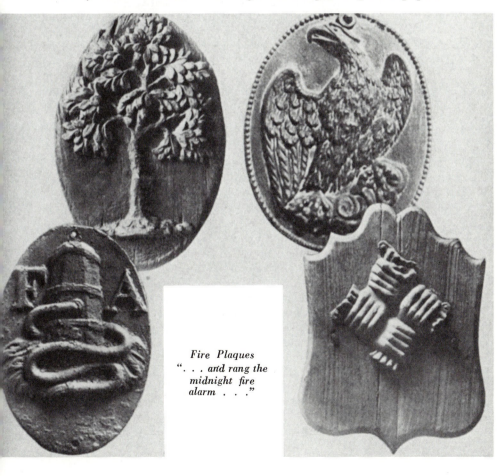

Fire Plaques
". . . and rang the
midnight fire
alarm . . ."

tion is now comparatively small, some Friends still consider it a bad omen to move into a new house on "Sixth Day" (Friday).

The early Swedes who preceded the English Quakers in the Philadelphia section had various legends and superstitions that were looked upon with disfavor by later settlers. Descendants of the first Scandinavians still repeat tales of phantom ships and of sailors carried away in the night by winged devils.

Welsh Quakers who followed William Penn in his search for religious freedom early acquired a 40,000-acre tract of land to the west of Philadelphia. This area became known as the Welsh Barony. Despite the fusion of other nationalities, it still retains a strong Welsh influence. One of the richest residential sections in the United States, this suburban territory lends a credulous ear to tales of haunted houses, lonely roads infested with ghosts, and spirits rising from dark graveyards.

The Welsh settlers were endowed with the native imagination of the Celt. Descendants of those in the remoter farmlands have retained a belief in the supernatural. Charms are supposed to provide immunity from disease, and are sought as a means to reconcile estranged lovers.

One of the early Welsh beliefs was that if a person suffering from a disease were to pass between the forks of a split tree, his malady would disappear in transit. This superstition is now in the limbo of forgotten things. Until about 1850, settlers of Welsh ancestry also believed that horned cattle uttered prayers upon their knees at midnight on Christmas Eve.

Several interesting legends have clung to the city and the memories of its inhabitants, and in a measure have become sectional traditions. One of these centers about the old Chalkley House, or Chalkley Hall as it is more popularly known, the residence of an old Quaker family in what is now Frankford. The legend described a tempestuous romance, disavowed by the Chalkley family, between one of the Chalkley girls and a suitor who failed to win the family's approval. The affair culminated in the suicide of the girl, who had been distraught over her misfortune. For many years, residents of the district declared, the wraith of the unhappy young woman hovered about the old mansion. Even with the advent of modern skepticism and the apparent disappearance of many ghostly traditions of the past, there are those who believe the girl's ghost still walks in Chalkley Hall. A local historian who had been chatting with the watchman of a factory nearby, was whimsically assured by the latter : "That Chalkley ghost comes around once in a while at night."

Unlike most other cities in its treatment of so-called "witches" in the seventeenth century, Philadelphia was not inclined to place much credence in the stories of witchcraft that were prevalent.

Old Ways and Old Tales

In 1683 Margaret Mattson and Yeshro Hendrickson were brought before the Provincial Council, in session at Philadelphia, on charges of witchcraft. William Penn presided at the trial. Lasse Cook, or Cock, an early Swedish settler in the Philadelphia area, acted as interpreter. Among the witnesses questioned was Henry Drystreet, who swore that he had been told, twenty years before, that Margaret Mattson was a witch and had cast spells upon several cows. A woman, Amnaky Coolin, told of an occasion when she and her husband were at home boiling the heart of a calf that had died. The Mattson woman came to the house and asked what they were doing. When they told her they were boiling flesh, she said, "You had better boil the bones." The verdict returned was : "Guilty of the common fame of being a witch, but not guilty in manner and form as indicated."

Since that day no official cognizance has been taken of witchcraft. The belief may still persist that hags ride through the air on broomsticks in Pennsylvania, but the police and courts do not interfere unless the broomstick falls upon someone's head.

Foods

LIQUID notes of the Negro oysterman's cry once trembled upon the chill air of old Philadelphia during the "R" months. Then, before the echoes of his voice had died away, there came in a different key the rousing tones of a lusty Negro, calling: "Here comes de hominy man f'um *wa-ay daown* b'low de Navy Yahd, a-comin' wid he's *hom*-min-ee !"

During the hot summer, as though to compensate for the absence of these hucksters and their wares, came the ice cream man, with his *"Tr-r-r-r-rah, la, la, la !* Here's lemon ice cream and vanilla, too !" And as the trundlebarrow with its cargo of delights appeared, dozens of children ran to meet it, equipped with cup and spoon. Welcome also were the cantaloupe man and the strawberry woman, who sang their songs of luscious fruits to receptive ears.

Still to be heard on the streets on a frosty morning is the rasping cry of "Horseradish, *Hor-r-r-se-radish !"* accompanied by a loud whirr, as the aged vendor grinds his condiment fresh for each customer on a portable machine operated by a foot pedal.

Philadelphians of earlier years waited anxiously for all the delicacies that add the festive touch to an ordinary meal ; but in recent years restaurants and well-stocked stores have made it easy for connoisseurs to obtain the food specialties that "tickle their palates." And there are many dishes of local origin or preparation for which Philadelphia has gained wide renown.

During the "R" months, from September to April, restaurants specializing in sea foods enjoy great popularity, and Philadelphia always has had many such eating places. Lack of adequate transportation facilities in the old days prevented the transport of oysters and other sea foods inland, thus limiting the fisherman's market to seaports and to river towns near the sea. Philadelphia thus became an important sea-food market, and Philadelphians during the years have retained their fondness for bivalves and shad.

Of the latter species of sea food, the Delaware shad is fast dwindling, and within a few years will have disappeared entirely from the market. The first shad of the season—in early spring—come from southern waters, but they do not compare in flavor with those caught later in the Delaware.

To many there is nothing that delights the taste more than a fine, fresh Delaware shad, nicely broiled over the coals, or planked, properly seasoned with salt, pepper, a piece of fresh butter, a dash of lemon juice, ornamented with sprigs of parsley, and flanked on either side by roe broiled a delicate brown. The shad is perhaps the only fish that has given its name to the cut of a garment — the shad-belly coat of the Quaker.

A dish long associated with Philadelphia is pepper pot, a Colonial soup which has become so popular that large canning factories now prepare it for export. The pepper pot of Colonial Philadelphia originally was made in such large quantities that the community kettle of tradition was employed. Whether or not the amount had anything to do with the quality is a moot question, but the fact remains that the soup became identified exclusively with the Quaker City. Women trundled their carts through the streets, crying, "Pepper pot! Old time pepper pot!" selling the product of their kitchens from door to door.

The recipe for this spicy dish was evolved in the early days to utilize beef tripe. It may well be imagined how stintingly the first colonists prepared every edible part of the imported beef. Finely cut cubes of tripe were used as the basis for this soup, with red peppers (possibly to "cover" the flavor of the meat), onions, potatoes, and carrots to give it body and variety. The broth was thickened with flour and small egg-dumplings, the whole being well seasoned and served piping hot.

The early Dutch and Swedes along the Delaware also contributed a prominent item to the list of dishes of Philadelphia fame. These settlers accepted many of the savory foods of the Indians as substitutes for those they had left at home, and concocted many dishes popular today. One of these delicious early foods was scrapple, which was called *pon-haus*.

Scrapple is made from the liquid of boiled pig's-head mixed with corn meal and highly seasoned, then recooked until it has acquired the proper consistency to be sliced when cold. This is a favorite local breakfast dish. It is fried to a crisp brown, and served with fried or poached eggs and fried potatoes. Philadelphia leads in its production. Though its manufacture has spread to other parts of the country, the early Colonial recipe alone has the zest really identified with scrapple. There are several meat-packing houses in the city, specializing in pork products, which prepare great quantities of scrapple every year. Many farmers in the eastern part of the State make their own.

And sticky cinnamon buns! Where can they be found better, in all their sweet "gooey" tastiness, than in Philadelphia, the city of their origin ? Made of sweet dough, the buns are generously sprinkled with cinnamon, currants or raisins, and sugar. The dough is spread out upon the baking board, rolled tight, and cut into sections from two to three inches long. The buns are baked slowly, so that the syrup formed by the heated filling will be absorbed by the dough, while a thin coating will be left on the outside.

Mince pie, which has become a popular dessert in many parts of the country, is another product that early found favor in Penn's city ; it is said that a Quaker family from England popularized mincemeat in Philadelphia in 1830.

In Philadelphia ice cream first made its appearance about 1782. More than a half century later an ingenious Philadelphian, Eben C. Seaman, invented an ice cream freezer operated by steam power, and this refreshing dessert became popular the country over. Philadelphia is now the home of the largest ice cream manufactory in the world, and its product is widely distributed. One feature that distinguishes the local product is the use of the powdered vanilla bean, rather than the extract.

From the beginning, Philadelphia has cherished a full pantry and a substantial table. That fondness for good food, and plenty of it, has not diminished with the years.

THE IMPRINT OF NATIONS

(Population figures based on 1930 Census)

THE varied characteristics of a majority of the nationalities of the world have blended with and balanced one another to form the personality of Philadelphia. Although many of them have settled in compact national communities established by compatriots who preceded them, yet the leaven of their customs and culture has permeated the life of the whole city.

Settlers of Colonial and Revolutionary times, emigrating chiefly from northern and western Europe and bound in many cases by a similarity in tongue and customs, found few obstacles to intermarriage ; thus they merged the characteristics of their respective nations into a homogeneous whole. Ceasing to think of themselves as Berliners, Londoners, or Amsterdammers, they became Philadelphians.

The Swedes, Dutch, English, and Germans were followed by immigrants from virtually all parts of Europe and Asia. Numerically strongest were the Irish, Russians, Jews, and Italians. From China, and in smaller numbers from Japan, came immigrants who are virtually unassimilable. Through the years there was a steady influx of Jews, reaching its peak during the early part of the twentieth century, many coming from Russia and Eastern Europe. A few Jews from other regions are believed to have preceded William Penn to Philadelphia.

The formation of special quarters by peoples not easily assimilated — the Italians, the Jews, and the Greeks — gives the city a certain cosmopolitan air. Sights and sounds of the Old World characterize these localities. European peasant customs and folkways, surviving the pressure or compensating for the meagerness of the new environment, frequently have left an imprint on the American-born children of immigrants.

The population of Philadelphia, according to the 1930 census, is composed of 69 percent native white, totaling 1,359,833 ; about 19 percent foreign-born white, totaling 368,624; and 11 percent Negro, totaling 219,599. The other groups comprise the remainder.

Closest knit of all the various nationalities and races are the Chinese. This is due, no doubt, to the disinclination of the whites to accept them socially, as well as to an innate desire on their part to

98

be left strictly alone. There are approximately 1,500 Chinese in Philadelphia, of whom about three-fourths reside on Race Street, between Eighth and Eleventh Streets.

Although small racial groups usually scatter over the city, the Greeks are an exception. Numbering only 3,415, they live for the most part in the vicinity of Tenth and Locust Streets.

Early settlers came principally to escape religious persecution. Hence, religion occupied much of their time and thoughts. Life was slow, earnest, and conservative ; and Philadelphia came to embody these characteristics. Not until the later groups arrived did the tempo of existence become accelerated.

The primary motive for later immigration was a desire for economic betterment. To that end the later contingents directed their talents and energies, and to them must go much of the credit for building industrial and commercial Philadelphia. With their Continental habits of life and un-Puritanical conception of morality, they did much to liberalize the outmoded Blue Laws which had made the Quaker City unique among great metropolitan centers.

Numbering 270,000 according to the 1930 American Jewish Year Book, the Jews represent a potent force in Philadelphia life. Representing, as they do, many nations, they can hardly be regarded as a distinct race. The fact remains, however, that though they differ

*Old Market on Second
Street at Pine*

from one another in physical characteristics, background, and home-land, they are united by the common bond of their religion.

Jews are found in the most densely settled sections of Philadelphia, largely in Strawberry Mansion, Logan, Wynnefield, and the area between Oregon Avenue and South Street from Third Street to Eighth Street. Other localities with a considerable Jewish population are the section bounded by Sixth and Eighth Streets, Poplar Street and Susquehanna Avenue ; the area around Fifty-eighth Street and Osage Avenue ; and the neighborhood of Fortieth Street and Girard Avenue.

Little is known of the Jews in Philadelphia prior to the Revolution, although the first Hebrew congregation, Mikveh Israel (Hope of Israel), was established here in 1747. Many prominent Philadelphia citizens and American patriots have been members of Mikveh Israel. Among them were Simon Gratz, merchant prince and philanthropist ; Isaac Moses, who subscribed three thousand pounds to the Bank of Pennsylvania so that the Continental Army might be provisioned for two months ; and Haym Solomon, banker and broker, who came to the Colonies from Poland and negotiated all Revolutionary War securities from France and Holland on his own personal security without loss of a cent to America. When Solomon died in 1784, the United States was indebted to him to the extent of $300,000. This debt, although acknowledged by the Federal Government, has never been paid.

Because the laws of many European countries forbade Jews to own land, the early Jewish immigrants had little agricultural knowledge. In 1726 a special act was passed in Pennsylvania permitting Jews to own land and engage in trade and commerce. This act was indirectly responsible for much of Philadelphia's industrial and commercial growth.

Numerous European countries had also denied cultural and educational advantages to the Jews, and, because of this, their appreciation of both became more acute. Since such restrictions were not maintained by William Penn, the Jews emigrated hopefully to the New World colony he founded.

Without the Jews, Philadelphia would still have an orchestra and an Academy of Music, but the impetus given to the musical movement in this city by members of the Jewish race cannot be denied. The Italians, too, with their passion for all forms of music, especially the opera, share in the credit for its local development. In the ticket lines at the Academy of Music there are always large numbers of Italians, their faces alight with anticipation.

The Italian population in Philadelphia numbers 182,368, of which nearly 70,000 are foreign-born. Apparently preferring the foods and customs of their homeland, these people do not assimilate as easily as some of the other groups, and are inclined to settle in sharply defined districts — notably South Philadelphia and, to a lesser degree, in sections of Chestnut Hill, Mount Airy, Germantown, and West Philadelphia.

Like the Irish, they are much interested in politics, and they formed an integral part of the huge Vare machine which dominated Philadelphia for a number of years. As has been the case with other large immigrant groups, they have been imposed upon by "ward-heelers," who attach themselves to the bewildered newcomers almost as soon as they arrive. These small-fry politicans help them to obtain naturalization papers, and as a result the vote of the immigrant usually goes to his "benefactor." Naturally light-hearted, and fond of good music, spicy food, and sour wine, this group has done much to soften the sterner ways of earlier Quaker and German settlers.

At the top of the Italian social scale are musicians, artists, physicians, jurists, and writers. Others work as barbers, vendors, and laborers. The restaurant business has attracted them, and Philadelphia contains a number of establishments specializing in the foods and wines of Italy.

The vast majority being of Catholic faith, they lend color to the city with religious festivals. Street parades in which sacred statues are carried frequently wind through the Italian quarter. Even in sports the Italian clings to the games of his fatherland. Bocce, a game related to bowling, is played extensively enough to warrant space on the sport pages of large daily newspapers, as well as in the Italian press.

Districts densely settled by Italians are those areas between Snyder Avenue and Bainbridge Street from Twenty-third to Seventh Streets, and the neighborhoods near Sixty-fourth and Carleton Streets and Fiftieth and Thompson Streets.

The German-born population in Philadelphia, numbering 37,923 in 1930, appears to assimilate easily. Intermarriage is common, and the average German is quick to adopt many American customs and to acquire a facile knowledge of English. The large numbers of "German-American" clubs and organizations in the Quaker City, however, indicate a strong attachment to the Fatherland.

The Germans flock to their 200 singing societies in the city, and seem glad to drop American ways for an evening devoted to songs of the Rhine country. This Teutonic love for community singing, indeed, has done much toward the development of music, especially of choral work, in this city. That the German in Philadelphia is reluctant to break away completely from the Old Country, its language, customs, and viewpoint, is further evidenced by the fact that there are two daily and two weekly newspapers printed in German.

Rigidly trained in his homeland to respect all forms of constituted authority, and imbued with the Teutonic ideal of "Church,

101

Home, and Children," the transplanted German makes a good citizen. Unspectacular by nature, he goes ahead with his plans in a determined manner which makes not for brilliant but for lasting accomplishments.

Philadelphia crime-news seldom features German names. Home-loving as it is, the German population has played a considerable part in gaining for Philadelphia its reputation as a "city of homes."

A large percentage of the German-born came to this city in the years following the Great War, when economic conditions abroad had become intolerable. Another wave of immigration from Germany followed the advent of Adolf Hitler as Reichsfuehrer. These immigrants included many of the Jewish faith who sought relief from laws depriving them of citizenship and (in many instances) property rights. This latter group contained a number of educators and scholars seeking a land where free expression of ideas would be tolerated. They have added in large measure to the cultural development of Philadelphia.

Strangely enough, the principal causes of the latest German immigration to Philadelphia were identical with those of the first — religious persecution and poverty. Warfare had torn Germany in the seventeenth and eighteenth centuries ; and from the Palatinate, bordering the Rhine, came these first immigrants. Most important among the early Teutonic settlers was Francis Daniel Pastorius, who came to Philadelphia in 1683 as a representative of the Frankfort Land Company. With him came a group which settled that section of Philadelphia now known as Germantown. The Teutonic love of home life is reflected today by this part of the city, Germantown, which is noted as one of the finer residential sections. Other German neighborhoods are in the vicinities of Fifth Street and Girard Avenue, Eighth Street and Lehigh Avenue, Twenty-ninth Street and Girard Avenue, and Olney.

Spicing the melting pot with Celtic aggressiveness are the Irish, to the number of 51,941 foreign born who keep in close contact with the hundreds of thousands of Irish descent among the city's population. Prime factors in the military and civil work of forming the new Nation, they are attracted by the hurly-burly of politics — perhaps because the element of competition in a political fight appeals to their traditional pugnacity, or perhaps because a successful politican must be a successful "mixer," a type to which the Gaelic sense of humor and love of conversation are peculiarly adapted. At any rate, the Irish have made themselves a power in shaping the political destinies of the Quaker City. Many societies named after Ireland's counties help immigrants to establish themselves and to keep in contact with friends from their native soil.

Although the majority of Irish came to Philadelphia after the great potato famine in Ireland in the middle of the nineteenth century, and during the early days of the twentieth century, a number resided here at the time of the Revolutionary War.

The city's Polish population, totaling 30,582 foreign born, is a stabilizing influence. Home-loving, hard working, and unobtrusive, they maintain in large measure the customs and language of their native country. Nevertheless, Poles prize American citizenship, and the great majority are either citizens or have applied for citizen's papers. Polish immigration on a large scale began in 1870, the main reason for its growth being political persecution in the homeland. Most Poles are members of the Catholic Church, and in Philadelphia their children are educated in parochial schools situated in the Polish districts. The Polish National Church, of recent origin in Pennsylvania, has grown steadily as a result of the large Polish immigration of late years.

Impetus was given to Philadelphia shipping, and to the textile and lace industries by immigrants from England, Scotland, and Wales, who were among the earliest groups to settle in the city. Bound close to one another and to America by a similarity of tongue and custom, they assimilate readily. Like the Germans, however, the English are intensely devoted to their homeland. The Empire and the things which it connotes seem to be forever in the foreground of their interest.

Of these foreign-born groups in Philadelphia, the English number 24,415, the Scots 11,313, and the Welsh 865. These groups, for the most part scattered throughout the city, are slightly predominant in the vicinity of Kensington.

Old Philadelphia — the Quaker City of Colonial, Revolutionary, and Civil War days — was much more influenced by the habits and viewpoint of the English than is the case today. In the early days, those of English birth or descent were in the majority, and the names of most of Philadelphia's leaders in the commercial and professional fields were of Anglo-Saxon derivation. Today, although not so important in industry and commerce as formerly, those of British descent still guard the forbidding portals of the city's "400." In the Quaker City Social Register, admittedly one of the most select in the country, the names are preponderantly of English origin.

Canadians, exclusive of the 636 French-Canadians living in the city, total 3,593. So similar are they to Philadelphians in thought, language, and custom that they can hardly be regarded as a foreign group. They do not reside in any particular section, nor do they flock into particular industries or professions.

Only 2,245 Swedes live in the city. They do not support a foreign-language paper, and are well assimilated. Descendants of the early Swedish settlers have lost their identity in the melting pot. Little remains today of Swedish influence save ancient churches, and grave-stones bearing the names of men who lived, loved, fought, and died in another and different Philadelphia.

The 970 Danes living here are almost lost in the city's swirl of humanity. Arriving in Philadelphia around 1890, most of them now have become an integral part of the American scene. Virtually the only remaining vestige of their homeland lies in their cookery, al-though there are no Danish restaurants in Philadelphia. The same is generally true of the city's 1,309 Norwegians.

The Russian population of Philadelphia, totaling 80,959, exclusive of Russian Jews, is a close-knit group that rarely mingles in a social way with other groups. Most of its members today work in oil re-fineries, leather plants, cigar factories, textile mills, and steel found-ries, but rarely in executive positions.

Mass immigration from Russia did not begin until 1905. Almost all the newcomers sought the New World to escape poverty, compulsory military service, and religious persecution aimed mainly at Russian Jews. Locomotive works, foundries, and shipyards provided employ-ment for most of them. For convenience sake they settled near their workshops, first in the area between Tenth Street and the Delaware River from Spring Garden Street to Girard Avenue. Later they in-habited the section between Point Breeze and Snyder Avenues, from Twenty-second to Thirtieth Street.

The peak in Russian immigration was reached in 1915-17. In 1921 the vanguard of "White Russians," those loyal to the Tsarist regime, reached Philadelphia from New York. Approximately 50 White Rus-sians are living here today, and (in contrast with the major Russian group) virtually all are engaged in either the arts or the professions.

Because of their disinclination to mingle outside their own circles, Russians have not become prominent in civic affairs. However, they have aided the artistic development of Philadelphia by their patron-age of dance and music recitals.

Coming to Philadelphia in great numbers during the latter part of the nineteenth century and the early part of the twentieth, Philadel-phia's 7,639 Rumanians plunged into the active life of the city and were soon assimilated. They readily adopted American ways and the English language, and chose to live in widely separated sections of the city rather than segregate themselves. This Americanization has become complete in all phases except that of cuisine, for they still prefer the foods of their mother country. Several restaurants cater to the Rumanian palate.

The Rumanian population tends toward the "white-collar" occu-pations, music, and the arts in general. A lesser number are laborers. Aside from their cooking, the one link Philadelphia Rumanians maintain with their homeland is the celebration of May 10 in com-

104

memoration of Rumania's independence. On this occasion folk dances are featured and native dress lends color to the affair.

Although Austrians arrived in Philadelphia as early as 1712, they were but a handful in number and scarcely influenced the city's thought. The majority came during the latter nineteenth and early twentieth centuries. At present, 10,707 live in Philadelphia. They are closely allied by tongue and customs to the Germans. No definite sections are inhabited by them, although the early settlers lived in the neighborhood between Fourth and Eighth Streets from Girard Avenue to Norris Street. Many now live in the section between Twenty-fifth and Twenty-eighth Streets from Spring Garden to Oxford Street.

Another group which had but little effect in shaping the city's life and traditions is the Yugoslavs, of whom there are approximately 1,394. Most of these are factory workers or, in the case of young women, domestics. Yugoslavs are concentrated in numbers in the vicinity of Twenty-fourth and Wolf Streets.

Czechoslovaks number 3,868. Many of these are Bohemians, generally of fair education. Many find employment in "white-collar" positions. They live mainly in the section between Spring Garden Street and Columbia Avenue from Front to Sixth Street.

Curb Market at Ninth and Christian Streets
"The Piazza del Mercato of Philadelphia"

Philadelphia's 7,102 Hungarians are scattered throughout the various trades and professions. They mix easily, and are readily assimilated. Hungarian and German are spoken by them, in addition to English. Those coming from a section near the Polish border also speak Polish. One Hungarian newspaper is printed in Philadelphia, with a two-page English supplement for American-born readers.

Many of Philadelphia's 3,415 Greeks seem attracted to the restaurant business above other commercial ventures. Greek domination is especially true of the smaller quick-lunch establishments, as devoid of elaborate cuisine as they are of tablecloths. The bulk of the Greeks came here between 1900 and 1910. They settled in the Richmond section, along Gaskill Street between South and Lombard Streets, and in the area between Eighth and Twelfth Streets from Locust Street to Spruce Street.

Philadelphia contains many other racial and national groups, but these are so few in number that their effect in molding the city's appearance, customs, and institutions have been negligible. Outstanding among these minority groups are the Armenians, who are devoted mostly to the rug business, and the Belgians, who engage mainly in the textile industry.

Negro Progress

THE story of the Negro in Philadelphia is a repetition of the saga of struggle marking his progress elsewhere. Here, however, he found the advantages of what in early days was a comparatively sympathetic environment.

A few Negro slaves were owned by the earliest Dutch and Swedes ; but when the Quakers came to found Penn's city, they looked with disfavor upon slaveholding, and many began almost immediately to agitate for its abolition. A State law providing for gradual emancipation was enacted in 1780, just 81 years before the outbreak of the Civil War. Those who could afford it purchased slaves for the purpose of freeing them, and then assisted the freedmen in adjusting themselves to their new life. Others participated in the operation of the Underground Railroad, a system which assisted escaping slaves to reach the North and the Canadian border.

Work of the first freedmen was limited to the domestic field, but by 1800 they were finding employment as seamen, mechanics, carpenters, wagonsmiths, and as skilled workers of other types. Despite racial oppression, they became home-owners, supported their own schools, contributed to beneficial societies, and financed their own business enterprises. A group duplicated in no other city was the guild of caterers, which had a monopoly on the catering business and

106

was so successful that some of its members reached affluence. The business, carried on from generation to generation, deteriorated only after modern youth became attracted to new fields.

In 1780 Philadelphia's Negro population of about 3,000 was concentrated in the area between Fifth and Ninth Streets from Pine to Lombard Street. The population doubled in the next 10 years, spreading westward across Broad Street to form a center of Negro business activity at Sixteenth and Seventeenth Streets, and a residential district in southwest Philadelphia. The spread took a northward trend in 1793, when about one-fourth of the Negro population was living between Market and Vine Streets. The trend continued northward, until now the north central section rivals South Philadelphia as a Negro residential center.

Today about 2,500 Negroes are employed in the government of the city and county, drawing annual salaries totaling approximately $2,-000,000. They include policemen, detectives, school teachers, clerks, inspectors, chemists, draftsmen, and janitors.

The mayoralty campaign of 1880 evoked the first sign of concerted action on the part of the city's Negro voters. Led by William Still, Robert Purvis, and James Forten, they revolted against the Republican Party. The Democrats rewarded them with appointments to the city police force. Negroes became increasingly political-minded thereafter, and today their vote is recognized as an important factor. Although members of the race served on the Common Council as early as 1893, James H. Irvin, elected councilman in 1935, has been the only Negro to sit in the new City Council.

A writer on Negro society of the nineteenth century cites the graciousness of manner and success in entertaining of the Negro matrons in Philadelphia. A knowledge of music was general. Musical instruments were found in every home and an interest and appreciation for melody and rhythm was cultivated. Often the first music lessons were given in a church. Still the center of social activity, the churches have taught the fundamentals of music to talented youth. In this manner the voice of Marian Anderson, now a marvel to music lovers the world over, was discovered.

As early as 1820 the African Methodist Episcopal Church in this city founded a publishing company, which still operates under the original charter. This institution, the A.M.E. Book Concern, is situated at 716 South Nineteenth Street. Near its former site on South College Avenue stands another important Negro institution, the Berean Church, built in the nineteenth century. The Bethel Methodist Episcopal Church, at Sixth and Lombard Streets, was built by Bishop Richard Allen in 1794; first of its denomination in the country, the church still stands on the original site. In 1791, St. Thomas' Church, first African Protestant Episcopal Church in

107

America, was founded by Absalom Jones. Originally on Second Street below Walnut, the church is now on Twelfth Street below Walnut. Both these men were responsible, in the main, for the formation of the first Negro religious groups in the country operating alone and independent of the white sects.

During the decade of 1860-70, there was a decrease of 17 percent in the Negro population of Philadelphia. Following the Civil War and emancipation, great hopes were entertained by Negroes for the rapid cultural and social advancement of their race. Nowhere was there a more fertile field than Philadelphia, seat of Quakerism in the United States. A growing spirit of liberalism toward the Negro was manifested here, many being disposed to grant him a chance to make his way in the world. Slowly but surely, petty hindrances were brushed away and the shackles of racial prejudice loosened. The Negro population increased by degrees, starting in 1870. In the following decade the increase amounted to 43.13 percent.

When the influx began, "old Philadelphians" — Negroes that had been serving aristocratic Philadelphia families for years — regarded the newcomers with disfavor, partly because Northern Negroes were better educated and their standard of living was much higher. This created among Negroes a class-consciousness that still exists.

Poor housing facilities and the rigorous Northern climate took its toll of these migrants. Census returns in 1880, erroneous in figures, seemed to indicate the race was dying out. But such was not the case. The death rate, 32.5 per 1,000 for the period from 1830 to 1840, remained at approximately the same level, 31.25 per 1,000 for the years 1884-90. Strong constitutions, improved living conditions, and better educational and medical facilities reduced the death rate to 24.42 per 1,000 by 1937.

Negro workers were hard hit during the depression that followed the Wall Street crash in 1929, and the business and professional men depending upon them for success suffered in their turn. Those in the medical field were affected with especial severity. Negro doctors, dependent almost entirely upon their own people for patronage, found thousands of these patrons unemployed and without funds. Both white and Negro workers discovered during this period the common bond of their economic status, and Negroes now form part of the membership of labor unions, in addition to their own many fraternal and social organizations.

Numerous social agencies are devoted to the interests of the race in the city, the principal one being the Armstrong Association, a member of the Welfare Federation. The city's Negro newspapers are the *Tribune*, established in 1884, and the *Independent*, founded in 1930.

108

GOVERNMENTAL MACHINERY

F AR exceeding even the optimistic hopes of William Penn, Philadelphia grew in area and governmental jurisdiction until the boundaries of the city coincided with those of Philadelphia County. This was accomplished by the absorption of many small towns that even as late as the middle of the nineteenth century were suburbs of the city.

Francisville, Belmont, Kensington, Northern Liberties, Richmond, Southwark, Penn, Manayunk, Bridesburg, Roxborough, Lower Dublin, Crescentville, Fish Town, Morrisville, Holmesburg, Haddington, Spring Garden, Blockley, Byberry, Delaware, Fox Chase, Germantown, Frankford, White Hall, Mount Airy, Franklinville, Mechanicsville, Hestonville, Kingsessing, Moreland, Moyamensing, Oxford, Tacony, Aramingo, Coopersville, Feltonville, Hollinsville, Chestnut Hill, Eastwick, Overbrook, Wynnewood, Oak Lane, Ogontz and Harrowgate — all of these villages and towns, together with Penn's original Philadelphia, compose the city of today.

Nevertheless, a legal fiction persists in treating county and city as separate entities, causing a somewhat complicated dual legislative and executive machine. For several years action has been proposed to consolidate the two coextensive governments, in order to simplify the set-up and to cut down expenditures.

Prior to February 2, 1854, when the Act of Consolidation went into effect, Philadelphia proper was bounded by South Street, Vine Street, the Schuylkill, and the Delaware. With the passage of the act, the boundaries of Philadelphia were fixed virtually as they are today. A part of Cheltenham Township, in Montgomery County, however, was annexed in 1916.

The principal law under which the present city government operates is the act of June 25, 1919, with a number of amendments, popularly known as the City Charter. Philadelphia has the "mayor and council" form of government. The Mayor, who is one of 73 officials elected by the voters of the city at large, is the chief executive, chosen for a term of four years. It is his duty to enforce the ordinances enacted by the 22 members of the City Council, elected by voters in the eight Councilmanic Districts (coinciding with State Senatorial Districts) into which Philadelphia is divided. In all, some 6,400 officials are elected in the various districts and wards.

109

City Hall Tower
"where Penn stands watchfu
guard o'er his city"

Under the Mayor are his thirteen assisting executive departments : Public Safety; Public Works; Public Welfare; Public Health; Wharves, Docks and Ferries; City Transit; City Treasurer; City Controller; Law (City Solicitor) ; Civil Service Commission; Receiver of Taxes; Supplies and Purchases; and City Architecture. The City Treasurer, City Controller, and Receiver of Taxes are elected for terms of four years.

The Director of Public Safety is the central head of the Police, Fire, Electrical, Maintenance and Repairs, Building Inspection, Elevator Inspection, and Steam Engine and Boiler Inspection Bureaus. Bureaus under the Department of Public Works include : City Property, Lighting and Gas, Water, Highways, Street Cleaning, and the combined department of Engineering, Zoning, and Surveys. The Department of Public Welfare directs the Bureaus of Charities and Correction, Personal Assistance, and Recreation.

Several other agencies function along specialized lines. They are the Sinking Fund Commission, Registration Commission, Gas Commission, Board of Pensions, Art Jury, Zoning Commission, and the Commission on City Planning.

The Commissioners of Fairmount Park, appointed by the Court of Common Pleas, have charge not only of Fairmount Park, but also of 25 small parks and squares, the Parkway, and Roosevelt Boulevard. This branch of the city government is virtually autonomous. It maintains the park guards—a special police force which is entirely independent of the Municipal Bureau of Police.

The Free Library system and the museums of the city are controlled by special boards of trustees.

In addition to the Magistrates' Courts, which are not tribunals of record, there are four trial courts : Common Pleas, Quarter Sessions of the Peace, Orphan's Court, and the Municipal Court. The Court of Oyer and Terminer and General Jail Delivery hears only murder trials.

The division of governmental authority between city and county is not distinct, some of the principal officers receiving dual salaries for similar duties in city and county governments. The City Treasurer is the County Treasurer ; the City Controller is County Controller ; the City Commissioners serve also as County Commissioners. This quality exists likewise with the Corner, District Attorney, Clerk of Quarter Sessions, Prothonotary, Register of Wills, and Recorder of Deeds.

Public education in Philadelphia is conducted under supervision of the Board of Public Education, the 15 members of which are appointed by a board of judges of the Common Pleas Court for overlapping terms of six years.

111

HUB OF COMMERCE AND INDUSTRY

PHILADELPHIA was born into a world still in the handicraft stage of economic development; the home was no less the producing than the consuming center of economic life in that slow-moving, candle-lit period when the prime motive force was the energy of man and beast. For many the basis of living was a subsistence standard in the narrowest meaning of the term; for a few there were some luxuries, but such luxuries as today's Philadelphia worker would deem commonplace.

The early settlement was on the fringe of the frontier. Its economy was a pioneer economy in large part, a basic struggle for the bare necessities of existence. With the passing years, Philadelphia has attained maturity in a world where the economics of plentitude have replaced the pioneer economy — a machine world in which the standard of living of the prosperous is so high that it would have astonished the founding fathers. Despite the productivity of the machine, however, many Philadelphians today live under conditions which are only a slight improvement over those existing in the days of the pioneers.

In Penn's time industry in the town was centered mainly in the home. Women and children carded, spun, and wove wool for clothing; they also produced knitted wear and made articles of leather and fur. Iron was melted and wrought, bricks were pressed in hand-operated molds, and stone was quarried by the men according to their individual needs.

Today Philadelphia is an industrial city. Thousands of factories meet the diversified needs of a technological civilization, and a modern transportation system distributes to every quarter of the world the commodities made here. It is a great and growing port through which flow the products and resources of a teeming hinterland: bituminous coal and anthracite, iron, steel, and other mineral products, together with the harvests of forest and farm — the diversified output of a giant and highly creative national industry. Great municipal piers for coastwise and transocean shipping, belt line and elevated-subway transportation systems, spacious manufacturing and storage plants, and a river alive with traffic attest the city's share in the forward thrust of America.

The city's economic destiny was determined by its location and by the industrious character of its people. It possessed the potentialities

112

of a manufacturing center and a port easily accessible from the sea, with harborage on a deep and wide river. The neighboring region was rich in timber, minerals, water power, and arable land. Being close to the sea, it had the assurance of a constant labor supply in the steady stream of immigration from the Old World. These natural advantages are today supplemented by the presence in the city of a large supply of skilled labor, and the fact that the city itself furnishes an excellent home market for the products of the industrial plants, more than 2 billion dollars being expended annually in the whole-sale and retail marts of business.

Philadelphia's first important industry, the manufacture of textiles, has remained its greatest. Its mills, the majority of which are in the Kensington and Frankford sections, produce 5 percent of the Nation's output in textiles. This industry originated with the German settlers, whose families produced woolen hose on home-made wooden frames, the product being sold for the equivalent of a dollar a pair. In another phase of textile manufacture, the making of rugs and car-pets, the city was a pioneer. The first woven carpet produced in the New World was made in Philadelphia in 1775, and by 1845 the industry had attained considerable magnitude and prosperity. The manufacture of knitted and hooked rugs, from strips of cloth torn off wornout garments, began with the city's founding.

The textile industry's 92,573 workers now maintain an average an-nual production with a value exceeding a quarter billion dollars. A great diversity of items is represented, such as clothing, lace, blan-kets and robes, flags and banners, print goods, tents and awnings, cordage, burlap and jute bagging, knitted goods, hats, uniforms, braids, tapes, and bindings.

The manufacture of hats, a specialized branch of textile making, had Colonial roots in Germantown. The high-crowned Germantown beaver hat, hand-felted and hand-blocked, adorned the head of many a Colonial aristocrat and was worn and admired even beyond the Alleghenies. Today another Philadelphia-made hat, the Stetson, is so widely known that it trade name has become a vernacular synonym for a man's headgear. The fac-tory in which it is made, in normal times, provides employment for 5,460 men and women and occupies a floor area of 25 acres. Multifold are the beavers, otters, muskrats, Belgian

Hosiery Worker
"a maker of silken sheaths"

113

hares, Scottish rabbits, and South American nutria whose fur comes to commercial use in this establishment.

Closely related to textile manufactures is the leather industry. Its expansion in Philadelphia has been stimulated by a plentiful supply of water soft enough to be used in tanning and a climate favorable to the proper processing of leather. Philadelphia-made shoes are in many places deemed a superior product, owing doubtless to local manufacturers' concentration on a higher quality of footwear.

In the preparation of glazed kid the city excels. It was a Philadelphian, Robert H. Foerderer, who perfected the first American process for making that type of leather which previously had been imported. As a consequence of its predominance in the leather industry, the city has become one of the Nation's leading markets for hides and peltries.

Although the city takes a large proportion of the country's production of hides, few of them are from animals slaughtered in Philadelphia. Its supply of meat and other products comes mainly from the packing houses of the Middle West and the Southwest. There was a time when the central city was dotted with abattoirs. Now, however, excepting two large slaughterhouses on Gray's Ferry Avenue, and one at Third Street and Girard Avenue, all are far from the city center.

The production of other articles of food is a highly diversified and widely scattered industry. Eight hundred and seventy-six firms are engaged in it, with an average annual production exceeding $200,-000,000 in value. Philadelphia scrapple and Philadelphia-made ice cream are two specialties that have a wide sale within the radius fixed by their perishable nature.

In the refining of sugar Philadelphia is second in the world. The first sugar refinery in the United States, established on Vine Street above Third in 1783, functioned for more than a century. Today there are three great refineries in the city, giving employment to about 2,477 persons.

From its earliest days, Philadelphia has produced liquors and malt beverages. The early colonists made sassafras beer, persimmon brandy, and small beer from Indian maize. As the city expanded, brewhouses and distilleries were established. Like the public houses, they were confined to the water front, but their products had a wide distribution. The early brewhouses and distilleries were the beginning of an important industry, and although the largest distillery is near the Delaware in South Philadelphia, many large plants have located on the outskirts or in the suburbs. After the period of "hibernation" enforced by the Eighteenth Amendment, the industry here prospered again.

The tobacco trade is also important on Philadelphia's commercial horizon. Cigars are the chief output of the city's 59 tobacco factories.

114

Snuff manufacture, of major importance in the nineteenth century, has declined in recent years.

A once important Philadelphia industry, the manufacture of cooking and heating stoves, has been curtailed. These stoves were turned out in great numbers for two centuries. In Colonial days the stoves were small "foot" models, taken along to the unheated churches of the time. Later, the Franklin and the so-called "cannon" types were Philadelphia specialties. The market was greatly reduced by the rise of oil and gas stoves for cooking, and of hot-air furnaces, hot water, steam, and vapor boilers, and oil-burning devices for heating. The former importance of this industry may readily be judged by the fact, that, even under these conditions, the city still produces more than $3,000,000 worth of stoves and furnaces annually.

Another Philadelphia industry that has languished is the carriage-building trade. It began humbly in a wheelwright's shop on Market Street near the water front, a few years before the Revolution. By the middle of the following century it had progressed to such extent that the local carriage makers and coach builders were capable of competing with and in some instances surpassing the craftsmen of Europe. In an age when the world of fashion drove behind spanking teams to its gaslit soirées, a barouche or a landau was the moving symbol of sound social position, and the task of supplying the vehicles was one of no little importance.

Carriages gave way before the relentless advance of the internal combustion engine, and the carriage builders turned to other pursuits. One branch of the industry still remains in the city, the manufacture of baby carriages — a vehicle conceived in the fertile mind of a Philadelphia carriage maker in 1831. They were first produced as miniature coaches for the children of the wealthy, but time has so democratized them that they have become an embarrassment to male parents the country over.

The city shares also in the automotive industry. The J. G. Brill Company, the world's largest maker of city transit equipment, and pioneer in the development of traction equipment from early horse-car days, is situated here. Another Philadelphia concern, the Budd Company, has built many of the modern light-weight streamlined trains which are revitalizing American railroad transport. It was here that the *Burlington Zephyr*, among the first of the streamlined trains, was designed and constructed.

An outstanding achievement of the Budd Company in 1937 was the completion of the first "desert dreadnought," a huge, light-weight, stainless steel bus trailer designed especially for passenger service in the Syrian desert. Styled for speed and built on principles similar to

115

Midvale Steel Workers
"Breaking up the Final"

those employed in the stainless steel streamlined railroad coaches produced by the same company, the bus has succeeded in cutting existing schedules more than a third.

It was built for the Nairn Transport Company, Ltd., and delivered to that company at Beirut. Because the length of the vehicle — 57 feet, 6 inches — was too great to permit turning of ordinary corners, it was necessary for the company to make advance studies of the road to New York and lay out special routes to get it through city streets. The trailer, drawn by a 150-horsepower Diesel tractor, is an air-conditioned sleeper with upper and lower berths. It was designed to make the 600-mile run between Damascus and Baghdad in 15 hours.

Philadelphia has also made an important contribution to steam rail transport through the Baldwin Locomotive Works which operated for many years on Broad Street at Spring Garden, but was later removed to Eddystone, south of the city in Delaware County. The first Baldwin locomotive, *Old Ironsides*, was built in Philadelphia in 1832, in the shops of Matthias Baldwin and David H. Mason, at Fourth and Walnut Streets. It was dubbed the "fair weather engine," because its weight of only five tons was not sufficient to give it traction on rails made slippery by rain. It puffed along valiantly on fair days, but during bad weather horses replaced it. From that uncertain beginning the Baldwin production has grown, until today its locomotives traverse the rails of almost every nation.

In shipbuilding, likewise, Philadelphia has figured largely. The vast Cramps' shipyard on the Delaware, until its closing in recent years, was the birthplace of fine vessels from the days of the sail to those of the turbine. Many of the country's war-craft were built in that yard, and some of the world's renowned pleasure craft took shape upon its way — among them Jay Gould's famed yacht *Atalanta*. Philadelphia was also the home of the first propeller steamer built in the United States. This steamer, the *Princeton*, was constructed at the Philadelphia Navy Yard in 1843. Two years earlier, the *Mississippi*, in which Commodore Matthew Calbraith Perry sailed to Japan where he negotiated a treaty opening the ports of Shimoda and Hakodate to United States commerce, was built here.

As it has contributed to speedier transportation, so has the city had a part in improving the world's means of communication. Two of its prominent manufacturing plants were pioneers in the radio industry, and some of the improvements which have given the air a voice had their origin in Philadelphia laboratories. In the related field of electrical equipment, the city has shared honors with Pittsburgh and Schenectady.

The manufacture of iron and its alloys is now concentrated around the sources of raw materials — the coal and iron mines west of the

117

Alleghenies. In Colonial days, however, Philadelphia was the leading iron producer of the Nation, and today it maintains a prominent position in the manufacture of light steel and non-ferrous products. Especially is the city a factor in the production of edged tools essential to high-speed machine manufacturing. Toolmaking in the city had an early beginning, the first saw in America having been forged in Philadelphia before the Revolution. Today the variety of tools produced is limited only by the requirements of the market. From the molten metal there eventually emerge machetes to cut the cane of Cuba, knives to behead the pineapple plants of Hawaii, and a great variety of cutting tools for the lathes, shapers, and planers of American industry.

In two other industries that are factors in modern life, the production of paper and printing, Philadelphia ranks among the first flight cities. Its 45 paper factories turn out products ranging from paper towels and railroad ticket stock to the finest bond and linen papers. The city's first paper mill was erected about 1693. Its natural corollary, the printing press, soon followed. In the United States today, only New York exceeds Philadelphia in the volume and variety of periodicals and commercial matter produced by its publishing houses and printing shops. In the allied fields of bookbinding, engraving, and lithography the city has many establishments.

In still another modern industry, the making of chemicals, Philadelphia claims a "first." From the Colonial retorts of Christopher and Charles Marshall emerged in 1793 probably the first American-made sulphuric acid. John Harrison, a pioneer in the manufacture of nitric acid, is also credited with having produced sulphuric acid at that time.

In 1789 Samuel Wetherill and his son Samuel, Jr., began the production of white lead, the first to be manufactured in the United States. In 1804 they erected a white lead factory. Prior to the death of Christopher Marshall, in 1797, the Marshall laboratory also was producing white lead regularly. Some years later this firm was making ether in commercial quantities; in the 1830's it added quinine and strychnine to its catalog. The Marshall laboratory is dwarfed in size now by many Philadelphia chemical plants, in which are produced a diversity of reagents and pharmaceuticals.

In 1839 a Philadelphian discovered that by using superheated sulphur instead of nitric acid, he could harden India rubber and still preserve its pliancy. The experimenter was Charles Goodyear. Aided by his brother-in-law, William De Forrest, and exhausting the financial resources of his entire family over a period of five years, Goodyear in 1844 perfected a vulcanizing process that is now followed in the rubber industry throughout the world, but he lost his patents for France and England.

118

In 1844 Samuel S. White, then only 22 years of age, embarked in the artificial-tooth manufacturing business at what was then 116 North Seventh Street, using his attic for a "factory" and a downstairs room for a "store." Up to that time, dentists carved crude teeth from blocks of porcelain — wretched imitations of nature's handiwork. Young White strove to make his dental work resemble the original as nearly as possible. His success was accelerated by the accidental discovery of feldspar as a base for porcelain, and within a short time he and two assistants were forced to seek larger quarters. Today there are a half hundred dentistry laboratories in Philadelphia, turning out approximately 83,000,000 artificial teeth every year.

An interesting sidelight on the history of Philadelphia's industrial development is afforded by the "Keely Motor Hoax," perpetrated by John W. Keely on credulous investors during the latter part of the nineteenth century. About 1872, Keely, who had a laboratory at 1422 North Twentieth Street, invited scientists to watch him demonstrate a machine which he asserted was motivated by a new and hitherto unknown force. By using a system of concealed rubber bulbs and tubes and employing compressed air as his power, Keely set a water motor in operation, the trick being executed so cleverly that it defied even the scientific scrutiny of the day.

Public interest and excitement was aroused, and before long a corporation was formed with $5,000,000 capital. The "invention" failed to show practical results during ensuing years, and interest in it died out. Meanwhile Keely had spent his money lavishly; he was at the end of his resources when a rich Philadelphia widow came to his assistance with $100,000.

In 1895, suspecting that she had been swindled, the widow appealed to Addison B. Burk, president of the Spring Garden Institute, and E. Alexander Scott, of the Engineers Club. These two investigated and found there was not the slightest evidence that Keely had discovered or developed a new force. Other investigators, searching the laboratory at a later date, unearthed the hidden attachments of Keely's "force-producing" machine. By that time, however, Keely was in his grave.

Imports and Exports

A S DEFINED for customs purposes, the port of Philadelphia is 88 nautical miles (about 101 statute miles) from the sea. The total water frontage is 37 miles, of which 20 are along the Delaware and 17 on the Schuylkill. Main activities are centered on approximately six miles of the Delaware, extending from Greenwich piers, three miles south of Market Street, to Port Richmond, about the same distance north of Market. There are 267 wharves of various sizes, including 84 individual sections of improved bulk-head. Rail service extending along Delaware Avenue, which parallels the river, has direct touch with all piers.

The port of Philadelphia had a shipping business of 32,378,567 tons in 1935, with an aggregate value of $958,491,268. All previous high records in tonnage and value were shattered by those totals. The principal raw and manufactured materials handled at the piers were anthracite, bituminous coal, sugar, chemicals, fruits, molasses, crude drugs, textiles, lumber, iron and steel, automobile parts, general merchandise, and petroleum and its products. Among these classifications, crude petroleum and petroleum products led by a wide margin.

By 1936 shippers in the foreign and domestic trades were showing even greater interest in the Philadelphia port. During that year custom receipts increased more than $4,000,000, the total estimated receipts amounting to $24,105,718 as compared with $28,574,914 for 1935.

Traffic on the Schuylkill, an important arm of the Philadelphia harbor, increased from 9,268,828 tons, with a value of $103,396,308, in 1934, to 10,066,667 tons, with a value of $116,047,297, in 1935. The bulk of the Schuylkill commerce is coastwise, and consequently does not come under either the export or import classification.

Since the first ships began plying between the Old World and the New, Philadelphia has been a center of maritime activity. The early colonization days saw Philadelphia elevated to a leading role in commerce and trade. Since then the city has kept well up among the shipping ports of the United States. In his charter, William Penn designated Philadelphia as the port and harbor of Pennsylvania, empowering the mayor, aldermen, and councilmen to erect quays and wharves to accommodate trade.

During the period preceding the Revolution, English statesmen saw in the Colonies an opportunity to expand the manufacturing and commercial marts of the King. In attempting to create a huge nation of agriculturists, Parliament offered bounties to the colonists for the exportation of agricultural products. What little was manufactured was shipped to England in English ships as raw material, to be returned to the Colonies in the form of finished products.

Thus the colonists were forced to till the soil for their livelihood. Their products were used first for their own maintenance, and second as a means of procuring money with which to meet their needs. As a last resort, to break the English stranglehold on American commerce, the Colonies banded together and refused either to purchase British goods or to export tobacco to the British Isles.

At the close of the Revolution, Philadelphia was far from prosperous. Its commerce was virtually ruined, and its manufacturers were forced to encounter disastrous competition from imported goods.

120

The collection of debts, suspended during the war, was again taken up. Court dockets were filled with suits, while goods flooded the market because of greatly reduced buying power.

When the Constitution went into effect, however, provisions were made for a custom house, commercial treaties, and duties on imports. With the revival of commerce it became necessary to increase the facilities of the port. Stephen Girard led the drive for much-needed improvements. Until his death Girard was a leading figure in the advancement of the port, and his will set aside a large sum of money to continue the work.

In the early years foodstuffs, as well as manufactured goods, were imported by the Colony. When European crops became acclimated and native crops developed, imports of foodstuffs grew smaller. Implements and tools as well as various manufactured articles, however, were regularly purchased abroad during the entire Colonial period.

The greater part of the imports from the mother country in 1721 was woolen manufactures, with wrought iron and nails next in importance. The others, in the order of their importance, were silk, leather goods, linen and sailcloths, cordage, pewter, lead and shot, brass and wrought copper, gunpowder, iron, hemp, and wrought silk.

The colonists early discovered that they could produce more than they could sell to England. Therefore they engaged in a surreptitious commerce, chiefly with the West Indies, exporting lumber of all sorts, fish, beef, pork, butter, horses, cattle, poultry, tobacco, corn, flour, cider, and even small vessels. This trade, however, was almost entirely ruined through the rigorous enforcement by Britain of the laws against smuggling, and the collection of duties in hard money.

The value of foreign trade, which was not quite $4,000,000 in 1791, had risen to more than $17,000,000 in 1796. The chief factor in this large increase was the life-and-death struggle between France and England, which began in 1793 and continued with few intermissions until Napoleon's fall in 1815. The superior naval forces of England gave her control of the seas, so that her enemies were compelled to depend upon neutrals to handle their trade. Because the United States was well situated in relation to the West Indies, and because it had long before established connection with them, it naturally had a large part of trade. Philadelphia's trade, however, was not confined to the West Indies, but extended to the Orient and to a majority of the ports of the world.

There was a general decline in American commerce during the War of 1812, and Philadelphia particularly was affected by the decreased tonnage. With the end of the war, and the realignment of national interests throughout the world, new commercial and shipping trends developed. European nations, their energy no longer dissipated by war, turned their attention to the protection of their

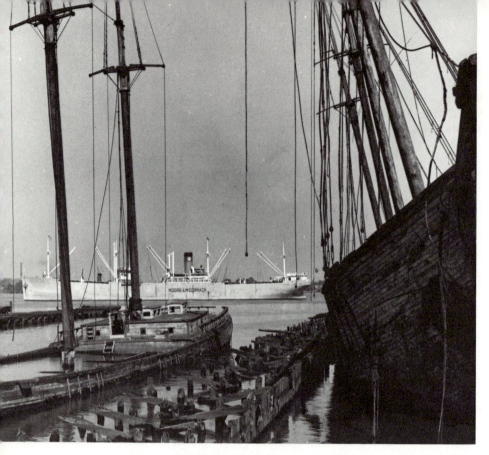

Old Ships and New
"the derelicts of seven seas"

manufacturing interests and the development of their commerce. With the general increase in European sailings, Philadelphia's shipping virtually came to an end. Some exports continued, however, and records indicate that grain, flour, iron utensils, flaxseed, soap and candles, lumber, pork, and beef left the port in Philadelphia bottoms.

By 1854 the exports had risen to a little more than $10,000,000, with imports close to $22,000,000. At this time preparations for the Crimean War occupied the attention of England, France, Italy, and Russia; consequently, the United States, and Philadelphia in particular, obtained an increased share of the carrying trade, which accounts for the sudden rise in the value of exports.

Exports and imports increased through many fluctuations from

1861 to 1900, the former increasing to $81,145,966. The imports doubled, climbing to a total of $49,191,003. From 1860 to 1875 there were only three years in which the balance of trade was unfavorable.

The year 1900 was notable in two respects. First, it set a new high mark for total exports ; and second, it established a new top not only in the exportation of manufactured goods but also in the importation of raw materials.

From 1860 to 1900 the outstanding developments of the export trade centered in the increasing importance of agriculture, the growing value of minerals, and the rise in volume of manufactured goods. Of the chief agricultural exports, only cotton showed a decrease in relative importance. Among the breadstuffs exported, wheat was first. The substitution of rollers for millstones in flour-making resulted in a sizable gain in the export of wheat. Also, instead of most of the wheat going out in the form of grain, as in 1860, more than half the export wheat, by value, in 1900, left the port as flour. Toward the close of the period, exports of livestock, mainly beef cattle, were valued at nearly $3,000,000.

The chief change in the import trade during the period from 1860 to 1900 was a decline in volume of manufactured goods. In 1860, these articles made up almost half the total value, but by 1900 they had declined to slightly more than one third. Wool and cotton exports made little advance over 1860, but silk showed a decided increase.

In 1915 the total of the foreign trade — combined exports and imports — at the port of Philadelphia reached $201,911,539. The total steadily increased until 1920, when the impressive figures of $733,-201,047 were achieved. The sharp upturn was due to the abnormal activity induced by the World War.

For the period of 1901-17 inclusive, exports reached a yearly average of $119,924,514 ; while from 1918 to 1924, the average was $181,817,267, despite the fact that a slowing down in the demand for our products followed in the wake of the war. This latter tendency continued until 1932, when bottom was touched at $42,461,145. The demand improved in 1933 and increased further in 1934, the exports for these two years being valued at $48,742,253 and $57,774,738. respectively.

The important exports in the year 1919 were food products, nonmetallic minerals, metals, and manufactures. Probably the outstanding feature in the heavy outgo was the remarkable increase shown in the value of manufactured goods, which had a combined worth in excess of $80,000,000. During the war, and for about a year after, the exportation of foodstuffs was heavy. There was a sharp drop in this classification in 1920.

While a marked increase was shown in 1933 and 1934 in Phila-

123

delphia's exports to South America, Canada, Asia, Union of South Africa, and New Zealand, the bulk went to Europe. Generally, the best customers were France, Great Britain, Japan, Germany, Belgium, the Netherlands, and Brazil.

Among the ports of the country, Philadelphia ranked fifth in exports in 1910, with 4.2 percent. In 1914 it was fifth with 2.7 percent. It became fourth in 1920, with 5.3 percent, dropping to eighth place in 1933, with 2.9 per cent. In 1934 it was still eighth, with 2.6 percent.

There was a notable increase in the import trade in the 1901-1934 period, with the yearly average from 1901 to 1917, inclusive, reaching $76,125,989. A much larger increase was reported for the years from 1918 to 1924, when the average jumped to $171,351,091. The peak year was 1920, with a total of $282,157,831. But from that time there was a decline to a low level of $89,780,480 in 1932, undoubtedly traceable to the depression which followed the Wall Street crash of 1929.

There were upturns in the dollar value of imports in both 1933 and 1934, the aggregate climbing to $103,468,886 in the former year and $111,056,443 in 1934. In the present century up to 1934, the port of Philadelphia ranked third in imports in 1910, 1914, 1920, 1933 and second in 1934, with the percentages, respectively, of 2.6, 5.9, 5.3, 6.2, and 6.0.

The port's foreign shipping, impressive as it is, represents only about one sixth of the tonnage carried by the ships which ply the river, the rest of the river traffic being devoted to coastwise, intercoastal and local shipping.

Agriculture

DESPITE real estate development, Philadelphia has approximately 13,889 acres of farmland within the city limits. The majority of these farms (the 1935 farm census listed 286) are devoted to the cultivation of truck crops. Many are owned by institutions; other represent country estates and private greenhouses. Some livestock is raised. The size of the farm holdings is not large enough to make power farming economical.

CRADLE OF AMERICAN FINANCE

O N A WARM spring day in 1754, four men sat around a table in William Bradford's Coffee House, sometimes called the Old London Coffee House, at the southwest corner of Front and High (now Market) Streets, Philadelphia. They were Robert Morris, Thomas Willing, Tench Francis, and Archibald McCall.

This was the opening day of Bradford's tavern and merchants' exchange. As the four drank their ale and occasionally glanced out the window at the craft upon the Delaware River, they were figuratively rocking the cradle of a giant — the cradle of American finance. They were launching a fiscal system that was destined not only to finance America's first four wars, but to rear the foundation for that colossal structure which is American finance today.

Second only to that of gunpowder was the part played by finance in molding the American Colonies into a Nation. Philadelphia, in the lean days when independence was at stake, had the only fiscal structure that was equal to the need. For the existence of this structure, the city and the Nation were indebted to a man who was to climax a glamorous financial and political career in a debtors' prison. That man was Robert Morris.

Born in Liverpool, England, Morris came to America at an early age. He was in his teens when he entered the counting house of Charles Willing (a name perpetuated in Willing's Alley, the city's old financial district), and only 21 when he helped found Philadelphia's first stock exchange in 1754. Immortalized as the father of American banking, Morris not only was the foremost financier of the Revolution, but helped to establish a mint and to found America's first banks — the Bank of Pennsylvania and the Bank of North America — in Philadelphia. Thomas Willing became the first president of the latter institution, serving for 10 years. He also headed the first Bank of the United States for the first 17 of its 20 years' existence.

It was largely through the leadership of a handful of its citizens that Philadelphia became the Nation's principal money center. As early as 1752 it had become the home of the first insurance company, although a limited amount of underwriting had been done even earlier. It maintained that leadership through succeeding decades, by the establishment of the first bank, the first United States Mint, the first saving fund society, the first building and loan society, and one of the first trust companies.

125

On such firm ground were they built that many of these original companies are still functioning, among them the Pennsylvania Company for Insurances on Lives and Granting Annuities, the Philadelphia Saving Fund Society, and the Philadelphia Contributionship for Insuring Houses from Loss by Fire.

More institutions of a fiduciary character were established within Philadelphia's borders in its early history than in any other American city. The scope and ramifications of many of the financial projects begun in this city more than a century ago have reached world wide proportions. Philadelphia today has more century-old companies than any other American municipality.

The record of the first century of America's financial development may be traced in the careers of three Philadelphia bankers — and behind that record lie the triumphs and the tragedies of their lives. Financial giants and chief supporters of the American wars of their times, Robert Morris, Stephen Girard, and Jay Cooke all knew not only the pinnacles of success but also the depths of sorrow and defeat.

Girard's sufferings were personal. His business life unmarred, he nevertheless knew the handicap of semi-blindness, suffered the loss of his only child, and saw his wife committed to a hospital for the insane. Morris and Cooke found their sorrows in financial failure. Deserted by many of those whose admiration they had won while scaling the heights, one Morris, went to debtors' prison with obligations estimated at $3,000,000, and the other, Cooke, saw the collapse of his financial empire precipitate the panic of 1873.

The seed from which the stock exchange movement grew was sown by Mayor James Hamilton on October 17, 1746, when he proposed that £150 be used to erect an exchange or public building for the purpose of barter. Willing, Morris, Francis, and McCall undertook its active promotion in 1753. The London Coffee House was opened in the following year by William Bradford, the printer, as "a licensed place to which will come and be centered the news from all parts of the world, an exchange upon which our merchants may walk, and a place of resort where our chief citizens of every department of life can meet and converse upon subjects which concern City and State." A considerable traffic gradually grew in bills of exchange, promissory notes, and early forms of negotiable capital. Members of the exchange were known as merchants and traders.

During the Revolution the coffeehouse was closed, and a rival institution known as the City Tavern, later called the Merchants' Coffee House, at Second Street near Walnut, took its place. From that time the Merchants' Coffee House was the favored gathering place for the traders. As stock brokerage developed into a separate business, the brokers finally obtained private quarters in the same establishment and formed an association.

This group, organized in 1790 and then known as the Philadelphia Board of Brokers, met regularly in the coffeehouse until 1834, when it moved into the newly completed Merchants' Exchange Building at Third and Walnut Streets. There it remained until July 1876, when it moved to Third Street below Chestnut. From 1888 to 1902 the exchange was in the Drexel Building, at Fifth and Chestnut Streets ; and then it returned to the Merchants' Exchange Building. On March 1, 1913, it moved to its present quarters, at 1411 Walnut Street.

The membership fee was raised at various times from $30, in 1790, to $50, $250, $300, $400, $500, $1,000, $2,000. In November 1868, it was increased to $5,000, and in 1881 to $10,000. By 1886 the income from operation of the exchange was sufficient to make it self-supporting. On December 8, 1875, its name was changed from the Board of Brokers to the Philadelphia Stock Exchange. In 1902 the membership was fixed at 225 ; in February 1923, it was reduced to its present number, 206.

In 1780 and 1781, more than a quarter century after the opening of Bradford's combined exchange and coffeehouse, Philadelphia established the first American banks. While the needs of peaceful trade dictated the founding of the stock exchange, it was war that sired these first two banks; both were established to finance the needs of America's armed forces in time of conflict.

The credit of Robert Morris was better than that of the entire country at the outbreak of the Revolution, and it was said that he gave his personal notes for $1,400,000 to finance Washington's army in its Yorktown campaign. This sum was later repaid by the Government. He was appointed Superintendent of Finance, on February 20, 1781, and retained office until 1784. Later reelected to the State assembly, he was a delegate to the Constitutional Convention and became one of the first United States Senators to be elected from Pennsylvania.

Through the efforts of Morris and his associates, the Bank of Pennsylvania was opened in July 1780, on Front Street north of Walnut. Its purpose was to borrow money to purchase rum, provisions, and transportation for the Continental Army. The two directors chosen to conduct that business were authorized to borrow on the credit of the bank for six months or less, and to issue to the lenders special notes bearing interest at 6 percent. Congress was to reimburse the bank from time to time for sums advanced, and all moneys borrowed or received from Congress were to be used to supply the needs of the Army and to discharge notes and expenses of the bank.

To start the bank, 10 percent in cash was required from the lenders. If money did not come in fast enough, the bond issuers were to lend a proportionate sum of their subscriptions in cash. Notes were to be taken by the creditors. They were to be paid off and cancelled, accounts settled, and the bank discontinued when Congress should complete its reimbursements. That was done, and the institution concluded its operations towards the end of 1784.

Morris' detailed plan for the Bank of North America was presented to the Continental Congress on May 18, 1781. Nine days later, Congress reported in favor of its adoption, and the charter was granted. The bank was organized on November 1 of that year, and began active operation on January 7, 1782.

Through the services of this bank, supplies were furnished to the Army, and the expenses of various branches of the Government were defrayed. Some of the most prominent financiers of the Revolutionary period were among its directors and supporters. When the so-called Whiskey Insurrection reached its climax in the western part of Pennsylvania in 1794, with an army of 19,500 men engaged in quelling the disturbance, the bank not only laid aside or renewed the notes of all persons in military service but also contributed cash to the expedition.

The Bank of North America was brought into being through the sale of stock, the first offering being 1,000 shares, tendered at $400 a share. The offering was well received, and was followed in a short time by another 1,000 shares, this time at $500 each. (This bank, on March 1, 1923, was merged with the Commercial Trust Company under the title of the Bank of North America and Trust Company, and on June 1, 1929, the new company was merged with the Pennsylvania Company.)

The institution was opened on the north side of Chestnut Street west of Third, where it remained for 65 years. Subsequently, as business expanded, it moved several times to other locations. The bank was brought under the National Bank Act in November 1864, thus becoming one of the few national banks that did not have the word "national" in its title.

Before retiring from public life at the expiration of his six-year term in the United States Senate, Morris became one of the largest real estate investors in the land. Envisioning a great country, expanding rapidly and attracting thousands of immigrant settlers, Morris in partnership with John Nicholson and James Greenleaf purchased thousands of lots in the new Federal City, then unnamed and existing on paper only, and took title to more than 15,000,000 acres in Pennsylvania, Massachusetts, and elsewhere.

He was the nabob of Philadelphia, with a mansion at 526-530 Market Street and a fine estate in "The Hills," later called Lemon Hill, and Fairmount Park. With the removal of the seat of National Government from New York to this city, he placed the Market Street residence at the disposal of President Washington, and took up quarters at the southeast corner of Sixth and Market Streets.

Then came the crash ! Although the sound of crumbling timbers did not press upon his ears until three years later, it was in 1794 that he made the flourish which at once crowned and destroyed his achievements. Selecting a lot on the south side of Chestnut Street, between Seventh and Eighth, for the site of an ornate palace, he enlisted Maj. Pierre Charles L'Enfant, engineer-architect who planned the city of Washington, to design it.

Three years later, he went to live in a mansion on the north side of Chestnut Street, at Eighth, a building which stood until 1934 and was known in its last half century as Green's Hotel. About this time, his creditors began action. Morris retired to his suburban estate, but finally was arrested under the Insolvent Debtors' Act, and confined in the debtors' prison, at Sixth and Locust Streets. Committed on February 16, 1798, he remained in prison until August 26, 1801 ; then, less than five years before his death, his release was obtained under provisions of the United States Bankruptcy Act of 1800.

"Morris's Folly," as the great palace upon which he had spent a considerable sum of money came to be known, was never completed. Upon his release from prison, Morris went to live with his family in the house then numbered 2 South Twelfth Street. Here he died on May 8, 1806. He was buried in the family vault of his wife's brother, Bishop William White, in the churchyard of Christ Church.

The first Bank of the United States had meantime become a factor in the city's banking activity. It was the materialization of Alexander Hamilton's idea, conceived in 1779, of a Government-organized and Government-controlled bank, based on landed security. The institution was chartered by Congress on February 14, 1791, and President Washington signed the bill on February 25. It was the limitation of the Bank of North America by its acceptance of a State charter narrowing its scope and reducing its capital from $10,000,000 to $2,000,000 that finally brought action on the plan for a Federal bank.

Two days after subscription books for the new bank were closed, a premium was being offered for the shares. A general meeting of stockholders was held in Philadelphia's City Hall on October 21, 1791, and four days later the directors selected Thomas Willing, president of the Bank of North America and former business partner of Robert Morris, as president.

By its liberal policy, the Bank of the United States stemmed a tide of loss and embarrassment resulting from the Coinage Act of 1793. This act decreed that all foreign silver coins, except Spanish milled dollars and parts of such dollars, should cease to be legal tender after October 15, 1797. Such foreign coins constituted a considerable part of the silver in circulation. The Federal bank, how-

Statute of Robert Morris at the Old Custom House
"Financier and Patriot"

ever, showed a willingness to receive French crowns and other silver coins at current rates of exchange, and it was not until 1857 that foreign gold and silver coins ceased to be respected as a medium of exchange. Despite a three-year controversy involving John Jacob Astor, Albert Gallatin, and many of the Nation's other financial leaders, Congress failed to renew the charter of the bank when it expired in 1811, and the institution was dissolved.

The prologue to the next test of American banking — the financing of the War of 1812 — had its setting on the deck of a fog-bound sloop at the mouth of Delaware Bay in June, 1776. On its voyage from the West Indies to New York, the *La Jeune Babe* had lost its bearings; and when its 26-year-old French master leaned over the rail to ask directions from a passing vessel, he was told that British men-of-war were hovering nearby. The young captain, instead of proceeding to New York, brought his sloop up the river to Philadelphia. Here he sold his interest in the vessel and opened a small store on Water Street. Thus the career of Stephen Girard as a sailor ended, and his career as a Philadelphia merchant began. In 1777 he married Mary Lum, daughter of a Kensington shipbuilder; and during the time the British occupied Philadelphia he ran a humble store in Mount Holly, N. J.

During the yellow-fever epidemics of 1793 and 1798, Girard first earned his reputation as a philanthropist. He contributed substantial sums of money, served as a manager of the Municipal Hospital, and performed the duties of a nurse when the plagues were at their worst.

The Revolution had turned the French mariner's course up the Delaware to Philadelphia, and the threat of a second war with England turned Girard's career into the banking field. Surveying the gathering war clouds, and foreseeing more of the depredations on neutral commerce which already had inflicted severe losses on him, Girard began recalling his ships and converting his property in foreign lands into American securities. In this manner he became the owner of a controlling interest in the first Bank of the United States. In the spring of 1812, when Congress failed to renew the charter of the Bank of the United States, Girard purchased the buildings and other assets and embarked on his career as a private banker, starting the Bank of Stephen Girard. During the struggle between Great Britain and the United States, the latter having failed utterly in its efforts to raise funds, Girard risked his entire fortune for the benefit of his adopted country. (Girard was born in Bordeaux, France.) With David Parrish and John Jacob Astor of New York, he took over the unsubscribed portion of the war bonds authorized by Congress.

Resuming his maritime ventures at the close of the war, and still actively engaging in banking, Girard accumulated a fortune then unequalled in America. He died on December 26, 1831, and his will became one of the most discussed instruments of its kind. More than $6,000,000 in cash and real estate represented the residue of his estate, after provision had been made for improving the entire eastern front of Philadelphia and for paying bequests to the State of Pennsylvania and the city of New Orleans for public uses. This residue was devoted to the founding of Girard College, "for poor white male orphans." The advancing value of central Philadelphia real estate, in which $3,000,000 of the total was invested, had increased the endowment in 1936 to more than $86,000,000.

In 1816, four years after Girard's debut as a banker and nearly a half century after the founding of the first American banks, the next major development in banking appeared in Philadelphia and in America — the founding of the first saving fund society by Col. Condy Raguet. Although Colonel Raguet turned his talents at various times to the callings of lawyer, merchant, volunteer soldier, writer on economic and financial subjects and, in 1822, United States consul at Rio de Janeiro, his most enduring claim to fame lies in his untiring efforts to spread the gospel of thrift.

In witness to the soundness of his principles stands the institution he founded in 1816 — the Philadelphia Saving Fund Society. With steady, measured strides, romantic in their very consistency and contempt of circumstance, the society rose to its present position of leadership among institutions of its kind in Philadelphia, and to favorable comparison with leading saving fund societies of the Nation. As early as October 1869, when it first occupied its present main office at Seventh and Walnut Streets, the society boasted 29,000 accounts, with deposits totaling approximately $6,380,000. Symbolic of its progress and growth is the architecturally renowned ultra-modern skyscraper built by Howe and Lescaze in 1932 at Market and Twelfth Streets, to house the society's mid-city branch.

The second Bank of the United States, which was destined to become a political football and parent of the Bank of the United States of Pennsylvania, was chartered in 1816. The ultimate collapse of the latter precipitated the panic of 1841.

Plans for the institution were submitted to Congress by Secretary of the Treasury Dallas in September 1814. The bank was to have had a capital of $50,000,000, three fifths to be subscribed by individuals and corporations and two fifths by the United States. The capital requirements later were reduced to $35,000,000. Unavailing efforts to modify the plan were instituted by John C. Calhoun and Daniel Webster. The bill was passed and approved by President Madison on April 10, 1816, and the bank was chartered to continue until March 3, 1836.

When, because of financial conditions following the War of 1812, the bank found no buyers for $3,038,300 worth of its stock, Stephen Girard subscribed the entire amount. Operations began on January 7, 1817. Nicholas Biddle became a director of the bank in 1819. In the same year, Langdon Cheves became its president. The bank, although virtually bankrupt, engaged in a vigorous effort to fulfill its obligations. Its efforts toward recovery, however, even at a time when the depreciation of paper money all over Europe had created a favorable financial condition in America through increased commercial exchange, prostrated the whole industry of the country.

Nicholas Biddle became president of the bank in 1823. Andrew Jackson, who assumed office as President of the United States in 1829, was hostile to the bank and to Biddle. Open conflict flared in the summer of 1829, with the refusal of Biddle to remove Jeremiah Mason, a friend of Webster, from the presidency of the Portsmouth branch, and with President Jackson's intimations that the charter of the bank was unconstitutional.

A new charter, applied for in 1832, four years before the expiration of the old one, was denied. Upon the expiration of the old charter in 1836, the institution became the Bank of the United States of Pennsylvania, under a State charter. The change was made without loss to either the Government or stockholders. A period of general expansion and over-trading, led to the failure of the State bank on September 4, 1841, and the crash spread disaster to business and trade throughout the Union.

Although the company that was to conduct it had been formed in 1812, it was not until 1836, two decades after the introduction of the saving fund idea, that Philadelphia's first trust business came into being. The Pennsylvania Company for Insurances on Lives and Granting Annuities was organized for the purpose indicated by its title. It carried on this business for a number of years, but in 1836 was authorized to accept trusts. Its development from that year forward was almost entirely along trust lines. The company's powers were further enlarged in 1853 to permit it to act as executor and administrator, and in 1872 it discontinued its original activities in the life insurance field.

The company's first dividend of 4 percent on the amount of capital then paid in was declared in July 1815. Thus was started a dividend record that today ranks among the best in American corporation history; beginning with that year, the Pennsylvania Company has made uninterrupted dividend payments for 122 years. The main office of the institution is at Fifteenth and Chestnut Streets.

Completing the local banking structure, the Philadelphia Clearing House Association came into being in 1858 as a voluntary, unincorporated organization enabling member banks to adjust their daily balances without the necessity and accompanying risk of transferring large sums of money through the streets. Its office is at 311 Chestnut Street, and it includes trust companies as well as National and State banks in its membership.

Third and last of the great Philadelphia bankers to uphold the city's position as the financial center of America was Jay Cooke. Son of Eleutheros Cooke, lawyer and member of Congress from 1831 to 1833, Jay Cooke left his home in Sandusky, Ohio, at 18, and found a clerk's job in the Philadelphia office of a packet line. A little later he entered the employ of the private banking house of E. W. Clark & Co., and in 1842, at 21, was admitted as a partner.

Hostilities in the Mexican War began three years later, and Cooke's firm negotiated a large part of the Government loans required to finance the conflict. He retired from the banking business for a time to specialize in negotiating railroad securities. His deals included the sale of the Pennsylvania State canals, but the peak of his career was to be reached some years later, with the outbreak of the Civil War.

The beginning of the war found the Government in great need of money. Prospects for preservation of the Union were dark when, in July, following the Battle of Bull Run, Cooke started to interest other Philadelphia bankers in the problem of a Government loan. Cooke had made the acquaintance of Salmon P. Chase, then Secretary of the Treasury, and after raising $2,000,000 in his first effort here, he went with Chase to New York. Bankers of that city were persuaded to lend an initial sum of $50,000,000. Jay Cooke & Co., with branch offices in New York, Washington, and later in London, then advertised and sold the bonds, from the proceeds of which the bankers were to be repaid.

The next big venture to which Cooke turned, the disposal of securities of the Northern Pacific Railroad, was his last. His firm was compelled to close its doors on September 18, 1873, and panic gripped the country. His failure was the more sensational because of widespread belief that the house was of great financial strength. Cooke turned over all assets to his creditors, and eventually succeeded in paying off all obligations. Indeed, by 1880 he had regained considerable wealth through fortunate investments in the Horn Silver Mine, Utah. He died on February 16, 1905.

Philadelphia's outstanding financier in the first part of the twentieth century has been Edward T. Stotesbury, manager and virtual head of Drexel & Co. since the death of Anthony J. Drexel, and a partner in the firm since its reorganization on January 1, 1882. Like his predecessors in the field, he lost no time in starting his business career. When he entered the employ of Drexel & Co. at the age of 17, he had already been employed in turn by Rutter & Patterson, wholesale grocers, and by his father's sugar refining

Girard Bank
"the hub of early commerce"

firm, Harris & Stotesbury. He was quick to master banking details.

Among the various affiliates of finance which had their American beginnings in Philadelphia, the first was fire insurance, which antedated even the formation of the stock exchange. This business, whose almost uninterrupted growth has placed it among the Nation's greatest enterprises, was begun by a group of men who met April 13, 1752, and organized the Philadelphia Contributionship for Insuring Houses from Loss by Fire. The first insurance issued by the company covered two houses on King Street, later renamed Water Street. The first directors were Benjamin Franklin, William Coleman, Philip Syng, Samuel Rhoads, Hugh Roberts, Israel Pemberton, Jr., John Mifflin, Joseph Norris, Joseph Fox, Jonathan Lane, William Griffiths, and Amos Strettell. The plan was that of mutual insurance, and the members were called "contributors." Policies were issued for a term of seven years, upon the payment of a deposit, the interest on which, during the continuance of the policy, belonged to the company. The "Hand in Hand" seal was adopted by the company in 1768.

Still leading the way, Philadelphia came forward just seven years later with the first scheme of life insurance established in the Colo-

135

nies. On petition of the Synod of Philadelphia, a charter was granted by the Proprietary government in 1759 to the "Corporation for the Relief of Poor and Distressed Presbyterian Ministers, and of the Poor and Distressed Widows and Children of Presbyterian Ministers."

The first United States Mint was established here in 1792, through the efforts of Robert Morris, Thomas Jefferson, and Alexander Hamilton. Hamilton, then Secretary of the Treasury, prepared the plan in 1790 and presented it at the next session of Congress. The act received President Washington's approval on April 2, 1792. Ground was purchased on the east side of Seventh Street, below Arch, and an old still-house that stood on the lot was demolished. An entry in the mint's account book of that time, dated July 31, 1792, shows that the materials of the demolished still-house sold for seven shillings and six pence. The structure that replaced it and housed the mint was the first building erected for public use under authority of the Federal Government. The mint later occupied a structure at the northwest corner of Chestnut and Juniper Streets, where the Widener Building now stands. Its present home is on Spring Garden Street, from Sixteenth to Seventeenth Streets.

The first coinage of the United States was silver half dimes, minted in October 1792. The use of four different rates of exchange at first caused much perplexity. In Vermont, New Hampshire, Massachusetts, Connecticut, Rhode Island, Virginia, and Kentucky the dollar was reckoned at six shillings ; in New York and North Carolina at eight shillings ; in New Jersey, Pennsylvania, and Maryland at seven shillings and sixpence ; and in South Carolina and Georgia at four shillings and eightpence. These differences were corrected by the Federal Government's passage of a law regulating the exchange rates.

The building and loan movement was largely an importation from England. It had its local origin in a tavern at what is now 4219 Frankford Avenue, where in 1831 leaders of the community formed the Oxford Provident Beneficial Association, the first organization of its kind in the United States. The par value of shares was set at $500 each, with no member holding more than five. Money received as dues was offered as loans to the highest bidder among the stockholders, who were entitled to borrow $500 for every share held. The first loan was made to Comly Rich, who borrowed $500 at a premium of $10. In 1854 the association brought its business to an end, some of its membership merging with a newer organization.

Although many of Philadelphia's ancient financial landmarks have been razed to make room for modern structures, the imposing edifice of the old United States Bank, on the south side of Chestnut Street west of Fourth, still stands. For many years it was used as the Custom House and by the Assistant United States Treasurer — an office abolished with the advent of the Federal Reserve System.

PUBLIC UTILITIES

AUTOMOBILES today traverse well-paved Philadelphia streets which conceal uncounted pipes and conduits supplying homes with water, gas, electricity, and telephone communication. An intricate yet carefully planned network provides conveniences now considered indispensable. When Philadelphia began to take on the aspect of a growing urban community, necessary improvements followed in due course; but development of public utilities to their present smoothly functioning status required many years of trial and effort.

Water

THE problem of a water supply was the first to occupy the early settlers. Individuals dug wells and pumped water for their own use, charging small sums for supplying their neighbors. In 1713 the Common Council drafted regulations authorizing owners of pumps to charge water rent. Not until 1756 did the city actually gain control of the water supply by buying up most of the private pumps in front of houses.

Philadelphians were forced to depend upon this means of water supply until 1800. A proposal to bring water from Spring Mill Creek had been rejected, but the movement for a central supply resulted in the city's commissioning Benjamin H. Latrobe, architect and engineer, to plan a water distributing system.

The result was a waterworks on the east bank of the Schuylkill River, at about Twenty-second and Chestnut Streets. Here water was raised from the river and sent by gravity through a six-foot aqueduct under Chestnut Street to a central enginehouse built on the spot where City Hall now stands. There the water flow was raised by means of a steam pump to an upper floor to gain pressure, and then distributed through wooden mains to the consumers.

The system was woefully inadequate. The reservoirs at Broad and Market Streets stored only a half hour's supply, and repairs were needed continually. In 1801 only 63 dwellings, four breweries, a sugar refinery, and 87 hydrants were using the system. The service was abandoned in 1815 when a new waterworks was constructed at Fairmount. This plant was constantly improved ; and, with the consolidation of the city in 1854, the plants of the various districts became parts of one large municipal system.

Purification of the water was still inadequate, however. Epidemics

137

of typhoid fever broke out frequently. In 1899 three experts were commissioned to plan an improved and extended water system. Their report led to the development of the present plan. By 1909 the entire city was supplied with filtered water, and the ravages of disease were lessened greatly.

Today there are 11 pumping stations, eight fresh-water reservoirs, and four raw-water reservoirs. The average daily supply of 325,-500,000 gallons comes from both the Schuylkill and Delaware Rivers, and the water is subjected to constant chemical and bacteriological analysis.

Gas

FOR several years after its introduction, gas as an illuminant was considered not only a novelty but a menace. The first hotels to employ it displayed large signs near every gas jet, warning their guests : "Don't blow out the gas." Many leading citizens doubted the feasibility of its successful use. Even Sir Walter Scott, from his home across the Atlantic, issued a diatribe against its employment. His castle at Abbottsford, however, was one of the first buildings to be piped for illuminating gas.

Agitation for city manufacture of gas for street lighting started early in the nineteenth century. There was opposition from many quarters; but in 1835 the city government authorized erection of the Philadelphia Gas Works as a municipally controlled project. An area of 7½ acres was set aside near Twenty-second and Market Streets, and a plant established there. By 1852 the total extent of pipes had reached 115 miles, and the plant had attained a maximum production of 962,000 cubic feet of gas in 24 hours.

About that time, it was found necessary to remove the gas works to larger quarters. The site selected was on the banks of the Schuylkill at Point Breeze. Meanwhile, constant improvements in the gas production process were being made.

The Northern Liberties Gas Company was chartered in 1838, supplying illumination to the Northern Liberties and Kensington districts. Gas works were also built in Manayunk, Frankford, Germantown, and Kensington.

In 1887 Philadelphia's new city charter eliminated the Gas Trust, as the city gas works under the trustee system was called. Duties of supervision devolved upon a Bureau of Gas, a division of the Department of Public Works. A decade later, after much wrangling on the part of the public both in and out of the courts, the United Gas Improvement Company, an interstate utility corporation, obtained a lease on the municipal gas works.

The lease covered a period of 30 years. Before its expiration an-

138

other lease was signed by the city in 1926 for an undetermined period, but either party could terminate the lease on December 31, 1937, or at expiration of any 10-year period thereafter, by giving to the other 18 months' notice of such intention. Under the terms of the lease, the Philadelphia Gas Works Company is designated as the operating concern. Supervision of the lease was placed in charge of a gas commission of three members. The city receives an annual rental of $4,200,000; the U. G. I. is paid an operating fee of $600,000 annually, plus an amount ranging from $200,000 to $500,000 for efficiency of management, the extra payment varying directly with the quantity of gas sold and inversely with the cost per 1,000 cubic feet. The prevailing rate to consumers is 90 cents per thousand cubic feet for the first 2,000 cubic feet, with relative reductions for quantities used in excess of this amount. All gas used by the city is paid for at wholesale rates.

Electricity

ELECTRIC service for the city of Philadelphia and adjacent territories — Delaware County and substantial parts of Bucks, Chester, and Montgomery Counties — is supplied by the Philadelphia Electric Company, which furnishes electric current to homes, factories, and industrial plants, and supplies street lighting to a majority of the cities, towns, and boroughs in this area. All electrical energy provided by the company is of the alternating current type, which can be transmitted much farther than the direct current type formerly supplied to central Philadelphia. The Philadelphia Electric Company also furnishes gas service to suburban sections near the city.

An area of approximately 1,547 square miles is served by the company. The population in this territory is 2,757,000, with slightly more than two million of those served residing in Philadelphia. Electricity is generated in the company's plants in Philadelphia and in its hydro-electric plant on the Susquehanna River at Conowingo. The latter is the second largest hydro-electric plant in the United States. Its location is four miles above tide water; the lake is a mile wide at the dam and extends eighteen miles up the river. This gigantic plant, opened in 1928, is connected with Philadelphia steam plants by means of 220,000-volt transmission lines, and its present capacity is 1,046,015 kilowatts. At its Plymouth Meeting substation, the largest outdoor substation in the world, the plant's 220,000-volt transmission lines inter-connect the Philadelphia Electric Company with two other companies — the Pennsylvania Power and Light Company and the Public Service Electric and Gas Company of New Jersey—the whole forming a pool which distributes more than two million horsepower in electrical energy.

The company furnishes energy for the operation of the Pennsylvania Railroad's electrified lines running between Perryville, Maryland, and the State line at Trenton, New Jersey; the line between the State Line and New York City ; the Chestnut Hill branch, and the Main Line as far as Paoli. All the electrified lines of the Reading Railroad running in the vicinity of Philadelphia, and the Philadelphia Rapid Transit Company, operators of the city's street car system, receive their electrical energy from the Philadelphia Electric Company.

Philadelphia's first electric service was supplied by the Brush Electric Light Co., which in 1881 installed street arc lights in the section of Chestnut Street between the Delaware and the Schuylkill Rivers. Then 26 neighborhood electric companies, all of them generating direct current, opened within the span of 18 years. In 1899 these plants were consolidated to form the Philadelphia Electric Company, the nucleus of the present company. In 1928 the Philadelphia Electric Company became an affiliate of the United Gas Improvement Company. A year later the Philadelphia Electric Company, which still operates independently, acquired the Philadelphia Suburban Counties Gas and Electric Company.

Telephone

ABOUT a quarter-century after the adoption of telegraphy for railroad communications, the world's first public telephone "system" was successfully demonstrated in Philadelphia — at the Centennial Exhibition of 1876. The device, consisting of two instruments connected by 500 feet of wire, was installed in the Exhibition's main building, where it lay neglected for six weeks — until an inquisitive visitor discovered its amazing potentialities.

The telephone, which has revolutionized transportation and communications the world over, was invented by Alexander Graham Bell, Boston elocution teacher, and sent to Philadelphia at the opening of the Exhibition. Bell himself was not urged to attend in person, and only by the promptings of a last-minute impulse did he board a train to bring him here. Neither he nor his contrivance provoked any attention until Dom Pedro de Alcantara, Emperor of Brazil, picked up the receiver and heard a human voice come from the transmitter at the other end of the 500-foot wire. "My God !" he exclaimed astoundedly to a crowd which included Sir William Thomson, then the foremost electrical scientist in the world. "It *talks!*"

Soon thereafter Bell's invention was first applied commercially in Philadelphia by an organization known as "The Telephone Company of Philadelphia." Later Bell's name was added. The first practical switchboard was housed in the second floor of 1111 Chestnut Street.

The first directory, which appeared in 1878, contained only 25 subscribers. Another, issued later during the same year, had 85 ; the third, put out the following year, contained the names of 420 subscribers.

Today the Bell Telephone Company has 42 central offices in the city handling 1,377,927 local and 79,362 toll calls daily. In 1937 there were more than 155,000 business telephones and approximately 191,-000 residence telephones in operation. The directory has grown to an issue of 400,000 copies.

The Keystone Telephone Company of Philadelphia came into existence Nov. 12, 1902. Five years later it absorbed the property of the Keystone State Telephone & Telegraph Company, extending its service to cities and towns in south New Jersey. Later it acquired the entire capital stock of the Eastern Telephone & Telegraph Company, and a majority of the stock of the Camden & Atlantic Telephone Company. The United Telephone Company, likewise, was absorbed in 1923.

The Keystone system operates six exchanges in Philadelphia, and 18 in nearby cities and towns. The company holds a perpetual charter from the State of Pennsylvania, and a perpetual franchise from the city of Philadelphia. It cooperates with the Bell system on telephone service outside the city.

TRANSPORTATION

PHILADELPHIA'S development from a compact little city to a sprawling metropolis made public transportation facilities imperative at an early date. Prior to the establishment of urban transportation facilities, however, there were only certain ancient dirt roads to depend on, such as Darby Road, Old York Road, and another that went north by way of Second Street. A Federal road was laid out in 1788 from Gray's Ferry to Southwark. Within city limits, the so-called streets were not much more than dirt roads either. According to the presentment of the Grand Jury in 1738, the streets were impassable. This was the beginning of a crusade to compel the paving of certain thoroughfares, notably Front, Sassafras, and High.

The first adequate public means of urban travel was supplied in 1831 by Joseph Boxall, who established a stagecoach line on lower Chestnut Street with an hourly schedule. "Boxall's Accommodation," as the line was called, was the only satisfactory public conveyance until July 1833, when an additional line was started by Edward Deschamps, to provide service between the Navy Yard and Kensington, via Second Street and Beach Street. This also proved successful, and within a short time lines were running on nearly every important street in the city.

The need of some better mode of transportation to outlying sections became pressing. The first locomotive made at the Baldwin Works in Philadelphia was "Old Ironsides," which had been placed on the Philadelphia & Germantown Railroad on November 23, 1832. Steam transportation had come to stay. There was a project to connect the Columbia Railroad and the Philadelphia, Wilmington & Baltimore Railroad, which led to the passage of the Act of April 15, 1845, by which the Schuylkill Railroad was incorporated.

In 1854 the Philadelphia & Delaware Railroad Company took out a charter to operate a steam railroad from Kensington to Easton. Failing to realize their ambition, the promoters envisioned the possibility of running a horse-car line from what is now Sixth Street and Montgomery Avenue, in Kensington, to the village of Southwark.

In 1856 preparations were made by the North Pennsylvania Railway Company to establish a line of passenger cars drawn by horses. On January 3 the company put such a line in operation on a route

142

about a mile and a half in length, extending from Willow Street along Front to Germantown Road, thence to Second Street, to Cadwalader, to Washington, to Cherry, connecting with what was known as the Cohocksink depot. These vehicles were 14 feet long, and seated 24 persons.

In April 1858, by Act of Assembly, the Philadelphia & Delaware Railroad Company became the Frankford & Southwark Philadelphia City Passenger Railroad Company, forerunner of the many traction and motor companies that have been incorporated to serve Philadelphia. Shortly before reorganization, the Philadelphia & Delaware Railroad Company, on January 21, 1858, ran its first horsecars from Kensington to Southwark, carrying 10,000 persons on 15 cars during the year. Such was the beginning of what long was known as "the Fifth and Sixth Street line."

For a time the cars were banned from operation on Sundays. Ministers complained that the noise interrupted Sunday worship ; but a Supreme Court decision held that operation on the Sabbath was not a breach of the peace, and thereafter the cars ran seven days a week. In 1857 the City Councils passed an ordinance permitting the car lines to operate sleighs in winter.

Strong opposition to street railways flared up and was slow in subsiding. Nevertheless, capitalists were stimulated by the success of the Fifth and Sixth Street line, and immediately began to project similar railways on Spruce and Pine Streets, Ridge Avenue, Second and Third, and other thoroughfares. Although the depression that followed the 1857 panic served to make the year 1858 a dull one generally in Philadelphia, the stagnation was not evident in railway circles. The West Philadelphia road, on Market Street, was the second to go into operation and was closely followed by the Tenth and Eleventh Street line on July 29. At that time, the Spruce and Pine, Second and Third, Green and Coates, and Race and Vine Street lines were in course of construction, and the Chestnut and Walnut Street Company was still engaged in beating down a bitter opposition. The fourth road to go into operation was the Spruce and Pine, on November 2. Among other events of this period was the opening on March 14, 1859, of the Girard College (Ridge Avenue) Railway.

In 1863, the Frankford & Southwark Company received authority to operate steam-driven cars over its route from Berks Street to Frankford. Their noisy engines, usually called "dummies," proved quite satisfactory. They ran for the first time on November 7, 1863, and survived about 30 years. Other attempts to use steam power were made by the West Philadelphia Passenger Railway Company and by the Haddington Line.

About this time the cable-car system began to be used successfully in some cities, and Philadelphia decided to experiment with it. The

Old Schuylkill Navigation Canal Lock in Fairmount Park
"Along its path the straining tow mules plodded"

Assembly passed an act permitting use of the cable, and in April 1883 a line was opened along Columbia Avenue from Twenty-third Street to Fairmount Park. This proved successful, and two years later the Philadelphia Traction Company opened a cable line along Market Street from Front Street to Forty-first Street. The system was used for 10 years, then was replaced by the electric trolley system.

In 1888 Frank J. Sprague developed in Richmond, Va., a successful electric street-car system, and again Philadelphia was eager to try an innovation. The Philadelphia Traction Company stepped to the fore and made practical use of the new method, operating in 1892 the first of such railways in Philadelphia. The route ran eastward from the Schuylkill River, with tracks on Catharine and Bainbridge Streets. During the next four years the 400 miles of horse and steam car lines in Philadelphia, with the exception of the Callowhill Street line, were electrified ; and on January 15, 1897, the last horse car was driven over the latter line, marking the end of this antiquated system in Philadelphia.

The rapid growth of the city made it necessary to evolve a speedier means of transportation. In 1901 the State Legislature enacted the legislation necessary to establish such a system (subway-elevated)

144

along Market Street, and six years later the first high-speed line began operation. In 1902 the Philadelphia Rapid Transit Company was incorporated, taking over all the transit companies in Philadelphia, with the absorbed companies acting as "underliers," a name by which they have since been known. They hold the leases of the systems and collect rent from the P.R.T.

With formation of the P.R.T. the transportation history of Philadelphia becomes the story of a single large system. The Market Street Subway-Elevated was opened in March 1907, from Sixty-ninth Street (Delaware County) to Fifteenth Street. In October 1908 the line was extended eastward to Delaware Avenue, and thence south to South Street. In November 1922 another branch extending north to Frankford was built by the city and the three branches became a continuous system.

In 1923 the first P.R.T. double-decked bus began operation, running from Broad Street and Erie Avenue to Frankford Avenue and Arrott Street. Trackless trolley coaches began operation in 1923 from Twenty-second Street and Passyunk Avenue to Delaware and Oregon Avenues.

The Broad Street subway, built by the city and leased to the P.R.T., began operation in 1928 under Broad Street from Olney Avenue to Market Street. Two years later it was extended to South Street. In 1932 the Ridge Avenue and Eighth Street spur was opened; and on June 7, 1936, the high-speed line over the Delaware River Bridge, linking Philadelphia and Camden, began operation. The latter line was built by the city under the direction of the Delaware River Joint Commission, and was turned over to the Philadelphia Rapid Transit Company for operation. It connects the Camden downtown section with the Eighth and Market Street subway station in Philadelphia.

Figures for 1937 showed the P.R.T. operating 2,150 trolley cars, 303 busses, 465 subway and elevated cars, and 8 trackless trolley coaches. In 1936 the system had a gross operating revenue of $34,732,768. It also operated about 930 taxicabs until February 1936, when the cab holdings were sold to another company.

The necessity for some form of transportation of supplies and commodities across the Delaware River was realized as early as 1695, when the court at Gloucester, N. J., authorized establishment of a ferry from the New Jersey shore to Pennsylvania. As traffic grew through the years, Philadelphia became more and more dependent upon these ferries. Until 1926, when the Delaware River Bridge was opened to traffic, ferries were the only means of direct public trans-river travel.

Besides the horsecars that were used during the early days of the city's public transportation, steam railroads played an important

145

part. The Philadelphia & Germantown Company as early as 1832 operated a steam railroad from Germantown to the Philadelphia depot at Green and Ninth Streets. The steam trains ran only in fair weather, the more reliable horse-drawn trains being depended upon to maintain the schedule in bad weather.

In 1834 the Philadelphia & West Chester Railroad was begun, providing steam-hauled transportation between the city and West Chester. Many companies were soon in operation, running trains within Philadelphia, and from Philadelphia to suburban points. Gradually a strong central company was formed, absorbing the smaller lines and providing a few great systems, thus increasing efficiency in both passenger and freight carriage.

The Philadelphia & Reading Railroad began operation in 1842, running trains between Philadelphia and Pottsville. The purpose of the new line was to provide some means of shipping from the coal regions to the industrial center of Philadelphia. The company developed swiftly and in a short time was one of the largest systems in this section.

The Pennsylvania Railroad, begun as the Columbia Railroad, was started in 1832. Its development also was swift. It branched into the western part of the State, carrying freight by means of a gigantic network of lines to Philadelphia. The Broad Street Station was erected in 1881, and the Suburban Station in 1930. A short time later, the Thirtieth Street Station—a huge and imposing structure— was opened to traffic.

The third great railroad system serving Philadelphia, the Baltimore & Ohio, was started in Baltimore. It was the first railroad in the United States to transport both passengers and freight. The company was incorporated in 1827, and started business in 1830. Beginning on a small scale, the railroad gradually developed a large interstate business, fulfilling its purpose of competing with the Erie Canal, New York's commercial route to Ohio's rich territory.

Philadelphia is without an airport for commercial flying. However, a WPA project started at Hog Island in 1935 will, when completed, provide the city with a municipal airport within 20 minutes' travel of Broad and Market Streets. The land for this airport was purchased by the city from the United States, after its usefulness as a wartime shipyard had ended. The Central Airport near Camden has served as Philadelphia's airport since September 1929. When the new post office was built at Thirtieth and Market Streets, a large flat roof was laid out upon it to provide a landing place for autogyros. It is planned eventually to have the autogyros carry mail to the airport, where it will be transferred to waiting planes for delivery to other cities.

146

Labor and Labor Problems

A LARGE part of labor in early Philadelphia was furnished by semi-servile whites, imported under bond for a term of years, and by Negroes sold into chattel slavery. Although Penn's city can claim a certain amount of credit for frowning upon the practice of bartering in human beings, that odious practice went on unchecked for years at the Delaware River wharf.

William Penn's ingenious advertising in England and on the European continent brought hundreds of artisans and mechanics to the new Province, where they hoped to find escape from economic and religious oppression. Indentured servants, redemptioners, and debtors swelled the ranks of those who came.

Indentured servants were those — men, women, even children — who, unable to pay their passage, signed a contract called an indenture before leaving the Old World. This contract bound the owner of the ship to transport such a person to America, and bound the emigrant to serve the owner or his assigns for a specified number of years after arrival in this country. Often the owner, upon reaching port, sold his rights in the contract to the highest bidder, or for whatever he could get as payment for passage. The redemptioner, on the other hand, signed no contract before embarking, but agreed with the shipping merchant to allow himself to be sold to the highest bidder if, at the expiration of a month, he failed to find someone to redeem him by paying the passage money. Others were debtors sold for a fixed time to cancel their obligations, criminals unable to pay their fines or willing to accept exile instead of prison or death, and inmates of poorhouses bound out for periods of servitude to defray the expense of their keeping.

The custom of selling criminals and indigents was brought about by the inadequate facilities of jails and poorhouses. Directors of the poor were empowered to bind men and women from the institutions for periods not exceeding three years, but terms of indenture for criminals varied. On one occasion a man who had stolen £14 was sold for £16, his punishment being 21 lashes and six years of bondage. Immigrant ships came regularly to Philadelphia from European ports, bearing paupers and criminals whose arrival the newspapers would announce somewhat like this : "Just arrived in the ship *Sallie*, from Amsterdam, a number of men, women, and children redemp-

147

tioners. Their times will be disposed of on reasonable terms by the captain on board." Parents sometimes sold their children in order to cover their own passage. Husbands and wives became separated, never again to meet. Sometimes the dreadful ships came up the Delaware with their human cargo depleted by disease, exposure, hunger, and ill treatment.

This traffic in humanity was carried on upon a vast scale. Agencies in European cities set up branches in Philadelphia. Scores of dealers, known as "newlanders" or "soul-drivers," invaded Germany and Switzerland, inveigling thousands into leaving their homes for a life of unsuspected slavery abroad. This continued until 1764, when a German society in Philadelphia was founded especially for the protection of redemptioners. Organized resistance also militated against the practice of bringing into Pennsylvania captured Tuscarora Indians from South Carolina, and selling them as bondmen.

In its more agreeable aspect, the term "indenture" was associated with apprenticeship. A boy, in order to learn a trade, was bound to his employer by an agreement known as an indenture. He usually was taken into the employer's family and treated kindly. After serving his apprenticeship, he often chose to remain with his employer as a journeyman.

The earliest artisan in Philadelphia commonly started with little more than tools. At first he went about from house to house, doing his work with raw materials provided by the householder. Afterward, it became more convenient for him to establish a shop in the town. As his business grew, he employed two or three journeymen, in addition to two or three apprentices. He also began to stock up with finished products made by the journeymen, and to sell them to customers. The position of the journeyman became changed. He held on to his tools, but lost ownership of the shops and the raw materials. He was therefore dependent upon wages for his living, while the retail merchant-employer looked to his investment and his managerial ability for remuneration.

The journeyman sought to protect the value of his skill by trying to prevent others from entering his trade, knowing his wages would be higher if there were fewer men with whom he had to compete. On the other hand, the demand for his work was greater than he himself could supply, and he was forced to train the unskilled worker in his trade. But he saw to it that the term of apprenticeship was as long as possible, thus delaying the apprentice in becoming his competitor. In spite of limitations and restrictions, the number of journeymen continued to grow. Immigration brought many recruits, and industry began to replace skilled workers with unskilled workers. Then the former started to organize into societies or trade unions, to protect themselves against the unskilled.

148

The first trade associations were organized as price-fixing groups which regulated particular trades. They guaranteed to the public products of high quality and fought against inferior ones. They were benevolent groups, which not only had a form of "insurance" for members, but also sought to educate apprentices. These associations sometimes included both masters and journeymen, for some of the mechanics believed their interests identical with those of their employers. For example, they believed that if prices of goods were high, wages would also be high. But mostly, the journeymen established separate mutual-aid societies — the division being on social, rather than economic, lines.

The Carpenters' Company of Philadelphia was founded in 1724 purely as a price-fixing association, so that the workman should have a fair recompense for his labor and the owner the worth of his money. It is probable that this company was composed solely of master builders.

The first authentic record of the organization of a single trade and the first strike of wage-earners in Philadelphia occurred in 1786. In that year the Philadelphia printers went on strike for a minimum wage of $6 a week. They won their demands, and the organization disappeared. In May 1791 the Journeymen Carpenters of the City and Liberties of Philadelphia struck against the master carpenters. This was the first strike for a 10-hour working day in this country, but the strikers lost.

The first continuous organization of wage-earners for the purpose of maintaining or advancing wages was that of the shoemakers of Philadelphia. The organization, instituted in 1792, existed less than a year. The shoemakers again organized in 1794 under the name of the Federal Society of Journeymen Cordwainers, and continued in existence until 1806. In that year, and twice in 1809, the shoemakers were indicted on charges of conspiracy. They were accused of unlawfully assembling to "unjustly and corruptly conspire, combine, confederate and agree together that none of them would work for any master who would thereafter infringe or break the unlawful rules of the boot and shoemakers." The judge, in instructing the jury, declared : "A combination of workmen to raise their wages may be considered in a twofold view : one is to benefit themselves ; the other to injure those who do not join the society. The rule of the law condemns both." The jury found the defendants guilty of a conspiracy to raise wages.

The American labor movement first manifested itself in Philadelphia in 1827, through a trade union demanding shorter hours of work. This was soon converted into a political party, primarily urging public education. This movement had for its keynote the desire for equal citizenship — the essentials of which were believed to be

149

leisure and education. The American wage-earners joined together for the first time as a class, regardless of trade lines, in a struggle against employers. All previous labor agitation had been confined to the limits of a single trade. In June 1827, 600 journeymen carpenters went on strike for a 10-hour day. Other trade societies became interested, and a general movement began for the shorter work day.

Out of this movement grew the first union of all organized workmen in any American city. The Mechanics Union of Trade Associations was formed in the latter part of 1827. All trade societies were invited to join, and those not yet organized were urged to do so. Its purpose was to establish a just balance of power — mental, moral, political, and scientific — among the various classes.

In May of the following year the union resolved to submit to constituent societies a proposal for the nomination of persons who would represent the working classes in the City Council and State Legislature. Political action was immediately endorsed by the various trade unions. From this date, though the political movement advanced, the Mechanics Union declined, and some time after November 1829 it went out of existence.

The Working Men's Party was formed in July 1828. From the start the new movement was obliged to fight for its existence against the machinations of professional politicians, who tried either to obtain control of the meetings or to break them up. As a result of the first campaign, eight candidates who were exclusively on the Working Men's Party ticket received from 229 to 539 votes each in the city, and about 425 votes in the county. All were defeated, but 21 candidates on the Jackson ticket — endorsed by the Working Men's Party —were elected. The mere number of votes polled did not by any means measure the influence of the first campaign. Indirectly, it brought from the candidates for Congress of both the older parties in the city an open acknowledgment of the justice of the working people's attempts to lessen the established hours of daily labor.

The paramount emphasis laid upon education shows that the workingmen's movement was a revolt primarily directed against social and political, rather than economic, inequalities. The workingman had achieved suffrage and believed that he should have leisure in which to educate himself for proper use of his franchise. An early report of the Philadelphia workingmen to the Legislature foreshadowed the general public school system, the manual training schools, the junior republics, and probably the kindergartens. This report was accompanied by two bills for the establishment of a public school system, and a combination of agricultural, mechanical, literary, and scientific instruction. A tax on "dealers in ardent spirits" was proposed as a means of raising the necessary money.

Before establishment of the Working Men's Party, there had been a movement to create public charity schools for the poor. But after the report of the party was published, the plan for charity schools was abandoned in favor of one for schools where children of rich and poor might be educated side by side. The public school system of today owes a large, if unrecognized, debt of gratitude to this effort of the working classes to exercise independently their citizenship. The abolition of imprisonment for debt was undoubtedly hastened by the strong and general support it received from the Working Men's Party. In Pennsylvania, as a result of attention directed to the evils of child labor in factories, legislative consideration was given the subject in 1832, and again in 1837.

Economic changes were causing the shift from mutual insurance to trade protection. The merchant-capitalist had gained control of the market and the productive process. Hand tools continued to be used, yet orders had become wholesale. Competition between masters in different communities became acute. The merchant-capitalist even resorted to the use of prison labor. This competitive pressure on the masters was passed on to the journeymen. Apprentice labor was then done by children and unskilled workers, and a great number of women entered industrial employment. In 1830 it was said that many journeymen printers of Philadelphia were out of work because of the employment of boys. In 1836, 24 of 58 societies of Philadelphia were seriously affected by female labor, to the impoverishment of whole families and the benefit chiefly of the employers. The Female Improvement Society—including tailoresses, seamstresses, binders, folders, stock makers, milliners, corset makers, and mantua makers —had been organized June 20, 1835. This was probably the first federation of women workers in the country.

During the 1830's the city central union form of organization appeared, two separate trades unions in Philadelphia springing up in close succession. The Trades Union of Pennsylvania, composed of delegates from the factory districts surrounding Philadelphia, was organized in August 1833, but disappeared four months later. The Trades Union of the City and County of Philadelphia was organized the same year and lasted only until 1838. It was composed of mechanics of the city, although later it was opened to factory workers and day laborers.

The 10-hour day movement, begun in June 1834, took on the aspect of a crusade in Philadelphia. Coalheavers and common laborers on the Schuylkill docks started it. Then followed a strike of 14 other unions. The excitement was intense ; organized processions marched through the streets to the tune of fife and roll of drum. The general strike ended in a victory for the trade unionists, a victory so overwhelming that its influence extended to many other towns.

In 1834 there were 6,000 trade unionists in Philadelphia. Delegates

151

Midvale Steel Works
"Melted Steel"

attended a national convention in New York in August 1834, when
the National Trades Union was formed. The third annual convention
of that organization was held at Military Hall in Philadelphia from
October 24 to 28, 1836. No later meeting was recorded. Education,
speculation in public lands, prison labor, the 10-hour day, and female
and child labor were the problems which concerned the organization
during its existence.

Labor and Labor Problems

The labor movement in Philadelphia was virtually wiped out after the panic of 1837, workers turning to politics and cooperation for relief. Exponents of Fourierism, based on the socialistic philosophy of Francois Marie Charles Fourier, succeeded in organizing a few isolated cooperative and social reform organizations during the forties and fifties. This movement failed to obtain the sympathy and support of the workers generally, because people were not inclined to live in communal colonies, sharing a common kitchen, common living quarters, and cooperative cuisine.

Local impetus was given to the formation of national unions during the industrial depression after the panic of 1857. The Machinists' and Blacksmiths' Union was formed the following year, the local taking the initiative in forming a national organization, as did the Philadelphia Moulders' Union in 1859.

In March 1860 the Machinists' and Blacksmiths' Union called a strike in the Baldwin Locomotive Works against a reduction in wages and payment of arrear wages in company stock. Although the strike was lost, the workers received nation-wide attention for battling against the then greatest shop in the country.

The first effects of the Civil War were a paralysis of business and the increase of unemployment. Prosperity returned after the passage of the legal tender act in 1862, but wage earners did not benefit by prosperity, because of low wages and the high cost of living. The most influential labor paper of that period, and one of the best ever published in the United States, was *Fincher's Trades' Review*, printed in Philadelphia from 1863 to 1866. The paper was a true mirror of the national labor movement.

During the war the local trades' assembly was the common unit of organization. The Philadelphia Trades' Assembly was organized in 1863 at the instigation of the Philadelphia Journeymen House Painters' Association. Within a year 28 local unions were affiliated.

With the upward sweep of prices in 1862, cooperatives were established by workingmen. The first substantial effort in this direction was that of the Union Cooperative Association of Philadelphia, the first to be formed, in December 1862. It expanded, and eventually established several branches in various parts of the city. In the field of trade unionism, the nationalization of markets gave birth to the national trade union. During the Civil War and Reconstruction period, the American labor movement developed its characteristic national features.

Four sets of causes operated during the sixties to bring about this nationalization : competition of products of different localities in the same market ; competition for employment between migratory out-of-town journeymen and locally organized mechanics ; organization of employers ; and application of machinery, which introduced a division of labor, splitting old established trades and laying them open to invasion of "green hands."

The most significant event in the local labor movement for many years was the organization of the Knights of Labor in 1869. Nine members of the old Philadelphia Garment Cutters' Association were among those who joined. It was a secret society, with an elaborate ritual. By 1873 more than 80 locals had been organized in or near Philadelphia, and the organization had become nation-wide in its scope. This rapid growth was due to several factors. In the seventies, trade unions were declining or disbanding because of the warfare which employers were conducting against them. As a result, workingmen were attracted to a society such as the Knights because of its secrecy, which was maintained until 1878. In addition, industrial unionism, as opposed to the craft distinctions of the older unions, was favored by the new organization, thus making eligible for membership all working people regardless of sex, race, or skill.

The membership was grouped in local assemblies on the basis of residence rather than of occupation or craft. Borrowing from the First International of Karl Marx the technique of centralized control and common action, the Knights developed their organization into a potent instrument for fighting labor's battles. Their chief weaknesses, however, were their refusal to enter the political field as a labor party, and a lack of aggressiveness in leadership. The society was brought into conflict with the craft unions of skilled workers, and this led to its ultimate submergence under the rising tide of the American Federation of Labor during the nineties.

In July 1877 members of the Brotherhood of Locomotive Engineers employed by the Pennsylvania and the Philadelphia & Reading Railroads joined the great railroad strike which had broken out over the country. The strike, directed against a wage reduction and the open-shop policies of the railroads, was broken by the State militia and the police.

The internecine war between the Knights of Labor and the craft unions during the eighties was manifested locally in 1888, when locomotive engineers and firemen enrolled in the brotherhood broke a strike of the Philadelphia & Reading Railroad employees, which had been called by the Knights of Labor. Refusal of the Knights to join the eight-hour day movement widened the rift with the American Federation of Labor and allied unions, so that by 1890 the former's membership and prestige had dwindled to almost nothing.

During the nineties and the first decade of the twentieth century the local labor movement was marked by the increasing strength of the federated unions, particularly those in the textile industry. Socialists had entered some of the unions. The Industrial Workers of the World emerged locally in this period, but made only small gains. The activity of the textile unions of Philadelphia since the eighties had paved the way for one of the most important textile strikes in the history of the city — the strike for a 55-hour work week in 1903. The city's entire textile industry was forced to close down when 75,000 workers went out. The strike lasted several months. In all but a few plants the workers lost the strike.

After the depression of 1907, business conditions improved slowly, and labor began to press the fight for improved standards of living. In 1909 the streetcar workers of the Philadelphia Rapid Transit Co., dissatisfied with their wage of 20 cents an hour, went on strike for a four-cent increase. The strike was defeated by the company's use of strikebreakers. A year later the P.R.T. employees struck again, with instructions from their leaders not to return to work until their union was recognized by the company and the wage rate increased from 20 to 25 cents per hour. Strikebreakers were brought in to run the trolleys and break up the strike. Virtual warfare ensued, much property being destroyed and many persons injured. The strike ended in defeat for the workers. A sympathy strike of 15,000 textile workers, called by the textile unions when the street-car men went out, gave considerable unity and impetus to the local labor movement for the next decade.

To meet the high cost of living that prevailed during the World War period, wages for labor generally were raised. Consequently, there was little unrest in local industry throughout the war years. In 1919 the textile workers won the 48-hour week. Collective bargaining helped to preserve stability in industrial relations until the depression of 1921, when the open-shop drive of certain manufacturers started a wave of strikes that has continued unabated up to 1937. The introduction of labor spies, "yellow-dog" contracts, and strikebreaking tactics has served to sharpen the struggle with each succeeding year.

On June 13, 1933, Congress passed the National Industrial Recovery Act to speed recovery, to foster fair competition, and to provide for construction of certain useful public works. Section 7a of the act provided that labor should have the right to organize and bargain collectively through representatives of its own choosing, and section 7b directed that the President should, as far as practicable, afford every opportunity for employers and employees to establish by mutual agreement standard maximum hours of labor and minimum rates of pay. In order to speed up achievement of the objectives of the NIRA, a blanket code was presented June 19. This code set maximum hours and minimum wages for labor.

Section 7a was hailed as a sort of Magna Charta for the workingman. Immediately, thousands of workers began drives for the organization of trade unions, for better wages and shorter hours. Thousands of Philadelphia workers — pocketbook makers, textile workers, painters, decorators and paperhangers, cab drivers, necktie workers, and actors went on strike.

But Section 7a did not always prove a boon to the workers. Employers were glad to seize upon the minimum wage and maximum hours set by the blanket code, and thereby lower wages to a minimum (if they had previously been higher) or increase the number of hours to maximum. Or they chose to interpret "organization of own choosing" as referring to the company type of union — and to refuse to recognize bona fide unions. And a labor board often spent its efforts persuading workers to return to shops without having their demands met.

An outstanding example of defiance of the NIRA was the case of the E. G. Budd Manufacturing Co. of Philadelphia. On November 14, 1933, 2,000 workers in this plant struck for a wage increase, union recognition, and a 35-hour week. The regional labor board reviewed the case and ordered an election to determine which organization should be the collective bargaining agency. The company defied the ruling, held a company union election, and hired outsiders to replace strikers. Feeling was so intense that Gen. Hugh Johnson, then National Recovery Administrator, gave personal attention to the case. Finally an election was arranged in which strikebreakers were permitted to vote as well as strikers. Vigorous protest arose from labor leaders in Philadelphia. The liberal press of the Nation condemned the company. However, a total of 5,762 votes were cast, the strike eventually ending in March 1934, with a defeat for the workers.

One factor which helped mitigate the industrial unrest in which Philadelphia, a "workshop city," naturally shared, was the Regional Labor Board, one of the 17 erected in 1933 as an adjunct to the N.R.A.

Under the chairmanship of Jacob Billikopf, who organized and directed the handling of the many cases brought before it, this board served for 19 months without compensation, adjudicating nearly a thousand disputes affecting more than 1,250,000 workers. Its novel technique, a panel system, was among the factors which contributed to the board's success and won it high praise, this system being later followed in many places. Representatives of industry, and an equal number of labor leaders were drawn upon in pairs to confer with disputants and arrange amicable settlements of the points at issue. Full sessions of the board were held weekly. Its effectiveness is shown by the fact that less than 10 per cent of the cases brought before it for settlement were forwarded to the national body in Washington for review.

Violence sometimes accompanied enforcement of the provisions of the NIRA. Two hosiery workers were killed during a hosiery strike, and many arrests were made. In May 1935 the NIRA was declared unconstitutional by the Supreme Court of the United States, but the National Labor Relations Act which set up a National Labor Relations Board became a law in July of that year. This act guarantees to employees the right to organize and to bargain collectively, and has aided in bringing about a better mutual understanding between capital and labor. Major Stanley W. Root, who had served as director of the Regional Labor Board, was named regional director of this new group.

The city body of American Federation of Labor trade unions in present-day Philadelphia is the Central Labor Union. In its 1935 directory that organization lists 187 locals of international unions and 20 Federal unions as affiliates. Thirty-four other unions, mostly in the railroad trades, are listed as unaffiliated. The secretary of the local American Federation of Labor estimated that some 225,000 workers were organized in A. F. of L. unions and probably about 15,000 in independent unions. Twenty unions received Federal charters during 1936.

The two best organized trade unions in Philadelphia at present are those of the clothing and the textile workers. Most of the original textile workers came to Philadelphia from England and Germany, with long traditions of unionism behind them. Until the period from 1921 to 1931, the textile industry was able to maintain strong unions. But like many other unions, they were unable to survive the depression of 1931. Some passed out of existence. Since the National Recovery Administration, some of the groups — especially the hosiery workers — have been able to strengthen their organizations greatly.

In September 1934, 28,000 Philadelphia textile workers from 200 mills joined in a nation-wide textile strike. The strikers' demands included a 30-hour week, pay increases, a closed shop, elimination of the "stretch-out" system, better working conditions and union recognition. By the end of the month, peace had been restored in all but 20 mills, where "lock-outs" affected 2,000 workers. It was at the request of President Roosevelt that the textile employees had gone back to their jobs. Arbitration followed, in which their demands were lost ; but at least one outcome of the struggle was the President's creation of the Textile Relations Board, which focused attention in particular upon the "stretch-out" system denounced by labor.

The Philadelphia department stores were the next to feel the effects, two years later, of a serious labor dispute. The trouble began in November 1936, with a walkout of warehouse drivers and other warehouse employees. The demand was for increased wages, better working conditions, and union recognition. The warehouse men soon were joined by clerks, stockkeepers and the sales force in a sympathy walkout. A temporary truce was agreed upon until after Christmas, when representatives of labor and the stores met with Mayor S. Davis Wilson's Labor Arbitration Board. Settlement of the dispute was finally arrived at in May 1937. This was one of 104 strikes settled by the board during the 16 months of its existence.

While settlement of the department store strike was pending, Philadelphia became the objective of a drive made by the Committee for Industrial Organization, or CIO, opposed by the American Federation of Labor because it sponsored industrial organization in opposition to craft unionism. It first appeared in the city on January 4, 1937, when it sponsored a strike of 1,800 employees of the Electric Storage Battery Company.

This strike was Philadelphia's first experience with the new "sit-down" technique. All the company's plants were effectually closed until February 24, when an agreement providing for a five-cents-an-hour wage increase and one week's vacation with pay was signed in Mayor Wilson's office.

The CIO thus came out the winner in this first tilt, and the result was the organization of the Philadelphia CIO Council in March 1937. Craft members and unorganized workers were now recruited at top speed, and within 60 days the CIO membership had shot up to 10,000.

A truck drivers' strike began July 24 following, in which the CIO and A. F. of L. affiliates clashed. A reign of terror in which a driver was dragged from his truck and stabbed, cabs and trucks were overturned and set afire, and much property damaged or destroyed, finally caused the Mayor after mobilizing additional police force to quell the violence, to declare a "state of emergency."

Settlement of the general strike was effected on August 4 through an exchange of letters between the Mayor and an attorney for the A. F. of L. union, despite which, violence and disorder ruled the city that evening and the following day. When the strike was called off, no contract had been drawn up with the employer with regard to contract haulers.

RELIGIONS

BEGINNING as a wilderness sanctuary for a persecuted religious sect, Philadelphia today is marked by hundreds of church steeples pointing high above surrounding rooftops. The graveyards in the shadow of these churches hold the mortal remains of Quaker, Dunkard, Catholic, Lutheran, Episcopalian, Presbyterian, Baptist, Jew — representatives of the many faiths to find refuge in Penn's city.

Many of the churches had their origin in meetings held outdoors, in tiny dwellings, in barns, fortresses — or even, across the Atlantic, in places as inaccessible as the catacombs themselves. But in Philadelphia there was no need to hide, so the spires of many religious edifices now write upon the sky America's guarantee of religious freedom.

Lutheran

THE LUTHERAN Church was established in the Philadelphia area before William Penn arrived in 1682. The early Swedish colonists on the Delaware were Lutherans. Some of these organized a congregation at Wicaco (now part of South Philadelphia) in 1638 ; at Tinicum in 1677 ; and in the Old Swedes' Church (Gloria Dei) in 1700. By the end of the eighteenth century, the descendants of the original colonists had become thoroughly Anglicized, and the Swedish Lutheran Church, Gloria Dei, became Episcopalian.

New groups of Lutheran immigrants began to come from Germany, some settling in and about Philadelphia, especially in Germantown, before the turn of the century. After 1710 the influx of German immigrants, half of them Lutherans, assumed larger proportions. Some of them gathered for worship in Germantown as early as 1726, and in 1730 they had erected St. Michael's. By 1733 another group was worshiping in a barn on Arch Street below Fifth. In 1742, with the arrival of the noted Dr. Henry Melchior Muhlenberg, German Lutheranism was definitely organized and assumed its place in the religious life of Philadelphia. The Ministerium of Pennsylvania, organized by Muhlenberg and others, is the oldest ecclesiastical organization of its kind in America, dating from 1747.

Since the close of the eighteenth century the Lutheran churches in Philadelphia have multiplied rapidly. There are now 155 in this area. Most of them are affiliated with the Ministerium of Pennsylvania and the East Pennsylvania Synod.

Friends—Hicksites and Orthodox

THE Society of Friends, or Quakers, was founded in England in the seventeenth century by George Fox. One of his followers, William Penn, obtained in 1681 the grant of Pennsylvania, and for 70 years the influence of the Friends predominated in Philadelphia.

The essential Christian doctrines of the Friends were in accord with those of their fellow Christians. Their distinctive doctrine was that the Holy Spirit spoke immediately to the individual, a precept often called the "Inner Light." The meetings were marked by silence, unless some individual was moved by the Spirit to speak. As a sect, Quakers emphasized spiritual baptism and communion rather than the outward rites, and maintained that war and oaths were inconsistent with Christianity.

In 1827 a controversy developed between two groups in the society. The Orthodox faction contended that the unsound doctrines of the Hicksites caused the difference; the Hicksites charged that the Orthodox were arbitrary in authority. The Hicksites apparently questioned the divinity of Jesus Christ, the doctrine of atonement, and the inspiration and authority of the Bible.

The Orthodox Friends' school in Philadelphia is Friends' Select School; the Hicksite Friends are represented by Friends' Central School. There are at present in the city 3,000 Orthodox Friends, with six meetinghouses, and more than 2,000 Hicksites, with four meetinghouses.

On March 30, 1937, the two groups met in joint session for the first time since the schism of 1827, when they gathered at the Hicksite Meeting House to plan for the Friends' World Conference.

Protestant Episcopal

THE first Church of England congregation in Pennsylvania was organized at the instance of Henry Compton, Bishop of London. Penn's charter specifically empowered the bishop to establish it. As early as 1695 a small group of churchmen of that denomination purchased a plot of ground on Second Street and erected Christ Church. Rev. Thomas Clayton, appointed by Bishop Compton, came from England to take charge, and within two years, under his active leadership the congregation had increased from 50 persons to 700.

After the death of Rev. Mr. Clayton, Rev. Evan Evans arrived in 1700 to take his place. Evans proved eminently fitted for advancing the cause of religion in the growing town. He organized many congregations and visited them frequently. His flock in Philadelphia increased rapidly. Four additional churches had been erected in the surrounding settlements by 1704. Rapid growth marked the Protestant Episcopal faith until the Revolution, at which time congregations were split by Whig and Tory sympathies.

At the close of the Revolutionary War the church was bereft of its clergy. Its ministers had been popularly suspected of being representatives of the British Government. The one minister remaining in Pennsylvania, one who had been a confidant of Washington and the trusted friend of patriot leaders, was the youthful William White. He dedicated all his energies to reconstruction of the religious heritage, exerting strong influence upon the work of reestablishing the spiritual and material forces of the Episcopal Church. His immediate task was to enlist and train native-born ministers. In 1783 he submitted to his vestry a proposal to form a representative body of the Episcopal churches in the State. This body met on May 24, 1784, and three years later White was elected to the episcopate.

In Colonial times most of the prominent non-Quaker Philadelphians were members of this church. At present, the Protestant Episcopal Church has many imposing edifices in Philadelphia. Christ Church and Gloria Dei are the oldest of this list, each having a long and rich historical tradition. The city's total number of communicants is 75,159.

Presbyterian

ALTHOUGH Philadelphia was destined to become an important center of Presbyterian influence, Presbyterianism in America antedates its first congregation in Philadelphia by more than half a century. A congregation existed in Virginia as early as 1614, and another was organized in New England August 6, 1629. But these were antedated by a church in the Bermudas founded in 1612.

In 1692 groups of Baptists and Presbyterians met in the old Barbados storehouse, Second and Chestnut Streets, to lay the foundation for both denominations. One group held morning services and the other met in the afternoon. This association continued for three years, until the arrival from New England of Jedediah Andrews. The congregation in the Barbados storehouse became strictly Presbyterian under his pastoral guidance, the Baptists withdrawing. The year 1698 is generally accepted as the date of the organization of the First Presbyterian Church of Philadelphia.

By 1704 the congregation had so increased as to be able to erect a building of its own on High (now Market) Street between Second and Third. Two years later the first presbytery met there. The number of Presbyterians had increased to such an extent by 1716 that the

161

presbytery felt justified in constituting the Synod of Philadelphia. The meeting for organization was held in First Presbyterian Church. It was here also, that the General Assembly of the Presbyterian Church in the United States of America was organized.

First Church continued as the sole Presbyterian church in the city until, in 1743, the Second Presbyterian Church was organized, with Gilbert Tennent as pastor. The formation of this church came as a direct result of the preaching activities of Tennent and George Whitefield at the time of the "Great Awakening." In 1762 Third Presbyterian Church was founded. Construction of the church building on Pine Street near Fourth was not begun, however, until 1766. When the present structure was erected in 1857, a section of the wall of the original building was retained. The fourth Presbyterian society to be organized was the Church of the Northern Liberties, established in 1813.

The close of the Colonial period, therefore, found Philadelphia Presbyterians with four distinct societies in four houses of worship. At present there are 108 Presbyterian churches and a Presbyterian population of 61,000 in the city.

Baptist

THE first permanent Baptist church established in Philadelphia and still existing is that known as the Lower Dublin or the Old Pennepek (Pennypack) Church. Organized in January 1688 by Rev. Elias Keach, it is termed "Mother of All Baptist Churches in Pennsylvania, New Jersey, New York, Delaware, and Maryland," although a Baptist congregation existed as early as 1684 at Cold Spring, near Bristol. Services of the present congregation are held in an edifice on Krewstown Road, near Welsh Road, in the Bustleton section.

The present First Baptist Church of Penn's city was founded in 1698 as a branch of that at Lower Dublin, and was not formally constituted until 1746. (Until 1698 services were held in the Barbados storehouse). The present house of worship is at Sansom and Seventeenth Streets.

The number of Baptists grew rapidly, and the city became the center of Baptist activities. Perhaps the most noted leader in the city was Rev. Dr. Russell H. Conwell, who became pastor of Grace Baptist Church in 1881. Largely by lecturing, Dr. Conwell raised more than $8,000,000, with which sum he founded Temple University and three great hospitals : Samaritan (now Temple University Hospital), Garretson, and Greatheart. From a little, debt-ridden mission, Grace Church became the Grace Baptist Temple at Broad and Berks Streets, with a seating capacity of 3,500. Out of a class of two or three young men meeting in the pastor's study grew the great

162

Temple University from which, at the time of Dr. Conwell's death in 1925, approximately 125,000 students had been graduated.

Among the larger Baptist churches, in addition to those mentioned, are : Alpha, York and Hancock Streets ; Chestnut Street, Chestnut Street west of Fortieth ; and Second, Second Street near Girard Avenue. The Baptist membership in the metropolitan area of Philadelphia numbers 46,162 white and approximately 50,000 Negro worshipers.

Mennonite

A GROUP of a dozen small bodies of Mennonites regard Menno Simons, a Dutch Anabaptist, as their founder. Most of them came to America from Holland, Germany, Switzerland, or Russia.

The first Mennonite colony was formed in Germantown in 1683 by some of the 13 original settlers. By 1708 they had built a little log meetinghouse on Main Street (now Germantown Avenue) above Herman Street. William Rittenhouse was the first pastor of the congregation. He is buried in the adjoining graveyard. In 1770 the present Mennonite Meetinghouse replaced the log structure.

Members of the sect believe in adult baptism, non-resistance, and practical piety, and are opposed to the judicial oath. The Mennonites (General Conference) have 800 members and three churches in Philadelphia ; and the Mennonite Brethren in Christ, with 400 members, also have three churches.

Brethren

I.   Brethren Church (Progressive Dunkards).
II. Church of the Brethren (Conservative Dunkards).

THIS religious group represents the Pietists who came from Crefeld, Germany, under the leadership of Peter Becker, and settled in Germantown in 1719. At 6611 Germantown Avenue is the meetinghouse which sheltered the mother congregation of the sect in America. The front section of the building was erected in 1770. The first Bible printed in this country in German came from the press of Christopher Saur, or Sauer, a member of this congregation.

These Germans were called Dunkers (baptizers), because of their belief in immersionism. Their communion was held in the evening, preceded by the rite of foot washing and the love feast. Simple, plain-living, devout Christians of the evangelical type, they are conservative regarding attire ; they are opposed to taking oaths ; and they advocate non-resistance and temperance.

The Progressives, who are more liberal in their customs and manners, and who believe that all ecclesiastical power should be lodged

163

in the local church, withdrew from the main body in 1882. They have 300 members and two churches here. The Conservatives have 1,500 members and five churches.

Reformed

THE Reformed Church in the United States, until 1869 known as the German Reformed Church, developed as a result of religious persecution in Germany and Switzerland. Many did not subscribe to the doctrines of Luther, finding the teachings of Zwingli and Calvin more acceptable.

When, in 1684, the first of these refugees came to America, the Reformed Church had its inception in the New World, although it did not become fully organized until 1725. The vast majority of the new settlers flocked to Pennsylvania, most of them proceeding inland beyond Philadelphia to what is now Montgomery County. The first German Reformed minister to arrive was Samuel Guldin, who preached in Germantown in 1718.

The First Reformed Church of Philadelphia, founded in 1727, was the first of this denomination in the city. Now at Fiftieth and Locust Streets, it is one of 27 Reformed churches in the Philadelphia area. Heidelberg, Broad and Grange Streets ; Trinity, Broad and Venango Streets ; and Grace, Eleventh and Huntingdon Streets, have the largest congregations.

Evangelical and Reformed

THE Evangelical and Reformed Church was formed in 1934 by a union of the Evangelical Synod of North America and the Reformed Church in the United States (German Reformed).

The Evangelical Synod traces its origin from missionaries of the Evangelical Church of Germany and Switzerland, who organized a synod in 1840 at Gravois, Mo. The first recorded communion service of the Reformed Church in the United States was held in 1725. The original German Reformed Church building was erected in Germantown in 1733, on the site now occupied by the Market Square Presbyterian Church. In 1747 a church was built in Philadelphia proper, on Race Street near Fourth. Members of both churches numbered 15,800 in 1937.

Roman Catholic

OF ALL who sought friendly shelter in Penn's Province, to none was it a more welcome haven than to the Catholics. Subjected to the lash of persecution elsewhere, they found a true refuge in Philadelphia. Here they could worship openly.

164

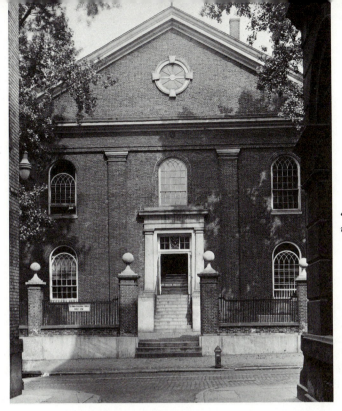

St. Paul's Protestant
Episcopal Church
"Here Stephen Girard
was married; here Edwin
Forrest lies"

Stenton House
"Home of
William Penn's
Secretary"

A chapel was established about 1729 in a private house next to the southeast corner of Second and Chestnut Streets. Although prior to this period Mass was celebrated in private homes by visiting Jesuits, this chapel marked the beginning of the Roman Catholic Church here.

Father Joseph Greaton, a Jesuit who arrived in Philadelphia in 1729, was the first to exercise his ministry in this humble place. Later, in the years between 1731 and 1733, the exact time not being clear, he built the tiny chapel of St. Joseph, oldest Catholic church in Philadelphia. The present building, which was erected in 1838, is the fourth structure on that site. Standing in Willing's Alley, between Third and Fourth Streets, and surrounded by the offices of large insurance companies, it is of lasting interest because of its association with Colonial and Revolutionary times.

Father Greaton's two successors were responsible for new edifices. St. Mary's, on Fourth Street north of Spruce, was erected in 1763 through the work of Father Harding. Father Molyneux opened a parish school there in 1782. Father Steinmeyer, a German Jesuit, who assisted Father Harding and Father Molyneux, was instrumental in settling difficulties between Catholics of German origin and those of Irish origin. In addition to his activities among the Germans in Philadelphia, he journeyed as a missionary through Pennsylvania, New Jersey, and New York. The colonists knew him as "Father Farmer."

After "Father Farmer's" death, the German Catholics felt the need of a church of their own, and in 1788 built Holy Trinity Church at Sixth and Spruce Streets. Of red and black glazed brick, this edifice appears now substantially as it did when first built.

In 1793 there arose a demand for a church in the northern section of the city. Opportunely, the Augustinians were seeking to establish their order in the United States, and to them was entrusted the project of erecting a new church. St. Augustine's was dedicated in 1801. The present structure, rebuilt in 1847, stands on the original site, on Fourth Street between Race and Vine.

Until 1808 the Catholic Church in Philadelphia had been under the jurisdiction of the Bishop of Baltimore. In that year, however, the city was proclaimed a separate diocese, and two years later Bishop Egan was installed as the first Bishop of Philadelphia.

In 1832 Bishop Francis P. Kenrick established, in an upstairs room of St. Mary's rectory on Fourth Street, what eventually became the diocesan seminary of St. Charles Borromeo. The first class consisted of five students. In 1871 the seminary was transferred to its present site in Overbrook. Toward the latter part of his 21-year administration Bishop Kenrick chose a site at Eighteenth and Race Streets for a cathedral. The first Mass was sung in the Cathedral of SS. Peter and Paul on Easter Sunday, 1862.

John Nepomucene Neumann, a Redemptorist, was made bishop of the diocese in March 1852. One of his first acts was to provide Catholic schools. At his death eight years later, they numbered nearly 100. Bishop Neumann has been proclaimed "Blessed" by the Church. This is a step preliminary to placing him on the calendar of saints.

In 1868 the Holy See divided the diocese of Philadelphia, establishing a new diocese at Scranton and another at Harrisburg. Philadelphia was elevated to the rank of a Metropolitan See in 1875.

His Eminence, Cardinal Dougherty, has been Archbishop of Philadelphia since July 1918. In 1921 he was created cardinal. The Catholic population of the archdiocese is estimated at 837,000.

Moravian

FOLLOWERS of the pre-Reformation faith of Johann Huss, the Moravian immigrants first settled in Georgia in 1735. They moved to Pennsylvania in 1740, built the towns of Bethlehem and Nazareth, and for some time adopted a form of communism to help them in their efforts to conquer the wilderness. Under Count Zinzendorf they cultivated a closely supervised spiritual discipline and endeavored to separate themselves from the world. The Moravian Church is broadly evangelical, and has a liturgy and an episcopal form of government.

The first Moravian church was built in Philadelphia in 1742, at Race and Broad Streets, through the efforts and ministry of Count Zinzendorf. The Moravians have 1,000 members in Philadelphia, with three churches.

Judaism

FROM a few scattered pioneers in 1720 to a total of 247,000 in 1936 — such is the growth of Judaism and the Jewish population in Philadelphia.

In 1747 the first congregation in the city was begun, later acquiring the name of Kahal Kadosh Mikveh Israel. It is believed to have held services in a small house in Sterling Alley, which ran from Cherry Street to Race, just below Front. The first synagogue was erected on Cherry Street between Third and Fourth and dedicated in 1782, with Rabbi Gershon Mendes Israel Seixas as first minister.

The services of Mikveh Israel closely resembled the Orthodox ritual of the Spanish and Portuguese Jews. Many of the early members were refugees from the Spanish Inquisition. The first Hebrew Sunday School in America opened in Philadelphia on March 4, 1838, as an adjunct to Mikveh Israel Congregation. Chief organizer of the school was Rebecca Gratz, noted for her talent and beauty, as well as for her strict adherence to the tenets of Judaism.

167

Mikveh Israel has had many noted members during its long history. Among them were Isaac Leeser, first American to translate the Old Testament into English, and editor of an important Jewish magazine, *The Occident*; Rabbi Sabato Morais, founder of the Jewish Theological Seminary of New York, a profound scholar and a doctor of laws of the University of Pennsylvania; Marcus Jastrow, author of the only Talmudic dictionary in English; Joseph Krauskopf, founder of the National Farm School, in Doylestown; Samuel Hirsch, nationally known religious orator; and Henry Berkowitz, founder of the Jewish Chautauqua Society. In 1860 Mikveh Israel was removed to Seventh Street above Arch. It is now located at Broad and York Streets.

The first synagogue of the German Jews was Rodeph Shalom, chartered in 1802. First worship was held in a building on Pear Street, later on Margaretta Street, then, in 1846, on Juliana (now Randolph) Street, which lies between and parallel to Fifth and Sixth. In 1870 the congregation dedicated a new synagogue at Broad and Mt. Vernon Streets. The present imposing synagogue was erected in 1927.

For some time this congregation was strictly Orthodox, but in 1866, under the direction of Dr. Jastrow, many innovations of the liberal wing of Judaism were adopted. With the coming of Rabbi Henry Berkowitz in 1892, the congregation definitely allied itself with Reformed Judaism, and is today one of the outstanding Reformed Congregations of America. In 1887 Rodeph Shalom built a school at 956 North Eighth Street. The Jewish Cultural Association also developed from this congregation.

The third synagogue in Philadelphia was known as Beth Israel, and held its first services in a rented hall near Fifth and Walnut Streets in December 1840. The synagogue is now at Thirty-second Street and Montgomery Avenue.

The Reformed Congregation, Keneseth Israel, largest in the city, was organized in 1847. Services were held in a hall at 528 North Second Street. At present the synagogue is on Broad Street above Columbia Avenue. The congregation supports a free library and reading room. There were about 10 synagogues in Philadelphia in 1875. At the end of 1935 there were 119.

Methodist Episcopal

METHODISM was introduced into Philadelphia in 1769 by Dr. Joseph Pilmoor, who preached his first sermon from the steps of the State House. His teachings, however, were not entirely new, for a year earlier Thomas Webb, a captain in the British army, had conducted services. Later, sermons were delivered by Dr. Pilmoor in open fields around the city. Dr. Pilmoor was assisted by Captain

168

Webb. Many were impressed by the latter's stern mien. The first regular meetings were held in a pothouse in Loxley's Court, between Arch and Cherry Streets.

The first Methodist Episcopal church in America actually was the present St. George's, Fourth Street north of Race. It was an unfinished building when purchased from the Dutch settlers in 1769, and remained floorless even up to Revolutionary times. During the British occupation the building was used as headquarters for cavalry.

Outstanding among Methodist Episcopal churches in this city are the Arch Street at Broad and Arch Streets ; Calvary at Forty-eighth Street and Baltimore Avenue ; and the First Methodist Episcopal of Germantown at 6023 Germantown Avenue. The church population of the Philadelphia Conference is more than 100,000. The Philadelphia membership ranges from 40,000 to 65,000 with 132 churches, 20 of which are for Negroes.

Universalist

ORGANIZATION of the Universalists in this city into a separate church came about as a result of a dispute arising in the First Baptist Church of Philadelphia. Its pastor privately upheld the doctrine of universal salvation. His views, becoming a subject of controversy, led to excommunication of himself and his followers. This ousted group called themselves Universal Baptists.

In 1770 a group gathered by the Rev. John Murry absorbed the greater part of the Universal Baptists, and the First Universalist Church of Philadelphia was formed. This body erected a church building on Lombard Street west of Fourth in 1793.

Today the principal Universalist Church in Philadelphia is the Church of the Messiah, at Broad Street and Montgomery Avenue.

Unitarian

THE First Unitarian Church of Philadelphia, first of all existing churches in America to take the Unitarian name, was organized in 1796 under Dr. Joseph Priestley, eminent scientist. Dr. Priestley came to Philadelphia in 1794 from Birmingham, England, and began preaching in this city.

John Adams, the Nation's second President, was a member of the Unitarian Church of Quincy, Mass. While he was President, he attended services at the First Unitarian Church in Philadelphia.

The present parish house of the First Unitarian Church, on Chestnut Street east of Twenty-second, was built in 1886. There is only one other church of this denomination in Philadelphia, the Germantown Unitarian Church at 6511 Lincoln Drive.

169

United Brethren in Christ

DURING the last half of the eighteenth century Philip William Otterbein, a missionary of the German Reformed Church, and Martin Boehm, of the Mennonite communion, feeling the need of a deeper spiritual life, conducted evangelistic services throughout Pennsylvania and the neighboring States. They gained converts rapidly, and in 1800 there was formed a distinct ecclesiastical body — the United Brethren in Christ. The church was a natural development of the spiritual needs of many German-Americans. Philadelphia today has 700 members of this faith, with four churches.

Christian Science

THE advent of Christian Science into Philadelphia was not a heralded event. The seedling was planted in the later years of the nineteenth century, and in 1906 work was begun on the erection of the First Church of Christ, Scientist, on Walnut Street west of Fortieth. The building was completed in 1910. From that date until its dedication in 1911 sufficient subscriptions were received to complete payment on its construction and to form the nucleus of a fund for the building of the Second Church of Christ, Scientist, at 5443 Greene Street, Germantown. There are four other churches, each with its own reading room. Jointly they maintain a city reading room in the Fidelity-Philadelphia Trust Building at Broad and Sansom Streets.

Spiritualists

SPIRITUALISM had its origin in the alleged spirit tappings heard by the Fox sisters of Hydesville, N. Y., in 1848. Through the work of the elder sister the sect spread rapidly.

There are five churches in Philadelphia: First Association of Spiritualists at Carlisle and Master Streets; Third Spiritualist Church at 1421 North Sixteenth Street; Universal Spiritualist Brotherhood Church at 3012 West Girard Avenue; All Saints Spiritual Church at 2026 Glenwood Avenue; and St. John's Spiritual Alliance Church at 805 West Lehigh Avenue.

Seamen's Church Institute

ALMOST a century ago a barge which had been converted into a floating church was towed down the Delaware River, moored to a wharf at Dock Street, and opened as a seamen's church. Arrival of the "floating church" aroused a great deal of interest, and throngs of visitors inspected this unusual structure.

Gateway of Old Christ Church
"Come to me, all ye who labor . . ."

After sufficient money was subscribed the church was consecrated by Rt. Rev. Alonzo Potter, and regular Sunday services were begun. This was the origin of what is now the Seamen's Church Institute. Work of the mission was transferred later to quarters at Catharine and Swanson Streets, and in 1878 to the Church of the Redeemer, Front and Queen Streets.

In 1920 the institute was incorporated as an independent interdenominational society for rendering every service possible to seamen, and was moved to its present location, Second and Walnut Streets. Within a year adjoining properties were acquired. In 1927 the M. Clark Mariner Home for Aged and Disabled Mariners was merged with the institute. More recently the Pennsylvania Seamen's Friend, which had operated a sailors' home at 422 South Front Street, transferred its work to the institute.

Miscellaneous

OTHER churches represented in Philadelphia are : Latter Day Saints, one church, 400 members ; Catholic Apostolic, one church 300 members ; Church of God in North America (General Eldership), one church, 116 members ; Congregational and Christian, eight churches, 1,800 members ; Christian Church Disciples of Christ, four churches, 1,900 members ; Dutch Reformed, four churches, 1,200 members ; Church of God, three churches, 150 members ; Seventh Day Adventists, seven churches, 2,500 members ; Evangelical Congregational, two churches, 389 members ; Reformed Episcopal, ten churches, 2,677 members.

Among the denominations represented in the Philadelphia Federation of Churches and not previously mentioned are : United Brethren, Christian Missionary Alliance, Covenanters, Methodist Free, Methodist Protestant, Pentecostal, Primitive Methodist, Reformed Presbyterian, Undenominational, and United Presbyterian.

Of the Orthodox (Eastern) Churches, the Greek Hellenic has one church and 3,000 members in Philadelphia ; the Russian (under the Patriarch of Moscow) has three churches and 2,266 members ; the Rumanian (under the Patriarch of Bucharest) has one church and 400 members ; the Independent Russian and the Albanian Orthodox have each one church and 500 members.

The Church of the New Jerusalem (Swedenborgian) has two churches in Philadelphia ; the Schwenkfelders, one. The Ethical Culture Society, with local headquarters at 1906 Rittenhouse Square, has a membership of 800. The organization known as Jehovah's Witnesses has headquarters at 1620 North Broad Street ; this group has no membership rolls, and meetings are held in private homes.

EDUCATION

THE Dutch and Swedes, Penn's predecessors in the "Grove of Tall Pines," laid the foundations for public instruction. Men who had to rely for survival almost entirely upon the strength of their backs and the brawn of their arms realized that continued progress and development depended upon how well the minds of their children were sharpened upon the whetstone of knowledge.

Accordingly, a school was established on Tinicum Island in 1642, with Christopher Taylor at its head. In 1657 Evert Pietersen conducted a school for Dutch children of new villages near Tinicum.

Penn thus found education established, in a small way, when he arrived here. One of his first acts was to direct the Pennsylvania Council to begin a school wherein the youth might be trained. Several enterprising tutors managed to obtain a few pupils from the wealthier immigrants. Enoch Flower, a teacher for 20 years, was summoned from England in 1683 to take charge of a school established by the council. Charges per quarter were four shillings to read English, six shillings for reading and writing, and eight shillings for reading and writing and "casting accounts." Flower also took pupils to board with him at £10 a year.

Founding of the Friends' Public School, now William Penn Charter School, was one of the important early steps leading to establishment of the public school system. The school was opened in 1689 on Fourth Street below Chestnut, and was chartered in 1697. Conducted by Quakers, it admitted pupils of every creed and gave instruction free to indigent children. George Keith was headmaster.

The University of Pennsylvania was founded in 1749 by Benjamin Franklin and a group of citizens interested in the "establishment of educational facilities for the youth of the Pennsylvania colony." Classes began in 1751 in a two-story brick building which had been erected for religious services at Fourth and Arch Streets. Franklin was the first president of the board of trustees.

The first charter was granted in 1753, and a second charter granting the right to confer degrees was issued in 1755. Later, the first medical school in America was established. In 1779 the charter became vested in "The Trustees of the University of the State of Pennsylvania," and professional schools, distinct from the college, were instituted.

173

Board of Education Administration Building

Penn Charter School
"The first established school of Philadelphia"

The first law school in the Nation was established in 1789 and three years later the college and the university were merged and incorporated under the title of "The University of Pennsylvania."

In 1829 the institution moved to Ninth and Chestnut Streets and thence to its present site at Thirty-fourth Street and Woodland Avenue, in 1872. The following year the college buildings, Logan Hall, Hare Laboratory and the main building of University Hospital were constructed. From this time forward, the institution expanded rapidly, adding new buildings and increasing the courses to such extent that the university today has a faculty numbering 1,333 and a student enrollment of about 15,000. The campus covers 106 acres and contains a total of 164 buildings. The total property value is about $35,000,000, and the endowment funds amount to $19,000,000.

Temple University was founded in 1884 by Dr. Russell H. Conwell, pastor of Grace Baptist Temple, Broad and Berks Streets. The institution began when Dr. Conwell started evening classes in his church for a small group of young men who desired to study for the ministry. From this modest beginning, the idea expanded so that opportunity for study was made available to poor students seeking higher education.

Today the university has more than 12,000 students enrolled. Its buildings occupy an entire block on the east side of Broad Street, from Montgomery Avenue to Berks Street. Other buildings include Temple University Medical College and Hospital at Broad and Ontario Streets ; the former Oak Lane Country Day School in Oak Lane; and the School of Art in Elkins Park. The university is maintained by two funds, one being obtained from student tuition, the other from periodic appropriations made by the State.

In 1761 the Germantown Academy was established in Bensell's (now School House) Lane, Germantown. It was sponsored by German settlers and English Quakers. It is the oldest school in the United States having a continuous existence in the same building. Twenty-three years after its founding the school obtained a charter as the Public School of Germantown, but an advertisement in the Pennsylvania *Gazette* of 1794 listed it as Germantown Academy, and that name has been retained.

These new schools did not, however, alleviate the sore need for educational facilities for poor children. The Declaration of Independence, written and signed in this city, proclaimed that all men were created equal and entitled to "life, liberty and the pursuit of happiness." Nevertheless, the problem of free education in Philadelphia received no adequate local attention until 1818. That year the Legislature passed an act setting up the city of Philadelphia as the first school district of Pennsylvania. New schools were opened, and a board of control was established to supervise them. Among the

175

institutions started then was the "Model School," which opened December 21, 1818.

This type school, originated in England by Joseph Lancaster, was used there to some extent. It provided for a headmaster and a group of monitors to act as teachers, each monitor handling 15 or 20 pupils. Under this arrangement it was possible to educate more children at smaller cost than under previous systems. A special committee which had been named to study this Lancaster plan reported upon it favorably ; 10 such schools were opened and a special building set aside for the eleventh.

Thus, the "Model School" was established and placed under the direct supervision of Lancaster, who crossed the Atlantic to take charge of it. It trained young men and women in the teaching profession, and its graduates received posts in the new school districts set up in the State by the law of 1834, which levied a tax to provide necessary revenue.

The advances made in the Legislature's act of 1834 were seriously threatened the following year when members of the Assembly were yielding to the pressure of those opposed to the new taxes. A masterly address by Thaddeus Stevens, "Father of the Pennsylvania Free Schools," completely turned the tide of sentiment.

In 1836 another law was passed, providing for the education of all children more than four years old. This was the first step toward compulsory education and one of the greatest strides in free public instruction. The new law also carried a provision for establishment of a high school in Philadelphia.

Accordingly, the board of control began erection of Central High School, on the east side of Juniper Street below Market, facing what was then Center Square. The school embodied all the dreams and ideals of the pioneers of free public education. It was a fine building, well staffed, and was surmounted by an astronomical observatory not surpassed anywhere in the country. Alexander Dallas Bache, great-grandson of Benjamin Franklin, was appointed first principal of the school in 1839. Franklin had not lived to see the fruit of his earlier campaigns for public education, but with Bache's appointment the tradition was carried on. During his three years at the school Bache organized a smoothly functioning unit and established a fine curriculum. The school's fame spread.

By 1853 business had moved westward from the Delaware until the school was almost surrounded by commercial establishments. The building was sold to the Pennsylvania Railroad, and in September 1854 Central High School moved to the southeast corner of Broad and Green Streets. In 1894 another building was erected on the southwest corner of the same intersection. Both buildings still stand but the earlier, which served as an annex, was condemned in 1937.

With the establishment of Central High School the board of control increased its activity and in 1848 opened a school of practice in conjunction with the Girls' Normal School in the old Model School building on Chester (Darien) Street north of Race. The popularity of this school of higher education for girls grew at such an amazing rate that by 1853 it became necessary to open a similar school to accommodate the overflow.

In 1859 the Normal School was closed and replaced by the Girls' High School, which in the second and third terms of its curriculum gave special instruction to those intending to become teachers. Students in the senior classes obtained practice by teaching the lower classes. The school was reorganized in 1861 and renamed Girls' High School and Normal School. Seven years later the word "high" was dropped, and it was renamed Girls' Normal School. It is now the Philadelphia Normal School.

Increasing registration and new requirements necessitated larger quarters, and in 1876 the school was moved to Seventeenth and Spring Garden Streets. Here it operated in conjunction with the Philadelphia High School for Girls until 1893, when its professional course having been extended from one to two years, and the Girls' High School course to four years, new facilities were required. The Normal School moved to Spring Garden and Thirteenth Streets, its present site, and the high school remained at Seventeenth Street.

Meanwhile, the school system improved steadily. The number of schools increased and teachers' salaries advanced. Then a campaign to simplify textbooks, courses, and methods of administration was launched.

By an act of Legislature in 1870, the name of the control board was changed to the Board of Public Education. Three years later the City Councils passed an ordinance creating a loan of $1,000,000 for the erection of additional school buildings. That same year, a clause in the new State constitution made provisions for education of children more than six years old, with $1,000,000 to be set aside yearly for that purpose. In 1895 the education of children became compulsory by legislative enactment.

In 1874 Quakers reorganized the William Penn Charter School, Fourth Street below Chestnut, and moved it to No. 8 South Twelfth Street. It occupied this latter site until 1925, when it was removed to School House Lane, Germantown, not far from Germantown Academy. This school claims direct descent from the old school of the same name. The Friends' Select School, Seventeenth Street and the Parkway, still under the direction of Friends' Meeting, also traces its origin to the old William Penn Charter School.

The mere enumeration of dates on which changes in the school system occurred can give little comprehension of the gradual rise of the educational idea to a broad and higher plane. Such factors as the consolidation of the city, in 1854, and the subsequent creation of separate school districts for each ward were quickly reflected in the viewpoint and morale of the administrative and teaching staffs. Similarly, creation of the office of Superintendent of Schools, about 1883, helped toward the establishment of a more professional standard throughout the city for all wards.

Such changes, however, were utterly inadequate to correct the abuses which had grown with the system itself, abuses due largely to the narrow selfishness of politicians. Ward leaders, members of City Councils, and even the small fry of the political world saw in the system a mere "grab bag." Teaching jobs were for sale at the political pay window, provided the applicant had a mere certificate showing qualifications for the work. There was no such thing as a list of eligibles to be drawn from in order, so political patronage far outweighed any excellence in the candidate for the schoolroom work, or the interests of the children themselves.

Real transformation of the educational picture began with the Act of 1905, by which the State reorganized the public school system and established the Board of Education for Philadelphia. This board was given the power of disposal of the money which Council was authorized to collect through a limited tax on real estate.

In Philadelphia and Pittsburgh, this limited power of taxation was transferred from Council to the Board itself by an act passed in 1911, which established a school code for the entire State.

The Philadelphia public school system today has an enrollment of about 272,000 day pupils. Adding to this the number attending evening schools, citizenship classes for mothers, and other extension activities, the total is about 300,000. The system requires the services of nearly 10,000 persons in the professional field. At present there are 4 practice, 14 senior high, 23 junior high, 3 vocational, 201 elementary schools and one industrial art school, one residential school, one demonstration school, and one normal school.

Negro Education

EDUCATION of the Negro in early days of the Colony was advocated by three groups — masters who sought to increase the efficiency of their slaves, sympathetic groups interested in the betterment of the race, and zealous Christian missionaries.

Of these three groups, the first was by far the most effective. Although it was undoubtedly selfishness that prompted the slave owners to pursue their policy of education, their efforts proved far more productive than those of the other groups. Their methods were based upon two forms — formal education in reading and writing, and industrial education to further the efficiency of the slave in his work.

The Quakers, however, strove not only to educate the Negro, but actually to free him from the bonds of slavery. They believed education would mean little to the Negro until he was free. Among the first Quaker leaders interested in emancipation were George Fox and William Penn. A definite scheme was advanced in 1713 whereby the slaves would be freed, educated, and returned to Africa in the capacity of missionaries among their own people.

In 1750 Anthony Benezet established a night school for Negroes in Philadelphia, and 20 years later he took the leading part in establishing a systematic method of education for the Negro. The Monthly Meeting of Friends in 1770 approved a proposal to establish a school for Negro and mulatto children. These were to be instructed in reading, writing, arithmetic, and other useful subjects. This school was continued for 16 years. Tuition was free, the school being maintained by subscriptions.

The first attempt of an organized body to educate the Negro was made by the Society for the Propagation of the Gospel in Foreign Parts, organized in London in 1701. Assisted by a private endowment, known as the Dr. Bray Fund, this society opened two schools in Philadelphia in 1760, and its educational work continued for nearly a century.

The period between 1830 and 1860 saw the greatest strides in the field of Negro education. Until 1830 only two schools for Negro children were supported by public funds, but in that year the board of control established another such school in Northern Liberties. In 1844 two more were opened, and others followed thereafter with increased frequency.

Meanwhile, the Negroes had begun a campaign of their own to educate members of their race. Societies were formed for that purpose, and libraries were opened. The close of the Civil War and the emancipation of slaves caused a veritable boom in Negro education. Previously Negroes had been refused admission to both Central High School and the Philadelphia Normal School, as well as to the University of Pennsylvania. When the bars were lowered, a large number of Negroes quickly took advantage of the opportunity to gain a higher education.

Parochial School System

IN THE parish of St. Joseph's, probably as early as the 1730's, was established the first parochial school in the city. In 1767 James White, a merchant, bequeathed £50 "toward a school house" — the first known bequest made to aid Catholic education in Philadelphia.

In 1781 St. Mary's Church took steps to pay off the old school debt and to buy new ground, presumably for another school building. St. Joseph's Society for the Education of Poor Orphan Children next entered the field, obtaining incorporation papers in 1808.

Later, the Germans of St. Mary's parish formed a church of their own, and immediately opened a school. This new church was known as Holy Trinity Church. The parish of St. Augustine was founded in 1796, and almost immediately began to provide facilities for the education of the parish children.

Parochial schools continued to be opened as the number of Catholics in the city increased and made new parishes necessary. Catholic education was accelerated in 1878, when the will of Thomas E. Cahill bequeathed almost $1,000,000 for the establishment of a Catholic high school. In 1890 the Roman Catholic High School was opened at Broad and Vine Streets. Today the school maintains an athletic field (Cahill Field) as a memorial to the founder.

At present there are seven Catholic High Schools and 127 parish elementary schools in Philadelphia. These are augmented by 10 schools conducted by Catholic charitable institutions.

Special Schools

PHILADELPHIA has a large number of special schools where trades, the arts, and various specialized vocations are taught. These include many preparatory schools, business schools, and schools of religion.

The Spring Garden Institute, Broad and Spring Garden Streets, was opened in 1851 to further educational facilities for young men and women. Reading rooms, night schools, and other features were included. Today the institute has a large number of students in the industrial crafts, manual training, and many fields of art.

Gratz College, Broad and York Streets, is the oldest school in the United States for the training of Jewish religious teachers. It was established in 1856 with a large bequest made by Hyman Gratz. Next door is Dropsie College, where Hebrew and cognate languages are taught to Jewish students and to any others interested.

The Mastbaum Vocational School, Frankford Avenue and Clementine Street, is conducted along the lines of the Smith-Hughes plan for vocational training. The two-year term provides vocational and academic training. Students enter directly from both junior high and senior high schools. Half the school day is spent in practical shop work, the other half in classroom study. Automobile mechanics, woodwork, textiles, electrical construction, stenography, bookkeeping, drafting, machine construction, vocational music, and vocational art are taught. A junior employment service is maintained for students.

In keeping with this progressive policy of making the schools fit

180

the actual needs of the pupils, several other special-purpose schools have been gradually integrated into the system. These include the Orthopedic School, the Shallcross School for Truants, and the Fleisher Vocational School.

Night schools have also proved an extensive and valuable addition to the board's ordinary activities, thousands of pupils, young and old, taking advantage of the opportunity thus offered them to pursue courses of commercial and cultural advantage.

Included among art schools are the Pennsylvania Museum School of Industrial Art, Broad and Pine Streets, opened in 1877 ; the Academy of Fine Arts, Broad and Cherry Streets, founded in 1805 and the oldest art institution in the United States ; and the Philadelphia School of Design for Women, Broad and Master Streets, founded in 1844 and incorporated in 1853.

Prominent among several theological seminaries in the city is the Eastern Baptist Theological Seminary, 1814 South Rittenhouse Square, which trains men as missionaries, preachers, and teachers. It is divided into three schools : theology, religious education, and sacred music. There are accommodations for married men and their families, as well as for single persons.

St. Vincent's Theological Seminary is conducted by the Vincentian Order, at Chelten and Magnolia Avenues, Germantown. This seminary educates young men as priests for Catholic missions. The Lutheran Theological Seminary, 7301 Germantown Avenue, was founded in 1864 to train ministers for the Lutheran Church. The seminary is augmented by a graduate school. The Reformed Episcopal Church conducts a seminary at 25 South Forty-third Street. Westminster Theological Seminary, Church Road and Willow Grove Avenue, Chestnut Hill, was formed as a result of a reorganization in modernistic direction of Princeton Theological Seminary, Princeton, N. J. in 1929. The course of study includes religious history, Bible study, and allied subjects. The Divinity School of the Protestant Episcopal Church, Forty-second and Locust Streets, was chartered in 1862. This institution maintains a graduate school.

Several private schools in the city, including Germantown Academy, Penn Charter, and many Friends' schools offer courses of study ranging from the early grades through college preparatory work. In any of these, pupils may enter at kindergarten age and continue through elementary grades, high school, and preparatory courses for college entrance. Thus the pupil's school life is continuous in the same surroundings and under the same system of education.

Most of the city's hospitals conduct nursing schools. High school graduates are accepted for a course of training which is augmented by actual hospital work. Thousands of young women yearly take advantage of these opportunities.

181

Many business schools are scattered throughout the city, where training is given in typewriting, stenography, bookkeeping, and general office practice. There are also a number of college preparatory schools such as Brown Preparatory School, Fifteenth and Race Streets.

Girard College, a school for the care and education of white, male orphans between the ages of six and eighteen, was founded in 1848 under the terms of the will of Stephen Girard.

The entrance to the institution's 42-acre plot of ground is at Corinthian and Girard Avenues. The present site and group of school buildings and dormitories are valued at more than $6,000,000. Control of the school is vested in a board of trustees of 12 members appointed by the judges of the Courts of Common Pleas of Philadelphia, and the Mayor and president of City Council.

Conditions for admission give preference (1) to boys born in the bounds of the old city of Philadelphia; (2) to boys born elsewhere in the Commonwealth of Pennsylvania; (3) to those born in New York City; (4) to boys born in New Orleans.

Founder's Hall, located just within the main gate, is regarded as a beautiful specimen of Grecian artchitecture. A sarcophagus just inside the door contains the remains of Girard.

The curriculum includes elementary, grammar, and high school courses as well as trade school and commercial courses.

Two schools in Philadelphia devoted to the teaching of the blind and deaf are the Pennsylvania School for the Blind, in Overbrook, and the Pennsylvania School for the Instruction of the Deaf, in Mount Airy. At the latter institution, deaf and dumb boys and girls are taught sign language and lip reading.

Universities and Colleges

IN ADDITION to the University of Pennsylvania and Temple University, there are several smaller colleges which are important factors in making Philadelphia an educational center.

La Salle College, in charge of the Catholic Christian Brothers, stands on an eminence at Twentieth Street and Olney Avenue. It was chartered in 1863 as an outgrowth of the old Christian Brothers Academy, founded in 1862 at 1419 North Second Street. In 1867 the college was moved to Juniper and Filbert Streets, and in 1886 to the old Bouvier mansion at Broad and Stiles Streets. Since 1930 it has occupied its present quarters, in more spacious surroundings, with fine new buildings and a large campus. The La Salle College High School, housed on the campus, offers a complete course in college preparation.

St. Joseph's College, Fifty-fourth Street and City Line Avenue, had its inception in the parish house of St. Joseph's Church, Willing's

Alley, in 1851. Classes were transferred to a building at Filbert and Juniper Streets in 1855, these quarters being used until 1860, when the college returned to old St. Joseph's. In 1876 the school was moved to new buildings at Seventeenth and Stiles Streets, and in 1927 to its present site. The old buildings at Seventeenth and Stiles Streets now house St. Joseph's College High School.

The Drexel Institute of Art, Science, and Industry was founded in 1891 by Anthony J. Drexel, who desired to open a new field of specific and fundamental education for young men and women. The school which is at Thirty-second and Chestnut Streets, maintains a cooperative course in engineering and business administration which allows its students periods of actual work in Philadelphia industrial plants.

The Philadelphia College of Pharmacy and Science, the first of its kind to be established in this country, was founded in historic Carpenters' Hall in 1821 as the College of Apothecaries. With the development of more scientific methods of compounding prescriptions, the school added courses in science and more advanced forms of pharmacy. In 1921 it received the right to confer the degree of bachelor of science, and in 1928 moved to its present building at Forty-third Street and Kingsessing Avenue. It was one of the first schools in the country to admit women students, this step being taken in 1876.

The Philadelphia College of Osteopathy, Forty-eighth and Spruce Streets, was incorporated in 1899. It offers a comprehensive course in osteopathy, augmenting its regular work with a hospital and a graduate school.

Regular medical colleges, notably Jefferson, Hahnemann, University of Pennsylvania, and Temple, have long served the medical world ably, by producing thoroughly trained graduates.

LITERATURE

PHILADELPHIA'S literary history dates from the earliest Colonial times. Was not William Penn himself in the way of being an author, with such expository-polemical works to his credit as *No Cross No Crown, Treatise on Oaths,* and *The Great Law or Frame of Government?* It was, however, during the second half of what is commonly distinguished as the Colonial period in the history of American literature that Philadelphia stepped into the foreground and became for a term of years the publishing and, to a large extent, the writing capital of the United States. This was the "Age of Franklin," as it is termed by literary historians, an epoch extending from 1727 to 1765 or thereabouts. It followed the darkly brooding era of Puritan witchcraft and theological writing, as exemplified in New England by such figures as Cotton and Increase Mather and by Jonathan Edwards in New Jersey.

If the age of witchcraft held much of the environing darkness of the primeval forest, the age of Franklin, on the other hand, was an increasingly practical one, foreshadowing and leading up to the American Revolution. It is an era instinctively associated with such productions as Franklin's *Poor Richard's Almanac* and the same author's *Autobiography* (although the latter was not published in its complete form until 1868).

With the dawn of the Revolution, there appeared the truly great personality — for he was a personality rather than a writer in the narrower acceptance of the term — of Thomas Paine, a humanitarian of world stature and a pioneer battler for the rights of man, who was to have his influence upon British thought and upon the course of the French Revolution of 1789. Such works as Paine's *Crisis, Common Sense,* and *Age of Reason,* pamphlets though they may be in essential nature, stand out here.

It is, in all likelihood, Franklin and Paine who first come to mind when one thinks back upon Philadelphia's literary past. If one skips from the Revolution to the mid-nineteenth century, Walt Whitman, poet of American democracy, and the tragic figure of Edgar Allan Poe loom large. Did not Whitman, in the declining years of his life, live in Camden, N. J., just across the river? And were not the poet's "good gray" beard and tossing mane a familiar sight in Philadelphia streets? And was it not, probably, in a house at 530 North Seventh

184

Street, that Poe sat in solitary contemplation of the bust of Pallas Athene above his chamber door — to pen the lines that were to make him immortal?

To this day Philadelphia continues to produce its due quota of writers — novelists, essayists, poets, historians, and scientific, travel and adventure writers. Such names as those of James Gibbons Huneker, Richard Harding Davis, Frank R. Stockton, Bayard Taylor, S. Weir Mitchell, Owen Wister, Christopher Morley, Agnes Repplier, Horace Howard Furness and his son, Horace Howard Furness, Jr., and John Bach McMaster are enough to lend luster to any city.

In addition to writers, Philadelphia has upon occasion provided literary material, as it did in the case of Theodore Dreiser's *The Financier*, based upon the career of a local capitalist, Charles T. Yerkes.

A S HAS been stated, literature, of a sort at least, began early in Pennsylvania ; and Pennsylvania meant Philadelphia, where the printing shops were situated. The printers themselves frequently were men of letters. Samuel Keimer, who set up a shop in 1723, is looked upon by many as the first Philadelphia publisher.

Scholarship rather than creation marked the Colonial literary output. This, perhaps, was not unnatural ; the colonists with their wives and children in "Penn's City" desired above all else not to lose contact with the Old World culture and civilization which they had left behind. And so we find, in the first days of the Commonwealth, Francis Daniel Pastorius, founder of Germantown, giving the public his encyclopedic *Beehive*.

That social questions, even at the outset, were not without their influence upon Pennsylvania writers, is shown by Pastorius' interest in the antislavery cause ; his efforts are said to have led to the founding of the first American abolitionist society.

Translations of classics also occupied a prominent place in the picture. William Penn's secretary, James Logan, of Scotch-Irish ancestry, made a rendering of Cato's *Moral Distichs* (1735) and one of Cicero's *Cato Major or Discourse on Old Age* (1744). The former was probably the first translation of its kind in America. Logan's manuscripts, copied by his wife, Deborah Norris, are now preserved in the Ridgway Branch of the Library Company of Philadelphia.

Philosophical, theological, and moral-didactic literature also flourished at this period, although not to the same degree as in New England ; the prevailing Quaker atmosphere appears to have exerted a mellowing influence, and the witch hunting, witch baiting of the Mathers, for instance, is gratifyingly absent for the most part. Nevertheless, the temper and cast of mind of the northern colonists were rather heavily theological, and it is not surprising if we find sermons

185

to have been a staple article of intellectual diet. Among the clerics whose pulpit exhortations were popular were the Muhlenberg brothers, Henry Melchior and Frederick Augustus Conrad ; William Tennent and his three sons ; George Whitefield, and Dr. William Smith.

In addition to the sermon writers of this time, there were a number of mystics, among them Johann Kelpius, Heinrich Bernard Koster, Dr. Christopher Witt, and Daniel Faulkner.

Yet another early Philadelphia clergyman deserving of notice is Rev. Jacob Duche, who gained notoriety by a letter which he wrote to General Washington in 1777, urging the Commander-in-Chief of the Continental Army to seek a reconciliation with the British. He was also the author (and publisher) of *Caspipina's Letters*, later reprinted in England.

John Woolman's journal of his own life and travels, which saw the light at this period, likewise won notice abroad.

Education vied with religion in the interest of the colonists : the first American treatise on school management is said to have been Christopher Dock's *Schulordnung.*

Though Colonial life may have been hard in many respects, and though it may still have worn a certain coating of theological gloom, it was by no means utterly joyless or lacking in humor, as may be seen from the satires and comedies of the Quaker, Gabriel Thomas. His writings were, it is true, rather looked down upon ; but they were passed from hand to hand and read with glee — when no austere member of the congregation chanced to be looking.

A LL of this, as may be seen, does not weigh very heavily in the literary scales. What we have so far is not so much a literature as the crude beginnings of one — or, it might be more accurate to say, the vestigial reflections of an older literature from beyond the seas. The appearance of Franklin's *Poor Richard*, destined to be America's household companion for more than a score of years, really marked the inception of a Philadelphia literature in the stricter sense of the word ; and even that is not pure literature, or literature of a high order.

The fact that the name of Franklin has been given to an entire period of our writing annals, means that he must have been an outstanding figure in more ways than one ; and it further implies that Franklin's home city, where his manifold activities were carried on, and where the greater part of his works were written and published, must have occupied the center of the literary stage for that period.

Franklin was indeed a personality that was to become familiar to two continents. His fat, round, beaming, bespectacled countenance was to mingle in the popular imagination of Europe and America with a mental picture of the "good doctor" with his kite, engaged in drawing

*The Poe House
"The House of
Melancholy"*

*Poe House Interior
". . . rapping at
my chamber door."*

the lightning from the heavens. For Franklin's scientific experiments and inventions, his skill as a diplomatic bargainer, his social successes in pre-revolutionary France and elsewhere, and his correspondence with the great of the world — the whole offset by a personal character which was at bottom a shrewd and calculating one — were to a large degree to overshadow his forays into the field of literature, and were to confer upon these sallies their quintessential flavor.

It is doubtful if Franklin ever took himself very seriously as a litterateur. The *Autobiography*, his most important work from a literary standpoint, appears to have been rather carelessly tossed off. While parts of it were published in France during 1791-98, it was not until 1868, from a manuscript obtained in France, that the first complete text was printed, under the editorship of John Bigelow. The *Autobiography* is a work which has been extravagantly praised and vigorously condemned. Charles Angoff, for example, author of *A Literary History of the American People*, considers Franklin a "two-penny philosopher," the first great exponent of the "lowbrow' point of view in American letters and precursor of the Rotarians and Kiwanians of today ; he sees in the creator of *Poor Richard* a thoroughgoing vulgarian, lacking in all literary grace.

It was in 1732 that *Poor Richard* made its bow, continuing to appear regularly thereafter (to the delectation of readers) for a quarter of a century. Here, in a way, was true American folk literature, an embodiment of that spirit of an almost fanatical, at times miserly, practicality which was so characteristic of the Pennsylvania colonist and, in a large degree, of the American colonist. "Early to bed and early to rise." "Take care of the pence, and the pounds will take care of themselves." This is unquestionably Colonial American to the bone ; and it is small wonder, then, that Franklin's name, despite a somewhat scant performance in the realm of literature proper, has fastened itself upon a literary era. His almanac sold three editions the first three months it was printed, and 10,000 copies annually during its quarter century publication.

It was one of Franklin's proteges, a young Scotch tutor named William Smith, who was responsible for publishing some of the earliest American poetry in a magazine which he founded at Philadelphia, and which was known as the *American Magazine and Monthly Chronicle for the British Colonies.* Among the poets to whom this publication afforded a hearing were Thomas Godfrey, Jr., Nathaniel Evans, and Elizabeth Graeme Ferguson.

AMONG Philadelphia writers of the Revolutionary period, Thomas Paine, "penman of the Revolution," is far and away the most important. It is true that most of Paine's life was spent under a cloud of deep opprobrium, in which slander of him as a man mingled with condemnations of his religious beliefs. The truth is, Paine's religious views have caused his greater claim to fame to be more or less overlooked. His real importance lies in the fact that he was the first modern internationalist ; his social views in general were far in advance of his time. He was one of the first, possibly the first, to advocate a system of governmental social security.

As for posterity's winnowed opinion of Paine, it appears to have been well summed up by Angoff, who says that Paine "probably did more to spread religious and theological enlightenment than any other one man who ever lived."

The Rights of Man, The Age of Reason, Common Sense, and *The Crisis,* as well as *Agrarian Justice,* a work in which Paine dealt with the problem of poverty somewhat in the manner of a Henry George — all of these are works of which Philadelphia well may be proud. *The Rights of Man,* though loathed by the Federalists, was a kind of Bible to Jefferson, Madison, and other forward-looking spirits. Written in answer to Burke's *Reflections on the French Revolution,* it had its repercussions in England and, especially in revolutionary France. The publication of *Common Sense* had made Paine the most influential political writer in America ; yet to many he still remained the "atheist' and "jailbird." A Trenton stagecoach driver declined to carry him, declaring that he, the driver, had already had one team of horses struck by lightning and did not care to take another chance.

Tom Paine, the Philadelphian whose unhallowed bones were carried to England by William Cobbett, has his revenge today, when from 5,000 to 10,000 copies of his works are printed annually in New York City alone.

There are a number of other men of this time of the "Founding Fathers" whose names have come down to us as associated in one way or another with literature. Most, if not all, of them were active in other walks of life, especially politics, and writing with them was

by way of being an expression of interests not essentially literary. John Dickinson, leader in the Constitutional Convention, was one of these. Francis Hopkinson, chairman of the Navy Board which designed

Thomas Paine
Precursor of Social Security.

189

the American flag, was another. Bishop Samuel Seabury was a leader of the church ; John Bartram was a botanist. Ralph Saundiford, Benjamin Lay, Anthony Benezet, Robert Proud, Morgan Edwards, Joseph Galloway, Thomas Coombe — these are no more than names (or not even so much as names) to the Philadelphian of today ; yet each in his own day was a distinguished citizen and contributor to the cultural life of the city, the Commonwealth, and the country.

There are, however, two names which emerge prominently from this obscurity of the past. One is that of Hugh H. Brackenridge, who shares with Charles Brockden Brown the honor of creating the novel in America. He, like Brown, was the author of a number of hair-raising, terror-inspiring tales, of the imported "Gothic Romance" school. Then, there was James Hector St. John de Crèvecoeur, author of an early romantically exaggerated account of America, which was greatly to influence the French and other Continentals in their conception of the transoceanic scene.

THE close of the Revolution found Philadelphia still the literary capital. Magazines, springing up, began to publish works of some of the foremost contemporary writers, not merely of Philadelphia but of the Nation. From about 1792 to 1812, Joseph Dennie and his circle were to confer upon the city a distinct literary aspect. Political pamphleteering, a carry-over from Revolutionary days, also continued and was sometimes of a violent character indeed.

Among the most colorful of the post-Revolutionary pamphleteers was William Cobbett, who is regarded by certain historians as one of the founders of American party journalism. A political refugee from the French Revolution, who had settled in Philadelphia as a teacher of English to his exiled fellow countrymen, Cobbett was extremely violent in his anti-republican prejudices, and was further possessed of a rare gift of vituperation. Advocating an alliance with England for a war against republican France, Cobbett braved the threat of tar and feathers and launched a publication known as *Porcupine's Gazette.* He finally became so obstreperous that President Adams thought seriously of deporting him ; but in 1800, he of his own accord left America for England.

Samples of the "incomparable Billingsgate" of this "Peter Porcupine," as he called himself, will be found in a number of old pamphlets, published in 1795 and later, such as *A Bone to Gnaw for the Democrats, A Kick for a Bite, A Little Plain English Addressed to the People of the United States,* and *A New Year's Gift for the Democrats.*

Among the magazines launched at this period was the *American Museum,* founded by Matthew Carey, in 1787. It numbered among its contributors such men as Franklin, Dr. Benjamin Rush, Jacob

Duche, and Philip Freneau, best of the American poets before Bryant and a pioneer exploiter of American Indian material.

The first American literary magazine really worthy of the name was *The Port Folio*, founded by Joseph Dennie in 1806. It ran until 1827, Dennie, under the name of Oliver Oldschool, Esq., being the editor until the time of his death in 1812. Begun as a weekly publication devoted to literature and politics, the new journal of "polite letters" had such contributors as John Quincy Adams, Charles Brockden Brown, and Dennie himself. A study of the influence exerted by Dennie and his followers has been made by H. M. Ellis, in *Joseph Dennie and His Circle*.

That Philadelphia, as well as America in general, was becoming less provincial and more cosmopolitan, is indicated by the space accorded in Dennie's *Port Folio* to reviews of foreign books. Indeed, beginning with Dennie, a line of cleavage may be recognized between the Revolutionary epoch and the one immediately following, which was marked by the establishment of the American Nation and the beginnings of a national literature. The period from 1750 or 1765 (authorities differ in their chronology, and there is no hard and fast demarcation) down to 1789-1792 was what might be described as the coffee-house era, marked by prolonged and impassioned discussion and debate on political and religious, but above all political, themes. With the adoption of the Federal Constitution and inauguration of the processes of orderly government, life tended to become more settled. There was a greater margin of leisure free from ideological preoccupations ; life became more refined, and there was room for a greater interest in pure literature and for culture in its broader aspects.

The first distinct movement to manifest itself in our national literature was romanticism, of which the first great exponent was to be James Fenimore Cooper, with Washington Irving as forerunner and pathbreaker. It is worthy of note that American romanticism, in a way, had its origins in Philadelphia, in the writings of Charles Brockden Brown, whose *Arthur Mervyn* is based upon the Philadelphia yellow-fever epidemic of 1793. The account which the author here gives us is unusually vivid, inspiring, at once, feelings of fear and of pity ; it is, moreover, essentially romantic in spirit and technique. Brown antedates Cooper by a score or more of years. He is further remembered, by students of literature at any rate, for his *Wieland* (1798) and his *Edgar Huntley, or Memoirs of a Sleep-walker* (1799). The degree of romanticism in his work is evidenced by the fact that in his *Wieland*, for instance, the author makes use of such plot elements as spontaneous combustion, ventriloquism, and religious mania. Brown was under the influence of the English horror school ; while his heroines, in their excessive lachrymose sentiment-

191

ality, are modeled after those of Richardson. He has been called the first professional man of letters in America.

If Philadelphia was for a time the literary capital of America, having taken this preeminence from Boston, it was, in the long run, to lose this title to New York City. Not, however, until Philadelphia had had the honor of publishing or being host to a Walt Whitman and an Edgar Allan Poe.

Prior to Poe and Whitman, Philadelphia had a number of writers who, while they could by no means lay claim to so stellar a place as the two great mid-century luminaries, had a certain importance of their own. One of these was John Fanning Watson, to whose *Annals,* published in 1830, Philadelphians are indebted for much fascinating and valuable information concerning their city, which would otherwise have been lost. It has become a standard work.

The proletarian-socialistic-humanitarian impulse was also coming to the fore. The most prominent representative here is George Lippard, journalist, author, reformer, lecturer, and a "Marxist before Marx," as someone has termed him. He is known today in fraternal circles as the founder of the Brotherhood of America (originally the Brotherhood of the Union). As a journalist he was a predecessor of the modern columnist, and his *Our Talisman* sketches have been compared to Dickens' *Boz.* In his *Bread Crust Papers* he coined the name, Thomas Dove Brown, which Poe was to revive. Lippard contributed a number of stories to the *Saturday Evening Post* and other magazines of the period ; and wrote a best-selling expose of Philadelphia vice, under the title of *Quaker City* ; and produced a number of books, including *The Nazarene* and *Blanche of Brandywine, The Pilgrim of Eternity, The Man with the Mask,* etc., while his proletarian sympathies come out in such a work as *New York, Its Upper Ten and Lower Million.* He has been described as "the poet of the proletariat."

Antislavery agitation, for one thing, played no small part in the published writings of the decades preceding the Civil War. This was especially true so far as newspapers were concerned ; the reflection in other fields was less noticeable.

During the conflict, and immediately before and after the Civil War, we find such writers of lesser note as Louisa M. Alcott (who left Philadelphia while a child), author of the perennially popular *Little Women* and *Little Men* ; Sarah Josepha Buell Hale, editor of *Godey's Lady's Book* and reputed author of the famous schoolroom classic of the nineteenth century, *Mary Had a Little Lamb* ; and T. S. Arthur (Timothy Shay in private life), author of the exceedingly bibulous play, *Ten Nights in a Barroom,* which was to the American temperance movement what Harriet Beecher Stowe's *Uncle Tom's Cabin* was to the abolitionist cause.

192

The period from 1815 on was marked by the rapid rise and development of an American periodic literature, in which Philadelphia had its full share. Worthy of note among local publications of the era are the famous *Godey's Lady's Book*, the colored fashion prints which are still sought after; the *Casket*, which later merged with the *Gentleman's Magazine* and was subsequently continued as *Graham's Magazine*; the *Salmugundi*; *Sartain's Union Magazine*; and, finally, the *Saturday Evening Post*, known the world over, which led to the formation of a distinctive school of professional writing in America.

It was the presence in the city of such magazines as the *Gentleman's* and *Graham's* that prompted Edgar Allan Poe to come here and settle with his frail little 16-year-old wife, Virginia Clem. The poet's ambition was to become a magazine editor. As to just where Poe made his home — or rather, as to all the places where he resided — while in Philadelphia, there is considerable controversy. More than a dozen houses have been identified as his place of residence. According to John Sartain's *Reminiscences*, the Poes first boarded at Fourth and Arch Streets. They also lived for a time in Sixteenth Street near Locust. Later, they had a little home in Coates Street (Fairmount Avenue) near Twenty-fifth, on the border of Fairmount Park. This at the time was an isolated spot, far from the city's center. From this dwelling they moved to the little "rose-covered cottage" set up against a large four-story brick house, which was occupied by a wealthy Quaker, Poe's landlord. If all reports are true, the Quaker was not overly fond, or overly proud, of his tenant. The cottage is now identified as the back-building of a house standing at 530 North Seventh Street. Poe left Philadelphia for New York in 1844, five years before his death.

While here, Poe contributed some of his best work to the *Gentleman's Magazine* and *Graham's*, and his poem, *The Bells*, famed for its tinkling, onomatopoetic melody, first appeared in *Sartain's Magazine*.

Just how much of the poet's work was actually first published, or wholly written, in Philadelphia is a matter of question. For example, while the first draft of *The Raven* was done in North Seventh Street, the piece was later rewritten and brought out in the *Evening Mirror* of New York, in 1845 (published in book form some months following). On the other hand, it was in Philadelphia that Poe put the finishing touches to certain manuscripts which he had begun elsewhere. It was in the Seventh Street house that *The Purloined Letter* was written, and several others of his works. The period of his Philadelphia residence, in short, would appear to have been the most prolific and the happiest in the poet's tragic life.

It has been remarked by critics that Poe shows no traces of any influence from the antislavery agitation of his time, although Philadelphia was something of a hotbed of abolitionist feeling, with the historic "Underground Railroad" functioning almost daily as a means of escape for the black fugitive. This, though, is not surprising, since throughout his work Poe manifests a complete unawareness of social problems of any kind.

As for Whitman, it was some eight years after the Civil War, in May 1873, that he came to Philadelphia. The "good gray poet" was fortunate enough to find those in Camden who were willing to care for him ; so he settled in Camden, where he made his home until his death on March 26, 1892.

The poet's distinguished visage was a familiar sight to Philadelphians of the 1870's and 1880's. Whitman would have his "Howdy" for all sorts of persons, deckhands, vagrants, those of either sex, of any color, age, or nationality. On the Philadelphia side, the author of *Leaves of Grass* would seat himself upon a chair provided by an Italian street vendor, and there he would munch peanuts and strike up friendships with horsecar drivers at the foot of Market Street. Often he would mount the stool on the front platform of a Market Street car and thus journey the entire length of the thoroughfare.

It was in Philadelphia that Whitman, in association with his friend and editor, Horace Traubel, was to find a publisher in David McKay, whose imprint appeared for years on the title page of *Leaves of Grass*.

Poe died in 1849, or more than a decade before the Civil War, while Whitman's life and work spanned the Civll War period. In the years following the struggle, Bayard Taylor, Frank R. Stockton, Henry George, Richard Harding Davis, and others continued to keep Philadelphia upon the literary map.

Taylor lived at West Chester, and it was Rufus Wilmot Griswold, editor of *Graham's Magazine*, who encouraged him to publish his first book of verse, *Ximena*. Taylor's significance in American literature may be said to be twofold. On the one hand, he was a good deal of a cosmopolitan. He traveled widely, and his travel letters appeared in two Philadelphia publications, the *Saturday Evening Post* and *United States Gazette*. He was the author of a translation of Goethe's *Faust* that ranks with Longfellow's *Divine Comedy* and Bryant's *Homer* as a standard rendering of a classic. His *Rhymes of Travel* and his *Eldorado* won for him a large circle of readers. On the other hand, particularly in such a work as his *Eldorado*, Taylor gave a definite impulsion to American regional literature.

Frank R. Stockton, born in Philadelphia in 1834, is proudly claimed by Central High School as its most distinguished literary graduate. Stockton's first book, *Ting-a-Ling*, was published in 1870 ; but it was with *Rudder Grange*, appearing in 1879, that his fame began. A long list of novels and short stories, including the enigmatic *The Lady or the Tiger*, followed.

Owen Wister, author of *The Virginian* and *Lin McLean*, is eminent among Philadelphia's novelists of the last years of the nineteenth and the early years of the twentieth century. A lawyer by profession, Wister found time to travel widely in various sections of the United States to gather material for his stories.

In the field of the essay, Agnes Repplier has for decades delighted readers of the *Atlantic Monthly* in particular, with her graceful eighteenth century flavored essays. The representative of an older and dignified literary tradition, she has had a faithful following ever since the publication of her first collection of essays, *Books and Men*, in 1888. Miss Repplier was born in Philadelphia of French parentage in 1858. She began by writing poetry, then turned to the essay form. She is today regarded by many as America's foremost contemporary essayist, and is the holder of honorary degrees from the universities of Pennsylvania, Yale, and Columbia.

As for the Quaker City poets of this period, they displayed an inclination for the purely esthetic as opposed to the controversial theme. Thomas Buchanan Read and George H. Boker exhibit this tendency.

Not to be forgotten among the figures of the late century era is Charles Godfrey Leland, an editor of distinction who at the same time was widely known as scholar and educator. Leland's editorial posts included the *New York Times*, the *Philadelphia Evening Bulletin*, and *Vanity Fair*. A wide traveler, he was the discoverer of the famous "lost language," the "Shelta" tongue. As an educator, he was responsible for the establishment of industrial training, based on the minor arts, as a branch of public school teaching. Among his works are *Hans Breitmann's Ballads*, a *Life of Abraham Lincoln*, *Algonquin Legends*, and several treatises on education.

A contemporary of Leland was Charles Leonard Moore, poet and essayist as well as business man, who devoted a score of years out of his life to literary work. He was a constant contributor to the original *Dial* magazine. Among his published works were *Atlas*, *Pocius*, and *Book of My Day Dreams*.

The closing year of the nineteenth century brought to Philadelphia's literary world a new figure who was to put a new life in the *Saturday Evening Post*, making it into the leading weekly, with the largest circulation of any magazine in the world. For 38 years George Horace Lorimer's name appeared at the masthead of this publication, and he became one of the most influential and best-known editors of his time. Lorimer was the author of *Letters From a Self-Made Merchant to His Son*, which became a classic of its kind. He published a number of other books.

By all odds the most important Philadelphia writer of the pre-war decade is James Gibbons Huneker, who as far back as 1900 was publishing *Chopin : The Man and His Music*, followed by *Overtones* (1904), *Iconoclasts* and *A Book of Dramatists* (1905). His vogue with the American intelligentsia continued after the war, with the publication of such brilliant books as *Steeplejack, Bedouins, Painted Veils*, and *Variations*.

Huneker's importance lies in the fact that he is America's foremost representative of the impressionist school of criticism, a school represented in England by Arthur Symons, and which may be said to have had its last journalistic flare with H. L. Mencken. It was as a Philadelphia music critic — and a critic of a kind the country had not seen before — that Huneker first brought himself into prominence. A commuter, as others have been, between Philadelphia and Manhattan, he was soon possessed of a reputation that was not bounded by the national frontiers ; for he was giving the world the most distinguished American criticism since Poe. His sparkling, studded, highly impressionistic style, his wealth of anecdote and epigram, his broad and genial erudition, his sensitiveness to the esthetic currents of his age, above all his cosmopolitanism — these were new to his countrymen. He brought to the latter, among other things, a "lust for life" as well as for literature, by introducing certain aspects of life which a hastily growing and democratic America had overlooked — the pleasures of the gourmet, for instance, the esoteric refinements of wining and dining.

Philadelphia newspapers in more instances than one have been a training school for literature. One case is that of Christopher Morley, noted essayist and novelist, who won his spurs on the staff of the Philadelphia *Evening Ledger*. Another example is Thomas A. Daly, who in addition to column-conducting in Philadelphia. has found time to publish such collections of whimsical verse as *Canzoni, Madrigali*, and *Songs of Wedlock*, written for the most part in the English of the Italian immigrant.

Something has been said previously of Philadelphia magazines. Their influence upon the literary life, not alone of Philadelphia but of the Nation, has from the start been notable. Just as a periodical like *Graham's*, back in the years preceding the Civil War, had attracted such contributors as Poe, Hawthorne, Bryant, and Longfellow, so the *Saturday Evening Post* and the *Ladies Home Journal* in the past half century have definitely shaped certain types of American writing, have served as a lure for many a budding talent, and therefore have had their not-to-be-doubted effect upon the national psychology.

And so it is not unfitting that one Philadelphia magazine editor, Edward Bok of the *Ladies Home Journal*, should in a manner bring an era to a close, in 1920, with his autobiography, *The Americaniza-tion of Edward Bok*, which received the Pulitzer award for that year. What, it may be asked, has this era so terminated ? Perhaps no bet-ter answer could be found than in Theodore Roosevelt's phrase, "the strenuous life," which, backed by "Teddy's" toothful grin, once echoed from coast to coast. This, it will be remembered, was the age of Orison Swett Marden and the gospel of "Success," of the Oliver Optic myth, perpetuating the nineteenth century canal-boy-to-presi-dent legend. The respected formula was : begin at the bottom and work up ; and this was the formula which Edward Bok carried out. The tradition is one which may be looked upon as having ended with or shortly after the World War. A new age was now in sight, with new problems to be faced, new adjustments to be made. It is there-fore not inappropriate that Bok's book should have come within a year or so after the signing of the Armistice.

True to the traditions of the man who has fought for and won suc-cess, Bok upon his death 10 years later left funds for the establish-ment of a number of awards for meritorious services, including the Philadelphia Award of $10,000 to the Philadelphian or person living nearby who each year does most to bring honor to his city.

IF WE LOOK at Philadelphia writing since the war, particularly at that which has been done since 1929, or the beginning of the "De-pression," and which is being done today, the outstanding aspects that we notice are a certain deepening introspection with regard to the native scene, on the one hand, and on the other, a certain broad-ening of social-literary interest, to include the problems of America and of the age.

Philadelphia has long been noted for its "first families," but that the members of these "first families" are capable at times of an ob-jective view of themselves is indicated by Francis Biddle's *The Llan-fear Pattern*, which is by way of being an unsparing expose of local insularity and the intellectual impotence of a new-rich type such as the novel places in the Chestnut Hill and Main Line regions. There is also Granville Toogood, whose first novel, *Huntsman in the Sky*, breathes a spirit of revolt.

There is an even more unlovely side of life, in Philadelphia as elsewhere, a side that is commonly cloaked by the euphemism of "underworld." It is this side of life that John T. McIntyre deals with, in his *Steps Going Down*, published in 1936.

Among other recent Philadelphia writers, novelists, and poets are Shirley Watkins, author of *This Poor Player* (1929) and *The Island of Green Myrtles* (1937) ; Roy Addison Helton, Edward Shenton, Mary Dixon Thayer, author of a number of well-known volumes of

Catholic verse, and the essayist Benjamin de Casseres. Shenton is an illustrator and editor as well as writer.

Like De Casseres, who left the city in his youth, others born or educated in Philadelphia have achieved reputations. This list would include such writers as H. D. (Helen Doolittle), John Cournos, Ezra Pound, Alexander Woollcott, and Gilbert Seldes.

There is a sense in which Philadelphia has been the "City of Scholars," and two of its leading representatives in this respect have been the Furnesses — Horace Howard Furness and his son, Horace Howard Furness, Jr. — editors of the famous "Variorum" edition of Shakespeare, which is considered the standard by authorities. In compiling this edition, the elder Furness gathered the largest Shakespearean library in the world. When he died in 1912, his work was carried on by his son, although the latter had prepared himself for a career as physicist and astronomer. Horace Howard Furness, Jr., died in Philadelphia in 1930. In his will, he left his father's and his own library to the University of Pennsylvania, with a fund of $100,-000 for its maintenance.

Another contributor to the field of literary scholarship was S. Austin Allibone, compiler of a critical *Dictionary of English Literature*. Not to be overlooked, either, is the somewhat fantastic Ignatius Donnelly (another graduate of Central High School, by the way), who spent the greater part of his life in trying to prove that Francis Bacon, and not one William Shakespeare, was in reality the author of Shakespeare's plays. He was the originator of the "great Baconian cryptogram," which in its day provoked a storm of discussion.

A Philadelphia critic, biographer and man of letters most of whose work has been done since the War is Albert Mordell, who first attracted wide attention with his treatise, *The Erotic Motive in Literature* (1919), pointing the application of psychoanalysis to creative writing. His biography, *Quaker Militant: John Greenleaf Whittier* (1933) was much discussed. Mordell has edited many books, but is perhaps best known by the articles and translations of Lafcadio Hearn, filling a dozen volumes, which he exhumed from newspaper files. His essay, *The Literature of Ecstasy* (1921) offered a new theory of poetry. His first work was a pamphlet, *The Shifting of Literary Values*, printed in Philadelphia in 1912.

In the modern age, one of the best-known native Philadelphia representatives of bookish lore is A. Edward Newton, whom the *New York Times* has termed "the world's most popular book collector." He is owner of a library, housed in his "Oak Knoll" home at Daylesford, Pennsylvania, consisting of more than 10,000 rare volumes. Hundreds of college students and other visitors come yearly to view this collection, which is especially noted for its completeness where the works of Dr. Samuel Johnson are concerned. Dr. Newton

198

(he is the holder of numerous honorary degrees) is author of such well known works as *The Amenities of Book Collecting, Dr. Johnson* (a play), *The Greatest Book in the World, A Magnificent Farce, This Book Collecting Game, A Tourist in Spite of Himself,* and *End Papers.* He is also known as a contributor to the *Atlantic Monthly.* In 1935, he was elected president of the Friends of the University of Pennsylvania Library, and was Rosenbach lecturer in bibliography at the University for the year 1935-36.

Known all over the world and from post-Revolutionary times for its surgeons, medical schools, and hospitals, Philadelphia, as might be expected, occupies a prominent place in the field of medical literature. One need but mention such writers as Jacob M. Da Costa, Samuel D. Gross, D. Hayes Agnew, George B. Wood, and William Pepper. In the allied province of the natural sciences, the names of Isaac Lea, Joseph Leidy, Edward D. Cope, and others are remembered.

Occasionally, as in the case of Dr. S. Weir Mitchell, we find science and literature joining hands. Dr. Mitchell was at one and the same time an eminent nerve specialist and a novelist of repute. In addition to his treatises on neurology, comparative psychology, and the like, Dr. Mitchell found leisure to write such tales as *The Red City ; Hugh Wynne, Free Quaker; Adventures of Francois,* and *A Diplomatic Adventure.* They found a wide audience — an audience which came to make almost as many demands upon him as did his medical practice.

In connection with medical writers, Dr. George Milbry Gould naturally comes to mind. In addition to editing medical, surgical, and biological dictionaries, medical encyclopedias, the *Medical News,* the *Philadelphia Medical Journal, American Medicine,* and the like, he published a number of purely literary works, such as the poetical volume, *Autumn Singer,* and two semi-philosophic works, *The Meaning of Life* and *The Infinite Presence.* He also helped prepare the *Life and Letters of Edmund Clarence Stedman.*

In legal writing, Eli Kirk Price and George Sharswood, who re-established the University of Pennsylvania Law School, have won distinction. In theology, the reputations of Phillips Brooks and Albert Barnes are but two of a number that have survived the past.

In connection with historical writing, the names of John Bach McMaster, Henry Charles Lea, and Ellis P. Oberholtzer stand out.

McMaster's best known work is his 8-volume *History of the United States,* which required many years of scholarly labor, and most of which was written while the author was professor of history at the University of Pennsylvania. McMaster introduced a new method into the study of American history, in accordance with which society is interpreted genetically, from the economic point of view.

199

He also wrote *Benjamin Franklin as a Man of Letters, The Life of Stephen Girard,* and *The United States in the World War.*

Henry Charles Lea, in addition to being a historian, was a publicist and man of affairs. He was, among other things, an early member and pamphleteer of the Union League Club of Philadelphia. As a leader in public life, he was the organizer and first president of the Municipal Reform Association, resigning from the Union League because he felt that the latter body failed to throw its influence on the side of better government. It was during the last 25 years of his life that he returned to historical scholarship and penned his 3-volume *History of the Inquisition,* published in 1888. This was followed by a number of other works dealing with the same or related periods of Spanish history.

Oberholtzer was the author of a *History of the United States Since the Civil War,* which entailed twenty years of work. He also produced a *Literary History of Philadelphia ; A History of Philadelphia and its People ; Robert Morris, Patriot and Financier ; Jay Cooke, Financier of the Civil War ; Abraham Lincoln ; Henry Clay ;* and *Memoir of John Bach McMaster.* He collapsed suddenly in the rooms of the Pennsylvania Historical Society in 1936 and died shortly after.

Special attention has been paid by many Philadelphia writers to local and State history. Joseph Jackson has written on *Early Philadelphia Architects and Engineers* and *American Colonial Architecture,* and is the author of an *Encyclopedia of Philadelphia,* as well as of treatises on *Market Street: America's Most Historic Highway* and *Dickens in Philadelphia.*

Possibly the most prolific of Philadelphia and State historians is Albert Cook Myers, who has written or edited a long list of works, including *Immigration of the Irish Quakers into Pennsylvania, Narratives of Early Pennsylvania, West New Jersey and Delaware,* and *The Boy George Washington.*

American Indian lore, travel, adventure, exploration — all these have been favored delving grounds. Among the travel and adventure writers, Elisha Kent Kane, Arctic explorer, and Dr. Israel Haynes may lay claim to prominence.

Innumerable literary contributions have come from the pens of Negro authors who have added histories, novels, poems, essays, short stories, biographies, dramas — in short, all types of writings — to the literary output of the city. Many of these works are valuable merely from a historical standpoint, while others are of meritorious literary value.

The first recorded literary work of this group was an account of the work of Richard Allen and Absalom Jones in saving lives and relieving the suffering of those afflicted with yellow fever in the epidemic of 1793. This first piece of literature (1794) was the joint production of Allen and Jones. From then until now there has been a steady stream of literature of various types.

One particularly interesting piece of work is *The Underground Railroad*, a history published by William Still in 1872. It is one of the most remarkable records in existence concerning the history of slavery. It is composed chiefly of letters written by fugitive slaves, sometimes while en route to Canada, sometimes after reaching their destination, and of letters written by different agents of the "Underground Railroad" to the secretary of the Vigilance Committee. These letters tell in the words of the fugitives themselves of the difficulties, sufferings, and fears of the runaway slaves, and of the many and varied devices employed by them to escape.

Prominent among present day writers are Henry B. Jones, Arthur Huff Fauset, his sister Jessie Fauset (Mrs. Herbert Harris), and Alain Leroy Locke. Jones is a writer of short stories, one of which, *Drums*, appeared in an issue of *Liberty* during November 1935. Under another name others of his stories appear frequently in pulp magazines. *For Freedom*, a biography of outstanding Negroes written by Arthur Huff Fauset, has been placed in the libraries of the public school system of the city. *There is Confusion, Plum Bun, Chinaberry Tree*, and *Comedy American Style* are four novels written by Jessie Fauset, first Negro woman to win the Phi Beta Kappa key at Cornell.

Locke's entire life has been associated with letters. After a brilliant record at Central High School he was graduated at 15, and in 1908 graduated "magna cum laude" from Harvard with membership in the Phi Beta Kappa. The only Negro thus far to win the Rhodes scholarship, he received the degree Litt. D. from Oxford University in 1911. He has devoted a great deal of time to magazine work, and his articles appear regularly in the best American periodicals.

One of the most interesting of literary clubs in Philadelphia is the Penn Club, organized in 1875 as an outgrowth of the *Penn Monthly*, a magazine published from 1870 to 1880. Headquarters of the magazine served as a meeting place for the Penn Monthly Association.

Another well-known literary group, the Franklin Inn Club, maintains a clubhouse at Camac and St. James Streets. It was organized in 1902, with Dr. S. Weir Mitchell as first president. Membership is limited to 100. Since its founding the club has been the gathering place of literary men of distinction visiting Philadelphia. Of about the same age is the Hathaway Shakespeare Club, a women's literary group which meets in various large hotels.

The Dickens Fellowship, similarly, is devoted to the works of Charles Dickens. This club holds meetings in rooms of the Musical Art Club, Seventeenth and Walnut Streets. Membership is approximately 800. The American Fiction Guild, a national association of professional writers has a local chapter in Philadelphia.

GROWTH OF THE PRESS

PHILADELPHIA'S newspaper tradition may be said to have begun in 1685, when William Bradford brought from England the first printing press used in the Colonies south of New England. Bradford became involved in political and social disputes in Pennsylvania, and in 1693 moved to New York. His business was revived in 1712 by his son Andrew, who in company with John Copson began publication in 1719 of the *American Weekly Mercury*. The *Mercury* was the first newspaper in the Middle Colonies and the third in the New World. *The Universal Instructor in All the Arts and Sciences and Pennsylvania Gazette* was the second newspaper established in Penn's city. It was first issued December 24, 1728, by Samuel Keimer, who had come to Philadelphia six years previously.

The most important actor in the early drama of printers' ink, Benjamin Franklin, came to Philadelphia in 1723 and applied to Andrew Bradford for work. The latter had nothing for him to do ; but William Bradford, happening to be in Philadelphia at the time, took Franklin to Samuel Keimer, who became Franklin's employer. (Franklin's unfavorable opinion of Keimer is aired in his autobiography.) In 1725 Keimer started publication of *Taylor's Almanac*. Almost immediately an advertisement in the *Mercury* characterized it as "a lying Almanac."

Soon after 1725 Andrew Bradford, who had dominated the printing business of the Province, began to face steadier opposition. Keimer still kept up his printing office and managed to do a little business, although he eked out an existence by some methods not strictly ethical. After publishing the weekly *Universal Instructor* for nine months, during which time it had only 90 subscribers, he became involved in debt. Unable to continue the paper, he sold it to Franklin and Hugh Meredith, who expunged the first part of the title, calling it the *Pennsylvania Gazette*. For a while it appeared twice a week, at 10 shillings per annum, and then was changed back to a weekly because of distribution difficulties. The energy and industry of Franklin and the improvement in the character of the paper created public interest.

In 1732 the partnership was dissolved, and Franklin continued the business on his own account. After his appointment as postmaster, the circulation of his paper increased ; the *Gazette* became very profitable. In 1748, engaged in public affairs, Franklin formed a connection with David Hall, under the firm name of B. Franklin & D. Hall. He sold his interest to Hall in 1765. The next year the paper was printed by Hall and William Sellers, and was issued regularly, although it suspended publication during the British occupation of Philadelphia.

Hall and Sellers dissolved partnership about 1805, and the new firm of Hall & Pierie was established. About 1815 or 1816 this latter partnership was dissolved, and Hall continued in operation with Samuel C. Atkinson as partner. David Hall died on May 27, 1821, and Atkinson took into partnership Charles Alexander, who at once determined upon a revolution in the character of the venerable paper. Proposals for the publication of a new weekly journal, to which they gave the name of *Saturday Evening Post*, were issued. The first number appeared on August 4, 1821. The proprietors, young and ambitious, endeavored to make the paper interesting to all classes. They encouraged rising talent by means of a "poet's corner," and gave attention to both foreign and domestic news. There was also a sufficient variety of news of general interest to attract persons outside of Philadelphia. The Atkinsons attended to business, and the paper gained in popularity and circulation. Its editor was Thomas Cottrell Clarke.

The *Hoch Deutsch Pensylvanische Geschict Shreiber, oder Sammlung Wichtiger Nachrichten aus dem Natur und Kirchen Reich* (translated literally, the "High German Pennsylvania Historiographer, or Collection of Important Intelligence from the Kingdom of Nature and the Church") was issued on August 20, 1739, by Christopher Saur, of Germantown, as a quarterly journal. Saur cast his own type and made his own ink.

The name of the publication was changed several times, becoming meanwhile a monthly publication, until, around 1766, the current name of *Berichte* was changed to *Germantauner Zeitung*, and it was issued weekly. It wielded much influence for a time and was removed to Philadelphia in 1777, where it continued until the following spring under a new name.

The *General Magazine and Historical Chronicle for all British Plantations in America* was begun by Franklin in January 1741. It lasted only six months. *The American Magazine or a Monthly View of the British Colonies* also appeared that year, published by John Webbe, who had engaged Bradford to print the work. Only two or three numbers were published.

The *Pennsylvania Journal and Weekly Advertiser*, third Philadelphia newspaper in the English language, was established in 1742. William Bradford, grandson of the first William and nephew of Andrew Bradford of the *American Weekly Mercury*, began its publication after he returned from England in 1742. The first issue was dated December 2. In 1766 his son Thomas became a partner in the business.

After Bradford's establishment of the London Coffee House in 1754 at what is now Front and Market Streets, the *Journal* office was removed to that building. No attempt was made to publish the *Journal* during the British occupation, but it was revived at the beginning of December 1778, and it appeared regularly until about 1793, two years after the death of Col. William Bradford. The *Merchant's Daily Advertiser*, founded in 1797, was succeeded by the *True American*, which began publication the following year. In November 1813 James Elliott and Thomas T. Stiles bought the paper. The latter became sole owner in 1815 ; Charles Miner became his partner in 1817 ; and then the paper purchased by Thomas Smith and Ebenezer Cummins, who five years later merged with the *U. S. Gazette* under the title *The Union United States Gazette and True American*.

The *Pennsylvania Evening Post* was the first evening paper in Philadelphia. It appeared just before the Revolution, and was issued three times a week on a half sheet of crown paper. This was the third evening paper in the Colonies. Its editor and publisher was Benjamin Towne. To follow the fortunes of Towne is to wade through some of the muddiest waters of early Philadelphia journalism. For business reasons Towne became a "patriot," but after Washington's defeat at Brandywine he began to curry favor with the British by printing long, almost jubilant, accounts of British successes. When Howe's army took possession of Philadelphia he went out of his way to praise the good manners of the invaders. Neither he nor his newspaper was molested.

When the British troops evacuated the city, Towne turned Whig again, and the *Evening Post* carried an equally fulsome account of the evacuation. Gen. Benedict Arnold, who became military governor of the city, made no movement against the printer, and the *Evening Post* continued, despite the indignation its owner had stirred up by his duplicity. Eventually, Towne was ordered to surrender to the authorities, but apparently was never tried.

In his efforts to recapture favor with the Whigs, Towne promised to publish a recantation written for him by Dr. John Witherspoon, member of the Continental Congress and a former subscriber. After reading Witherspoon's article, however, the publisher refused to make good his promise, but the "Towne Recantation" found a reading public through numerous other journals in the Colonies. Presented in the first person, the recantation read in part :

> . . . I am not only proscribed by the President and Supreme executive council of Pennsylvania, but that several other persons are for reprobating my paper, and allege that instead of being suffered to print, I ought to be hanged as a traitor to my country.

> . . . I never was, nor ever pretended to be a man of character, repute or dignity. I was originally an understrapper to the famous Galloway in his infamous squabble with Goddard, and did in that service contract such a habit of meanness in thinking and scurrility in writing that nothing exalted . . . could ever be expected from me . . .
> . . .Finally, I do hereby recant, draw back, eat in and swallow down, every word that I have ever spoken, written or printed to the prejudice of the United States of America, hoping it will not only satisfy the good people in general, but also all those scatterbrained fellows, who call one another out to shoot pistols in the air, while they tremble so much that they cannot hit the mark.

Towne died on July 8, 1793, having published for a time before his death a paper, *All the News for Two Coppers*, which he carried about the streets himself.

The *Pennsylvania Evening Post* started as a tri-weekly on January 24, 1775, being published on Tuesdays, Thursdays, and Saturdays until January 7, 1779, when it became a semi-weekly. On August 3, 1781, its title was changed to the *Pennsylvania Evening Post and Public Advertiser*, and two years later it became a daily under the title the *Pennsylvania Post and Daily Advertiser.* It continued as a daily for six years, until 1789, under this latter name and still under Towne's proprietorship. It was the first paper to print the Declaration of Independence.

The *Pennsylvania Chronicle and Universal Advertiser* first appeared on January 26, 1767. It was published by William Goddard. The *Pennsylvania Packet or General Advertiser* was first issued on October 28, 1771, by John Dunlap. This latter journal warmly supported the cause of the Colonists against Great Britain in 1775-6; at this time it was published semi-weekly with postscripts similar to the "extras" of today being issued whenever important news was received from abroad or from the other Colonies. While the British occupied Philadelphia, the *Packet* was printed at Lancaster, but resumed printing in Philadelphia on July 4, 1778. That day John Dunlap published an editorial — very rare in those days — on the evacuation of the city by the British troops. On September 21, 1784, the *Packet*, which had theretofore been issued three times weekly, was converted into a daily. Shortly afterward the title was changed to the *American Daily Advertiser*, and then to *Dunlap & Claypoole's American Daily Advertiser* — this when David C. Claypoole, Dunlap's apprentice and later partner, became sole owner. Dunlap died on November 27, 1812, and was buried with military honors in Christ Church graveyard, Fifth and Arch Streets.

The excellent work of J. Thomas Scharf and Thompson Westcott, constantly referred to by students of Philadelphia's history, contains an erroneous statement regarding *Claypoole's Daily Advertiser.* Scharf and Westcott confounded this publication with Towne's *Pennsylvania*

Evening Post. Historical research by the American Antiquarian Society proves that the *Pennsylvania Evening Post,* not the *Daily Advertiser,* was the first daily newspaper published in America. The *Daily Advertiser* was continued by David C. Claypoole until September 30, 1800, when he sold it to Zachariah Poulson, Jr., for $10,000. Under Poulson the *Advertiser* prospered for 30 years, although it never attained a large circulation. Always respectable, never brilliant, and strictly Whig, Poulson was 78 years old and in feeble health when, on December 28, 1839, he bade farewell to journalism. The *North American and the United States Gazette,* the outgrowth of a number of journals of various degrees of importance, was first issued under that name on March 26, 1839, at 63 Dock Street. Its first publishers, S. C. Brace and T. R. Newbold, soon gave way to William Welsh, last survivor of a group that had acquired the paper in an effort to elevate newspaper morality. Before the end of 1839 it absorbed Poulson's *Daily Advertiser,* and in 1840 it acquired the *Commercial Herald.* Welsh also purchased the *Philadelphia Gazette,* an afternoon paper.

On October 1, 1845, Welsh sold the *North American* to George R. Graham and Alexander Cummings. It joined with the New York *Tribune* in revolutionary efforts to obtain fresh news. In 1846 the two newspapers hired the pilot boat *Romer* and beat the regular

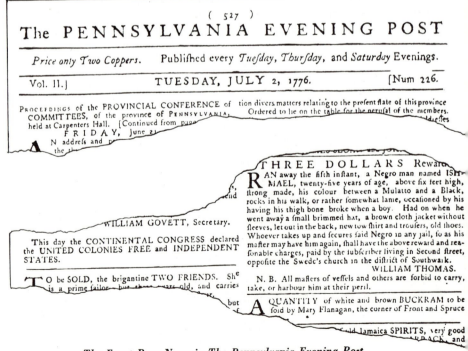

The Front Page News in The Pennsylvania Evening Post

packet with foreign news by several days — the first stirrings of the modern attitude towards news gathering.

At the beginning of 1847 the *North American* and the *United States Gazette* were prosperous Whig papers of similar character and standing. Neither could hope for any material increase in prosperity while the other existed. Morton McMichael conceived the idea of consolidating the two rivals, and this was accomplished on July 1, 1847, when they combined under the name of the *North American and United States Gazette.* Born in Burlington County, N. J., McMichael was to write his name in bold letters across the early history of Philadelphia journalism. Educated at the University of Pennsylvania, he became editor of the *Saturday Evening Post* in 1826. In 1831 he was editor-in-chief of the *Saturday Courier,* a new enterprise, and with Louis A. Godey and Joseph C. Neal he began publication in 1836 of the *Saturday News.* In 1844 the *Saturday Gazette* was published, McMichael and Neal being associate editors. The weeklies have long since ceased to exist, but the *North American* (it resumed this name in May 1876) survived until 1925 — the oldest daily newspaper in America.

The *Inquirer,* the first number of which bore the name *Pennsylvania Inquirer,* made its appearance on June 29, 1829, at 5 Bank Alley, near the Merchants' Coffee House. It came at an auspicious time, since Duane's *Aurora,* the principal Democratic newspaper, was then in a weakened state and had vainly sought to sustain itself by absorbing the *Franklin Gazette.* One of the editors of the merged *Aurora and Gazette,* John Norvell, was dissatisfied with his prospects for the future, and induced John R. Walker, a young printer, to join him in the publication of the *Pennsylvania Inquirer.*

In November of that year, 1829, the new journal passed into the hands of Jesper Harding and was merged with the *Democratic Press.* Harding changed the *Pennsylvania Inquirer* from a morning to an evening journal, featuring editorials — chiefly political — didactic articles, literary reviews, dramatic criticisms, poetry, and fiction. It contained little news, as news is known today, and its advertisements were displayed blatantly.

Upon their amalgamation on July 1, 1930, the *Morning Journal* and the *Inquirer* became known as the *Pennsylvania Inquirer and Morning Journal,* retaining this name until June 2, 1834, when it absorbed the *Daily Courier* and changed its title to the *Pennsylvania Inquirer and Daily Courier.* Under this caption it soon took its place in the Whig party as rival and opponent of the *United States Gazette,* so that upon absorption of the latter on January 1, 1842 it again changed its title, this time to the *Pennsylvania Inquirer and National Gazette.* In October 1859 the paper was acquired by William W. Harding, son of Jesper Harding, and on April 2, 1860 its name was changed to the Philadelphia *Inquirer*. The old custom of seeking yearly subscribers was abandoned, and the price was reduced to two cents a copy. A large increase of circulation was obtained through the establishment of the carrier system and street sales. Its eyewitness reporting of Civil War battles added greatly to its prestige. It was among the first newspapers to introduce the stereotyping process.

In 1889 the *Inquirer* became the property of the late James Elverson, Sr., upon whose death in 1911 it passed to his son, the late Col. James Elverson, Jr., who made it one of the most successful morning newspapers in the country. After the colonel's death in 1929, it became conservative in tone, under Elverson's sister, Mrs. Eleanor Patenotre, widow of a French citizen. It was sold in 1930 to the Curtis-Martin Newspapers, Inc., but was returned to the Patenotre interests a few years later. In 1936 it was acquired by Moses L. Annenberg, former circulation manager for William Randolph Hearst and publisher of the New York *Morning Telegraph*. Under Annenberg its style of news reporting was recast into the "human interest" mold.

Among Philadelphia's oldest and largest newspapers (until 1934) was the *Public Ledger*, born March 25, 1836. Its publishers declared at the outset that they could keep on printing at a continued loss for "one whole year." A half century later the fact had become established that no one could tell whether a new journal would succeed or fail in less than two years of experimentation. A. H. Simmons, one of the *Ledger* publishers, gathered around him a staff of enthusiastic men. The new paper announced : "We shall give place to no religious discussions, nor to political discussions involving questions of merely partisan character. The *Ledger* will worship no men, and be devoted to no parties."

The firm of Swain & Abell published the *Ledger* until December 3, 1864, when it was sold to George W. Childs, who followed the course laid out by its founders. He devised new features, introduced new machinery, and moved the paper to better quarters at Sixth and Chestnut Streets. It was next acquired by the Adolph S. Ochs interests, and finally by Cyrus H. K. Curtis, who afterwards formed the Curtis-Martin Newspapers, Inc. When the morning *Ledger* merged with the *Inquirer* in 1933, the newer *Evening Public Ledger* (established in 1914) was continued under the direction of John C. Martin, the step-son-in-law of Curtis, who died before the merger.

The *Evening Bulletin* first saw the light of day on April 12, 1847, with the resounding title of *Cummings' Evening Telegraphic Bulletin*. Its publisher was Alexander Cummings, who also published *Neal's Saturday Gazette*. In 1856 the name was changed to *Daily Evening Bulletin*, and in 1870 to *Evening Bulletin*. Acquired in 1895 by the late William L. McLean, the *Evening Bulletin* is still in the hands of the McLean family.

Weekly newspapers published on Sunday gradually disappeared, as each of the morning dailies began to blossom forth with an ambitious Sunday edition. One of the most prominent of the early weeklies was *Taggart's Sunday Times*, published on Walnut Street near Eighth. Others were the *Mercury, Sunday World, Republic, Transcript*, and *Dispatch*.

One of the first Philadelphia dailies to issue a Sunday edition was the *Press*, edited by Charles Emory Smith, onetime Postmaster General and United States Ambassador to Russia. It was a propaganda sheet, financed by steel interests in western Pennsylvania. The *Press* was subsequently absorbed by the Curtis-Martin publications. This firm also bought and scrapped the *Evening Telegraph* and the *North American*.

The Philadelphia *Record*, bulwark of the liberal element in Pennsylvania, is a descendant of the *Public Record*, which first appeared in 1870 as a humble imitator of the *Public Ledger*. In 1877 William M. Singerly took hold of the paper and made it a phenomenal success, both financially and editorially. Its name was changed to the Philadelphia *Record* in 1877. It attained a large circulation, and the price was lowered to one cent in the face of dire predictions. A strong supporter of the Democratic Party, the *Record* was particularly popular with workingmen.

Success of the *Sunday Press* opened the eyes of other publishers to the possibilities of a Sunday issue. The *Record* therefore issued an eight page Sunday edition — so simple were the journalistic demands of that period — and for years it was sold at three cents a copy, while other Sunday papers were selling at five cents. Singerly was a versatile promoter, but apparently he overreached himself, for his various properties eventually went into receivership. The paper was then acquired by the John Wanamaker interests. In 1928 J. David Stern, publisher of the *Evening Courier*, of Camden, N. J., gained control of the *Record*. Under him the circulation and advertising increased and the paper developed into an influential organ of liberalism.

The *Times* was a prominent Philadelphia morning newspaper from 1875 until it was merged with the *Public Ledger* on August 16, 1902. Until its purchase in 1901 by Adolph S. Ochs, then owner of the *Ledger*, it had been published by Col. A. K. McClure, a prominent figure in Philadelphia civil and political life. The *Times* was Democratic in its editorial policies. It was a penny paper, with a Sunday edition that sold at five cents. During most of its existence it was published in its own building at the southwest corner of Eighth and Chestnut Streets.

The *Evening Telegraph* was first issued on January 4, 1864, at 108 South Third Street. It was a four-page paper, seven columns to the page, and was sold at two cents a copy. At the close of the first year it was enlarged to eight pages of six columns each, and the price was increased to three cents. The original proprietors were J. Barclay Harding and Charles E. Warburton, the former a son of Jesper Harding, whose name has figured conspicuously in the history of Philadelphia journalism. After Harding's death, in 1865, the paper passed to the sole control of Warburton, Harding's brother-in-law, and later to Warburtons son, Barclay H. The *Telegraph*, Republican in policy, was absorbed by the *Evening Public Ledger* in 1918.

The *Evening Times* first appeared in 1908, being published by Frank A. Munsey, millionaire magazine owner. It went out of existence June 16, 1914. Another now defunct evening newspaper, the *Daily Evening Item*, was an outgrowth of the *Sunday Item*, founded in 1847 by Thomas Fitzgerald. The *Item*, which continued to issue a Sunday edition after becoming a daily, ceased publication in 1913.

On May 18, 1925, the Public Ledger Company began the publication of a tabloid newspaper called the *Sun*. It was issued each weekday morning, and was profusely illustrated with news pictures. The *Sun* ceased publication on February 4, 1928.

Another tabloid, the *Daily News*, which had been established about the same time (March 31, 1925) as the *Sun*, continued in existence, and survives today. First proprietor of the *Daily News* was the late William Scott Vare, long a dominant factor in Pennsylvania politics. Vare entered the newspaper publishing business in order to advance his prospects as U. S. Senatorial candidate in the 1926 campaign. Following his election to the Senate, and his subsequent repudiation by that body, he sold a half interest in the *News* to Bernarr MacFadden. Vare died in 1934, and the newspaper finally was taken over by Lee Ellmaker.

The list of foreign-language newspapers in Philadelphia comprises publications in Spanish, Italian, Hungarian, German, Armenian, Yiddish, Russian, Lithuanian, and Ukrainian. There are two weeklies, now issued by and for Negroes — the Philadelphia *Tribune* and the Philadelphia *Independent*, but at the end of the first decade of the nineteenth century the *Caret*, the *Chat*, the *Citizen*, and the *Pilot* were among the several newspapers being published by this group.

The city has a long tradition of journalistic attainment. In its newsrooms have been trained such prominent writers as Christopher Morley, poet, essayist, and novelist ; James Gibbons Huneker, critic and molder of many a budding genius ; and Richard Harding Davis, novelist and war correspondent. Benjamin Franklin, with his *Poor Richard's Almanac*, early wielded wide journalistic influence. Thomas Paine, Revolutionary pamphleteer, issued from Philadelphia presses an appeal for liberty of thought and action which resounds even in modern times.

210

Radio

MORE quickly than it had ever before taken up a new activity, Philadelphia seized radio in the latter's babyhood and did much to bring it to its present stage of perfection. Almost immediately after the first broadcasting stations began operating, the roofs of the city became a wire entaglement reminiscent of No Man's Land. Newspapers issued weekly supplements full of instructions for building receiving sets, and almost every boy with the least mechanical bent was soon tinkering with the necessary apparatus.

Families gathered around crystal sets while the young "operator" manipulated a "cat's whisker," extracting sounds approaching that of the human voice of phonographic music. "Keep the young folks at home," advertised the early manufacturers of radio receivers, and for a long time that is what radio did.

As the manufacture of high grade receiving sets grew apace, Philadelphia became the home of two of the largest producers, with another just across the Delaware River in Camden.

Transmitting Station of WCAU "And the night shall be filled with music"

Department stores took the lead in setting up broadcasting stations. In the early twenties every large department store was advertising over the air. When the large national networks were formed, Philadelphia stations were connected with each chain. Individuals entered the field, and it was not long before radio had proved its value as an advertising medium. Newspapers began to regret the publicity they had given to what turned out to be their greatest competitor, but public interest made it necessary for them to run a daily time table of broadcasts. Experiments were being carried on all over the country, and novelties were being presented every day. In Philadelphia began many practices that are now universal. The first radio record of a football game, Penn-Cornell; the first children's program, Uncle Wip; the first remote dance-music program, by Charlie Kerr's Orchestra; the first street interviews — these and many other radio "firsts" were born in the much cudgelled brains of the city's program directors and publicity men.

Today there are nine broadcasting stations in Philadelphia: WCAU, with a power of 50,000 watts, is the Columbia outlet; WFIL and KYW are connected respectively with the Red and Blue networks of the National Broadcasting Company; WIP represents an inter-city network; and WDAS, WPEN, WRAX, WHAT, and WTEL are independent stations.

STAGE AND SCREEN

T HE muse of the stage descended upon Philadelphia under a cloud of suspicion. Her doubtful reputation had preceded her. To the Quaker mind, moved by religion to the practice of austerity and fixed in it by necessity, she was a hussy to be guarded against. Her allurements were suspected as an evil likely to ruin the weak and turn the virtuous from thrift and hard work. It was an attitude fostered by the spirit of pioneer economy that left no surplus for the luxury of art.

But charity, another Quaker trait, required that the lady be given the benefit of the doubt ; her presence was tolerated until it attracted a meager success, and then she was outlawed. In time a rising prosperity brought with it the sparse beginnings of a leisure class, and the muse was readmitted to the city's precincts. There she flourished, to the glory of the American theatre and the delight of her admirers.

A slight adversity made a good beginning. Philadelphia and the drama have been long boon companions ; only a few other American cities ranked higher as theatrical centers. It outranked New York during the early part of the nineteenth century, and could with reason dispute Boston's claim to the title of "Athens of the New World," at least as far as the drama was concerned. The greater physical growth of New York and the free expression permitted by its civil authorities have since raised the New York stage to preeminence, but that city's theatre has drawn heavily upon Philadelphia for acting talent and authorship. This city has given to the stage such notable actors as the Drews and the Barrymores, Edwin Forrest, James E. Murdoch, and Joseph Jefferson ; among the playwrights and critics it has nurtured are John Luther Long, Richard Harding Davis, George Kelly, Clifford Odets, and George Jean Nathan.

In talent and appreciation the city has contributed heavily to the motion picture industry, whose rise in Philadelphia, as elsewhere, curtailed the legitimate theatre. Some of the earliest moving pictures ever exhibited were projected in Philadelphia from a machine invented by a Philadelphian. The Lubin Studio, pioneer in this field, was a Philadelphia enterprise.

In recent years the city has sought a new dramatic importance through the rise of a little theatre movement aiming to correct what

213

its leaders deem the failure of the commercial theatre to interpret the American spirit. The groups are free to experiment with new forms and new material, their receipts being secondary to artistic integrity. Their stages have been the proving grounds for some successes of the commercial theatre, whose producers take over the experimental drama which has demonstrated its box-office appeal. However, in practice, most of these groups have confined themselves to presentation of plays already given by professional players.

Within the little theatre movement there is a distinct group which employs the stage as a forum for the expression of a revolutionary economic philosophy rather than as an artistic medium — a group of pioneers in workers' theatres. In Philadelphia its audience has been meager and its resources slender throughout a brief but exciting history.

The early difficulties under which the theater labored in Philadelphia have not wholly disappeared. The urge to censorship is still extant, often prevails, and usually adds to the trivial and salacious the allure of forbidden fruit. Such cases are exceptions, however. On the whole, Philadelphia and the theatre get on well together.

History of The Theatre

DESPITE opposition of the Quakers, attempts to establish theatres were made persistently during the earliest years of the eighteenth century. On three different occasions between 1700 and 1713, laws were passed by the Provincial Assembly prohibiting "stage plays, masks and revels," and each time the laws were repealed by popular demand.

There is no record as to when the first local theatrical performance was held, but in the *American Weekly Mercury* of 1724, mention was made of a "Roap Dancing" at the "New Booth on Society Hill," and in the Pennsylvania *Archives* of the previous year there is mention of "comedians in town." In a letter dated 1723, James Logan, then mayor of Philadelphia, stated with distress that a company of itinerant players had "set up stage just without the verge of the town" and that "the sober people of the city" wanted him to suppress the plays, a situation embarrassing for him because Governor Keith of Pennsylvania Province was in the habit of attending them.

The city apparently was without any form of theatrical entertainment until 1743, when *Punch and Joan*, a puppet show, was presented "At the Sign of the Coach and Horses," on Chestnut Street against the State House. In 1742 the first picture show was given in the city when a "Magick Lanthorn" was exhibited at Joseph Barber's Temple Bar on Second Street.

The first actors' performance recorded in Philadelphia's history

214

took place in August 1749, when a company of players enacted Addison's *Cato* in William Plumstead's warehouse on Water Street. The building has been razed, but evidence of the distaste with which the performance was regarded exists in the journal of one John Smith, which is now in the Ridgway Library. Smith sets forth : "John Morris and I happened in at Peacock Bigger's and drank tea there, and his daughter being one of the company going to hear the tragedy of *Cato* acted, it occasioned some conversation, in which I expressed my sorrow that anything of the kind was encouraged."

Smith's sorrow was assuaged on December 30 of that year, when the Common Council took steps against this invasion of frivolity. Its minutes for that date include this paragraph :

> The Recorder then acquainted the board that certain persons had taken it upon themselves to act plays in this city, and, as he was informed, intended to make a frequent practice thereof; which, it was to be feared, would be attended with very mischievous effects, such as the encouraging of idleness and drawing great sums of money from weak and inconsiderate people, who are apt to be fond of such entertainment, though the performance be ever so mean and contemptible. Whereupon the board unanimously requested the magistrates to take the most effectual measures of suppressing the disorder, by sending for the actors and binding them to their good behavior, or by such other means as they should judge most proper.

Thus bound, the luckless actors departed for New York. In the company was Nancy George, the first Philadelphia girl to desert the respectability of home for the glamour of the stage. In his *Annals of Philadelphia*, John F. Watson quotes an aged Negro, Robert Venable, as saying that "many persons fell out with Nancy George because she went there to play." What the players performed, other than *Cato*, is unknown ; the newspapers of the time took note only of their departure.

Five years later another company, led by Lewis Hallam, was fortunate enough to attract the favor of Mayor Plumstead, and under his protection they enacted Rowe's tragedy, *The Fair Penitent*. For five more years the drama languished ; then David Douglass re-organized Hallam's company and won the good will of Governor Denny by promising to perform a benefit for the Pennsylvania Hospital. Douglass could not obtain a building in the city for a theatre and had one constructed secretly outside the city limits, at what is now Hancock and South Streets. Opened June 25, 1759, and known as the Society Hill Theatre, this playhouse was the first to be built in Philadelphia.

On the opening of the new theatre, aroused church leaders appealed to the Assembly, which passed an act proscribing the drama in and near Philadelphia. Governor Denny delayed the enforcement of the act, and the Society Hill Theatre was kept open until December 1759. Its players performed *Tamerlane, King Lear, Romeo and Juliet, Richard III, Lord Chalkstone, George Barnwell*, and *Lethe*. Meanwhile, Douglass kept his promise to Governor Denny : *Hamlet* was enacted for the benefit of the Pennsylvania Hospital on February 27. This was Philadelphia's first *Hamlet* and its first benefit performance.

The liberal element in the city gained strength as commerce expanded and external influences modified the townsmen's severe tastes. By 1766 it was possible for Douglass to build another theatre, this time nearer the city, on South Street west of Fourth. The Pennsylvania *Gazette* and the Pennsylvania *Chronicle* now deigned to accept his advertisements. In the new playhouse, which became known as the Southwark Theatre, the first American tragedy, *The Prince of Parthia*, by Thomas Godfrey, Jr., was performed April 24,1767.

Douglass' company had a varied repertory, and the Southwark was a flourishing playhouse until the Revolution forced it to close. The theatre was reopened during the British occupation, and Tory ladies united their talents with those of Lord Howe's officers in performances for the benefit of the widows and orphans of soldiers.

After independence had been attained, the society of the new Republic's capital took up the theatre in earnest, and when George Washington himself attended a performance at the Southwark, the poor muse was at least draped with the mantle of respectability. Even so, many a good Philadelphian believed the mantle cloaked a lady who still was no better than she should be.

Approval of the polite world resulted in a project for a new theatre large enough and fine enough to be a fitting playhouse for the country's capital. The project was realized in the Chestnut Street Theatre, opened at Sixth and Chestnut Streets in 1794. Here, in the flickering candlelight from a "profusion of chandeliers," as many as 2,000 persons attended some performances.

In this age of political ferment the muse grew topical. *The Slaves of Algeria* was a trenchant prelude to the skirmishes with the Barbary corsairs, and the President was mildly rebuked for his shilly-shallying with England by the authors of *Embargo, or Every Man Has His Own Opinion*.

By 1809 the drama had so far outgrown its humble beginnings that a second playhouse became a profitable possibility, and the Walnut Street Theatre was built. This theatre is the oldest existing playhouse in the United States. Its interior has been refashioned to fit modern tastes and supply modern conveniences. In its old age change has assailed it ; burlesque queens have trod the boards where once walked such great artists as Edwin Forrest and Mrs. John Drew, Edmund

Kean, Edwin Booth, Francis Wemyss, Fanny Kemble, Charlotte Cushman, and George Arliss. It has housed vaudeville and a group of Yiddish players.

The first Chestnut (Chesnut) Street Theatre was destroyed by fire in 1820. A second, which replaced it, was built in 1822 and lives in theatrical history as "Old Drury." It opened with *The School for Scandal* and had a brilliant career. There Barnum, wedding ballyhoo to art, presented Jenny Lind, "the Swedish Nightingale ;" Laura Keene, Forrest, Booth, and Jefferson also played there. The theatre was razed in 1855, in the belief that the new Academy of Music would absorb its patronage ; but the Academy proved too large — it engulfed the average play in deadening space. A third theatre was therefore erected, on Chestnut Street west of Twelfth.

Its opening on January 26, 1863, was marked by the first instance of ticket "scalping" in Philadelphia. Seats were sold at auction for *Virginius*, starring Edwin Forrest. One "scalper" purchased 500 tickets. When the box office opened, it was surrounded by a milling crowd of disappointed playgoers for whom there were no seats. The police barely averted a riot over a practice which the public has since come to tolerate. There Joseph Jefferson presented his *Rip Van Winkle* to a delighted public ; Daly's stock company and E. L. Davenport, tragedian, frequently occupied its stage. The last performance was given on October 18, 1910. A few years later the theatre was razed and an office building erected on the site.

One of the older of the Philadelphia theatres, the Arch Street, has passed into oblivion. It was opened October 1, 1828, with a comedy *The Honeymoon* ; a farce, *Three and the Deuce* ; and the reading of a prize address by "a gentleman of the city." This auspicious beginning was of no avail ; the salaries paid to actors were extraordinarily high for that time, and the playhouse closed December 24 for lack of funds. A series of sporadic openings and premature closings marked its history until Mrs. John Drew took it over in Civil War times. Her genius kept it open until 1892. Within the next 10 years it was a German theatre, and then a Jewish theatre ; and from 1902 to 1907 was known as Blaney's Theatre. It became a Jewish theatre again in 1915 and so remained until 1934, when it closed for the last time. In 1935 the building was razed.

The Garrick, at Chestnut and Juniper Streets, which opened in 1901 with Richard Mansfield playing the lead in *Monsieur Beaucaire*, was razed in 1937. The playhouse was identified with many famous stars and attractions. Among the former were Mrs. Patrick Campbell, John Drew, Ethel Barrymore, Walter Hampden, George M. Cohan, Otis Skinner, Jane Cowl, Jeanne Eagels, Fred Stone, David Warfield, Alla Nazimova, and Helen Hayes.

217

Walnut Street Theatre
"*Ghosts of Kean, Booth, Bernhardt and Drew haunt the Green Room*"

The First Chestnut Street Theatre
"*Amid a 'profusion of chandeliers' Thespis reigned in 1794*"

Personalities of the Stage

PHILADELPHIA has made an important contribution to the drama in actors and actresses born or reared in the city : Edwin Forrest, James E. Murdoch, the Jefferson, Davenport, Drew, and Barrymore families, Rose Eytinge, Francis Wilson, Ed Wynn, Frank Tinney, Janet Gaynor, Jeannette MacDonald, George Bancroft, Vivienne Segal, Constance Binney, W. C. Fields, Walter C. Kelly, Eddie Quillen, Eleanor Boardman, to name some of the better known.

Edwin Forrest (1806-1872) was born at 51 George (now South American) Street. One of Philadelphia's most famous actors, he first appeared in juvenile roles for a Thespian society. His first appearance on a regular stage was made at the Walnut Street Theatre, and his last appearance as an actor was in the role of "Richelieu" at the Globe Theatre, Boston, April 2, 1872.

He made his debut as a star at the Chestnut Street Theatre on July 5, 1826, in Othello, and was one of the first American actors to invade the English stage. Forrest made two tours in England, the first in the Spring of 1836, the second in 1845. Criticism of his performances abroad created resentment on this side of the Atlantic. This feeling persisted, and a few years later it resulted in one of the most remarkable tragedies connected with the stage. William Macready, an English actor, came to this country with an English company to present Shakespearean plays. Macready arrived in the spring of 1849. In May of that year he opened as Macbeth, at the Astor Place Theatre, New York. In revenge for the treatment accorded Forrest in London, the gallery audience hissed Macready and his company. A tumult followed, and was continued in the street, where fighting broke out and soon assumed the proportions of a riot. Twenty-two men were killed and several hundred injured.

In 1822 at the age of 16, and for many years thereafter Forrest toured the country. After Forrest's return to his home he bought a brownstone mansion on Broad Street and retired. In 1860 he was persuaded to return to the stage, but failing health marred his last appearance. He died December 12, 1872, broken and unhappy, his sensitive nature shattered by the tumult which had resulted from his trip to England.

His will provided for the establishment and maintenance of a home for aged actors. The Edwin Forrest Home, at Forty-ninth Street and Parkside Avenue, is comparatively new, but from 1876 until a few years ago the home was maintained on the actor's estate in Holmesburg. The institution is a sanctuary for actors and actresses more than 60 years old, or those unable to continue their profession because of infirmities.

Another organization for stage folk, the Charlotte Cushman Club, formerly had a clubhouse at 1010 Spruce Street and now maintains a room at the Bellevue-Stratford Hotel, where actresses who are taken ill while in the city are cared for.

James Edward Murdoch was born January 25, 1811. Before his death at 82 he had played at the Haymarket in London for 110 nights, devoted himself to a prolonged study of Shakespeare, and published a monograph on the cultivation of the voice. He had also studied voice culture in Germany, Switzerland, and Italy. His greatest roles were those of Young Mirable in *The Inconstant*, Charles Surface in *The School for Scandal*, Rover in *Wild Oats*, and Don Felix in *The Wonder*.

Joseph Jefferson, born at Spruce and Fifth Streets, February 20, 1829, grew up in the atmosphere of the theatre. His mother, father, and grandfather were stage folk, and he appeared on the stage as a baby. He played many comedy parts in Philadelphia as a youth, but his outstanding success was the title role in *Rip Van Winkle*, which he played for years. In 1849 he toured the South. In 1861 he made a tour of Australia, and four years later appeared at the Adelphi in London. The noted dramatic critic, William Winter, rated him among the greatest actors of all time.

Long in the annals of the Philadelphia theatre is the name of Davenport, nine generations of whom have appeared before theatrical audiences in England and America. At one time 10 members of the family were on the stage simultaneously. Fanny Davenport, sister of E. L. Davenport, played many of "the divine" Sarah Bernhardt's roles in America, and her niece of the same name appeared in *Topaze* a few years ago. Harry, son of the illustrious E. L. and now in Hollywood, is perhaps the most unusual of this family, because of his long career behind the footlights which began in Philadelphia in 1871 when he was just five years of age. He still treasures the first money he earned on the stage in Philadelphia.

Mrs. John Drew was the matriarch of Philadelphia's second great theatrical family and one of the greatest of American actresses. Born January 10, 1820, in London, she came to America at the age of seven, and as a young girl played at the Walnut Street Theatre in support of Booth. She married John Drew, her third husband, in 1850. After his death she managed the Arch Street Theatre for 30 years and then moved to New York, appearing there in a few all-star revivals. Finally she returned to Philadelphia to live with her son. She died in Larchmont, N. Y., August 31, 1897.

John Drew, the younger, was born in Philadelphia November 13, 1853, and made his first appearance at the Arch Street Theatre in 1873 in *Cool as a Cucumber*. He joined Augustin Daly's company in New York, and remained with it for years. He played 70 parts with Daly and in support of Booth, Fanny Davenport, and other stage notables. Later Drew joined Charles Frohman. He died in 1927 while touring the West with the comedy revival, *Trelawney of the Wells*. Petruchio, in *The Taming of the Shrew*, was his favorite role.

Of all the stars Philadelphia has given to the theatre, none have shone more brightly than the members of the Barrymore constellation — Ethel, Lionel, and John, children of Georgiana Drew and Maurice Barrymore. John was born in Philadelphia February 15, 1882. In his youth he studied art, and professed a distaste for the theatre ; but he had appeared in *Camille* with Ethel and Lionel while the three still were children. By 1903 he was playing the male lead in Richard Harding Davis' *The Dictator* — a role which took him to London in 1905.

For 10 years his star rose steadily. His portrayal of the title role in *Peter Ibbetson* sent critics into superlatives, and when he returned to the higher realm of Shakespearean repertory their praise continued. In 1921 his *Hamlet* was a sensation in America, and in London a critic said Barrymore seemed to have "gathered in himself all the Hamlets of his generation." He has also portrayed on the screen leading roles in such successes as *Don Juan, Dr. Jekyll and Mr. Hyde, Moby Dick, Manon Lescaut, General Crack, Svengali, Grand Hotel,* and *Rasputin*.

Ethel was born in Philadelphia on August 15, 1879. Her success has been, if less spectacular, more solid than her younger brother's, and the range of her acting has been limited only by the vehicles available. Her portrayals of Lady Teazle in *School for Scandal* and the leading roles in *Captain Jinks, Mid-Channel, Our Miss McChesney, Declassé,* and *The Constant Wife* have left an indelible impression upon the theatre in America and England. She was somewhat less successful on the screen in *The Nightingale, The White Raven,* and *Rasputin*.

Eldest of the Barrymore trinity is Lionel, born in Philadelphia April 29, 1878. At 15 he was playing small parts in a company with his uncle, Sidney Drew, and later appeared in *The Rivals*. His first real success was in support of his uncle, John Drew, in *The Mummy and the Humming Bird*. After years of trouping he renounced the stage and turned to painting. In 1918 he returned to the stage and achieved great success in *The Copperhead*, a play of Civil War time. His screen career began with D. W. Griffith in the old Biograph studio in New York. Recognition as a screen actor was slow in coming, but in a long string of films — *The Mysterious Island, The Lion and the Mouse, Body and Soul, A Free Soul, The Man I Killed, Grand Hotel, Arsene Lupin, The Yellow Ticket,* and others — his fame has grown with every role.

Francis Wilson, born in 1854 of Quaker parents in Philadelphia,

221

is best remembered as a comedian in many comic operas. But he also achieved success several times in his own plays. He died in New York on October 7, 1935. Ed Wynn, popular comedian, was born in Philadelphia in 1886. He made his first appearance in vaudeville as a lad of 15. Later he played in such Broadway successes as *The Perfect Fool, Simple Simon, The Laugh Parade,* and *The Grab Bag.*

W. C. Fields was born in Philadelphia in 1879. As an actor and juggler he appeared in England, France, and Germany, and from 1915 to 1921 was in each successive edition of Ziegfeld's *Follies.* His film career began with D. W. Griffith in 1925. He proved a great screen comedian and has scored increasing success in *Sally of the Sawdust, It's the Old Army Game, Two Flaming Youths, Mrs. Wiggs of the Cabbage Patch, David Copperfield, Poppy, The Man on the Flying Trapeze,* and others.

Charlotte Greenwood's career has also been divided between the stage and the newer medium of the films. Born in Philadelphia in 1893, she first attracted attention in the Winter Garden production, *The Passing Show,* and has appeared in many popular films.

Other native Philadelphians to acquire prominence in the dramatic field were August, Charlotte, and Charles Durang, Eph Horn, McKean Buchanan, Robert Butler, Harry A. Perry, Eliza Logan, Celia Logan, Herman Vezin, Henry Langdon, Mrs. Oscar Beringer, Minnie Palmer, Hugh J. Ward, George Frederick Nash, Jack Norworth, Margaret Dale, Charles Hopkins, Ethelin Terry, Margaret Lawrence, Evelyn Herbert, George Gaul, Frances Carson, and Emma Haig.

Playwrights

PHILADELPHIA'S writers for the stage have done their share in the advancement of the theatre. The real beginning of American dramatic literature was made with Edwin Forrest's offer of prizes for original plays. In 1759 Thomas Godfrey, Jr., wrote America's first play, *The Prince of Parthia*; and 1801 had seen the performance of Charles Jared Ingersoll's verse tragedy, *Edwy and Elgwia,* based on English history; Mordecai Noah, David Paul Brown, and James Nelson Barker were early Philadelphia playwrights. Forrest's contest brought out John Augustus Stone, whose *Metamora,* Forrest's greatest vehicle, still survives; and Robert Montgomery Bird, three of whose plays, *Oraloosa, The Gladiator,* and *The Broker of Bogata,* were among those awarded Forrest prizes.

George Henry Boker — once called the handsomest man in America — one of the founders of the Union League and sometime minister to Turkey and Russia, wrote *Calaynos, Anne Boleyn,* and *The Betrothal.* His masterpiece, *Francesca da Rimini,* in which Lawrence Barrett first made his mark, was successfully revived by Otis Skinner in 1901.

222

John Luther Long, born in Hanover, Pa., in 1861, wrote the short story, *Madame Butterfly*, in 1900. David Belasco sensed its dramatic possibilities, and collaborated with Long in writing the play of the same name. Later the play was used as a basis for the Puccini opera, *Madama Butterfly*. *The Darling of the Gods* followed, with Blanche Bates and George Arliss costarring. The Belasco-Long collaboration ended in 1904 with *Andrea*. Other Long plays were *The Dragon Fly*, *Dolce*, *Kassa*, and *Crowns*.

Ernest Lucy, who made Philadelphia his home, wrote *Chatterton*, in which Julia Marlowe starred.

John T. McIntyre's imaginative comedy of a dream world, *A Young Man's Fancy*, was produced in 1919 and was praised in some quarters for its poetic charm.

That there can be depth and interest in common things was the conviction of Edward Childs Carpenter, another Philadelphia dramatist, born in 1872. He submitted his *Barber of New Orleans* in a prize contest conducted by the New York *Globe*, and the play was produced by William Faversham in 1908. He wrote a half dozen plays, his most successful being *The Bachelor Father*, produced by Belasco in 1928.

Elliot Lester, born in Philadelphia in 1894, deserted the profession of teaching at Temple University when his first play, *The Mud Turtle*, achieved success, and he followed this with *Take My Advice*, a criticism of contemporary life.

George Kelly has established himself in the vanguard of American dramatists whose plays demand serious consideration. Born in Philadelphia in 1887, he played for five years in vaudeville, where his brother Walter, "The Virginia Judge," had long been popular. His first plays were sketches, and his most successful three-act play, *The Show-off*, was an amplification of one of these with its plot laid in Philadelphia. It was produced in 1924. His satire of the little theatres, *The Torch Bearers*, was a success ; and in 1926 he turned to serious drama, writing *Craig's Wife*, winner of a Pulitzer Prize. *Behold, The Bridegroom* in 1928, and *Philip Goes Forth* in 1930, were less popular. His comedy, *Reflected Glory*, was produced in Philadelphia in January 1937.

Langdon Elwyn Mitchell, son of the author-physician, Dr. S. Weir Mitchell, was born in Philadelphia in 1862, and became well known as a playwright. He wrote *In the Season*, produced at St. James Theatre, London, in 1893, and dramatized Thackeray's *Vanity Fair* under the title *Becky Sharp*, a play produced by Mrs. Fiske in 1899 and later put on the screen in colors. His *Pendennis* was produced by John Drew in 1916, and *The New York Idea*, his most successful dramatic offering, in 1906.

223

Other Philadelphia playwrights were Richard Harding Davis and Thomas Fitzgerald, the latter known for many satisfactory plays during the closing years of the nineteenth century.

The city's latest claimant to dramatic fame is Clifford Odets, who rose from the obscurity of a stock player with the Group Theater in New York. In three days he wrote *Waiting for Lefty*, a one-act play that met with tremendous success. He followed in rapid succession with *Awake and Sing, Till the Day I Die, Paradise Lost*, and *Golden Boy*. His plays, anti-Fascist in content, in instances reflect the alleged degeneracy of middle-class society in the changing social order.

Existing Theatres

THE city's modern legitimate theatres have housed a full share of the outstanding dramatic performances of the present century.

The Walnut Street Theatre, Ninth and Walnut Streets, (see Tour, *Where the City Fathers Walked*) believed to be the oldest existing playhouse in America, still follows its ancient traditions though with lagging footsteps. Those who have appeared on its stage run the gamut from circus performers to the greatest names in the history of the American theatre. Remodeled many times since its erection in 1808, an aura of its former greatness still lingers round it.

The Forrest, on Walnut Street at Quince, named for Edwin Forrest, was opened May 1, 1928, with *Under the Red Robe*, a light opera. Designed for spectacular musical and dramatic productions, the theatre has a large and excellently equipped stage. The building is fireproof, and has a seating capacity of approximately 2,000.

Keith's, on Chestnut Street between Eleventh and Twelfth, was built under the personal direction of B. F. Keith, and was opened November 2, 1902. By the will of Andrew Keith, son of the founder, the theater was bequeathed in equal shares to William Cardinal O'Connell, of Boston, and the president and fellows of Harvard College. It was a vaudeville house until September 1928, when the Shuberts made it a home for drama and musical comedy. Later it became a motion-picture house. It was the first so-called "million-dollar theatre" in the country ; on its stage have appeared Sarah Bernhardt, Lillian Russell, Maggie Cline, Will Rogers, Sophie Tucker, Belle Baker, Chic Sale, the Dooleys, and Charlie Chaplin.

The Chestnut Street Opera House at 1021 Chestnut Street, is one of the oldest playhouses in America still in operation. It was opened in 1865, and during its career has been the scene of hundreds of dramatic and musical successes. Today the theatre is equipped to show motion pictures as well as to present stage attractions. It is the home of the American Theatre Society, an organization which has been very successful in presenting plays under a subscription plan.

The Broad Street Theatre, at 261 South Broad Street, for upwards of a half century one of Philadelphia's most noted theatres, dates back to 1876. It has changed ownership many times. The Kiralfy Brothers, who built this playhouse of Moorish design, called it the Alhambra Palace. For a time it was the home of the McCaull Opera Company, and its stage was the scene of several of the earlier Gilbert and Sullivan successes. It was in this theatre, in 1888, that Julia Marlowe made her debut. In 1895, the Nixon-Zimmerman interests gained control of the Broad, and under their management many of the great stars of Broadway, including John Drew, Viola Allen, Alla Nazimova, Maude Adams, Sarah Bernhardt, and Mrs. Patrick Campbell played here. With the depression and the inroads made by the motion-picture theatres, the Broad lost a prestige it was never to regain. It closed after the 1935-36 season, was razed in the fall of 1937, and its site is a parking lot.

The Erlanger Theatre, built by the Erlanger interests at Twenty-first and Market Streets in 1927, was devoted largely to musical comedy, and presented some of the front-rank stars of the day, among them Fred Stone, Will Rogers, Helen Morgan, Fred Allen, and W. C. Fields. Occasionally motion pictures have been shown there.

The Locust Street Theatre, on Locust Street near Broad, was opened in March, 1927, as a motion-picture house. Not until 1931 did it change to legitimate drama, the first play being *The Greeks Had a Word for It*. The theatre is of Gothic design.

The Shubert, on Broad Street below Locust, was built in 1917-18, and for a time was the leading house of the Shubert interests in Philadelphia. Among the many productions presented here were *The Student Prince, Sinbad* (with Al Jolson in the starring role), and *The Vagabond King*. The house is now devoted to burlesque.

The first Negro theatre in the city was the Standard, South Street east of Twelfth, which opened September 8, 1888. It remained a legitimate theatre until 1934 when it became, as it is now, a motion-picture theatre. In 1912 the first Negro moving picture theatre, the Keystone, was opened at 937-41 South Street, but it closed in 1934. In 1919 the Dunbar Theatre, now the Lincoln, opened at Broad and Lombard Streets, with an all-Negro cast in the play *Within the Law*. For several seasons this theatre which was named for Paul Laurence Dunbar, a famed Negro poet, ran only legitimate dramas. Later, however, it was taken over by other interests, and it became a moving-picture house. It was opened in September, 1937 as a Jewish Theatre.

The Bijou, on Eighth Street above Race, opened November 4, 1899, was the first Philadelphia theatre with a continuous vaudeville bill. Upon the opening of the Keith Theatre on Chestnut Street in 1902, a stock company occupied the Bijou. In 1907 vaudeville was resumed, giving way to burlesque in 1910.

225

The Trocadero, at Tenth and Arch Streets, has been a burlesque house for about 30 years. The theatre occupies a site originally used by a playhouse devoted to the presentation of Negro minstrels.

The Little Theatres

THE American theatre, moved by the demand for profits, has derived new energy from the little theatre movement, the success of which is twofold : it provides a medium of self-expression for thousands of talented players, and serves as a testing ground for playwrights who might be denied a hearing by professional producers.

In uncounted barns, dwellings, warehouses — wherever a stage may be erected — earnest members of little theatre groups nowadays are busy experimenting with new dramatic forms and new material. From the obscurity of these groups emerge some of the current drama's first playwrights and some worthwhile plays. Philadelphia has not been laggard in the movement. In the city and its environs are more than 200 little theatre groups, many independent, others associated with some school, college, church, or other institution.

Foremost among them is the Hedgerow Theatre, in Rose Valley — not within the city limits, but within its cultural orbit. It began in 1923, with no assets other than a decrepit gristmill and the enthusiasm of its director, Jasper Deeter, who had abandoned a successful career on the professional stage to found the Hedgerow. The company lives a communal life. The work of the group, even the menial domestic work, is performed by the members, and the profits are shared equally. The actresses of an evening may on the morrow be found in the garden hoeing peas ; the actors may combine a talent for acting and for stage carpentry.

The group remodeled the building which houses the theatre. It seats 168 and is open 50 weeks each year, six nights a week from April to October, and three times a week during the winter. The company has a wide and increasing repertory. Plays which have had their premières at Hedgerow include *Cherokee Night*, by Lynn Riggs ; *The D. A.*, by Bayard Veiller ; *Plum Hollow*, by Alvin Kerr ; *Wolves*, by Romain Rolland ; *King Hunger*, by Andreyev ; and *Winesburg, Ohio*, based on the collection of short stories of the same name by Sherwood Anderson. In 1934-35 the group toured the country, and gave 76 plays before an aggregate audience of 120,000.

Another group, the Stagecrafters, began in 1929 with 17 members. It now has 350, all residents of Germantown or Chestnut Hill. After four years in a remodeled blacksmith shop at 8132 Germantown Avenue, the group erected a new building at the same location. This playhouse was opened October 12, 1936, with the production of

226

Robert Sherwood's *The Petrified Forest.* Plays are presented on the second Thursday and Friday of each month, from November through April.

The Alden Park Players are an organization of residents of the Alden Park Apartments, a group of apartment buildings in Germantown, adjoining Fairmount Park. It was organized in 1930 and has had the enthusiastic support of other residents of the apartments. The group has produced many Broadway successes, often under professional direction, in a theatre which is set up each winter over the apartment swimming pool.

The Chestnut Hill Players perform in a renovated barn at Allen's Lane and McCallum Street. Subscribers to the number of 150 make this playhouse self-sustaining. Its repertory has included plays by Molnar, Ibsen, Shaw and Barrie.

A converted barn at 4821 Germantown Avenue houses the Germantown Theatre Guild, which in its three years of life up to 1936 had produced 170 plays, many of them experimental or with a limited audience appeal.

One of the city's older and more successful theatrical groups is Plays and Players, organized in 1911 by Mrs. Otis Skinner. The company produces dramas, operas, and ballets in its own well-equipped theatre at Seventeenth and Delancey Streets. A self-sustaining organization, it maintains club rooms and a theatrical library.

The Showcrafters, organized in 1934, utilize a small second-floor dance hall at Bridge Street and Frankford Avenue. Their theatre, triangular in shape, seats few spectators, but its members have done well with some of the lighter Broadway successes.

An organization which has had the inspiring assistance of Jasper Deeter is the Theatre League, a group of young people producing some of the advanced plays in an old garage at 2034 Chancellor Street. Its equipment is improvised, but it has had considerable success with some important plays, among them *The Sisters' Tragedy, It's the Poor that Helps the Poor, Cradle Song, Marriage Contract,* and *Pillars of Society.*

The city's youngest little theatre group, the Quince Street Players, is another which emulates Hedgerow. Its resources are communalized, and the members share the meager profits of their productions. Their theatre, at 204 South Quince Street, is an unadorned second-floor loft accommodating few spectators.

The most successful, financially, of all the little theatre groups in or near Philadelphia is the Players Club of Swarthmore, the majority of whose members are employed in the city. The club, which grew out of a benefit minstrel show presented in 1911, has its own clubhouse and theatre, with a large and well-equipped stage and a commodious auditorium.

The Mask and Wig Club of the University of Pennsylvania has attained a high reputation throughout the eastern United States for its musical plays, written and acted by members. At Temple University a similar organization, the Templayers, produces plays written by its own members or by accepted dramatists.

It is impossible to distinguish strictly between the little theatre groups and those which might be more properly classified as amateurs. The little theatre stages are not always occupied by experimental or significant drama, and on occasion the amateur groups make a genuine contribution to the theatre. Some of the more important of these borderline groups are : The Lincoln Drive Players, performing at the Unitarian Church, Germantown ; Neighborhood Center Players, 428 Bainbridge Street; Torresdale Dramatic Club, parish house of All Saints Church ; Old Academy Players, 3544 Indian Queen Lane ; and Three Oaks Dramatic Club, Germantown Women's Club building on Washington Lane. The Neighborhood Center Players are especially noteworthy for the inspiration given to playwriting by the yearly contests they foster. They are one of the few little theatres which frequently include new and untried plays in their productions.

The Workers' Theatre

AKIN to the little theatre groups in facilities, but distinct in emphasis and direction, the Workers' Theatre has attempted to present plays which would arouse class consciousness. For ten years, after the World War, a number of groups presented such drama in Philadelphia, but their productions generally died aborning because of a lack either of funds or experience.

In 1926 a group led by Alfred Sobel organized the Workers' Theatre Alliance, and the movement began to assume some consciousness of its direction. In the face of the same disheartening difficulties which had dampened the ardor of its predecessors, the Workers' Theatre Alliance succeeded in presenting several provocative one-act plays: *The Sisters' Tragedy*, by Richard Hughes ; *Victory*, by John Laessen and Simon Felshin ; *The Second Story Man*, by Upton Sinclair ; and *Mr. God Is Not In*, by Harbor Allen. The last named play was an acid satire on organized religion.

The Vanguard Group of players took up the laborers' torch in 1928 at the point where the Workers' Theatre Alliance had met defeat. Jasper Deeter was the Vanguard's first director. Only one play, *The Miners*, was presented before dissension between the players and their director caused production to be suspended. The Vanguard Group was reorganized under Harry Bellaver, also of Hedgerow, and

228

such plays as *What Price Coal?*; *Last Days of the Paris Commune*; *Bound East for Cardiff*; *The Big Stiff*; and *The Unemployed* were presented.

Another group, organized in 1926, is the Labor Institute Drama Guild, a part of the educational and cultural program of the Labor Education Center (formerly the Labor Institute), at 415 South Nineteenth Street. Among its early presentations, given in Yiddish as well as in English, were *The Clock That Struck Thirteen*, adapted from a story by Sholem Aleichem; and *Bebele*, by Perez Hirshbein; also such dramatizations as *Money*, by Michael Gold; and *The Everlasting Song*, by Mark Arnstein.

Theatre Crafts, a group of 40 semi-professional actors, was organized in 1932. Its membership included Clifford Odets; Abner Biberman, who afterwards joined the Theatre Union in New York; and Ted Burke, director of the group.

In presenting plays of social protest, Theatre Crafts was unique among little theatre groups. Its repertory consisted of only two plays : *Precedent*, which dealt with the imprisonment of Tom Mooney in San Francisco, and John Golden's *Gods of Lightning*, a dramatization of the Sacco and Vanzetti case.

To foster greater cooperation between the little groups, the New Theatre (organized in 1934) sponsored a theatre festival in 1936. This marked the third conference of the New Theatre League, at which the Philadelphia center acted as host to more than 100 delegates from similar organizations throughout the country.

With the broadcast of a scene from Albert Bein's *Let Freedom Ring*, in March 1936, the New Theatre made its radio debut. In addition to their dramatic activities, these players also maintain a Film Section, which from time to time has made available to its audiences, at low prices, such screen plays as *Ten Days that Shook the World*, *Broken Shoes*, *Poil de Carotte*, and *Thunder Over Mexico*. Outstanding achievements in the dramatic field were the presentation of *Black Pit* at the Erlanger Theatre, *Too Late to Die* at the Locust, and the only Philadelphia performance of *Let Freedom Ring*, at their own theatre on North Sixteenth Street.

Puppet Shows and Marionettes

P UPPET shows in Philadelphia date back to 1742. In 1781 Charles Willson Peale, the famous painter, exhibited at his home (Third and Lombard Streets) a series of transparent scenes showing events which occurred during the War for Independence.

In the winter of 1786, puppet shows were given on the third floor of a house near Second and Pine Streets, and were directed by Charles Dusselot, a young ex-officer in the French Guards of Louis XVI. A

229

skilled mechanic, Dusselot introduced variety in his shows and succeeded in representing sea fights, a water mill, and various mobile figures. The puppet plays included *Poor Soldier*, in which the songs of Norah and Darby were sung behind the scenes by Mrs. Dusselot and others.

Today, 1937, Philadelphia has revived the ancient and piquant art of puppetry and in cooperation with the Board of Education is demonstrating its ingenuity to various trade unions, settlement houses, schools, hospitals, and other institutions without facilities for the production of the legitimate drama. On the eighth floor of the Y.W.C.A. building, at Eighteenth and Arch Streets, such ancient favorites as *Punch and Judy, Dr. Faustus, Little Black Sambo,* and the more modern Marx Brothers have their headquarters. These puppet shows were begun in January 1936, with plays written by the staff, and figures and costumes created in the workshop. This is a WPA project, part of the Federal Theatre program.

Minstrels

T HREE generations of Philadelphia theatregoers have enjoyed the songs and comedy of what is known as Negro minstrelsy. The claim that this form of entertainment had its inception in this city in 1842 is based upon the statement of William Whitlock, who that year appeared in the Walnut Street Theatre with Master John Diamond.

Buckley's Serenaders are known to have given a minstrel show in Musical Fund Hall in 1849, and four years later a member of the troupe, known as Sam Sanford though his name was Lindsay, opened his "Opera House" on Twelfth Street below Chestnut. He moved his entertainers to Cartee's Museum, Eleventh Street and Marble Alley, in 1854, and this new "opera house" was a home of minstrelsy, under successive managers, for 55 years. Manager Robert F. Simpson changed the name of the house to Carncross and Dixey's in 1862, in honor of two of the most popular minstrels in the troupe.

Lew Simmons and E. N. Slocum opened the "Arch Street Opera House," on Arch Street west of Tenth, in 1870, and that same year Carncross, together with Dixey and Simmons, opened the American Museum, Menagerie and Theatre, on the northwest Corner of Ninth and Arch Streets. Three homes of minstrelsy were thus operating successfully for some time, an indication of the popularity of the song and laugh brand of stagecraft in Philadelphia. Stage stars such as Raymond Hitchcock and Eddie Foy had their start on the Quaker City's minstrel stages.

Frank Dumont succeeded Carncross upon the latter's retirement from the theatre in 1895, managing the Eleventh Street house until

230

1909, when he took over the theatre at 10th and Arch, which he operated until his death in 1919. Emmet J. Welch, ballad writer and singer, was his successor, Welch's Minstrels carrying on the old traditions. A fire in 1929 damaged the playhouse, and in 1931 the onetime old home of sentimental ballads gave way to the raucous automobile, being demolished to provide a parking lot.

Hedgerow Theatre
Where stars are born

The Cinema in Philadelphia

P HILADELPHIA was a pioneer city in moving pictures. In 1860 Dr. Coleman Sellers made the first photographs of motion, and the machine which he devised for showing them was patented in 1861 as "a new and useful improvement in the mode of exhibiting stereoscopic pictures of moving objects." The apparatus was looked upon as merely an interesting toy. It was, however, the first step in motion pictures, and 25 years later its principles were employed by Edison.

On February 5, 1870, Henry R. Heyl displayed at the Academy of Music an invention which he called the "phasmatrope," described as "a recent scientific invention designed to give to various objects and figures upon the screen the most graceful and lifelike movements." His machine was a converted projecting lantern, in front of which was a large revolving disk containing 16 openings near the edge, into which lantern slides were arranged. A disk is still used on motion-picture projectors and in recent television apparatus.

The first motion pictures from flexible films were cast upon a screen at Franklin Institute by C. Francis Jenkins in 1894 ; the first in a Philadelphia theatre were exhibited at Keith's Bijou in 1896. Two years later a Philadelphia optician, Sigmund Lubin, opened a studio for making motion pictures on the roof of a building on Arch Street near Ninth. In the following year these and others were shown at Betzwood, and in 1899 Lubin opened at Seventh and Market Streets a motion-picture theatre — probably the first in the United States. For 15 years Lubin continued as a producer, with studios at Nineteenth Street and Indiana Avenue.

Jeanette MacDonald, the movie star, was born in Philadelphia the early part of the twentieth century, and attended West Philadelphia Girls' High School. Her first job was in the chorus of a Ned Wayburn show in 1920, and success in other musical comedies followed. Her film career began in 1929 in *The Love Parade*, with Maurice Chevalier.

Another Philadelphia screen actress is Janet Gaynor, born here on October 6, 1907. *Seventh Heaven*, in which she appeared in 1926, brought her fame ; and she was subsequently starred in *Sunny Side Up* (the first musical comedy written expressly for films), *The Man Who Came Back, Daddy Long Legs*, and *The Farmer Takes a Wife*.

Constance Binney, born in Philadelphia in 1900, made her first stage appearance 17 years later in New York's Bijou Theatre, in *Saturday to Monday*. In 1920 she made her first appearance on the screen.

Vivienne Segal, born in Philadelphia in 1897, began her film career in 1929, after some experience on the stage. She has appeared in many films, including *Song of the West, The Bride of the Regiment,* and *Viennese Nights.*

Other Philadelphia-born cinema players include Eleanor Boardman, star of *The Auction Block,* and George Bancroft, typifier of rugged force in numerous screen roles.

With more than 150 moving-picture theatres in the city, Philadelphians have no lack of facilities for viewing the latest products of the film industry. Eleven of these theatres, situated in the downtown section of the city, are "first run" houses : Aldine, Arcadia, Boyd, Earle, Erlanger, Fox, Karlton, Stanley, Stanton, and Trans-Lux. In addition, the Europa shows the best of the Continental films, and for several years the Mastbaum, at Twentieth and Market Streets, largest house in the city, displayed "first run" pictures of exceptional merit.

The interest in current news was the inspiration for the Trans-Lux Theatre, which opened on January 1, 1935. The exterior of the building superimposes cubic masses of blue upon silver in a distinctive design. The News Theatre, 1230 Market Street, was opened in 1937.

Memorial Arch at Valley Forge
Dedicated to the thirteen original colonies.

233

MUSIC

MUSICAL progress and appreciation in Philadelphia have kept
faith with the long-haired Hermits of the Wissahickon who,
at the city's first concert in 1703, wrung somber strains from the
viol, the oboe, and the trumpet. It is not difficult to resurrect that
scene of long ago — the music-starved Colonials tapping their feet
in tempo with the kettledrum; the half-austere, half-exalted expression upon the faces of the musicians ; the lack of symphonic
richness. From this early recital at the ordination of Justus Falkner
in Old Swedes Church, musical endeavor in Philadelphia has marched
down an ever-widening path, emerging finally into the broad highway
of accomplishment.

Music in modern Philadelphia is symbolized by the renowned
Philadelphia Orchestra and the Curtis Institute of Music. Under the
driving force of Leopold Stokowski's genius, the former has come to
be recognized as one of the great symphonic organizations of the
world. Philadelphia's musical tradition, however, does not entirely
center about the orchestra and the Academy of Music in which it
plays. Numerous singing societies, choral groups, orchestral clubs,
and organization of various kinds reflect the musical tendencies of
its people.

That Philadelphia was a musical center as early as Colonial times
was due partly to its geographical location midway between Boston
and the capital of southern secular music, Charleston. This fortunate
circumstance helped it to absorb musical influences from each, while
developing its own appreciation.

The city's next modest step in music, following the Hermits' concert in 1703, was the purchase and installation in Christ Church, in
1728, of its first organ. In 1743 Gustavus Hesselius was manufacturing
spinets and organs in the city, and this date marks the beginning of
the history of the American pianoforte.

The American Company opened the Southwark Theatre on November 14, 1766, giving as its first performance *Thomas and Sally*, or,
The Sailor's Return. Philadelphia was in the forefront operatically
when other cities were experimenting with crude band concerts, and
was also the first city in the country to present a really ambitious
concert, which took place May 4, 1786. A "grand concert" with 230

234

vocal and 50 instrumental performers was given on that date at the German Reformed Church in Race Street.

Choral and secular music, meanwhile, had been developing at a rapid pace. By the latter part of the eighteenth century, and in the early years of the nineteenth, many Philadelphia musicians were devoting a major part of their time to the advancement of choral music in churches and independent societies. Publication of books dealing with hymn singing and choral selections increased.

In 1852 a drive was organized to obtain money for construction of the Philadelphia Academy of Music. The sum of $400,000 was raised, and five years later the Academy was formally opened. In February 1857 the building saw its first opera, *Il Trovatore*. This presentation conclusively demonstrated the Academy's worth to Philadelphia music lovers. The acoustics was declared the finest in the United States, and even today the Academy is distinguished for its acoustic excellence.

Another event of importance was the arrival, in 1907, of Oscar Hammerstein. He built, at Broad and Poplar Streets, the gigantic opera house known as the Metropolitan. Hammerstein scoffed at

The Academy of Music
"Where rich memories are born"

warnings that the venture would fail because the building was too far from the center of the city. Whether or not the location was a vital factor, the house, despite its spacious stage and elaborate appointments, was not successful. To the bitter disappointment of himself and local music lovers, Hammerstein was able to present opera for only two years. Later, however, the Metropolitan was the scene of intermittent operatic productions.

The twentieth century ushered in a new era in Philadelphia music. In the years to follow, the city surged forward in a magnificent musical advance that ultimately placed it among the leaders as a world musical center.

Philadelphia Orchestra

THE Philadelphia Orchestra was organized in 1900, as an outgrowth of the defunct Philadelphia Symphonic Society, which had been founded in 1893, with William Wallace Gilchrist as its leader. The orchestra's first concert was held November 16 under the baton of Fritz Scheel. During the winter of 1900-01 a series of six concerts was given in the Academy of Music, and in the spring of 1901 the orchestra, still under Scheel's direction, gave a concert for the benefit of the soldiers and sailors of the Philippine campaign.

These concerts were received with so much favor that a movement was set afoot to establish the orchestra on a permanent basis.

Up to that time, Philadelphia music lovers had to get along with a few concerts given each year by touring symphony orchestras, or else go to New York. Finally, through the efforts of Alexander Van Rensselaer and a committee composed of John H. Ingham, Oliver Boyce Judson, Edward S. McCollin, John C. Sims, Henry Wheelen, Jr., Oscar A. Knipe, and Dr. Edward I. Keffer, the Philadelphia Orchestra Association was formed. Scheel was engaged as the regular conductor ; and although the early years of the orchestra's existence were marked by financial difficulties, public-spirited citizens from time to time aided with generous contributions.

Scheel died in 1907. After an exhaustive search throughout Europe, Carl Polhig, Royal Court Conductor of the King of Württemburg, was engaged as conductor. Polhig's leadership over a period of five years, however, was not especially impressive.

The year 1912 was important in the development of the orchestra. Leopold Stokowski, who had been conducting the Cincinnati Orchestra, was engaged to lead the Philadelphia organization. A man of artistic temperament and spectacular methods, the maestro began a long series of experiments with new symphonic works, new methods of instrument arrangement, and new styles of presentation. In the 20 succeeding years the fame of Stokowski spread throughout the world.

236

MUSIC

Among his innovations was the arrangement of the orchestra personnel on a level platform instead of in the conventional amphitheatre. He became noted, also, for his rebukes to noisy and to late-arriving patrons. On one occasion, during the season of 1926, he chided tardy arrivals by opening the concert with an "orchestra" composed of a cellist and a violinist, permitting the other orchestra members to straggle in two or three at a time. In 1929 he rebuked patrons who had hissed a Schonberg number by suggesting they surrender their seats to others who would appreciate good music.

A few years later, when orchestra patrons criticized the appearance of modern compositions on the programs, the blond conductor arranged a program with a division between "regular" and "modern" numbers, virtually inviting those who disliked the new music to leave. On still another occasion he interrupted a concert to upbraid a few members of the audience, maintaining that their applause of a Bach transcription disturbed the delicate mood inspired by the music.

Stokowski's conductorship ended with the close of the 1935-36 season. He had decided to devote more time to musical research and to experimentation in connection with motion pictures. In the spring of 1936 the orchestra made a nation-wide tour. Stokowski was the chief conductor, while Saul Cohen Caston and Charles O'Connell alternated on the podium as associate conductors. However, the 1936-37 season saw a new conductor, Eugene Ormandy, with Stokowski acting as musical director and conducting a limited number of concerts.

Closely affiliated with the orchestra is the Youth Movement in Music, instituted by Stokowski with two concerts for youths, which he directed, in 1933. In response to his appeal for some sort of organization among the younger music lovers, clubs were formed and placed under the guidance of orchestra members. Their purpose was a discussion and exchange of ideas on singing, drama, and orchestration.

The Concerts for Youth Committee, of which C. David Hocker is chairman, acts in an advisory capacity to the movement. The committee arranges auditions for unusually talented youngsters. One of those selected at an audition was Eugene List, who later obtained a position with the Philharmonic Society of New York, and was engaged for an extensive tour of Europe. The youth concerts are well attended, and the 100 youth clubs had a membership of more than 1,000 in 1937.

Curtis Institute of Music

FOUNDED in 1924 by Mary Louise Curtis Bok, the Curtis Institute "endeavors, through contemporary masters, to inculcate into students of today the great traditions of the past." It provides free tuition, individual instruction by world-famous artists, financial assistance, and also arranges preparatory stage and radio performances for students of merit.

Student soloists, ensemble groups, and the Curtis Orchestra participate in approximately 25 programs each season. They are broadcast from the institute auditorium and from Philadelphia's radio studios over a national network. Students also appear before educational and civic organizations within a hundred-mile radius of the city. Some of them are permitted, at the discretion of the school, to accept professional engagements.

Admission to the institute, which is situated on Rittenhouse Square, is limited to those whose inherent musical gift shows promise of development to a point of professional quality. Auditions are held within a month after application for enrollment, the final decision as to the suitability of the applicant resting upon talent shown in the examination.

Since Curtis Institute was founded, 246 students have been graduated. Among these were Helen Jepson, Rose Bampton, Conrad Thibault, Charlotte Symons, Samuel Barber, Wilbur Evans, Benjamin de Loache, Boris Goldovsky, Edwina Eustis, Edna Phillips, Shura Cherkassky, Sylvan Levin, Eugene Lowenthal, Agnes Davis, and Ira Petina.

Other Musical Groups

FOR a number of years orchestral concerts were given in an open-air pavilion on Lemon Hill in Fairmount Park. The orchestra consisted of about 50 musicians, many of them members of the Philadelphia Orchestra. The programs were made up generally of semi-popular works of great composers, arranged to appeal to different gradations of understanding and appreciation. These concerts were popular and well attended, a gathering of more than 10,000 having been estimated on one Sunday. Since the auditorium could accommodate only a fraction of this number, thousands were forced to find seats on the surrounding lawns.

Among the conductors who appeared at Lemon Hill from 1922 to 1925 were Thaddeus Rich, Richard Hageman, Willem Van Hoogstraten, Henry Hadley, Alexander Smallens, Nahan Franko, and Victor Kolar. Other musical celebrities to appear at the Lemon Hill concerts included Olga Samaroff, Elsa Alsen, Elly Ney, and Rence

MUSIC

Thornton. The concert season at Lemon Hill lasted for seven weeks during July and August. These concerts were supplanted by the Robin Hood Dell programs, begun in 1930.

During the seventh (1936) season at the Dell, operas and ballets were presented in addition to "straight" concerts, with Jose Iturbi as musical director of these concerts which are a cooperative venture on the part of members of the Philadelphia Orchestra. The Dell, a natural amphitheater which accommodates 6,000, is also in Fairmount Park, and most of the musicians are members of the Philadelphia Orchestra. Concerts are scheduled for six nights each week during the season. If inclement weather interrupts the schedule, performances are held over until weather permits.

The Philadelphia Grand Opera Company, organized in 1926, affiliated itself two years later with the Curtis Institute of Music, providing graduates of the institute with an opportunity to appear in grand opera. The late William C. Hammer, a trumpeter, was one of the founders ; Artur Rodzinski was its first conductor. No performances have been given by this group in recent years.

The Savoy Opera Company, founded in 1901 by the late Dr. Reginald Allens, presents Gilbert and Sullivan operas exclusively. The group is sponsored by the School of Music of the University of Pennsylvania, and the proceeds of its performances go to the school. The operas are usually given with a cast and chorus of 100 or more.

Philadelphia's keen appreciation of music also reveals itself in the existence of many other groups. The Stringart Quartet, a well-known chamber music ensemble organized in 1933, seeks to advance the more obscure classical music. This group is composed of Leon Lawisza and Arthur Cohn, violinists ; Gabriel Braverman, violist ; and Maurice Stad, violoncellist. The quartet annually presents a number of subscription concerts in Philadelphia and vicinity.

The Strawbridge & Clothier Company Chorus was founded in 1885 by a group of employees. Since 1905 Dr. Herbert J. Tily, who was made president of Strawbridge & Clothier in 1927, has directed the chorus. Dr. Tily has written much of the music sung by the group, including a number of well-known cantatas. The chorus gives an annual concert at Robin Hood Dell, as well as performances in the Strawbridge & Clothier store during the Christmas and Easter seasons.

Victor Herbert, renowned composer of light operas, wrote many numbers especially for this group. Long identified with Philadelphia music, Herbert is best remembered for his annual engagements at Willow Grove Park, just north of the city. These extended over a period of 20 years. His first contact with the Philadelphia public dates back to the time when he gave concerts in Washington Park on the Delaware. He also appeared here in the old days as conductor of the Philadelphia Operatic Society. In 1916, at the request of Dr. Tily, he came to the city and gave at the Metropolitan Opera House a concert which included only his works. Many of his compositions were presented for the first time in Willow Grove Park ; others were started or completed during his stay there.

The Keystone Quartet, whose personnel has remained unchanged since its formation in 1918, is composed of employees of the Pennsylvania Railroad. This group has been heard in all parts of the world, both on the radio and in personal appearances. The quartet has broadcast frequently on short wave transmission to Europe, and in 1930 took part in the first television broadcasting of this kind.

The Orpheus Club of Philadelphia, one of the oldest singing societies in the city, was organized in 1872. Composed of professional and business men, the chorus numbers about 70 voices. Concerts are given three times a year at the Academy of Music. The American Opera Guild, organized in 1935, promotes musical appreciation among American singers of talent and provides training facilities for them. The guild plans to present operas in English, with local singers. Operas will be staged and rehearsed in Philadelphia before the company goes on tour.

Philadelphia is the home of the oldest German singing organization in the United States — the Maennerchor Society, founded in 1835. The Mendelssohn Club, founded in 1874 by Dr. William Wallace Gilchrist, gives a number of special performances each year in conjunction with the Philadelphia Orchestra. The Canzonetta Chorus, organized in 1920, gives two performances yearly in the ballroom of the Bellevue-Stratford Hotel. During the Lenten season it offers a number of concerts in which sacred music is featured. Lit Brothers' department store maintains a chorus of employees, giving annual concerts for charity at the Bellevue-Stratford.

Valuable training in music and drama is also offered by the Settlement Music School, 416 Queen Street, which was founded in 1908 and incorporated in 1914. The present school was erected in 1917 from funds donated by Mrs. Edward W. Bok. Each student is required to pay a reasonable tuition fee, but only a few are able to pay for the full cost of instruction.

Celebrities

TO THE concert artist and musician, Philadelphia offers a life ideally adapted to study. The traditions of the city are inspiring, and Philadelphians are especially sympathetic to the musical student. Many world-renowned artists were born and educated, or have lived here.

240

MUSIC

Josef Hofmann, celebrated pianist and dean of the Curtis Institute of Music, resides in Merion Penna. Born in Poland in 1876, Hofmann at an early age attracted the attention of the composer Rubinstein. When only 10 years old, Hofmann toured the United States and was acclaimed a child prodigy. Today he is recognized as one of the greatest living pianists. Hofmann, now an American citizen, has been associated with the Curtis Institute since its inception in 1924.

Mme. Olga Samaroff, at one time the wife of Leopold Stokowski, was born in San Antonio, Texas, in 1882, and made her American debut as a pianist at Carnegie Hall in 1905, with the New York Symphony Orchestra, under the direction of Walter Damrosch. Since then she has given many concerts either alone or with such artists as Kreisler and Zimbalist, and with the Kreisler Quartet. At present, Madam Samaroff is associated with the Philadelphia Conservatory.

Harl MacDonald, one of the most promising of modern composers, is professor of music in the University of Pennsylvania's Department of Music. Born in Boulder, Colorado, in 1899, MacDonald has composed many symphonies, modern in treatment and often dissonant and barbaric in style and rhythm.

One of the outstanding opera singers of today, Dusolina Giannini, was born in Philadelphia in 1902, of Italian parents. For years her father conducted a small opera house known as Verdi Hall, in South Philadelphia, where she and her sister Euphemia learned to sing the songs of Italy under the tutelage of their parents. Ferruccio Giannini himself had been an opera singer, and he soon recognized the great possibilities in Dusolina's voice. He took his daughter to Mme. Marcella Sembrich, under whom she was trained for an operatic career. She made her debut at Berlin in 1925 in *Aida*, and in 1936 she created a sensation in New York. Later in 1936 she toured Europe, her star gaining brilliance with every appearance.

The baritone, Nelson Eddy, rose to national prominence from the newsroom of a Philadelphia newspaper. In 1933 Eddy sang in *Parsifal* with the Philadelphia Orchestra. Eddy was born in Providence, Rhode Island, in 1901, and came to Philadephia fourteen years later. While working as a newspaper reporter, he studied singing under the late David Bispham, making his first theatrical appearance as a minor character in *The Marriage Tax* in 1922. Success followed on the concert stage, in grand opera, in the motion pictures, and on the radio. Among films in which he has appeared are *Dancing Lady*, *Naughty Marietta, Rose Marie*, and *Maytime.*

David S. Bispham himself was one of the greatest operatic baritones this country ever produced. For years he sang many of the leading baritone roles with the Metropolitan Opera Company, creating a number of notable parts. After his retirement from the operatic stage he devoted himself to vocal teaching, a field in which he also won signal success. Bispham, whose parents were Quakers, was born in Philadelphia January 5, 1857.

Another of the city's noted contemporary singers is Marian Anderson, a Negro, whose success began with her first professional appearance — as contralto soloist with the Philadelphia Philharmonic Symphony Society. A recital in New York followed. Competing against 300 singers, she won the New York Philharmonic contest and later went abroad to begin a series of tours and courses of study. Of the same age as Dusolina Giannini, Miss Anderson is hailed as having one of the rarest contralto voices in modern times.

The music critic who possibly did more than any other man in America to "discover" such musical geniuses as Strindberg and Stravinsky was the Philadelphian, James G. Huneker. Born here January 31, 1860, Huneker studied music in New York and Paris, and then became assistant to Rafael Joseffy, teaching at the then newly founded National Conservatory. Afterwards, becoming a "steeplejack of the seven arts," as he whimsically termed it, he wrote for the New York *Morning Recorder* and *Advertiser*, and then joined the staff of the *Sun* as dramatic critic, art editor, and special writer. Following an extended tour of Europe, Huneker in 1918 became connected with the New York *Times* as music critic. When death ended his brilliant career in 1921, he was with the New York *World*. During a part of this time he traveled weekly to Philadelphia to conduct a column in the Philadelphia *Press*. His published volumes of epigrammatic appreciation of art and letters included *Mezzotints in Modern Music, Melomaniacs, Overtones, Iconoclasts, Book of Dramatics,* and others.

Among other Philadelphians prominent in the music world are Josephine Lucchese, soprano ; Wilbur Evans, baritone ; Henri Scott, basso ; Nicholas Douty, tenor ; Edward Ellsworth Hipsher and Guy Vincent Rice Marriner, directors; Alexander McCurdy, Jr., Russell King Miller, and Norris Lindsay Norden, organists ; Samuel L. Laciar, music critic ; and Dr. James Francis Cooke, composer.

PAINTING AND SCULPTURE

A LTHOUGH Philadelphia's early days were notable for utilitarian rather than artistic achievement, this city long has occupied an enviable position as a shrine of the arts. During the city's early settlement there was neither the money, time, nor inclination for anything but practical accomplishment. Then, gradually, with the growth of trade, there emerged a class with the necessary time and money to indulge in cultural pursuits. Those who appreciated "the true and beautiful" found expression for their appreciation in the collecting of rare treasures and in patronizing painting and sculpture. The more utilitarian crafts such as the making of silverware, pewterware, and furniture also were encouraged.

In the field of furniture-making particularly, Philadelphia achieved real distinction. Its late eighteenth century cabinetmakers evolved an ornate style known as "Philadelphia Chippendale" for the reason that it was derived in part from the engravings published by Thomas Chippendale in his *Cabinet Maker's Directory* of 1754-1755 and 1761. The market provided by a large and increasingly prosperous merchant class, and the unofficial boycott on foreign goods which existed in the American colonies as early as 1761 in protest against the odious import taxes on British wares, combined to place domestic goods at a premium and to develop a pride in fine local workmanship. On the other hand, loss of contact with the center of current taste was evident in a continued vogue of the florid Chippendale style until well after the close of the Revolution, whereas in England the classic Adam style had been launched some years earlier.

The work of four early cabinetmakers, represented at the Pennsylvania Museum of Art — Benjamin Randolph, Jonathan ᐧGostelowe, Thomas Tufft, and Edward James — exemplifies the unique features of early Philadelphia furniture craft.

Such painting as was done, particularly at the beginning of the eighteenth century, was practiced by men who had little if any preliminary training. Spoken of as limners (a corruption of the old English term "illuminer," or decorator of manuscripts), they traveled from town to town with a stock collection of portraits complete except for the faces. It usually required but one sitting to fill in the individual likeness.

243

The Historical Society of Pennsylvania has in its possession what are probably among the earliest paintings done in Philadelphia. They are three portraits (of Robert Morris and of the artist and his wife) by Gustavus Hesselius, who came to Philadelphia from Sweden in 1711. Hesselius, the first organ-builder in the Colonies, executed a number of portraits and designs for churches.

Other early painters included John Meng; William Williams, Benjamin West's first instructor; Matthew Pratt, who worked as West's assistant for a time; and James Claypoole, a miniature painter who also served as Sheriff of Philadelphia for several years. Pierre Eugène du Simitière, artist and naturalist, became one of the curators of the American Philosophical Society; and Joseph Wright, who modeled miniature heads in wax, was appointed by President Washington as first draughtsman and die-sinker in the United States Mint. Among their contemporaries were Henry Bembridge, John Wesley Jarvis (one of the first American artists to study art anatomy), Robert E. Pine, and Jean Pierre Henri-Louis.

The first painter of consequence born on American soil was Philadelphia's celebrated Benjamin West (1738-1820). A Quaker, whose sect tolerated no pictures save family portraits, West spent most of his life in England.

The reasons which took West to London also actuated many other American artists. New York, Boston, and Philadelphia, in West's day, offered little encouragement to any sort of artist other than the itinerant portrait painter. The lack of art museums, of artistic companionship, and of any real interest in the arts drove Americans to seek fame and fortune abroad. London at that time was the hub of the civilized world, with Hogarth, Reynolds, and Gainsborough at the height of their fame. And an abundance of art lovers and patrons contrived to give the town an atmosphere particularly stimulating to aspiring artists.

Ultimately, West acquired an eminent position in London as a painter and teacher. He was favored with the royal patronage, and became a founding member, and later president, of the Royal Academy. He was always ready to assist young American artists, financially as well as didactically. Among his students or protégés were Gilbert Stuart, Copley, Malbone, C. W. Peale, Matthew Pratt, and Thomas Sully.

West's chief claim to interest today probably lies in his canvas, *The Death of* (General) *Wolfe*, in which the figures are clad in clothes of the period, instead of the classical robes with which painters at the time commonly arrayed their historical subjects.

Of the famous Peale family, which includes several painters, Charles Willson Peale (1741-1827) is probably most outstanding. His studies of Revolutionary patriots are on permanent exhibition at the

Pennsylvania Academy of the Fine Arts, which he helped to found. His son Rembrandt (1778-1860) at the age of 17 executed a portrait of Washington, from whom he obtained three sittings. Another son, Raphael (1774-1825) devoted his energies principally to still-life subjects. Still another, Titian (1800-1885), occupied himself with the delineation of animal life. He executed most of the plates in the first and fourth volumes of Charles Lucien Bonaparte's *American Ornithology*. James Peale, brother of Charles, is known for his many miniatures and portraits in oil. He served during the Revolution as an officer in the Continental line.

Patriotism and painting marched hand in hand during the Revolution, when the artist packed his palette and brushes in his camp baggage and started off to war. One of Charles Willson Peale's best known portraits of Washington was painted when the artist was a captain with the general. The canvas was begun at Valley Forge, continued at New Brunswick a day or two after the battle of Monmouth, and finished later in Philadelphia.

Because portrait painting was at the height of its popularity in England during the eighteenth century, American painters, whose viewpoints were derived from the mother country, likewise devoted themselves to this branch of art. After the Revolution, a number of artists from various parts of the world were attracted to the young republic. All were eager to attempt likenesses of George Washington, who perhaps served as the subject of more paintings, etchings, and lithographs than any other man of his time. A ship docking at the port of Philadelphia from Canton, China, during this period, brought paintings of Washington done on glass by an eminent Chinese artist.

The most distinguished delineator of President Washington was Gilbert Stuart (1755-1828), who is credited with 124 studies of his subject and who probably worked on about 1,000 different canvases. A colleague of West's, and a student of anatomy under Dr. William C. Cruikshank, Stuart never acquired the power of handling large canvases with the fluency and grace of Reynolds and Gainsborough; but within the compass of a single portrait he was distinctly successful.

Stuart, who was born in Rhode Island, set up a studio in Philadelphia late in 1794, soon after his return to America from a long period of study abroad. His sojourn in this city is memorable by reason of the brilliant series of women's portraits he completed here, and for the three famous studies of Washington done during the latter's old age — all executed either in Philadelphia or in nearby Germantown. For the first, a bust portrait identified as the Vaughan Type, Washington sat during the winter of 1795. The second, a life size standing portrait known as the Lansdowne Type, was completed in the spring of 1796.

A short time later, Stuart moved his studio to Germantown, where in the autumn of 1796 Washington sat for the now familiar "Athenaeum Head," which is unfinished as to the stock and coat, but is a highly idealized representation of the first President's features during his declining years. Stuart took the painting with him to Boston when he moved there in the summer of 1805. He died in Boston 23 years later.

Stuart's color is still alive and fresh. His portraits reveal a feeling for form, as expressed in the modulation of values, and a notable capacity for character analysis. It is probable that he will always rank among America's finest portrait painters.

The era of the new republic also produced William Birch, miniature painter and engraver, who is known for the development of a red-brown enamel which he used as background in his miniatures ; Bass Otis, the first American lithographer, whose work was prophetic of the multitude of colored pictures which were to come tumbling from the presses of Currier & Ives ; and James Sharples, painter of the French-influenced pastels w :ich hang in Independence Hall. Some time during the years between 1801 and 1807, the city also served as host to Edward Green Malbone, as skilled a painter of miniatures as Stuart was of portraits.

William Birch's son, Thomas (1779-1851), also achieved distinction as an engraver, producing jointly with his father the much-prized *Views of Philadelphia*. His most important work, however, was done in landscapes and marine subjects.

Washington Crossing the Delaware, the study of Lafayette in Independence Hall, and a full-length portrait of Queen Victoria which the artist was commissioned to paint for the Sons of St. George of Philadelphia, are among the most important works of Thomas Sully (1783-1872). Born in England, Sully came to America at the age of nine and in 1808 settled in Philadelphia, where he remained for the rest of his life. His painting technique was largely self-taught, although he was undoubtedly influenced by Stuart and Lawrence. He was a prolific portraitist; and was onetime president of the Pennsylvania Academy of the Fine Arts, which possesses today a number of fine specimens of his work.

Among the minor painters of post-Revolutionary Philadelphia were John Neagle, whose series of American theatrical portraits now line the walls of the Players Club in New York City ; Robert Fulton, known as the designer of the first successful steamboat ; Benjamin Trott, the miniature painter ; Samuel Jennings, whose canvas, *The Genius of America*, hangs in the main room of the Free Library ; John Joseph Holland, landscape and scene painter ; John James Barralett, engraver, and John Lewis Krimmel, whose work anticipated the Düsseldorf School. Adolph Ulric Wertmuller, a Swedish painter who settled in Philadelphia in 1794, is celebrated chiefly for his canvas *Danae*, which he was forbidden to exhibit publicly because it was a nude. Private exhibitions of the painting, however, netted the artist a handsome income.

Philadelphia was the birthplace of the pioneer American sculptor, William Rush (1756-1833). A wood carver by profession, Rush developed great skill in designing figureheads for ships. His *River God* for the ship *Ganges* is said to have been revered by the Hindus who came in boatloads to see it. The Pennsylvania Academy, which he helped to establish, possesses an interesting memento of Rush in the plaster cast made from the original portrait of himself which he carved in a pine knot.

Had time permitted, Rush would doubtless have attempted marble instead of confining his efforts to wood and clay. However, he was rather indifferent to the material used. Of more significance, he insisted, was the artist's ability to visualize the figure in the block. Removal of the surface he regarded as merely mechanical; often when time was lacking he would hire a wood chopper and stand by giving directions where to cut. Rush had ideas in abundance, a sense of grace, and much facility.

Another early Philadelphia marine painter was James Hamilton. Like his predecessor, Thomas Birch, Hamilton also painted landscapes that are much prized today.

With the interest in the mezzotint stimulated by the work of John Sartain, who became associated with *Graham's Magazine* in 1841, the use of illustrations grew in vogue as a distinctive feature of American periodicals. Other engravers of this early period were Cephas Grier Childs, Daniel Claypoole Johnson (the "American Cruikshank"), James Barton Longacre, and William Mason. Felix Darley's pen and ink sketches were in the manner of the best English illustrations of the time.

Painting in Philadelphia continued to reflect Continental tendencies. The assault on the stilted classicism of West and David, which led to French Romanticism and indirectly stimulated the rise of the anecdotal schools of Düsseldorf and Munich, deluged the United States with an avalanche of story-telling pictures soaked in German sentimentality. This type of painting, exploited by a number of Philadelphia artists whose names are now forgotten, was enormously popular, for it was intelligible even to those who knew little about art. During this period, an extraordinarily rapid increase in the fortunes of persons of little culture led to the foundation of many private collections by ambitious owners for whom the anecdotal picture held greatest appeal.

247

Another Continental movement, the landscape painting school of Corot and Turner, helped shape one of the first native developments in American art. Applying the style of their European masters, American landscape painters turned to the scenic loveliness of America for their subject matter.

Foremost among the city's scenic painters of this period were William Trost Richards (1833-1905) noted for his marine paintings; and the Moran brothers, Thomas, Edward, and Peter. A member of the Pennsylvania Academy, Thomas Moran was the first important artist to paint scenes of what are now our national parks, such as the Yellowstone.

Outstanding for their historical paintings were Emmanuel Leutze, a native of Germany, who spent many years in Philadelphia, and who executed the well-known painting, *Washington Crossing the Delaware*; Peter F. Rothermel, painter of the colossal *Battle of Gettysburg*; and James R. Lambdin, known for his portraits of the Civil War period.

With the renascence of Romanticism, France became increasingly dominant in shaping the artistic ideals of Europe, and, in turn, of the United States. Particularly profound in their influence on American painters, because of their preoccupation with outdoor phenomena, was that group of independents known as the Impressionists. Their movement gave impetus to a trend among American artists which was apparent from the second half of the nineteenth century — the great trek to Paris.

The realistic approach began with Courbet, but with increasing insistence made itself felt in art toward the end of the last century; it is manifested in the straightforward works of Thomas Eakins (1844-1916). Although he was in the vanguard of the American movement to Paris, where he studied under Bonnat and Gérôme, Eakins returned to America to paint the subjects of his native land in a style peculiarly his own. Possibly because he had grown up amid the prevailing red brick row houses of Philadelphia and its tree-shaded streets, in a period when houses and clothes were sombre and oil or gas afforded a meager illumination, Eakins painted his canvasses in colors that were dark and warm. Moreover, most of the paintings he had seen in his youth had been in that tradition, and when he went abroad impressionism had barely begun.

Indeed, not only impressionism but most of the leading tendencies of French art passed him by completely — the cult of the exotic and the Oriental, the return to the primitive, the increasing subjectivism, the decorative bent, the trend toward abstraction, the restless search for new forms and colors. Unlike many of his contemporaries who either became expatriates or drew a veil of pretty sentiment over America's crudities, Eakins, while revolting against its puritanism,

248

accepted his environment with the same robust affirmation as did Walt Whitman.

Eakins' influence would be difficult to trace. His work had few elements to make it popular ; it called for too fundamental a knowledge to attract imitators. However, he exercised an unmistakable power over his students at the Pennsylvania Academy, from which his expulsion, because of prudish objections to his insistence on reality in the life class, provoked a student parade of protest on Chestnut Street.

Eakins' early pre-occupation with science — his chief interest next to painting — was demonstrated again and again in his work. He encouraged a study of anatomy before drawing the human figure, and emphasized that space and form relationships should be determined by perspective. Even his color was rationalized. To learn the fundamentals of the human figure, Eakins studied at Jefferson Medical College, and probably knew more about the structure of the body than any other artist of his time. His medical studies inspired the sensational *Gross Clinic* hanging in Jefferson College ; also, the *Agnew Clinic* at the University of Pennsylvania, which when first exhibited aroused a storm of protest and indignation.

There is evidence that Eakins' name will also be remembered for his success with the camera. Like Eadweard Muybridge, he experimented with motion ; but where Muybridge studied movements from different positions at the same time, Eakins concentrated on progressive action seen from one position. In 1884 he conducted experiments at the University of Pennsylvania demonstrating the muscular action of horses and athletes. His viewpoint was that of the motion picture ; and his lecture, using the zoetrope, at the academy in 1885, was possibly the first exhibition in the United States of motion pictures taken from a single angle.

Mary Cassatt (1845-1926), among the most distinguished Americans to follow the leadership of Degas, Manet, Cézanne, Monet, Renoir, Morisot, and Pissarro, spent most of her life in France. Born in Pittsburgh, the daughter of a well-to-do banker, she was taken to Paris at the age of five. Upon returning to the United States five years later, the family settled in Philadelphia, where Mary studied at the Academy of the Fine Arts. In 1868 she went to Europe, where she found study more profitable in the galleries than in the academies. So captivated was she by Correggio that she remained in Parma eight months. She admired the discriminating firmness of Holbein, the insistent purity of Ingres, she copied Parmigiano ; her own color prints benefited by her response to the compositional novelties of the Japanese wood-block printers that took Paris by storm in the early seventies.

However, the work of Degas had the greatest influence on her. His manner can be traced throughout all her work. Regarded primarily as a painter of mother and child subjects, Mary Cassatt was actually an artist of considerable versatility. The color etchings which supplement her paintings testify to the scope of her inventiveness.

Daniel Ridgway Knight, a Philadelphia painter who won international distinction with his large and typical French Salon picture exhibited at the Philadelphia Centennial in 1876, likewise passed the greater part of his life abroad. The Philadelphians, Earl Stetson Crawford and Elisha Kent Wetherill, whose work shows a decided Whistler influence, were also Paris-trained.

Like other artists of the period, the Negro painter, Henry Ossawa Tanner (1859-1937) spent much of his life in Europe. Coming to Philadelphia from Pittsburgh in 1870, he later studied under Thomas Eakins at the Academy of the Fine Arts. His Biblical paintings attracted attention immediately, and the late John Wanamaker purchased several, one of which, *Christ Learning to Read*, hangs in the Philadelphia store. Two of his paintings were purchased by the French Government and hung in the world-famed Luxembourg Galleries in Paris. Others of his works hang in the Metropolitan Museum in New York *(Destruction of Sodom and Gomorrah)*; Memorial Hall in Fairmount Park *(The Madonna Annunciation)* ; the Carnegie Institute ; the Wilstach collection ; the Chicago Art Institute ; the Los Angeles Art Gallery ; and many other places. About 1899 Tanner left Philadelphia for Paris where he accomplished much of the work which achieved for him universal fame as a painter of Biblical scenes.

Cecilia Beaux, one of the academy's most successful students, painted chiefly in France. Characterized by forthright brushwork and feeling for audacious design, her canvases suggest a kinship with Sargent's. Her work has a masculine power and vigor, without any suggestion of stylistic imitation or technical affectation.

The sculptors for whom nineteenth century Philadelphia is noteworthy similarly made their pilgrimage to Paris. Howard Roberts, whose first important work, *La Première Pose*, was shown at the Centennial Exhibition, pioneered in promoting the ideals of the modern French school in this country. The American Indian was first utilized as a sculptural subject by John J. Boyle, a native of New York, who is represented by *The Stone Age* in Fairmount Park ; he also modeled the heroic-size statue of Franklin which stands alongside the old post-office building on Chestnut Street near Ninth. Joseph A. Bailly, a native of Paris who opened a violin studio in Philadelphia at the age of 25, is known for his figure of Washington and for other works.

Alexander Milne Calder is best known for his gigantic bronze of William Penn atop City Hall. His son, Alexander Stirling Calder, has executed some of the Parkway's most important sculpture. A statue of Dr. Samuel Gross, now in Washington, D. C., and the six heroic figures adorning the Witherspoon Building at Juniper and Walnut Streets are among his outstanding studies.

Edmund Austin Stewardson was a sculptor of great promise whose career was terminated by his death at 32. He lived to complete only one work, *The Bather*, but this is accounted a fine specimen of American art. The highly acclaimed *Fountain of Man* was produced by the academy's long-time teacher, Charles Grafly, also esteemed for his portrait busts and bronze groups. The Meade Memorial in Washington, D. C., *The Symbol of Life, Pioneer Mother*, and *In Much Wisdom* are among his most important works.

The turn of the century ushered into prominence such artists as Edwin Austin Abbey, Violet Oakley, Maxfield Parrish, Joseph Pennell, Howard Pyle and George Walter Dawson.

Abbey, who spent the last years of his life doing murals for the State Capitol at Harrisburg, attracted international attention in 1882 through his illustrations for Goldsmith's *She Stoops to Conquer.* Violet Oakley, who began her professional career with illustrations for books and magazines, is noted for her murals and for her portraits and designs for stained glass. Maxfield Parrish, whose work is a familiar decoration in countless homes, is noted for his delicacy of line combined with individuality of color effects. Pennell and Pyle were writers as well as illustrators. The former achieved distinction as etcher and lithographer, the latter for his drawings of American Colonial life. Dawson has attracted much attention by his landscape and botanical water colors.

With the onset of the movements ushered in by the New York Armory show of independent artists in 1913, several factors combined to decrease Philadelphia's importance as an art center. The academy, which had driven out Eakins and which had earlier set aside separate visiting days for ladies when the nude statues on view were swathed from head to foot in all-concealing draperies, refused to recognize post-impressionism except in pained surprise. The institution accordingly came to be looked upon with more and more impatience.

On the other hand, the work which this institution, the Pennsylvania Academy of Fine Arts, has accomplished is by no means to be underestimated. Not only has it performed well its task of teaching art students the technical essentials of their craft — those things which can be taught ; but it has also furthered artistic endeavor by giving European scholarships, and is, moreover, the home of a number of valuable painting and print collections, such as the Henry C. Gibson and Edward H. Coates collections.

For more than 40 years Hugh Breckenridge (1870-1937) exerted tremendous influence upon the pupils who studied under him at this

Rodin's "The Kiss"
"The warm breath of life in cold marble"

252

institution. Some of the most widely recognized artists of modern American art studied under this instructor, who was one of the first American artists to introduce the methods of the modern French school. Included in the list of artists who have been trained at the academy are such reputable figures as Robert Henri, George Luks, John Sloan, and Edward W. Redfield. Redfield's landscapes and snow scenes are found in important collections throughout the country.

However, with the rise of New York City as an art market, the more enterprising inhabitants of Philadelphia's Bohemia deserted Camac Street and moved on to Greenwich Village. Other painters forsook Philadelphia to develop the landscape possibilities of New Hope, Pennsylvania, and of Arden, Delaware.

A number of Philadelphia painters and sculptors, however, have continued to work in an older tradition, and have found the placid cultural atmosphere of the city congenial. Daniel Garber teaches at the Academy of the Fine Arts, and paints decorative canvases of the scenes around New Hope ; largely American trained, he owes much, however, to the French Impressionists. Albert Rosenthal, painter and etcher, who studied under his father Max Rosenthal, noted lithographer, has made copies of historic portraits for the city's collection in Independence Hall and for the Historical Society of Pennsylvania.

Some of the country's most distinguished men have sat for portraits by Lazar Raditz, Robert Susan, and Cesare Ricciardi, whose work is well represented at the Graphic Sketch Club. Robert W. Vonnoh, Birge Harrison, his brother Thomas Alexander Harrison, W. Elmer Schofield, Maurice Molarsky, and the late Adolphe Borie are others whose works are included in important collections. Birge Harrison and Schofield in particular have won considerable reputation as landscapists. Like Redfield, both have exhibited widely, and are holders of numerous distinguished prize awards.

Philadelphia's sculptors, generally, have carried on well. The modern athlete not unnaturally has inspired much of the work of Dr. R. Tait McKenzie, who in addition to being a sculptor is research professor of physical education at the University of Pennsylvania. Two of his compositions are on the University campus : a heroic statue of the youthful Franklin, and a figure, likewise heroic in size, of Rev. George Whitefield. Among his other works are the Dr. White Memorial, in Rittenhouse Square, which has been praised for the strength and originality of its composition ; and the *Alma Mater* figure at Girard College.

Albert Laessle and Samuel Murray have also distinguished themselves in sculpture. Laessle, who teaches at the Academy of the Fine Arts, executed the Pennypacker Memorial. His *Billy* in Rittenhouse Square and his *Penguins* in Fairmount Park are examples of his humor and skill in the treatment of animal subjects.

253

Murray is represented by statues of Commodore Barry and Joseph Leidy on the Parkway. *The Prophets*, over the entrance to the Witherspoon Building, is another of his creations.

In connection with sculpture, the presence in the city of the Rodin Museum is evidence of Philadelphia's artistic consciousness and taste. It is one of the few great Rodin Museums in the world, the original being in Paris. On the Parkway and in Fairmount Park are such works as the equestrian statue of Washington by Rudolph Siemering, Fremiet's *Jeanne d'Arc*, Frederic Remington's *Cowboy*, *The Pilgrim* by Augustus Saint-Gaudens, *Duck Girl* by Paul Manship, and sculptures by Daniel Chester French, Einar Jonsson, Charles Grafly, Beatrice Fenton, and others. In addition, there are the Paul Bartlett statues of Robert Morris and McClellan; Karl Bitter's statue of Dr. William Pepper; and, in Rittenhouse Square, a copy of what is possibly Barye's best work, *The Lion and the Serpent*.

New tendencies and interests current in American art are reflected locally in Julius Bloch's proletarian themes, Benton Spruance's scenes of the city, Earl Horter's etchings, Franklin C. Watkins' striking canvases, and the sculptures of Boris Blai and Wallace Kelly.

Outstanding artists in their respective fields are Nicola D'Ascenzo, noted for his stained glass work and murals, and Samuel Yellin, master metal craftsman. Yellin received the Bok Award in 1925 for his distinguished work in decorative iron.

Straws in the wind seem to indicate that a more vigorous art atmosphere is emerging in Philadelphia. A small but flourishing group of art clubs is fostering local talent by affording to members facilities for exhibition. Opportunity is being given students to observe the fresh currents in contemporary art through exhibits staged by several enterprising modern galleries.

It is significant that Philadelphia's great museum on the Parkway is supplementing its rich historical treasures, such as the Elkins and the John G. Johnson collections, with frequently varied shows which present a cross section of the latest modes in painting and sculpture. The Pennsylvania Museum of Art, as this institution is now known, was founded in 1876. It has a total collection of nearly 60,000 paintings, sculptures and art objects. Operated in connection with the museum is the School of Industrial Art, occupying a spacious location at Broad and Pine Streets. And at Merion, just outside of Philadelphia, is the Albert Barnes private collection of modern paintings, the finest in the country, in connection with which courses of art instruction are regularly given.

Memorial Hall in Fairmount Park houses the extensive Wilstach collection of paintings, which contains fine specimens of the various schools and periods. Independence Hall, the Historical Society of

PAINTING AND SCULPTURE

Pennsylvania, and the Union League contain valuable collections of portraits by early American masters.

In the field of art instruction Philadelphia has the long-established school of the Pennsylvania Academy of the Fine Arts ; the Moore Institute of Art, Science, and Industry ; the School of Fine Arts at the University of Pennsylvania; and the Stella Elkins Tyler School of Fine Arts at Temple University. The Graphic Sketch Club's evening classes, under the patronage of Samuel Fleisher, provide free competent training in art for those who are employed during the day, and afford an outlet for the creative energy of numerous others to whom art is only an avocation. The interesting recent development, the Cultural Olympics, organized for school children in Philadelphia and suburbs, seeks to center upon the arts something of the enthusiasm that is bestowed upon athletics.

Artists who find difficulty in disposing of their works may now have recourse to the annual spring "Clothes Line Show" in Rittenhouse Square, where paintings, drawings, etchings, and water colors are strung between the trees, while attending painters in their bright-hued smocks provide a touch of Parisian atmosphere. This unusual exhibit, held in May, is attended by many visitors, the prices paid for pictures ranging from $1 to $15.

Perhaps the most vital recent agency in developing popular esthetic appreciation has been the WPA Federal Art Project in Philadelphia. In utilizing the ability of unemployed painters and sculptors to produce mural and easel paintings for schools, recreation centers, and other public buildings, the WPA has provided sustenance, preserved morale, and conserved valuable skill. Hardly less significant, it has also encouraged a lively curiosity concerning the fine arts among thousand to whom this field has hitherto meant little or nothing.

Mosaic in lobby of Curtis Publishing Company Building
"The Dream Garden"—after Maxfield Parrish

255

ARCHITECTURE

FOUR towers tell the story of Philadelphia. As architecturally different from one another as the ages which fashioned them, they and their contemporary structures indicate the local physical conditions, the economic and cultural progress of their time, and the changes in the art and science of building design. The first tower, that of the State House or Independence Hall, almost an exact restoration of the original tower which was built in 1750, is of brick with a wooden belfry. Fashioned after the Georgian style of England but adapted to the needs of the early Colony, it reflects the city's early growth and its part in the struggle for independence. The tower of the old Merchants' or Stock Exchange Building, completed in 1834, a stone lantern in the style of a Greek temple, tells of the days of the new Republic. The third tower, that of City Hall, 1894, of massive masonry, solid and tall, portrays the city's growth to a metropolis of world importance. The Philadelphia Saving Fund Society building, completed in 1932, is a tower of steel, concrete, chromium and glass — modern materials for a modern age. It tells of today — an age of search, of challenge, of the testing of new ideas.

Independence Hall was erected embodying architectural features contributed by Andrew Hamilton, a famous lawyer and holder of various offices in the Province. Dominated by its handsome bell tower, a masterpiece of Colonial architecture and craftsmanship, it is a symbol of early Philadelphia. Unlike the situation in other early American Colonies, the settlers of Philadelphia did not experience a great struggle against hardships. Relations with the Indians were amicable, and commerce flourished. True, some of the colonists spent the first winter in caves on the banks of the Delaware River, but as clay was locally abundant and brick had been favored for city residences in the homeland, houses were built of brick almost from the beginning. It is to this material that Independence Hall owes much of its charm.

From the earliest days, men of means, including many personal friends of William Penn, as well as skilled workers and craftsmen, came here to live. Capital of one of the last of the major Colonies to be settled, Philadelphia grew rapidly, soon taking its place as a leading city of the New World, both in wealth and culture. This late start is amply expressed in its architecture. Whereas the buildings of the older Colonies reflected an early English Renaissance style — some of it going back to the Tudor period — the State House tower and most of Philadelphia's building designs were inspired by the later Georgian style.

However, early Philadelphia felt architectural influences other than the English Georgian. There still remain a few structures having their roots in the early Swedish settlement of the mid-seventeenth century. These, the relics of a colony settled in lower Philadelphia before the coming of William Penn, are Bellaire, or the Singley house; the Cannonball, or Bleakly house; and the Schetzline, or Swedish Glebe house. Old Swedes' Church, or Gloria Dei, built about 1700 on Swanson Street south of Christian Street, has only a slight Swedish flavor, evident in the rake of its eaves and the simplicity of its tower. The chief contribution of the Swedes to Philadelphia's architecture was log construction. It was natural that they should build of logs, as their native country used this type of construction extensively, whereas England, with limited forests, used wood sparingly. The Dutch supremacy on the lower Delaware, which superseded that of the Swedes, was but short-lived, and today there is no remaining architectural evidence of their influence, unless we accept the Dutch stoep and double door.

Just as the influence of the Swedes upon the life of the colony was overshadowed by that of the English, so were Swedish architectural influences soon eclipsed by the Georgian. While the State House tower is indicative of the important part England played in the shaping of the early colony, the Georgian style of architecture was adapted to suit local conditions. Its design, however, is rooted in the Italian Renaissance of the fifteenth and sixteenth centuries, the superb Palladian window in the tower being traceable to the Renaissance buildings of Palladio in Vicenza. The Renaissance style, spreading over Europe like a slow wave, reached England about two centuries later, where its highest development was called Georgian. England altered the Italian Renaissance style to suit its needs, and it is the Georgian style modified in the Thirteen Colonies which popularly is called Colonial architecture. Stone, much in favor in England, was here generally supplanted by brick, with white-painted wood, soapstone, and marble for decorative trim, especially for buildings within the city.

Colonials who gazed upon Philadelphia from the belfry of the State House beheld a neat, compact, and orderly scene. The city, stretching north and south along the Delaware and westward for about a mile, presented a pattern of red brick pierced by the white spires and cupolas of Christ Church, Old Swedes' Church, St. Peter's Church, and the Pennsylvania Hospital.

Nearby a diagonal highway extended toward Germantown. Here

Francis Daniel Pastorius and his German colonists had built their homes, structures which retain Germanic traits such as the Germantown hood or pent roof, which extended from the face of the dwelling to protect the first story from sun and rain.

Along the streets of Philadelphia, surrounded by gardens and fine shade trees, were neat shops and dwellings, of red brick with white trim, often of wood painted white. The street pattern designed by William Penn consisted of large rectangular blocks cut through by alleys. Only a small section of the Penn plan had been developed. The heart of the "towne" extended from the busy port on the Delaware but a short distance along High Street, now called Market Street. Here stood Philadelphia's quaint first buildings, mostly of brick, but occasionally frame, stone or log construction.

At Second Street, in the center of High stood the Town Hall, of brick and wood, with small dormer windows in the steep roof. Just in front was a small prison. Behind were the market stalls. In those early days when William Penn, James Logan, Edward Shippen and, soon after, young Benjamin Franklin, frequented the neighborhood, there stood here all the important buildings. Besides the Town Hall, there were the old London Coffee House, at Front and Market Streets; the Masters' Mansion, built in 1704, also at Front and Market Streets; the Friends' Meeting House, at Second and Market Streets; and the Royal Standard Tavern close by. Such was the picture of Philadelphia as a new merchant town.

The State House was started in 1731 and first occupied in October 1735. Its fine tower was built in 1750 ; the bell, now known as the Liberty Bell, hung in 1753 ; and the upper part rebuilt by William Strickland in 1828. Built of bricks of clay from the nearby riverbanks, wood from Penn's forests, and marble from nearby quarries, the structure portrays the spirit of the days during which the idea of independence was growing. The State House has changed only in name. Today, Independence Hall and its tower still reflect the dignity, wealth, and cultural life of the early community.

Several local factors influenced Philadelphia's early building. The abundance of forests and the arrival of competent carpenters with the first group of settlers made for elegant wood craftsmanship with its fine detail. The severity of Quakerism, with its abhorrence of frivolous embellishments, was an influence for simplicity and vigor. Even the homes of the well-to-do showed a fine sense of fitness and restraint. As the American historians Charles and Mary Beard point out:

> There were riches in Colonial America, but few fortunes were great enough to allow that lavish display which separates the arts from the business of working and living. For such reasons as these the noblest examples of Colonial architecture revealed the power of re-

258

straint and simple beauty, commanding the admiration of succeeding generations and attracting servile copyists long after the conditions which nourished the models had passed away forever.

The towers of the Colonial public buildings and churches, such as Independence Hall and Christ Church (built between 1727-47 ; Dr. John Kearsley, architect), are successful adaptations in brick and wood of their predecessors — the stone towers of Sir Christopher Wren, James Gibbs and Nicholas Hawksmoore in England. The more severe economic conditions in the Colonies made advisable a reduced scale in their buildings and a strengthening of the horizontal lines. The broad lines of the Morris house, at 225 South Eighth Street, erected in 1786 by John Reynolds, and the north facade of the State House are outstanding examples.

Modern Philadelphia contains fine examples of Georgian Colonial architecture other than those in the shadow of the Independence Hall tower. Germantown, Frankford, and Kingsessing, originally separate towns, are sections of present-day Philadelphia, where fine early domestic architecture may be seen. The Stenton and Chew houses are notable examples. Following the English custom of wealthy men having country homes, Philadelphia's men of means built mansions along the beautiful Schuylkill River. Of these, Mount Pleasant, Lemon Hill, Woodford, Woodlands, Solitude, and others are still standing. The houses were erected as completed structures, and the resultant shape was simple and rather boxlike. Even the poorer country homes in and near Philadelphia were built in this form. Indeed, when an owner prospered and made additions to his house, each unit retained the boxlike pattern, and the final result was a succession of increasingly larger but similar sections. The Livezey house in upper Wissahickon Valley is an excellent illustration.

Mount Pleasant, one of the most pretentious country homes of the period, was begun in 1761 by John MacPherson, a sea captain from Scotland, who amassed a fortune in the practice of privateering. He lived in manorial splendor, entertaining the most eminent personages of the day with munificent hospitality. The central feature of a group of surrounding, dependent buildings, Mount Pleasant is situated in Fairmount Park, on the east bank of the Schuylkill River, a slight distance north of the Girard Avenue Bridge. The exterior of this two-and-a-half-story Georgian mansion is of massive rubblestone masonry covered with reddish buff rough-cast plaster, above a high foundation of hewn stone. The principal feature of the river facade is a slightly projecting central portion with quoined corners, corniced pediment above the Palladian window of the second story, and a superb pedimented doorway in harmony with the pedimented motive above. The interior wood finish is very fine ; gracefully tooled cornices, and pilasters, and heavy pedimented door-

259

Independence Hall

Old Stock Exchange

Vivid Living Symbols of the Changing Eras Which Gave Them Being

City Hall

Philadelphia Saving Fund Society Building

heads are of excellent design. Two small outbuildings, and two barns complete the group, making the house the central feature of a picturesque group of buildings possessing the manorial effect of the old Virginia mansions along the James River.

Pennsylvania, so named because of its abundance of forests, containing principally pine, oak, hickory, and chestnut trees, built its rural structures of stone and brick, whereas New England, having large areas strewn with stone left behind by the great glaciers, built almost exclusively of white pine. The reasons for these apparently inconsistent courses were twofold. The glacial deposits of the north were mostly a granitelike stone too difficult to be handled easily. Furthermore, lime for cement was very scarce in the New England Colonies. White pine was not only plentiful, but it weathered well and was readily adaptable to building purposes.

In Pennsylvania, particularly near Philadelphia, there was, and still is, an abundance of excellent field stone — a gneiss-mica schist, usually very durable. This stone weathers well, is easy to cut, and although predominantly gray, has a variety of hues. It is quarried along a line running, roughly, northeast from Media to Trenton. The Philadelphia area is plentifully supplied with lime. There was also a local supply of fairly good light gray marble which was used for trim. Besides the abundance of lime and building stone, the stone tradition for the better-class English home was strong with the early colonists.

If the quaint old houses of Elfreth's Alley — the eastern end of Cherry Street — may serve as a criterion, the workers' dwellings, while smaller and less pretentious, were very much like the city homes of the well-to-do. For both rich and poor, fireplaces served as the only means of providing heat; outside pumps supplied water. In these modest dwellings, but two rooms deep, every room received ample daylight and ventilation — an advantage to which modern housing projects are now returning. It was well into the nineteenth century before speculative builders began their rows of long narrow houses whose gloomy inner rooms were poorly served by narrow courts or skylights.

A discussion of Colonial architecture must include mention of the Carpenters' Company and historic Carpenters' Hall, its headquarters. Begun 20 years after the State House tower, but not completed until 1792, its design is somewhat more sophisticated. It was in 1724, however, less than a half century after the coming of William Penn, that the master carpenters of Philadelphia formed the Carpenters' Company, a guild or society somewhat like the Worshipful Company of Carpenters in London. The Philadelphia company, extant today, is important for the influence it exerted upon fine architecture and workmanship — not in Philadelphia alone but throughout the Colonies. James Porteus, an early member, established the nucleus for a valuable builders' library. Professional architects did not exist in Philadelphia in those days; gentlemen architects — men whose cultural attainments included some knowledge of architecture — collaborated with the master builders in designing their structures.

Robert Smith (1722-1777), Philadelphia's foremost builder-architect of Colonial times, was born in Scotland and came to this city at an early age. His first recorded projects were Nassau Hall and the president's house at Princeton University. In Philadelphia, his St. Peter's Church, completed in 1761, still stands little changed except for the addition of the spire. It is noted for its fenestration and the beauty of its interior appointments. Smith submitted designs for Carpenters' Hall and later headed its building committee. About 1771 he made extensive repairs on the spire of old Christ Church. Old Pine Street Presbyterian Church, now virtually rebuilt, and Old Zion Lutheran Church were designed by him, as was the Walnut Street Prison. (The original Zion Lutheran Church and Walnut Street Prison are no longer standing.)

The Colonial Georgian style continued for a period after the Revolution, when the forces that engendered this style had ceased to exert their influence. Many fine dwellings, such as the Sellers-Hoffman house in West Philadelphia; the Upsala, Loudoun, and Wister houses in Germantown; and the Morris and Wharton houses in central Philadelphia were built soon after the Revolutionary War, evidencing the prosperity of that period.

Another example of post-Revolutionary Georgian architecture is the group of buildings at Fort Mifflin, projected by the British shortly before the Revolution. These buildings rank with Independence Hall and the Pennsylvania Hospital in interest and charm of grouping. The fort, at the southwestern extremity of Philadelphia, just above Hog Island, was laid out in 1771 by Capt. John Montressor, an engineer. Work was finally started in 1773 but proceeded slowly. Unfinished at the outbreak of the Revolutionary War. it was hastily completed in 1777 by the Committee of Safety. In 1793 Maj. Pierre Charles L'Enfant, who later laid out the city of Washington, planned the fine buildings within its moat and walls and the repairs on the fort. Progress was slow, but in 1798 the fortifications were finally rebuilt in stone under the direction of the French military engineer, Col. Louis de Toussard, along the plans prepared by L'Enfant. In 1904 the fort was dismantled and allowed to fall into decay, but in 1915 it was declared a national monument, and finally, in 1930, it was restored according to the original plans of L'Enfant.

During the early nineteenth century the Georgian Colonial style gradually declined. But even while the cannon of the Revolution were resounding around Philadelphia, the seeds of a new architectural style were being sown. The new nation, strongly in sympathy with the Greek War for Independence, 1821-29, developed a strong interest in the civilization of ancient Greece. Many towns were given Greek names, and Greek structures sprang up all over the country. As Howard Major, in *The Domestic Architecture of the Early American Republic ; The Greek Revival,* says:

> After the separation from England, America naturally turned more to the Continent than heretofore and particularly to the ancient republics of Greece and Rome for inspiration in architecture as in government, and so became the inheritor of their free institutions and traditions and more eagerly assimilated the results of archaeological research.

The so-called Greek Revival was a spontaneous return to Classic influence throughout the Western World. The subsequent widespread interest in classicism had its greatest influence in America. Thomas Jefferson, leader of the new democracy and a "gentleman architect" of no small ability, was a dominant influence in the development of the Classic Revival, although his designs were of Roman rather than Greek inspiration. He confined his efforts largely to his native State of Virginia ; the buildings for the University of Virginia, the State Capitol at Richmond, and his home, "Monticello," offer ample evidence of his skill.

The Greek Revival did not assert itself until after 1800 and did not cease its manifestations until just before the Civil War. The old Merchants' or Stock Exchange Building, as it is now known, at Third and Walnut Streets, crowned by the second of the four towers — a circular templelike superstructure of six columns—is symbolic of this period — the era of national emergence. The semicircular facade of the building itself, with its tall, fluted Corinthian columns, is truly imposing. (William Strickland was the designer.) Today, unfortunately, market sheds crowd its base. The opening of this building was a great event, and at the time of its dedication in 1834 parties were given continuously for a week.

Unlike the red brick of Colonial Independence Hall, the old Stock Exchange is constructed of marble. Marble and stone were thought more appropriate for the new monumental structures. However, brick continued in use for houses, with marble porches and details of classic design. Houses, churches, and public buildings of this age took on the form, or at least the details, of Greek temples. Four, six, or eight columns, usually Doric or Ionic, formed the portico; these, topped with an entablature and wide pediment, composed the usual Greek Revival facade. In one respect, the Greek architecture of the early Republic is not so divorced from that of the Georgian period: both styles are classic, but the Revival goes directly back to Greece for inspiration.

Often the exterior result was remarkably fine, as in Thomas U.

264

Walter's Girard College (1833-1848) with its huge, peripteral Corinthian colonnade; the old Custom House (1819-1824), designed by Latrobe and completed by Strickland, with its heavy north and south facades in the Greek Doric style; and the First Bank of the United States (1797), designed by Samuel Blodget, the oldest bank building in America and said to have the first marble facade in this country. Numerous churches with typical colonnaded facades, such as that of the First Presbyterian Church (1820), John Haviland, architect, were erected. Indeed, Philadelphia has many of the oldest public and ecclesiastical buildings of Greek design in the country.

In domestic architecture, it was to country living that this style most readily lent itself. In Philadelphia the Greek influence on houses was superficial, being confined mostly to exterior details of marble and interior details of wood. With the rapid growth of the city, the row house came into favor, the better rows having such names as Carlton, Franklin, Washington, and Rittenhouse. On the south side of Spruce Street, between Ninth and Tenth Streets, is a row of red brick dwellings, each two having a common marble portico of three Greek Ionic columns. No. 715 Spruce Street, built about 1820, has an entrance in the style of the Greek Revival period, and the Philadelphia Contributionship, at 214 South Fourth Street, offers another interesting example — domestic in spirit but built for commercial purposes.

An interesting characteristic of the Greek Revival period is the change in construction of pitched roofs. Whereas in Colonial times the roof overhung the end walls to form the eaves, later the walls rose higher than the roof to form a parapet, the chimneys being built as part of the wall. This feature may be seen in the old Custom House, old Wills Eye Hospital (1832), the Aquarium (1815), and in other public buildings and dwellings.

Hundreds of commercial buildings supplanted the Colonial structures in the neighborhood of the Stock Exchange. These simple business structures, usually three, four, or five stories high, were characterized by sturdy, square, classic piers of stone on the first floor, with the upper stories of traditional plain red brick and little or no adornment. An exception is the 138 South Front Street structure, the Egyptian design of the first story being due to the influence of Thomas U. Walter's design for the debtors' gaol, now a part of Moyamensing Prison. During this period Nicholas Biddle was waging an unsuccessful fight with Andrew Jackson for the survival of his Second United States Bank. Stephen Girard was sending ships from the nearby docks to the world's corners. The city was a hive of industry and commerce. These many similar structures, esthetically unassuming, befitted the commercially expanding Philadelphia.

The Stock Exchange tower marks the period in which America

began developing its own architects — professionally trained men. The important architects of the Greek Revival and the years immediately thereafter were Benjamin Henry Latrobe, William Strickland, Robert Mills, John Haviland, and Thomas U. Walter. Of the work of Latrobe and Mills, little remains in Philadelphia. Latrobe, born in England in 1764, arrived in Philadelphia in 1798. Soon after his arrival, he designed the Bank of Pennsylvania, which stood on Second Street just above Walnut. This building, inspired by the Temple of the Muses near the Ilissus, outside Athens, is considered, generally, the first structure of Greek design in America. Another important work of Latrobe during his six years in Philadelphia was the domed Waterworks Building (1799-1801) on the present site of City Hall. One of the architects of the Capitol at Washington and designer of the Baltimore cathedral, Latrobe was also an engineer.

Latrobe is credited with introducing the Gothic style to America, a tendency that asserted itself some years later and then degenerated in the Victorian era. His Bank of Philadelphia, executed under the supervision of his pupil, Robert Mills, in 1807, was a Gothic structure of brick and marble. It stood on the southwest corner of Fourth and Chestnut Streets, with a wide, high entrance arch on Fourth Street.

The previously mentioned Custom House, on Chestnut Street between Fourth and Fifth Streets, built for the Bank of the United States and so used until 1844, while generally accredited to Strickland, was designed by Latrobe. Although Strickland supervised the construction of this building, Latrobe prepared the plans. He and Mills were among the competitors who submitted designs, which had to conform to the Government's requirements. Mills submitted a design fronted by six Greek Doric columns; Latrobe went further and proposed an imitation of the octastyle front of the Parthenon. His plan seemed to meet with the approval of the directors, but due to financial difficulties at the time, work was delayed. In the meantime, Latrobe left for New Orleans, and the undertaking was resumed under the direction of Strickland. Although the principal room is a departure from Latrobe's plan, the rest of the design follows his original drawings. Latrobe died in New Orleans in 1820 while supervising the construction there of the waterworks.

While Latrobe lived in Philadelphia he had as his pupils Strickland and Mills. Mills (1781-1855), a native of Charleston, S. C., designed the connecting wings of the State House group in Philadelphia in 1813. He was appointed architect of public buildings in Washington in 1836, supervised the erection of several major buildings, and was the architect for the Washington Monuments in Washington and Baltimore.

William Strickland (1787-1854), born in Philadelphia, recognized as a leading architect, was also an engineer, landscape painter, author, and engraver. His first building, the Gothic Masonic Hall — the "Pride of Philadelphia" — dedicated in 1811, showed a lack of understanding of Gothic as a system of construction. This structure was outstanding as an example of the Gothic Revival which, while less extensive, was virtually contemporaneous with the Classic period. In 1819 the building was destroyed by fire. An interesting print, a copy of which may be seen at the Philadelphia Library Company, on Locust Street west of Thirteenth, shows the structure in flames. The temple had only a veneer of Gothic details: crenelation, small turrets, and lancet windows. The high and square wooden tower, with its cornices and spire, was more Georgian than Gothic. There is still standing on the road between Reading and Pottsville a quaint little red and white church that presents an excellent example of this naïve fusing of the Colonial and Gothic modes. Another example less far afield is St. Mary's Church (erected 1763, enlarged 1810, remodeled 1886), on South Fourth Street in Philadelphia.

Strickland's many works included the first Custom House (1818), situated on Second Street below Dock, a simple, three-story brick and marble building (now demolished); the United States Mint (1833), also demolished; Merchants' or Stock Exchange Building; United States Naval Asylum (1827-1848); Arch Street Theatre (1822), demolished in 1936; Blockley Almshouse (1834); and several churches. In 1828 he undertook major restorations of the State House. His final and most important work was outside Philadelphia — the Tennessee State House at Nashville, where he lies buried. Its tower, or lantern, is similar to that of the old Philadelphia Stock Exchange.

John Haviland, born in England in 1792, is noted chiefly for his prisons — in Philadelphia, the Eastern State Penitentiary (1829). His first important work, however, was the First Presbyterian Church (1820), on South Washington Square, designed in the Greek manner. He was also the architect responsible for the design of the old Franklin Institute, erected in 1826 on Seventh Street south of Market, and the much altered Walnut Street Theatre (1809), northeast corner of Walnut and Ninth Streets. Upon his death in 1852, he was buried in a crypt in St. George's Greek Catholic Church (1822), on Eighth Street above Spruce, also his design.

Thomas Ustick Walter (1804-1887), a native of Philadelphia, received his early knowledge of building from his father, mason contractor under Strickland for Latrobe's Bank of the United States. The son studied architecture at the Franklin Institute under Strickland, with whom he was employed for about two years. His major work — one of the noblest examples of the Greek Revival — is his Girard College building, begun in 1833, which utilizes the Corinthian order. Others are Moyamensing Prison (1831), old Wills Eye Hospital (1832), Preston Retreat (1837), and the Nicholas Biddle mansion,

267

in Andalusia, Bucks County, erected in 1794 and remodeled by Walter in 1835. As United States Architect succeeding Robert Mills, he designed the present dome and the extension of the wings of the Capitol at Washington. He was professor of architecture at Franklin Institute and later a lecturer at Columbia University. Walter prepared many of the detail designs for the present City Hall and until his death worked on them as assistant to John McArthur, the architect of City Hall.

Toward the end of the 1830's there was a general lull in building, and by 1850 a reaction had set in from the chaste influence of the Greek Revival. As the Civil War approached, the Greek flame had entirely burned out, and from this point on taste in architecture declined considerably.

Influencing factors in the third architectural period were national in scope. The country was rapidly expanding, frontiers were being pushed forward, and commerce and industry had developed to the point where huge fortunes were being made. This was the age of industrial expansion — an age which wrought havoc with the arts. Its architectural manifestations extend roughly from the end of the Greek Revival period to about the close of the nineteenth century.

The architectural profession was not equipped to express the problem of an expanding commerce, nor were the industrial captains particularly concerned with esthetic values. The spirit of the age was not one to evolve a fine architectural expression. It may well be said that the low estate to which building design fell was entirely in keeping with architecture's function of expressing the spirit of the age. As in other cities, land and building speculators added to the confusion of the rapidly growing metropolis. The lust for wealth and the resultant neglect of human values brought squalid, unsanitary living conditions for those who toiled. Rows of drab dwellings sprang up. With the development of machinery there came a rush of "jig-saw" embellishments completely lacking in taste and restraint. Buildings that pretended to architectural ostentation aped the current fashions of Europe.

The somber picture of Philadelphia's architectural "Dark Age" has, however, a few bright spots. The middle of the century saw the development of interest in the Gothic. A spirit of romanticism, already evident in England, which was exhibiting a renewed interest in Gothic architecture, assumed here various forms, some of which were admirable, others very poor. Two fine churches of this period still exist in Philadelphia : the Church of St. James the Less (1846), at Falls of Schuylkill, a fine reproduction of St. Michael's Church, at Long Staunton, England — a small thirteenth century English village church — and St. Mark's Church (1847) on Locust Street west of Sixteenth, both by John Notman, St. Clement's Church (1859) at

268

Chew House, Germantown

"Where the Continentals l o s t their lives, and Major Andre his heart"

Doorway of Mt. Pleasant (Mt. Pleasant Mansion)

"A traitor's wedding gift"

Twentieth and Cherry Streets, likewise by Notman (1810-1865), and the Academy of Music (1857), Broad and Locust Streets, designed by Napoleon LeBrun, are also among the better structures erected during this period.

LeBrun (1821-1901), of the firm of LeBrun & Runge, was a pupil of Thomas U. Walter. He designed, in addition to the Academy of Music, such Philadelphia churches as the Cathedral of SS. Peter and Paul (1846), on Eighteenth Street north of the Parkway, and St. Augustine's Church (1847), Fourth Street below Vine.

For the Centennial Exhibition of 1876, Memorial Hall, of Renaissance design; nearby Horticultural Hall, built of glass and steel with Moorish embellishments; and many Victorian buildings were erected. These presented an assortment of building styles, exhibiting the diversified eclecticism of the age.

The Victorian era introduced buildings of brown and green stone, square turreted, with mansard roofs of slate. Their vertical lines contrast sharply with the horizontal lines of Colonial times. The mansard roof, actually a top story with slightly sloping walls, was introduced from France. This was a period of high ceilings, tall, narrow windows, and poor taste in detail. Structures of this type include the Union League building (1865), College Hall (1871) of the University of Pennsylvania, and the many gaunt, turreted mansions in and around the city. Dark woodwork, overcarved and overstuffed furniture, long, gilt mirrors, and gloomy hangings gave to the interiors of the homes an effect at once opulent and dismal.

The French Renaissance style, notable for its many columns and profuse ornamentation, was used in Philadelphia construction for several large buildings. City Hall (1871-1901); the old Post Office building (1873-1884), on Ninth Street from Chestnut to Market; and the Victory Building (1873), Tenth and Chestnut Streets, are examples of this style.

Buildings combining designs of many periods were erected, with startling results. They were usually of heavy masonry, although the red brick tradition of Philadelphia continued to assert itself. Besides the heavy Victorian Gothic and the French Renaissance, there were Romanesque interpretations and suggestions of Moorish mosques and Venetian palaces, garnished with a profusion of ornate details of cast iron and wood. Frequently, buildings expressed no style or function whatsoever, or else they exhibited a strange mixture of several styles. Broad Street Theatre (1876), of Moorish effect, and the many buildings of the old banking district, particularly Chestnut Street between Third and Fourth Streets (a museum of architectural oddities) are typical. The extravagant buildings designed by Furness & Evans are highly individualistic structures touched with Gothic. Broad Street Station (1880-1894), the Academy of the Fine Arts

(1876), and the library of the University of Pennsylvania (1891) are their better known works.

Considered one of the great architects of his age, Henry Hobson Richardson (1838-1886) designed truly fine buildings in the Romanesque style. While none of his structures were erected in Philadelphia, his followers built here the Central High School (1902), on Broad Street at Green; the Market Square Presbyterian Church (1886), in Germantown; and other structures. None of these is comparable, however, to the work of Richardson.

City Hall tower, completed in 1894, marks the close of the city's third architectural period — an era fraught with national conflicts and marked by rapid industrial development. Rising 547 feet, it was at the time of its completion the tallest tower in the country with the exception of the Washington Monument (Washington, D. C.), which is about eight feet taller.

It is surmounted by a huge, bronze statue of William Penn contemplating from on high the cold gray of his once quaint and charming red brick "towne." The tower itself is an epitaph to the age of masonry. Even while it was being erected, advances in the technique of steel and concrete construction were pointing the way to a new architecture.

The modern period of American architecture dates historically from the Columbian Exposition at Chicago in 1893. The great "White City," as the fair was called, gave impetus to a revival of the broad, classic facade and to "grand" concepts of planning. Louis Sullivan's individualistic Transportation Building, however, was the rebel of the fair. It pointed away from classic eclecticism toward a fresh interpretation of design. Two schools of architecture received impetus from the Chicago fair : the traditionalists, who adapt to present-day needs the designs of an older civilization, and the modernists, who seek a new expression for the materials and techniques of today.

Rising above the central city skyline, the Philadelphia Saving Fund Society building — its huge, neon letters "PSFS" visible for miles around—casts its shadow over the classic Wanamaker Store. Last of the four towers which express the city's architectural ages, it is truly a challenge to Philadelphia's traditionalism. Designed by Howe & Lescaze and completed in 1932, it is one of America's outstanding examples of the so-called International style — a style whose exterior architecture frankly expresses its construction and use. As an intellectual concept it represents the courage of the modern age.

Another example of functional architecture is the Carl Mackley housing group in Frankford (1934), designed for the Philadelphia hosiery workers by Kastner & Stonorov and William Pope Barney. The four long units, planned as a complete residential community, are extremely simple in detail. The steel and glass foundries of the

Philadelphia Navy Yard are still further examples of functional design.

Nationally known architects other than Philadelphians have erected buildings here. Foremost among those of the traditional school was the New York firm of McKim, Mead & White. In Philadelphia, this firm designed the bank and office building of the Girard Trust Company (1908) and the clubhouse of the Germantown Cricket Club (1891). These and the John Wanamaker Store (1910), designed by Daniel H. Burnham, of Chicago, architect of the Union Station in Washington, are representative of the best buildings erected in Philadelphia at the turn of the century.

The Provident Mutual Life Insurance Company building (1928), by Cram & Ferguson, of Boston, and the new Pennsylvania Station (1933), by Burnham's successors — Graham, Anderson, Probst & White — follow in this tradition. The Parkway, with its fountains and monumental edifices, most notable of which is the Pennsylvania Art Museum (started in 1918 and officially opened in March 1928), by Philadelphia's Zantzinger & Borie and Horace Trumbauer, is a direct outgrowth of the broad planning of the Chicago World's Fair.

Today there is a tendency in buildings of classic inspiration toward simplification of details, particularly in the elimination of heavy, overhanging cornices which, as in the case of the Manufacturers Club (1914), at Broad and Walnut Streets, tend to cut off daylight from the too narrow streets. The Federal Reserve building (1935), designed by Paul Philippe Cret ; the Central Penn National Bank (1928), at Fifteenth and Sansom Streets, by Davis, Dunlap & Barney ; Girard College Chapel (1933) by Thomas & Martin ; and the new Post Office (1935), by the firms of Rankin & Kellog, and Tilden, Register & Pepper, are fine classic structures notable for their exterior simplicity.

Among the city's finest modern buildings, but following neither the "imperial" design nor the functional style of the Philadelphia Saving Fund Society building, are the University of Pennsylvania dormitories (1895) of English Jacobean architecture by Cope & Stewardson ; the Museum of the University of Pennsylvania, started in 1896 — a beautiful, low, broad building in the Romanesque style of San Stefano at Bologna — designed by Charles Z. Klauder, Stewardson & Page, and Wilson Eyre & McIlvaine ; the Church of St. Andrew (1936), a Gothic design by Zantzinger, Borie & Medary ; the Church of the Holy Child (1930), in Romanesque design, by George I. Lovatt ; and Rodeph Shalom Synagogue (1928), of Moorish architecture, designed by Simon & Simon.

Lewis Mumford, referring in his *Sticks and Stones* to America's grand classic facades, says:

> Our imperial architecture is an architecture of compensation; it provides grandiloquent stones for people who have been deprived of

272

bread and sunlight and all that keeps man from becoming vile. Behind the monumental faces of our metropolises trudges a landless proletariat, doomed to the servile routine of the factory system.

This statement is in accord with architecture's reflection of contemporary society and is applicable to Philadelphia. We still live in an age where the extremes of wealth and poverty are reflected in grandiose architecture on the one hand and slums on the other.

The blighted areas of Philadelphia, the worst of which extend north and south of the central city zone and west from the Delaware River, consist mainly of small, overcrowded, and insanitary "bandbox" houses, many on the verge of collapse. Indeed, several dwellings have fallen down in recent years, indicating the acuteness of the hous-

Home of Robert Morris
"Whose strong box financed the Revolution"

ing problem in Philadelphia. The worst conditions exist in the sections where the Negro population of the city is housed. The thousands of depressing rows of attached houses for which Philadelphia is notorious are largely the work of unenlightened land subdividers and speculative builders. Built in long, narrow plots, only the front and back rooms receive ample daylight and ventilation, the middle rooms being served by air shafts or skylights. While the Carl Mackley Houses and other projects erected by the Public Works Administration point the way to what can be done, the housing solution awaits local initiative.

It has been said that "The most beautiful part of Philadelphia is outside of Philadelphia." The city's suburbs have a charm of architecture that is mellowed by tradition. While the forces of the Greek Revival, Middle, and Modern periods have left their imprint upon suburban structures, as upon those of the metropolis, the strain of early simplicity and charm has never been broken. There are several factors which account for the existence of an indigenous architecture in the Philadelphia area : strength of tradition ; the abundance of excellent local field stone which is used for homes, churches, public buildings, barns, and mills ; the fact that early buildings were so firmly constructed as to continue to assert themselves through the succeeding generations, and possibly the fact that the men of wealth who own the great estates around Philadelphia have a true appreciation of the fitness of the early stone houses for country living.

The low lines of these homes, suggesting comfort, utility, and durability, combine with the local material of which they are built to portray graciousness of living. Contrasts of gray stone and white-painted wood, of fine touches of detail against simple surfaces, the use of whitewash over stone, and the accent of horizontal lines are the major characteristics of the suburban house, both large and small. Simple doorways, low roofs from which rows of small dormer windows and heavy stone chimneys project, fine interior paneling, low fireplaces, and beautiful stairways are of refined and traditional taste, indicating a deeply rooted conservatism.

At almost any point where the main pikes leading toward Philadelphia dip to cross the many creeks, the simply built stone houses of the worker, and sometimes the mills of former days may be seen. The interesting little town of Glen Riddle, in Delaware County three miles southwest of Media, still retains the atmosphere and charm of an early mill village.

There are other interesting old towns in the four counties surrounding Philadelphia which have preserved much of their atmosphere : King of Prussia, near Valley Forge ; Newtown, Buckingham Valley, Spring Valley, and Doylestown, in the rich farm country of Bucks County ; and West Chester, with its old, red brick dwellings.

274

Swimming Pool at the Carl Mackley House

Carl Mackley House
"Labor's answer to the Housing Problem"

Founder's Hall, Girard College
Dedicated to the education of Philadelphia orphans

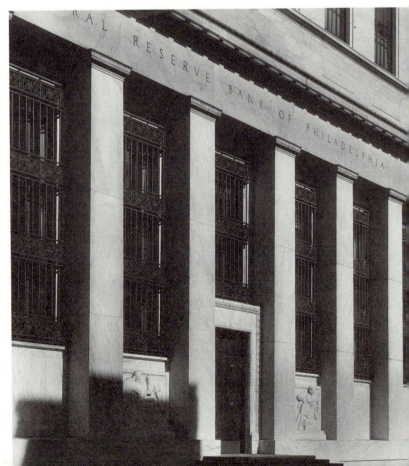

Federal Reserve
Bank Building

ARCHITECTURE

Among the fine old structures are many stone barns and houses, particularly in Bucks County and the Whitemarsh Valley ; Washington's Headquarters at Valley Forge (1742-1752) ; the charming old Pennsylvania German church at Trappe (1743) ; St. David's Episcopal Church (1715) at Radnor, influenced by an earlier architecture than the Georgian ; and the Town Hall at Chester, built in 1724 and restored in 1920. Notable in the period of the Greek Revival is the Biddle home, "Andalusia," built in 1794 and rebuilt in 1835, in Bucks County, and the Wetherill house, "Locust Grove," near Protectory Station, built by James Vaux in 1776 and rebuilt in 1845 by Dr. William Wetherill.

In the present period suburban Philadelphia has witnessed the erection of many fine structures for Swarthmore, Bryn Mawr, Haverford, and other nearby colleges. Fine churches, too, have been constructed. Outstanding among these is the imposing two-towered Church of the New Jerusalem at Bryn Athyn ; the older Gothic section was designed by Cram & Ferguson and completed in 1919, and the later, but still incompleted, Romanesque additions are Raymond Pitcairn's work. Others are Bryn Mawr Presbyterian Churh (1928), by Walter T. Karcher and Livingston Smith ; the Gothic Valley Forge Chapel (1903-1932), by Zantzinger, Borie & Medary ; and Brazer, Frohman & Robb's classic First Presbyterian Church (1921) at Chester. The new Delaware County Courthouse (1932), the work of Clarence Brazer, is a classic marble structure.

As the architectural profession matured, organizations were formed to broaden its influence. In 1869 the Philadelphia Chapter of the American Institute of Architects was founded, and the T Square Club in 1883. Both of these institutions have been a major cultural force in the architectural development of the city. In 1890 under Theophilus P. Chandler the University of Pennsylvania organized a department of architecture. It is now one of the leading architectural schools in America.

A picture of architecture in Philadelphia would be incomplete without mention of the influence of Paul Philippe Cret. Born (1876) and educated in France, he came to Philadelphia in 1903 to teach at the University of Pennsylvania. His knowledge of design and his ability to convey his ideas to his students brought to Pennsylvania its reputation as one of the foremost schools of architecture in the country. He collaborated with Jacques Greber of Paris on the design of the Philadelphia Parkway and helped to plan the city's parks and to design numerous bridges and buildings. The architecture of the Philadelphia-Camden bridge (1926), Ralph Modjeski, engineer, was designed by Cret. In 1931 he received the "Philadelphia Award." Favoring although not confining himself to classic interpretations, he has brought freshness of design to defy the critics of classicism, as

277

seen in his Rodin Museum and Federal Reserve Bank in Philadelphia and his many other important structures in this country and abroad.

Philadelphia is a vast and spreading city from whose central skyscraper region extend areas of drab homes and factories, interspersed with the spires of the many hundreds of churches. Numerous green parks and tree-shaded streets lend softness to this harsh pattern. Fairmount Park, covering 3,845 acres, is the largest park within any American municipality. The city's two rivers and several creeks are spanned by scores of fine bridges, and beyond the periphery of the city are the beautiful suburban homes of traditional Colonial stone architecture for which this region is justly noted. This is Philadelphia today.

In buildings of poor as well as of good design are traced the phases of Philadelphia's life : the peaceful colony under Quaker dominance; the proud new Nation whose finest city was Philadelphia ; the age of expansion ; and the present period — all have left their imprint upon the city's face. That much of the city is ugly cannot be denied. No architect is to be exonerated for erecting monstrosities, but society itself must bear the blame for an era of ugly edifices. The best of Philadelphia's structures were erected in its youth ; the present shows signs — indeed definite proof — of an awakening.

OLD PLANS AND NEW

PHILADELPHIA is one of the few large cities of the world that was systematically planned before it was born. Today its central section retains the geometrical arrangement of straight streets laid out by Thomas Holme in 1682.

Holme, who had served in Cromwell's army, later became a Quaker and was chosen by Penn as his surveyor-general. He arrived in the Province four months before the founder. On the site selected by Penn's commissioners early in 1682, Holme immediately began to lay out the town on broad and adequate lines, guided by the plan Penn had submitted to him. After clearing enough land for his purpose, he divided it into rectangular blocks extending west from the Delaware River and north from Cedar (now South) Street to Valley Street (now Vine).

The plan fixed Cedar Street as the southern and Valley Street as the northern boundary of the town; High Street (now Market) ran from river to river, with Broad Street bisecting it. Now between Thirteenth and Fifteenth Streets, Broad Street originally was situated more nearly at Twelfth Street, having been relocated in 1733. Penn named most of the east-west thoroughfares after trees — Pine, Locust, Walnut, Chestnut, and Sassafras; most of the north-south streets were numbered.

At several points in the plan — on lower High Street, on Second Street south of Pine and at other points as new streets were laid out as the city grew — the roadways were widened to provide space for open market places. The market at Second and Pine Streets, with its quaint "headhouse," still stands. Wide and winding Dock Creek, flowing from Third Street into the Delaware River, and breaking the rectangular regularity of the town, was spanned in early days by a drawbridge. Later the creek bed was filled in, and Dock Creek became Dock Street.

The Penn plan is probably based upon that of ancient Babylon, with its system of rectangular blocks. From the outset the characteristics of a great city were apparent. The two main streets, intersecting each other at the town's heart, formed a gigantic cross that divided Philadelphia into four quarters. Where the two streets came together, a 10-acre plot was reserved for Center Square, also relocated in 1733 and now the site of City Hall. Here, from 1799 to 1829, stood the old Philadelphia Water Works, surrounded by a fine park, with its

279

interesting pump house designed in the Greek Revival style by Henry Latrobe. (A painting of it by John Kremmell, as it appeared in 1812, is in the Academy of Fine Arts.) Old wooden pipes from this water system have been unearthed in the course of excavation work for the Philadelphia subway system.

Four parks, of about eight acres each, were included in the plan, one in the center of each quarter of the city. These are Franklin Square, at the approach to the Delaware River Bridge ; Washington Square and Rittenhouse Square, the latter relandscaped in 1913 by Paul Philippe Cret ; and beautiful Logan Circle, on the Parkway. As a precaution against such a conflagration as had almost destroyed London in 1666, Penn's plan also provided for large city blocks, so that houses, although built in even rows, would have ample space at the back and sides.

Bordering the northern edge of Penn's new city were large tracts of land known as the "Liberties." These areas were reserved for the use of the people who settled in Philadelphia. Surrounding Philadelphia and the "Liberties" were the grants of land sold to individuals and to land companies, such as the large estates along the Schuylkill River and the grants of Germantown, Passyunk, Blockley, Kingsessing, and Frankford. The grants sold to companies developed into communities. These and other neighboring towns, such as Southwark and Moyamensing, numbering 24 altogether, were gradually incorporated into Philadelphia until the city's boundaries became coterminous with those of Philadelphia County.

These former towns still maintain in some degree their original identity, even though the gridiron system of intersecting streets has been extended like a huge network over virtually the entire city. In the light of present planning knowledge, it would have been well to preserve these early communities by maintaining parks or "green belts" between them, thereby breaking up the monotony of Philadelphia's pattern and providing parks and open spaces accessible to all.

Several such dividing parks do exist. Cobbs Creek Park, along the western boundary of Philadelphia, and Tacony and Pennypack Parks, in the northeastern part of the city, are each several miles long. Fairmount Park divides West Philadelphia from North Philadelphia and Germantown, and the Wissahickon separates Roxborough from Germantown.

Philadelphia planning owes much to the far-sighted Stephen Girard, whose will, dated February 16, 1830, set aside $500,000 for the following purposes :

    1. To lay out, regulate, curb, light and pave a passage or street, on the east part of the city of Philadelphia, fronting the river Delaware, not less than twenty-one feet wide, and to be called Delaware Avenue,

extending from South or Cedar Street, all along the east part of Water Street squares, and the west side of the logs, which form the heads of the docks or thereabouts . . . to completely clean and keep clean all the docks within the limits of the city, fronting on the Delaware: — and to pull down all platforms carried out from the east part of the city over the river Delaware on piles or pillars.

2. To pull down and remove all wooden buildings . . . that are erected within the limits of the city of Philadelphia — and also to prohibit the erection of any such buildings within the said city's limits at any future time.

3. To regulate, widen, pave and curb Water Street, and to distribute the Schuylkill water [system] therein.

A further provision of $300,000 to the Commonwealth of Pennsylvania "for the purposes of internal improvement by canal navigation," to become effective only after the passage of legislation enabling the city of Philadelphia to proceed with the Delaware River front improvements, is evidence of Girard's shrewdness. Penn's plan provided for a grand boulevard along the Delaware River, but it was not until Girard's will set aside a fund for developing Delaware Avenue that this plan began to take shape.

As Philadelphia grew beyond the limits of Penn's plan, diagonal roads such as Gray's Ferry Road, Moyamensing, Woodland, Baltimore, Lancaster, Ridge, and Germantown Avenues, Roosevelt Boulevard and, finally, the Parkway, were included within the system of rectangles. These are the main highways leading from the city, and, since they converge toward the center of Philadelphia, they provide ready ingress and egress. They do, however, make for ever-increasing congestion as they approach the central city. The recently completed ring road or bypass, as it is popularly called, connecting these highways at the points where they pass out of Philadelphia, has eased this congestion.

The Parkway serves not only as one of the most important highways leading into the heart of the town, but also as a magnificent setting for many of the city's monumental buildings. The Fairmount Park Art Association commissioned Paul P. Cret, Horace Trumbauer, and C. C. Zantzinger to prepare its plan. Some years later Jacques Greber of Paris enlarged upon this plan, and its realization was effected by Mayor John E. Reyburn.

The Parkway starts at City Hall and continues to the Art Museum on the hill above the Schuylkill, where once stood the reservoir for Philadelphia. About midway is Logan Circle. Since little control has been exercised over the shapes and sizes of buildings along the Parkway, there is little harmony of style in the structures that line it.

Location of the buildings, likewise, has become indiscriminate. Franklin Institute, the Board of Education's administrative building,

281

and the comparatively small Boy Scout building stand in a row which runs off at a tangent to the Parkway. Across the Parkway and parallel to it is the beautiful Rodin Museum. Skyscrapers crowding its southeastern extremity destroy the effectiveness of the boulevard's majestic sweep. While the Parkway does expedite the flow of traffic, it also creates three-street intersections — an unfortunate circumstance caused by superimposing a diagonal street upon a system of rectangles.

Although convenient for the center of the city, except that most of the streets are now too narrow, the prevailing gridiron pattern has not been entirely satisfactory for the outlying sections. Continuous straight streets are not only monotonous ; they are needlessly wasteful, expensive, and dangerous. City planners agree that the concentration of the main flow of traffic in a few very wide streets would be better.

The blocks which Holme laid out would be somewhat too large for present-day use. They have been divided by narrow streets and byways which, in the more congested parts of the town, have for the most part become noisy and dirty service alleys. Some, however, have developed into quaint and beautiful little thoroughfares. Among these are the quiet tree-lined Clinton Street between Ninth and Eleventh Streets ; sections of Delancey, Panama, and Camac Streets ; Elfreth's Alley and other small streets near the city's center. In North, South, and West Philadelphia these smaller thoroughfares serve merely as an added convenience to the real estate subdividers, who have given to the city its long, monotonous rows of houses.

City planning is more than the laying out of streets. The relation of industrial to residential areas ; the location of public buildings, bridges, and tunnels ; the proper design of parks and recreational areas ; the flow of traffic by road, rail, air, and water ; housing and the migration of population — all these are phases of city planning. The Philadelphia City Planning Commission is engaged in studying these problems, giving to the city much valuable guidance and advice.

Among the improvements contemplated are removal of the "Chinese Wall" of the Pennsylvania Railroad along Market Street from Fifteenth Street to the Schuylkill River ; beautification of the Schuylkill below the Fairmount dam, with broad drives along both shores ; continuation of the Locust Street subway through southwest Philadelphia ; removal of the Market Street Elevated railway, a tunnel having already been constructed beneath the Schuylkill River and as far west as Thirty-second Street; construction of a subway to serve Germantown, and extension of the South Broad Street subway. An alternate plan for extension of Philadelphia's high-speed railway system provides for connections with the suburban systems of the Pennsylvania, the Reading, and the Baltimore & Ohio Railroads.

A "ring" subway connecting South, West, North Philadelphia and the Northeast, cutting across existing and proposed lines might be suggested. This would relieve congestion at the center of the city, where all high-speed lines now converge. It would give better access to the University of Pennsylvania, to the University and Commercial Museums, Convention Hall, the Arena, and to points in Fairmount Park.

Another contemplated improvement is the eventual elimination of slums, especially those south of Pine Street and east of Broad. Plans made by the Tri-State Regional Planning Board, covering sections of Pennsylvania, Delaware, and New Jersey, have also been of value in planning for the future. The Philadelphia Housing Association, a research body founded in 1909, submits valuable findings which point the way to better housing conditions.

While the Parkway, Fairmount Park, and many outlying sections of Philadelphia are truly beautiful, and many of the central streets are very fine, little can be done about the present cramped condition of the street system. The expense involved in making radical changes would be prohibitive. In a few cases, as at City Hall Annex and the Commercial Trust Company building at Fifteenth and Market Streets, sidewalk arcades have permitted the widening of streets.

The lower Schuylkill River and the city's 20 miles of Delaware River frontage are a disgrace. The two rivers, once beautiful streams but now little more than open sewers, can be cleaned up. Slums can be cleared, better housing can be provided as cheaply or even more cheaply than at present, and factories and "nuisance buildings" can be zoned out of residential neighborhoods. Possibilities for improvement of the city are almost illimitable. It can be made a safer and more healthful city, so that commerce may be widely benefited and the citizens themselves may enjoy more beauty and comfort.

SCIENCE

The Pioneers

THE building of homes in the virgin wilderness occupied much of the attention of American colonists until the beginning of the eighteenth century. Then a few individuals turned to more intellectual pursuits — to problems of science and philosophy. As early as 1690 William Rittenhouse (1644-1708), great-grandfather of the illustrious David Rittenhouse, built America's first paper mill on the banks of the Wissahickon, near Germantown, and within a few score of years such figures as James Logan, David Rittenhouse, John Bartram, and Benjamin Franklin were to achieve distinction in various branches of science ; they were to help establish Philadelphia as one of the chief centers of learning and culture in the American Colonies.

Although James Logan was noted as a man of public affairs, serving as Governor of the Province of Pennsylvania for nearly two years, he was also the first American investigator of physiological botany. Born in Ireland in 1674, Logan became a member of the Society of Friends, and in 1699 in the capacity of secretary he accompanied William Penn to America. A man of broad culture, his translation of Cicero's *De Senectute* was published by Benjamin Franklin in 1744. The results of his botanical studies were made public at Leyden, Germany, in an essay entitled *Experimenta et Melitemato de Plantarum Generatione* (1739). This essay, which dealt with the fructification of Indian corn, constituted a valuable contribution to the science of botany.

More prominent in the annals of botany is the name of John Bartram. Although he followed Kelpius in the science, Bartram is generally considered the first great American botanist. That his fame overshadows that of his contemporaries, may be due to the fact that he left a lasting memorial to his name in Bartram's Gardens in West Philadelphia.

Bartram's people came from England in 1682 and thus were identified with the early settlement of Philadelphia. He himself was born in 1699 on a homestead in Chester County, and from boyhood manifested a keen interest in botany and tree surgery. In September

284

1728 he purchased a small tract of land on the west side of the Schuylkill River, on the road to Darby, where he built a stone house and laid out his gardens.

In the autumn of each year he traveled widely throughout North America, carrying on research and field work in the wilderness, and bringing back enormous collections of rare and valuable plants. Some he kept for his own gardens, others he gave to his friends.

Upon his death, in 1777, his work was taken over by his son, William, who had inherited many of his father's tastes.

Preeminent among American pioneers in astronomy was David Rittenhouse (1732-96). Setting up as a clockmaker in Norristown, young Rittenhouse diligently studied the sciences, with particular attention to astronomy. He discovered independently the method of fluxions or the rate of conduction of energy by radiation ; and in his ignorance of what Leibnitz and Newton had done in this field, he believed himself to be the original discoverer. In 1763 he was appointed to determine the position of the Pennsylvania-Maryland border. This task, arduous and involving numerous intricate calculations, was performed mainly with instruments made by Rittenhouse ; and later his findings were accepted substantially by Mason and Dixon. His construction of an orrery and his brilliant part in the observation of the transit of Venus, in 1769, greatly enhanced his reputation at home and abroad. The observations were important, in that they supplied a basis for computing the earth's distance from the sun. He observed the transit of Mercury in the same year. Many other contributions to astronomy followed.

Rittenhouse was prominent also as a man of public affairs, serving as a member of the General Assembly and of the first State Constitutional Convention in 1776. He was the first State Treasurer (1777-89), first director of the United States Mint (1792-5), and professor of astronomy at the University of Pennsylvania (1779-82). He became secretary of the American Philosophical Society in 1771, a vice-president of that body in 1786, and on January 7, 1791, was elected its president, continuing in that capacity through consecutive re-elections until his death. He contributed many papers to the American Philosophical Society on astronomy, optics, magnetism, and other subjects, and in 1795 was selected as a foreign member of the Royal Society of London.

One of the outstanding figures of Colonial times was Benjamin Franklin (1706-90), who achieved eminence as a scientist, statesman, author, publisher, inventor, and linguist. It was as a pioneer in the field of electricity that Franklin accomplished his work most useful to science. When not occupied with his business and public affairs, he carried on extensive experiments and research in electricity. He published the results of these experiments in 1749 in an essay entitled

285

Observations and Suppositions Towards Forming a New Hypothesis for Explaining the Several Phenomena of Thunder-Gusts.

In 1751 he published a paper on *Experiments and Observations on Electricity, Made at Philadelphia in America.* This treatise created a sensation in Europe, and was praised by the Comte de Buffon and by Sir William Watson of the Royal Society. In the face of much incredulity, Franklin's work demonstrated conclusively that lightning and electricity were manifestations of the same force. Not long after the appearance of his paper, Franklin conducted the famous kite experiment, which confirmed his hypothesis. Meanwhile, the Royal Society, which had previously ridiculed his theory, elected him a member. In the following year, the society honored him with the Copley medal.

At Franklin's suggestion the American Philosophical Society was formed in 1743. In 1769 he became president of the organization, holding this post until his death. He continued to occupy himself with scientific problems, invented a new stove, perfected Philadelphia's street-lighting system, and was a potent influence in the founding of the noted Union Fire Company. His scientific writings included 63 papers on electricity and many others on varied subjects. Franklin was so universally esteemed that honors were accorded him in Europe as well as at home. He was made a foreign associate of the French Academy of Sciences in 1772, and was elected a member of the Spanish Royal Academy of Sciences in 1784.

Other Philadelphia pioneers in science were John Fitch, among the early experimenters with steamboats; Thomas Say, entomologist, one of the founders of the Academy of Natural Sciences; James Pollard Espy, father of meteorology; Dr. Robert Hare, chemist; Alexander Wilson, ornithologist; Charles Willson Peale, naturalist and founder of one of the first museums in America; Thomas Nuttall, botanist; Dr. Benjamin Smith Barton, naturalist; Gerard Troost, mineralogist and one of the founders of the Academy of Natural Sciences; Constantine Samuel Rafinesque, naturalist; and Joseph Priestley, who had discovered oxygen while still living in England.

Industrial Science

WITH the opening of the nineteenth century, Philadelphia gave impetus to the expansion of industry through numerous inventions in the field of applied science. Manufacturing had grown rapidly in proportion to the development of new machines and new technique.

Oliver Evans (1755-1819), inventor of what may be regarded as the first automobile, a steam-driven amphibian dredging machine, had begun the manufacture of steam engines. He had also taken out patents for cotton and wool carding machines.

Patents for grain-threshing machines were granted to Samuel Mullikens, of Philadelphia, as early as 1791. Dr. Robert Hare invented the first electric furnace in 1816 ; and in the same year Dr. Charles Kugler exhibited his new gas lamp. In 1824 William Horstmann adapted the Jacquard loom for American industry ; and in 1832 the first successful American locomotive, "Old Ironsides," was built by Matthias Baldwin.

Foremost among Philadelphia inventors and scientists of the last 50 years were Dr. Elihu Thomson, Frederick Winslow Taylor, Coleman Sellers, Herman Haupt.

Born in 1853 at Manchester, England, Elihu Thomson at the age of five came with his parents to Philadelphia. Here he later taught in the high schools. Dr. Thomson, a pioneer in electrical science, is credited with the invention of the resistance method of electric welding and the three-phase armature winding of dynamos, besides making important discoveries in the field of electrical production and distribution. In the winter of 1876-77 he constructed the first electric dynamo made in Philadelphia at the Franklin Institute while a lecturer at old Central High School, Broad and Green Streets. Twelve years later he received the Grand Prix in Paris for his inventions. He died March 13, 1937, at his home in Swampscott, Mass.

Probably one of the most significant figures in the history of industrial science and invention of modern times was Frederick Winslow Taylor (1856-1915), the father of scientific management in industry and business. Taylor's name is synonymous with modern methods of mass production. When the Soviet Government recently inaugurated the Stakhanovite movement for greater efficiency in industrial production and business management, it was merely applying the principles formulated by Taylor in the latter part of the nineteenth century and used since then in all large-scale industries and business organizations in America and abroad.

Born in Germantown, Taylor was educated at Phillips Exeter Academy, Harvard University, and Stevens Institute of Technology. He received his M. E. from Stevens in 1883 and received his degree of Doctor of Science at the University of Pennsylvania in 1906. Entering the employ of the Midvale Steel Company in Philadelphia, he held jobs ranging from laborer to chief engineer. In 1889 he began his work of organizing on a basis of efficiency the management of various kinds of manufacturing establishments, among them the Midvale Steel Company, Cramp's Shipbuilding Company, and the Bethlehem Steel Company. Using the exact methods of science, Taylor computed just how many operations were required to perform a given job with a minimum of wasted time and motion. He invented the Taylor-White process of treating modern high-speed tools, for which he received a gold medal at the Paris Exposition of 1900 and the Elliott-Cresson gold medal of the Franklin Institute. He obtained patents on about 100 inventions. Taylor was president of the American Society of Mechanical Engineers in 1905.

Coleman Sellers (1827-1907) is best known for his invention of the first kinetoscope and photographic motion pictures. Sellers patented his invention in 1861. Improvements made later by Thomas A. Edison on Sellers' invention opened the way for development of the motion-picture industry. Dr. Sellers also invented a machine for rifling gun barrels, an automatic stop for bolt cutters, and improvements in presses for putting railway wheels on their axles.

Herman Haupt (1817-1905), an American engineer, was director and chief engineer of the Pennsylvania Railroad from 1847 to 1861, during which time he superintended the construction of the Hoosac Tunnel, almost five miles long, under the Hoosac Mountains at Hoosac, Mass. During the Civil War he was superintendent of military railroads for the Federal Government, and afterwards became general manager of the Northern Pacific Railroad. He was the inventor of a drilling machine and of a method for the transportation of oil from the well.

Prominent among contemporary Philadelphia inventors was Frederick Eugene Ives, experimenter in television, who has made important contributions in this new field. On April 7, 1927, Ives conducted the first practical demonstration of television, by transmitting the image of President Hoover from Washington to New York over facilities provided by the American Telephone & Telegraph Company. He died May 28, 1937, in Philadelphia.

Scientific Institutions

FOREMOST among local scientific societies, and first of its kind in America, is the American Philosophical Society, which has occupied its present home in Independence Square since 1789. The Society was founded in Philadelphia in 1743, with Thomas Hopkinson as president. An outgrowth of Franklin's Junto, the society might well claim 1727 as its natal year. The original Junto was reorganized in 1766 as "The American Society Held at Philadelphia for Promoting Useful Knowledge." In 1769 this society was merged with the earlier American Philosophical Society.

Franklin, who served as president until his death, was succeeded by David Rittenhouse. Other incumbents were Thomas Jefferson, Dr. Caspar Wistar, Peter Du Ponceau, Dr. Nathaniel Chapman, Dr. Franklin Bache, Frederick Fraley, Alexander Dallas Bache, Gen. Isaac Wistar, Dr. Edgar F. Smith, Dr. Robert Patterson, Chief Justice Tilghman, Judge John K. Kane, Robert M. Patterson, Dr. George B. Wood, Dr. W. W. Keen, Prof. William B. Scott, Charles D. Walcott,

Dr. Henry Norris Russell, Roland S. Morris, and Dr. Francis X. Dercum. The society's library is rich in Frankliniana and early scientific lore, as well as in other historical and scientific treasures. The proceedings of its meetings are published.

At the beginning of the nineteenth century, with the American Philosophical Society enjoying a position of eminence throughout the world, and Philadelphia recognized as the seat of scientific culture in America, there could be found only a scant handful of men who thought that the field of natural science offered any opportunity for intellectual endeavor.

The Botanical Society, founded in 1806, was doomed to a brief and, but for one exception, an unproductive existence. The exception was the publication of a work by Benjamin Smith Barton entitled *Discourse on Some Principal Desiderata in Natural History.*

The Academy of Natural Sciences, conceived during informal discussions among such ardent naturalists as John Speakman and Dr. Jacob Gilliams as early as 1809, was fully organized under its present name in 1812. In addition to Speakman, Dr. Joseph Leidy and Gilliams, to whom is due much of the credit for the forming of the organization, Nicholas B. Parmentier, John Shinn, Jr., Dr. Gerard Troost, Dr. Camillus MacMahon Mann, and Thomas Say were cofounders of the institution, which was to become one of the most active influences in the world of natural science.

Members of the academy have acquitted themselves with honor and gallantry in many far-flung expeditions ever since the time when Thomas Say accompanied Long to the Rockies in 1819-20. Two members participated in Wilkes' Antarctic expedition of 1838, and the academy outfitted the Arctic expeditions of Dr. Elisha Kent Kane in 1853 and Dr. Isaac Hayes in 1860. Most outstanding of the many explorations sponsored by the academy, however, was that of Rear Admiral Robert E. Peary to the North Pole.

The academy's collections are counted among the finest in the world. The conchological collection, started by Thomas Say, numbers more than a million specimens. Botanical research has resulted in the accumulation of another million specimens in that field. Its collections of birds, minerals, and European neolithic fossils are world-renowned.

Franklin Institute, founded in 1824 at a meeting of citizens in Congress Hall, is the oldest organization in the United States devoted to the promotion of applied sciences and mechanical arts. Prominent in and primarily responsible for the founding of the institution were Samuel Vaughan Merrick, later head of the Southwark Iron Works, and Dr. William Hypolitus Keating, son of a French baron and prominently associated with the University of Pennsylvania.

289

In 1825 the cornerstone of the institute building, which was on the east side of Seventh Street below Market, was laid, and in 1826 the structure was completed. Classes were started immediately after the founding, William Strickland teaching architecture and Dr. Keating, chemistry. The classes were continued until 1924. The institute was the precursor of the first city high school.

For many years the institute held exhibits of American manufactures. It still conducts considerable scientific research through its various committees and through the Bartol Research Foundation at Swarthmore, founded in 1921 by Henry W. Bartol, life member of the institute.

The new home of the institute on the Parkway was completed in 1933. Dedicated as a memorial to Benjamin Franklin, this building contains the offices, library, and auditorium of the institute, as well as a scientific and technological museum. It also houses the Fels Planetarium. The museum has many exhibits and collections showing development in the various fields of applied science.

In the field of archeological exploration and preservation the University of Pennsylvania Museum is predominant. Founded as the Archaeological Association in 1888, it was given its present name in 1892. Among the best known of this museum's ventures was the so-called Babylonian Expedition of 1888. Failing to make arrangements in London to prevent illicit excavations in Babylonia and Assyria, the committee in charge of this expedition determined to use its efforts to divert antiquities to the United States. After much haggling, the collection of Joseph Shemtob was purchased for much less than it would have cost to obtain a similar one by excavation. The collection, now housed in the museum, together with another purchased by Dr. Harper, consisted of several hundred pieces, and constituted what was then the greatest gathering of Babylonian and Assyrian relics in the United States.

In 1895 the museum sponsored an exhaustive ethnological survey of Borneo conducted by William H. Furness, 3d, and H. M. Miller. Its recent activities have included the search for evidences of early man in the southwestern United States ; a study of the old Mayan empire at Piedras Negras, Guatemala ; explorations in Tell Billa and Tepe Gawra in Mesopotamia, Ravy in Persia, and Cyprus.

Lectures, classroom instruction, visual education by means of museum specimens, and a complete reference library are provided by the Wagner Free Institute of Science, at Seventeenth Street and Montgomery Avenue. The institute conducts free lecture courses, supplemented by class work in engineering, organic and inorganic chemistry, botany, zoology, physics, and geology. Certificates are awarded to students who complete a four-year course in any of these

Serenity

Natural Habitat Exhibits in the Academy of Natural Sciences

The Aerie

subjects. The institute has a museum of 25,000 specimens in mineralogy, palaeontology, petrology, corals, birds, and mammals.

The American Entomological Society was founded in 1859 to investigate the habits of insects. It publishes the monthly *Entomological News*.

The Pennsylvania Horticultural Society, oldest in the country, was organized November 24, 1827, with Horace Binney as first president. The latter has been active in promoting and encouraging the study of flowers, vegetables, fruits, plants, and trees. Its 3,600-volume library and its offices are at No. 1600 Arch Street. Supported mainly by the endowment of a former president, William L. Schaffer, the society has a nominal dues-paying membership of 3,700. It aids greatly in the forming of garden clubs.

The Penrose Research Laboratories, as a subsidiary of the Zoological Gardens, conduct studies in comparative pathology and nutritive values. The laboratories were established in 1901.

The Morris Arboretum and the Botanic Garden, both maintained by the University of Pennsylvania, are engaged in plant study. The arboretum, bequeathed to the university by the late Miss Lydia Thompson Morris, occupies a 170-acre estate in Chestnut Hill, and is one of the beauty spots in the United States. Lying between Hamilton Walk and the grounds of the Philadelphia Hospital is the Botanic Garden, comprising nearly four acres of trees and flowers. Six greenhouses shelter a collection of orchids, palms, aroids, ferns, and succulents, which have proved of value in the teaching and research work of the University of Pennsylvania's botany department.

Fitch's Steamboat "Perseverance"
The progenitor of the S. S. Queen Mary

MEDICINE

MEDICAL practice in Penn's city had its beginning with Jan Peterson, Swedish barber-surgeon, who administered to the ills of the early Dutch and Swedish settlers long before the city was laid out. John Goodson, a chirurgeon to the Society of Free Traders, came from London to Chester (then Upland) early in Pennsylvania history. He was practicing in Upland in 1682, and moved to Philadelphia after the coming of William Penn.

Struggling in a fog of uncertainty and ignorance, Philadelphia's earnest medical pioneers laid the foundation for future greatness in the field of medicine. Hardy warriors, they fought valiantly against the epidemics and plagues which swept the young city every few years. Included in this advance guard were John Kearsley, Thomas Graeme, Lloyd Zachary, John Morgan, William Shippen, Jr., Thomas Bond, Benjamin Rush, Phineas Bond, Adam Kuhn, and Thomas Cadwalader. Dr. Cadwalader was one of the early physicians to apply modern scientific methods to an autopsy, and the first to employ electricity in the treatment of disease, especially paralysis.

Among first practitioners were Thomas Wynne, Thomas Lloyd, and Griffith Owen, all three of whom arrived from Wales in 1682 and held the first consultation in Philadelphia shortly thereafter. Dr. Owen performed the first professional operation — amputation of a gunner's arm shattered by a cannon ball fired as a salute on the occasion of William Penn's second coming to Philadelphia — in 1699.

The earliest physicians provided the impetus to medical advancement which led to the establishment in 1732 of a hospital department in the Philadelphia Almshouse. Twenty years later the Pennsylvania Hospital was founded. Benjamin Franklin, man of marvelous versatility, aided in the fight for its establishment with his inimitable flair for publicity.

During the city's formative years there was no institution offering instruction in the medical arts and sciences until the founding of the Medical School of the College of Philadelphia in 1765. The first medical degree of Colonial days, Bachelor in Physic, was conferred upon graduates of this school in 1768. The degree of Doctor of Medicine did not come into existence until 1789.

The first half of the nineteenth century witnessed a quickened interest and a practical growth in medical education facilities. In 1820

293

Dr. Jason Lawrence founded the Philadelphia Anatomical Rooms, later known as the Philadelphia School of Anatomy. Jefferson Medical College was founded in 1825, Pennsylvania Medical College in 1840. The founding of these schools broke the ice of uncertainty surrounding the medical profession, and many more schools sprang up throughout the city. Franklin Medical College and the Philadelphia College of Medicine had their inception in 1846. By this time Philadelphia had gained a reputation as the medical center of the United States, and the city's renown in this field has continued to grow with the years.

Advocates of the homeopathic doctrine aided in the founding of the Homeopathic Medical College of Pennsylvania. Untiring efforts on the part of supporters of women who clamored for admission to medical schools resulted in the founding, in 1850, of the Female Medical College of Philadelphia, later known as the Women's Medical College of Pennsylvania.

To meet the need of the growing demand for specialization, the Philadelphia Polyclinic and College for Graduates in Medicine was established in 1889. The school proved highly successful, and Temple University followed with the opening of a department of medicine. Medical science was at last leaving its swaddling clothes and abandoning its ancient superstitions to become more nearly a science.

The profession of dentistry arrived as an offspring of medicine. The Philadelphia College of Dental Surgery was founded in 1852. Upon recognizing the demand for study in this field, the Philadelphia Dental College, now a part of Temple University, was founded. This was in 1863, preceding by 15 years the opening of the University of Pennsylvania's dental department.

Pharmacy had made but a timid appearance in Philadelphia before the Revolution, and for some time afterward only a few apothecaries were available. One of the first apothecaries in America was David Leighton, whom Dr. John Morgan brought to Philadelphia after the latter's sojourn abroad. However, many years elapsed before Philadelphia won distinction by founding the first American institution of that science, the Philadelphia College of Pharmacy, in 1821.

Colonial Medical Practice

A N INCIDENT in the life of Dr. William Shippen, Jr., shows to what extent medical research in early Philadelphia was hampered by the ignorance and superstition of both layman and physician. When, in his search for knowledge to aid in alleviating suffering, he dissected a human body in 1762, a storm of protest broke throughout the city. He was threatened with physical violence, and an at-

294

tempt was made to destroy his home. Nevertheless, the intrepid physician continued his efforts to probe the unknown. Dr. Shippen was in advance of all his contemporaries in the study and knowledge of obstetrics, and in 1762 he established the city's first private maternity home.

A close associate and friend of his, Dr. John Morgan, has been called the "founder of American medicine" as a result of extensive research work. To Dr. Morgan goes the credit for effecting a division between medicine and surgery, realizing, as he did, that each specialty required its own type of practitioner. When he returned from his studies abroad, he founded, in 1765, America's first school of medicine. (Dr. Shippen was professor of surgery and anatomy in this school, which later became part of the University of Pennsylvania.) Dr. Morgan made invaluable contributions to the study of the origin and formation of pus, and his views on scientific surgery are approved even today by medical men everywhere.

Early Philadelphians were the originators of many valuable methods of treatment, especially in the field of surgery. Dr. Thomas Bond created a flurry of speculation in medical circles in 1756 when he performed the city's first recorded lithotomy (bladder operation) at the Pennsylvania Hospital. It can well be imagined what pain was suffered by the patient, without benefit of anesthesia; but the operation was successful, and medical science thus moved another step forward. Dr. Bond also perfected a splint for fractures of the lower end of the radius. He discovered the medicinal value of mercury, and was the first in the Colonies to advocate the use of hot and cold baths in medical treatment.

Another prominent practitioner in early Philadelphia was Dr. Philip Syng Physick, "the father of American surgery" and inventor of a number of surgical appliances and instruments. Among his creations were the urethrotome, the seton for ununified fractures, ligatures for vessels, and the tonsillotome. Dr. Hugh L. Hodge invented a pessary and obstetrical forceps; Dr. S. D. Gross a transfusion apparatus, foreign body extractor, bullet probe, artery forceps, tourniquet, and splints. Dr. Gross conducted the first systematic course of lectures on morbid anatomy given in the United States.

Dr. Benjamin Rush, also a Philadelphian, is conceded to have been one of the greatest clinicians that this country has ever produced. Besides being an acknowledged leader in the field of medicine, he was an essayist, orator, philosopher, and statesman, and a highly successful teacher.

The first medical textbook in America was published in 1811 by a Philadelphian, Dr. Caspar Wistar, whose anatomical specimens form the nucleus of the present Wistar Museum. William P. C. Barton, nephew of Dr. Benjamin Smith Barton and successor to the latter

Laboratory—Sharp & Dohme, Inc.
Man versus disease

as professor of botany at the University of Pennsylvania, wrote the first American Materia Medica, *Florae Philadelphicae Prodromus* (1815), containing a botanical, general, and medical history of the medicinal plants indigenous to the United States.

Philadelphia has suffered its share of major epidemics. The first recorded plague occurred in 1699, when yellow fever exacted a toll of 220 lives. In the early days vaccination was little known and less used, but an epidemic of smallpox in 1730 induced Philadelphia medical men to experiment in the field of prevention. When another epidemic broke out, six years later, there was vociferous objection to vaccination, although by this time it had been successfully used in England. However, the value of inoculation was demonstrated by the fact that only one of 129 persons submitting to the treatment succumbed to the malady. Another invasion of the dread disease in 1756 further tended to fortify the arguments of those in favor of preventive measures. Finally, in 1773, an inoculation hospital was opened in Philadelphia.

During the terrible yellow-fever scourge of 1793, of the Philadelphia physicians who fought the epidemic heroically one stood out conspicuously — Dr. Benjamin Rush. Fighting blindly, he finally evolved a treatment which, though in no sense a cure, nevertheless did much to ease the suffering. Each day he treated an average of 125 persons stricken by the deadly "Yellow Jack." The epidemic spread rapidly from Water and Front Streets to surrounding areas and raged for six long weeks. Thousands fled the city. Those who remained wandered through streets heavy with the acrid smoke of burning wood and gunpowder, used in an effort to halt the scourge. With the coming of cold weather the plague subsided, but only after 4,000 deaths had been recorded.

Later Efforts

AMONG those Philadelphians who helped make medical history during the latter part of the eighteenth and early nineteenth centuries were John K. Mitchell (1798-1858), first to describe neurotic spinal-joint diseases and their treatment ; Dr. George Bacon Wood (1797-1879), and Dr. Franklin Bache (1792-1864), collaborators on the *United States Dispensatory* ; Nathaniel Chapman (1780-1853) and Matthew Carey (1760-1839), founders of the *Philadelphia Journal of the Medical and Physical Sciences,* later called *American Journal of the Medical Sciences ;* Dr. Samuel George Morton (1799-1851), author of valuable papers on craniology, palaeontology, and phthisisography ; William Wood Gerhard (1809-72), specialist in pulmonary diseases ; and Elisha Kent Kane (1820-57), physician and arctic explorer.

Dr. Crawford Williamson Long (1815-78) was a pioneer in the use of ether ; Dr. Joseph Pancoast (1805-82), Dr. Joseph Leidy (1823-1891), Dr. James Tyson (1841-1919), Dr. William Pepper (1843-98), and Dr. Jacob M. DaCosta (1833-1900) contributed much to the steady march of medical progress. Dr. Silas Weir Mitchell (1829-1914), termed the "father of American neurology," was almost equally well known as a novelist and poet.

Outstanding physicians of a later day include Dr. John B. Deaver (1855-1931), a surgeon noted for his success in appendectomy ; Dr. George Edmund de Schweinitz, recognized as one of the country's outstanding eye specialists ; Dr. Solomon Solis-Cohen, professor emeritus of clinical medicine at Jefferson College, who delivered the first systematic course of lectures on *Therapeutic Measures Other than Drugs* in an American school ; and Dr. Chevalier Jackson, developer of the world-famous bronchoscope and now occupying the chair of bronchoscopy at Temple University. Dr. Jackson is also inventor of the esophogoscope.

The crippling scourge of infantile paralysis is now somewhat less dreaded as a result of the efforts of Dr. John A. Kolmer, head of the Temple University medical staff. Dr. Kolmer experimented with monkeys for three years before perfecting a treatment at the Research Institute of Cutaneous Medicine. His studies and persistent work in immunization and vaccine therapy stand today as the most important achievements toward prevention and cure of infantile paralysis.

Dr. William B. Van Lennep (1853-1919), one of the founders of the American College of Surgeons, was acknowledged by his contemporaries as being among the greatest American teachers of surgery. Another noted surgeon, Dr. William W. Keen (1837-1932), achieved his greatest fame through his work in the treatment of war wounds.

Dr. Rufus B. Weaver (1841-1936), famous throughout the country, performed one of the greatest anatomical feats the world has known. Within a period of seven months he dissected and mounted a complete human cerebro-nervous system from the remains of Harriet Cole, a colored scrub woman at Hahnemann Hospital. The students to this day refer to it as Harriet. The white nerves are suspended on the heads of protruding pins ; the eyes fixed to meet the gaze of the many visitors. This work, the only one of its kind in the history of medicine, is preserved in a fireproof vault in the Rufus B. Weaver Museum of Hahnemann Medical College. Early in his career Dr. Weaver astounded the medical profession by identifying, from their buried remains, the bodies of 3,000 Confederate soldiers who had been killed at Gettysburg.

Dr. Louis A. Duhring (1845-1913) was an outstanding skin specialist. An ailing Philadelphian once traveled to Vienna for treatment by a noted Austrian dermatologist. The Vienna doctor told him he had gone to much unnecessary trouble since Philadelphia had in Dr. Duhring one of the world's best skin specialists.

Pediatrics has been greatly advanced through the efforts of two notable Philadelphians, Dr. John P. Crozer Griffith and Dr. Charles Sigmund Raue. Dr. Raue is chief of the department of pediatrics at Hahnemann, and St. Luke's and Children's Hospitals. Dr. George W. MacKenzie, highly revered by members of his profession, is noted for his work as an ear, nose, and throat specialist. To Dr. MacKenzie, who teaches not only students but also physicians, was awarded the gold honor medal by the University of Vienna for his contributions to medical science.

Dr. Francis Colgate Benson, Jr., a pioneer in the adaptation of radium to medical purposes, organized this country's first separate department for the use of radium in medicine and surgery.

The progress of health among the school children of Philadelphia has been greatly furthered by the work of Dr. Walter S. Cornell, head of the medical inspection department of the Philadelphia Board of Education. His department's yearly reports serve as models for public school systems throughout the Nation.

Although Negroes did not become active in the medical field until late in the nineteenth century, members of the race have made many valuable contributions to medical knowledge. The first accredited doctor to appear upon the scene was Dr. Nathan F. Mossell, the first Negro student to enter and graduate from the University of Pennsylvania's medical school. Graduating from that institution in 1882, he began practicing that same year and is now (1937) rounding out 55 continuous years of medical service to his people. The following year Dr. James Potter finished his medical course in the same university and began a practice which lasted until his death in 1929. During the last decade of the century Drs. A. E. White, Thomas J. Stanford, George R. Hilton, and Wilbert D. Postels began their work. Early in the new century (1906) Dr. Henry M. Minton, now (1937) superintendent of Mercy Hospital, started his practice. He has given a great deal of time towards the cure of tuberculosis, and is dispensing physician to the Henry Phipps Institute, an agency for the prevention and treatment of this disease. Among well-known, present-day doctors are Drs. J. Q. McDougald, successful surgeon ; John P. Turner, police surgeon and first Negro member of the Board of Education ; and Virginia M. Alexander, who in connection with her practice, maintains a private hospital.

Hygiene and Hygiene Legislation

G OVERNMENTAL action in the field of health preservation came when laymen and medical men alike sought to devise some means of preventing the recurrence of conditions similar to those prevailing at the time of the yellow-fever epidemic in 1793. Agitation along this line culminated in the 1794 Act of Assembly which created a Board of Health. Full authority was given the board to make and enforce all rules and regulations deemed necessary for conducting effective quarantines.

Health authorities received wider powers from the State Legislature in 1895. An act of that year required the prompt reporting of contagious diseases, the isolation of patients, and the quarantining of houses where contagious cases existed. It regulated the school attendance of children living in such houses, required the disinfection of persons and clothing, and instituted compulsory vaccination to prevent smallpox. The law provided heavy penalties for violations.

Philadelphia's first water works was begun in 1799, with the erection of a powerhouse and a receiving fountain along the Schuylkill River, south of Market Street. In 1818 the first pumps were installed in the section then known as "Faire Mount" along the Schuylkill, north of Market Street.

Until 1884 Philadelphia's sewer system consisted of less than 30 miles of sewers. The first intercepting sewer was constructed in 1884, its purpose being to prevent pollution of that part of the Schuylkill River within the city limits. Eighteen hundred miles of sewers drain the city today.

Steps toward systematic control of the city's milk supply were taken in 1888, when the city made an appropriation for the employment of a milk inspector. Today it maintains a special division of milk inspection, with a chief inspector and a large staff of assistants. Food inspection has been handled with much greater efficiency since the division of bacteriology, pathology, and disinfection was established in 1895. This division performs an invaluable service by confiscating impure and tainted foodstuffs.

As for hospitalization, there is no resemblance at all between the insanitary and miasmic pesthouse of Colonial Philadelphia and the 74 spotless and scientifically equipped institutions of today.

Overcrowded conditions in the city's first hospital resulted in the establishment of the Pennsylvania Hospital in 1751. This institution's department for the sick and injured has remained at Eighth and Spruce Streets ever since completion of the hospital, construction of which was begun in 1755. The department for mental and nervous diseases, commonly known as Kirkbride's, is in West Philadelphia. The various buildings are scattered over an immense plot of ground

300

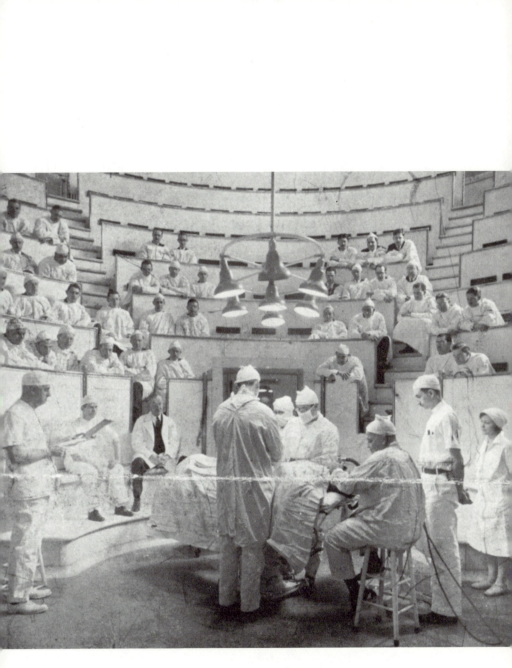

Men in White

Operating room in Hahnemann Hospital

bounded approximately by Market Street, Powelton Avenue, Forty-second Street, Haverford Avenue, and Forty-ninth Street. Construction of the buildings to house the mental and nervous department was begun in 1836. Kirkbride's was for many years a model for mental institutions all over the world. Pennsylvania Hospital was the first in America to establish a department of psychiatry. In 1928 ground was broken at Forty-ninth and Market Streets for the erection of a modern psychiatric institute.

Philadelphia General Hospital, an outgrowth of the city's early almshouse, is admittedly one of the finest and largest institutions of its kind in the United States. The hospital was separated from the almshouse by a legislative act in 1919. A group of old buildings, which for half a century housed the indigent insane, and physically ill, was metamorphosed into the gigantic General Hospital at Thirty-fourth and Pine Streets. The main buildings were completed and first occupied in 1928. Additional buildings were added in 1929, 1930, and 1933, in which last named year the cost of buildings and equipment approximated $8,000,000. The hospital is modern in every detail and has 2,500 beds.

The School of Medicine of the University of Pennsylvania, founded in 1765, was the first American medical school connected with a university. Headquarters are in the Medical Laboratory Building at Thirty-sixth Street and Hamilton Walk, and the various department buildings radiate from that point. From the small Surgeon's Hall, open in 1765 at Fifth Street near Walnut, the school has grown to vast proportions. Since its founding more than 16,000 students have received medical degrees from the school, and approximately 500 students are currently enrolled. The courses of instruction include every branch of the medical profession.

The Graduate Hospital of the University of Pennsylvania, at Nineteenth and Lombard Streets, provides post-graduate courses in all branches of medicine. The Medico-Chirurgical (Medico-Chi) College and Hospital merged with the University of Pennsylvania in 1916. The Philadelphia Polyclinic and College for graduates in medicine and the Diagnostic Hospital merged with the university in 1918 and 1926, respectively.

Jefferson Medical College, at Tenth and Walnut Streets, has been noted since its inception for its distinguished clinicians and the inclusiveness of its clinical teaching. The college and clinical buildings, recently constructed, house one of the most modern medical colleges in the United States.

There are two hospitals operated by and chiefly for Negroes. Douglass Hospital, Lombard Street near Sixteenth, was established in 1895, the first of its kind in Pennsylvania. In addition to ward, private, and semiprivate facilities the hospital maintains a special X-ray room for diagnosis with modernly equipped pathological and histological laboratories. It has a bed capacity of approximately 100. Mercy Hospital, Fiftieth and Woodland Avenue, opened on February 12, 1907, receiving its charter the following March. It maintains a 110-bed capacity and is supported by State aid and through the community fund. Both institutions maintain a training school for nurses.

The Homeopathic Medical College of Pennsylvania was consolidated with the Hahnemann Medical College of Philadelphia in 1869, under the latter name. The college, on Broad Street north of Race, is the oldest homeopathic medical school in existence. The Hospital of Philadelphia merged with Hahnemann in 1885. Completely reorganized in 1916, many new and desirable educational improvements were effected. The present 20-story structure was completed in 1928. Every available aid for the diagnosis and treatment of disease is found in this modern college and hospital.

The Jewish Hospital Association, at York and Tabor Roads, was founded in 1865. This institution has from the beginning been "dedicated to the relief work of the sick and wounded without regard to creed, color, or nationality."

An unusual medical institution is the College of Physicians and Surgeons now located at 15 South Twenty-second Street. A prototype of the Royal College of Physicians of London, it was instituted in Philadelphia in September 1787. In its earlier years this scientific body was active in the maintenance of public health and morals. In recent years, however, its largest measures have been devoted to the discussion of scientific matters. Its valuable library occupies a prominent position among medical libraries of the world.

A noteworthy forward step in medical progress was taken with the establishment of the Philadelphia School of Occupational Therapy in 1918. Under the auspices of the National League for Woman's Service, the school aims to develop the formula of "occupation under medical prescription" as treatment for both mental and physical ailments.

SOCIAL SERVICE

"Do good with what thou hast, or it will do thee no good."

SOCIAL service has by no means been laggard in its contribution
to the picture of general achievement in Philadelphia. Despite
its widely flung area and density of population, the city manages
to take reasonably good care of its destitute.

Even the wealthy, golfing or riding to hounds in the sun-drenched
suburbs far from the city's slums, regard their charities seriously.
The annual Charity Ball of the socialites is as much a part of Philadelphia tradition as is the thrift of Benjamin Franklin or the prodi-
gality of Robert Morris.

The family relief situation in Philadelphia was probably at its
worst during the early days of the Colony, when members of needy
families were forced to beg upon the streets. There was no differen-
tiation between those who could not work and those who would not
work. Charitable organizations, such as they were, carried on their
work independently of one another, so that confusion and inefficiency
resulted. Pauper laws, brought from England by the Quakers, were
invoked in the cases of individuals seeking aid. A trace of these laws
remains today in those Philadelphia hospitals which require an oath
of poverty from a charity patient.

The first almshouse in Philadelphia was established in 1713, by the
Society of Friends, on the south side of Walnut Street between Third
and Fourth. It was devoted exclusively to the care of indigent members of the Quaker faith.

The first municipal almshouse was completed in 1732, and was
operated under supervision of the city government. Known as the
Philadelphia Almshouse, it maintained a hospital department and
accommodated the sick and insane as well as the poor. It was situated
in a green meadow at Third and Spruce Streets. Its hospital department developed into what is today the Philadelphia General Hospital.
In 1767 a new almshouse with larger accommodations was opened
at Eleventh and Pine Streets.

With the passing of the years, and the steady growth of the city's
population, a corresponding increase in the number of dependents
necessitated a larger institution. On March 5, 1828, an act was passed
providing for an almshouse, hospital, and other buildings "on a site
not exceeding two miles from Broad & Market Sts." In the vicinity

304

of what is now Thirty-fourth and Spruce Streets a large tract of land was purchased, and on it were erected the buildings of the Blockley Almshouse. Completed in 1834, the institution was operated by the city for many years.

The oldest prison organization in America, the Pennsylvania Prison Society, was established in 1787. This society aids and advises prisoners in the problems facing them during their confinement and after their release.

The first private charitable institution in the city was the Magdalen Society, founded in 1799 for the reformation of fallen women. Bishop William White, of the Protestant Episcopal Church, was its first president.

Through the efforts of Ann Parrish, a member of the Society of Friends, the first organization for temporary assistance of the distressed was formed in 1793, following the epidemic of yellow fever, which had caused great suffering and privation among the poor. Assistance was given to the sick, and in the winter wood and food were distributed to the needy.

In 1815 the Second Presbyterian Church erected a two-story building at Eighteenth and Cherry Streets, dedicating it to the care of orphans. Thus the Orphans' Society of Philadelphia was formed. The society carried on its work at the original address until 1872, when the encroachment of business houses and the corresponding rise in real estate values forced its removal to Sixty-fourth Street and Haverford Avenue.

One of the pioneer organizations for poor relief was the Union Benevolent Association, founded in 1831 by David Nasmith and Rev. Thomas G. Allen, an Episcopal clergyman. In 1868 the Orphans Guardian was established under the guidance of Dr. Samuel Hirsch, rabbi of the Congregation Keneseth Israel. It was restricted to a policy of aiding only the needy in its own congregation until 1891. Then its scope was enlarged to noncongregational activities. Under the Guardian plan, one family became a "big brother" to a poorer family, aiding it financially, spiritually, and educationally.

The Philadelphia Society for Organizing Charity and Repressing Mendicancy was formed in 1879. Third of its kind in the country, its name was shortened later to Philadelphia Society for Organizing Charity. A central office was established, with trained workers devoting all their labors to the alleviation of poverty and sickness. This idea of centralization and unification has been developed with the years, until at present most of the funds for relief purposes in Philadelphia are collected in one large drive conducted annually by the United Campaign of the Welfare Federation.

Today the poor and feeble of Philadelphia are far less unfortunate than those of 1700, who dared not go to bed sick, for fear of being

305

removed to prison once they had become well. Now they can obtain medical treatment in charity wards in the city's hospitals or in hospital clinics. In addition to the hospital clinics, special health clinics are maintained for low-income and needy families.

There is also an organization known as the Marriage Counsel, with offices at 253 South Fifteenth Street, which helps young married couples, or those contemplating marriage, to a better understanding of what companionship in married life involves. Counsel, in terms of the individual's needs, is given at one or more personal interviews. The Maternal Health Centers and the Pennsylvania Birth Control Federation have offices at the same address.

A committee of the latter organization operates the National Health centers with four clinics in the city. Since the first of these clinics was opened in Philadelphia in 1929, nearly 20,000 women seeking reliable medical information on marital problems have been instructed by these clinic physicians. The aim of the organization is to make medically directed birth control information available to under-privileged mothers who have no reliable means of limiting their families. Social agencies of all kinds cooperate in referring patients to the clinics.

Philadelphia has also helped lead the way toward socialized medicine in the State through the C. Dudley Saul Medical Service, organized in June 1935, which provides low-cost medical treatment to a large number of subscribers. This service was started in conjunction with the Newspaper Guild of Philadelphia and Camden. Members of the service pay a monthly fee of $2, for which they receive necessary medical attention and are entitled to three months' hospitalization a year. Dependents are also served at a rate less than half the ordinary fees. Many minor ailments that might develop into serious illnesses are cared for under the monthly payment plan without additional expense.

The Philadelphia Department of Public Health conducts 12 tuberculosis clinics. This department also provides eye dispensaries for those otherwise unable to procure treatment. Many neighborhood organizations, such as the Big Brother Association and the Germantown Community Center, conduct clinics on a free or nominal fee basis. The Visiting Nurses Association has skilled nurses traveling through the poorer districts, ministering to those in need of bedside care.

Foremost among the community service ventures is the United Campaign, a joint drive held by the Welfare Federation and the Federation of Jewish Charities each spring to obtain funds for the maintenance of the city's social agencies. Altogether, 141 charitable institutions are supported by this United Campaign.

The Federation of Jewish Charities, organized in 1901, which supports 53 Jewish charitable institutions in Philadelphia, was established in order to eliminate the many benefits, ticket sellings, bazaars, fairs, and other methods of collection. Among the institutions aided by the federation are Mount Sinai Hospital, Bureau for Jewish Children, Jewish Hospital Association, National Farm School at Doylestown, Jewish Seaside Home for Invalids at Ventnor, N. J., Young Men's and Young Women's Hebrew Associations and the Jewish Sheltering Home for the Homeless and Aged.

The Welfare Federation of Philadelphia performs a similar clearing house function for other social agencies in the city. Operating in much the same manner as the Federation of Jewish Charities, its purpose is to eliminate the waste of a number of solicitation drives by combining them and by setting up a single unit for collecting and allocating funds and interpreting agency programs to the public.

Numerous groups are devoted to the welfare of the city's youth. The Boy Scouts, Girl Scouts, Campfire Girls, Catholic Young Men's Association, Boy Council of Philadelphia, and other youth organizations aid the young to obtain healthful recreation and social development.

The Bureau of Recreation of the Department of Public Welfare, in City Hall, sets up and manages neighborhood playgrounds, recreation centers, and swimming pools. Forty-one playgrounds and 38 swimming pools are maintained by the municipal bureau. Also included in the municipal Department of Public Welfare are the Bureau of Charities and Correction and the Bureau of Personal Assistance. There are many city-wide organizations engaged in bettering community life and establishing a friendly attitude among the various peoples of Philadelphia.

The Philadelphia Conference on Social Work holds an annual meeting at which representatives of social organizations discuss ways and means of improving the latter's activities.

Constant coordination in social service is achieved through the Social Service Exchange to which virtually all public and private agencies engaged in welfare and relief work subscribe. In the central index maintained by the Exchange are listed the names and addresses of all persons known to any of the social agencies of the city, thereby permitting each agency to avoid duplicating relief or service and at the same time to coordinate its activity on behalf of a particular family with that of other agencies concerned.

The Bureau of Municipal Research is a civic agency designed to collect and classify facts regarding the powers and duties of municipal departments, and to seek ways and means of coordinating and expediting the functions of government. There are also within Philadelphia various agencies whose functions include the sponsoring of

307

legislation designed to increase the effectiveness of child education and to eliminate child labor.

Agencies such as the Armstrong Association and the Whittier Center strive to better the conditions and culture of the Negro, through education and other channels.

The American Penal Labor Association, the County Prison Officials Association of Pennsylvania, and the Philadelphia Criminal Justice Association seek to curb crime, to alleviate suffering among the families of imprisoned criminals, and to return discharged prisoners to normal occupations.

The Philadelphia Zoning Commission, Better Homes in America Association, Philadelphia Housing Association, and other organizations seek to produce a model residential, commercial, and industrial community. Marking the city off into zones of residential, business, and factory sections is the duty of the Zoning Commission. Through this method, an apportionment of sections is sought to facilitate business and restrict certain residential sections, for the protection of real estate investments and municipal improvement areas.

*   *   *

In 1927 Charles Edwin Fox, then District Attorney, ordered an investigation into the background of four young bandits responsible for the Olney Bank robbery, in which a policeman was shot and killed. County Detective Merryweather, assigned to the case, turned in a startling analysis of the factors contributing to the excessive criminal delinquency among youths between the ages of 16 and 21.

The lack of recreational facilities and of parental education, combined with bad housing and the use of political "pull," was given as a cause tending to sidetrack these youths into a life of crime. With this information before him, Fox took steps to alleviate this shocking condition. The Crime Prevention Association was formed, with Detective Merryweather as executive director. It began operating June 1, 1932. Simultaneously a police department crime prevention bureau was set up.

Merryweather obtained the second floor of a South Broad Street building. He installed pool tables, games, and other forms of recreation, and within a few days the street corners of the neighborhood were virtually clear of youthful loungers. An "unofficial parole" system and card index file were put into effect, with first offenders and repeaters segregated. Thus a close contact was maintained with youths of criminal tendencies. In order to remove the implied stigma the name was later changed from Crime Prevention Association to the Philadelphia Council of Older Boys' Clubs.

Numerous clubhouses have been established throughout the city. That their work has proved beneficial is indicated by recent figures

Preston Retreat
"A child was born . . ."

showing an 11 percent decrease in crime among the older boys in the city. Among the organizations which strive to keep youths off street corners and provide them recreational facilities are the Big Brother Association, Bethany Brotherhood Club, Board of Education Physical and Health Education Division, and the boys' clubs in most communities. The Y. M. and Y. W. H. A., Y. M. C. A., and neighborhood settlement houses, as well as playgrounds, swimming pools, and other facilities, help to swell the total of recreational, educational, and character-building agencies in Philadelphia.

Community service is materially aided by the great number of settlement houses, where social problems are discussed, community group meetings held, and a social life provided for young and old. Not only do these settlement houses aid in the social scheme of the community, but during periods of suffering and want they strive to alleviate cold and hunger by means of soup kitchens and other forms of relief.

Many of these houses have combined all the phases of worthy charities heretofore carried on under separate roofs, and today provide reading and recreational rooms, day nurseries, and health clinics. Some conduct classes where persons may learn trades, or increase their material education in art or commerce.

The Association of Philadelphia Settlements promotes efficiency among settlement houses throughout the city, unifying them in a common purpose. Through mutual exchange of experiences and through discussion groups, it helps solve their problems.

The Board of Education supervises more than 500 special classes for cardiac sufferers, deaf, tubercular, and feeble-minded children, and for those who have defective vision or impediments in their speech.

For adults whose physical handicaps bar them from regular positions, agencies in the city provide training in the vocations adapted to their limited capabilities. These agencies also furnish such aids as braces and artificial limbs, either free or at a nominal charge. The Shut-In Society provides reading matter and arranges for visitors, or correspondents for those confined to their homes.

The Red Cross maintains a library of Braille books for the blind. The Philadelphia Free Library on the Parkway also has a large collection of such volumes, which it mails, postage-free, to any part of the State. The Blind Relief Fund of Philadelphia is an agency for collecting money to aid the poor and aged blind.

The Philadelphia League for the Hard of Hearing provides a community center to promote sociability and recreation and to maintain an employment service for the deaf. This society also conducts a school of lip reading.

For 15 years Philadelphia has had a Junior Employment Service for persons who are more than 18 and who have completed high school. The service is operated in conjunction with the Board of Education, and school records of applicants are transferred to the service. Classes are formed for the unemployed, and medical and psychological examinations are facilitated. During 1936 registrations numbered 57,256, with 2,757 placements.

The Catholic Women's Alliance founded in 1916, and the Friendly Sons of St. Patrick instruct immigrants in American principles and aid them to obtain work.

For men and boys interested in recreation, or seeking living quarters, the Y. M. C. A. offers a friendly atmosphere at comparatively low rates. The central building, at 1421 Arch Street, accommodates about 1,283 single persons and 55 married couples. There are seven Philadelphia branches of the "Y" — at Fifty-second and Sansom Streets, 1007 West Lehigh Avenue, 1724 Christian Street, 117 North Fifteenth Street, Forty-first Street and Westminster Avenue, Lehigh and Kensington Avenues and Ninth and Spring Garden Streets.

The Catholic Y. M. A., at 1819 Arch Street, conducts a dormitory, where Catholic men may board at moderate rates. This association was formed during the World War to provide accommodations for service men. It was continued after the Armistice as a society to care for homeless men and boys. Its purpose is to furnish education, recreation, food, shelter, and clothing.

The Luther Hospice, at 157 North Twentieth Street, is a Christian boarding home for students and business men of all denominations. The Salvation Army Men's Hotel and the United Service Club maintain sleeping quarters for workingmen and enlisted men, respectively.

The Salvation Army also has one of the most diversified forms of relief of any organization. The Philadelphia headquarters is at 701 North Broad Street, in a building provided by the will of John Wanamaker. This property is to be the Salvation Army's so long as that organization occupies it. If the Salvation Army vacates the property, it will go to the Y. M. C. A.

From its headquarters the army distributes family relief in the form of food, clothing, shoes, and other necessities. It also maintain a transient bureau at 705 North Broad Street, where free lodging and food are provided. At 1224 Parrish Street is its social service department, where cast-off clothing and shoes, and second-hand furniture are reclaimed and sold at nominal prices. Here approximately 125 men, remaining permanently or until they can better themselves, receive room and board, with a small salary.

The Salvation Army also maintains a children's home at 5441 Lansdowne Avenue and a day nursery at 224 South Third Street, where children are cared for during the day while their mothers work. The army also distributes fuel to the needy during winter months, and

311

in the summer provides a camp vacation for underprivileged children and their mothers.

Philadelphia offers many residences for women and girls, especially for those who have to support themselves. The Catholic Women's Club, at 306 South Thirteenth Street, maintains quarters for Catholic business and professional women ; the Coles House, at 915 Clinton Street, cares for Protestant women.

The Dominican House of Retreats, at 1812 Green Street, also maintains a boarding house for women. For the Protestant girl who is homeless, or dependent upon a low-paying job, Esther Hall, at 2021 Mt. Vernon Street, provides shelter. The Friendship Home, at 1939 North Twenty-second Street, is for Negro girls ; the Rebecca Gratz Club, 532 Spruce Street, is for Jewish women ; and St. Isaac's House, at 3311 Haverford Avenue, a non-sectarian institution, furnishes living quarters for working girls and women.

The Y. W. C. A. of Philadelphia also provides living quarters in its large central club residence, at Eighteenth and Arch Streets, and its eight branches throughout the city. The accommodations and rates are much the same as those of the Y. M. C. A.

The Girls' Friendly Society, organized in England in 1875 and introduced into this country in 1886, is an organization designed to aid young women who are earning their way in the world, offering them recreational advantages and instructing them in general subjects. The society is operated under the auspices of the Episcopal Church. There are at present 47 branches of the Girls' Friendly Society in Philadelphia, with a total membership of 2,500. Central headquarters is at 202 South Nineteenth Street.

For the aid of seamen there are a number of agencies. Foremost among these is the Seamen's Institute at 211 Walnut Street, with a branch in Port Richmond at 2815 East Cambria Street. Originally begun as a "floating church," the institute was moved ashore and gradually enlarged, absorbing many other similar institutions. The institute can accommodate 327 men. In addition to sleeping quarters, it has a restaurant and reading, recreation, and work rooms. Classes in seamanship are also conducted.

The Lutheran Seamen's Home, at 1402 East Moyamensing Avenue, and the Lutheran Seamen's Mission, 1226 Spruce Street, care for seamen, regardless of nationality, creed, or color. Other organizations are the Pennsylvania Seamen's Friend Society at 201 Walnut Street ; the Seamen's and Landsmen's Aid Society at 332 South Front Street ; and the Norwegian Seamen's Church of Philadelphia at 22 South Third Street.

Many of Philadelphia's less fortunate children are helped by numerous civic, charitable, or welfare organizations throughout the year. In summer great numbers of those living in congested or slum areas are removed from the heat of the city to healthful camps in the country, where they enjoy from one to three weeks reveling in health-giving air and sunshine. Others go to camps at the seashore or mountains.

Many of these associations in Philadelphia conduct one or more such camps. The number is swelled by those of the Boy Scouts, Girl Scouts, Camp Fire Girls, religious societies, universities, Y. M. C. A., large industrial organizations, boys' clubs, and settlement houses.

Philadelphia likewise has numerous orphan homes supported by religious institutions, private agencies, foundations, and popular subscription. They care for children of any race or creed. For physically handicapped children, who cannot attend school as normal children do, there are special classes and schools.

Outstanding among local welfare institutions is Girard College at Corinthian and South College Avenues. Founded under the will of Stephen Girard, the college was first opened in January 1848. It provides a home and precollege education for the normal white boy who is either totally orphaned or whose father is dead. Boys are admitted to the college between the ages of 6 and 10, and discharged between the ages of 14 and 18.

The Catholic Children's Bureau, at 1706 Summer Street, is the central office of the diocesan institutions caring for needy children. All applications for admission and discharge are made at this office. Children are accepted by court commitment or on private application. Besides placing children in institutions, the bureau also places them in private boarding homes.

The Mothers' Assistance Fund, at 260 South Broad Street, is the administrative agency which provides public aid to dependent children in their own homes from funds derived equally (until January 1, 1938) from municipal, State, and Federal sources. Aid to dependent children (formerly known as Mothers' Assistance) is given in the form of monthly cash payments to mothers with young children, after a careful investigation of eligibility and need. Under the State Public Assistance Law children must be under 16 and must have been deprived of paternal support through the death, absence from home, or disability of their fathers. The Federal Social Security Board participates in one-third of all payments not exceeding $18 monthly for the first child and $12 monthly for each additional child. (The law provided that after January 1, 1938, the program of aid to dependent children, as well as all other forms of public aid to persons in their own homes, should be the responsibility of a County Board of Public Assistance, to be financed entirely by State appropriations, supplemented by special Federal grants-in-aid.) Since 1934 the activities of the Mothers' Assistance Fund have included the administration of State pensions for the blind and State old-age

313

assistance, which is granted to needy persons 70 or more years of age.

The Bureau for Colored Children, at 712 North Forty-third Street, places dependent and neglected Negro boys and girls under 16 years of age in homes.

During the darkest days of the depression of the early 1930's, Philadelphia awoke to the realization that her charitable and welfare groups, largely of a privately endowed nature, were unable to cope with the problem of relief and unemployment. In a desperate effort to meet the situation, a group known as the "Lloyd Committee," and headed by the late Horatio Gates Lloyd, was formed. Funds were raised by popular subscription, and relief was temporarily broadened.

In 1932 the General Assembly of Pennsylvania passed three measures — the Woodward act, the second Talbot act, and the Emergency Relief Sales Tax act, these becoming the cornerstone of relief in the days to follow. The Woodward act created the State Emergency Relief Board, and authorized the setting up of county boards to administer aid locally. The Philadelphia County Relief Board was thus instituted, and the first appointments were made in August 1932.

From September 1, 1932, to February 28, 1933, emergency relief was financed by State revenue derived from a one percent tax on gross income from sales. Further support for Philadelphia's needy families was given in May 1933, by creation of the Federal Emergency Relief Administration. This State and Federal cooperation continued until December 1935, when Federal funds were discontinued and emergency relief became solely the responsibility of the State.

The emergency relief program was financed for a time by the sale of tax anticipation notes, secured by revenue from several levies imposed at a special session of the Legislature. Three levies included allowance for an increase in the State tax on property from one to four mills, an increase in the tax on corporate loans, extension of the inheritance tax to cover joint transfer, and a 10 percent tax on liquor sales at State stores.

From September 1932 to May 1936, the Philadelphia County Relief Board disbursed funds totaling $101,000,000, the average grant per case for the latter part of 1936 amounting to $7.47 per week, the average family being three persons.

At a special session in the spring of 1936 the Legislature provided $45,000,000 for emergency relief in Pennsylvania for the period between May 1936 and January 1937. In Philadelphia approximately 161,000 persons were on direct relief at the beginning of 1937. When on July 1, 1937, the Philadelphia County Relief Board went out of existence, more than 205,000 families had been assisted at one time or another. This work is now carried on by the Philadelphia County Board of Assistance.

In determining individual or family eligibility for relief, a thorough investigation is made of financial status, including income, if any, family resources, and the ability of relatives to aid. One of the basic requirements of eligibility for employment relief is the registration of all employable members of the family at the State Employment Office. The method of making investigations and determining needs stresses the responsibility of the applicant to assist in establishing his own eligibility by furnishing documentary and other information. Relief grants, limited to maximum amounts based on family size and the essential budget items allowed, are issued weekly in cash. Information obtained through periodic reinvestigations or reported voluntarily by relief families makes possible the adjustment of grants in accordance with changing needs and the prompt discontinuance of relief to persons no longer eligible.

Through the instrumentality of the Works Progress Administration program, inaugurated under the Federal Emergency Relief Appropriation Act of 1935, employable persons on the Philadelphia relief rolls were enabled to earn their livelihood and to so regain self-respect. The WPA program was designed to replace the less adequate machinery of work relief previously set up under the Civil Works Administration in 1933 and the Local Works Division in 1934. The many useful public works and cultural projects of the WPA have provided gainful and salutary occupation for thousands of Philadelphians who otherwise would have lost both skill and morale through living in enforced idleness on the dole.

Among the long established organizations to shoulder greatly increased responsibility during the depression was the Family Society, which provided food, clothing, and shelter for more than 15,000 families. Founded in 1878 for the purpose of maintaining needy families as units, the society throughout the years has fought constantly for the alleviation of want. Another group to stand the test of time is the Society of St. Vincent de Paul, established here in 1851. Neglected children in various Catholic parishes are placed in suitable homes, and each summer the society conducts a fresh-air camp in Chester County for children in the poorer sections.

Philadelphia has more than 60 homes for the aged, conducted by many organizations and churches. They are within the city as well as in surounding suburbs. Retired and needy actors are cared for at the Edwin Forrest Home for Actors, at Forty-ninth Street and Parkside Avenue. Mechanics also conduct a home, as do many veterans' organizations.

The Bureau of Legal Aid, maintained by the municipal government until 1933, has been superseded by an organization known as the Legal Aid Society of Philadelphia. Its offices are at 4 South Fifteenth Street, and it is supported by the Community Fund. The Philadelphia Voluntary Defender Association, at the same address, provides similar

315

free legal service, except that its interests are restricted to criminal cases only. The association, organized in 1933, with Maurice B. Saul as president, Francis Fisher Kane as secretary, and Thomas E. Cogan as defender began operating April 14, 1934. This association is likewise maintained by the Community Fund.

Philadelphia Skyline As Seen from the Art Museum

★

★

★

★

★

★

POINTS of SPECIAL INTEREST

to the CITY'S GUESTS

★

★

★

Old Gate at Independence Square

INDEPENDENCE SQUARE GROUP

Independence Hall, Congress Hall, Old City Hall, American Philosophical Society Building. Bounded by 5th, 6th, Chestnut and Walnut Sts.

INDEPENDENCE SQUARE

WITHIN the confines of a comparatively small plot of ground known as Independence Square stands a group of red brick buildings enshrined in the hearts of patriotic Americans. Revered by liberty-loving people the world over, these structures, their beauty and simplicity undisturbed by modern progress, are mute reminders of heroic times and intrepid men.

Long before the Revolution the old square was the meeting place of Philadelphia's citizenry. To this outdoor rendezvous they came in hundreds and thousands whenever trouble threatened. Here, both indoors and outdoors, many of the events that culminated in American independence took place—events now regarded as having led to one of the greatest contributions ever made toward establishing an ideal of free government.

From a small wooden astronomical observatory in the rear of Independence Hall, John Nixon, a member of the Revolutionary Committee of Safety, made the first public announcement of the Declaration of Independence. He read the immortal document in full to a tense throng of citizens on July 8, 1776. More than a decade earlier, on October 25, 1765, Philadelphia merchants had met in the square and adopted a resolution to boycott British merchandise — a stern retaliation against the obnoxious Stamp Act. On October 16, 1773, several weeks prior to the Boston Tea Party, Philadelphia patriots gathered here to devise measures for turning back the tea ship *Polly.*

Its early name of State House Yard was given the plot of ground at the time when it was purchased (in 1730) as the site for a state house. The yard, near the then western limits of the city, at first extended from Chestnut Street halfway to Walnut ; the remaining lots on Fifth, Sixth, and Walnut Streets were acquired at various times prior to the Revolution. Successive acts, the first in 1736, ordered the ground south of the State House to be retained as a public green forever ; but the American Philosophical Society building, which still stands, encroached upon it, as did the Quarter Sessions Courthouse, which was removed in 1902.

319

The square was entirely restored in 1875. In 1915-16 it was again reconstructed, and 56 gas lamps of antique pattern, one for each signer of the Declaration of Independence, were installed. The four-acre rectangular tract measures 396 by 510 feet.

In Colonial times the square was surrounded by a brick wall seven or eight feet high, with an immense central gateway and wooden door on the Walnut Street side. Prior to 1812, the city of Philadelphia reduced the height of the wall to three feet along Fifth and Sixth Streets and placed upon it an iron railing fixed into stone coping. The wall paralleling Walnut Street, however, was not reduced to a corresponding height until 1813. At that time an iron gateway, flanked by marble posts surmounted by lamps, replaced the large double wooden doors which opened inwardly. These gates were removed in 1876 and have been replaced by a low brick wall.

In the center of the square stands a bronze statue of Commodore John Barry. The work of Samuel Murray, this statue is a gift to the city from the Friendly Sons of St. Patrick, of which organization Barry was a member. It was erected in 1907 at a cost of $10,000. An iron chain which once surrounded the statue was stolen one night in 1910 and has never been replaced.

Among the trees in the square are 13 red oaks, one for each of the original Colonies, planted by the National Association of Gardeners on October 11, 1926. The roots of each tree are nurtured in soil brought from the State the tree represents. The Independence Square fountain, with separate drinking outlets for humans, birds, and dogs, originally stood in the Centennial Exhibition grounds in Fairmount Park. It is maintained by the Sons of Temperance Society, and a special guard keeps it supplied with ice during the summer months.

Measures to protect the buildings in the square against fire have been taken in response to public insistence. The present dry-head sprinkler system consists of a network of pipes extending to all the buildings. In the event of fire, the pipes release a downpour that covers the exteriors with water deemed sufficient to check the blaze until firemen arrive. The system is tested in semiannual drills. Two truck companies, five engine companies, one pipe-line squad, and a rescue squad take part in these drills. Employees participate in weekly fire drills.

The city of Philadelphia acquired the entire property of the Independence Square group in 1816, receiving a formally executed deed from the State upon the payment of $70,000. More than 500,000 persons annually visit the National Museum housed in the buildings of the group.

Independence Hall

On Chestnut St. midway between 5th and 6th. Open daily 8:45 a.m. to 4:30 p.m. Admission free. Visitors and teachers can obtain the services of a guide upon application to the curator.

MANY episodes entitle Independence Hall to lasting fame. Within its walls, on July 4, 1776, the Declaration of Independence received the signatures which made it official. Here, on June 16, 1775, the Congress had given Washington command of the undisciplined, inadequately armed Continental Army which later became the weapon that defeated England. Here, on July 9, 1778, the Articles of Confederation were ratified, welding the Thirteen Colonies into one union. And here, on September 17, 1787, the Constitution was drawn up as the Nation's basic law, superseding the Articles of Confederation, which the swift march of events had outmoded.

The convention at which the Constitution was framed had been called ostensibly to revise the Articles of Confederation and was held behind closed doors. This subterfuge was necessitated by reluctance of the various States to place governmental authority in the hands of a central body. The secrecy had the effect of forestalling any vigorous action on the part of the general public toward inserting provisions that would be inimical to the interests of the leaders.

Construction of Independence Hall was begun in 1732, and in 1736, while still in an unfinished condition, it was occupied by the Provincial Assembly, which used it continuously until May 10, 1775, when the Second Continental Congress took possession. It was before the latter body, on June 7, 1776, that Richard Henry Lee, obeying the instructions of the Virginia Assembly, moved the resolution :

> That these United Colonies are, and of right ought to be, free and independent States; that they are absolved from all allegiance to the British Crown, and that all political connection between them and the State of Great Britain is, and ought to be, totally dissolved.

At that same moment, Britain's German mercenaries were riding the high seas towards the seething Colonies, and fortifications were sprouting along Boston harbor (Charlestown). The pressing need of organizing military forces took several of the delegates away from their legislative duties.

Lee's first speech on the resolution reveals some idea of the high purpose that actuated the Congress. Said Lee :

Barry Statue and Independence Hall
"Father of the American Navy"

> Let this happy day give birth to an American republic.
> The eyes of Europe are fixed upon us; she demands of
> us a living example of freedom . . . If we are not this
> day wanting in our duty to our country, the names of the
> American Legislators of '76 will be placed by posterity
> at the side of these . . . whose memory . . . forever
> will be dear.

The absolutely secret debate and the meager records kept by the beleaguered delegates account in part for conflicting versions of the exciting events. Three days of deliberation upon the resolution ended with its postponement until July 1, to allow various Provincial conventions time to meet and adopt an authoritative stand. Meanwhile, a committee headed by Thomas Jefferson was chosen to draw up the Declaration of Independence "in case the Congress agree thereto."

July 1 was a hot, sultry day. Through open windows of the old State House came a plague of flies to harass the assembled delegates, and the air outside pulsated with heat waves and the emotions of an aroused populace.

Towards the close of the first day the vote showed nine Colonies favoring the resolution. The final vote, postponed to the next day, was unanimous, due partly to the spectacular efforts of several delegates. Memorable among these was Caesar Rodney, who, suffering from a life-long affliction, rode 80 miles on horseback from Dover, Del. He arrived, half-dead from pain and fatigue, in time to break the deadlock in the Delaware delegation.

This was on July 2. July 4 is celebrated as Independence Day because on that day Jefferson's draft of the Declaration was made official by the signatures of John Hancock, the Speaker, and Charles Thompson, the Secretary. However, this was not before Jefferson had watched in misery while Franklin and Adams performed forensic surgery upon his brain child, deleting, as a concession to the southern Colonies, the section on slavery, and curbing his rhetorical flights.

Most historians agree that the delegates did not immediately affix their signatures. Considerable confusion, resulting from divergent accounts by Jefferson and Thomas McKean, both present at the time, later arose on this point. Historical evidence, in contradiction of Jefferson's letters, points to the fact that the delegates' signatures were not affixed to the Declaration until August 2, when a copy had been engrossed on parchment. At that time Franklin, in the midst of the solemn hush that followed the signing, remarked dryly : "Gentlemen, we must now all hang together, or we shall most assuredly hang separately."

On July 8, after the Declaration had been printed on broadsides for distribution among the Colonies, public announcement of the document was made ; the great bell in the State House tower rang in a new era of history.

The LIBERTY BELL, in the rear of the first floor corridor, is identified in popular imagination with the ideal of freedom. The great and famous of all lands have paid it homage. But it was not always thus. This now priceless symbol of liberty was regarded as a worthless nuisance by the early authorities· It was originally cast in 1751, at the cost of £60, 14 shillings, and five pence, by Thomas Lister, in London's Whitechapel. The bell, weighing 2,080 pounds, arrived in Philadelphia late in August 1752. While being tested, it cracked under the impact of the clapper. Two ambitious men, Pass and Stow, undertook to recast it. The town wags derided the mortified workmen when the new bell, rung in April 1753, complained in a sour, discordant voice of the presence of too much copper. However, its tone was such as to satisfy the most exacting critics when, in June of the same year, it had been again recast and hung in the State House belfry.

Then followed a virtual epidemic of bell ringing. The huge clapper, like a termagant's tongue, was rarely still. It rang for state purposes ; it rang to summon congregations and to announce meetings ; it sometimes rang for no good reason at all. Residents in the vicinity of the State House became irritated at its perpetual clangor. In a petition to the authorities they begged to be saved from what they described as a "lethal weapon," declaring : "From its uncommon size and unusual sound, it is extremely dangerous and may prove fatal to those afflicted with sickness."

The Liberty Bell acquired its name in 1776, when it pealed forth its triumphant notes. One year later, as evidence of the strong sentiment then attached to it, the bell was removed when British troops approached the city. It was carted to Allentown under military escort and hidden under the floor of the Zion Reformed Church.

Following British evacuation, the bell was brought back and suspended from its beam. The windows of the belfry were covered with sounding boards to achieve a better tonal effect. For many years it did yeoman service. In 1824 it pealed a welcome to Lafayette, when a gala reception for him enlivened Independence Hall. Its voice died when the metal cracked during a somber accompaniment to the funeral procession of Chief Justice John Marshall on July 8, 1835.

Years of inglorious neglect followed. Its thunderous voice muted and its heroic labors forgotten by fickle humanity, the bell was offered in part payment for a new one ordered by the city fathers from John Wilbank, a Germantown bell founder. Wilbank cast and delivered the new bell, but found prohibitive the cost of hauling the Liberty Bell from the State House.

"Drayage costs more than the bell's worth," he finally declared, and he left it there.

INDEPENDENCE SQUARE GROUP

The incensed city fathers haled Wilbank before a magistrate for failing to remove the old bell. The magistrate decreed that Wilbank should pay the costs of the suit, but suggested that if the bell maker offered the burdensome relic to the city authorities as a gift, they might accept. They accepted, but with little enthusiasm.

The old bell's peal for freedom, however, had penetrated to the ears of the oppressed peoples of the world — imperceptible waves of sound and meaning that found an echo. These peoples came in multitudes, touched the bell with trembling hands and wept tears of mingled joy and sorrow at sight of the cold, dark metal whose mighty tongue had given forth peals of defiance to oppressors. Simultaneously, the city fathers and the local populace awoke to a shamed realization of their callousness. Today the Liberty Bell's value cannot be measured.

The bell was shipped around the country for many years, but its trip in 1915 to the Panama-Pacific Exposition at San Francisco aroused so many misgivings that descendants of the signers of the Declaration of Independence demanded that it never again be moved from Independence Hall. However, another trip was made in 1917, when the bell was removed for the Philadelphia Liberty Loan street parade. It has come now to its final resting place, in the building where its voice rang loudest.

Special precautions have been taken to safeguard the bell. In 1929, its supporting yoke having been dangerously weakened by dry rot, one-inch steel bars were inserted to strengthen it. The bell is mounted upon a truck encased in a removable pedestal, and in the event of fire it can be towed out of the building by one man in less than two minutes.

Encircling the crown of the bell is the prophetic lettering from Leviticus XXV. 10 : "PROCLAIM LIBERTY THROUGHOUT ALL THE LAND UNTO ALL THE INHABITANTS THEREOF."

The surface of the bell, which is larger than is generally supposed, is pitted and uneven on the outer walls as well as in the barrel, evidence of the inexperience of Messrs. Pass and Stow. The gaping crack zigzags from lip to lettering. The parted edges are held in place by large round bolts. The chipped and ragged lip discloses the vandalism of souvenir collectors and the inescapable misadventures attendant upon longevity.

The first real attempt to assemble a historical art collection for Independence Hall was made in 1854 when, at the sale of Charles Willson Peale's effects, the city acquired more than 100 of his oil portraits. Peale, whose museum occupied the second-floor chambers of Independence Hall from 1802 to 1826, studied art under Hesselius, Copley, and West, masters of that day. Possessing talent as a portrait painter, he set for himself the patriotic task of preserving the likenesses of the heroes of the day. These formed the nucleus of the present National Portrait Gallery.

In 1873 this collection, together with numerous relics and curios that had been accumulating for years, was taken over by the city as the National Museum. Credit for this is due mainly to Frank M. Etting, who was most active in urging the restoration of Independence Hall, and who became chairman of its board of managers when restoration was accomplished. The museum has grown to occupy approximately two acres of floor space in the several buildings constituting the group. Tasteful arrangement has enhanced the attractiveness which patriotic feelings lend to the exhibits

To the right as the building is entered from Chestnut Street is the room where the Pennsylvania State Constitution was framed and adopted. It was also used as a JUDICIAL CHAMBER of the Supreme Court of Pennsylvania from 1743 to 1776.

Left on the first floor is the DECLARATION CHAMBER. A fine pedimented panel framing a facsimile of the Declaration of Independence is set between the fireplaces that flank the small platform at the end of the room. The crystal chandelier in this room, brought from Waterford, Ireland, in 1745, is the only one of the original chandeliers remaining. Lining the walls of the chamber are several pieces of furniture once used by the signers of the Declaration. The portrait of Washington by James Peale hangs over the chamber entrance and is surrounded by facsimiles of flags carried by Continental troops. The room contains the SILVER INKSTAND SET made by the famous Philip Syng, goldsmith, and used by the signers of the Declaration.

The Liberty Bell is near the rear door on this floor. Second in interest to the bell are the paintings in the National Portrait Gallery. The major portion of the celebrated collection is on the second floor of Independence Hall. Conspicuous in the collection is the painting, *Penn's Treaty with the Indians*, by Benjamin West, and three portraits of Washington by his contemporaries, Robert Edge Pine, Rembrandt Peale, and James Peale.

The second floor contains three rooms : the CHAMBER OF THE CLERK OF THE ASSEMBLY, the BANQUET CHAMBER or LONG ROOM, and the COUNCIL CHAMBER, where the Provincial Governors of Pennsylvania and their councils sat from 1748 to the time of the Revolution.

The West Wing of Independence Hall is known as the COLONIAL MUSEUM and contains collections relating to the periods of discovery, permanent settlement, and activities of the Colonies up to the outbreak of the Revolutionary War. This wing was built in 1735, and its

326

first floor was used as an office by the Secretary of the Province until 1776.

On the first floor of the West Wing is the COSTUME COLLECTION. Here are a brocaded dress worn during Revolutionary War times, a suit of boy's clothes of the period of 1750, a fashion doll of the eighteenth century, and many other articles of clothing worn during that era. On one side of the room is a collection of old spinning wheels. The second floor of the west wing was occupied as a committee room until 1783. Then it was fitted up for the Supreme Court of the State of Pennsylvania. The building is a restoration erected in 1897.

The East Wing is used as a museum. It was built in 1735. The first floor, which is now one large room with a small hallway, was formerly divided into two rooms, assigned respectively to the Registrar General and the Recorder of Deeds of the Province. Examples of military equipment, including a service sword owned by Gen. Anthony Wayne and a drum carried in the Revolution, are on exhibition. There is a fine collection of eighteenth century firearms, among which is the George Washington rifle and the musket which belonged to General Wayne. In the center of the room is a small Spanish cannon, sometimes called a falconet, used in Europe in the sixteenth century.

An exhibit of china, porcelain, pottery, and glassware is on the second floor of the West Wing. Included in the collection are a cup, saucer, and soup plate used at the wedding of George and Martha Washington, and a platter used by the Washington family at Mount Vernon. Here also is a sixteenth century brewing jar brought to America by William Penn ; a pitcher used by Washington ; a jar which belonged to Mrs. John Adams ; glassware used by Patrick Henry ; an early butter crock ; and pitchers used by Washington and Lafayette. This room was occupied by the Philadelphia Library Company as a place of deposit for its books from 1739 to 1773.

Congress Hall

S.E. corner 6th and Chestnut Sts. Open weekdays 8:45 a.m. to 4:30 p.m. Admission free.

IN CONGRESS HALL, during the turbulent decade between December 6, 1790, and May 4, 1800, some of the early scenes in the pageant of America's national history were enacted. Here Washington delivered his second inaugural address ; the Army and Navy assumed a creditable footing ; the Mint was born ; the first Bank of the United States was instituted ; Vermont, Kentucky and Tennessee were admitted to statehood ; and the celebrated Jay Treaty of Commerce with England was promulgated. Here John Adams was inaugurated as the second President of the United States, and Washington delivered his famous Farewell Address to the American people.

Congress Hall stands on ground purchased in 1736 as a site for a Philadelphia County building. Construction began in 1787, two years after the Pennsylvania Assembly had appropriated $3,000 for that purpose, and in 1789 the hall was ready for use.

The first session of Congress had been held in New York City, but most of the Colonies regarded the arrangement as temporary, and sought for themselves the commercial advantage and the prestige attendant upon a capital city. Considerable acrimonious debate was indulged in, especially in the Senate.

Stealing a march, the Pennsylvania Assembly, on March 4, 1789 (the same day the new Government met in New York for its first session), instructed the State's Congressional representatives to exert themselves to obtain for Philadelphia the seat of the National Government, offering for that purpose any of Philadelphia's public buildings, particularly the newly erected county building.

The House of Representatives passed a resolution favoring Pennsylvania, but Robert Morris' activities in the Senate met with abuse and ridicule. The bill finally passed was a compromise measure designed to smooth ruffled feelings. The land along both banks of the Potomac, "neutral territory" later to be known as the District of Columbia, was designated as the National Capital, beginning with the year 1800. Meanwhile, Philadelphia became the temporary capital.

The newly woven fabric of government was subjected to severe tests, but its essential strength, based upon enthusiastic popular support, was sufficient to withstand them. Gravest of all was the diplomatic joust with France, when her privateers strained friendly relations by practicing hostilities upon American commerce. As a result of these clashes President John Adams issued a proclamation, dated July 13, 1798, depriving French consular officials of their right to function. The new Government displayed similar resolution in dealing with the Whiskey Insurrection and in conducting the Indian campaign, made famous by St. Clair's defeat and Wayne's success.

The exterior and interior of Congress Hall, restored in 1913 by a committee of architects appointed by the city and rededicated on October 25 of that year in the presence of President Wilson, are substantially as they were during the occupancy by Congress. Numerous exhibits are on display.

The first floor consists of a single chamber, with a vestibule running along the front and a double staircase leading to the gallery. Here the House of Representatives met. On view in this chamber is Joshua Humphreys' model of what is thought to be the ship *Americana*, de-

328

signed in 1777 and presented to John Paul Jones. Here, too, is a plaster model of Thomas Jefferson, cast more than 100 years ago. Also on view is a statuette in terra cotta of Lafayette, cast in America from a Staffordshire, England, pottery figure, at the time of Lafayette's last visit to America in 1824. Two of the original fireplaces still remain, also some eighteenth century implements, such as a foot stove, candle mold, hearth shovel, and fire tongs.

In the vestibule is the regimental flag carried by troops under Gen. Philip John Schuyler during the Revolutionary War, also a flag believed to have been carried during the Battle of the Brandywine.

The SENATE CHAMBER is in the rear of the second floor. The President of the Senate occupied a platform on the south side of the room. At first this room had no gallery, but at the suggestion of James Monroe, one suitable for the use of the public, running along the north side of the chamber, was constructed in 1795. In the center of the room in front of the speaker's rostrum is a life-size wood carving of Washington by William Rush. Among the personal effects is one of Washington's Masonic aprons. There is also the original commission making George Washington Commander in Chief of the Continental Army, and the muster roll of Washington's bodyguard. Other exhibits include original letters written by men of the Revolutionary period and a Washington life mask, cast from the original owned by J. Pierpont Morgan.

In the hallway of the second floor is an exhibition of early American pewter. Conspicuous in this collection is a molasses jug used by Washington and Lafayette while in (Widow Ford's) winter headquarters. Also on view are plates, an inkstand, and a chocolate pot.

In the first room to the right is a collection of furniture and silverware of the Revolutionary period, including the chair used by Lafayette when he was the city's guest in 1824 ; the sofa used by Washington's family in the Executive Mansion on High (now Market) Street ; the drop-leaf table which Washington used while living at the Frederick Wampole farmhouse at Tawamencin, Pa., during the winter sojourn at Valley Forge ; Jefferson's card table ; a collection of eighteenth century spoons ; an eighteenth century sperm oil lamp ; and a teapot used by Daniel Webster. Other objects of interest are Thomas Jefferson's cane ; numerous watches of the Revolutionary period ; and a collection of spectacles, including the silver-rimmed pair worn by George Washington.

In the second room to the right, UNITED STATES COIN ROOM, is a collection of American coins found during the demolition of the first United States Mint building on North Seventh Street. They are the only specimens in existence of planchets and slugs in gold, silver, and copper from which our first coins were made. There also is a boot

329

Congress Hall
"The place of Washington's Farewell Address"

Old City Hall
*"Where the city's statutes and ordinances were
first passed"*

scraper and other items from the old Mint building. A collection of early bank notes and a Presidential series of bronze medals from Washington to Theodore Roosevelt are also on exhibition.

In the first room to the left is a collection of early surgical instruments, including a number of eighteenth century lancets. Also on view is an early American jewel box ; a silver loving cup which belonged to Caesar Augustus Rodney, nephew of the Delaware delegate to the Continental Congress whose ride is one of the dramatic episodes in America's history ; a fruit basket made in London in 1763 ; a coffee pot used by Robert Morris ; George Washington's pocket compass ; Martha Washington's toasting fork ; a powder horn and bag used in the Battle of Kings Mountain ; and the ale mug of Admiral John Paul Jones.

Old City Hall

S.W. corner 5th and Chestnut Sts. Open weekdays 8:45 a.m. to 4:30 p.m. Admission free.

PHILADELPHIA'S Old City Hall was built at Fifth and Chestnut Streets in 1791, in architectural harmony with the earlier structures of the Independence Square group. Intended as the seat of the municipality, the Supreme Court of the United States met here during the last decade of the eighteenth century. The judicial branch of the Federal Government, after assembling in New York City in 1789 and framing a simple code of rules, began sessions for the first time in Philadelphia's Old City Hall.

The first Chief Justice of the United States was Washington's appointee, John Jay, who later arranged with England the important commercial treaty which bears his name. The first case of note to come before the Court was the "State of Georgia v. Brailsford and others," concerning a bond, given by persons alleged to be aliens, which was sequestered by the State of Georgia.

Virtually all the cases to come before the Court during its occupancy of Old City Hall were of a type that distinguished the rights of the citizens from those of the States. At this period the Justices served also as circuit judges whenever the Supreme Court was not in session.

City Council met in the building until 1854, although the Mayor's office was moved in 1816 to Independence Hall, purchased that year by the city. After 1800, with the removal of the State capital to Lancaster and transfer of the Federal Government to Washington, Philadelphia became less prominent in the affairs of Pennsylvania and the Nation.

Doorway of the American Philosophical Society Building
Portal of Savants.

Old City Hall, like Congress Hall, is in scale with the central unit, their similar crowning cupolas balancing the central tower. The identical theme of their architecture makes these two almost twin structures.

To the left as one enters Old City Hall is the OFFICE OF THE MAYOR. The only article left in this room from the time the first mayor occupied the building — Matthew Clarkson, who served during the yellow-fever epidemic of 1793 — is a built-in wall clock imported from England in 1789. It has remained in its original position since the day of installation. A collection of Indian objects including arrowheads, tomahawks, wooden and stone implements used in the preparation of food, blankets, ornamental decorations of beads, and musical instruments are on display.

In the MAYOR'S COURT ROOM on the first floor are several articles of antique furniture and a large collection of ancient firefighting equipment used by Philadelphia's early firemen ; also a section of an old water main excavated at Ninth and Market Streets, and Franklin's perpetual calendar which was presented to him in 1774 by James Moody of London.

In the vestibule on the side of the stairs leading up to the second floor is a large piece of the elm tree under which William Penn is believed to have negotiated a treaty with the Indians. Here also is a miniature model of the old battleship *Pennsylvania* constructed at the Philadelphia Navy Yard. Several relics reminiscent of the days when the Indians were on the warpath include an Indian scalp, a scalp lock, a scalping knife, and a tomahawk. There are also some pieces of ancient fire-fighting apparatus.

On the second floor is the SUPREME COURT CHAMBER. There are four other rooms which were occupied by the Common Council and Select Council and by various departments of the city government.

Throughout these rooms on the second floor are interesting exhibits of scientific instruments. Of especial attraction is the transit, one of the three with which astronomical observation in the New World was made in 1768. Other exhibits include ancient locks and keys, scales, iron chests, a cradle, a model of Christ Church, and part of the original pew used by George Washington in Christ Church.

The second floor also has a room devoted to old-time Quaker relics and costumes, a rather rare and unusual exhibit which satisfies the keen curiosity shown by many visitors in anything pertaining to the early Quakers.

333

American Philosophical Society

On the 5th St. side of Independence Square, just south of Chestnut St. Open weekdays 9:30 a. m. to 4:30 p. m. ; Saturdays 9:30 a. m. to 12 noon. Closed Saturdays from June to September. Admission by appointment.

MELLOWED by a Colonial charm of architecture and setting which belies its eminent rank in the realm of learning, the century-and-a-half-old home of the American Philosophical Society stands on the east side of the square, symbolizing a scientific tradition interlocking Colonial and modern times.

It was built on a lot in Independence Square and presented to the society in 1785 by the Commonwealth of Pennsylvania. Funds for the building were raised by Benjamin Franklin and his associates. The society shelters a group founded by Franklin in 1727, and its membership rolls list 12 Presidents of the United States.

The first of these was George Washington ; the most recent, Herbert Hoover. The others were John Adams, Thomas Jefferson, James Madison, John Quincy Adams, James Buchanan, Ulysses S. Grant, Grover Cleveland, Theodore Roosevelt, William Howard Taft, and Woodrow Wilson. Cleveland, Roosevelt, and Taft became members while in office.

Fifteen of the signers of the Declaration of Independence ; 18 signers of the Constitution of the United States ; 12 Associate Justices of the Supreme Court of the United States ; and five Chief Justices of the United States were or are members of the society. Of 23 American winners of Nobel Prizes, 11 are on the membership rolls.

The society's collection includes a copy of the original draft of the Declaration of Independence, in Jefferson's handwriting ; Jefferson's desk chair ; portraits and busts of a number of distinguished Americans, including a Stuart portrait of Washington ordered in 1799 ; a clock made by David Rittenhouse ; and the instruments he and his associates used in recording the transit of Venus across the sun on June 3, 1769. Among nearly 15,000 pieces of Frankliniana are Franklin's first battery and his ingenious "stepladder library chair." One of the finest of scientific library collections was maintained in this building until it outgrew the original structure's facilities. It is now in the Drexel Building just opposite, in room 222. Manuscripts, paintings, and other treasures exhibited by the society are valued at millions of dollars.

Interior of Independence Hall

Architecture of the Group

ANDREW HAMILTON, recognized as the original designer of old Independence Hall, is believed to have drawn his inspiration for the hall from James Gibbs' *Book of Architecture*, which was published in 1728. At least, there is a striking resemblance between a drawing in Gibbs' book and the historic shrine. Independence Hall, however, represents a more elaborate design than Gibbs' drawing. The idea of grouping the State House with the other two buildings into a harmonious unit is similar to the scheme used in the construction of the Pennsylvania Hospital.

The warmth of the red brick used in their construction effectively contrasts with well-studied marble and white-painted wooden details. The dominant feature of the group is the former State House, occupied in 1735, though work on the interiors lasted for several more years. The fine tower was built in 1750 ; a steeple was added in 1753 but removed in 1781. In 1828 William Strickland completed the present bell tower and steeple, a close copy of the original. By that time the old structure had long been known as Independence Hall.

The handsome Chestnut Street facade attains its dignity by the stress of horizontal lines and repetition of finely proportioned windows and blue soapstone panels. Soapstone belt courses connect the keystones of the first-floor windows and the second-floor sills. The entrance, approached by four steps, contains a high, simple doorway, which is deeply recessed. Where the pitch of the roof breaks into a flat gambrel, a balustrade connecting the quadruple end chimneys repeats the line of the beautiful cornice. Four drain spouts and the quoined corners are the only vertical accents. At each end of Independence Hall are unusual triple-arched chimneys, each with a small bull's-eye window beneath. These circular windows were originally used for the State House clock dials. The clockworks were in the center of the attic with connecting rods to each dial. Details of ornament that usually pass unnoticed are the grotesque keystones with carved heads, over the windows on three sides of the top story of the brick tower.

The tower gives access to Independence Hall from the square. Its exceptionally beautiful Palladian window above the Doric tower entrance, the setbacks of the upper wooden sections, the small domed cupola set upon a larger one, and the slim steeple and weathervane make this old bell tower one of outstanding beauty.

Connected with Independence Hall by covered arcades are two hip-roofed wings. The original East Wing, completed in 1735, and the West Wing, in 1739, had no provision for reaching the upper stories by an interior stairway, the only access to the second floor being by the tower staircase. Both were altered in 1813. The two arcades and

336

the outside stairways of the wings were removed at that time, and two-story buildings, designed by Robert Mills, were erected in their places. In 1896 the wings were razed, and new structures the size of the originals but with interior stairways were erected, with arched arcades again joining them with the main building. Their two stories rise to the height of but one story of the State House.

The American Philosophical Society Building, erected in 1789, is the only private building on Independence Square. Standing as it does in its position so close to Old City Hall, its exterior is in keeping with the rest of the group.

The most outstanding interiors architecturally are those of Independence Hall—the entire ground floor, the bell tower, and the long banquet hall on the second floor. The chief features of the central hall are the engaged fluted Roman Doric columns supporting the mutulary entablature which surrounds the hall, the pedimented wall tablets and the entrance to the Declaration Chamber on the east side, the triple archway to the Judicial Chamber to the west, and the fine pedimented main entrance with its heavy wrought-iron hardware. The pediments above the main door and the entrance to the Declaration Chamber are unusual. Between the curved scrolls at the top are heads with leaf crowns and beards. A fine arched opening leads to the tower that once housed the Liberty Bell. This bell tower is the most beautiful interior of the entire group. Its open staircase and Palladian window are masterpieces of Georgian Colonial design and craftsmanship.

The west room is the Judicial or State Constitution Chamber. Here are Doric pilasters of design similar to the columns of the central hall. The speaker's platform, extending across the west wall, somewhat larger than that in the Declaration Chamber, has been completely restored. Six small steps at each end approach the large, white, paneled desk which serves as the rail of the platform.

To the east of the central hall is the Independence Assembly Hall, now known as the Declaration Chamber. It is similar in architectural treatment to the entrance hall, but has piers and pilasters in place of columns. At the far end of the room is a small platform two steps above the floor upon which rests the speaker's desk. Behind the desk within a large monumental pedimented panel is set a facsimile of the Declaration of Independence. On either side of the platform is a broad fireplace. The heavy mantels are supported at the ends by scroll brackets decorated with acanthus leaves.

The most interesting room on the second floor is the Banquet Chamber or Long Room, notable mainly for its proportions, its long row of nine windows, its fine doorways, and its simple end fireplaces.

Congress Hall, completed in 1789, was found to be too small, so in

337

1793 it was lengthened by about 27 feet. The entrance doorway, approached by five steps, is framed within an arch supported by Doric pilasters of rough gray marble. The double wooden doors in four narrow sections are painted white. Above the arch is carved a coat of arms of Pennsylvania, and above this on the second story level is a fine wrought-iron balcony. The main feature of the ground floor is the room containing the speaker's rostrum and the small circular raised platform which seated the first House of Representatives, both of which have been restored. Aside from the copy of the original glass chandelier, the interior is simple in detail. The arched windows, chaste entablature, and simple gallery are the chief features. The smaller Senate room above, only slightly richer in detail, has an ornamental plaster ceiling of Adam design.

Old City Hall, or Towne Hall, Fifth and Chestnut Streets, is a two-story structure similar in design to Congress Hall, but smaller. On the first floor is the Mayor's Court Room, which is entered through paneled double doors, having a large single fan light above. The atmosphere of the room is restrained and dignified. The long axis of the chamber runs at right angles to the entrance. Opposite the doors and beneath a broad arch is the speaker's rostrum set within a bay and guarded by a delicate railing. Three handsome, rounded, headed windows form a backdrop. On the opposite side of the platform and above the entrance is a balcony, running the length of the chamber. A delicate, old pewter chandelier, now wired for electricity, depends from the ceiling. Doors in either side of the speaker's platform lead to the courtyard. The witnesses of the walls, ceiling, and wood trim is relieved by the mahogany-stained floor and the handsome hand rail of the rostrum.

On the second floor are several rooms. In these the old fireplaces have been replaced by mantelpieces over a modern heating system. It was in the south room of this floor that the Supreme Court met.

Benjamin Franklin's Chair
Presto! It Became a Library Stepladder.

338

CARPENTERS' HALL

*In Carpenters' Court, extending south from
Chestnut St., between 3d and 4th. Open
weekdays 9 a. m. to 4 p. m. Admission free.*

AS INDEPENDENCE HALL was the forge on which the sword
of liberty was shaped, so Carpenters' Hall—two squares east,
and home of one of the Colonies' first crafts guilds—was the
foundry in which the chains of British oppression were converted into
the steel weapons of resistance.

It was here, in 1774—and by a singular coincidence, on July 4—
that the Committee of the City and County of Philadelphia appointed
a subcommittee to prepare plans for a Provincial conference.

It was here, in spite of hints by the Royalist press that the necks
of both participants and abettors "might be inconveniently lengthened," that the First Continental Congress assembled on September
5, 1774.

The Society of Carpenters was organized in 1724 by master carpenters of Colonial Philadelphia for the dissemination of architectural instruction, and assistance of needy members of the craft. The
craftsmen's guild was incorporated in 1790 as the Carpenters' Company of Philadelphia. Members began construction of the hall in
1770, and although the guild held its first meeting there the following January, the structure remained unfinished throughout the turbulent Revolutionary period. It was not completed until 1792.

Meantime, years of suffering under the heel of oppression had been
capped by numerous outrages against Colonials on the part of British
Regulars. Finally the advent of arbitrary taxation fanned the smolder-
ing flame of protest so that it spread to local legislative assemblies.

Convinced that the time was ripe for action, leading patriots urged
that the Colonies call a convention and voice their united protests.
The meeting was called for September 5, and its sponsors, in order to
avoid interference with the session of the State Assembly in the State
House, chose Carpenters' Hall as their meeting place.

Three years later, when British troops occupied the city, the hall
was converted into a barracks. Grimly reminiscent of that chapter in
its history is the bullet-riddled metal ball, now displayed in the hallway. Once a part of the weather vane atop the cupola of the building,
this ball was used as a target by Redcoats intent on improving their
marksmanship. In 1787 the building was occupied by the Commissary
General of Military Stores of the Continental Army.

The communal value of the building was by no means limited to
its wartime service, however, for it served with nearly equal prominence in the advancement of trade, finance, and culture. Subsequent
to its evacuation by the British, it quartered a meeting called to for-

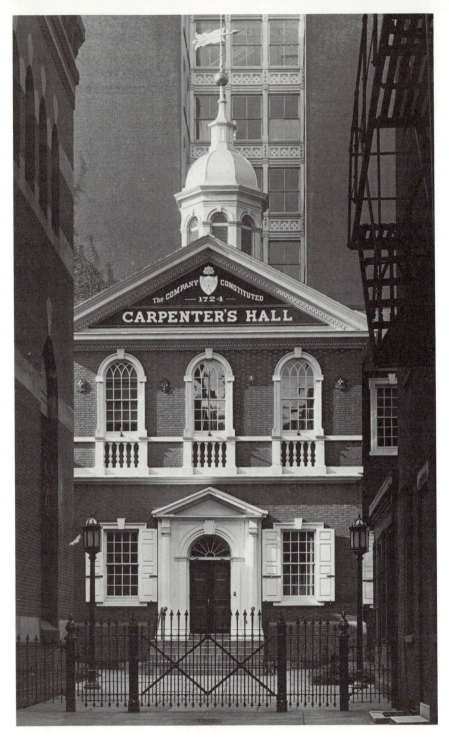

Carpenter's Hall

mulate plans for encouraging American manufacture of linens, woolens, and other textiles. That meeting laid the groundwork of the great textile industry in Philadelphia today.

In the field of letters, it is a matter of record that the great collection of the present Free Library of Philadelphia had its nucleus in the volumes that lined the bookshelves of Carpenters' Hall between 1773 and 1790.

It was in Carpenters' Hall that the first Bank of the United States set up its headquarters in 1791. In addition, this historical old meeting hall has sheltered at various times the Bank of the State of Pennsylvania, the United States Law Office, United States Custom House, Apprentices' Free Library, Franklin Institute, and the Society of Friends.

The high character of the Carpenters' Company explains in large degree the excellence of the architecture of this section, of which the company's own hall, as well as the old State House, built by Edmond Woolley, a member of the company, are distinguished examples.

The structure is built in the form of a Greek cross, with four projecting gable ends and a central cupola. It is constructed of brick, laid in Flemish bond, with glazed headers. The main entrance is approached by five steps leading to the pedimented doorway with a fanlight. Three fine arched windows, with stone balustrades below, rest on a horizontal belt course of white woodwork at the second-floor level.

The front part of the building contains a vestibule and stairs leading to the second floor, which is not open to the public. The rest of the first floor is one large room, in the rear of which is a huge doorway. This door, the finest architectural detail of the interior, was originally the front entrance. The original floor lies under the present floor, and the fireplaces have been removed.

In the southwest corner of the room are eight of the Windsor chairs occupied by members of the First Continental Congress. Arms of the Carpenters' Company, with the inscription, "Instituted 1724," are woven into two silk banners hanging on the east and west walls.

Also on view are the original minutes of the First Continental Congress, portraits of members, original manuscripts and important letters relating to the Revolutionary struggle, Stuart's painting of Washington, and the original painting of Patrick Henry addressing the first Congress. Among the unusual exhibits is the waistcoat worn by Robert Morris.

The historic events which took place within its walls rather than the somewhat meager furnishings which remain as mementos of those stirring days provide the real interest in this storied old structure.

341

With a fine reverence for their old hall, the Carpenters' Company in 1857 withdrew permission to use it for trade and commercial purposes, restricting usage almost wholly to the needs of its own organization, but permitting inspection by visitors during fixed hours. For nearly 170 years the company has maintained the hall at its own expense.

BETSY ROSS HOUSE

239 Arch St. Open weekdays 9 a. m. to 5 p. m., Sundays 11 a. m. to 5 p. m. Admission free.

THE flourishing but highly controversial legend of Betsy Ross and the first American flag makes up in sentiment what it lacks in proof. The first public intimation of the Betsy Ross story came from William J. Canby, a grandson of the seamstress, in an address before the Historical Society of Pennsylvania on March 14, 1870. Affidavits signed at the time by members of the Ross family state that this story had been long familiar to them. They are presumed to have delayed its public announcement because of its conflict with their antimilitaristic Quaker principles. Nearly all the affidavits stated that their ancestress lived in the house which is now 239 Arch Street. No other number was mentioned by them.

George Canby, after the death of his brother, William, sought among Government archives for evidence to convince skeptics, but without result.

Unverified statements, attributed to Betsy Ross by her descendants, avow that George Washington, in company with Robert Morris and Col. George Ross, went to the home of Betsy Ross on a morning in June 1776. The story dwells minutely upon the feelings of awe, reverence, and patriotic excitement that filled her when Washington produced a rough design for a flag sketched on paper, with the design showing six-pointed stars, and asked if she could piece it together out of bunting. She replied that she could, but indicated that a five-pointed star could be made with a single snip of the scissors. When she had demonstrated this, Washington and his companions approved its use. By the next day, having sacrificed a good deal of her sleep to work at her task, Betsy finished the first American flag.

This version is upheld in a volume entitled *Betsy Ross, Quaker Rebel,* by Edwin S. Parry, descendant of Betsy Ross. The book's jacket calls it "The final answer to the controversial question, 'Who made the flag ?' "

An opposite stand is taken by Joseph Jackson, author of the *Encyclopedia of Philadelphia* and other historical works ; Albert Cook Myers, historian ; Ellis Paxson Oberholtzer, officially identified with

342

the Historical Society of Pennsylvania ; and other authorities. They maintain that no one knows just where the first American flag was made, or who made it. Jackson declares that the story of Washington's visit to Betsy Ross is "pure imagination, uncorroborated by the slightest evidence."

He further insists that 239 Arch Street was not the dwelling place of Betsy Ross, but that her house stood at 233 Arch Street. He bases his belief partly upon the listings in two city directories issued in 1785 — the first to be published of Philadelphia — but does not impugn the good faith of those who hold the opposite view. Diligent search has failed to produce incontrovertible proof of where Betsy Ross lived in 1776.

In Macpherson's Directory of 1785 John Claypoole, third husband of Betsy Ross, was listed as occupying 335 Arch Street. The dwelling was on the north side of the street, and house numbers then increased consecutively east. All numbers in subsequent directories increased west. The next city directory issued was Biddle's, in 1791, which listed the Claypoole house as 91. It retained that number until 1858, when it was changed to the present number — 241, an address one lot removed from what is generally considered the onetime abode of Betsy Ross.

So far as the purported "Home of Old Glory" is concerned, Macpherson's Directory listed a Widow Ford as occupying 336 in 1785. The number was changed to 89 in 1791, and in 1858 to the present 239 Arch Street. After this dwelling was selected as the Flag House, 241 was torn down to lessen the hazards of fire, perhaps adding a touch of irony to what may well have been an error in research. The house at 239 Arch Street was selected, as Jackson says, "in some manner not now easily learned."

Even Jackson, while pointing out the error, makes a mistake in fixing the Betsy Ross address as 233. He identifies the 83 of 1785 with the 233 of today, though Macpherson's Directory lists a certain Sellers as living at 339, and it is that number which in 1791 became 83, and finally 233. Jackson selected the name and address of Alexander Wilcocks as his "key to the situation." Wilcocks lived at 325 Arch, between Third and Fourth Streets, while the Claypooles resided between Second and Third. Obviously, Sellers is the logical key man, as he lived four doors east of Betsy Ross Claypoole in 1785, occupying the address for more than a quarter century.

Meanwhile, because it filled a genuine patriotic need, the story that the first American flag had been stitched together at 239 Arch Street by Betsy Ross became part of the legendary history of the United States, in defiance of all the acid tests of historical research.

The house was built about 1700. It has two stories, an attic, and an additional two rooms in the basement. Extending across the front is a large coved hood, and above it are two second-story windows topped with a heavy cornice. A single dormer window extends from the third-story attic. The exterior is of stone faced with brick, of Flemish bond construction, set with black headers typical of the masonry walls of the eighteenth century. Part of the rear is constructed of field stone, apparently because its use was more economical than brick.

The most interesting architectural features of this patriotic shrine are its small windows and its doors. It also has an attractive, blue-tiled fireplace which, except for a few broken tiles now replaced, is just as it was when imported from Holland. Cupboards in the central passage are interesting chiefly for the HL hinges.

In the basement, floored with brick, are the original kitchen and dining room. The kitchen, in the rear, has a huge elliptical arched fireplace of brick, containing a hanger for open-fire cooking. Leading from this room to the rear yard is a short flight of steps. At the front a steep, brick-arched opening leads to the street pavement.

The back room on the first floor is the reputed scene of the discussion with Washington regarding the design of the flag. And it was in this room that the industrious Betsy, with nimble fingers, is alleged to have sewed the first flag of the United States. The front room is used as a novelty shop and contains a small, simple fireplace, with wood paneling above and to the left. Winding stairways lead to the basement and to the upper floors ; large double doors lead into a court.

The rooms on the second floor are three in number: fair sized rooms in the front and rear, and a small room off the central hall. The front room is fitted with a fireplace and paneled closets ; at the rear is the children's room, furnished with antiques reminiscent of the days of Betsy Ross. The front stairs leading to the third floor have the original handrail, with fine, carved spindles. The third floor contains one large room with a very small fireplace, and a small plain room opening off the hall.

Neglected for many years, the Flag House became a center of renewed interest only within comparatively recent times. A group of New Englanders interested prominent men in becoming directors of a movement which raised more than $100,000 through the sale of more than a million memberships, to buy and restore the shrine. In December 1936 A. Atwater Kent, socially prominent Philadelphia manufacturer, offered to spend at least $25,000 for the restoration of the house. His offer was accepted by City Council, and the property was rehabilitated under the architectural direction of Brognard Okie.

In the task of renewing the "Birthplace of Old Glory," old floors, old boards, and old nails were saved wherever possible ; three fireplaces, long hidden, were revealed. A stairway in the front of the house, long since removed, was replaced, and a door leading from the yard into the basement kitchen was restored. Where replacements were necessary, material was obtained from old homes in the neighborhood — those corresponding with the period of the shrine. A mantel was brought from one old house then being demolished ; bricks and window glass were obtained from other Colonial homes. The first floor front was rebuilt, a doorway was transferred from the western to the eastern corner of the building, and a new window was installed.

In addition to the rejuvenation of the shrine, the work of rehabilitation included the addition, in the rear, of the heating plant and a ladies' rest room, at a cost of $7,000. For construction of this, brick of the Revolutionary period was used.

For many years only two rooms were open to the public, but visitors now are permitted to explore all eight rooms in the house. In some can be viewed the actual belongings of Betsy Ross. All the furniture is of the Revolutionary period, or good reproductions. Bunting, said to be similar to that used in making the first flag, is preserved in a glass case.

The Flag House is maintained with funds raised by the sale to the general public of souvenirs of all kinds, such as postcards, Liberty Bells and other mementos. These may be purchased on the premises.

THE POWEL HOUSE

244 S. 3d St. Eastbound trolley on Chestnut St. to 3d.

THE POWEL HOUSE, which was occupied by Philadelphia's last pre-Revolutionary mayor, still presents much the same outward appearance as when its distinguished owner lavishly entertained notables of this country and eminent guests from abroad.

A three-story structure of red brick, it is flanked on the south side by a garden recently restored in part. Low, broad steps with a wrought-iron railing lead to a wide Colonial doorway.

The building dates from about 1765, at which time it was regarded as pretentious. The street door opens into a wide reception hall, where the noble arch is a dominant feature. A rich wainscoting of solid mahogany and mahogany spindles on the banisters embellish the staircase. Every room is of proportions unusually large for a town house.

The reception room, first floor front, has been restored as a memorial to Mrs. Cyrus H. K. Curtis, through whose generosity the original "Survey of the Old City" was made. The dining room is also completed. The drawing room, the original of which is in the Pennsylvania Museum, is being restored by carefully copying details of the original woodwork.

345

Originally the Powel House was surrounded by extensive grounds magnificently landscaped, with rare fruit trees and shrubbery in profusion, and costly statuary lining the walks and paths. When Powel was elected mayor of the city in 1775, the house and garden became the scene of numerous meetings of men high in public life. Members of the American Philosophical Society, to which Samuel Powel belonged, sometimes came there.

Washington was a frequent guest ; there are constant records in his diary of his taking both dinner and tea with the mayor and Mrs. Powell in their Third Street home. Lafayette and many foreign diplomats and personages of importance also were entertained there. When the British forces occupied the city during the winter of 1777-78, the Earl of Carlisle, British High Commissioner, was quartered in the Powel house. The nobleman wrote home in laudatory terms of his stay here.

Often called the "Patriotic Mayor," Powel headed Philadelphia's government until 1789. The last mayor under British rule, he was also the first under a free government. His father had been one of the richest members of the Carpenters' Company and the first operative builder in Philadelphia. His wife was the former Elizabeth Willing, who did as much as her husband to make the Powel home famous for its hospitality.

In those days the neighborhood was considered the most fashionable in the city, and originally there were only three dwellings in the square between Spruce Street and Willing's Alley. Charles Willing, former mayor and father of Mrs. Powel, lived at the corner of Willing's Alley. With the passage of time, however, a number of dwellings replaced the Powel gardens, until finally only the backyard remained.

In 1931 the Philadelphia Society for the Preservation of Landmarks purchased the Powel House and the house next door. The second was demolished, and the garden now occupies its site. This change has done much to restore the appearance of the old dwelling to its original beauty.

The Powel House is important not only because it was one of the most beautiful dwellings of the pre-Revolutionary period, but because it is considered the last dwelling in Colonial Philadelphia where Washington was a frequent guest.

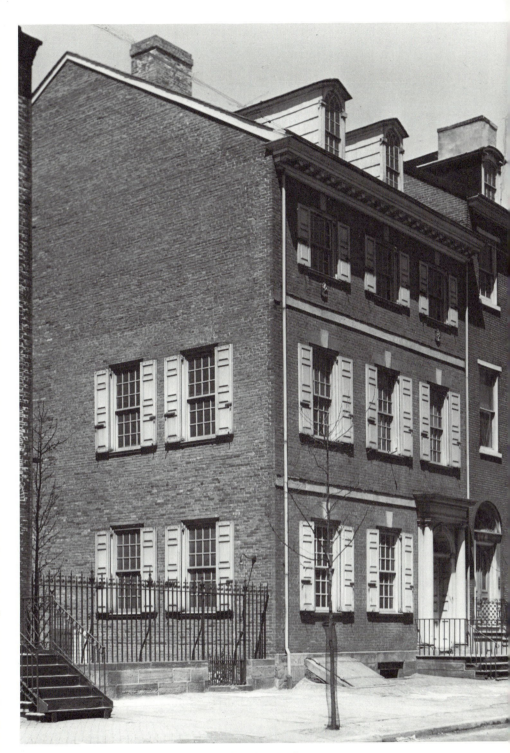

The Powel House

ACADEMY OF MUSIC

Broad and Locust Sts., three blocks south of
City Hall.

FEW American buildings hold richer echoes of the past than does Philadelphia's venerable Academy of Music. Across its spacious stage has passed a pageant of the Nation's history — political as well as musical.

For generations it has been the focal point of the city's cultural life, and the auditorium has resounded to the music of great orchestras, the eloquence of Presidents and poets, the lyric ardor of the world's finest voices, and once, in a strange metamorphosis, to the clamor of a circus menagerie.

King Edward VII of England visited the academy when he was Prince of Wales, and the memory of that brillant occasion is kept alive by the "Prince of Wales Box," on the balcony floor to the right. Dom Pedro, Emperor of Brazil, was a visitor here on several occasions while attending the Centennial Exhibition in this city.

The vaulted ceiling has resounded to cheers for Clay and Webster and Blaine ; it has echoed the impassioned voices of William Lloyd Garrison denouncing the iniquity of slavery, and of Robert G. Ingersoll demanding freedom for the human mind ; it has echoed, too, the oratory of scholarly Edward Everett and John B. Gough.

Many Presidents of the United States, from James Buchanan to Herbert Hoover, have spoken from its stage. Grover Cleveland and his bride were feted in the auditorium by an assemblage whose brilliance dazzled even the participants; there were 1,500 persons present, including foreign ambassadors, at a dinner costing $25 a plate, an enormous sum in those days.

On the academy's boards Edwin Booth and Tomasso Salvini acted. Gallery gods thrilled to the incomparable tones of Adelina Patti ; to the voices of Albani, Campanini, and Caruso ; to the magnetic charm of Christine Nilsson. The gilded caryatids have looked down upon the writhing grace of La Argentina; and they have preserved their immobility in the face of the astonishing sight of an indoor football game. There in the very citadel of culture !

To list the actors on the world's stage who have passed through its entrance would be almost to call the roll of modern history. The academy has seen them all : personages and near-personages, political pygmies strutting their little hours, and the authentic great — Lloyd George and Clemenceau, Charles Evans Hughes, the Earl of Birkenhead, Prince William of Sweden, Galli-Curci, Paderewski, Josef Hofmann, Roald Amundsen, Jane Addams, John McCormack, Dr. Charles H. Mayo, Rev. Harry Emerson Fosdick, Elman,

348

Heifetz, Kreisler, Ole Bull, Rubenstein, Chaliapin, Viscount Cecil — the list is well nigh inexhaustible.

Versatility has been the ruling note in the academy's long life. The first motion pictures ever thrown upon a screen were exhibited there. Not long after the World War the Hagenbeck-Wallace circus filled the auditorium briefly. Dances, debutantes' teas, lectures, card parties, musicales, and even boxing and wrestling matches have occupied the auditorium or the second-floor foyer ; and in that foyer many aspiring young musicians have made their first public appearance.

The splendors of its past are veiled behind a drab exterior. The building, designed by Napoleon Le Brun, was completed in 1857 and was opened with a grand ball which eclipsed in size and brilliance any event held up to that time in Philadelphia. It had been five years building, and there had been many periods of delay while funds were being collected to finance the $400,000 project. The first opera offered there, *Il Trovatore*, was presented on February 25, 1857, with Gazzaniga, Aldini, Brignoli, and Amodio in the cast. To this day, opera and concert music have remained the mainstays of the academy's varied repertoire. In the Philadelphia Orchestra season, music lovers with more devotion than worldly goods form block-long queues in Locust Street, often standing in line for hours to obtain low-priced gallery tickets.

Solidly constructed of brownstone and red brick, the sullen exterior is unmitigated by the large, arched windows on the Broad Street and Locust Street facades.

The huge Corinthian columns of the auditorium were designed in elliptical sections, to provide as unobstructed a view of the stage as possible. The four steep balconies ; the huge crystal chandelier (originally in the old Crystal Palace in New York) ; the painted ceiling ; the use of baroque ornamentation ; the caryatids ; and the lavish use of gold, cream, and red plush coloring all blend to create a gay and intimate atmosphere.

An interesting feature is the acoustical pit under the floor of the auditorium, built in the shape of an inverted elliptical dome. The pit and the domed ceiling of the auditorium were designed to obtain acoustical excellence. Today, however, engineers doubt that the academy's marvelous acoustics is attributable to this construction.

Extraordinary precautions have been taken to prevent the huge chandelier from falling. It hangs from a separate iron structure above the ceiling, and is suspended by several cables, so that if one should break there still would be no danger.

Olive gray walls adorned with Ionic pilasters and columns ; numerous mirrored doors ; window openings delicately paneled in the

349

manner of the eighteenth century ; and brilliant crystal chandeliers form the decorative scheme of the fayer.

THE FREE LIBRARY

Logan Square and the Parkway (Vine St. between 19th and 20th). Bus "A" from Reyburn Plaza ; Routes 21 and 33. Open daily, 9 a. m. to 10 p. m.; Sundays, 2 p. m. to 10 p. m., except during June, July, August, and September. Closed on legal holidays, except Election and Armistice Days.

Outstanding features: rare and original editions, collections, and treatises ; documents, newspaper and magazine files ; collections of music ; cuneiform tablets ; and books for the blind.

THE FREE LIBRARY, one of the most imposing buildings along the Parkway, was erected at a cost of $6,300,000. It is constructed of Indiana limestone with a granite base and is of the French Renaissance style. The design of the facade follows closely that of the Ministry of Marine building in Paris, and is distinguished by a long row of Corinthian columns above the first floor.

Within the building are a number of spacious rooms well appointed for their particular purposes. The entrance hall and great stairway are of marble and impressive both in size and dignity.

The library contains a large lending department and a comprehensive reference department. It also possesses many rare books, some of them long out of print, and many priceless original editions. There are also special departments arranged to facilitate study and research.

Shelf space has been provided for 2,000,000 volumes. The circulating department contains 110,000 books, about 30,000 being available on open shelves. In Pepper Hall alone, there are 36,000 reference books dealing with a wide variety of subjects and including a splendid collection of Judaics and Hebraics. There is also a novel "circulating library" in the form of a collection of more than 2,000 cuneiform tablets which scholars are permitted to examine in the privacy of their own homes. The reference department conducts a business and statistical service, and it has a collection of Philadelphia directories dating from 1785, as well as telephone directories of every city in the United States of more than 100,000 population.

Another interesting feature is the library for the blind, which contains 21,000 volumes of embossed type. These volumes were provided by the Pennsylvania Home Teaching Society for the Blind, the Library of Congress, and the Southeastern Pennsylvania Chapter, American Red Cross. This department also maintains a collection of 9,319 "talking book" records which combine the features of a portable radio and a phonograph. The records are reproductions, in the speaking voice, of entire volumes. Books and records, with return postage, are mailed free to blind persons living in eastern Pennsylvania, New Jersey, and Delaware.

Collections of connoisseurs and bibliophiles have been added to the library from time to time. Examination of these volumes is permitted, but the rarer books may not be removed from the building.

Among the departments of special interest are those devoted to law, music, children and public documents.

The law department contains the Hampton L. Carson collection illustrating the growth of the common law. It consists of 8,000 books and includes more than 100 manuscripts and 8,000 prints. Another collection is that donated by Henry R. Edmunds which deals with admiralty law. Simon Gratz presented a number of volumes devoted to State trials, while a collection covering early American law was received from William Brook Rawle.

In the music department more than 52,000 items are catalogued, including 12,597 bound biographies and opera, orchestral, and organ scores, all of which are available for home use. In addition, there are 1,389 books of biography, dictionaries, encyclopedias, and textbooks, and 39 current musical periodicals for reference use, together with thousands of unbound pianoforte numbers, numerous phonograph records, and several hundred player piano rolls. Here also is the Edward A. Fleisher collection of chamber music consisting of more than 4,100 items. Mr. Fleisher also presented to the Free Library one of the world's largest collections of orchestral music, of more than 2,522 numbers for full orchestra, 1,700 numbers for string orchestra, and 1,686 concertos, each of which is complete with conductor's score and all necessary parts for its performance.

The following outstanding collections are also of major interest: David Nunes Carvalho, collection of manuscripts and documents relative to handwriting; John Frederick Lewis collection of Oriental manuscripts, medieval manuscripts, books on engraving, early printing and manuscripts; John Frederick Lewis collection of portraits, containing some 88,000 portraits arranged under the names of the sitters.

A department devoted to children contains on open shelves more than 8,000 books available for home use, 700 reference books, and 2,500 books devoted to work with children. There are also many picture books and a number of volumes printed in large type for children with defective vision.

The public documents department is for reference use only. It

351

contains all documents distributed to public libraries by the Federal Government and the various States and the more important documents issued by foreign countries, as well as publications of organizations such as the League of Nations. It also contains a number of film-volumes issued by the National Recovery Administration and the Agricultural Adjustment Administration publicizing the activities of both these organizations, and accounts of hearings on the codes of fair competition. A municipal reference division contains documents dealing with municipal affairs in this and other nations, and much unofficial material relating to civic affairs.

The periodical department receives currently 3,223 publications of general or specialized interest. It has 47,600 bound volumes and an extensive index and check list. The newspaper files embrace 235 publications.

An extension department provides library service at seven hospitals and three prisons and also conducts traveling libraries and neighborhood service through 102 local agencies, such as community centers, fire stations, industrial plants, schools, and summer camps.

Outstanding among the diversified collections and exhibits are the John Ashhurst collection of title pages and printers' marks, and a treasured group of old Bibles, pamphlets, manuscripts and what is said to be the world's largest book: *Investigations and Studies in Jade*. This book, which required 20 years to complete, is illustrated in colors, the work of many famous Chinese artists.

The Rosenwald collection, 3,000 books on printing, engraving, book collecting, portraiture, and book plates, is available for reference under certain restrictions. The collection was lent by Lessing J. Rosenwald. The extensive Isaac Norris medical library is also available for reference use under certain restrictions.

There are also exhibition galleries for paintings and prints, a catalogue department, a binding department, a shipping department, and a photostat room where the public may have photostats made at cost. There is also a large reading room and additional reading facilities on the roof, where an enclosed portion offers protection against the vagaries of the weather.

The free library system in Philadelphia was established under a charter granted in 1891, with a board of trustees as the governing body. Operating expenses are provided by appropriations made by City Council and by income from such funds as have been donated.

The free library in this city was opened in three rooms in City Hall on March 12, 1894. A year later it was moved to 1217-21 Chestnut Street, and on December 1, 1910, it was removed to the northeast corner of Thirteenth and Locust Streets. The present library on the Parkway was opened on June 2, 1927. The city's free library system embraces 31 branches, three deposit stations, and 112 other agencies, included in which is the H. Josephine Widener Memorial Branch *(open daily, 9 a.m. to 5 p.m., Sundays and legal holidays excepted).* The Widener Memorial Branch is situated at the northwest corner of Broad Street and Girard Avenue and contains more than 500 works of incunabula representing more than 300 different presses in Belgium, France, Germany, Holland, Italy and Switzerland. It also possesses many lantern slides comprising biography, history, literature, travel, and other educational subjects.

FRANKLIN INSTITUTE

Winter St., at 20th St. and Parkway. Limited parking permitted at all times on Winter St. and 20th St. sides of building.
MUSEUM—Open Wed., Thur., Fri., Sun. 2 p. m. to 10 p. m. Sat. and holidays, 10 a. m. to 10 p. m. Adm. 25 cents. Closed Mon., Tues., Christmas and Independence Days.
FELS PLANETARIUM—Winter Street entrance facing the Parkway. Demonstrations accompanied by 45 - minute explanatory talks : weekdays at 3, 4 and 8:30 p. m. Sat., 12 noon, 3 p. m. and 8:30 p. m. Sun., 3, 4 and 8:30 p. m. Closed Christmas and Independence Days. Adm. 25 cents.

THE FRANKLIN INSTITUTE, which includes the Fels Planetarium, houses a diversity of exhibits such as has seldom been seen under one roof. The contents of this imposing building represent man's persistent efforts to wrest from nature an ever-increasing knowledge and use of her laws. The exhibits illustrate his cautious groping for scientific truth and his efforts at practical application.

The Franklin Institute, named to honor Benjamin Franklin, is the oldest organization in the United States devoted to the study and promotion of mechanical arts and applied sciences. It was founded in 1824 by Samuel Vaughan Merrick, who later headed the Southwark Foundry, and Dr. William H. Keating, one of the leading scientists at the University of Pennsylvania. The institute held its first exhibition in the fall of the same year at Carpenters' Hall. It met with immediate success, and the following year the association erected a building on the east side of Seventh Street, below Market, where it remained for more than a century.

During the ensuing upsurge of scientific accomplishment, the institute's hall became a recognized assembly place for scholars from all over the world.

The present building, begun in 1930 and opened in 1934, represents the culmination of the combined efforts of the institute itself

Franklin Institute by Night
"The Layman's Temple of Science"

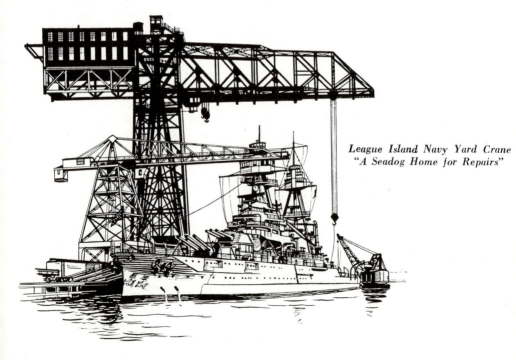

League Island Navy Yard Crane
"A Seadog Home for Repairs"

and the Benjamin Franklin Memorial, Inc., an organization sponsored by interested citizens. The museum, the first of its type in this country, is modeled after the Deutsches Museum of Munich, Germany. John T. Windrim was the architect of the building. It is of classic design ; having two symmetrical and almost identical facades, the principal one—on the Twentieth Street side—facing Logan Circle. The central portico consists of six massive Corinthian columns supporting a heavy entablature. The exterior is of light buff limestone with a granite base. The structure is not yet completed (1937).

The museum of the institute has the following departments : astronomy, marine engineering, graphic arts, electrical communications, physics, chemistry, aviation, railroad engineering, medicine, a miscellany of manufacturing exhibits, and the Fels Planetarium.

Exhibits are housed in spacious chambers. It is virtually impossible to give a comprehensive representation of all the exhibits, since even a casual survey would consume about 15 hours. Every item has been chosen carefully, arranged attractively, and constructed simply and ingeniously. Particularly fascinating are the numerous experimental exhibits which may be operated by the visitor or the guide, thus serving to fix in the mind the scientific principles involved.

Immediately within the heavy bronze doorway of the Twentieth Street entrance is a large hall. The painted canvas ceiling of Renaissance design, profusely decorated in colors of red, blue, and gold, was imported from England. Four steps lead from this hall to the outstanding architectural feature of the building—the octagonal Benjamin Franklin Memorial Chamber. The quiet dignity of this large hall, its design inspired by the Pantheon in Rome, is a suitable setting for the heroic statue of Franklin which is to be placed here. Foreshortening of the setbacks within the large coffers of the dome creates an illusion of height greater than actually exists. The following representative list of exhibits, a small part of the total, is arranged in the order suggested by the institute for visitors.

An official greeter, a six-foot mechanical man, was installed in 1934. Nattily dressed in a brass-buttoned blue uniform trimmed with gold braid, the robot salutes each visitor passing through the Twentieth Street entrance. "Egbert," so named at the time of his arrival, also bows, and in the manner of the perfect host, says, "How do you do ? I am very glad to see you. I hope you enjoy your visit."

"Egbert" is set in motion by the interruption of two invisible rays focused on photoelectric cells. Visiting patrons unknowingly pass through the beams, and the robot's seeming independent action makes it appear to be a living being. "Egbert" was designed by

355

F. R. Marion, a New York engineer, and it is Marion's voice that issues from a phonograph concealed in the mechanism.

HALL OF ELECTRICAL COMMUNICATIONS: Exhibits here give a comprehensive history of electricity and its practical application, from the first experiments to modern times. The nature of frictional electricity is shown with various types of friction machines, among them one used by Benjamin Franklin.

The properties and effects of electromagnetism are shown with various types of apparatus. The action of a simple transformer is demonstrated, showing the mechanical force due to currents in an adjoining coil and the attraction of an iron rod to a magnetic field.

The telegraphy group contains one of the earliest forms of telegraphic recorders. A complete portrayal of telephonic communication includes a machine which records the "looks" of the voice. Radio transmission and reception are demonstrated with exhibits including the early "rock crusher" spark transmitter, the latest receiving sets, and loud speaker comparisons.

HALL OF MECHANISMS: Here is vividly portrayed the development of many modern mechanical devices—vacuum cleaners, sewing machines, locks, air brakes, reapers, plows, cash registers, and numerous others. In almost every case the new is contrasted with the old. An especially effective exhibit in this room is a modern bank vault entrance weighing 35,000 pounds, contrasted with the small hand-made type of safe of 100 years ago.

A sectional view of a modern adding machine shows the intricate maze of levers between the operator's button and the adding and printing devices. An automatic mechanical woman, constructed by Maelzel more than a hundred years ago, writes three verses and draws four pictures.

A five-ton cross section exhibit of the cables used to support the Philadelphia-Camden bridge reveals the myriad of fine wires that compose the finished cable. The first steam coining press, used in the United States Mint in 1836, is shown in operation stamping out souvenir coins.

HALL OF PRIME MOVERS: Exhibited here are numerous mechanisms which utilize nature's power sources to do the work of mankind. Various types of steam engines and turbines are on display: a quarter-size scale model of the Newcomen steam engine, the world's first successful piston engine; a half-size model of the Watt steam engine (1782), the first to use the principle of steam expansion; the walking-beam engine built by the Franklin Iron Works in 1847.

Typical of early devices using animal power as a prime mover is the dog treadmill exhibit. Nearby is a complete hydraulic power plant with many accessories. So-called "perpetual motion" machines

356

are represented with a model of the machine of the notorious Redhefer and one of the more notorious Keely.

PAPER MAKING AND GRAPHIC ARTS: Exhibits in this section are among the most extensive in the museum. They present a visual history of the arts of paper making and printing from their inception up to the present day. Upon entering the room, one sees displayed at the right and left the most up-to-date typesetting machines used for the printing of books and newspapers. The monotype which casts single types in justified lines, and the intertype, a linecasting machine of the latest design, are shown.

One exhibit, entitled "How a Newspaper is Printed," gives a thorough visual explanation of the processes used. A press built by Cottrell shows the mechanics of four-color printing.

Various old hand presses show by comparison the tremendous advance made in the printing field. A unique exhibit of engraving and matrix making is that showing the Lord's Prayer, containing 253 characters and spaces, engraved in a space one-sixth of an inch square.

The paper-making display includes an exhibit showing how pulp is made. A working scale model of a Fourdrinier paper-making machine shows the complete process.

ELECTRICAL ENGINEERING AND HALL OF ILLUMINATION: The generation of electrical energy and its uses are portrayed here. A number of early dynamos include Joseph Saxton's magneto-electric machine and Edison's original bipolar direct current generators for three-wire distribution driven by a steam engine.

A large collection of direct and alternating current motors give an insight into the principles of operation and development. Among other exhibits in this room are experimental generators, transformers, and arc lamps used by Elihu Thomson in his experimental work; a collection showing the development of the watt-hour electric meter ; a group of recording and indicating instruments ; and 25 types of relays.

Especially interesting and revealing are the exhibits devoted to the development of illumination, tracing its history from the primitive pine-knot torch to modern lighting units. A series of striking settings compare the halting progress of early lighting with the rapid advances of recent years. Exhibits are arranged successively, showing first the "rush lights" and "Betty lamps" used by this country's early settlers in their log cabins ; then the whale-oil lamps of Colonial times; then the candle fixtures of the Louis XV period ; then the open-flame kerosene lamps and gas lights of the early Victorian era ; then the incandescent carbon filament lamp of today ; and finally a glimpse into the future, when artificial illumination may supplant sunlight entirely in all new buildings.

Exhibits seeking to convey the value of proper lighting as an aid to good sight include the "sight-light" demonstrator which proves the importance of sufficient light ; a display treating with the problem of "white" light and "artificial sunlight" in relation to color discrimination and matching ; and a number of instruments designed to record the physical characteristics of various light sources.

LOCOMOTIVE ROOM: Exhibits include a number of early locomotive models, steam and electric. Comparison of the old with the new reveals the great strides made in locomotive development. The "Rocket," built in England in 1837 and weighing slightly more than eight tons, has run 310,164 miles. Nearby is the "60,000," a modern 3-cylinder compound heavy duty engine built in 1926 by the Baldwin Locomotive Works. It weighs 350 tons. This exhibit has been arranged to move a short distance on a real railroad bridge in response to manipulation of the controls. Degrees of ensuing stress and strain on the bridge are recorded on instruments in the hall below the engine.

HALL OF AVIATION : Dominating this room is the Lockheed-Vega airplane in which Amelia Earhart spanned the North Atlantic. (She was lost in the Pacific in July 1937 on a round-the-world flight.) A number of exhibits review the history of airplane development, beginning with Orville Wright's trial flight in 1903 when he rose a few feet above the ground at Kitty Hawk, North Carolina, and leading up to the round-the-world flights of today. A mural by William Heaslip accurately depicts Wright's first successful flight. Among the actual aircraft on exhibit is the only existing Wright Brothers V plane still capable of flying. It was first flown in 1912. Also on view is a faithful reproduction on a 1 to 15 scale of Col. Charles A. Lindbergh's famous *Spirit of St. Louis.*

The fundamental principles of flight are demonstrated with the aid of several wind tunnels. A model of an airplane engine runs under its own power and turns a 14-inch propellor 6,000 revolutions a minute.

MEDICINE, SURGERY, AND DENTISTRY : This section has many exhibits, all designed to show the contributions made by chemistry, physics, and mechanics to the development of medical science.

An early model of the Drinker respirator, designed to furnish artificial respiration over long periods of time, can be operated so that a doll within the machine seems to breathe. This exhibit is supplemented by a rubber model of human lungs illustrating the principles of breathing.

The principles of the electrocardiograph are shown in an exhibit in which the observer serves as subject. Other exhibits show the value of X-rays and other scientific phenomena as applied to the problems of human health.

358

Numerous medical and surgical instruments are displayed in a glass case. This collection, changed from time to time, includes reproductions of instruments found in the ruins of Pompeii ; a series showing the development of the stethoscope ; surgical instruments used during the Civil War ; and devices for the hard-of-hearing. A dentist's office of 1860, as well as one of today, is shown.

HALL OF ASTRONOMY : The astronomy room is equipped with two telescopes, a 10-inch refractor, and a 24-inch reflector. Shown also is a scale model of the 200-inch telescope which will go into operation on a western mountain peak in 1940, and a sample of the glass of which the mirror is made. An old 8-inch telescope, installed in Central High School in 1839 and a source of education for many generations of Philadelphia students until 1900, has been added to the collection.

Other exhibits, too numerous to mention, are displayed in the *HALL OF CHEMISTRY, HALL OF RADIATIONS, MARINE TRANSPORTATION ROOM, AND THE FRANKLIN PRINTING SHOP* (an authentic reconstruction of a printing shop of Franklin's time, with printing presses used by Franklin).

The institute has a scientific library known as PEPPER HALL, which houses more than 100,000 volumes. The library's wall and Corinthian pilasters are painted yellow, with details in buff ; the door, windows, and bookcases are of walnut. A nicely executed cornice completely surrounds the base of the institute's acoustically treated BOARD ROOM, a simple and dignified circular chamber in light buff shades.

Its research department includes two laboratories ; a periodical devoted to the discussion of scientific questions has been published monthly since 1826.

The board room, lecture room, and library are reached by means of a stairway of monumental proportions at the right of MEMORIAL HALL. This, the lecture hall, designed along the lines of the old Franklin Institute, is a dignified room in the Doric order, tinted gray, buff, and green. Its walls have been treated with a special plaster which makes it doubly soundproof. All the walls throughout the building are padded or insulated with punctured steel sheets backed by rock wool.

Fels Planetarium

T HE FELS PLANETARIUM, gift of Samuel S. Fels, a Philadelphian, was the second of its kind in the United States. Its vivid demonstration of the motion of the heavenly bodies has made it of outstanding interest among the institute's exhibits. The apparatus consists of a hemispherical metal dome 68 feet in diameter, and a projector shaped like a huge dumbbell, composed of thousands of small devices—lights, shutters, gears, and lenses—all precisely timed and spaced. The planetarium, entered through a semi-circular entrance hall of travertine walls and red marble trim, consists of the dome of the heavens rising above a silhouette of the Philadelphia skyline. Echoes usually occurring in circular auditoriums have been eliminated by using a dome of perforated sheets of stainless steel and padding the walls with mineral wool.

Lights are extinguished, and the dome becomes the dark blue sky of a moonless night. The demonstration of the planetary system — the phases of the moon and the positions of the stars and constellations during the annual journey of the earth—proceeds with convincing verisimilitude. Phenomena that require years to complete are condensed into a brief hour.

The heavens can be depicted as they appear from any part of the earth, at any time in the past or future. So many phenomena can be demonstrated that the topic of the demonstration is changed monthly.

THE PENNSYLVANIA MUSEUM OF ART

Parkway at 25th St. "A" bus at Reyburn Plaza. (Open free, daily and Sunday: 10:30 a. m. to 5 p. m.).
Important exhibits: Period rooms of the English, French, and American schools; art of the Middle Ages; cloisters, furniture collections and contemporary exhibitions of art.

THE PENNSYLVANIA MUSEUM OF ART, one of the most imposing buildings in the city, is situated at the extreme upper end of the Parkway, near the east bank of the Schuylkill River and at the southernmost end of Fairmount Park.

This museum, the chief repository of art in Philadelphia, is the architectural product of Zantzinger & Borie and Horace Trumbauer. Its exhibits present a comprehensive view of the history of art from ancient times to the present day.

Originally conceived as a $5,000,000 project, the museum represented a cost of $25,000,000 when it was opened in 1928. Although not entirely completed up to 1937, it reflects as fine an interpretation of Grecian architecture as any structural effort of modern times.

On the summit of a rock-terraced hill known as Olde Faire Mount, the building is constructed of Minnesota, Mankato, and Kosota stone — stones of similar type, having a warm, golden hue. The roof. covering an expanse of about four acres, is of blue tile with gilded ornaments at the corners and edges.

From its high place on the hill the structure affords a beautiful view of the Parkway and overlooks the imposing Washington monument on the Parkway Plaza, in the immediate foreground.

The approach to the museum, across the Plaza circle, is up a

360

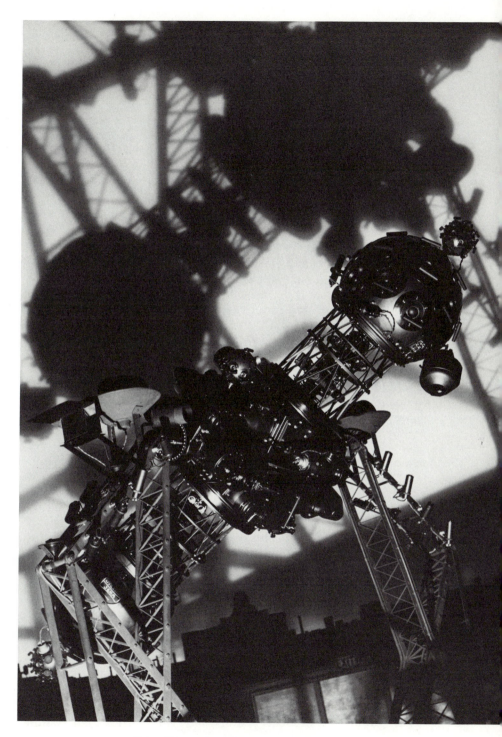

Zeiss Planatarium Instrument in the Fels Planetarium
". . . the stars in their courses proclaim . . ."

series of 68 broad stone steps which rise in five levels to an expansive forecourt paved with flagstone, that leads to another flight of 26 steps to the main entrance.

On either side of the five series of steps, cascades of water descend with a rush that suggests unending motion. And in the forecourt a great fountain lends color and charm. This fountain was erected in 1932 with funds bequeathed by Henry M. Phillips, an original member of the Fairmount Park Commission and its president from 1881 to 1884.

The museum is built in three great wings : the main or west wing, along the western edge of the courtyard ; the north and south wings extending east, bordering either side of the court.

Maintaining a fidelity to classic precedent, the design of the museum facade incorporates a certain subtlety of construction such as was practiced by the ancient Greeks for the purpose of creating optical illusions and to soften the starkness of absolutely straight lines. The walls were built slightly convex, and other lines were made to appear straight to the eye by curving them—rows of columns follow an imperceptibly curved line ; the roof peaks and the steps of the main approach are convex.

Within the pediment surmounting the northeast facade are 13 freestanding, life-size figures designed by C. Paul Jennewein and John Gregory. They were executed in chrome and gold glazes and occupy a tympanum 70 feet wide at the base and ranging to 12 feet in height. They are considered an outstanding example of the ceramic art in colors. The mythological figures, according to the sculptors, signify sacred and profane love, the two underlying forces which are basic in the development of art and civilization in every age. Among the figures represented are Jupiter, Venus, Aurora, Cupid and Adonis. They, together with the figures of a lion, a mighty serpent and an owl, all made from polychrome terra cotta, symbolize the influences which produced western culture.

The massive main entrance of the building represents a compromise between modern exigency and adherence to Greek art. Ancient Greek temples were built without windows or doors, entrance being through a large central opening. The Pennsylvania Museum of Art was built with this in mind — the unadorned, severe looking opening of great breadth rising to the heights of the portico pillars. This opening, however, has been enclosed with many panels of glass which admit light to the interior court. This glass primarily serves the purpose of excluding the wintry winds and the summer heats.

Just within the glass-enclosed entrance is the Great Hall. Within the hall the polychrome decorations of the columns and entablature correspond with the external treatment, where gilded ornamentation and scarlet, yellow, blue, and green colors are used so effectively, following the precedent of ancient Greece. The imposing grand staircase, which faces the entrance and dominates the hall, leads to a colonnaded gallery on the second floor.

As one enters the Great Hall, one of the first things to greet the eye is Augustus Saint-Gaudens' *Diana*, a splendid example of American sculpture. This statue once graced the pedestal atop the old Madison Square Garden, in New York. It was presented to the museum in 1932.

Adorning the walls of the Great Hall and the adjoining rooms, as well as throughout the building, are a number of beautiful and priceless examples of the age-old art of tapestry. Tapestries of the finest weave, some dating back to the fifteenth century and many of modern design, are contained in this extensive collection.

Among those to be seen in the Great Hall is an exquisite piece of modern work showing American troops, on the way to France, passing Indepenence Hall. It is a Gobelin made in France and was designed by G. L. Jaulmes. It was presented to the museum by the French Government in recognition of the welcome extended to French artists by the city of Philadelphia.

Included among the more valuable tapestries on view are an Arras tapestry from France, made in 1400 and showing a boar hunt ; a Coptic tapestry, from Tournai, Belgium, about 1600 ; an Esperance, from Tournai, 1475 ; *Scene of Courtly Life in France*, 1490 ; *Deposition of Christ*, Brussels, 1510 ; Beauvais tapestry showing Italian village feasts, 1736.

The Arras tapestry, sometimes called the "tapestry of 1,000 flowers," hangs in the medieval section of the Romanesque Court ; the Coptic is in the same section. Gothic Hall, in the medieval section, has the "Courtly Life" and the Esperance tapestries.

Although the Philadelphia Art Museum is not mellowed with age so far as its physical aspects are concerned, it has achieved eminence as a repository of priceless art and rare treasures that date back hundreds of years, some to the eleventh century. Masterpieces from the hands of the great artists of the ages and of virtually every recognized school may be seen ; handiwork of some of the foremost craftsmen in furniture may be viewed ; superb tapestries, fine marbles, great clocks, prized doors, specimens of architectural art of every race and clime are exhibited. And all of these treasures are laid out in chronological order, thereby revealing the evolution of the broad field of art in simple fashion.

On the first floor is exhibited the John G. Johnson collection of art which comprises masterpieces representing the most important

East Wing of Art Museum
"The grandeur that was Greece, the glory . . ."

phases in the history of painting. It is the largest single collection in the world that is chronologically listed, except that in the British Museum.

Johnson, a noted lawyer as well as a distinguished art collector, left his collection of 1,280 pictures to the city when he died in 1917. The collection has been kept intact, in accordance with the provisions of his will, and was on exhibition at the Johnson home, 510 South Broad Street, until several years ago, when the house was abandoned temporarily. The collection was moved to the museum, where it is rotated, only 300 pictures being on view at any one time.

Included in this collection are representative works of the Italian, Flemish, Dutch, Spanish, German, French, and English schools, executed by the skilled hands of the world's great masters.

Johnson began his collection in 1881 and during the ensuing years acquired works by such famous painters as Jan Van Eyck, founder of the Flemish fifteenth century school ; Rogier van der Weyden, founder of the Brussels school ; and Hieronymous Bosch, whose satirical art forms a connecting link between the Flemish and Dutch schools. In fact, the collection comprises paintings of distinction done by such famous artists as Pieter Bruegel, the elder ; Rembrandt, Rubens, Aelbert Cuyp, Pieter de Hooch, and Adriaen Brouwer. Works of Botticelli, the Florentine master ; Fra Angelico, Francesco Pesellino, Pietro Lorenzetti, Luca Signorelli, Carlo Crevelli, Antonella Da Messina, Giovanni Bellini, Titian, Tiepolo, Cosimo Tura, Canaletto, Marieschi, and Francesco Guardi, of the Italian schools, are also in this collection.

The German primitives are represented by Lucas Granach, Master Wilhelm, and Bartholomaeus Bruyn, the elder ; while the French school is represented in primitive and modern work by Simon Marimon, master of Moulins ; Francois Clouet, Corneille de Lyon, Poussin, Chardin, Gericault, Delacroix, Manet, Monet, Corot, Millet, and others, with the English school having Hogarth, Sir Joshua Reynolds, Thomas Gainsborough, Turner, Constable, and Crome. The Spanish painters are well represented in a group which includes three very fine panels by El Greco.

Among the better known works are *St. Francis Receiving the Stigmata*, by Van Eyck ; two panels showing *Christ on the Cross with the Virgin and St. John*, by Van der Weyden ; *The Shepherd Fleeing from the Wolf*, by the elder Bruegel ; *Saint Francis*, by Fra Angelico ; four exquisite predelle panels and some other fine work by Botticelli, including : *Portrait of Lorenzo Lorenzano, Last Moments of the Magdalene, Noli Me Tangere, Feast in the House of Levi*, and *Christ Preaching ; The Virgin and Child with Saints*, by Pesellino ; *Pieta*, by Crevelli ; *Madonna and Child*, by Bellini.

On the second floor, the central section contains the Joseph Lees

Williams collection of Persian rugs, and collections of china and bric-a-brac, and jasper medallions of Wedgewood.

In the south wing is part of a Romanesque cloister of the eleventh and twelfth centuries and a Catalan cloister from Saint Genis des Fontaines, construction of which started in 1086. About one third of the original structure was brought here, together with stones taken from adjacent territory, sufficient to complete the erection. Beyond the cloister is the medieval art gallery devoted mainly to early German and Spanish art. Next to this gallery are numerous Gothic-Romanesque details, such as fine stained-glass windows, including the Crusaders' windows (roundels) which are gem-lined and made of full-blown glass, with polychrome mother-and-child theme. In the adjoining room is a Gothic chapel, interesting in that it has a vaulted roof and buttresses at each end. The chapel wall is about 40 inches thick, and the exterior stone is laid in pleasing pattern, while the interior is of rough gray stone.

In this section there are numerous examples of Romanesque sculpture — the triple-arched portal from Saint Laurent les Augustins, a Burgundian abbey of the twelfth century, and a traceried doorway of about 100 years later ; a wainscoted French room of the sixteenth century French Renaissance period, which is hung with interesting paintings and tapestries ; two Italian Gothic rooms from Florence and Venice and various specimens of Gothic art. Here, too, one finds an interesting reminder of the romance of old in the figure of *The Knight on Horseback*, who eternally rides in the Romanesque Court. This "knight" is merely a suit of tournament armor bearing the mark of Lorenz Colman, armorer to Emperor Maximilian. It was brought from the imperial collection at Vienna and dates back to 1500. The horse, festooned with armorial trappings for tournament use, bears the arms of Freiherr Behaim von Schwarzenbach, a German or Austrian of the seventeenth century. In addition to the trappings, the "knight" is armed with a lance, fully prepared for the joust.

A number of exhibits of secular rooms are to be found in the west wing, including a French-Gothic room that is wood-paneled with linen fold motif on the walls and a polychrome floor of fleur-de-lys pattern ; a Florentine-Gothic gallery with flagstone floor and paintings in the Giotto tradition by Giovanni di Paolo ; a room from a Venice house, completely furnished and including a fireplace, a Savonarola bed or tea chair, and a floor with crushed stone imbedded in cement, dating back to 1493.

In this west wing there are five galleries devoted to an exhibition of American art which includes works by Sully, Peale, Sargent, Eicholtz, Stuart, Thomas Eakins, Mary Cassatt, Charles Rosen, Arthur B. Charles, Daniel Garber, and other representative artists of the seventeenth, eighteenth, nineteenth, and twentieth centuries. This exhibit also contains a number of miniatures, a group of eye miniatures, a large statue of Washington, busts by Charles Grafly, Serge Yourievitch, and Alexander Portnoff, as well as such furniture as a Queen Anne chair, a splat-back chair, a Chippendale lowboy, and an Empire style sideboard.

The north wing has two Italian Renaissance galleries of the fifteenth and sixteenth centuries. The former contains paintings by —Antonello Da Messina, Lorenzo Lotto, and Jacopo di Barbari, and sculpture by Bertolodo as well as terra cottas ; furniture, and tapestry ; the latter has a stone chimney piece in the style of Sansovino ; chairs, paintings, tables, large wrought-iron candleholders, and paintings by Cariani Guardi, and others. Immediately adjoining is another Italian fifteenth century Renaissance room, with doorways and ceilings from Rome, Venice, and Pesaro ; a fireplace of carved wood and a flagstone floor. A beautiful plaque, *The Virgin Worshipping the Child*, by Della Robbia, is set in the wall. Two large altarpieces are the work of Masolina da Panicale, and the several paintings by Botticelli and Fra Angelico. One of the masterpieces in this room is the low-relief *Madonna and Child* by Desiderio da Settignano.

The German (Austrian) Renaissance period is represented by a sixteenth century exhibit from Stiegerhof (Nagerschigg) in Carinthia, Austria, which includes a white marble fountain, a French table of the same period, templated ceiling, an interesting tile stove and casement windows, as well as a painting by Hans Maler.

The French Renaissance room of the fifteenth century is still incomplete, but it has some fine examples of wood carving, a drawbridge table, a child's high chair and a high-backed chair from the Chateau de Cussac. Although the French gallery is not yet permanently placed, it has some good eighteenth and nineteenth century representation in paintings by Delacroix, Courbet, Chasserian, Corot, Jongkind, Millet, and Gericault. It also has some bronze animals by Barye and several pieces of furniture typical of the period, as well as an attractive Louis XVI interior from the Hotel Letellier, Paris (1789), showing parquetry floors, paneled and mirrored walls, overdoor bas-relief, heavy Empire ornamental furniture, bric-a-brac, and china of the luxuriant period of Louis XVI.

More humble and homelike is the Dutch room with wooden floors, walls, and ceilings ; casement windows of stained glass design, tiled fireplace, alcove bed, and a painting by Jerborch. This room was taken from a house called "Het Scheepje" (the little boat), in Haarlem, Netherlands, which was built by Dirk Dirick. Paintings in the Dutch gallery of the seventeenth century are by Jacob Ruysdael, De Hooch, Steen, and Hobbema.

A Tudor room from Red Lodge, West Wickham, Kent, England,

dates from 1529 and contains elaborately carved, oak paneled walls, brick and stone fireplace, large windows, velvet drapes, period furniture, and a painting by Antonio Moro. The small English gallery includes several pictures by George Moreland, such as *Old Coaching Days, Fruits of Early Industry and Economy*, and *The Happy Cottagers*. There is also a painting by Richard Wilson of *Westminster Bridge*. This gallery also shows a London interior of 1760, with plastered, painted walls, period furniture, and a fireplace of marble and metal. In this wing there are five galleries for current exhibitions of art.

Close by is an exhibit of three beautifully paneled old rooms brought complete from the Sutton Scarsdale House, Derbyshire, England, and dating back to 1724. The bedroom, in the style of Christopher Wren, contains a gilt marble table of Georgian style, porcelain vases, damask drapes, brass candelabra, and a side chair of the William and Mary period. Another room, in the style of William Kent, has a mahogany console dating from 1745; English pottery, and a vase from Delft, Holland ; and the third room, at one time a dining room and done in the style of Wren, contains numerous pieces of furniture that have no logical connection with the period, but are noteworthy because of other details. In this room is a grandfather clock made in London in 1700 which still keeps excellent time and chimes the hours. All these rooms have original fireplaces, paneled oak walls, ceilings, cornices, floors, door frames, knobs, and locks brought from England direct to the museum. Paintings in the rooms include Gainsborough's *A Classical Landscape*, Reynolds' *Edmund Burke*, Raeburn's *Portrait of a Gentleman*, Constable's *The Locke*, Crome's *Blacksmith's Shop, near Hingham, Norfolk*, and portraits by Romney. Here, too, may be seen Hogarth's *Assembly at Wanstead House* ; *Going to the Hayfield*, by David Cox ; *The Storm*, by John Linnell ; *Burning of the Houses of Parliament*, by Joseph M. W. Turner ; *Sir Walter Scott*, a portrait, by Sir John Watson.

In this same wing there is an interior of the Derby House (1799), Salem, Mass., with a secretary-bookcase of the Sheraton style, a Hepplewhite side chair, a tall clock, a mahogany sofa, and a painting by Francis Wheatley. There is also a room from Wrightington Hall, Lancashire, England (1748), with a Carlton House desk, Sheffield candlesticks, silver inkstand, Chippendale chair, an elaborately carved fireplace with Chelsea porcelain figures on the mantelpiece, a curtain cornice, and carved wood covered with old damask.

Next comes the German-Dutch kitchen — a room from the Muller House (1752), at Millbach, Lebanon County, Pa. The furnishings were given by J. Stogdell Stokes. It has wooden beamed ceilings ; plain plastered walls ; a picture of *A Mennonite Woman*, by Jacob Eicholtz ; pewter plates ; slip and Sgraffito ware ; large, stone fireplace fully equipped with large iron kettle and other cooking utensils ; a wooden stairway ; a long, crude wooden table ; long, narrow benches about six inches wide ; an iron candelabrum — and an old musket over the fireplace.

From the same house is the adjoining bedroom exhibit with its rare wood trimmings, small pane windows, wicker basket, wooden cradle, small bed, crude wooden table, plain straight-backed chairs, cross-stitch mottoes, painted wooden chests with primitive decorative motifs, a triangular cupboard, and quaint pictures on the walls.

Still another old Pennsylvania room in this section is that from the Powel House, Philadelphia (about 1765). It has paneled, painted pine walls ; a bas-relief ceiling, and a white marble fireplace. It contains two wing chairs, two tables, a secretary, sofa, and candlestick, all Chippendale style ; two silver coffee pots, four wall mirrors, and a great clock.

For a time, with the help of Works Progress Administration funds, work was in progress which would have greatly increased the present exhibition facilities of the museum. In the autumn of 1937, it was announced that the WPA phase of the work would be gradually discontinued.

Art Museum and Old Water Works
Gazing Placidly Across the Schuylkill River

GIRARD COLLEGE

*Corinthian and Girard Aves. Broad St. Sub-
way northbound to Girard Ave.; westbound
Route 15 trolley to college.
Important exhibits: Murals by George
Gibbs ; Girard statue by Gevelot ; sarcophagus containing Girard's remains ; Girard's
furniture and other relics.*

THE COLLEGE, enclosed within a 10-foot stone wall and pleasantly situated in a park-like setting in the midst of a populous
residential section, is outstanding among institutions of its kind.
"To rest is to rust," was the motto of Girard. And that is the keynote of the institution which carries on progressively the work of its
taciturn founder.

Established under the will of Stephen Girard, mariner merchant,
banker, and philanthropist, the college received a legacy conserva-
tively estimated at about $6,000,000. Farsighted real estate investments
made by Girard, and careful management by the trustees, have increased the value of the estate far beyond expectations. The trust fund
today amounts to approximately $87,000,000.

The curriculum includes a comprehensive manual training course,
grammar, and high school courses. The senior high school offers
a full college preparatory school course, and one to two years junior
college work is provided, at the discretion of the college authorities,
to a limited number after graduation. The college is a home as well
as a school to the students, whose entire maintenance and care are
assumed by the trustees.

Construction of the first five buildings of the college was begun in
1833. On January 1, 1848, the school was opened on its present site,
then known as Peel Hall Farm, with 100 boys. By 1936 the student
body numbered 1,730, and the college group embraced 29 buildings,
including Founder's Hall, an armory, containing also music and
recreation facilities, library, a high school, an infirmary, a mechanical
school, dormitories, and officials' residences. Light, heat, and
power are furnished by a central plant at the western end of the
grounds. The college staff exceeds 600. During the 90 years of its
existence more than 12,000 youths have gone forth from its guarded
portals, many to occupy places of importance in the world.

The college campus embraces 42 acres of land extending south-
west along South College Avenue from Nineteenth Street and Ridge
Avenue to Twenty-fifth and Poplar Streets, north to North College
Avenue, east to Ridge Avenue at Twentieth Street, and southeast to
Nineteenth Street.

Entrance to the college is at Corinthian and Girard Avenues. This entrance, just east of the middle of the campus, is attended by gate-men who admit visitors through a small lodge east of the gate.

Within the walls and directly ahead from the gate is the main building, known as Founder's Hall. The structure was designed by Thomas U. Walter and is recognized as being an excellent reproduction of a Greek temple. Supporting the structure, and surrounding it, are 34 fluted Corinthian columns rising from a broad-stepped base. At the ends are wide and simple pediments. The building is roofed with marble tiles. Just inside the main entrance to Founder's Hall is a life-size statue of Stephen Girard sculptured by Francois Victor Gevelot. A sarcophagus, close by the statue, holds the remains of the founder. Opening from the vestibule are the directors' rooms and the Girard Museum wherein are housed the founder's furniture and many other relics.

While Founder's Hall, set in the framework of a broad expanse of beautiful lawn decorated with flowers and shrubs, is the most monumental building on the campus, the new chapel, located west of the main gate, is equally impressive, presenting as it does a dignified exterior with an interior of rare beauty. The chapel, dedicated in 1933, was designed by Thomas, Martin & Kirkpatrick. Bearing in mind the ban imposed by Girard against sectarian training, the architects departed from all known orthodox ecclesiastical styles of architecture, yet retained sufficient spiritual beauty to make it "a joy forever." The chapel is of classical design, wedge-shaped, and built after the Doric style. Within recesses on each of the exterior side walls are 10 massive columns. At the choir end of the building and at the opposite or gallery end, four and six additional columns, respectively, are similarly recessed. The leaded windows are so delicately colored as to be effective from both the exterior and the interior; the great main doors are of cast aluminum.

Inside, the dominant feature is a carved ebony desk surmounting a rostrum of black Belgian marble with lighter marble forming a mosaic. A great organ and an echo organ are placed above the ceiling. A novel mechanism broadcasts quarter-hour chimes across the expansive campus. The chapel has a seating capacity of 2,400.

Parallel with the chapel, but located immediately east of the main gate, is the college library. This structure, which was built with funds remaining from the allotment that had been provided for the erection of the chapel, is a square two-story building of white Vermont marble. It is modern Greek in style, and presents an unusually dignified appearance. The building was dedicated in the spring of 1933 ; it contains more than 30,000 books.

The high school building, west of the front entrance near the south wall, was begun in 1914 and completed in 1916. Farther west, beyond the chapel, is a modern armory which contains a drill hall

Founder's Hall at Girard College
"Portico and Stately Corinthian Columns"

Stephen Girard Sarcophagus at Girard College
"Doth the tomb pen up the spirit?"

110 by 220 feet, classrooms, company rooms, and supply rooms for a cadet battalion of four companies. The instrumental music activities also center in this building, with facilities for band and orchestra group and individual instruction.

At the southwest corner of the grounds are the dormitories for the youngest boys, a group of six houses accommodating 25 each. A governess presides over each of these houses. To the east of this house group is the mechanical school, which includes departments for instruction in carpentry, printing, drafting, forge and sheet metal practice, machine shop practice, pattern making, electrical construction, painting and auto mechanics.

Along the north wall, about the middle of the grounds, are the laundry, bakery and shoe repair shop. Just beyond to the east is a commodious dining and service building wherein is housed the department of domestic economy. It also includes a series of dining rooms for the five houses of the oldest boys, all of which are served from a central kitchen.

Comparatively new homes (with garages) for the president, the vice-president and the superintendent of household occupy a wedge-shaped tract of land at the easternmost end of the grounds.

In addition to the many buildings within the college area, there are three playgrounds in the armory, five outdoor playgrounds, a drill field and a playing field, two swimming pools, and two gymnasiums.

The subtle eccentricities of the great philanthropist whose heart and mind provided this unique institution for the protection and education of orphan boys—boys whose fathers alone have died—were born in a philosophy of good that, despite much adverse criticism, has accomplished the fruitful results for which Girard hoped. He wanted his wards to be educated and guided in inclination and habit in order to assume their rightful places in the world; he intended that they be taught the purest principles of morality in an atmosphere of tenderness such as other boys might expect at home. And to assure the carrying out of the broad, general purposes of his program, he stipulated in his will that no denominational or sectarian doctrines might be taught to the students. He further stipulated that no person must influence the boys in this respect, and he specifically barred clergymen of all denominations from the college.

There was, however, no lack of reverence intended in these regulations, since Girard, himself, was a courageous, God-fearing man. The Bible, indeed, was the first book carried into the college. Girard's insistence on strict adherence to his wishes in respect to moral training was due solely to his peculiar love for humanity, which endowed him with unusual consideration for all, regardless of creed. Neither denominationalism nor sectarianism has a place in the college, and neither must there be any influence exercised against his religious beliefs while in school, nor hinder a student, upon the attainment of mature reasoning, from holding such religious tenets as he may prefer.

At the age of 14 Girard ran away from his home in France because of ill-treatment by his stepmother. He obtained work as a ship's cabin boy. By the time he was 23 he had won a master's license. His ship plied between New York, New Orleans, and the West Indies. In 1776, after narrowly escaping capture by British frigates patrolling the American shores, he took refuge in Philadelphia where he later opened a small store. Rising successively through the states of merchant, shipowner, and banker, he acquired a large merchant fleet and established trade with all the leading ports of the world.

Girard's preeminence as a great humanitarian began with the yellow-fever epidemic in Philadelphia in 1793. He contributed liberally of his material wealth and risked his own life by working among the victims of the pestilence. He frequently carried out and helped bury the dead, and labored many long nights in the overcrowded hospitals.

During the second war with England, Girard helped the Federal Government finance the national defense with ships and money.

Although born a Roman Catholic, Girard developed a peculiar philosophy from his study of Voltaire and other French writers. Always a contributor to the Catholic Church, he nevertheless joined the Masonic fraternity. He believed in a Supreme Being, but insisted upon the right of a man to follow the dictates of his own conscience.

He died in Philadelphia in 1831 and was buried in the cemetery of Holy Trinity Roman Catholic Church, Sixth and Spruce Streets. His remains eventually were disinterred and removed with much ceremony to the sarcophagus in Founder's Hall, where they were laid at final rest with full Masonic rites.

United States Mint
"Where silver and copper become 'the coin of the realm'"

UNITED STATES MINT

*Spring Garden St., from 16th to 17th
Sts. Northbound trolley 16th St. (Open
weekdays from 10:00 a. m. to 12 m.; Saturdays 9:30 to 11 a. m.; admission free).*

THE PHILADELPHIA MINT is the oldest and largest of the
three United States mints. Here it is possible to observe the
process of minting, from metal in a molten state to the finished
product — coins ready for circulation.

The mint coins 65 percent of the specie used in this country, as
well as a large amount of coins for South and Central American
nations. It also makes Army and Navy medals and "proof" coins,
which may be purchased. The Bureau of the Mint not only coins
money for the Government, but also assays precious metals for private
owners at fixed rates and collects statistics on the production of these
metals in the United States. The mint can turn out 1,250,000 coins in
an 8-hour workday.

The first mint in the country was established in Philadelphia in
1792, after agitation on the part of Thomas Jefferson, Alexander
Hamilton, and Robert Morris had influenced Congress to pass an
enabling act. The flag raised over the mint was the first displayed on
a Government-owned building.

First set up at 37 North Seventh Street, the mint was moved to
Juniper and Chestnut Streets in 1833, and to its present quarters in
1901. It has been operated as a bureau of the Treasury Department
since 1873, when passage of the Coinage Act made its operations subject to conditions imposed by Congress. Prior to 1873 it was under
the supervision of the Director of the Mint at Philadelphia.

As the mint service grew in its operations and other mints and as-
say offices were opened, the supervisory heads of these institutions
were called superintendents, all under the supervision of the Director
of the Mint, whose office is in Washington.

Every process in the mint is attended with safeguards to ensure the
least possible loss in precious metals. The metals are weighed at the
beginning and end of each operation. Steel-grated floors scrape valuable dust from workmen's feet. Gloves, machine wipers, and hand
towels are gathered up and burned, and the ashes are washed in a
special bath that separates metal from waste.

The metals — gold, silver, copper, nickel, tin, and zinc — received
at the mint are cast into ingots. The content of the ingots depends
upon the type of coin to be cast. Silver coins are made of silver
alloyed with copper in the ratio of one part copper to nine parts
silver bullion; nickel coins of 75 percent copper and 25 percent

375

nickel ; bronze coins of 95 percent copper and 5 percent tin and zinc.

The ingots are run through rolling mills until they have been reduced to the required thickness. The sheets pass through a cutting press, where blank discs are stamped out. They are then passed through an annealing furnace to anneal, or soften, them before they go to the coining presses. The discs are revolved in barrels filled with a burnishing solution and then dried in centrifugal drying machines.

After each of these steps the coins are weighed. If found too heavy, they are shaved to the proper weight ; if too light, they are rejected.

Next, the blank discs are put through machines, which mill the edges, then stamp the designs and the lettering in one operation. Finished coins pass on belts before inspectors, whose task it is to detect any flaw. Those which survive the rigid tests are placed in bags and held in the mint vaults awaiting distribution to the various Federal Reserve Banks, which order them through the Treasury Department in Washington. Rejected coins are returned to the refinery to be melted for recasting into ingots. All silver coins, with the exception of dimes, are weighed separately. If the coins are found to be outside the legal weight, they are condemned. The weight of the dimes is verified by frequent test weights, but not all pieces are weighed separately. In addition, all silver coins are weighed in $1,000 lots before being bagged for circulation.

All these operations may be observed from glass-enclosed galleries along the sides of the various rooms.

The mint building is of solid granite, rectangular in shape, and designed in the Italian Renaissance style. A loggia with four Ionic columns supporting the entablature is directly above the triple-arched entrance. The first story is horizontally rusticated, the upper two smooth-surfaced. The entrance hall with six vaulted bays is finished in white marble with ceilings enriched by gold mosaics. Piers and pilasters are of the Doric order. Seven circular mosaic murals within the arches of the walls depict the early development of coinage. They were designed by Tiffany & Co. A monumental staircase rises opposite the entrance. On the second-floor landing is a striking pedimented doorway leading into a large, high, octagonal exhibit room with a domical ceiling, from the center of which hangs a magnificent crystal chandelier. The walls are faced with red Virginia marble.

Relics preserved in the mint include record books dating from 1792 ; the original of a letter from President Buchanan to the Director of the Mint ; the first hand press and scales ; facsimiles of Presidential medals and of medals presented to Col. Charles A. Lindbergh and Rear Admiral Richard E. Byrd ; and specimens of service medals.

★

★

★

★

★

★

ROADS and RAMBLES

in and around THE CITY

★

★

★

City Tours

Philadelphia's City Hall is the starting point for all city tours. The courtyard at the intersection of the two axial streets, Broad and Market, is the heart of the city.

All traffic passing City Hall swings a half circle around the building. Pedestrians, however, may walk through archways built into the four sides of the structure. The archways lead north and south on Broad Street and east and west on Market Street. A large compass dial is cemented in the center of the courtyard. The cardinal points are plainly marked, and broad arrows point to the corresponding axial streets. Thus, west on the compass dial may be used as a guide to the West Market entrance, which is marked by a red-and-gold sign on the west arch. The East Market, South Broad, and North Broad Street arches are similarly designated.

City Hall and Skyline
"The Heart of the City"

HEART OF THE CITY

PHILADELPHIA'S CITY HALL (1) *(open weekdays, 9:30 to 5; 9 to 11; closed Sun.; adm. free)*, and the buildings in its proximity are, in some measure, symbolic of the metropolis as a whole. A walk around City Hall brings into view many types of structures, each representing a definite phase of the city's varied activities.

The granite mass of City Hall, one of the largest municipal buildings in the world, rises from Penn Square, which covers an entire city block in the crowded heart of the metropolis. The courtyard of the mid-Victorian structure encloses the actual intersection of Broad and Market Streets, main axes of the city as planned by William Penn, and still the chief north-south and east-west thoroughfares.

Rising 510 feet above the street and topped by a 37-foot statue of Penn, its hand outstretched in benediction over the city he founded more than 250 years ago, City Hall tower is the highest building point in Philadelphia.

This temple of local politics represents an outlay of $26,000,000, and its construction, attended by much bitter criticism and more than a hint of bribery and corruption, dragged on for almost a third of a century. Some parts of the building still lack finishing touches.

Thomas U. Walter, architect of Girard College and of the United States Capitol extensions, prepared plans for City Hall in 1842. Nothing further was done until December 1868, when City Council passed an ordinance providing for the erection of municipal buildings in Independence Square. However, in a referendum on August 5, 1870, the citizenry defeated this proposal. In its stead the voters chose the present site, then known as Center Square, at one time the site of the municipal waterworks. A commission created by the Legislature to handle construction of all municipally owned edifices took charge of the City Hall project on August 27 of the same year. The body continued functioning for 30 years. It was dissolved on July 1, 1901, and city authorities took command in the final weary drive for completion of the building.

John J. McArthur, Jr., the chief architect, gave nearly 20 years of personal service to construction of City Hall. His bust rests in a niche high up on the grand stairway on the south side of the building. Alexander Milne Calder spent 15 years on the sculptural and

379

statuary work. His huge statue of Penn was hoisted to the top of the tower in 1894.

The immense masonry structure is treated in a debased French Renaissance style. Columns, pedimented windows and a variety of sculpture embellish the four similar facades of white granite and marble. The total effect is gray, heavy, and somber. Accent was placed on the four main entrances centering on the facades and on the four corner entrances by extending them from the main wall. The corner stairways extend through five stories in octagonal spirals, their huge granite blocks cantilevered from the wall.

Interiors of interest are the mayor's suite, with its gilded ceiling and great chandelier ; the finance committee room, with its matched panels of Circassian walnut ; Council Chamber, Conversation Hall, and the Supreme Courtroom, which, like the mayor's office, are decorated in the heavy, classic style with columns, pilasters, and paneling of colored marble and granite.

The four-faced tower clock, a colossal mechanism with illuminated dials which are visible for a great distance, has been Philadelphia's official timepiece since 1899. Shortly after the clock was installed the city inaugurated a custom which still continues. Every evening at three minutes of nine the tower lights are turned off, and then turned on again on the hour. This enables those within observation distance, though unable to see the hands, to set their timepieces.

In early days City Hall had a private water supply. A pipe line more than five miles long connected the water system to the Belmont reservoir in Fairmount Park. Before filtration of the city's supply became general, persons who worked in the building were permitted to carry home bottles of reservoir water filtered by a special plant in the building. When the building was electrified, considerable drilling was necessary to run wires through the granite walls and the three miles of corridors.

One of the greatest feats of underpinning ever attempted was accomplished in 1934 when the weight of the mammoth structure was shifted to new foundations — thus permitting the Market-Frankford Subway-Elevated to run in a straight line underneath the building instead of circuitously — a hazardous task, as some of the basement walls are 22 feet thick, with single blocks weighing from two to five tons. Huge steel "needle" beams were threaded through the old masonry, and the final transfer of weight was effected by an intricate arrangement of steel wedges. The new foundations are 20 feet below the old.

The task of beautifying the City Hall area began in 1931, and work was completed July 1935. Bare plots in the corners of the courtyard were gradually given the appearance of heavily wooded miniature parks. The two largest plots are in the northeast and northwest corners, with a slightly smaller patch in the southwest corner. In the southeast corner are two relatively small patches.

All the beds are bordered by dwarf barberry, a compact form of Japanese hedge which presents an attractive foliage. Privet honeysuckle occupies the beds bordering the east-to-west walks. Other plants growing here include azalea, dwarf box ilex, the spreading English yew, Japanese holly, and sumach. A compass in the center of the courtyard acts as a guide to pedestrians emerging from the subway.

Beautification of City Hall itself was begun in the autumn of 1936, when a large crew of WPA workers started the gigantic task of cleaning the million square feet of stone composing the building's exterior. Twenty tons of pipe and 25,000 feet of lumber were used in the scaffolding, erected to a height of 150 feet. Fifty thousand gallons of specially prepared paste were used in one of the largest cleaning jobs ever attempted.

Despite its size, City Hall is too small to accommodate all municipal offices. CITY HALL ANNEX (1a), standing at Juniper and Filbert Streets, was completed in 1927. The structure is 15 stories high, of Italian Renaissance design, with a light gray limestone veneer covering the steel and concrete. The first three stories of this building are in Doric style, and the last two in the Ionic style. The middle 10 stories are without embellishment. The building was designed by Philip H. Johnson. A vaulted open arcade with 11 arches runs along Filbert and Thirteenth Street sides of the building.

At the northeast corner of Juniper and Market Streets, facing City Hall, is the 24-story salmon-colored MARKET STREET NATIONAL BANK BUILDING (1b), a modern office building.

Opposite City Hall (to the southeast), covering an entire city block on the site formerly occupied by the old Pennsylvania Railroad warehouse, stands the main store of Philadelphia's merchant prince, the late John Wanamaker.

THE WANAMAKER DEPARTMENT STORE (2) is a distinguished example of the trend toward cultural and civic enterprise as an adjunct of commercial activity. Designed by Daniel Burnham, its broad surfaces are unusually well treated in Italian Renaissance style with huge Doric pilasters and columns at the base.

Rising 12 stories above the street, with three more floors below, the store has spacious aisles and attractive displays. The whole structure is built around a Grand Court, six stories high. Concealed in the court's walls are the 30,000 pipes of one of the world's largest organs. Hundreds of persons throng the court to listen to the 15-minute recitals given hourly. During the Christmas season, carols are sung.

381

Also sheltered within the court is the gigantic "Wanamaker Eagle" of shining metal, a popular meeting place for Philadelphians. "Meet me at the Eagle" has become a common phrase to many residents. Ionic and Corinthian architectural details suggest a palatial atmosphere. A dome rises 150 feet above the main floor and is supported by a series of Italian and Greek marble arches. At the south end of the court is a gallery holding the console of the organ and space for the seating of bands and orchestras.

The policy of the store is to promote originality in decorative designs each year. The Grand Court is decorated seasonally in recognition of Christmas and Easter. The Easter decoration exhibits two great canvases by Michael de Munkacsy—*Christ Before Pilate* and *The Crucifixion*—and through the year calendared events are recognized with suitable decorations.

Rich paintings, tapestries, and fabrics, furniture, and rare objects brought from the far corners of the earth abound in the store. In Egyptian Hall on the second floor is the superb painting, *The Conquerors*, by Pierre Fritel. Greek Hall, on the same floor, in pure Greek style, is paneled in mahogany inlaid with satinwood.

On the fifth floor is the Eighteenth Century House, its rooms furnished and decorated with authentic pieces of that period.

Several rooms of a Virginia mansion designed by Thomas Jefferson are faithfully reproduced in the Old Colony House on the sixth floor.

On the seventh floor on the Chestnut Street side, entered through an imposing iron grille, is the Wanamaker Art Gallery. It houses representative art works of five schools — English, French, Flemish, Italian, and Dutch. Included are canvases from the Salon des Artistes Francais and the Société Nationale des Beaux Arts, and some excellent pieces of statuary.

Adjacent is the Wanamaker Men's Store, occupying seven floors of the LINCOLN-LIBERTY BUILDING (3) on the east side of Broad Street between Chestnut Street and South Penn Square. The Men's Store was opened in 1932. The 26-story structure is a modern office building, surmounted by a tower from which a deep-voiced bell booms the hours.

Across Broad Street is a low-domed structure built in 1908 for the century-old GIRARD TRUST COMPANY (4). It was designed by the architectural firm of McKim, Mead & White, and inspired by the Pantheon in Rome. Several additions were necessitated by the company's growth. Its latest acquisition, erected in 1930, is the adjoining 30-story Girard Trust Company Building, on the southwest corner of Broad Street and South Penn Square. Designed by the same architects, it is faced with white marble and is of a dignified, classic design.

On the southwest corner of West Penn Square and Market Street, directly facing the western facade of City Hall, is a squat structure housing the MITTEN BANK (5). Directly in back of it looms the 22-story Commercial Trust Building, another bank and office building.

Across Market Street and extending to Filbert is the BROAD STREET STATION (6), of the Pennsylvania Railroad. Erected by the railroad in 1880, it was at that time one of the largest railroad stations in the United States. Built of brick, terra cotta and granite, it is a highly individualistic interpretation of Gothic architecture, designed by the firm of Furness & Evans.

Additions have been made to this old five-story landmark, but the northern part of the building is still in its original condition. In 1892 foundations were laid for elaborate additions including a 10-story office building. The improved building was opened in 1894 and remains unchanged, with the exception of the train shed, which was destroyed by fire in 1923. Railroad officials are contemplating demolition of the building and train shed.

Beyond the northwest corner of City Hall, at Broad and Filbert Streets, lies the open sweep of REYBURN PLAZA (7), an area acquired by the city under ordinances between 1909 and 1934. From time to time, by special permit, various public functions are held here — addresses, concerts, mass meetings, and ceremonials. The band shell was erected with private funds.

Stretching northwestward from the plaza, the wide smooth Parkway leads directly to the Pennsylvania Museum of Art *(see Points of Interest)*.

On the east side of Broad Street at Filbert, facing the plaza, is the MASONIC TEMPLE (8), headquarters of the Pennsylvania Masonic order *(see City Tour 5)*.

The BULLETIN BUILDING (9), home of the *Evening Bulletin*, is at Juniper and Filbert Streets. The *Bulletin*, established in 1847 as the *Cummings Telegraphic Evening Bulletin*, has grown to be the largest daily newspaper in Pennsylvania.

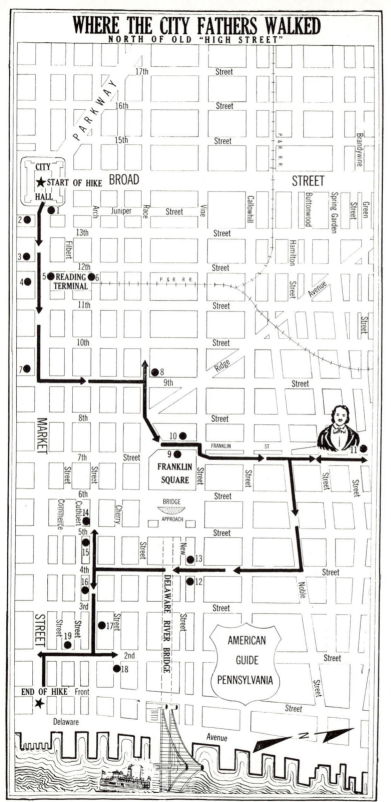

WHERE THE CITY FATHERS WALKED
NORTH OF OLD "HIGH STREET"

1. City Hall

2. Wanamaker's Department Store

3. Philadelphia Saving Fund Society Building

4. Department Store of N. Snellenburg & Company

5. Reading Terminal

6. Reading Terminal Market

7. The Federal Building

8. Chinatown

9. Franklin Sq.

10. Zion Lutheran Church

11. Edgar Allan Poe House

12. St. George's Methodist Episcopal Church

13. St. Augustine's Roman Catholic Church

14. The Friends Meeting House

15. The Christ Church Burial Ground

16. The Arch Street Friends Meeting House

18. Elfreth's Alley

17. The Betsy Ross House

19. Christ Church

WHERE THE CITY FATHERS WALKED

City Tour 1

North of Market (Old High Street) East of Broad

FROM the heavy Victorian mass of CITY HALL (1) *(see Heart of the City)* the tour proceeds east on Market Street.

On the southeast corner of Market and Juniper Streets stands WANAMAKER'S DEPARTMENT STORE (2) *(see Heart of the City)*.

At Twelfth Street, on the southwest corner, is the PHILADELPHIA SAVING FUND SOCIETY BUILDING (3) *(glass-inclosed observatory, 35th floor, open weekdays, 9:30 to 4:30; adm. 25¢, children under 12 years of age accompanied by an adult, free; additional fee of 10¢ for use of telescope).*

Rearing its black and chromium-ribbed bulk above the lesser structures of Philadelphia's varied skyline, this pillar of stone, glass, and chromium stands forth as a monument to modern architectural achievement.

New as it is, it has become generally known as "12 South 12th Street," the address of the office building entrance. The Market Street entrance is for the bank only.

The PSFS building is one of the best examples in America of the so-called modern International style of architecture. The aim of the architects, Howe & Lescaze, was so to construct the interior as to offer ideal working conditions. Broad surfaces of glass admit sunlight; restful colors reduce eye strain; and wide escalators and fast elevators speed communication between floors. It was the second office building in America to be air-conditioned. Of particular interest is the fact that the vertical structural members of the exterior have been built on the outside of the walls to eliminate interior surface obstructions.

The architecture expresses its commercial purpose. Horizontal courses of windows and stone are cut by light accents, stone covering the vertical structural members. Highly polished gray and black granite on the lower stories contrasts with the light-colored limestone of the rest of the building.

An enormous window composed of 25 huge panes of glass encloses the 52-foot high entrance hall on the Market Street side. The lofty lobby of gray and black Belgian marble contains a modern double escalator of chromium giving access to the second-floor banking room. Near the banking room is a course of black marble under a high window of heavy plate glass, which runs along two sides of the building. The only warm note in this room of glass walls and large surfaces of light gray and black Belgian marble is given by the large light-reflecting panels of the acoustically treated ceiling. Business in the banking room is transacted over open counters, the customary glass partitions being absent.

The entire building is conspicuously free of ornamentation. All metal fixtures and the sign and the doors are of stainless steel ; the window frames are of aluminum.

Built in 1932 on the early site of the William Penn Charter School, this skyscraper contrasts strangely with the old Quaker meetinghouse next door ; typifying Philadelphia's past and present.

The DEPARTMENT STORE OF N. SNELLENBURG & CO. (4) occupies the entire frontage on the right side of Market Street from Twelfth to Eleventh.

On the northeast corner of Twelfth Street is the READING TERMINAL (5), principal station of the Reading Company and terminal for a number of bus lines.

The building, erected in 1893, is an eight-story structure of brick and cream terra cotta, designed in heavy Italian Renaissance style. A broad shed protects the main entrance. The top story forms the architrave of the broad, rich entablature, and a balustrade crowns the structure.

In the rear of the station, at Twelfth and Filbert Streets, is the READING TERMINAL MARKET (6), largest indoor market in the city and a center for the sale of farm products, rare edibles, and sea foods.

The FEDERAL BUILDING (7), on the southwest corner at Ninth Street, is one of the centers of United States governmental activities in Philadelphia (1937). It was formerly the city's main post office and is now a branch post office, and the home of the Federal Court and several governmental departments.

The building, erected in 1872, occupies the site of the old University of Pennsylvania buildings, one of which was the so-called "Presidential mansion" built by the State of Pennsylvania for the use of Washington, but never occupied by him.

Constructed of limestone and granite, the design of the Federal Building was influenced by the Louvre in Paris. Each story is divided by a heavy entablature supported by Ionic pilasters and columns. Above the center of the Ninth Street facade is a huge mansard dome, a large slated superstructure with tall flanking chimneys.

The Market and Chestnut Street sides are similar in design to the Ninth Street facade. On the Chestnut Street sidewalk stands a statue by Boyle commemorating Franklin as Postmaster General.

NORTH OF OLD HIGH STREET (CITY TOUR 1)

It was from this site, then an open field, that Benjamin Franklin flew his famous kite into a thunderstorm, and touching a knuckle to the brass key at the end of the hempen line, demonstrated the accuracy of his belief that lightning and electricity were the same.

The low coping that surrounds three sides of the Post Office is the meeting place of the life-weary of Philadelphia, who bask in, and follow, lizard-like, the moving sun, feeding their companions, the pigeons.

Plans were announced in 1937 for the demolition of this building and the erection of a new structure to house the Federal Courts in the city.

L. from Market St. on 9th to Race ; R. on Race.

Along Race Street, between Ninth and Tenth, is Philadelphia's CHINATOWN (8), a block of three- and four-story buildings, erected more than a hundred years ago as dwellings. The dormer windows of the attics, the swing signs, and skeletal fire escapes, intertwining the decorative iron balconies, give the street a bizzarre effect.

The Far East Restaurant is one building in the block that gives an Oriental flavor to the row of ramshackle and neglected stores and restaurants. The recessed balcony with Chinese inscriptions painted on plaques between the windows, the curved roof, with upturned scrolls and reclining dolphins and dragons, add the only touch of the Orient to the drab street.

Placid Chinese, the younger in western dress, tend novelty store, and serve in restaurants. The older generation, clinging to the robes of the East, lounge about the sidewalk, smoking, their long silver-bowled pipes.

Retrace on Race St. to Franklin.

The tour passes FRANKLIN SQUARE (9), which occupies the block between Race and Vine, Sixth and Franklin Streets, and faces on the wide approach to the Delaware River Bridge.

The park, one of five originally outlined by William Penn in his city plan, was at one time the center of a fashionable residential section. With the expansion of the city, however, the wealthier citizens moved out to leave the neighborhood to decay and disrepute. Some of the brown stone houses along Franklin Street still retain traces of the austere respectability that once permeated the area.

On the left side of the square, between Race and Vine Streets, is the ZION LUTHERAN CHURCH (10). It is constructed of brown sandstone in Gothic style, with a slate steeple and six buttresses on each side. The congregation of this church was organized in 1742 by Henry Melchior Muhlenberg, the patriarch of the Lutheran Church in America. In its first church building at Fifth and Appletree Streets, the Evangelical Lutheran Ministerium of Pennsylvania was organized on August 14, 1748. In Old Zion, the second church, at

Fourth and Cherry Streets, Congress met on October 24, 1781, for a thanksgiving service after the victory at Yorktown. The national funeral services for George Washington were held in Old Zion on December 26, 1799. It was at these services that Gen. "Light Horse" Harry Lee pronounced his famous tribute : "First in war, first in peace, first in the hearts of his countrymen." Memorial services for Gen. Lafayette were held in Zion Church in 1834. The present edifice was erected in 1870 upon the site of the former burial ground.

R. from Franklin St. on Vine ; L. on 7th.

At 530 North Seventh Street (beyond Spring Garden Street) is a small cottage haunted by the ghost of a genius who lived there and knew tragedy during his stay. This is the EDGAR ALLAN POE HOUSE (11) *(open daily 9 to 5 ; adm. 25¢)*, where from June 1842 to May 1844, the "Prince of Melancholy" lived and worked on some of his best-known stories.

With Poe during this time was his tragic child-wife, Virginia, who inspired much of his darkly romantic poetry. During the time he occupied this cottage Poe was dependent upon his meager earnings as a free-lance writer, and he and Virginia often endured acute privation. Here one evening while singing for Poe, Virginia suffered the rupture of a blood vessel in her throat. That accident was partly responsible for her death three years later.

The building is a single three-story structure of red brick with a steep roof slanting toward the front. It is devoid of ornamentation. An interesting feature is the squareness of the four windows in the front of the top story. The cottage was without fitting designation until 1927, when, through the philanthropy of Richard Gimbel, it was restored to its former appearance, and a museum of Poe's works installed. Here, in "The Rose-Covered Cottage," Poe wrote *The Raven, The Gold Bug, The Black Cat, Masque of the Red Death, The Pit and the Pendulum*, and other celebrated works. Many important manuscripts and all first editions are on display. Use of the library on the premises is restricted to research students, who must make special arrangements through the caretaker.

Retrace on 7th St.; L. on Noble; R. on 4th.

Just north of the Delaware River Bridge approach on the left at New Street is ST. GEORGE'S METHODIST EPISCOPAL CHURCH (12).

Old St. George's Church is American Methodism's oldest and most historic edifice. Its style of architecture is American Georgian. The cornerstone was laid in 1763, and the edifice was dedicated and occupied in 1769. It is a square structure, with two square doorways separated by a stone memorial. The huge pediment above the third floor formed by the gable is pierced by a semi-circular window.

The deep affection in which it is held today was well illustrated

St. George's Methodist Church
"In the shadow of modernity . . ."

when its demolition was threatened by the original plans for the
Delaware River Bridge. Protests raised by Methodists throughout
the country, accompanied by a barrage of petitions and letters, caused
a change in the plans. Now the church stands in the shadow of the
great bridge that once threatened its existence.

The walls and roof were built by seceding members of the Dutch
Reformed Church, who, not being able to finish or meet the obligations of their enterprise, were jailed for debt, and the edifice was
offered at public auction. Among the bidders was a young man
of feeble intellect but wealthy parentage, and his bid of £700 was
accepted. The young man's father, unwilling to admit that his son
was mentally infirm, paid the money.

He immediately sold the church to Miles Pennington, agent for
the Methodist Society, and Capt. Thomas Webb, famous in Colonial
times as a Methodist evangelist. Captain Webb preached there very
frequently. He delivered his sermons attired in the full regimentals
of a British officer, with a patch over his eye and his sword laid
across the pulpit. Throngs were attracted by his powerful personality.

Old St. George's Church, one of the evangelical outposts of Methodism in America, contributed to the fusing of the newly developed
country with its new religious doctrine. It was in this house of prayer
that Bishop Francis Asbury, the Methodist apostle to America, de-

389

livered on October 28, 1771, his first sermon on this side of the Atlantic. At this church the first conference of American Methodism, held on July 14, 1773, was attended by 10 ministers, six of whom took appointments.

Under the direction of a committee of parishioners, in 1837 a basement was dug to provide adequate space for Sunday School purposes.

Today, in a small room are still to be seen the desk and chairs used by Bishop Asbury. Much Revolutionary tradition is associated with the old church.

On the walls of the church are three marble memorial tablets, one on each side of the pulpit platform and one on the south side under the gallery. Upon these tablets are chiseled the names of all the pastors who served at St. George's since 1769. Among them are four bishops of the Methodist Episcopal Church : Francis Asbury, Richard Whatcoat, Robert R. Roberts, and Levi Scott. Rev. John Dickins, an early pastor of St. George's, founded the Methodist Book Concern of the United States.

On the right, near Race Street, is ST. AUGUSTINE'S ROMAN CATHOLIC CHURCH (13), which was erected on the site of the original edifice, built in 1796 by the Hermits of St. Augustine. The building was destroyed by fire in 1844 and rebuilt in 1847.

The present building was designed after the manner of the churches of Sir Christopher Wren. Constructed of red brick with limestone doorway and trim, the building shows strength of character in the tall tower with its heavy white quoins centering on the facade. The interior, heavily ornamented, is Corinthian in design.

R. from 4th St. on Arch.

The FREE QUAKER BUILDING (14) is on the southwest corner at Fifth Street. It was erected in 1783 by those Friends who defied the principles of the sect and took up arms in the Revolution.

This two-story building is enriched by the delicacy of the pediment above the main doorway and flat stone arches above the windows. Flemish bond brickwork with black headers adds color to the building.

The CHRIST CHURCH BURIAL GROUND (15), on the southeast corner of Fifth Street, contains Benjamin Franklin's grave.

The burial ground was established in 1719 in what was then the outskirts of the city. The tomb of Franklin and his wife is situated at the cemetery's northwest corner, and is marked by a flat stone with the simple inscription : "Benjamin and Deborah Franklin," and the date, 1790. In the same lot lie the remains of Franklin's son, Francis F. ; his daughter, Sarah Bache ; Sarah's husband, Richard Bache ; and John Read, Franklin's father-in-law.

Elfreth's Alley
"Candlelight and cobblestones"

Benjamin Franklin's Grave
"Like the cover of an old book, its
contents torn . . ."

Near Franklin's grave the brick wall was removed in 1858 and an iron railing substituted, so that the hallowed spot might be viewed readily from Arch Street. In 1911 bronze tablets recording Franklin's achievements were attached to the wall. These were gifts of the late Cyrus H. K. Curtis.

Other graves within this two-acre enclosure hold the remains of many men and women who devoted their lives to the cause of civil and religious liberty, among them four signers of the Declaration of Independence : Benjamin Rush, distinguished physician who founded Dickinson College and the Philadelphia Dispensary ; Francis Hopkinson, noted composer ; Joseph Hewes ; and George Ross. Also buried here are three commodores of the United States Navy—Thomas Truxton, Richard Dale, and William Bainbridge — and the first Treasurer of the United States, Michael Hillegas.

Christ Church Burial Ground, in the business section of modern Philadelphia, was purchased by the vestry of Christ Church for the modest sum of £72. When the original wooden fence around the grounds began to fall apart in 1772, a brick wall was constructed. More than a century and a half later the wall was rebuilt, much of the old material being used again. A Bible, a prayer book for soldiers and sailors, and other items of historic interest were sealed in a copper container in the rebuilt wall, dedicated in 1927.

Retrace on Arch St.

On the right, midway between Fourth and Third Streets, is the ARCH STREET FRIENDS MEETING HOUSE (16). The building was erected in 1804 on ground granted by William Penn and originally used as a cemetery. The house has served continuously for the Yearly Meeting of (Orthodox) Friends. The grounds constitute a colorful garden of trees and flowers.

For about 70 years no one has been interred there, but within the century preceding that more than 20,000 persons were buried in the grounds — many of them victims of the yellow-fever epidemic of 1793.

The first person buried there was the wife of David Lloyd, one of the early Governors of the Province of Pennsylvania. William Penn stood at her grave and spoke in appreciation of her character and piety. In the yard also rest the remains of James Logan, Penn's distinguished secretary, who later became Governor of the Province, and Lydia Darrah, heroine of the Revolution.

The broad, low, red brick building, devoid of all ornamentation, is typical of the Quaker architecture of the times. The simple facade is relieved only by a large central pediment and the three small entrance porticos. Behind the building is an old Colonial watch box.

A big room in this old Meeting House was the scene of many early Quaker gatherings. The original key is still used, and the original deed from Penn is preserved by the Meeting.

392

The ground floor contains three large meeting rooms, and end rooms with galleries on three sides. Benches are made of wood from trees cut down to clear the site. On the second floor, in the center, roof beams are made of hand-hewn timbers.

Today the Arch Street Meeting House is one of the most frequently used in the Philadelphia area, many of the Society's social functions being held there.

On the left side of Arch Street between Second and Third is the BETSY ROSS HOUSE (17), where the first flag is said to have been made *(see Points of Interest)*.

L. from Arch St. on 2d.

ELFRETH'S ALLEY (18) is that portion of Cherry Street between Second and Front.

Another remnant of Colonial days, only lightly touched by Time's effacing hands, is Elfreth's Alley. To the alley — it is an alley in name only now, and the name is but little known — there still clings the aura of the candlelit eighteenth century and the whisper of great names.

The alley is an echo of yesteryear. Within sound and sight of the commercial bustle of Delaware Avenue and the humming traffic of Delaware River Bridge, its houses are still the prim, brass-knockered, white-doored brick dwellings of Colonial Philadelphia.

Tradition has it that Benjamin Franklin and Talleyrand both resided in houses in the alley. If either did, it was for such a brief period that history failed to record the stay. That Stephen Girard lived there is certain. Detained in Philadelphia when the British blockade prevented departure of his merchantmen, Girard took lodgings in the house at 111 Elfreth's Alley.

Talleyrand resided in Philadelphia for two years, and there is evidence that a group of French émigrés lived in the alley for a time, but whether or not the astute diplomat was among them is uncertain. These émigrés were from San Domingo, whence a scourge of yellow fever had routed them.

For age alone, the houses of the alley would be notable. Three standing there, among the oldest in the country, were saved from demolition in 1933 through intervention of the Philadelphia Society for the Preservation of Landmarks, acting upon the plea of Mrs. D. W. Ottey, a resident of the alley. In Mrs. Ottey's house, at 115, may be seen a fine Colonial mantelpiece, constructed when the house was erected in 1720. Many of the present-day dwellers in the alley retain and treasure the fine woodwork and handmade glass installed by the Colonial builders.

The exteriors of the houses are typical of the Philadelphia Colonial type. Two stories in height, their red-brick fronts line both sides of the little street uninterrupted by any discordant newer buildings.

393

The windows are wood-shuttered ; the entrances are arched white doorways, approached by two or three stone steps. Of special note are several simple but well executed pedimented doorways. In better repair, this street could be one of the show places representative of the old Philadelphia.

The alley takes its name from the Elfreth family, whose name in old documents is variously spelled Elfreth, Elfrith, Elfrey, and even Elfrit. The first of the name to come to Philadelphia was Jeremiah, a blacksmith, who arrived from England in 1690. He wished to establish a wharfage and shipbuilding business and acquired land for the purpose. Public clamor thwarted him, however, when it was learned that his land had previously been reserved for a public dock by the Penns. His nephew, Henry, bought property for a wharfage business on what is now Cherry Street, near Front, and prospered. He married Sara, daughter of John Gilbert, merchant, and came into possession of his father-in-law's property, known as Gilbert's Alley. He renamed it Elfreth's Alley.

To stimulate an appreciation of the alley's historic associations, the people residing on it have formed the Elfreth Alley Association and hold open house at their dwellings each year on the first Saturday in June.

Retrace on 2d St.

On the right, south of Arch Street, is old CHRIST CHURCH (19), first Protestant Episcopal church in the Province. Here Washington, Franklin, and other leaders sought spiritual guidance for their service in the cause of freedom and democracy. John Penn, last male of his line, is buried near the steps of the pulpit.

Still preserved, and marked by bronze tablets, are the pews occupied by the Penn family, by Washington, Adams, Franklin, Lafayette, Robert Morris, Hopkinson, Rush, and Betsy Ross. Washington worshiped here regularly during the seven years of his residence in Philadelphia, and the door to the southeast of the nave, through which he was accustomed to enter, is known as the Washington Door. The Washington pew is number 58, and that of Franklin, number 70. Members of the Continental Congress attended a service of fasting and prayer in Christ Church, shortly after the Battle of Lexington.

Still to be seen are the eight bells that added their volume to that of the Liberty Bell on July 8, 1776, when the Declaration of Independence was first read to the public. These same bells were removed to Allentown along with the Liberty Bell when Howe's army advanced upon Philadelphia. They were brought back after the British had evacuated the city.

In addition to their primary function of calling worshippers to service and their jubilant announcement of the Nation's birth, the Christ Church bells were sounded on the eve of marketing days. On

394

such occasions residents of outlying villages would journey part way to the city to listen to their silver-voiced symphony. These bells are referred to in Longfellow's *Evangeline*. The bells were purchased in England for about £560 through a committee, of which Franklin was a member.

The church was established by a group of 36 English churchmen under a provision inserted in King Charles' charter to Penn at the instance of Rt. Rev. Henry Compton, Bishop of London. The first structure was erected in 1695 and was succeeded by the present building, begun about 1727 and completed in 1754. St. Peter's Church was erected at Third and Pine Streets in 1761, as a chapel of ease of Christ Church, and St. James's Church was built in 1809. The three were known as the United Churches. Later, however, each became a separate corporation.

The red brick edifice is a Colonial adaptation of Georgian architecture in the general style of Sir Christopher Wren's churches in London. It is generally agreed that the structure was built under the direction of Dr. John Kearsley, one of the vestrymen. Though all but lost among the drab buildings that surround it, the church cuts a salient contour in Philadelphia's skyline as seen from the Delaware River.

The profusion of decoration, which renders the church almost baroque in its architectural design, is unusual for old Philadelphia. A feature of the east facade is a large Palladian window in which is a memorial to Bishop White. Over the window is a heavy entablature with a rounded frieze. Rows of fine arched windows in both the first and second stories, separated by brick pilasters and enriched by delicately patterned keystones, ornament the sides of the church. The baroque effect is due largely to the detail of the entablature and balustrades, which are surmounted by flaming colored urns. Much of the detail work, especially the cornices, arches, and pilasters, is of beautifully molded brick.

In sharp contrast with the ornateness of the main structure, rises the massive and severe stone tower, its walls four feet thick and faced with Flemish bond brick. The tower, adjoining the western end of the church, supports a wooden belfry, incongruously light for the mass of the tower. Above this is the steeple. The tower was completed with proceeds from the Philadelphia Steeple Lottery and other lotteries, which in the early days of the city were an accepted means of financing public improvements.

The crown which originally capped the spire was replaced by a mitre, after the Rt. Rev. William White became Bishop of Pennsylvania in 1787. This was in line with previous action of church officials, immediately following the signing of the Declaration of Independence, in authorizing their ministers to abandon the prayer for the

King of England, and to phrase in its stead a prayer for the new government.

Prayer books that have been preserved show the erasure of the reference to "our most gracious sovereign Lord, King George," and the substitution of the words: "all in authority, legislative and judicial, in these United States." Likewise, the vestry took down several coats of arms of English kings that had adorned the walls of the church. Some of these have been replaced recently.

Within the church are the communion silver presented by Queen Anne in 1708 ; the Kearsley Cup, made in Cologne not later than 1610 and presented to the church by Dr. John Kearsley ; and numerous other mementos of the institution's early history. The central chandelier dates from 1749. The original organ, recently supplanted by the Curtis memorial organ, was installed in 1728. The organ stands in the curved back portion of a balcony that runs along three walls. The cream and gold pulpit was erected in 1769. The Lord's Table, built by Jonathan Gostelowe, a vestryman, after the Revolution, now is enclosed beneath a new altar installed as a memorial to Rev. Dr. Edward Y. Buchanan, brother of President Buchanan. The octagonal baptismal font, constructed in 1795, is five feet in height, composed of black walnut, and resembles in style the old-fashioned wooden pepper box with revolving top, used to grind peppers. A plain iron ring encircles it.

The interior was altered in 1834 under the direction of Thomas U. Walter, architect of the United States Capitol dome. In 1881 it was restored to an approximation of the original arrangement. Although the baroque note is less in evidence, the opulence of the exterior is sustained within the church. Large fluted Doric columns with entablature "impost caps" support the arches and separate the nave from the side aisles. The Palladian window above the altar was the first stained glass window in Philadelphia. Another interesting feature is the wineglass pulpit which stands near Washington's pew. It is a sexagonal goblet-shaped pulpit in rich cream color with gilt decoration. The front face is decorated with a sunburst. White wooden paneling with brown trim adds a note of richness to the enclosed pews.

The remains of several illustrious early Americans repose in family vaults in the churchyard. The family vault of Robert Morris, patriot-financier of the Revolution, stands at the head of the new Morris Garden of Remembrance. Near the southwest door is the grave of Gen. Charles Lee, of the Continental Army, and close by, until 1840, was that of Gen. Hugh Mercer, who fell in the Battle of Princeton in 1777. The churchyard also contains the graves of Peyton Randolph, President of the First Continental Congress ; Commodore Nicholas Biddle; and James Wilson, a signer of the Declaration of Independ-

Christ Church Doorway

"Here Seven Signers of the Declara-
tion of Independence Sleep Serenely"

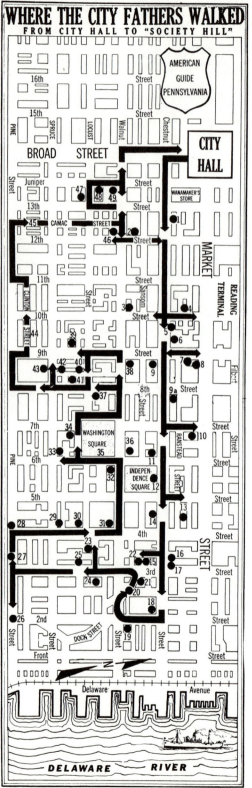

WHERE THE CITY FATHERS WALKED

FROM CITY HALL TO "SOCIETY HILL"

1. Adelphia Hotel
2. The New Century Club
3. Jefferson Medical College and Hospital
4. The Mercantile Library
5. The Federal Reserve Bank of Philadelphia
6. The Federal Building
7. Leary's Book Store
8. Gimbel Brothers Department Store
9. Benjamin Franklin Hotel
9a. Site of Green's Hotel
10. Old Franklin Institute
11. Ledger Building
12. Independence Hall
13. The Philadelphia Bourse
14. The Old Custom House
15. Carpenters' Hall
16. The First National Bank of Philadelphia
17. The Bank of North America
18. Custom House
19. Krider Gun Shop (Drinker House)
20. Dock Street
21. Stock Exchange Building
22. The Girard National Bank
23. St. Joseph's Church
24. St. Paul's Protestant Episcopal Church
25. The Powel House
26. Second Street Market
27. St. Peter's Protestant Episcopal Church
28. Old Pine Street Presbyterian Church
29. St. Mary's Church
30. Shippen Wistar Residence
31. Philadelphia Contributionship
32. Penn Mutual Life Insurance Company Building
33. Holy Trinity Roman Catholic Church
34. The First Presbyterian Church
35. Washington Square
36. Curtis Publishing Company
37. Residence of Robert Morris
38. Walnut Street Theatre
39. Bonaparte House
40. Musical Fund Hall
41. St. George's Greek Catholic Church
42. The Cemetery of Mikveh Israel Congregation
43. Pennsylvania Hospital
44. Clinton Street
45. Camac Street
46. The Artists Union
47. The Historical Society of Pennsylvania
48. Library Company of Philadelphia
49. Rosenbach Galleries

ence. Bishop White, first bishop of Pennsylvania and long presiding
bishop of the United States, is buried in front of the chancel rail.
His episcopal chair stands beside the altar.

R. from 2d St. on Church ; L. on Philip.

On the right side of Philip Street, known in Colonial days as
Grindstone Alley, is a plaque, attached to the side of the Philadel-
phia branch building of the First Camden National Bank and Trust
Company, which marks the site of the old headquarters of the Union
Fire Company.

L. from Philip St. on Market.

At Front Street, on the southwest corner, is the site of the Old
London Coffee House, where the first stock exchange in America
originated. Attempts to organize an exchange were made in Philadelphia as early as 1746.

Retrace to 2d St.

Take Market Street subway westbound at the Second Street station,
leaving the train at either the Thirteenth or Fifteenth Street station.
Signs in the underground concourse direct the traveler to stairways
leading to City Hall.

City Tour 2

From Market Street (Old High Street) To Society Hill, East of Broad

S. on Broad St. from City Hall ; L. on Chestnut St.

AMID the specialty shops and department stores which line Chestnut Street, one of Philadelphia's busiest shopping thoroughfares, a shining copper marquee sets apart the ADELPHIA
HOTEL (1), just beyond Thirteenth Street on the left. The building
was erected in 1914 from the plans prepared by Horace Trumbauer.
It is 21 stories in height and contains 400 guest rooms. It is constructed of brown brick with cream terra cotta on the upper and
lower stories, in French Renaissance design.

R. from Chestnut St. on 12th.

The NEW CENTURY CLUB (2), 124 South Twelfth Street, organized on February 8, 1877, and chartered in the following month,
is the oldest women's club in Philadelphia and the third oldest in
the United States.

In 1877 married women were not allowed to hold property in their
own name, and therefore the application for a charter was signed by
single women only.

Great as have been the advances in according privileges to women
in the lifetime of the New Century Club, the marked growth of

399

women's club movements has been greater. This pioneer club of its kind has namesakes throughout the country, while the membership in the general club movement now exceeds 3,000,000 women.

The New Century Club is the outgrowth of the Women's Committee of the Centennial, which issued a small paper, the *New Century*, in honor of the dawning new century of American independence. The Centennial over and the committee desiring to continue its work, it hit upon the idea of forming a women's club, an almost unheard of and not at all popular venture at that time. The first president was Mrs. S. C. Hallowell, and the first meeting place was in a hall on Girard Street east of Twelfth. The members furnished the rooms with articles from their own homes. From this modest beginning the club has grown into a membership exceeding 600.

The first cooking class in Philadelphia was established by the club in its headquarters.

The State Federation of Pennsylvania Women was organized at the New Century Club in 1895.

Retrace on 12th St.; R. on Chestnut; R. on 10th.

JEFFERSON MEDICAL COLLEGE AND HOSPITAL (3), on the right side of Tenth Street from Sansom to Walnut, was organized in 1825 as the medical department of Jefferson College, then at Canonsburg, Pa. In 1838 by a special act of the Legislature it became a separate institution. Today it is one of the most highly rated medical schools in the United States.

Retrace on 10th St.; cross Chestnut.

The MERCANTILE LIBRARY (4), 14 South Tenth Street *(open weekdays 9 to 9, except July and August, when closing hour is 6, and legal holidays, 5)*, is preeminent in the scope of its collection of more than 300,000 volumes. Light novels and abstruse treatises, books long out of print, and books and periodicals fresh from the press crowd its shelves.

Among its treasures are special collections of Civil War history, Irish history and Irish literature; old almanacs, newspapers, and records; a pastel of Walt Whitman, done from life by J. P. Silver; and a portrait of Washington by Rembrandt Peale.

The building, erected in 1859, originally designed by John McArthur to house the Franklin Market, was purchased from the Pennsylvania Railroad Company in 1867. Although never used as a market house and since altered to meet the requirements of the library, which took possession of it in 1869, the structure has served as a model for several other market buildings. The classic red brick facade with its large and decorative arch above the triple-arched windows of the second floor has at least the merit of expressing on the exterior the curve of the vaulting of the interior stack room.

An unusual air of freedom prevails; congeniality replaces the

400

restraint called for in most libraries. In addition to a chess room, which has gained a wide reputation as a meeting place of chess enthusiasts, there are a smoking room and a conversation room. Current newspapers and periodicals from cities and towns throughout the country are on file.

Owned and maintained by the Mercantile Library Association and conducted without State aid, the institution is supported by endowments and the membership dues of its 2,600 members — who pay an annual fee of $5 each. Library services are free to members and nonmembers alike, but borrowing privileges are extended to members only.

The library had its origin in the zeal for intellectual improvement that made itself felt after the War of 1812. The city's cultural leaders wanted a new circulating library, but the necessary public funds were lacking. So, on November 10, a meeting was held in Masonic Hall on Chestnut Street to consider the establishment of a Mercantile Library Association. The meeting was called and attended by the city's leading business men, and they issued a public notice inviting merchants and merchants' clerks to meet at the Mayor's office on November 17 to discuss the subject. At this meeting a committee was appointed to draft a constitution. Robert Waln, whose shipping business had been established in this country by his father early in the eighteenth century, was chairman of the committee.

The constitution was adopted at a meeting held on December 1, and a committee of 15 was appointed to secure subscribers to it, with instructions to give public notice of an election of directors when 100 were obtained.

The new library was warmly welcomed, for 300 members enrolled themselves, and on January 10, 1822, they met in the Merchants' Coffee House, formally organized the Mercantile Library Association and elected the first board of directors.

The aim of the group was to serve its members not only with the average reader's selection, but also with records, almanacs, and books helpful in their businesses. The library formally opened in a second-story room at 100 Chestnut Street, on March 5, 1821, with less than 1,000 books and pamphlets. The collection at first was marked by quantity rather than quality, but the passing years have brought the library to eminence in both respects.

Retrace on 10th St.; L. on Chestnut.

On the northeast corner at Tenth Street is the FEDERAL RESERVE BANK OF PHILADELPHIA (5). As the seat of the Third Federal Reserve District, the bank serves a territory embracing 48 counties of Pennsylvania, nine counties of New Jersey, and the entire State of Delaware.

The great volume of banking transactions originating in this highly industrialized region has made the bank a correspondingly large insti-tution. This marble building, where about one thousand are employed, houses an organization that began business in a suite of two rooms at 408 Chestnut Street on November 16, 1914. Since before the World War, the bank has served as the fiscal agent of the Government.

The building, designed by Paul Philippe Cret, rises six stories in height. It has a frontage of 170 feet on Chestnut Street, 144 feet on Tenth. Ramps to the basement loading platforms lead in from the Tenth Street side.

The design of the building, which is a free adaptation from Grecian forms, is admirably subordinated to function. The result is both har-monious and individual.

The entire facade is of Vermont blue-white marble. The lower half, with its 14 square piers, supports an unusual entablature, there being no architrave. The frieze is wide and unornamented, except at the corners. The massive upper stories are set back several feet. Sculptured reliefs flanking the simple entrance and the heavy eagle above the cornice are the chief decorations.

The main entrance, on Chestnut Street, leads to a vestibule with bronze doors and side grilles which embody the symbolic griffon, guardian of treasuries ; the two-faced Janus, looking to the past and to the future; and the seal of the Third Federal Reserve District. From the vestibule, revolving doors give access to an inner lobby, whence the main banking room is reached through bronze and glass bays. The end wall of this lobby bears the coats of arms of the States composing the banking district — New Jersey, Pennsylvania, and Delaware.

The main banking room is a well-lighted, high-ceilinged room, divided into offices by bronze and glass partitions. The ceiling of white plaster is supported by a number of colored marble pillars of severely plain design.

In the lofty executive room on the left of the entrance hall are 16 huge piers of dark Levanto marble and delicate rails and partitions, also of imported marbles. The simple classic ceiling is decorated with a cornice border in delicate colors and the silver-colored official coat of arms of the United States in the center.

The building has an air-conditioning system. The lighting system is of the indirect type, with fixtures in bronze which carry out the sym-bolism found in the entrance.

Its grimy next-door neighbor is the FEDERAL BUILDING (6) *(see City Tour 1)*.

L. from Chestnut St. on 9th.

LEARY'S BOOK STORE (7), 9 South Ninth Street, was founded in 1836, at Second and New Streets, and is the oldest book store of its kind in the United States. Here bookworm, casual reader, and student browse undisturbed through rows and stacks of books and pamphlets — books of every size and color, some fresh, some dog-eared and worn, some bearing on their flyleaves the pen-and-ink sentiments of those who owned them in an earlier day. A wide range of subjects is covered and a score of languages represented.

The store, regarded as a landmark for many years, occupies the only space in the Ninth Street facade of the GIMBEL BROTHERS DEPARTMENT STORE (8), used for purposes other than those of Gimbel Brothers. In 1925 the book store was moved from the site, which it had occupied since 1877, for about a year during enlargement of the Gimbel store, which now occupies almost the entire block, Market to Chestnut Streets and Eighth to Ninth Streets.

Retrace on 9th St.; L. on Chestnut.

On the southeast corner is the BENJAMIN FRANKLIN HOTEL (9). The "Ben Franklin" occupies the site of the old Continental Hotel, the scene of many historic and colorful episodes. Edward VII, then Prince of Wales, and Charles Dickens, who found Philadelphia "a handsome city but distractingly regular," were guests at the Continental. In one of its rooms Thomas Buchanan Read wrote his dramatic *Sheridan's Ride.*

On the northeast corner at Eighth Street is the SITE OF GREEN'S HOTEL (9a), now an open-air parking lot. Gathering place of politicians, sportsmen, artists, and writers from the time of the Centennial year, 1876, until the advent of prohibition, Green's Hotel represented an era in the life of Philadelphia — an era of good living and easy spending that reached its height in the "gay nineties." Famous for its bar and barroom, the hotel was highly esteemed also for the quality and diversity of its food —with emphasis on the sea food.

When the hotel was first opened in 1866 by Thomas Green, the former home of Edward Shippen, Chief Justice of Pennsylvania in Colonial times, was made part of it. The room in which Peggy Shippen and Benedict Arnold were married was preserved intact by Green.

After several changes in management, the trustees of the Green estate transferred the property to a New York syndicate in 1923. However, changing times and changing habits, and especially the uselessness of its famous bar, caused the place to lose its popularity.

It was sold at sheriff's sale on August 7, 1934, and the following month demolition work was started.

L. from Chestnut St. on 7th.

The old BUILDING OF THE FRANKLIN INSTITUTE (1), at 15 South Seventh Street, was the first official home of the great scientific institution on the Parkway *(see Points of Interest).* Six broad soapstone steps, flanked by two iron lamps, lead to the auster, dignified facade of this simple, two-story, Doric structure of gray marble.

Four sturdy piers support a heavy entablature containing a frieze of simple wreaths. This old building is an example of the Greek Revival period. Designed by John Haviland, it was completed in 1826, but has fallen into disrepair. Its demolition has been considered a number of times, but public opposition has prevented it.

Retrace on 7th St.; L. on Chestnut.

On the west side of Sixth Street below Chestnut is the entrance to the LEDGER BUILDING (11), home of the *Evening Public Ledger.* *(Open weekdays 9 to 4; guides provided, adm. free.)*

In the square on the right is INDEPENDENCE HALL (12) *(see Points of Interest).*

L. from Chestnut St. on 5th.

The PHILADELPHIA BOURSE (13), right, between Ludlow and Ranstead Streets, is the center of maritime business in Philadelphia. The building was erected in 1895 as a meeting place for trade organizations. It is occupied now by the Philadelphia Shipping Exchange, a number of shipping agents, and the Grain Exchange.

Retrace on 5th St.; L. on Chestnut.

The OLD CUSTOM HOUSE (14), on the right, midway between Fifth and Fourth Streets, now grimy and weather-worn, housed the second Bank of the United States from 1824-1837. The structure is of Greek Revival design. The architect, Benjamin H. Latrobe, used the Parthenon as his model. A statue of Robert Morris, who helped to finance the Revolutionary War, stands in front of the building.

Just beyond 320 Chestnut Street, on the right, is a small alleyway leading to CARPENTERS' HALL (15) *(see Points of Interest).*

The FIRST NATIONAL BANK OF PHILADELPHIA (16), 315 Chestnut Street, was chartered by act of Congress in 1863 and issued the first national currency. It is a two-story granite building of Greek design, built in 1865.

At 305 is the BANK OF NORTH AMERICA (17), whose first president was Robert Morris. This was the first bank chartered by the Continental Congress — on December 31, 1781. The present building, erected in 1893, is a Roman classic adaptation in light brown stone and red granite. The Doric order is employed on its first floor, Ionic on the second.

At Second and Chestnut Streets the new CUSTOM HOUSE (18) rises high above the surrounding buildings. Here are the offices of the Collector of the Port of Philadelphia and numerous Army and Navy and other Federal department offices.

The building, a large red brick and limestone edifice, is a modernized version of a classic design. The contrasting red and white of these materials is intended to harmonize with the structures of old historic Philadelphia. A tall cruciform tower rising over the center of the building terminates in an ornate enclosed water tank.

The chief interior feature is the circular rotunda of the ground floor. Eight black columns support a balcony and dome with unusual shell designs set within the coffers of the dome. The details, including the balcony of the rotunda, the spiral stairways, and the triple entrace doors are of aluminum. The building, designed by Ritter and Shay, was erected in 1933.

R. from Chestnut St. on 2d.

On the northeast corner at Walnut Street stands a small, gray building, on the site where the first white child in Philadelphia was born. The original building has been replaced by one which today houses the old KRIDER GUN SHOP (19), with its collection of antique firearms in the windows. Built by the Drinker family in 1751, this building displays a marker commemorating the birth. The marker gives John Drinker as the child's name.

R. from 2d St. on Dock.

DOCK STREET (20) is the produce center of Philadelphia. While most Philadelphians sleep and other streets are silent — from shortly after midnight (and as early as 8 p. m. in summer) until 8 in the morning — this strange byway throbs with the pulse of trade. The clatter of horses' hoofs and the rumbling of heavy trucks mingle with the gruff roars of drivers and the trade talk of shippers and merchants in this bypath of the city's modern scene. Carrots and cabbages, apples and grapes, and every edible root, leaf, and fruit from persimmon to artichoke lie in piles on street and sidewalk.

The street, three blocks long and forming a misshapen S, carries on a billion dollar business annually. It is the sidewalk pantry of half a million kitchens. Hundreds of trucks nightly are unloaded and loaded to rush the day's food throughout Philadelphia and its outlying districts, sometimes as far as 100 miles away.

Dock Street is built upon the filled-in course of Dock Creek, once a winding inlet of the Delaware River, on which Indians paddled canoes and white men sailed barges. In the early days the creek was spanned by a drawbridge. Until 1784 there was only the waterway,

Drinker House
"On the Site Where Philadel-phias First White Child was Born"

with markets along its banks, upon which boats unloaded their produce. Today a paved roadway overlies the bed of the creek, but it is still an inlet — an inlet for vast amounts of produce, arriving on freighters. They come up the Delaware with delicacies gathered from far-away fields and orchards — oranges from Florida and California, bananas and pineapples from Cuba, strawberries from Georgia, peanuts and sweet potatoes from other southern States, and apples from Virginia.

The importance of this small street to Philadelphia was painfully demonstrated during a truck drivers' strike in 1935. Virtually all the fresh vegetables and other commodities supplied by the merchants of Dock Street were tied up, and business was at a complete standstill. The truck drivers' union, realizing the strategic value of this little street, refused to allow any produce to leave it. Prices soared while fruits and vegetables rotted where they had been dumped from ships and farmers' drays. But Philadelphia could not long forego fresh food, and the strike was settled within a few days.

Shortly after noon, Dock Street slumbers. The shop doors are closed and the street virtually deserted. "Evening" comes early on Dock Street.

At Third Street, left, is the old STOCK EXCHANGE BUILDING (21). Wide and winding Dock Street serves as the eastern approach to this building of old Philadelphia. The semi-circular Corinthian colonnade above the first floor, the entablature and the unusual tall crowning cupola of alternate columns and windows embellish this beautiful gray stone structure, which was designed by William Strickland and completed in 1834.

L. on 3d St.

The GIRARD NATIONAL BANK BUILDING (22), 116 South Third Street, is the oldest bank building in the country. It was completed in 1797, designed by Samuel Blodget, and originally was the home of the Bank of the United States. Stephen Girard purchased the building in 1812 and conducted a private bank there until 1831. It is now the Philadelphia headquarters of the American Legion.

Except for the rich wooden entablature and pediment, the exterior of the building is of Pennsylvania blue marble. It is designed in the Corinthian style, with six free-standing fluted columns supporting the pediment. The main room is two stories high with a circular rotunda. Eight Corinthian columns support the balcony and above these rise 40 small Corinthian columns supporting the low dome with its large skylight. The original fireplace is in the southeast corner room of the second floor.

Continue on 3d St.; R. on Willing's Alley.

In Willing's Alley stands ST. JOSEPH'S CHURCH (23), oldest Roman Catholic church in Philadelphia. A German pastor of St.

406

To Society Hill (City Tour 2)

Joseph's is said to have been the first to refer to Washington as "Des Landes Vater" — "The Father of His Country."

Beneath an archway, a curiously wrought iron gate opens from Willing's Alley into a large paved courtyard, along the inner side of which stands the church. The present structure, in spite of its record of constant reconstruction, retains a few mementos of the vicissitudes to which the Catholic Church was heir in its early days in Philadelphia.

The original edifice was erected in 1733, enlarged in 1821, and rebuilt in 1838. Additions have since been made. Today the unpretentious brick building, with large, rounded, stained-glass windows, is so surrounded by the offices of insurance companies that little is visible of the exterior beyond two bays of side windows. Its red-brick wall, with white wood trim, has little decoration, except for a marble bust of Father Felix Joseph Barbelin, S. J., rector of the church for 25 years, and a tablet to his memory. As for the ornate interior, a curved balcony at the sides and back, and Ionic columns which support the arch above the altar, constitute the only architecturally significant features.

The Jesuit priests in charge of the parish live in a dwelling on the right side of the courtyard. The doorway of this house is distinguished by a little wicket through which a lay brother, before opening the door, may inspect those seeking admittance. The large lamp hanging beside it illumines all after-dark callers. The interior offers little of historical note. The portion of the rectory adjoining the church, including the sacristy, is the only part of the original building that remains, and this section has been completely renovated. The few archaic fireplaces that have been preserved are on the upper floors, which are closed to visitors.

Of considerable interest is a canvas on one of the rectory parlor walls. This, Benjamin West's first large and important work, was presented by the painter to the Jesuits of Conshohocken. The painting — a woman in conventional scriptural dress giving a child a drink from a little bowl, while an old man stands beside her and an angel hovers near the child — was formerly believed to portray the Holy Family, and for many years hung over the main altar. When it was discovered that the artist intended to commemorate the adventures of Hagar and Ishmael in the desert, the picture was removed from a position which was considered inappropriately conspicuous.

The land on which St. Joseph's stands was purchased and a modest chapel was erected in 1722. It was built to resemble a private house, because English law then forbade the erection of a Catholic church or chapel. In 1722 Father Joseph Greaton, of the Jesuit Order, was sent from Baltimore, and on arriving in the city, he donned the garb of a Quaker lest he provoke outbreaks of intolerance. Before a year

407

had passed, he had resumed his clerical robe. A chapel, with its own pastor and a regular congregation, could not long pass unnoticed, and the following year the situation began to excite comment. Father Greaton's activities were referred to the Provincial Council and discussed at two meetings, but the matter was allowed to rest, and the priest continued his work undisturbed. During the anti-Catholic riots of 1844, when houses were burned to ashes and churches were set afire, St. Joseph's escaped unscathed.

The church today is a center for the devout who work in the old business center of the city. They frequently visit here during the luncheon hour or after work. A narrow areaway provides access to the church from Walnut Street, in addition to the main entrance to the courtyard from Willing's alley.

Retrace on Willing's Alley.

On Third Street opposite the alley is ST. PAUL'S PROTESTANT EPISCOPAL CHURCH (24), a red and white brick structure set back between two poplar trees and surrounded by a neatly designed brick wall. Large limestone spheres surmount the wall's eight brick posts. Originally erected in 1761, the building was extensively altered in 1832 by William Strickland, who virtually rebuilt the white woodwork interior. Edwin Forrest, tragedian, is buried in the churchyard.

R. from Willing's Alley on 3d.

The POWEL HOUSE (25) is at 244 South Third Street *(see Points of Interest).*

L. from 3d St. on Pine.

Standing in the center of Second Street and facing on Pine is the HEADHOUSE OF THE SECOND STREET MARKET (26), a quaint two-and-a-half-story structure with heavy octagnal cupola and steep gable ends. There is a tasteful use of marble trim in the belt course and window sills. Edward Shippen and Joseph Wharton began the structure, August 1745, by building stalls at their own expense. They received rents until they were repaid the principal and interest of the advanced money. This site has been a market place since the days of Penn.

The cupola was probably used as a lookout tower for locating fires. (Fire engines were kept downstairs and the second story was long the headquarters of the volunteer Hope Fire Engine Company.) The first building was erected in 1745. About 1800 the present headhouse was built, and in 1814 the market was extended to South Street.

Retrace on Pine St.

On the southwest corner at Third Street is ST. PETER'S PROTESTANT EPISCOPAL CHURCH (27), a simple and dignified structure of red brick, designed by Robert Smith. One of the older churches in the city, it is surrounded by an old cemetery and by lawns and tall trees within brick walls and iron fences.

St. Joseph's Roman Catholic Church
"In the Quiet of Willing's
Alley . . ."

St. Peter's Church
"Whose rear pulpit caused
consternation"

At its western end rises a five-and-a-half-story square tower surmounted by a simple wooden spire from which rises an octagonal lantern topped by a ball and cross. The austerity of the tower, with its corner piers and suggestion of a crenellated top, is relieved by the finely designed windows, rising one above the other.

The chief feature of the eastern side of the exterior is a large Palladian window with 237 panes. The fine arched windows on the sides and rear light the interior balcony — the first such arrangement used in America. All of the windows have brick arches and white marble sills, spring blocks, and keystones. An unusual feature is the location of the organ and altar at the eastern end and the reading desk and lofty pulpit at the western end — a rare arrangement which compels the rector to conduct part of the service at each end of the church, with an accompanying shift in seats by the congregation. The organ, rising to the height of the ceiling, blocks the Palladian window.

St. Peter's was erected in 1758-1761 as a branch of Christ Church, and for many years both were under the same rectorship. Washington, on his frequent visits to Philadelphia, often attended services in this church, and the pews used by him, by Governor Penn, and by Benjamin Franklin have been carefully preserved. The sacristy displays a number of relics significant in the church's history.

At Fourth Street is the OLD PINE STREET CHURCH (Third Presbyterian) (28). A number of documents and portraits reminiscent of the days when the Nation was young are preserved in the church.

Founded on its present site in 1768, this church remains today a well-known place of public worship, although racial population changes have caused 30 Protestant churches in the vicinity to close their doors in recent years. An endowment fund enables the church to carry on in the face of decreasing attendance.

The site was used as a place of worship prior to the founding of Old Pine Street Church. Members of the First Presbyterian and other churches constituted a congregation which worshipped in a small edifice known as the Hill Meetinghouse, erected in 1764 when the group received letters patent to the site. Previous to that time, when he was refused permission to preach in any of the churches in the vicinity, George Whitefield had preached from a platform erected on this spot.

The present church, built in 1837, is of late Greek Revival design. It has a huge raised portico with four pairs of fluted Corinthian columns. One of the walls of the original building of 1768 still stands as part of the present structure. Various alterations have been made, including the raising of the roof and floor, and the addition of an entrance porch and columns.

Rev. George Duffield, D. D., first chaplain of the church, who was

410

also chaplain of the First Continental Congress and the Pennsylvania Militia at the time of the Revolution, was so well known for his fiery revolutionary spirit that the British placed a price on his head. During British occupation of Philadelphia the church was used as a hospital, and the pews were burned for fuel.

Old records show that many members of the church served the country in times of war. Sixty-seven served in the Revolutionary Army, outstanding among them being Gen. John Steele, personal aide-de-camp to Washington in New Jersey. Later General Steele was in charge of the military unit assigned to protect Martha Washington during her stay in Norristown. During the Civil War 130 members of the congregation carried arms. In the upper vestibule a tablet bears the names of 18 who died in action.

Among the many famous men who attended services at the venerable church was John Adams, second President of the United States. His diary contains many references to "Duffield's Meetings." Many early historic figures connected with the church are buried in its grounds ; among them are Dr. Duffield : General Steele ; Col. William Linnard, Quartermaster of the United States Army in the War of 1812 ; Mrs. Mary Nelson, in charge of the Philadelphia powder magazine in the War of 1812 ; and William Hurrie, bell ringer at the State House, who probably rang the Liberty Bell on the first day of America's independence. One hundred Hessian soldiers were buried here. The Sunday school, begun in 1814, is the oldest in Philadelphia.

R. from Pine St. on 4th.

ST. MARY'S CHURCH (29), 244 South Fourth Street, is the second-oldest Roman Catholic church in the city. Built in 1763 and enlarged in 1810, it presents a facade of red brick with white marble trim, a fusion of Colonial and Gothic styles. The interior consists of one large rectangular room with balconies on three sides. With the appointment of a bishop for this country, in 1808, St. Mary's became the first cathedral. Commodore Barry and several members of the Continental Congress are buried in the churchyard.

At Locust Street on the southwest corner is the SHIPPEN RESIDENCE (30), built about 200 years ago by Dr. William Shippen and his brother Joseph, on land granted them by the Penns. When, in 1798, the famous Dr. Caspar Wistar established his residence in the house it became the scene of the celebrated Wistar parties. Parties are still held here in memory of the hospitable doctor. The building, typical of the Colonial town house, was built in 1752 and adjoined the Cadwalader house on the south. These two structures of red brick laid in Flemish bond with white trim and shuttered windows have been converted into one building in recent years. The garden of the house at one time extended to old St. Mary's Church.

On the left at 212 is the PHILADELPHIA CONTRIBUTIONSHIP (31), which houses an old insurance company.

The structure, designed by Thomas U. Walter and erected in 1836, follows the style of the Greek Revival period. The outstanding feature of the red brick and white marble exterior is the porch, which is approached from both sides by curved stairs. Four fluted marble Corinthian columns support a heavy entablature. Double windows in either side of the porch have slightly projecting hoods following the line of the porch cornice. The second-story windows call attention to their pilasters and lintels. Three dormer windows framed by pilasters, scrolls, and low pediments rise above the third-story cornice.

The keynote of the interior is one of severity, with the ground floor consisting of two small rooms and one large room, in the center of which rises a gracefully curved staircase.

L. from 4th St. on Walnut.

On the right between Fifth and Sixth Streets is INDEPENDENCE SQUARE *(see Points of Interest).*

On the southeast corner of Sixth Street, now occupied by the PENN MUTUAL LIFE INSURANCE COMPANY BUILDING (32), is the site of the old Walnut Street Prison. The British, who took over the jail during their occupancy of Philadelphia, herded all of Washington's troops who fell into their hands into this prison. Many of the captured Continentals died after enduring unspeakable treatment. The British commandant responsible for these conditions was later tried and hanged in England. On the southern portion of this lot a Debtors Prison was erected, and for a time Robert Morris, financier of the Revolution, was incarcerated there.

L. from Walnut St. on 6th.

On the northwest corner at Spruce Street is HOLY TRINITY ROMAN CATHOLIC CHURCH (33), in the graveyard of which Stephen Girard was buried. His remains were later removed to a sarcophagus in Founder's Hall at Girard College. A grave here is said to be that of Evangeline, heroine of Longfellow's poem. The poem reads :

> Still stands the forest primeval ; but far away from its shadow,
> Side by side in their nameless graves, the lovers are sleeping.
> Under the humble walls of the little Catholic churchyard,
> In the heart of the city, they lie, unknown and unnoticed.

Retrace on 6th St. ; L. on S. Washington Square.

The FIRST PRESBYTERIAN CHURCH (34), facing on the square, was erected in 1820 following the plans of John Haviland, who designed it after the Temple on the Illisus near Athens. It is one of the best examples of the Greek Revival style. The structure has fallen into disrepair since the congregation left it several years ago to merge with that of the Christ Calvary Church near Fifteenth on Locust Street.

412

Philadelphia Contributionship

*"The Home of the 'Hand-in-Hand',
founded in 1752"*

WASHINGTON SQUARE (35), extending along Walnut Street from Sixth to Seventh Streets, once was a Potter's Field for Philadelphia. Here, during the Revolution, hundreds of Continental soldiers were buried after death released them from the horrors' and torture of the British prison. Here, too, were interred thousands of the victims of the yellow-fever plague that ravaged the city in 1793. In 1825 the ground was leveled and converted into a memorial park.
Continue around Washington Square to Walnut St.

CURTIS PUBLISHING COMPANY PLANT (36), across Walnut Street from the square *(5 tours daily ; free)*, is one of the world's largest foundries of the printed word and home of the *Saturday Evening Post*, father of all five-cent weeklies. It occupies a vast 12-story boxlike building bounded by Walnut and Sansom and Sixth and Seventh Streets, with the main entrance on Sixth Street.

The exterior design of the huge Curtis plant, the cornerstone of which was laid in 1910, represents an attempt to establish harmony with the Independence Square group across Sixth Street. The architect, Edgar Seiler, succeeded in achieving a certain amount of dignity by the use of marble in the lower and top stories. Various bits of detail, such as the oval design work in the frieze and the keystones, are distinct adaptations from Independence Hall. The 14 huge Ionic columns on the lower facade are white monoliths weighing 21 tons each.

The entrance lobby is dominated by a large, especially processed glass mosaic, executed by Louis C. Tiffany, distinguished New York artist and decorator, from an elaborate sketch, *The Dream Garden*, by Maxfield Parrish.

The dining room for female employees contains 16 panels from the brush of Parrish, and his large pastel mural, *The Florentine Fete*. The original painting of *The Dream Garden* hangs in the executive dining room. The luxurious directors' room features tapestries and furniture of the Adam period, a deep piled rug and vase of Chinese origin, a carved table of Carrara marble, and originals of drawings used in the company's publications.

The plant covers 23 acres of floor space. Four thousand workers are employed in three shifts. Operating day and night, it is a notable example of organized efficiency and modern mechanical development. Special steel construction eliminates vibration, and the editorial rooms are shut off from the clamor of the mechanized departments by an elaborate system of soundproofing. Giant multicolor presses. in a single lightning operation, produce 16-page units, vividly colored and printed on both sides with the aid of an exclusive wax-spraying process. In all, there are 200 presses, each weighing many tons and costing many thousands of dollars. The total output is 17,000,000 magazines each month. Figures showing paper, fuel, and ink consumption read like recordings of astronomical distances.

To Society Hill (City Tour 2)

Each of the five daily tours requires about one hour, but this time is sufficient to obtain only a bare idea of the breadth, scope and intricacy of this huge production center.

L. on Walnut St.; L. on 8th.

At 225 South Eighth Street is a Colonial structure that was once the city RESIDENCE OF ROBERT MORRIS (37). Although built shortly after the Revolution (in 1786) the house is completely Georgian Colonial in character. Faced with brick laid in Flemish bond with black headers, the building has a severely simple facade of broad horizontal lines accented by the second and third-floor belt courses and a beautiful cornice. Two windows flank the central doorway, with its fluted pilasters, dainty fanlight, and simple broken pediment.

Retrace on 8th St.; L. on Walnut.

At Ninth Street, in the gray building on the right, is the WALNUT STREET THEATRE (38), built in 1808 and the oldest existing theatre in the city. Here during the prime of the theatre's life appeared most of the stage stars of a century.

The building now bears little resemblance to the original as designed by John Haviland, but the early classical atmosphere of the interior has been retained.

Renovation and remodeling have given a modern aspect to the ancient playhouse, and its name has been changed several times, but it still occupies the original site, and the mellowness of great stage traditions clings to it.

It was opened in 1809 as a circus and later as a combined theatre and circus. Philadelphia entertainment seekers thronged to the "New Circus" for four years during the management of Pepin and Breschard.

After its early circus days, the playhouse assumed a new dignity and a new name, the Olympic, when it was converted into a theatre for the presentation of legitimate stage productions. This new phase of its existence began New Year's Day, 1812, with a presentation of Sheridan's comedy, *The Rivals*. A musical farce, *Poor Soldiers*, was the second on the theatre's list of stage performances. The Olympic was renamed the Walnut Street Theatre in 1820 and, except for a brief period during which it was called the American Theatre, that name has clung.

Edwin Forrest, later eminent as a tragedian, made his first appearance here at the age of 14. Edmund Kean, another outstanding tragedian, played at the Olympic frequently. Louisa Lane, later to become Mrs. John Drew, made her first stage appearance in this theatre at the age of 7, in the cast of Shakespeare's *Richard III*.

415

Many of the greatest names in theatrical history are linked with the Walnut. Edwin Booth, whose father, Junius Brutus Booth, had previously appeared there, was for many years part owner of the house. Indeed, every actor or actress of note who appeared in this country during the nineteenth century trod the boards of this theatre.

At the height of their popularity, Sarah Bernhardt, Ellen Terry, and Sir Henry Irving played the Walnut. Here appeared Richard Mansfield, Lily Langtry, John Drew, DeWolf Hopper, David Warfield, and Maude Adams. Otis Skinner, Ethel Barrymore, Julia Marlowe, James K. Hackett, Walter Hampden, George Arliss, and Grace George in more recent years have sustained this theatre's fine tradition.

For 16 consecutive years, during the Christmas holidays, Chauncey Olcott appeared here before enthusiastic audiences. In 1905 Mme. Schumann-Heink, beloved songstress of two generations, appeared here in the opera, *Love's Lottery*. Douglas Fairbanks began his successful theatrical career at the Walnut in 1906, and his autographed picture still hangs in the lobby.

The playhouse suffered the same decline that threatened all legitimate playhouses with the development of the "movies," the "talkies," and the radio. In 1920 heirs of Edwin Booth and John Sleeper Clarke sold the establishment to James Beury, who restored it to its high estate for a few seasons. It was formally reopened on December 27, 1920, with George Arliss in *The Green Goddess*.

Since 1932 the theatre has changed management several times, passing through brief eras of movies, vaudeville, and stock.

Doorways leading into the auditorium from the foyer and the curtained screen or "stand-up" rail are Colonial in detail. The massive globular crystal chandelier hanging immediately before the proscenium was removed from the old Bingham House when that hotel was torn down.

The balcony has been rebuilt with steel supports, but the stage remains substantially the same as during the early circus days, when its boards creaked under the feet of performing elephants. Most of the roof is borne by the original wooden trusses which once vibrated to the roars of trained lions.

L. from Walnut St. on 9th.

At 260, south of Locust Street, is the BONAPARTE HOUSE (39), residence for two years of Joseph Bonaparte, brother of Napoleon. Some of the mural canvases Joseph brought with him from France adorn the walls of the dining room. The house was built in 1812.

Retrace on 9th St.; R. on Locust.

MUSICAL FUND HALL (40), 808 Locust Street, is the oldest music hall in the United States. Built in 1824, it once echoed to the liquid notes of Jenny Lind. Here, too, William Makepeace Thackeray lectured during his visit to Philadelphia. In June 1856 it was the scene

416

of the first Republican National Convention. Today the building presents a forlorn appearance, out of keeping with its colorful past.

The building, a three-story structure of Italian Renaissance design, is constructed of light buff brick and terra cotta with a marble base, and the cornice and central pediment of copper. Pilasters of the composite order decorate the upper two stories.

R. from Locust St. on 8th.

South of Locust, on the right, is ST. GEORGE'S GREEK CATHO-LIC CHURCH (41). This church, erected in 1822, was designed by John Haviland, who patterned it after the same model (the Athenian temple on the Illisus) which he had used two years before for the First Presbyterian Church on Washington Square. Its huge porch with fluted Ionic columns at the top of seven marble steps supports a massive denticular entablature, surmounted by a broad pediment. A great paneled doorway of wood, painted to simulate bronze, leads to an interior lavishly painted in blue, gold, and white. The most arresting feature is a choir screen with a central pedimented entrance containing a painting of the "symbolic eye."

R. from 8th St. on Spruce.

The CEMETERY OF MIKVEH ISRAEL CONGREGATION (42) occupies a small parcel of land at Spruce and Darien Streets. The ground was granted to Rabbi Nathan Levy by John Penn in 1783, and it contains the graves of numerous Philadelphians of the Jewish faith. The most famous grave is that of Rebecca Gratz, the original of Sir Walter Scott's heroine, Rebecca, in *Ivanhoe*.

It was through Washington Irving, whose fiancée, Matilda Hoffman, was an intimate friend of Rebecca Gratz, that Miss Gratz became the inspiration of Scott's medieval romance. On a visit to England, Irving met Scott and learned that he was contemplating the writing of a novel with Jews among the principal characters. Irving told him about the lovely Philadelphia friend of his fiancée. After the appearance of *Ivanhoe* in 1819, Scott wrote his American col-

Mikveh Israel Cemetery "Resting place of Rebecca Gratz, Immortalized by Scott's 'Ivanhoe'"

league : "How do you like your Rebecca ? Does the Rebecca I have pictured compare well with the pattern given ?"

Miss Gratz made important contributions to the development of her native city's philanthropies. In her twenty-first year she was elected secretary of the Female Association for the Relief of Women and Children in Reduced Circumstances. In 1815 she helped found the Philadelphia Orphans' Society and in 1838 succeeded in organizing the Hebrew Sunday School Society, the first organization of its kind in the United States. Her efforts were largely instrumental in the establishment of the Jewish Foster Home in 1855.

On the opposite side of Spruce Street is the PENNSYLVANIA HOSPITAL (43), oldest hospital in the United States. The original buildings offer quaint contrast to the newer, sanitary structures of the institution.

Although the Philadelphia General Hospital, originally the Philadelphia Almshouse, antedates the Pennsylvania Hospital as an institution, the former was not used as a hospital until after the latter was founded in 1751.

A perusal of the old records of the hospital serves as a pleasant reminder of some of the customs of the times. The old Managers (many of them Friends) designated the months of the year by number in the minutes of their meetings. This custom was followed until recent days, entries such as First Month or Fifth Month adding a quaint touch to the modern records.

The prime mover in establishing the Pennsylvania Hospital was Dr. Thomas Bond, who for years had urged the necessity of such an institution. Until 1751, however, he received nothing more substantial than sympathy for his cause. In that year he appealed to Benjamin Franklin, who immediately espoused the idea and vigorously championed it with pen and voice, winning a charter from the Provincial Assembly and support from private citizens.

An organization meeting of 36 contributors was held on May 1 in the State House, and 12 managers and a treasurer were elected. In September a meeting was held in Widow Pratt's Royal Standard Tavern, High (now Market) Street near Second. Here it was decided to open the hospital in a private house on the south side of High Street. The first patient, a Margaret Sherlock, was admitted on February 11, 1752 ; she was likewise the first discharged as cured. The medical staff at that time was composed of Dr. Lloyd Zachary, Dr. Thomas Bond, and Dr. Phineas Bond ; Joshua Crosby was president of the board of managers, and Benjamin Franklin, clerk.

Purchase of the block now occupied by the hospital, except for the Spruce Street front, was agreed upon by the board on September 11, 1754, and on May 28 of the year following, the cornerstone of the first building was laid. Before the end of December 1756, all patients

William Penn Statue, Pennsylvania Hospital
"Where Quaker Quiet Still Prevails"

and furniture from the temporary hospital on High Street had been removed to the permanent building. The lot facing on Spruce Street was deeded to the hospital by the Penn family on November 10, 1767.

Within the brick-walled and iron-paled enclosure, extending from Eighth to Ninth and from Spruce to Pine Streets, an odd atmosphere prevails ; it carries the imagination back to the time when gentle comforters, many with faces framed in Quaker bonnets, tiptoed along the spacious corridors of the original brick buildings, which still are intact.

From the beginning the Pennsylvania Hospital took care of the insane, who were housed on the ground floor of the east wing. In those days there was no enclosure about the hospital, and passers-by made a practice of congregating at the windows and teasing the unfortunates. In addition, crowds milled through the hospital corridors, ogling the patients and interfering with the duties of the staff. This condition was eventually alleviated when a high fence was erected around the hospital grounds, and an admission fee of four pence was charged. In 1791, however, the managers resolved to refuse admittance to all persons except those vouched for by themselves, the medical staff, or the steward.

With the growth and expansion of the hospital's activities, the proper care and handling of mental cases became a problem. Consequently, a farm was purchased west of the city (at what now is Forty-fourth and Market Streets in West Philadelphia) and a special department, known as the Pennsylvania Hospital Department for Mental and Nervous Diseases, was created. In 1841 the buildings were completed, and mental patients were transferred there. This institution since has become generally known as "Kirkbride's," in tribute to Dr. Thomas S. Kirkbride, chief resident physician through its first 43 years, and one of the early specialists whose ideas in the handling of the mentally deficient form the basis of modern treatment.

Many features perpetuate the Pennsylvania Hospital's fame as an historic shrine. In front of the Pine Street facade are the great iron scrollwork gates, creation of some nameless early master craftsman, that once guarded the main entrance and exit at either terminus of a horseshoe drive. In 1824 Marquis de Lafayette, seated in an open barouche drawn by six dappled horses, drove through this gateway on a visit to the hospital. The gates then remained closed for more than a century, and a story was invented that their closing was a tribute to the visiting nobleman. Actually, the gates were closed because the main entrance had been moved to the Eighth Street side.

Behind the Pine Street gates stands a statue of William Penn that once graced the estate of Lord LeDespencer, friend of Franklin, at High Wycombe, England. It was discovered and purchased by John Penn in a London junk shop in 1804.

420

To Society Hill (City Tour 2)

Revered not only as the work of a renowned Colonial artist, but also for its profound message of inspiration for the healer and hope for the ailing, Benjamin West's painting, *Christ Healing the Sick in the Temple*, commands attention. It hangs in the main office. Fellow members of the Society of Friends had appealed to the Quaker artist for a contribution for the hospital. Being then of meager financial means, West offered to paint a picture for the institution. When the picture was exhibited in London, the British Institute of Philosophy offered the artist 3,000 guineas for it. He accepted with the stipulation that he be permitted to make a replica for the hospital. Proceeds from an exhibition of the second painting in Philadelphia were sufficient to finance the care of 33 patients.

A plaster model of the hand of Benjamin West holding a brush is on display in the lobby of the hospital.

Meteorological records preserved in the archives report the daily temperature and weather conditions of the city for a century and a half. Students of meteorology consider these records of great value, and the Federal Weather Bureau has made a transcript for its files. The hospital library contains the oldest collection of medical books in the country.

No architect was employed in the construction of the hospital. The planning was carried on by the building committee of the Board of Managers, of which Samuel Rhoads, a builder, later to become mayor of Philadelphia, was chairman. The plans called for a main structure fronting on Pine Street and connecting with wings on the east and west.

The old main building is a large, handsome structure, with two-and-a-half-story wings. White, wooden, octagonal cupolas, with delicate circular-headed windows, surmount the wings. The dome of the eastern cupola is bell-shaped. Recent additions which were applied in 1929 to the fronts of the wings are unfortunate, their design detracting from the harmony of the whole.

A balustraded stoop leads up to the doorway with its handsome semi-circular fan and side lights. On each side of this doorway are two large arched windows. Above are six marble Corinthian pilasters, two stories high, supporting a beautifully detailed entablature at the eaves, from which springs a pediment containing an unusual oval-shaped window with a horizontal panel in its center. The rich red coloration of the second and third-story brick panels, separated by blue-gray marble pilasters, forms a gay color pattern, perhaps the most striking feature of the building.

Surmounting the hip roof is an unusual square-paneled white superstructure of wood, above which is a low belvedere platform, originally intended to be topped by a dome. Owing to difficulties of design, however, the dome was omitted. The absence of the central

421

dome is thought by some to give the building an unfinished appearance, which, at the same time, strengthens the building's personality.

The interior has much fine wood finish. Fluted Ionic columns support a mutulary Doric entablature of the high, broad hall. This leads back to a double open staircase with well-designed bracket stringers and heavy newels and balusters. The staircases lead to the library on the second floor and to the circular amphitheatre on the third floor. Under the blue dome of the amphitheatre are three circular tiers of seats for those watching operations.

A fanlight over one of the windows in the record room contains a ground glass reproduction of the seal of the hospital, and it is believed the other windows once had similar fans which were somehow destroyed. The record room originally was the apothecary shop.

The east wing was the first part of the hospital erected. A small "elaboratory," or north house, was completed in 1768, the west wing in 1796, and the central building in 1805. Some of the original buildings still bear insignia of the old insurance companies.

The newer buildings of the Pennsylvania Hospital, particularly those along Spruce Street, are out of harmony with the older structures and mar the simplicity of the original plan. The Eighth Street side of the nurses' home at the southeast corner of Eighth and Spruce Streets boasts two very fine fanlights above the doorways.

Retrace on Spruce St. to 8th ; R. on 8th ; R. on Pine ; R. on 9th.

CLINTON STREET (44), running from Ninth to Eleventh Streets and lined with time-hallowed residences, is much the same as it was a hundred years ago. It has resisted modernization and retained the flavor of the period when prancing bays drew the carriages of sweet-faced Quaker ladies on their rounds of calls.

When the street was opened, wealthy families moved there to escape the din of traffic-laden Market and Chestnut Streets in the "center" of the city. They were highly successful in their effort to maintain the street as an exclusive residential section, for property was sold under penalizing restrictions. Included in all property transfers was a paragraph permitting demolition of any structure that fell short of prescribed standards.

Most of the houses now standing were built shortly after the street was opened in 1836. Although the Federal style in architecture was then on the decline, the dignity and charm of these houses, with their carefully designed doorways and the contrast of white trim against red brick, enhanced by overhanging shade trees, made this one of the most charming streets in the city. Seen through the denuded trees in winter, the cupola of Pennsylvania Hospital forms a striking focal point at the eastern end of the street. The thoroughfare once was owned by the hospital and the Philadelphia Almshouse, the latter then at the southeast corner of Clinton and Eleventh Streets.

422

Camac Street
"Le Quartier Latin of Philadelphia"

Clinton Street
"The Street Where Time Stood Still"

After the street was opened Philadelphia social life was centered largely in these two blocks. Evenings, by the light of sparkling crystal chandeliers, furbelowed maids and their beaus changed partners with their elders in the figures of the quadrille.

On the whole, wealthy residents kept the street dignified and respectable ; yet "ye towne crier" stalked its pavements on his rounds, and the shrilling strawberry women, the raucous-voiced fish peddler, the sing-songing hominy man, and the soot-covered chimney sweep followed close on his heels. Since it was in the "suburbs," skirted by open fields, there were times when runaway hogs invaded the street. Then neighborhood youngsters ruffled the dignified silence with gleeful shouts as they cornered the squealing porkers and rode them "bareback."

The Clinton Street boarding home for young women, now known as Coles House, was opened in 1872, at 913-915, by the Young Women's Boarding Home Association members of the Protestant Episcopal church, to provide living quarters for young Protestant business women and students. At the northeast corner of Tenth and Clinton Streets, the site now occupied by a hotel, stood, in 1868, the Clinton Street Presbyterian Church.

On May 22, 1936, residents revived the old-time brilliance of Clinton Street with a pageant called the "Windows of Old Philadelphia." The street was roped off at both ends, and costumed society and club folk impersonated Charles Dickens, Jenny Lind, P. T. Barnum, the Cushman sisters, and other notables who figured at one time or another in the street's history. Sketches reminiscent of the early days, including scenes from *Pickwick Papers*, were presented in an outdoor theatre in the rear of the United Service Club, 901 Clinton Street. First floors of vacant houses were outfitted with furnishings typical of the early nineteenth century, and costumed celebrants portrayed the activities of those days.

Among the distinguished residents of present-day Clinton Street is Agnes Repplier, Philadelphia essayist.

L. from Clinton St. on 11th ; R. on Pine ; R. on Camac.

CAMAC STREET (45), a narrow thoroughfare between Twelfth and Thirteenth Streets, running from Pine to Walnut, is the concentration point for the Bohemian life in the city, and its sides are sprinkled with art clubs, luncheon clubs, studios, and garishly designed taprooms.

The street is more of contemporary than historic interest. Home of one of the oldest art colonies in America, it has survived three violently contrasting eras in a century and a half. Originally a seat of staid respectability, it drifted into a chaotic depravity — four blocks of degeneracy, gangsterism, and crime. Then came art. Today the street's pungent atmosphere seems thinning into the commonplace.

424

To Society Hill (City Tour 2)

Camac Street was named after Turner Camac, wealthy Irish land-owner who came to Philadelphia in 1804 to take over the management of properties inherited by his wife. Long ago it was a typical old Philadelphia thoroughfare. Though narrow, it was neat and clean, lined with fine, small early-American houses with picturesque third-story windows, attractive doorways, and well-kept little gardens in the rear.

The street kept its respectability until about 1880. Then came a period of decline, and it degenerated into one of the meanest and most disreputable streets in the city. Until 1900 it was the scene of brawls by day and crimes by night, requiring at times an entire squad of the city's police to maintain order. For 20 years the street, lined with brothels and taverns, rotted in a mire of debauchery. Unkempt derelicts of every sort frequented its dark corners and hideaways.

The turn of the twentieth century brought the next marked change in Camac Street. The city fathers officially took a hand in transforming it, and the Poor Richard Club, interested in restoring the flavor of old-time Philadelphia, began a campaign of resuscitation. Various clubs of the arts and crafts moved into the old houses. Studios and galleries took the place of dens and gaming houses, and painters and builders were put to work at restoration. Doorways were retouched to bring out their onetime beauty, shutters were painted a bright cobalt blue, and windows were brightened with flower boxes. The darkness of Hell's Highway was efficiently buried, and it was once again safe to walk through the street after dark.

At 255 South Camac Street is the house in which Mrs. John Drew lived in the 1850's when she was playing stock in the city theatres.

Only artists and writers are accepted as members of Le Coin d'Or, 251 South Camac Street. This club aims to preserve the atmosphere of the Latin Quarter and of the cafes of the French capital.

At 239 South Camac Street is the Yachtsmen's Club, founded for the various clubs of Barnegat Bay. Over the entrance are displayed the club's flag and colors. In the trophy room is the famed James Gordon Bennett Bermuda Challenge Cup, won by Commodore Charles Lagens in the races of 1908, 1909, 1910, 1912, 1913. The Poor Richard Club once had its headquarters in this building.

The Sketch Club, oldest art club in the United States, is at 233-35-37. This club played a major part in the rejuvenation of the street, for when it moved its headquarters there in 1902, other art and business groups followed. Outgrowth of the proposal of George F. Bensell, illustrator for a society of artists, the club held its first meeting at the Academy of the Fine Arts in 1860. A charter was secured in 1889, and for a few years the group met in a building on the present site of Broad Street Station. The Sketch Club gained prominence during the World War by selling $3,700,000 worth of Liberty Bonds. Many noted

425

American artists of the last 50 years have been members, among them Joseph Pennell, Thomas Anshutz, Nicola D'Ascenzo, R. Blossom Farley, Nathaniel Little, Weyman Adams, and Richard Bishop. The club has a magnificent library of art works, including many cartoons. A rathskeller, richly furnished with hand-carved chairs, and chess and billiard rooms are maintained for the relaxation of the members. The public may view the art works only during the club's free exhibitions, held at various times during the year.

Across the street, at 213, is the Princeton Club, a social organization of Princeton University alumni.

The private dwelling at 206 South Camac Street presents a curious spectacle. Its front and side walls, bordering on a narrow alley, are plastered with a hodge-podge of early documents, including a facsimile of a letter in Penn's handwriting, a number of pages from old newspapers, a print portraying the opening of the Centennial Exhibition, old theatre programs, and old German inscriptions. High on a wall of the building is an old fire plaque, reminder of the days when fire protection was in the hands of private companies.

Men well known in literary fields have been members of the Franklin Inn Club, 205 South Camac Street. George Gibbs, novelist ; Owen Wister, author of *The Virginian* ; R. Tait McKenzie, sculptor ; S. Weir Mitchell, author of *Hugh Wynne* ; Horace Howard Furness ; and Samuel Scoville, Jr.—all are or have been members of this group. The clubhouse is a reproduction of a Colonial building, rebuilt and refurnished in the Georgian style of that era. The low steps leading to the door are flanked by iron rails, severe but with a simplicity appropriate to Colonial architecture.

At the north end of the street, just below Walnut, is the home of the Meridian Club, a luncheon group of professional and business men.

Four or five little eating houses dot the street on both sides, each with characteristic novelties. One is decorated to resemble a pirates' den, another presents marionette shows for its guests. All afford the layman a glimpse of bohemianism of the Greenwich Village type, a bit artificial, but colorful, nevertheless.

The south end of the street more closely resembles a typical Philadelphia thoroughfare.

R. from Camac St. on Walnut.

The ARTISTS UNION (46), 1212 Walnut Street, is the baby among Philadelphia's art organizations. The school maintained by the union offers evening classes in painting, sculpture, life drawing, commercial design, and art appreciation. Its experimental galleries exhibit some of the most forthright painting and sculpture currently produced in Philadelphia.

Retrace on Walnut St. ; L. on 13th.

426

To Society Hill (City Tour 2)

At Locust Street is the HEADQUARTERS OF THE HISTORICAL SOCIETY OF PENNSYLVANIA (47). *(Open daily 9 to 5 except Sun. and holidays ; July and August open 9 to 4 Mon. to Fri. ; adm. free).* Salvaged from the musty hideaways and obscure pigeonholes of historical oblivion, collections of thousands of time-yellowed documents, archives, books, and newspapers — the chronicles of Pennsylvania's illustrious past — are carefully preserved in the building.

This red brick structure with marble trim, is an adaptation of the traditional Philadelphia Colonial style. Six huge Ionic columns with heavy entablature and balustrade form the portico, on either side of which is a Palladian window.

A group of citizens formed the society in 1824, and chose for its first home the residence of Thomas I. Wharton, 130 South Sixth Street. The organization later moved to the Athenaeum Building, 219 South Sixth Street. In 1882 the society purchased a plot of ground at Thirteenth and Locust Streets, but it was not until 1910 that the present home, designed by Addison Hutton, was opened. The structure is four stories high and was built at a cost of $230,000, of which $150,000 was appropriated by the Commonwealth.

Here the dramatic story of Pennsylvania is told in 200,000 bound books, 300,000 pamphlets, 3,000,000 manuscripts, and 3,500 bound volumes of newspapers. Many important collections of original manuscripts, kept intact, are invaluable for making historical surveys. Notable among these manuscripts and books are the Charlemagne Tower collection of Colonial laws, the Cassel collection in German, Watson's *Annals of Philadelphia,* papers dealing with the life of Lincoln, and numerous publications of Franklin, William Bradford, Christopher Sauer, Robert Hall, and William Penn. The world-famous Simon Gratz collection of historical manuscripts also is here.

On the museum's second floor is a writing desk once used by William Penn. In the Gilpin Library, which contains imprints, some of the rarest items of Americana in the country are housed. Other interesting curios are: an old clock once owned by David Rittenhouse, early Philadelphia clockmaker, statesman, and astronomer; the telescope carried by John Paul Jones at the time of the capture of the *Serapis;* Washington's tea caddy, silver watch, camp knife, and fork; Penn's shaving bowl and razor; James Logan's silver watch; George Fox's burning glass; the wampum belt presented to Penn by the Indians; some of the Washington and Lincoln furniture ; and a fine collection of early maps of Philadelphia and Pennsylvania, including the original Holme's map of Pennsylvania.

The walls of the building are hung with an exceptionally fine collection of oil paintings. Included are Charles Willson Peale's portrait of Franklin, one of Gilbert Stuart's paintings of George Washington, and Rembrandt Peale's portrait of Washington. There

427

is also the Kennedy collection of more than 600 water colors of Philadelphia buildings no longer in existence.

The structure sheltering these treasures is built of red brick with marble trim and is an adaptation of the traditional Philadelphia Georgian Colonial style. Six huge Ionic columns with heavy entablature and balustrade form the portico. Palladian windows are on both sides. Reading rooms having tinted wall surfaces with white classic trim are on the first floor.

R. from 13th St. on Locust.

On the right, at Juniper Street, is the HOME OF LIBRARY COMPANY OF PHILADELPHIA (48), oldest circulating library in America. Founded in 1731 by the Junto Club, of which Benjamin Franklin was one of the moving spirits, the company has had a continuous existence. Today its library, the result of years of collection, contains a wealth of valuable and historic books. One of its volumes, printed in Cologne in 1532, contains an account of Cortez's conquest of Mexico and of the Aztecs whom he vanquished. Sir Humphrey Gilbert's rare *Discoveries of a Passage to Cataia*, the oldest book published in English about America, is also in the library's collection. A clock once belonging to William Penn, the writing table of James Logan, Benjamin Franklin's electric wheel, and the desk at which John Dickinson wrote his famous *Farmer's Letters* also are on display.

The site ·for the library was purchased in 1880 for $60,000, and work began immediately under the direction of its architect, Frank Furness. The building is a two-story red brick structure with a brown stone base. Its design is Victorian Gothic. The double curved flight of steps with wrought-iron balustrade was taken from the old building. Above the main entrance there is a niche with a statue of Benjamin Franklin.

R. from Locust St. on Juniper ; R. on Walnut.

At 1318-1322 are the ROSENBACH GALLERIES (49) *(open 9:30 to 5 weekdays ; closed every Sat. and Sun. during July and Aug. ; adm. free)*, a treasure house of art objects collected over a period of 100 years by the Rosenbach family. The galleries were opened in 1897 by Philip H. Rosenbach who was later joined by his brother, Dr. A. S. W. Rosenbach, noted bibliophile and authority on art.

Excellent arrangements of rare and antique period furniture, in authentic settings complete with tapestries and rugs, china, pewter, glassware, and silver, make these galleries a mecca for art enthusiasts. Paintings, prints, and a large collection of books, many printed before Columbus sailed on his historic voyage ; original manuscripts including that of Dickens' *Pickwick Papers*, and three Shakespeare First Folios indicate the richness of a collection to delight bibliophiles.

The Meigs House, at 1322, a division of the galleries, contains 13

428

paneled rooms. The Georgian dining room, with eighteenth century pine paneling, displays a fine crystal chandelier, a complete dinner service of old china, an Abner Reeder collection of sterling silver (1797), and an antique Sheffield plate tray (1820). A walnut and mahogany Chippendale card table with ball and claw feet is covered with fine needlepoint, woven into an old gaming design.

A room with pine paneling from the old Red House, Topsham, Maine (built before 1770), is furnished entirely in maple. One of its exhibits is the earliest known working model of a locomotive (designed by Matthew Murray of Holbeck, Leeds, England, in 1812). The English room, with its eighteenth century Spode dinner service and complete Coalport service, shows Chinese influence.

Old pewter, a set of Bennington ware bowls, and a Hitchcock settee of 1810, decorate the Pennsylvania German room. A choice array of Venetian and Bohemian glass, a pair of Renaissance bronze candlesticks, and an antique Chippendale bookcase, once owned by Edwin Keene, Bishop of Ely; a Carolinian chest of olive wood lined with cedar (it stood in Windsor Castle until the death of George IV in 1830), a fine Savonnerie rug, an old Chinese porcelain bowl, and a set of eight Hepplewhite chairs with an uncommon plume design are in other rooms.

A room from Hanover Square, London, contains a pair of eighteenth cetury mirrors from the collection of the Duchess of Rutland. Another pine paneled room (valued at $9,500) came from the Dower House of the Duchess of Northumberland, Darlington, England.

Another room has Gothic carved-oak paneling, in the linen-fold style of the fifteenth century. A small engraving by Paul Revere, representing the Boston Massacre and valued at $3,650, is hung in a room whose paneling was taken from one of the oldest dwellings in Philadelphia.

The rail of the mahogany stairway in the Meigs House is beautifully carved and the wall is closely hung with old English sporting prints.
Retrace on Walnut St.; R. on Broad to City Hall.

429

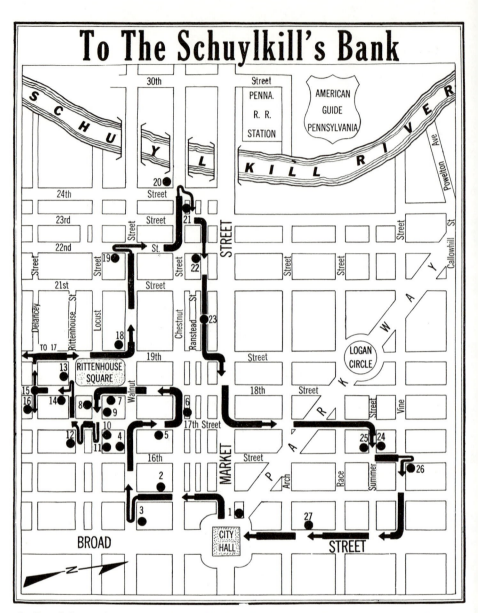

To The Schuylkill's Bank

1. Broad Street Station
2. Central-Penn National Bank
3. Philadelphia Stock Exchange
4. Walnut Street
5. First Baptist Church
6. American Baptist Publication Society
7. Penn Athletic Club
8. Curtis Institute of Music
9. Warwick Hotel
10. Hannah Penn House
11. St. Mark's Church
12. Print Club
13. Eastern Baptist Theological Seminary
14. Philadelphia Art Alliance
15. Delancey Street
16. Plays and Players Theatre
17. Philadelphia School of Occupational Therapy
18. Holy Trinity Church
19. English Village
20. Baltimore & Ohio Station
21. Barracks of the First City Troops
22. College of Physicians and Surgeons
23. Lantern Lane
24. Headquarters of the State Fencibles
25. D'Ascenzo Glass Works
26. New Theatre
27. Pennsylvania Academy of the Fine Arts

To the Schuylkill's Bank

City Tour 3

W. from City Hall on Market St.

AT Fifteenth Street, on the right, is the Pennsylvania Railroad's BROAD STREET STATION (1) *(see Heart of City).*

L. from Market St. on 15th.

On the northwest corner of Sansom Street is a branch office of the CENTRAL-PENN NATIONAL BANK (2), one of the finest examples of bank architecture in Philadelphia. Davis, Dunlap & Barney, designers of the building, won the 1929 gold medal awarded by the Architectural League of New York.

The exterior of the narrow three-story building is of gray French stone. Set within the impressive facade are two fluted columns with modified composite capitals which support an entablature, in the frieze of which is a handsome sculptured panel. Sculptured stone medallions embellish the upper story, one above each of three windows. Pilasters similar to the columns of the facade support the entablature on the Sansom Street side. On the frieze are two sculptured panels by Leo Friedlander, symbolic of American Prudence and National Wisdom.

A wide, arched, glazed doorway, reaching almost to the ceiling, opens into the two-story-high banking room. The inside of the arch and the scroll-pedimented door at the far end of this room are trimmed with green Tinos marble, which provides a striking contrast to the wall color. French marble is used for the face of the banking screen, and pink Tennessee marble for the floor. This imposing structure was built for the American Bank and Trust Company, which merged with the present occupant.

L. from 15th St. on Walnut.

The PHILADELPHIA STOCK EXCHANGE (3) is at 1411 Walnut Street *(open 10 to 3 Sat. 10-12 ; adm. to visitors' gallery by permission of secretary on second floor).* The building on the present site was erected in 1912.

Retrace on Walnut St.

The building known only as 1616 WALNUT STREET (4), a 24-story structure of cream-colored brick, completed in 1930, won its designers, Tilden, Register & Pepper, a diploma from the Twelfth International Buildings Congress held at Budapest in September 1930. The lobby is distinguished for the dextrous use of bronze and aluminum and the concealed lights in the grill, visible only on the inside.

R. from Walnut on 17th.

The FIRST BAPTIST CHURCH (6), erected in 1899, on the southeast corner of Seventeenth and Sansom Streets, is the direct successor

431

of an earlier Baptist church erected at Second and Chestnut Streets in 1698. Its historical room, rich in mementos of early Philadelphia, may be visited by special arrangement.

The design of the brownstone structure is based upon Byzantine and Romanesque traditions. The entrance motif consists of three elaborately carved arches. The auditorium is in the form of a Greek cross, the arms being arched by barrel vaults from the crown of which springs a circular dome. Byzantine stained glass fills the 12 panels of the dome. Along three sides range stained glass windows. Edgar V. Seeler was the architect.

L. from 17th St. on Chestnut.

At 1703 Chestnut Street is the HEADQUARTERS OF THE AMERICAN BAPTIST PUBLICATION SOCIETY (6), which was organized on February 25, 1824. The printing plant, which is situated at Juniper and Lombard Streets, was built in 1896. It distributes more religious literature than any other publishing house of that denomination.

L. from Chestnut St. on 18th.

At Eighteenth and Walnut Streets is the first view of RITTEN-HOUSE SQUARE, with its inviting pool and flower beds. The shrubbery here forms an attractive background for the Art Alliance's annual outdoor exhibition of sculpture, and for the Flower Mart over which socially prominent patronesses preside each year. Since 1928 the Clothes Line Art Exhibit has been held here each spring. Some of the city's most famous clubs, hotels, churches, and apartment buildings border the square.

Facing Rittenhouse Square is the handsome BUILDING OF THE PENN ATHLETIC CLUB (7) at 225 South Eighteenth Street. Founded in 1923, the club has become one of the city's foremost recreational centers, offering its members resident quarters and a widely varied program of social activities.

L. from 18th St. on Locust.

At 1726 Locust Street, on the right, is the CURTIS INSTITUTE OF MUSIC (8).

"To hand down through contemporary masters the great traditions of the past — to teach students to build on this heritage for the future." This is the expressed purpose of the Curtis Institute of Music.

How well the Institute has succeeded in fulfilling its aim is revealed in the names of former students who have won places in fine symphony orchestras and opera companies throughout the Nation, or as soloists in concerts and recitals.

The Institute was established in 1924 by Mary Louise Curtis Bok, widow of Edward W. Bok, journalist, and daughter of the late Cyrus H. K. Curtis, publisher and philanthropist, in whose honor it was named. Today it ranks among the finest schools of music in the

432

world. Affording, as it does, the opportunity of studying under such distinguished musical masters as Josef Hofmann, Elizabeth Schumann, Emilio de Gogorza, Efrem Zimbalist, Léa Luboshutz, Louis Bailly, Felix Salmond, Carlos Salzedo, Fritz Reiner, and Ernst Lert, and the well-known music critic, Samuel Chotzinoff, a scholarship to Curtis is the golden dream of countless youthful musicians. The famed pianist Josef Hofmann, Mus.D., is the Director.

But the realization of this dream is not easy. Applicants are given auditions, and only those exhibiting an inherent musical gift which "shows promise of development to a point of professional ability" are accepted. The way is open to anyone, for no tuition fees are charged, and the Institute often pays the living expenses of students from outside of Philadelphia.

To those fortunate enough to pass the entrance examination comes the thrill of playing upon instruments of the Institute's collection— actually using them for practice, students' recitals, and public appearances.

Every branch of musical study is included in the curriculum. Besides individual instruction in one or more instruments or in vocal training, classes are held in ensemble work, theory, harmony, composition, conducting, and allied subjects. Students also participate in numerous nation-wide radio programs each season, and in public concerts scheduled by the Institute.

After students are graduated, the Institute guides their early efforts and permits them the continued use of its instruments and its extensive library, which was greatly augmented in October 1936 by the acquisition of the Charles H. Jarvis collection of 1,700 volumes of musical scores.

Many of the Institute's graduates have attained first rank in the musical world. Among Curtis Institute graduates are Samuel Barber, composer, who won the Pulitzer musical awards for 1935 and 1936 and was acclaimed enthusiastically in Rome as Music Fellow in the American Academy for the same years; Gian Carlo Menotti, composer of the successful one-act opera *Amelia al Ballo;* Helen Jepson, operatic soprano; Rose Bampton, internationally known mezzosoprano ; Charlotte Symons, soprano with Metropolitan connections ; Irra Petina, mezzo-soprano ; Natalia Bodanya, Metropolitan soprano ; Shura Cherkassky, world-renowned pianist ; Henri Temianka, violinist ; Alexander McCurdy, organist and choirmaster of the Second Presbyterian Church, Philadelphia, and Instructor of Organ at Curtis Institute ; and the Curtis String Quartet, composed of Jascha Brodsky and Charles Jaffe, violinists ; Max Aronoff, viola player, and Orlando Cole, violoncellist.

Curtis Institute is housed in four buildings, three of which are former residences. The Indiana limestone building at the corner,

433

*Doorway of St. Mark's
Church
"The Crucifixion, in Gold
and Vermillion"*

*First City Troop Armory
"Headquarters of Philadelphia's Light Cavalry*

once the home of George W. Childs Drexel, is designed in the manner of the Italian Renaissance. In the interior is a fine hall, with wood paneling, high windows, and large fireplaces, and a library heavily paneled in wood, with a painted ceiling by Edwin H. Blashfield.

Casimir Hall, designed by Horace Wells Sellers, was built for the Institute in 1927. The exterior and interior iron work is by Samuel Yellin. This small auditorium, used for solo and ensemble recitals, is simply paneled in wood, indirectly lighted, and has an acoustically treated ceiling. 1720 Locust Street, the former home of Theodore Cramp, forms another unit of the Institute. Inside is an impressive marble staircase with iron railing. This building houses also the phonograph, radio, and recording studios, and the Institute's cafeteria.

Many fine paintings and other works of art are exhibited in the buildings. A very fine piece of sculpture is the Bourdelle head of Beethoven. In the studio used by Dr. Hofmann is a bas-relief portrait of Mme. Marcella Sembrich, the noted opera singer, who was a member of the faculty from the opening of the Institute until her death.

On the left at 1715 is the WARWICK HOTEL (9), where the Acorn Club, a social club for women only, has its headquarters. A group of 10 women organized the club in 1889.

The HANNAH PENN HOUSE (10), on the northeast corner of Seventeenth Street, is the headquarters of the Republican Women of Pennsylvania and the Philadelphia County branch of the same organization. It was so named because its sponsors believed Hannah Penn, more than any other woman, "embodied the spirit and ideals of the Republican woman."

The walls of the main hallway are decorated with a series of murals by the well-known Philadelphia artist, Violet Oakley, depicting the *House of Wisdom*, a story of the rise of education and knowledge.

The building contains 35 rooms, including a special ballroom. The assembly room and the dining room are available for private affairs. The structure, formerly the town house of Charlton Yarnall, banker, was acquired by the present occupants in 1927.

Left, at 1625, is ST. MARK'S CHURCH (11), built of brownstone in the Gothic style. It is notable for an elaborately carved doorway and richly decorated interior. The cornerstone was laid on April 25, 1848, and the church was completed and consecrated the following year.

Retrace on Locust St.; L. on 17th; L. on Latimer.

The PRINT CLUB (12), 1614 Latimer Street, *(open weekdays 9:15 to 5, Sat. 9:15 to 1; adm. free)* was the first American club of its type. It was founded in 1912 by a group of collectors and lovers of prints who met at the home of Mrs. Alice MacFadden Eyre.

The quarters include two large galleries, executive offices and an

435

attractive garden. Exhibitions, changed approximately every three weeks, include the works of members and non-members. Many print clubs in other cities have patterned themselves after the Philadelphia organization, and receive its encouragement and advice.

The club has been sending exhibitions to schools and other institutions in Philadelphia and its environs since 1922. Classes from both public and private schools visit the club to hear lectures on current exhibits. The original membership of 149 has grown to 767.

Retrace on Latimer St. into Rittenhouse Sq.

At 1808-18 South Rittenhouse Square, facing the park, is the EASTERN BAPTIST THEOLOGICAL SEMINARY (13), founded in 1925. This institution occupies an important place in the religious and educational life of the Baptist denomination. In its three schools, the School of Theology, the School of Christian Education, and the School of Sacred Music, the seminary trains preachers, missionaries, and also teachers who intend to devote their lives to Christian service. The students number approximately 200 annually.

Retrace on Rittenhouse Sq.; R. on 18th St.

The PHILADELPHIA ART ALLIANCE (14), 251 South Eighteenth Street *(open weekdays 10:30 to 9; Sunday 1 to 6; June, July and Aug., 10:30 to 6; adm. free)*, one of the city's finest art centers, represents virtually all the arts. Its five galleries, in which exhibitions are given, have introduced to Philadelphia a distinctive list of paintings, sculpture, and applied arts, culled from collections both in this country and abroad. One gallery is devoted exclusively to exhibitions of member artists. Special displays concentrating upon water colors, prints, oils, crafts, photography, or sculpture are arranged periodically. During the summer, work done by members of the alliance is on view. It is estimated that 40,000 persons visit the galleries each month.

With the formation of the Circulating Picture Club, a lending library of original paintings by noteworthy American artists, the Art Alliance created a medium for extending its cultural influence. By paying a $10 annual fee, each member of this department (and the membership includes not only individuals but clubs, hospitals, schools, libraries, and universities) may select and borrow eight original paintings during the year. One month is the usual time limit for which the painting may be held, although if unusual interest is evinced, the borrowing period may be extended.

The Art Alliance has ventured into fields other than the graphic arts. Its sponsorship of plays and films of exceptional merit constitutes a significant part of the activities. Chamber music concerts also are held under its auspices, and the committee of the alliance presents 5 o'clock talks weekly by authoritative speakers on subjects of cultural interest.

To the Schuylkill's Bank (City Tour 3)

A lending library of books and magazines on art, music, and the drama is conducted for members, and lectures and demonstrations are given to advance understanding of the ballet, and other forms of the dance.

There is a sales and registration bureau, a play-writing contest and experimental work to encourage and develop actors, writers, and artists. There are 300 small theatres in Philadelphia with a personnel of more than 50,000. The alliance is forming a Little Theatre to get these together in one common group, to find out their needs, and to help develop and place the talent of its members. Every two years the alliance holds an open air exhibit of sculpture in Rittenhouse Square.

Among the associations and projects which the Art Alliance sponsors are the Art League, the sculpture at the annual Philadelphia flower show, and the Intercollegiate Dramatic Alliance.

The alliance was organized in 1915 under the leadership of Christine Wetherill Stevenson. The present building has been occupied by the alliance since 1925. It was erected in 1906, after designs by Frank Miles Day, as a private residence for Samuel Price Wetherill. This square three-story-and attic building, Renaissance in character, is of Indiana limestone with a hipped roof. Except for the arched Roman doorway, flanked by fluted and banded columns and surmounted by two handsomely carved tablets, the lines are simple.

Sculptured and ornamental plaster bands decorate the arched ceil-

Rittenhouse Square
"Morning Coats . . . Holy Trinity
Church . . . and Pigeons"

ing of the long hallway that ends at the ornamental iron gates of the old dining room. Above these gates is a bas-relief of the founder, Mrs. Stevenson.

On the right of the hall is the most striking feature of the interior, the staircase which rises by a single broad flight of heavy oak treads to a spacious landing, where it divides and continues in reverse direction to the second floor. A richly colored leaded Palladian window, providing light for the stairs and both halls, extends across the entire width of the landing. The front rooms are used as art galleries. Club room are on the first and second floors, administrative offices on the third.

L. from 18th St. on Delancey.

Stretching across the heart of the city in a broken course between Spruce and Pine Streets, DELANCEY STREET (15) is characterized in places by residential blocks, and in other places runs through poverty-ridden sections. The section between Eighteenth and Twenty-second Streets, however, is one of Philadelphia's most fashionable and exclusive streets. It is still called, on some of the older signs, De Lancey Place.

Here are residences of many families whose names are an integral part of the city's history, the stock in trade of society editors. Unpretentious but dignified are the facades of red brick and white marble, with spotless white steps and finely wrought iron rails. White wood or marble doorways and wooden shutters painted white or green complete the exteriors, except for an occasional flower box. Although few of the houses follow exactly the same design, the general effect is harmonious.

Commercial life is excluded from this charming, tree-shaded street. The residents have banded together to prevent business firms from encroaching upon it ; they are active in bringing about improvements by planting evergreens and vines, and in other ways enhancing its attractiveness. The only large building along this section of the street is the headquarters of the Southeastern Pennsylvania Chapter of the American Red Cross, southwest corner of Twenty-first and Delancey Streets.

East of Eighteenth, however, the street takes on a sharply different aspect. Between private garages that once were stables, a variety of activity goes on. One of the most unusual establishments is a dog "laundry," in reality a beauty parlor where manicures and even permanent waves are given canine pets.

The transition at Eighteenth Street serves to emphasize the quiet charm of the residential blocks — to express by means of visual contrast their intangible, yet perceptible, atmosphere of simple beauty.

In the "Old Towne" in the neighborhood of Front and Second

438

Streets, Delancey Street retains a number of quaint, old, brick houses of authentic Colonial design, the models for the more recent dwellings farther west.

At 1714 is the PLAYS AND PLAYERS THEATRE (16). In this little playhouse amateur thespians produce numerous stage presentations for the enjoyment of several hundred subscribers. The club, founded in 1911 by Mrs. Otis Skinner, was housed until 1922 at Eighteenth and Chestnut Streets. It is considered one of the oldest Little Theatre organizations in the United States. The well-equipped and tastefully appointed theatre on Delancey Street, intimate and comfortable, seats approximately 300.

Retrace on Delancey St.; L. on 19th.

The PHILADELPHIA SCHOOL OF OCCUPATIONAL THERAPY (17), at 419 South Nineteenth Street, has for its primary purpose the training of women in the profession of occupational therapy. This organization has undertaken the task of reconditioning, rehabilitating, and reeducating the mentally and physically disabled by means of recreation and manual occupations. The school also sponsors a curative workshop which accepts patients free of charge and treats them under physicians' guidance. Although the purpose of the shop is primarily therapeutic and not vocational, patients sometimes earn small sums through the sale of articles made while under treatment.

Retrace on 19th St.; L. around Rittenhouse Sq.; L. to Walnut.

HOLY TRINITY CHURCH (Protestant Episcopal) (18), on the southwest corner at Walnut Street, was opened for worship in 1859, at a time when Walnut, Spruce, and nearby streets were developing into a select residential center. Past rectors of the church, among them A. H. Vinton, Phillips Brooks (later Bishop of Massachusetts), Thomas A. Jaggar, William N. McVicker (later Bishop of Rhode Island), and Floyd W. Tomkins, have been eminent scholars and orators as well as outstanding clergymen. It was during his service here that Phillips Brooks wrote the carol, *O Little Town of Bethlehem.* The brownstone church and the fine rectory adjoining on the west are of Gothic design. Handsomely carved pews and a chancel grace the dignified interior.

Left on Walnut St. to 22d; L. on 22d.

On the left, between Walnut and Locust Streets, is the charming ENGLISH VILLAGE (19), an interesting arrangement of attached dwellings built around a central flagstoned court which is accented with shrubbery. Building operations began in 1923 and were completed the following year. The architect was Spencer Roberts. The stuccoed houses, with tall mansards, are slightly Elizabethan in flavor.

Retrace on 22d St.; L. on Chestnut.

The BALTIMORE & OHIO STATION (20), on the west side of Twenty-fourth Street, is a red-painted brick structure with ornamental

439

members of cast iron. A relic of Victorian days, it is transfigured by night into a vague mass suggestive of a haunted castle. It is pierced by dormer windows. A squat clock tower and marquees add to the bizarre effect of the structure.

R. from Chestnut St. on 24th ; R. on Ranstead.

An atmosphere reminiscent of medieval fortresses envelops the BARRACKS OF THE FIRST CITY TROOP (21), on the southwest corner at Twenty-third Street. The barracks is given an impression of heaviness by the square tower, loophole windows, menacing battlements, and broad gateway and portcullis. The ground floor serves as a riding hall.

L. from Ranstead St. on 23d ; R. on Ludlow.

The COLLEGE OF PHYSICIANS AND SURGEONS (22), on the southeast corner at Twenty-second Street, is the home of the oldest existing medical society in the United States. Founded in 1787 by John Redman, its first president, and other prominent physicians of that period, the society's building holds numerous exhibits of interest to the medical profession, including the skeleton of the so-called "Kentucky Giant." The society maintains a comprehensive library, considered second only to that of the Army Medical Library at Washington, D. C. The present building was completed in 1909.

LANTERN LANE (23) opens on Ludlow Street between Nineteenth and Twentieth Streets. The houses were erected in 1922. Wrought-iron gates give entrance to the brick courtyard around which are grouped 16 houses. The facades are stuccoed in pastel tones with rows of colored tile across the front. At the second floor windows are gayly colored shutters and wrought-iron balconies.

*L. from Ludlow St. on 19th ; R. on Market⎮; L. on 17th and R,
on Summer.*

On the left at 1615 Summer Street is the HOUSE OF THE STATE FENCIBLES (24), organized in 1813. During the Civil War the Fencibles participated in the Peninsular Campaign, the Battle of Gettysburg, and many other important battles. On exhibition in the headquarters are relics recalling the role which the organization has played in many military campaigns.

Across the street, at 1604, is the D'ASCENZO GLASS WORKS (25), a large studio Nicola D'Ascenzo and his son established in 1920. There they create the numerous stained glass designs which have made the D'Ascenzo name world-famous. Among the Philadelphia examples of their artisanship are the doorways of the main entrance of Rodeph Shalom Synagogue, Broad and Mt. Vernon Street ; the windows in the Church of the Holy Child at Broad and Duncannon Streets ; and the chancel windows and mosaic in the Unitarian Church, Germantown.

L. from Summer St. on 16th.

440

The NEW THEATRE (26), 311 North Sixteenth Street, Philadelphia's newest experimental theatre, organized in 1934, serves as a dramatic school, theatre workshop, and production center. With a budget of $2,000 and a large supply of energetic labor, this enterprising group succeeded in remodeling an abandoned church into a theatre building with the only double revolving stage in Philadelphia. Membership of the group has increased until today it has a production unit of almost 100 persons.

Retrace on 16th St.; L. on Vine; R. on Broad.

On the southwest corner at Cherry Street is the PENNSYLVANIA ACADEMY OF THE FINE ARTS (27) *(see City Tour No. 5).*
Continue on Broad St. to City Hall.

THE LONGEST STRAIGHT STREET
Through the Melting Pot
City Tour 4

PICTURESQUE patches populated by foreign groups give South Philadelphia an Old World flavor. Phalanxes of pushcarts, some piled high with china and trays, with men's mittens, with pins and pencils, and flypaper, others heaped with grapes and bananas and berries, clutter some of the streets. The aroma of strange viands permeates the air. There is the persistence of peasant folkways—weddings, funerals, and christenings conducted with all the ceremony which custom demanded in European villages.

South Philadelphia is the home of one of the greatest Negro populations in the North. The Irish, who have long been the dominant element in the section, are represented by an array of political organizations and athletic clubs. Until a decade or so ago, synagogues, bearded orthodox rabbis, and devout women in shawls and wigs recreated the atmosphere of an Old World ghetto.

A slice of Locust Street, between Tenth and Eleventh, is largely Greek. Conversations over the thick, black coffee and native foods at the restaurants may be in the idiom of the Ionian Isles. At Eastertide bakery windows display bread with colored eggs baked, shell included, in the crust. A Greek workers' club, on South Eleventh Street, decorated in keeping with the Hellene's unabashed love of gaiety, is a center of activities.

The heart of Little Italy throbs at Eighth and Christian Streets—the scene of numerous gang murders in the days of prohibition. Streets are lined with undertakers' establishments, displaying elaborate candlelit coffins, music stores plastered with bravely colored chromos of the reigning sovereigns of Italy, and poultry markets, smelling of their cackling wares. An Italian daily newspaper is pub-

441

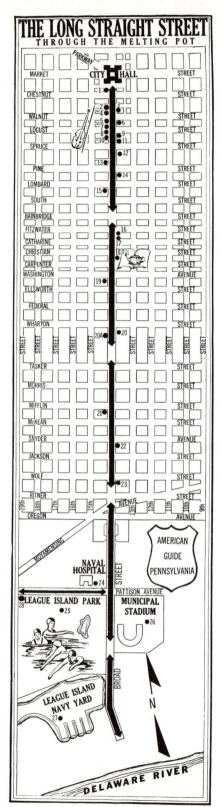

THE LONG STRAIGHT STREET
THROUGH THE MELTING POT

1. Girard Trust Company

2. Union League

3. Fidelity-Philadelphia Trust Company

4. Manufacturers and Bankers Club

5. Bellevue-Stratford Hotel

6. Ritz-Carlton Hotel

7. Art Club of Philadelphia

8. Academy of Music

9. Walton Hotel

10. Shubert Theatre

11. Site of Old Broad Street Theatre

12. Chambers-Wylie Memorial Presbyterian Church

13. Philadelphia Textile School and the School of Industrial Art

14. Y. M. and Y. W. H. A. Building

15. Lincoln Theatre

16. Broad Street Hospital

17. St. Theresa's Roman Catholic Church

18. Ridgway Library

19. United States Marine Corps Building

20. Combs Conservatory of Music

20a. Broad Street Baptist Church

21. St. Agnes Hospital

22. South Philadelphia High School

23. Methodist Episcopal Hospital

24. Naval Hospital

25. League Island Park

26. Municipal Stadium

27. League Island Navy Yard

28. American Swedish Historical Museum

lished at Eighth Street, and there are numerous fraternal associations and bocce clubs.

More evident, however, than their color and quaintness is the paralyzing poverty of South Philadelphia's Negro and foreign sections. The cobbled streets and uneven brick sidewalks, many reminiscent of Revolutionary days, are usually littered with dirt, rubbish, and torn newspapers. There are a few shopping districts, notably South Street, which sparkle with showy wares, but the prevailing note, particularly in the older quarters, is dull and depressingly minor in key.

Slum areas splotch the scene like open sores, exhibiting the unlovely aspects of all slums. Neglected children swarm about dingy alleyways. Ramshackle hovels, built without benefit of bathtubs, huddle forlornly together. Through broken window panes, sometimes patched with paper, an ancient iron bedstead is occasionally outlined or a chipped bowl and pitcher—and society pays the usual price of its apathy in a high mortality, disease, and crime rate.

S. from City Hall on Broad St.

The route leads through a swirl of concentrated commercial activity. Skyscrapers, some of considerable architectural distinction, line both sides of constantly thronged Broad Street, "the longest straight street."

The GIRARD TRUST COMPANY BUILDING (1), is on the northwest corner of Chestnut Street. *(See Heart of the City.)*

Entirely of marble, the structure is notable for its huge Ionic columns, which support entablatures and pediments on both the Broad and Chestnut Streets facades, and for its distinctively simple, broad dome. Within the Broad Street pediment is a sculptured relief of two sailing ships and a profile of Stephen Girard, the work of the sculptor Weiman.

On the southwest corner at Sansom Street is the HOME OF THE UNION LEAGUE (2), traditional citadel of the Republican Party in Philadelphia. The league was formed during the Civil War by a group of men who offered their services both as individuals and as an organization to President Lincoln in the struggle to keep the Union intact. Many Republican Presidents have addressed the members in the Lincoln Room, and the organization has been host to most of the notable Republican figures in the country.

The massive, ornate structure of red brick and brownstone, erected in 1865, exhibits the florid taste typical of the Victorian era. The large rooms are highly decorated, and the staircase in the hall is heavy with pompous ornamentation.

On the northeast corner at Walnut Street is the 30-story FIDELITY-PHILADELPHIA TRUST COMPANY BUILDING (3), containing a bank and business offices. It is one of the largest buildings in the city, built in 1927-28 and designed by Simon & Simon.

443

At the northwest corner is the MANUFACTURERS AND BANK-ERS CLUB (4). The club was founded by a group of prominent manufacturers, who in 1908 took formal possession of the site, then occupied by the old Bellevue Hotel, a favorite dining place of Phila-delphia's elite. Today the club's membership includes some of the most successful business men in the State.

One of Philadelphia's oldest and most important hostelries is at the southwest corner of Walnut Street — the BELLEVUE-STRAT-FORD (5), opened September 20, 1904. Its construction and arrange-ment have been copied by many other leading hotels in the country, including five of the best known in New York City. Opposite the Bellevue-Stratford, and of a name world-famous, is the RITZ-CARL-TON HOTEL (6), built in 1912 and enlarged in 1914.

On the same side as the Bellevue-Stratford and but a little farther south, at Chancellor Street, is the ART CLUB OF PHILADELPHIA (7), erected in 1886.

The building, a four-story structure, is of French Renaissance design, constructed of brick and limestone with tile roof. Originally a private residence, the interior has been altered, for the purpose of the club, by Zantzinger, Borie & Medary. The delicate stone design, the over-hanging balcony at the corner of the third floor, and the huge chimney give the building a French chateau effect.

The membership includes not only artists, but also a numerous representation of business and professional men.

On the southwest corner at Locust Street is the ACADEMY OF MUSIC (8) *(see Points of Interest)*.

On the southeast corner at Locust Street is the WALTON HOTEL (9), which has been the scene of many notable functions.

The SHUBERT THEATRE (10), on the right at No. 250, features "glorified burlesque."

The SITE OF THE BROAD STREET THEATRE (11), on the left, will bring a reminiscent sigh to most of the theatre lovers who pass by. It was one of the oldest playhouses in the city, having been built in 1876. The theatre was demolished in 1937.

On the left, below Spruce Street, is the CHAMBERS-WYLIE MEMORIAL PRESBYTERIAN CHURCH (12). This Gothic temple, where many prominent Philadelphians worship, was founded May 5, 1825. Rankin & Kellogg designed the building.

The building occupied since 1893 by the PHILADELPHIA TEX-TILE SCHOOL AND THE SCHOOL OF INDUSTRIAL ART (13), on the northwest corner at Pine Street, was built in 1826 for the Penn-sylvania Institute for the Deaf. The first school provides complete technical instruction in the textile industry, and courses in various fields of industrial art are offered by the other.

The building, plastered in buff, has a broad two-story facade with

444

a colonnade supporting the pedimented gable end of its projecting central section. The walls of the original building and most of the foundation are of roughhewn stone, plastered over. Furness & Evans designed the large addition at the rear in 1876.

The Y. M. AND Y. W. H. A. BUILDING (14), southeast corner at Pine Street, houses the largest Hebrew athletic and social organizations in the city.

The LINCOLN THEATRE (15), on the southwest corner at Lombard Street, was once a popular Negro theatre.On June 1, 1937, it was taken over by the Hebrew Actors Union, Inc., for the presentation of Yiddish plays.

At South Street is the heart of the Philadelphia Negro business section.

At Fitzwater Street, on the southeast corner, is the BROAD STREET HOSPITAL (16), built in 1911 and enlarged in 1928.

ST. THERESA'S ROMAN CATHOLIC CHURCH (17), northeast corner at Catharine Street, was founded in 1853. The building is a classic brownstone structure of Roman Doric design with four pilasters supporting a pediment.

RIDGWAY LIBRARY (18), left, between Christian and Carpenter Streets (open weekdays, 1 to 5), is housed in a solid granite building. With its three porticos—the center one with eight Doric columns, the other two, each with four similar columns—this building gives the impression of three Greek temples joined by a common facade. The columns support a denticulated cornice surmounted by broad, low, graceful arches with decorative scrolls. The severe and simple design of the interior is classic Greek. To the right of the large central hall, virtually bare of decoration, a broad staircase leads to a balcony.

This library, which occupies an entire city block, was the gift of Dr. James Rush. When he died in 1869 he left a trust fund of more than $1,000,000 for the erection of a building to house a library of generous proportions. At the rear of the main hall is the tomb of the founder. The library contains about 170,000 volumes and excels in Americana of the Revolutionary period, particularly in material devoted to Pennsylvania. It possesses a collection of geological literature second only to that of the library of the United States Geological Survey.

The UNITED STATES MARINE CORPS BUILDING (19), on the southwest corner at Washington Avenue, is the headquarters of the quartermaster's department of the Marine Corps.

The COMBS CONSERVATORY OF MUSIC (20), is on the left at 1331. It is one of the best-known schools of music theory and practice in the East, and its pianoforte department has achieved an enviable reputation.

The BROAD STREET BAPTIST CHURCH (20a), is on the

445

southwest corner at Reed Street, and at Mifflin Street, on the right, is ST. AGNES HOSPITAL (21). The hospital buildings and grounds cover an entire block.

SOUTH PHILADELPHIA HIGH SCHOOL (22), on the left, from Jackson Street to Snyder Avenue, is part of the public school system.

METHODIST EPISCOPAL HOSPITAL (23), on the southeast corner at Wolf Street, is one of the oldest hospitals in South Philadelphia. It received its first patients in 1892. A new building was added in 1924.

The NAVAL HOSPITAL (24) is on the right at Pattison Avenue. Built at a cost of $3,200,000, its 12 stories contain most of the devices of modern medical science. The building, designed by Walter T. Karcher and Livingston Smith, was opened April 12, 1935, to care for ailing United States Service men and has accommodations for 650 beds. Twenty-two acres of well-kept lawn surrounding the building provide ample space for exercise and recreation.

Ridgway Library
"The Classic Touch of Ancient Greece"

Through the Melting Pot (City Tour 4)

LEAGUE ISLAND PARK (25), bounded by Eleventh and Twenty-first Streets and Pattison and Government Avenues, has an entrance on Broad Street. This was the site of the Sesqui-Centennial Exposition of 1926. The completion of the park in 1923 brought to a close one of the most remarkable works of reclamation ever undertaken by municipal engineers.

Nearly 300 acres of low-lying marshland were brought to grade, covered with topsoil, sodded, planted and laid out with walks and drives. Buildings were erected, and a natural body of water, once popularly known as "Twin Lakes," was converted into a bathing place. The beautifully landscaped beaches are visited on hot summer days by thousands. During the winter, when conditions permit, there is ice skating.

The MUNICIPAL STADIUM (26), at Terminal Avenue, is one of the structures erected in 1926 for the Sesqui-Centennial Exposition. Simon & Simon were the architects. The large horseshoe of buff brick and gray limestone was the scene of the Dempsey-Tunney fight in 1926 and of the Army-Navy football games in 1936 and 1937. It has a seating capacity of 102,000 for football and 126,000 for boxing. Seventy-seven tiers of seats rising from a low field side wall are enclosed by an arcaded exterior wall.

The LEAGUE ISLAND NAVY YARD (27), at the southern end of Broad Street *(open to visitors, Sat., Sun., and holidays, 1 to 4 p. m.)*, epitomizes in many ways the history of American sea power.

Authorized the same year as the Navy Department, 1798, it is filled with stirring martial memories. It has served as a base of supplies in all the Nation's wars.

In the days of Commodore John Barry the ships of America's infant Navy were berthed at the Philadelphia yard (then at the foot of Federal Street), and there the frigates that held the seas against French privateers were supplied and outfitted. There, likewise, were built the vessels that Commodore Stephen Decatur hurled against the Barbary corsairs. When the American doctrine of the freedom of the seas was enunciated in 1812, the Philadelphia yard built, outfitted, or repaired many of the stout, oaken vessels which defended that doctrine against the might of Great Britain's Navy. One of those ships, the venerable *Constitution*, was towed past the yard in 1931 on a memorial cruise—a strange contrast to the modern, fast, hard-hitting ships of steel then lying at the yard.

With the passing of wooden warships the old yard passed too. It was not suited to the construction of iron vessels, which became the backbone of naval power after the epic fight between the *Monitor* and the *Merrimac*. The yard, on whose ways 35 fighting ships had been constructed, was abandoned in 1862, and a new plant was constructed on League Island. Philadelphia, eagerly alert and anxious to retain

447

the business which accrued from the location of the yard there, purchased the 923-acre island for $310,000 and presented it to the Federal
Government. The plant and site of the yard are now valued at $100,-
000,000.

The first project at the new yard was the construction of vessels
for the Federal Navy during the Civil War, when so many ships were
built that the United States became the dominant sea power for the
ensuing decade. After the war the yard languished, but it had a brief
resurgence when the Spanish-American War focused attention upon
the Navy. During the World War the yard was greatly expanded, its
facilities were modernized, and many large ships built, outfitted
or repaired. League Island also became a training base for thousands
of youths destined to man the vessels which patrolled the mine-strewn
seas around Europe and guarded troopships against submarine attack.

The yard, third largest in the country, derives much of its importance from its advantageous situation on the Delaware—at the edge
of a great metropolitan center where skilled labor is plentiful, and
within a short freight haul of steel mills and coal mines. It is the
Navy's only fresh-water yard, and thus the only one where the Gov--
ernment's steel ships are safe from the rapid corrosive effects of salt
water.

There are three drydocks. The largest, which can accommodate
ships up to 1,000 feet in length, has a water capacity of 53,108,000
gallons and is equipped with two of the world's largest electric cranes.
Each crane is 230 feet high, with a lift of 350 tons. Vessels are repaired
and outfitted at a pier which provides dockage for two capital ships.

During the World War the emergence of air power as a factor in
naval strength led to the addition of a naval aircraft factory and a
flying field with a hangar accommodating eight seaplanes. The field,
named for Capt. Henry C. Mustin, a distinguished naval officer, has
become one of the yard's more important adjuncts, and probably its
most spectacular. It is used as a testing ground for ships and a training station for navy pilots and observers.

The aircraft factory is one of the largest of its kind in the world.
All the parts of the ill-fated dirigible *Shenandoah* were manufactured
here and later assembled at Akron, Ohio. During the war the factory
employed 5,000 workers an dturned out many seaplanes.

The Navy Yard is probably the epitome of Philadelphia's industrial structures of modern design. The new aircraft factory and
hangars and several structures of the ship-building section, especially
foundry shop No. 20 with its setback upper section entirely of glass,
are noteworthy.

Docked at the yard as a permanent exhibit is the old cruiser
Olympia, Admiral George Dewey's flagship when his victory at
Manila in 1898 made the United States a world power. The destroyer

Through the Melting Pot (City Tour 4)

Jacob Jones, victor in many an exciting clash on the precarious sea lanes of 1917, and now decommissioned, lies at anchor in the yard. It is one of a dozen destroyers here, their steel hides spotted with rust. The light cruiser *Philadelphia* was launched at the yard in 1936, and the *Wichita*, a 10,000-ton cruiser, on November 17 the following year.

Retrace on Broad St.; L. on Pattison Ave.

The AMERICAN SWEDISH HISTORICAL MUSEUM (28), at Nineteenth Street, was erected in 1926 during the Sesqui-Centennial Exposition. It was originally named the John Morton Memorial Museum in honor of the man who cast the deciding vote in the Pennsylvania delegation when the Declaration of Independence was adopted. Morton was of Swedish extraction. This museum, when it is completed in 1938 for the 300th anniversary of the arrival of the Swedes here, will contain 16 rooms. John Nyden, of Chicago, was the architect.

Another Swede, John Hanson, was elected on November 5, 1781, as President of the Continental Congress. He took office under the Articles of Confederation prior to the Constitution, and presided over Congress for a full term of one year, resigning because of illness.

Many important souvenirs and mementos of Morton and Hanson, in addition to documents and relics pertaining to Jenny Lind, the

American Swedish Historical Museum
Philadelphia's Tribute to Leif Ericsson

"Swedish Nightingale," to John Ericsson, inventor of the steamship propeller-screw, and to other Swedes vitally identified with American history, are in the museum collections.

Ericsson's memorial will serve to recall the part played in the Civil War by his famous ship, the *Monitor*, in its battle with the Confederate ironclad *Merrimac* in Hampton Roads. The *Princeton*, built in 1849 in accordance with his designs, was the first ship with engine and boilers below the water line. Other inventions followed, and the principle of the armored turret ship which he employed in the *Monitor* and in which he tried to interest the world seven years before the Civil War, has been employed ever since on naval craft in constantly developing form.

The American Sons and Daughters of Sweden erected this memorial in honor of Sweden's famous citizens who have contributed some lasting service to America's development. Each room is dedicated to that field in which the person did his or her greatest work. Thus, the John Ericsson room is dedicated to inventions and engineering ; the Jenny Lind room to music ; the Frederica Bremer room to records of women's movements ; and the Swedenborg room to science, philosophy, mysticism, etc.

Retrace on Pattison Ave. ; R. on Broad St. to City Hall.

Where Houses Stand in Regiments

City Tour 5

NORTH BROAD STREET begins at City Hall in commercial bravura. Its first notes are blatant. Automobile marts spread gleaming billboards and show windows along its sides. Furniture stores, drug stores, a few cigar stores are among the commercial enterprises of this street on which a mortuary chapel or undertaking establishment appears in nearly every block.

Rows of stodgy, aloof, brownstone houses stand among the commercial houses of lower North Broad Street, but to the north of Roosevelt Boulevard the yearning for more gracious living which swept post-war America finds expression in popular-priced gray stone duplex homes, a compromise between shortage of space and the boredom of the row house. In winter the glass-enclosed porches of these homes diffuse the glow of gas logs and the rose and amber of shaded lamps. Summer finds the street vivid with the striped awnings and painted furniture on its porches, the clumps of hydrangeas and old-fashioned flowers in small gardens crowded upon short-banked front lawns.

450

1. Masonic Temple
2. Pennsylvania Academy of the Fine Arts
3. Scottish Rite Temple
4. Philadelphia Bureau of Fire
5. Hahnemann Hospital and Medical College
6. Roman Catholic High School for Boys
7. Broadwood Hotel
8. Record Building
9. Regiment Armory
10. Elverson Building
11. Terminal Commerce Building
12. Site of the Old Baldwin Locomotive Works
13. Spring Garden Institute
14. Central High School
15. Temple Rodeph Shalom
16. Post No. 2 Memorial Hall, G. A. R.
17. Site of the Caledonian Club
18. Philadelphia Normal School and School of Practice
19. Philadelphia Aerie No. 42
20. Lu Lu Temple
21. Salvation Army
22. Church of Our Lady of the Blessed Sacrament
23. Metropolitan Opera House
24. H. Josephine Widener Memorial Library
25. Majestic Hotel
26. Moose Hall
27. The Patriotic Order Sons of America Building
28. Clubrooms of the Knights of Columbus
29. The Moore Institute of Art, Science and Industry
30. Irish-American Club
31. Headquarters of Jehovah's Witnesses
32. Temple Keneseth Israel
33. Universalist Church of the Messiah
34. Temple University
35. Grace Baptist Temple
36. 108th Field Artillery Armory
37. National Headquarters of the American Federation of Hosiery Workers
38. Dropsie College
39. Gratz College
40. Mikveh Israel Synagogue
41. North Broad Street Station
42. Philadelphia National League Baseball Park
43. North Philadelphia Station
44. Masonic Home for the Aged
45. Temple University Hospital
46. Temple University Medical College
47. Home for Aged Widows and Wives of Free Masons and the William L. Elkins Masonic Orphanage for Girls
48. Holy Child Roman Catholic Church
49. Clarkson Park
50. Jewish Hospital
51. Widener Home for Crippled Children
51a. Site of the Butler Place
52. Shibe Park
53. Wagner Free Institute of Science
54. Girard College
55. Lankenau Hospital
56. Eastern Penitentiary
57. Philadelphia High School for Girls
58. Wills Hospital
59. United States Mint
60. Friends Meeting House
61. Co-operative Center
62. Philadelphia Branch of the Y. M. C. A.

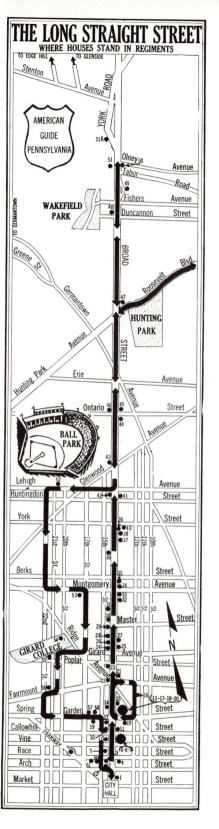

THE LONG STRAIGHT STREET
WHERE HOUSES STAND IN REGIMENTS

N. on Broad St. from City Hall.

The MASONIC TEMPLE (1) *(open clear days only, 10:30 to 2; adm. free)*, standing in quiet massive dignity on the northeastern corner at Filbert Street, headquarters of the R. W. Grand Lodge of Free and Accepted Masons of Pennsylvania, is a great granite structure, an adaptation of Romanesque style. The cornerstone was laid on June 24, 1868 ; the building was designed by James H. Windrim, the rooms constituting an architectural museum. Oriental Hall, a lodge room on the first floor, is designed in the Moorish style after the Alhambra in Granada, and is formed of more than 20,000 pieces of fiber and plaster board screwed to the walls and ceiling. The grand master's apartments are in the northwestern angle, across from the banquet hall. The apartment consists of four communicating rooms, their style and architecture in keeping with the exalted office.

The library, situated on this floor, is an interesting room filled with books on Masonic lore. The hall, Byzantine in style, has columns fluted with bold Corinthian capitals. The inscriptions on the frieze and the twenty allegorical figures are in recognition of the virtues derived from Education. Latin texts are in the friezes beneath the ceiling cornice. The north wall pictures the departments of human knowledge : Medicine, Philosophy, Poetry, History, Astronomy, Mathematics ; the south side pictures the sources of real or normal happiness : Charity, Peace, Industry, Internal Trade, International Commerce, Reflection.

Beginning on the east wall and continuing on the west are the ancient cities as centers from which we received our learning : Rome, Alexandria, Corinth, Athens, Byzantium, Ravenna. In the remaining division of the western wall are symbols of the two great qualities enjoined by the Masonic order : Fidelity and Virtue. An important relic of Masonic history contained in the library is the Lafayette Masonic apron embroidered by Madame Lafayette and worn by George Washington during the laying of the cornerstone of the National Capitol. A bust of Voltaire, reproductions of the works of Houdon, and a portrait of Franklin by Fred James, Philadelphia artist, are valuable relics also in this room.

Other ceremonial rooms are on the second floor. The Ionic Hall on the southeast corner follows the Greek order of architecture — light and elegance. Columns of ivory tone with capitals of gold. Panels, in Pompeian brick, together with the walls of light blue and a ceiling representing the midday sun surrounded by planets and zodiac signs, complete the Greek idea and symbolize Free Masonry. The room contains many portraits of past grand masters of the Grand Lodge of Pennsylvania.

The Norman Hall is characterized by designs of the Norman period, with green and gold leaf, and the Renaissance Hall, grand chapter hall of Royal Arch Masonry, is in buff and red. The most agreeable of the lodge rooms is Corinthian Hall with its octagonal entrance chamber in green, cream and gold. The main room is in subdued tones of blue and gold with an attractice coffered ceiling. The caryatids above the altar, copied from the porch of the maidens at the Acropolis, are poorly done.

Fragments from Greek mythology of the spiritual life are in practical representations in the panels of the large frieze running around the four enclosing walls. Ivory is the general decorative scheme from floor to cornice, gold being used to accentuate all to a higher value. The ceiling is in blue, studded with stars above a lattice balustrade placed upon a cornice, similar to the open or un-covered hall of the ancient Greek temple.

The Egyptian Hall, with its 12 huge columns on the four sides sur-mounted by capitals, is modeled after Luxor, Karnak, Philae, and other temples. The columns have panel ornaments as in Egyptian temples. The massive furniture is also Egyptian in style, and the master's throne of gilded ebony is flanked by sphinxes. The blue ceil-ing, with the sun in the east, and the frieze of the cornice, represent-ing the seasons and the 12-hour day, give significance to the Egyptian influence.

The entire building is rich in symbolic and architectural interest. It is open only on clear days in order to safeguard the valuable rugs which cover the floors.

One block beyond the Masonic Temple, on the left at Cherry Street, is the PENNSYLVANIA ACADEMY OF THE FINE ARTS (2). *(Open daily, except Christmas, 10 to 5 ; adm. free to permanent ex-hibitions. Adm. 25¢ to spring and fall exhibitions, except Sun. and Fri., when free).*

Notable exhibits include a portrait gallery of early Americans, historical paintings and sculpture, and a comprehensive collection of American art, with notable representation of several European schools.

The history of this institution begins with the history of the United States. With the Revolution successfully ended, intellectual leaders of the new Nation cast about for means of building a new culture that would reflect the aspirations and achievements of America. Phila-delphia, stronghold of commerce, political activities, philosophy, and art, seemed at that time to be, logically, the hub from which the spokes of cultural advancement should extend. In this city the clamor-ing for a real native art began as early as 1791, when Charles Willson Peale circulated a proposal for the establishment of a school, in which young artists might receive training.

453

Academy of Fine Arts
"The Louvre on Broad Street"

Not until 1805, however, did Peale's plan crystallize into definite action. At that time a group gathered in Independence Hall and drew up and signed a petition to establish the Pennsylvania Academy of the Fine Arts. The charter was obtained in 1806. Thus was born the first art organization in the United States.

The academy, first housed in a building on Chestnut Street between Tenth and Eleventh, where the Chestnut Street Opera House now stands, was removed to its present site in 1870. The building which now houses the academy was completed six years later. It was planned by Furness & Evans, designers of the Broad Street Station of the Pennsylvania Railroad and the University of Pennsylvania library. The works of this firm have an individuality of design ascribable to no recognized style of architecture, although in the academy building certain Gothic characteristics are apparent.

The massive exterior of red brick and limestone, with polished granite columns, is of the Victorian period in concept. For more than 60 years a huge five-ton statue of the goddess Ceres, brought from Greece in 1828 and presented to the academy by Commodore Daniel Patterson, stood guard in a niche above the entrance to the building. In August 1937, after an existence of 2,300 years, the statue began to crumble. There was no way to save the figure, so drill and chisel were brought into play and the ancient statue was demolished.

Through the years the academy has grown in stature, becoming more and more widely recognized as a sponsor of native American art.

Although there is no set policy governing purchases, the great majority of works acquired are of native origin. The faculty is composed chiefly of native citizens.

The galleries of the academy contain one of the finest collections of American historical portraits to be found in this country. Included are studies of George Washington by Gilbert Stuart, Charles Willson Peale, and Rembrandt Peale. Although Stuart's Washingtons are the best known, the works of the others are of equal importance.

Other famous personages of the Revolution presented on canvas include Benjamin Franklin, painted by Charles Willson Peale ; Benjamin West, by Matthew Pratt ; and James Claypoole, by Charles Willson Peale, all in K gallery. A portrait of Washington by Gilbert Stuart is exhibited in L gallery, and two others by Rembrandt Peale and Charles Willson Peale in gallery K. Later studies of Francis Scott Key, by Charles Willson Peale; Henry Clay, by Rembrandt Peale; and a large collection of Stuart's other works are also included.

The Hudson River school, a group of landscape artists who settled along the Hudson River about 1875, is represented by William Hunt's *Flight of Night*. Hunt was a well-known member of this group.

The Temple Collection, founded in 1880 by Joseph E. Temple, is best exemplified by the painting, *New England Woman*, by Cecilia Beaux.

The John Lambert collection, established in 1913 with an endowment of $50,000, uses the income of the trust to purchase the works of young artists who have not had sufficient encouragement.

The Lambert collection hangs in the west central gallery. Included in the group are *The Seine, Paris* by Samuel Halpert, *Bell* by Clyde Snyder, *Cornwall Cliffs* by Margaret Huntington, *An Actress as*

Cleopatra by Arthur B. Carles, and *Holidays* by Horace Giles. One of the most distinguished paintings is *The Fisherman* by John R. Connor.

One of the foreign groups is the Henry C. Gibson collection, presented to the academy in 1896. This represents the famous Barbizon school of painting.

The Edward H. Coates collection represents the French and American schools. It was presented to the academy in 1923 by Mr. Coates as a memorial. The *Tragic Muse* by Violet Oakley, *February* by William T. Richards, and the *Grand Canal* by Thomas Moran are included here.

The Gilpin Gallery, formed in 1850, includes a fine study of William Ewart Gladstone, done at 10 Downing Street, London, official town residence of the British Prime Minister, by John McClure Hamilton. This gallery also includes 23 specimens of dekadrachms (Greek silver coins) presented by George H. Earle, the father of the Governor of Pennsylvania.

In the school office hangs the small Fields collection, containing the *Virgin and Child* of Gozzoli and a small *St. John the Baptist* by Veronese.

Aside from the galleries and the fine school maintained by the academy, a permanent fellowship and a summer school are among its activities. The fellowship is composed of the alumni of the school and is designed to further the art of America. Annual prizes are offered by the fellowship for the best work by a student done within 10 years after his or her matriculation, including two medals awarded in the water-color exhibit, two prizes in black and white, and three medals and three money prizes in oils and sculpture. The fellowship maintains exhibits that are kept moving from school to school in the Philadelphia district for the purpose of bringing regular academic students into close contact with artistic expression. The summer school is at Chester Springs, 35 miles northwest of Philadelphia.

The SCOTTISH RITE TEMPLE (3), on the southwest corner at Race Street, is a focal point of Masonic activities in Philadelphia.

The building, designed by Horace W. Castor and completed in 1927, is a massive seven-story, gray limestone structure of Greek Doric design. Above the one-story base, pierced by three doorways — the monumental main entrance in the center — rise eight broad pilasters to the sixth story. Narrow window-like openings between the pilasters form vertical accents. The huge entablature is colored with gold, green, and blue terra cotta, the architrave having a blue fret design.

The building contains 103 rooms devoted exclusively to the interests of Masons. The main lobby, known as the outer court, is entered through a vestibule within the main entrance of the building. The outer court leads to the inner court and the main part of the building. The inner court, a soundproof room, was arranged for the use of the Consistorial bodies.

The temple stage extends 40 feet behind the curtain and runs the entire width of the building. The stage lights and other lighting connections of the building are controlled by a huge switchboard containing 4,400 switches with 16 presets, and weighing eight and three-fourths tons.

The building was dedicated to George Washington. A portrait of the first President by Charles Willson Peale hangs over the fireplace in the reception room. On the north wall of the outer court is a bronze tablet containing the names of the Masons under whose supervision the building was constructed.

R. from Broad St. on Race.

The modern headquarters BUILDING OF THE PHILADELPHIA BUREAU OF FIRE (4) is right, at 1328 Race Street. This bureau represents a far cry from the private fire protection offered by early insurance companies. Identifying plaques of these companies remain on the fronts of some of Philadelphia's old buildings.

The fire bureau building designed by the city architect, John Molitor, and erected in 1925, stands on ground that has been occupied by the Fire Department of Philadelphia since 1875. It is a dignified structure of red brick with limestone trim, a Gothic adaptation. Its triple, lancet arched entrance, with grotesque figures of firemen carved into the capitals of the piers, and the corbeled arches at the eaves enhance the effect of the structure. All the administrative offices of the bureau, as well as the offices of the chief engineer and of the Firemen's Pension Fund, are in this building.

On the premises is stationed a fire-fighting force especially trained and equipped to cope with fires in the tall buildings of the central city section. The force is augmented by a rescue squad with specialized functions, which operates only on multiple alarms, or in cases of emergency.

Personnel of the bureau consists of the chief engineer, one deputy chief, 11 battalion chiefs, one fire-school instructor, 90 captains, 94 lieutenants, six marine engineers, six pilots, 12 marine firemen, and 1,600 hosemen and laddermen. There is one captain of the fire school.

The present efficient fire-fighting system contrasts sharply with the turmoil of the volunteer days, when bitter rivalry reached such a height that it was found advisable to create a paid fire department, which started to function March 15, 1871, with 22 engine companies and 5 truck companies. These were selected from the 117 volunteer organizations, and so much controversy was aroused that five additional companies were added to the paid organization in 1872. The

Fire Prevention Division and the Firemen's Training School for officers and new members are two of the most valuable additions made to the department in recent years.

Retrace on Race St.; R. on Broad.

The oldest homeopathic medical college in the United States is on the left, just north of Race Street. This, the HAHNEMANN HOSPITAL AND MEDICAL COLLEGE (5), was merged with the Hospital of Philadelphia in 1885 and moved to its present site. In 1928 the old building was razed and replaced with a modern 20-story structure. The building is of Gothic design, the work of H. Hall Marshall. Normally 500 students are enrolled in the college. The hospital can accommodate 700 patients.

The hospital faces on Broad Street. The college entrance is on Fifteenth Street.

The ROMAN CATHOLIC HIGH SCHOOL FOR BOYS (6), on the northeast corner at Vine Street, is the oldest of the high schools supplementing the Philadelphia parochial school system. The building, a gray limestone structure in Victorian Gothic style, has an ornate tower rising to a dome. It was built in 1886.

The BROADWOOD HOTEL (7), on the southwest corner at Wood Street, has hotel facilities, gymnasium and swimming pool. A 12-story red brick and limestone building in Italian Renaissance design, the work of Andrew Saur, it was built in 1923.

The Philadelphia *Record* is published in the RECORD BUILDING (8), on the southeast corner at Wood Street. The eight-story terracotta structure is topped by an overhanging cornice and has broad window areas on each floor.

Just beyond, and on the same side of Broad Street as the Record Building, is the 103rd REGIMENT ARMORY (9). Built in 1883 to house the military organization previously known as the Gray Reserves, the building is also the home of the Walter M. Gearty and the Yeomanettes posts of the American Legion.

This fort-like structure, rising three stories from a gray granite base to a crenelated top, was designed by James H. Windrim.

The Philadelphia *Inquirer* is printed in the tall and imposing ELVERSON BUILDING (10), on the northwest corner at Callowhill Street *(tours through the plant daily, 2:30 to 9)*.

The building, a huge Italian Renaissance structure faced with white terra cotta details rises in a series of setbacks to a graceful, central clock tower with a lantern and small golden dome. The rear five-story section, extending to Fifteenth Street, is of buff brick. Large front windows on the first story, on the Broad Street side, reveal the color-plate presses in action.

The building, which was erected in 1924, was designed by Rankin, Kellogg, & Crane.

458

The TERMINAL COMMERCE BUILDING (11), northeast corner at Callowhill Street, houses a large railroad freight depot and a number of offices and manufacturing units. This massive 13-story building of yellow brick and light brown terra cotta, with Egyptian ornamentation in colored terra cotta, was designed by William Steele & Sons and built in 1930.

On the left, just below Spring Garden Street, is the SITE OF THE OLD BALDWIN LOCOMOTIVE WORKS (12). The buildings, razed in 1937, covered about 20 acres. Here was the famous plant where a large portion of America's "iron horses" were produced. In 1928 the company removed to Eddystone, south of the city, leaving the red brick structures deserted.

On the northeast corner at Spring Garden Street is the SPRING GARDEN INSTITUTE (13), still housed in the original building, dedicated in 1852.

The first story of the Victorian structure on the Broad Street corner is of brown stone, and two upper floors are of light buff plaster. A small green domed tower rises above the center of the facade. The adjoining building on Spring Garden Street is three stories high and is constructed of brown brick in Italian Renaissance style. It was the first school in the United States to provide courses in manual training. It now offers day and night classes in electrodynamics, pattern-making, auto mechanics, home economics, dressmaking, and interior decorating.

The second oldest high school in the United States, CENTRAL HIGH SCHOOL (14), on the southwest corner at Green Street, is rich in traditions. The present building was erected in 1900 at a cost of $1,500,000. The original red brick structure, now used as an annex, is across the street.

The TEMPLE RODEPH SHALOM (15), southeast corner at Mt. Vernon Street, is an excellent example of Byzantine architecture. Designed by Simon & Simon and begun in 1927 for a Jewish conservative congregation, the building is of Indiana limestone. The interior is notable for its great painted dome supported by massive painted pendentives. Within is the arch of the ark, with its copper and glass inlaid iron doors. Red Tennessee marble columns, with carved white marble capitals, support a canopy.

R. from Broad St. on Fairmount Ave.; R. on 12th St.

The home of POST NO. 2 MEMORIAL HALL, G. A. R. (16), at 667 North Twelfth Street *(open daily, 10 to 3, closed Sat. in summer; adm. free)*, contains numerous relics of the Civil War, including the first Confederate flag captured by a Philadelphia regiment, handcuffs and shackles found in the possession of John Wilkes Booth, and a collection of flags, cannon, and rifles.

R. from 12th St. on Spring Garden.

459

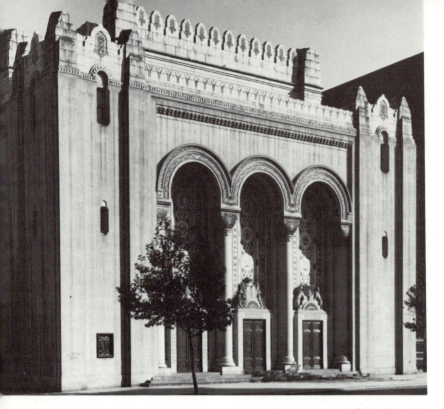

Rodeph Shalom Synagogue
*"They Built a Temple to
Jehovah . . ."*

Observatory—Central High School
*"We will keep the watches of
the night"*

WHERE HOUSES STAND IN REGIMENTS (CITY TOUR 5)

The SITE OF THE CALEDONIAN CLUB (17), which was established in 1859, is on the northeast corner at Thirteenth Street.

The PHILADELPHIA NORMAL SCHOOL AND SCHOOL OF PRACTICE (18) is on the northwest corner at Thirteenth Street. It is four-story, gray granite structure of Italian Renaissance design with a broad arched entrance after the Richardson Romonesque influence. The building, erected in 1893, was designed by Joseph W. Anschutz.

Adjacent to it is a large building of Saracenic architecture, with curious pointed domes. This is the LU LU TEMPLE (19), Nobles of the Mystic Shrine.

The building is a profusely decorated buff brick and terra-cotta structure of Moorish design. Coupled marble columns, cusped arches, and lavishly carved ornaments form an all over pattern on the facade. A huge green dome, surrounded by four similar domes, tops the structure. The building was erected in 1903.

PHILADELPHIA AERIE NO. 42 (20), Fraternal Order of Eagles, built in 1907, is at 1336 Spring Garden Street. The order, organized in Seattle in 1898, has as its prime motive mutual protection against illness and death. Recreation, companionship, and the desire to aid others less fortunate are other objectives of the organization.

R. from Spring Garden St. on Broad.

The Philadelphia HEADQUARTERS OF THE SALVATION ARMY (21) are at 701 North Broad Street. The building is a Victorian structure of brick, built in 1887 and designed by J. B. McElpatrick. The organization maintains an Anti-Suicide Club, where persons contemplating self-destruction are assured of a sympathic hearing, spiritual and sometimes financial assistance.

The Roman Catholic church for Negroes — occupied by them since 1907—called the CHURCH OF OUR LADY OF THE BLESSED SACRAMENT (22), is on the left just north of Fairmount Avenue.

On the southwest corner at Poplar Street is the METROPOLITAN OPERA HOUSE (23). The Metropolitan of today is little more than the tomb of the musical glories of another generation. The discoloration of the light brick and limestone exterior emphasizes the air of somberness that has enshrouded the massive building during recent years.

In its heyday, 1908 to 1913, operatic stars of the first magnitude graced its stage, and wealthy and socially prominent Philadelphians filled the horseshoe boxes and the orchestra and dress circle seats. The house has been dark most of the time during recent years, except for sporadic theatrical and operatic productions and one period of four years when motion pictures were presented intermittently. On occasion, religious and political affairs have been held here.

Oscar Hammerstein came to Philadelphia in 1907 and built the opera house, then known as the Philadelphia Opera House, on the

461

Dome of Lu Lu Temple
"Scimitars . . . Fezes . . . Bagdad"

site of the former O'Harrah mansion. Comment in musical circles at the time ran to the effect that "social Philadelphia will never go uptown." Society's playground was centered south of Market Street. Hammerstein proceeded serenely enough with the new project, however, and when the doors of the house opened for a presentation of *Carmen* on November 17, 1908, social Philadelphia attended in a body.

Philadelphia audiences responded whole-heartedly to Hammerstein's presentations for two seasons. But, faced with a $400,000 mortgage which he saw no way of clearing, he abandoned hope of making a success of the house. It was taken over by E. T. Stotesbury as an adjunct of the Metropolitan Opera Company of New York, and the name of the theatre was changed to the Metropolitan Opera House. For three successive years opera was presented there each Tuesday evening with such luminaries as Enrico Caruso, John McCormack, Tetrazzini, Nellie Melba, Frieda Hempel, Mary Garden, Geraldine Farrar, Louise Homer, Antonio Scotti, and Mme. Schumann-Heink.

Since then the house has been intermittently devoted to a variety of purposes. It was leased to Fred G. Nixon-Nirdlinger, theatrical producer, in 1913. In 1920 the lease was taken over by the trustees of Lu Lu Temple, Nobles of the Mystic Shrine, who now own the building.

In order to accommodate Morris Gest's production, *The Miracle*, in the winter of 1926-27, the theatre was redecorated to simulate a cathedral. Evangelistic services were conducted here in 1930, and it was used by the world-famous Freiburg Players for the presentation of their Passion Play in 1931.

The heavy marquee is in keeping with the structure's French Renaissance style of architecture. The ornate white, gold, and brick-red auditorium is in the over-ornamented classic manner. The stage is the largest of any theatre in the city, and the seating capacity — 3,791 — the second greatest.

A branch of the Free Library of Philadelphia, the H. JOSEPHINE WIDENER MEMORIAL LIBRARY (24), is on the northwest corner at Girard Avenue.

Designed by George Herzog and built in 1887, the brownstone structure has a chateau-like appearance. It is decorated with turrets, dormers, and arched galleries. A horseshoe stairway leads to the broad arched entrance.

On the northeast corner at Girard Avenue is the MAJESTIC HOTEL (25), a building reconstructed from the home of William L. Elkins in 1905. The original structure was built in 1892.

On the left, at 1314 North Broad Street, is MOOSE HALL (26), the Philadelphia home of the Loyal Order of Moose. The hall consists of three brownstone buildings, formerly dwellings, which were built in 1914 after designs of Carl P. Berger.

THE PATRIOTIC ORDER SONS OF AMERICA BUILDING (27) is at 1317.

The CLUBROOMS OF THE KNIGHTS OF COLUMBUS (28) are at 1324. The building, a four-story Victorian brownstone structure, was originally erected as a private home.

THE MOORE INSTITUTE OF ART, SCIENCE AND INDUSTRY (29), southwest corner at Master Street, was founded in 1844. Formerly known as the Philadelphia School of Design for Women, its present name dates from 1932. The Philadelphia School of Design was the first school in the United States to offer designing courses for women.

The institute has been at its present address since 1881. The corner house of the mid-Victorian brownstone dwellings that form the school group was at one time the home of Edwin Forrest, noted Shakespearean actor.

The IRISH-AMERICAN CLUB (30), a social and patriotic association, maintains quarters at 1428 North Broad Street. It is a narrow, four-story brownstone building.

The Philadelphia HEADQUARTERS OF JEHOVAH'S WITNESSES (31) is at 1620. This group achieved notoriety as a result of its aversion to saluting any flag.

TEMPLE KENESETH ISRAEL (32), one of the best-known Hebrew cultural and educational organizations in the country, is on the right between Columbia and Montgomery Avenues. This temple of a Reformed Jewish congregation was founded by Rev. Joseph Krauskopf, Hebraic educator noted for his devotion to charitable causes.

The building, erected in 1892, was designed by Louis C. Hickman and Oscar Trotscher. It is an Italian Renaissance structure of buff brick and gray limestone with a tall campanile above the left side of the facade. The center is surmounted by a huge silvery dome.

UNIVERSALIST CHURCH OF THE MESSIAH (33) is on the southeast corner at Montgomery Avenue. The Gothic gray granite structure with limestone trim, erected in 1890, was designed by Hazel, Hurst & Huckel.

The main building of TEMPLE UNIVERSITY (34) is at the northeast corner of Montgomery Avenue.

The story of the birth and growth of Temple University forms one of the most inspiring chapters in the history of higher education.

In 1884 Dr. Russell H. Conwell, pastor of Grace Baptist Temple, Broad and Berks Streets, envisioned a mighty institution that would provide a liberal education for all who desired it. Today, on the spot where his dreams first placed it, stands Temple University —

464

Mitten Hall, Temple University
"Founded on 'Acres of Diamonds' "

Rear of Temple University Dormitories
"College Life . . . with a Touch of Home"

recognized as one of the country's leading seats of higher learning.

From a small group of young men, studying under Dr. Conwell's direction each evening in his home, the university has grown until it now has a student body of 12,000.

The university's climb to its present degree of development, although rapid, was attended with difficulty. Dr. Conwell's congregation supported him, but in many quarters he met with rebuffs. Within four years the original student body of less than 10 had grown to 590. At this time, 1888, Dr. Conwell obtained a college charter, and three years later the college received the right to confer degrees. Until then it had operated exclusively as a night school.

The Theological School was opened in 1893, and in 1901 an evening course in medicine was added. In the same year Samaritan Hospital, which has now become Temple University Hospital, was brought within the provisions of the charter, and a school of pharmacy was opened. In 1907 a charter was issued changing the name from Temple College to Temple University, and during the same year the Philadelphia Dental College, one of the oldest schools of dentistry in the United States, was absorbed by Temple.

Born in South Worthington, Mass., in 1843, Dr. Conwell received his higher education at Yale. Even while devoting much of his time to the college he was gaining wide fame as a lecturer. The lecture, *Acres of Diamonds,* which he delivered thousands of times throughout the country, inspired millions and brought large financial returns. This money was used to further the development of Temple. Dr. Conwell received the Bok Award in 1923.

At the time of the founder's death in 1925, enrollment at the university had reached 10,000. It had expanded to seven professional schools, three undergraduate schools, three hospitals, a high school, and an elementary laboratory school ; for a time a special course in aviation was offered.

Dr. Conwell was succeeded as president of the university by Dr. Charles E. Beury, his associate for many years, who continues to improve the standards and fulfill the ambitions of the founder. During President Beury's administration the university's assets have been increased between $6,000,000 and $7,000,000 and all of its departments awarded grade-A ratings.

Most of the newest and largest buildings, of modern collegiate Gothic design in gray field stone and limestone trim, are in the vicinity of Broad Street and Montgomery Avenue. A few are scattered in other parts of the city.

Conwell Hall, northeast corner of Broad Street and Montgomery Avenue, houses the administrative offices and the School of Commerce. This hall, built before the founder's death, is the first unit of the proposed Tower group, which, when completed, will consist of five skyscraper buildings. It is distinctive for its crenelated turrets on the Broad Street facade. Adjacent on the north is Carnell Hall, completed in 1929 and named for the late Dean Laura Carnell. In the same block, and likewise facing Broad Street, are older buildings which house Teachers' College, College of Liberal Arts and Sciences, and evening schools.

Mitten Memorial Hall, northeast corner of Broad and Berks Streets, completed in 1931 as a recreational center, has a broad facade with three high bays in the center. At the corner of the building, in a carved niche of Gothic design, is a sculptured stone image of the Temple "Owl," traditional symbol of the university. Within the building is a lofty, spacious auditorium. In addition to lounge and auditorium, Mitten Hall contains a dining room, a cafeteria, and other club conveniences.

Right, on Berks Street, a half block away, is the Thomas D. Sullivan Memorial Library, dedicated in 1936, its four high Gothic traceried windows separated by buttresses. The southern end of the wall on Watts Street discards the Gothic and is a frank treatment of the tall vertical piers of the stackroom. Exposed hammerbeam trusses support the roof of the reading room on the second floor.

The School of Medicine building, Broad and Ontario Streets, opposite the Temple University Hospital, was dedicated in 1930. The structure is built of brick and limestone. The Georgian characteristics are mainly evidenced by its triple arched entrance, pedimented center windows above the entrance and round top windows of the entire sixth floor between the wings. William H. Lee, architect of Mitten and Carnell Halls and Sullivan Library, was likewise the designer of this building. One of the outstanding departments of the hospital is the Bronchoscopic Clinic, directed by Dr. Chevalier Jackson, who perfected the use of the bronchoscope.

The Oak Lane Country Day School was acquired in 1931 and became the laboratory division of Teachers' College. Other schools now include those of Chiropody, Oral Hygiene, Music, Law, Secretarial Training, and various specialized courses.

Today the remains of Russell H. Conwell rest within the shadows of the institution, itself the finest monument to the lifework of this patriot, preacher, educator, and friend of mankind.

GRACE BAPTIST TEMPLE (35), where Dr. Conwell was pastor for years, is on the southeast corner at Berks Street. The granite Romanesque structure, designed by Thomas Lonsdale, was completed in 1893. Above the two center doorways is a huge fan-shaped window. The edifice is surmounted by a green dome.

The 108TH FIELD ARTILLERY ARMORY (36) is on the left at 2110. This was the first regiment of State militia to use the name "National Guards."

The NATIONAL HEADQUARTERS OF THE AMERICAN FEDERATION OF HOSIERY WORKERS (37) is at 2319, on the right. The remodeled facade of the building is of modern design in buff plaster and glass brick.

DROPSIE COLLEGE (38), just below York Street, on the right, is a school of cognate learning, established in 1907 in accordance with the will of Moses A. Dropsie. The college asks no tuition fee, but each applicant for admission must have a B. A. degree, a knowledge of the Hebrew language, and an acquaintance with modern languages. The school cooperates with all other colleges which offer courses in Semitic law and languages. The two-story gray limestone building of Italian Renaissance style was designed by the architect, Tachau, and built in 1911.

GRATZ COLLEGE (39), around the corner from Dropsie College, is the oldest Hebrew educational institution in the United States. Founded in 1895 under a trust fund established in 1856 by the will of Hyman Gratz, it specializes in the teaching of Hebrew law. Gratz College encourages its students to take postgraduate courses at Dropsie.

The college has occupied the present site since 1909. The building was designed by Pilcher & Tachau in Greek Revival manner.

The oldest Hebrew congregation in Philadelphia, and the second oldest in the United States, is the Congregation Mikveh Israel. The MIKVEH ISRAEL SYNAGOGUE (40) is on the southeast corner at York Street.

The present building, erected in 1909, was designed by Pilcher & Tachau. It is a monumental limestone structure of Italian Renaissance design with three large arched doors between four pairs of engaged Ionic columns. Between these columns are arched niches. The interior is Georgian in blue, gold, and gray. The barrel-vaulted foyer is also Georgian.

The NORTH BROAD STREET STATION (41) of the Reading Railroad stands on the northeast corner at Huntingdon Street. Built in 1929 after plans by Horace Trumbauer and constructed of light buff Indiana limestone on a granite base, the building resembles a Greek temple with its colonnade of 12 Ionic columns facing Broad Street.

The PHILADELPHIA NATIONAL LEAGUE BASEBALL PARK (42), extending from Huntingdon Street to Lehigh Avenue on the left, was opened in 1887. It is the home of the major league team known locally as the Phillies. The seating capacity is 18,500. Boxing and wrestling shows and football games are also held in this park. It is an enclosure of red brick and corrugated iron, painted green.

The NORTH PHILADELPHIA STATION (43) of the Pennsylvania Railroad is·on the northwest corner, at Glenwood Avenue. Designed by A. C. Shand, and built in 1900 it is a gray limestone and terra-cotta structure in Italian Renaissance and French Chateau style.

The MASONIC HOME FOR THE AGED (44), on the southeast corner at Ontario Street, is one of the many charitable institutions maintained by Masons. The three-story building of brown brick and limestone in Renaissance style, was designed by Philip Johnson and erected in 1924.

TEMPLE UNIVERSITY HOSPITAL (45) (formerly Samaritan Hospital), on the northeast corner at Ontario Street, and the TEMPLE UNIVERSITY MEDICAL COLLEGE (46), facing it on the left, are operated by the university.

Broad Street, Germantown Avenue, and Erie Avenue intersect a few blocks beyond. Around this intersection the once prevalent brownstone-front dwellings are slowly giving way to modern shops.

Roosevelt Boulevard intersects at 4400 North Broad Street.

R. from Broad St. on Roosevelt Blvd.

The Roosevelt Boulevard, one of Philadelphia's happier civic developments, named in honor of Theodore Roosevelt, is a refreshingly verdant parkway. It is a main traffic artery through northern Philadelphia and forms a part of the Lincoln Highway between Philadelphia and New York.

The lawns and woodlands of HUNTING PARK (a), right, at the intersection of Old York Road and the Boulevard, give to a large area along the highway a forest grace and felicity. The ground was a race track from the time of the opening in 1818 until 1854, when it was dedicated as a park for the people of Philadelphia. A music pavilion, tennis courts, a lake, and a carrousel are in the park, which is under the jurisdiction of Fairmount Park Commission.

The Boulevard, from Old York Road to Pennypack Circle, consists of three roadways. The four-lane artery in the center is separated from the two-lane, one-way roadways on either side by pleasing strips of shade trees, shrubs, and grass. Traffic on the center highway is restricted to private cars; commercial vehicles use the outer lanes. From Pennypack Circle to City Line the Boulevard is laid out in two one-way roads, each two lanes in width.

At Adams Avenue and the Boulevard, right, is the FRIENDS' HOSPITAL FOR MENTAL AND NERVOUS DISEASE (b). The first building on this site was erected in 1817. It is a private institution founded in 1813 under the auspices of Philadelphia Quakers.

Next to it at Adams and Fisher's Avenues on the right, and covering an area of 43 acres, is OAKLAND CEMETERY (c) opened in 1881.

On the left, at Adams Avenue and the Boulevard, the giant department store and warehouse of SEARS, ROEBUCK & CO. (d), which was built in 1920, rises in terra-cotta tiers. A tour of this branch of the country's largest mail order house provides an exciting glimpse into the technique of a highly efficient industry—girls dashing about on roller skates and collecting goods from a giant conglomeration of bins; merchandise whizzing through chutes; thousands of workers performing, in carefully allotted time, the minutely specialized tasks involved in filling mail orders.

The SHRINERS' HOME FOR CRIPPLED CHILDREN (e), on the

469

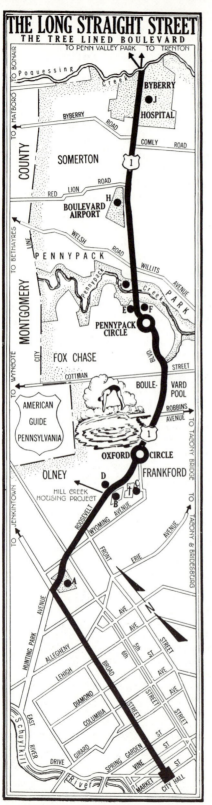

a. Hunting Park

b. Friends' Hospital for Mental and
    Nervous Diseases

c. Oakland Cemetery

d. Sears, Roebuck & Co.

e. Shriners' Home for Crippled
    Children

f. Baptist Home

f. Evangelical Home for the Aged

g. Pennypack Park

h. Boulevard Airport

j. Philadelphia Hospital for Mental
    Diseases

left at North Pennypack Circle, was established in 1926. Maintained by Lu Lu Temple, Nobles of the Mystic Shrine, it cares for crippled children, free of charge.

On the right at North Pennypack Circle is the BAPTIST HOME (f), for aged and infirm members of that faith, and on the northeast corner at Strahle Street is the EVANGELICAL HOME FOR THE AGED (f).

The Boulevard crosses PENNYPACK PARK (g) *(see City Tours 18 and 19)*, one of the largest units of the Fairmount Park system.

At Red Lion Road, left, is the BOULEVARD AIRPORT (h), a passenger-carrying air center used by sightseeing planes as a terminus for air tours of the city.

The PHILADELPHIA HOSPITAL FOR MENTAL DISEASES (j), at Southampton Road and the Boulevard, marks the end of the outgoing trip. The hospital, operated by Philadelphia County, with assistance of a State appropriation, is the largest institution of its kind in Pennsylvania. The women's and children's buildings are on the left, the men's on the right.

Retrace on Roosevelt Blvd.; R. on Broad St.

On the northeast corner of the Boulevard and Broad Street are the HOME FOR AGED WIDOWS AND WIVES OF FREE MASONS and the WILLIAM L. ELKINS MASONIC ORPHANAGE FOR GIRLS (47).

Broad Street north of Roosevelt Boulevard becomes the business section of Logan, with its many shops lining both sides of the street.

At Duncannon Street, on the northwest corner, is the HOLY CHILD ROMAN CATHOLIC CHURCH (48), erected in 1909. Its design is adapted from the Norman style. Constructed of Mount Airy granite, the church edifice and the rectory and school, between which it stands, form a harmonious composition.

The most noteworthy features of the interior are the reredos of the main altar and traceried west window. The light from the red and blue stained glass, composed in the manner of thirteenth century French windows, filters through the delicate tracery to produce a purple glow.

The chancel is richly adorned with stone and marble. On the high altar, executed in gold-veined Sienna marble trimmed with gold-veined black marble, is a six-foot ebony crucifix of filigree with gold corpus. The golden Sienna marble font in the octagonal baptistry has a finely carved bowl supported by eight decorative angels symbolizing the eight beatitudes.

On the right, beginning at Fisher's Avenue and continuing to Tabor Road, is CLARKSON PARK (49), separating Old York Road from Broad Street and coming to a point where the two streets meet.

At the point is a monument erected in memory of George McKenzie Poinsett, a native of this neighborhood, who was killed in action at Vera Cruz, Mexico, April 21, 1914. The memorial was erected by the Logan Improvement League.

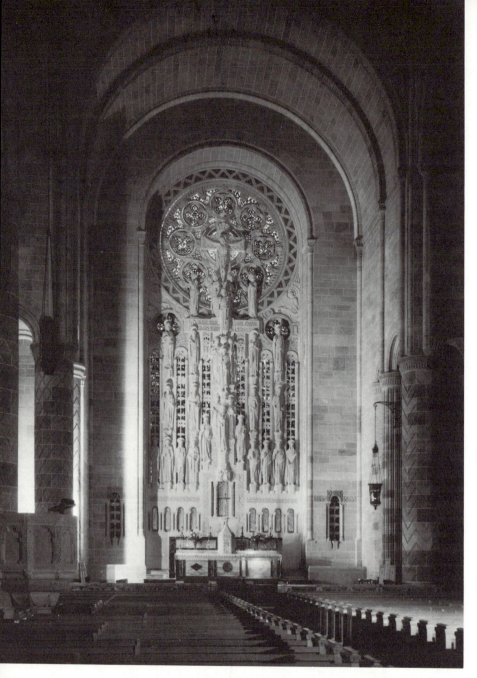

Main Altar, Church of the Holy Child
"I will enter unto the altar of God"

WHERE HOUSES STAND IN REGIMENTS (CITY TOUR 5)

At Old York Road is the JEWISH HOSPITAL (50). The first building, designed by Furness Hewett, was erected in 1871. Fresh vegetables for the use of the institution are grown in an extensive garden in the rear.

The WIDENER HOME FOR CRIPPLED CHILDREN (51), on the southwest corner at Olney Avenue, cares for and attempts to teach useful occupations to the afflicted. The rolling lawns of this spacious charitable institution extend two blocks on Broad Street and three blocks on Olney Avenue. Designed by Horace Trumbauer, it was built in 1904.

L. from Broad St. on Old York Rd.

Approximately 100 yards to the left of Old York Road, about midway between Olney Avenue and Nedro Avenue (about half the distance above the 5700 block), is the SITE OF THE BUTLER PLACE (51a) which was built about the middle of the eighteenth century. Pierce Butler, Senator from South Carolina, purchased it as a country home in 1790. In 1910 it became the home of Owen Wister, author of *The Virginian.*

With Senator Butler's death in 1822 the house passed to his sister Frances (or Sarah). Upon her death, 10 years later, the house became the property of the Senator's grandson, Pierce Butler, who married Fanny Kemble, novelist, daughter of Charles Kemble, actor.

At the close of the Civil War, her oldest daughter, Sarah, inherited the house. A short time afterward Sarah became the wife of Dr. Owen Jones Wister, of Germantown. At about this time, the original acreage was cut down by other heirs disposing of their shares, and finally, in 1925, the estate and isolated farm, surrounded by blocks of city dwellings, gave way to the trend of the times. The old homestead, outhouses, and stables were torn down. Streets were cut through and the property was divided into lots.

The estate, originally some 20 acres in extent, was believed to have been owned and occupied originally by a French family of the name of deBenneville.

Retrace on Old York Rd.; R. on Broad St.; R. on Lehigh Ave.

Extending from Twentieth to Twenty-first Streets is SHIBE PARK (52), home of the Philadelphia American League Baseball Club, the Athletics, who have captured nine American League championships and five World Series under the leadership of Connie Mack. The park, opened in 1908 at a cost of $654,000, seats 33,000.

L. from Lehigh Ave. on 22d St.; L. on Montgomery Ave.

The WAGNER FREE INSTITUTE OF SCIENCE (53), at Seventeenth Street *(library open daily 10 to 9; museum open Wed. and Sat. 2 to 5; adm. free),* was founded by William Wagner in 1855 to give instruction on scientific subjects to persons who, like himself, were unable to obtain a formal education. Wagner, a retired merchant, originated the school in a series of lectures he gave in his home, Elm Grove, opposite the present building. The edifice, built of plastered brick, with a massive pediment above the facade, is of classical revival design. It was opened in 1865.

Museum exhibits, which are used primarily by students, include 25,000 specimens in mineralogy, paleontology, petrology, conchology, geology, and zoology.

On display are some of the fossil remains of the huge "thunder lizard," an amphibious dinosaur which roamed the flooded plains around Canon City, Colorado, millions of years ago.

The institute maintains a comprehensive reference library *(open weekdays 10 to 9)*. School teachers and their classes are invited to tour the museum in groups, and may, by special appointment, visit the displays when the museum is closed to the general public. A public circulating library occupies a wing of the building.

R. from Montgomery Ave. on 17th St.; R. on Girard Ave.

GIRARD COLLEGE (54) lies behind the high stone wall at Corinthian Avenue *(see Points of Interest)*.

Also at this intersection, left, is LANKENAU HOSPITAL (55), formerly known as the German Hospital, founded in 1860. Joseph Lankenau's election to the presidency of the institution in 1869 resulted in many improvements. The hospital maintains a deaconesses' home, children's hospital, old folk's home, and a school for girls, all housed in the Mary J. Drexel Home, a building erected on the grounds in 1888.

L. from Girard Ave. on Corinthian; R. on Fairmount.

On Corinthian Avenue, before reaching Fairmount Avenue, the high gray walls of the EASTERN PENITENTIARY (56) rise above the roofs of some of the surrounding dwellings. The entrance gate to the prison is on Fairmount Avenue.

L. from Fairmount Ave. on 22d St.; L. on Spring Garden.

On the left at Seventeenth Street is the building of the PHILADELPHIA HIGH SCHOOL FOR GIRLS (57), the first public secondary school for girls in Philadelphia. Next door to the school is the WILLS HOSPITAL (58), one of the leading eye hospitals of the world. It was built in 1932. Opposite the hospital, on the right, is the UNITED STATES MINT (59) *(see Points of Interest)*.

R. from Spring Garden St. on 15th.

On the southwest corner at Race Street is the FRIENDS MEETING HOUSE (60), built in 1856. This is the headquarters of the Friends Yearly Meeting and houses administrative offices.

The building is a two-story, red-brick structure with an attic and two shallow side wings. The front and rear facades are similar, with their three large double entrance doors and large window. Simple pediments surmount the facades and the two side wings. A simple

474

cornice extends around the entire building. The meetinghouse is set within a large brick court surrounded by buildings of later date.

The structure contains two auditoriums for worship. The larger auditorium, facing Race Street, is open to the public on Sunday evenings during the winter months, as the Race Street Forum. A library containing about 2,000 volumes and pamphlets is maintained.

At 1506 Race Street, near the corner, is the CO-OPERATIVE CENTER (61), devoted to co-operative trading.

L. from 15th St. on Arch.

Midway between Fifteenth and Broad Streets is the central building of the PHILADELPHIA BRANCH OF THE YOUNG MEN'S CHRISTIAN ASSOCIATION (62), built in 1929.

R. from Arch St. on Broad to City Hall.

HISTORIC GERMANTOWN
City Tour 6

IN GERMANTOWN are many mansions which were old when the British occupied Philadelphia, homes whose quiet-colored walls have looked upon the gallantries of the King's officers and the coquetries of Tory maids. These are houses full of years and memories and a quiet dignity. Built in an age when privacy was deemed the essence of a home, they are set in spacious gardens and the common world is shut out by high stone walls. Today they still have a quality of aloofness, deepened rather than diminished by the years. Aged vines embower their walls and gateways, and the heavy window draperies of an older day shield their interiors from the glances of the curious.

The past is revered in Germantown, perhaps, because it is so closely linked with the present. The Battle of Germantown was fought among these very homes and gardens. Many of the houses bear the marks of cannon and musket balls.

Yet, not all Germantown cherishes yesterday; on its northern fringe, where it merges with Chestnut Hill, youth is served and serves in turn the commands of imperious today. The street scene moves to a jazzier tempo. The common sight here is not of age, but of debutante and subdebutante in tweeds and flat-heeled shoes. It is a section of Philadelphia peopled by Americans conscious of their own modernism, who find distinction in a present of hard work and hard play rather than in the recollection of past glories.

N. from City Hall on Broad St. to Butler (3800 north) ; L. on Butler ; on Germantown Ave.

Just north of Wayne Junction, left, with its rim of railroads and nineteenth century brick factory buildings, rises Negley's Hill, sur-

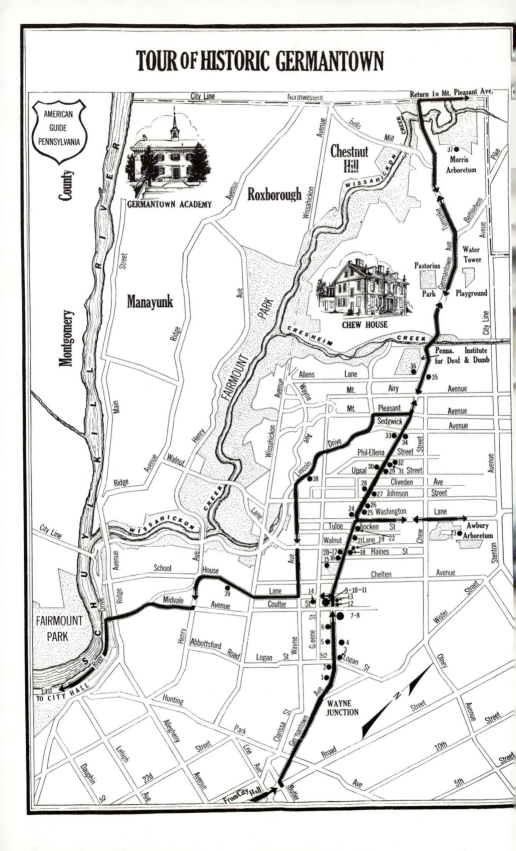

TOUR OF HISTORIC GERMANTOWN

AMERICAN GUIDE PENNSYLVANIA

County

Montgomery

GERMANTOWN ACADEMY

Roxborough

Chestnut Hill

Manayunk

CHEW HOUSE

FAIRMOUNT PARK

Morris Arboretum

Return To Mt. Pleasant Ave.

Water Tower

Pastorius Park

Playground

Penna. Institute for Deaf & Dumb

Allens Lane

Mt. Airy

Mt. Pleasant

Sedgwick

Phil-Ellena Street

Upsal Street

Cliveden Ave

Johnson Street

Washington Lane

Awbury Arboretum

hocken St

Walnut Lane

Haines St

Chelten Avenue

Lane

Coulter

Midvale Avenue

Abbottsford Road

Logan

FAIRMOUNT PARK

To CITY HALL

WAYNE JUNCTION

From City Hall

N

Historic Germantown (City Tour 6)

mounted by LOUDOUN (1), one of the fine old mansions for which Germantown is famous.

Patrician white pine trees and a terraced garden frame the two-and-a-half story structure, with its gabled roof, hipped at one end, and its ivy-covered walls of irregular stone, plastered over. Although the house was erected after the Revolution by Thomas Armat, whose descendants occupy it, the handsome leaded fanlight above the paneled front door and a pillared portico with a simple wooden pediment and wooden columns express the Colonial spirit.

On the left, at 4840, is the SITE OF THE WAGNER HOUSE (2), which was built in 1747 and used as a hospital after the Battle of Germantown. The house was demolished in 1915, and a row of dwelling houses was built upon the site.

On the right at Logan Street is Hood's Cemetery, known also as the LOWER BURIAL GROUND (3). The oldest tombstone here is

---

1. Loudoun
2. Site of the Wagner House
3. Lower Burial Ground
4. Kunders House
5. Gilbert Stuart House
6. Germantown Historical Society
7. Grumblethorpe
8. Watson House
9. Germantown Friends Meeting House
10. Germantown Friends Library
11. Morris House
12. Market Square Presbyterian Church
13. Market Square
14. Germantown Academy
15. Vernon Park
16. Germantown Branch of the Y. W. C. A.
17. Town Hall
18. Germantown High School
19. Green Tree Inn
20. Wyck
21. Germantown Mennonite Church
22. Keyser House
23. Awbury Arboretum and Park
24. Johnson House
25. Concord School House
26. Upper Burial Ground
27. Chew Mansion
28. Upsala
29. Billmeyer House
30. "Sparrowjack's House"
31. First Church of the Brethren
32. St. Michael's Lutheran Church
33. Luthern Orphanage
34. Lovett Memorial Library
35. Lutheran Theological Seminary
36. Pennsylvania School for the Deaf
37. Morris Arboretum
38. Germantown Unitarian Church
39. William Penn Charter School

marked 1708. Crossbones and the words, "Memendo Mory," a mis-
spelled Latin phrase meaning "remember we must die," have been
chiseled on another ancient gravestone built into the cemetery wall
on Logan Street. William Hood, who amassed a fortune in Cuba,
provided for the erection of the marble wall, balustrade, and gateway. He and his wife were buried just inside the gates of the cemetery.

At 5109 is the old KUNDERS HOUSE (4). The street numbers
are confusing at this point, 5100 on the right being directly opposite
5000 on the left.

The Kunders house stands on the spot where Thones Kunders,
original settler, built his first house in the New World in 1683. Part
of the north wall of the dwelling is believed to be a remnant of the
wall of the original structure.

The building, constructed of stone and plaster and three stories in
height, has been remodeled several times. Small wrought-iron balconies to each of the second-story windows and one to the center window of the third floor are recent additions. At the right of the Colonial
doorway there is a bay window of English style.

Here were held the first meetings in Germantown of the Society
of Friends, and from this house, in 1688, came the first public protest against slavery in America. This was contained in a paper written by Daniel Pastorius and signed by him and three others.

GILBERT STUART HOUSE (5) is at 5140 Germantown Avenue.
Occupied at times by some of Germantown's most prominent families,
including the Shippens, Bringhursts, and Wisters, the house is most
famous for its connection with Gilbert Stuart, the early American
painter. Here he painted a full-length portrait of Cornplanter, famous
Indian chief ; and here, in 1796, he did one of his well-known portraits of George Washingtion. While posing, Washington was entertained by the daughters of Benjamin Chew, to whom the President
gave full credit for any success he achieved as a sitter. The portrait,
property of the Athenaeum, is now being exhibited at the Boston
Museum of Fine Arts. The house is a two-story-and-attic building,
with dormer windows and brick chimneys at either end.

For a time Stuart used the barn in the rear of the property as a
studio. It later served as a manufacturing shop and as a schoolhouse.
Possibly because of the crows that are among the numerous birds
frequenting the place, it has become known as "The Corvy."

Only tulip trees and hydrangeas remain today of the old garden
where Washington used to lounge between sittings.

A Colonial building of rough gray stone at 5214 Germantown
Avenue houses the GERMANTOWN HISTORICAL SOCIETY (6)
(open weekdays 1 to 5 ; adm. free). The building contains the
society's collection of relics, china, portraits by Charles Willson Peale,

478

and a library of works on Germantown. The house, three stories in height, built about 1772, was known successively as the Conyngham, the Wister, and the Hacker house. It was renovated in 1927 and taken over by the society.

The estate's brick wall, draped with vines and roses, encloses a garden bordered with box and other evergreens.

At 5267 is GRUMBLETHORPE (7), the Wister "Big House." When built by John Wister in 1744, it was the first summer home in Germantown. Originally constructed of timber and native stone, it was altered in 1808, and today the rubblestone building, now pebble-dashed in front, reflects both the earlier and the more sophisticated later architecture.

The once fine gardens in the rear of the house were developed by Charles J. Wister, grandson of the builder and one of the leading horticulturists of his day. Some of the fruit trees have been productive for almost two centuries ; a beautiful specimen of the purple beech graces the garden, and a gingko tree in front of the garden is one of the largest female species in the country. Wister, who was interested in mineralogy and astronomy as well as botany, built an observatory in the yard in 1835 ; four feet of the original wall still stands.

In her sprightly diary, Sally Wister described the entertaining persons and events revolving around the Wister house in the days when the British occupied Philadelphia. One of Sally's most whimsical stories centers on the *British Grenadier*, a life-size figure painted on a wooden panel, supposedly by Major Andre, for the *Meschianza*, the pageant held by British officers in May 1778 as a farewell to Sir William Howe. The panel, once displayed in the hallway of the house, was used by Sally's father, Daniel Wister, and a number of American officers visiting his home, to deflate the ego of one Major Tilly, who boasted his anxiety to meet the British in battle. The panel was placed near the front door in the dim light of a lantern, and Tilly was summoned. A hidden officer demanded to know if any rebel officers were in the house. Tilly fled through a rear door and was making for Washington's camp when he fell into a mill pond. His fellow officers overtook him and explained the deception.

Some of the incidents related about the house, however, are grim. During the Battle of Germantown the British General, James Agnew, was brought to the house bleeding profusely from mortal wounds and was laid on the floor of the west parlor. His blood soaked into the boards, and the stain remains, despite the scrubbings of one and a half centuries.

A few doors beyond Grumblethorpe, at 5275-77, is the WATSON HOUSE (8), where Washington is said to have spent one or two nights. The British held a court martial in the upstairs parlor. During the fever epidemic of 1793 Thomas Jefferson, then Secretary of

State, and Edmund Randolph, Attorney General, took refuge here.

Although there is no record of the date of the erection of this building, its association with Revolutionary War events gives it an air of antiquity. It is a two-and-one-half story building of plaster with a slag shingled roof.

Between 1824 and 1868 this and the adjoining dwelling served as headquarters for the National Bank of Germantown, and parts of the old vaults may still be seen. The house is named for John F. Watson, the historian, who was cashier of the bank for 34 years. While a resident there, Watson compiled the *Annals of Philadelphia*.

On the left, just north of Coulter Street, which it faces, is the GERMANTOWN FRIENDS MEETINGHOUSE (9), set far back from the street, with a playground and graveyard separating it from the Germantown Friends School on the same premises. The present building was erected in 1871 on land conveyed to the meeting in 1693 by Jacob Shoemaker. A meetinghouse has existed on this site since the completion of the first stone building in 1705.

Daniel Pastorius, who was born September 26, 1651, and died September 27, 1719, is believed to be buried in the graveyard, although the exact location of his grave has never been determined.

On a small plot of ground adjoining the meetinghouse grounds is the GERMANTOWN FRIENDS LIBRARY (10), a comprehensive reference library much used by the residents of the community.

The MORRIS HOUSE (11), at 5442 Germantown Avenue, retains its delightful gardens and fine orchards and vineyards.

The house was built in 1772 by David Deschler, a wealthy India merchant. This two-story-and-attic plastered gray stone structure with white trim has a pedimented doorway with recessed heavy paneled door flanked by engaged Tuscan columns. Between the end chimneys are two pedimented dormers with round-topped windows. Twenty-four panel windows on the first and second floors have frames with molded sills. The cornice has modillions and dentils.

A large hall extends through the center of the house, widening beyond the front room to contain a graceful stairway. White wood paneling in all the rooms and halls rises to the height of the chair rail. Fireplaces faced with dark Pennsylvania marble, overmantels, and woodwork exemplify Colonial craftsmanship. Many pieces of the original furniture, china, and silverware remain.

Here, in 1793, when a fever epidemic was ravaging Philadelphia, President Washington found refuge. At that time the first President and his family attended services in the Market Square Church, almost directly across the square from the house.

The present MARKET SQUARE PRESBYTERIAN CHURCH (12), facing on the square from the eastern side, was erected in 1888, upon the site of a Dutch Reformed church established in 1733. It

480

retains some relics of the early edifice, including a bell, brass angels, a weathercock, and a steeple which was perforated by bullets when the Paxton Boys descended upon Germantown in search of the Conestoga Indians who fled Lancaster County after members of their tribe had been massacred.

MARKET SQUARE (13), on which the church fronts, in the early days of the community was Germantown's market place, the site of its stocks, its jail, and its firehouse. In recent years the plot has been transformed into a plaza, with tree-shaded lawns. A memorial to the Civil War dead stands in the square.

L. from Germantown Ave. on School House Lane.

At Greene Street is one of the oldest schools in the United States, the GERMANTOWN ACADEMY (14). It was founded as the Germantown Union School in 1760. The buildings that compose the school group, like numerous others in the vicinity, were used as a hospital for British soldiers after the Battle of Germantown. Some of the British dead were buried in the grounds. The crown of England still surmounts the spire over the belfry which contains a bell brought to the city in 1774 in the *Polly*, a British tea ship which the citizens of Philadelphia prevented from docking. The bell was carried back to England and was reshipped in 1784.

The local dressed stone of the two-story, six-room schoolhouse is veiled with ivy. Except for the modillions in the cornice, the facade is bare of ornament. Recent additions in the Colonial spirit have been made so skillfully that it is difficult to distinguish old from new. The years have wrought few changes in the appearance of Germantown Academy, and the original building is still in use.

Retrace on School House Lane ; L. on Germantown Ave.

Between School House Lane and a point slightly north of Chelten Avenue is one part of Germantown's business and amusement sections.

Just north of Chelten Avenue, on the left, is VERNON PARK (15), extending west to Greene Street. Some of the holly trees in the park are noteworthy. The mansion in the park's center was built in 1803 by James Matthews and later was purchased by John Wister, who named it in honor of Washington's home, Mount Vernon. At one time it housed a branch of the Free Library of Philadelphia and later was the headquarters of the Site and Relic Society of Germantown.

City Council's Committee on City Property, on March 29, 1937, approved the leasing of historic Wister house to the Germantown Community Council for $1 a year. The council, which represents 40 civic, educational, and social organizations in Germantown, agreed to put the house in good condition, using $925 collected for the purpose and a $7,000 WPA grant. The structure will be used as a community center, with art exhibitions and similar events to be held there.

481

Germantown Academy
"Its steeple still wears the crown of England"

The library is now housed in the Carnegie Library building on the north side of the park. A battle monument, a memorial fountain, a shaft to Pastorius, a band pavilion, and an open plaza are also on the grounds. The GERMANTOWN BRANCH OF THE YOUNG WOMEN'S CHRISTIAN ASSOCIATION (16) is on the northern border of the Park.

Germantown's TOWN HALL (17), a striking white building surmounted by a tall spire, is on the left at Haines Street.

482

The building is three stories in height and constructed of white sandstone with steel construction and granite base. Above the six Ionic columns of the semi-circular porch is a denticulated cornice and above this a railing. The building was completed in 1923 by John Molitor. It was dedicated in 1925 and supplanted the old Town Hall, which was used as a hospital during the Civil War. The clock and the bell in the tower were formerly in Independence Hall.

GERMANTOWN HIGH SCHOOL (18), one of Philadelphia's finest school buildings, sets back in a wide plot of well-kept lawn, studded with trees and interlaced with cement walks, at High Street, right.

Just north of High Street, adjoining the First Methodist Episcopal Church, right, is the old GREEN TREE INN (19), famous in the early days of Germantown as a rendezvous for sleighing and coaching parties. The building now is the parsonage of the church. Established in 1748 by Daniel Pastorius, grandson of the founder of Germantown, and maintained by him until his death in 1754, the inn was carried on under the direction of his widow. Here, in 1759, a group of citizens gathered to form the Germantown Union School, later Germantown Academy. Lafayette was a guest here, and a picture in the hall portrays his reception. The two-and-a-half story structure of field stone is of Colonial design, with three small plain dormers with segmental-topped windows and a six-paneled Dutch door.

WYCK (20), on the left at Germantown Avenue and Walnut Lane, is said to be a remnant of the oldest house in the community. Two and a half stories high, with a one-story kitchen wing, Wyck is a combination of two houses once divided by a paved wagonway. Horizontal trellises, beribboned with vines, accentuate the length of the 80-foot fronts of white plaster and rubble masonry. Luxurious ferns, drooping willows, and rare shade trees, including the famous Spanish chestnut planted by Washington and the white walnut grown from a slip planted by Lafayette at Belmont upon the occasion of his farewell visit to America, embower the house in foliage.

In the garden, roses bloom riotously in late spring mingling their fragrance with that of the hawthorn and lilac. A rose so old as to defy identification, a Burgundy rose, meadowsweet and crepe myrtle, pink lilies of the valley, purple and white drop, chimonanthus, which bloom at Christmas, fuchsias, oak-leaved hydrangeas, and hardy phlox make the garden among the loveliest in all Germantown.

The property, still in the hands of the family whose ancestors cleared the land, was used as a hospital during the Battle of Germantown. Reminders of that time, in the form of dark bloodstains on the floor, have withstood the years.

On the right, a few yards north of Herman Street and just north of Wyck, is the GERMANTOWN MENNONITE CHURCH (21), with a

483

The Wyck House
"A symphony of shutters and shadows"

Germantown Mennonite Church
Where a Picturesque Sect Worships

burial ground on the south side of the building. Built in 1770, the edifice, oldest Mennonite church in America, retains the original pews and furnishings, including a table on which, it is said, an early protest against slavery in America was written.

A tall tulip tree towers above this simple structure of gray field stone with painted white woodwork. A pediment forms a hood above the entrance door, on either side of which is a shuttered window of 24 small panes. A 16-pane window without shutters centers above the door. Between this window and the eaves is a date stone marked 1770.

On the northeast corner at Tulpehocken Street, set above the sidewalk and flanked by a wide garden, is the KEYSER HOUSE (22), built in 1738 by Dirck Keyser. It is believed to be the first two-story dwelling erected in the community and is one of Germantown's oldest houses. Keyser, a Mennonite, was one of the original settlers. He came to America from Amsterdam in 1688.

R. from Germantown Ave. on Washington Lane.

AWBURY ABBORETUM AND PARK (23) a picturesque and inviting spot, with its spacious gardens and woodland, stretches away to the right east of Chew Street. When the city took over the 40 acres of the old Awbury estate, it constructed in the grounds an artificial lake and stream, planted additional trees and shrubs, and provided seats along the paths and drives that interlace the woods and meadowland. Now and then turns in the drive bring into view old houses, reminders of the years past and typical of Germantown.

Retrace on Washington Lane; R. on Germantown Ave.

The gray stone JOHNSON HOUSE (24), at the northwest corner of Germantown Avenue and Washington Lane, now housing the Germantown Women's Club, was the center of fierce fighting during the Battle of Germantown. The house was erected in 1768 by John Johnson for his son and the latter's bride, the former Rachel Livezey. The extensive gardens, planted by the first mistress of the house, hold a wealth of hardy perennials along with familiar shrubs such as calycanthus, snowball, and Persian lilac, a glorious fig tree, and large beds of lilies of the valley.

Typical of Colonial Germantown's architecture is the solidly constructed native ledge stone house, two-and-one-half stories high, with a gabled roof. On the front facade two dormer windows intersect the large end chimneys, and a brass knocker and wrought-iron hinges decorate the split Dutch door. The interior of the house retains Colonial charm. The floors, woodwork, fireplace, and many of the windows are original. Much of the furniture is antique, and in the corner cupboards is the old china used during the pre-Revolutionary period.

In the battle, soldiers used as a breastwork the stone wall that separated the garden from that of the house next door. A northwest wall still bears marks of bullets and cannon balls. It is said that while the fighting raged, milkmaids carried their tasks to completion, despite warnings to seek safety. Thus, after the battle, British soldiers who ransacked the house found refreshments awaiting them.

On the right, a few yards north of Washington Lane, is the CONCORD SCHOOL HOUSE (25), set above the avenue and fronted by a four-and-a-half-foot stone wall. It was built in 1775 for the use of children who found it difficult to travel to the Germantown Union School during the winter months. The simple Colonial edifice is in fairly good condition.

Adjoining the school on the north is the old UPPER BURIAL GROUND (26). This is surrounded by a high stone wall, but parts of it may be seen through the narrow gate. The oldest gravestone is dated 1716. One grave is the resting place of three officers and six men killed in the battle.

The CHEW MANSION (27) *(private)*, on the right, surrounded by grounds occupying the entire block between Johnson and Cliveden Streets, was the scene of one of the most desperate phases of the battle.

In its first stages Washington's attack was successful. On the morning of October 3, 1777, the Continentals advanced under cover of a heavy fog and drove the British before them. The main assault had swept past the Chew house and was moving on towards the heart of Germantown when Washington discovered that five companies of British infantry had barricaded themselves in the Chew house and were threatening his force from the rear.

Maxwell's brigade was told off from the American reserves to storm the house, but the hot fire of the British within halted the attack. Cannon were brought up and the door was blown in. Men were sent forward to fire the mansion, but were shot down in the Chew grounds, and a messenger with a flag of truce and a demand for surrender suffered the same fate.

The heavy walls of the Chew home withstood bullets and cannon balls, and the Americans withdrew from Germantown. This they were forced to do because their own ranks had been thrown into confusion by one commander, General Stephen, who was confused by a dense fog ; and another, General Greene, whose troops came up too late to fit into Washington's plans.

After the battle, the Chew family, absent at the time, returned to the house and repaired the damage, but the building still bears marks of the encounter.

The house is one of the finest examples of domestic architecture in local Colonial style. The plans were made by Chief Justice Benjamin Chew, who began construction of the building in 1761. A Doric doorway, with pediment, dignifies the front entrance. The limestone belt course at the second floor level, the heavy modillioned cornice, projecting water table, and the fine roof line give a sense of quiet stability in contrast with the broken effect of the chimney, the dormer windows, urns, and pediments above the second floor.

The heavy masonry front of the two-and-a-half-story house is of faced Germantown stone quarried within one hundred yards of the house ; the other walls are of rubble masonry, plastered and marked to simulate dressed stone. The two wings were originally connected by quadrants. Behind the house, connected by an underground passage, a stable in virtually its original condition still shelters the old family coach.

Off the large central hall are small front rooms used as offices. All of the walls of the first story are beautifully wainscoted and have dentilated cornices. Mahogany top moldings on the stairway wainscoting and balustrade afford effective contrast with the white woodwork.

The estate was once the seat of romance. Four beautiful daughters entertained suitors in the house and walked with them in the garden. A few faded souvenirs treasured by the Chew family commemorate the romance of Peggy Chew and the ill-starred Major Andre, who was among the town's most popular beaus when the British Army was in Philadelphia.

Directly across Germantown Avenue from the Chew house is UPSALA (28), one of the finest examples of post-Revolutionary architecture in Philadelphia. The British were encamped on the site of this house for some time, and a tablet set in a large boulder in the front of the property lists the names of American officers killed in the battle that raged about this spot.

The ivy-covered house, standing amid verdant lawns, with a white fence running along the street border of the property, presents a peaceful picture. This two-and-a-half-story square gabled residence belonging to the Johnson family was begun in 1798 and was three years in the building. The pedimented porch of Upsala is mentioned by authors of books on architecture as one of the finest in America. At the top of three stone steps is a square platform with slender, fluted Doric columns. Engaged columns flank the high, fairly narrow stairway. The front of the house is veneered with three-inch ashlar of dressed Germantown stone, applied to a rubble wall ; the rear wall is plastered and has quoined corners, covered by a grapevine. The beauty of the interior is particularly marked in the delicately ornamented mantelpieces, fine cornices of Roman design gracefully modeled in plaster, paneled wainscoting throughout the house, and good wood finishes. The house contains three of the most prized hand-carved mantelpieces in America. Upsala belongs to a later period than most of Philadelphia's Colonial homes. The delicate design of the mantels and interior woodwork, the broad sweeping curves of the graceful staircases with their simple dark wood handrail and square molded balusters, definitely show the influence of the Adam style in their design.

Henry N. Johnson, one-time resident of Upsala, was an enthusiastic horticulturist, fond of cultivating grapes. Concord, Isabella, and Catawba vines to this day decorate the sunny walls of the house. In a small greenhouse attached to Upsala are a few old white jasmines and a century-old white camellia, which used to bear a hundred flowers at once.

The BILLMEYER HOUSE (29), on the right, north of Upsal Street, bears many scars received during the assault on the Chew house. A tablet in the front of the building marks the spot where Continental officers held a council of war to determine the best means of attacking the barricaded Chew home. Erected in 1727, the Billmeyer house is an interesting example of an early Germantown two-family stone dwelling. Steps on the outer side lead up from the pavement to each doorway, with simply designed wrought-iron balustrades and two seats placed back to back on the stoop.

Opposite the Billmeyer house is "SPARROWJACK'S HOUSE" (30), which received its name from John Bardley, an occupant, whom City Council engaged to procure English sparrows to combat a plague of caterpillars.

The Billmeyer House
"A battle-scarred veteran of the Revolution"

Historic Germantown (City Tour 6)

On the northeast corner at Montana Street stands the FIRST CHURCH OF THE BRETHREN (31), mother church of the Dunkard sect in America. From 1760 to 1770 a wooden building housed the congregation while the present stone church was being erected. This latter building was remodeled in 1896 and again in 1915. The burial ground in the rear has been neatly kept and holds the dust of 2,000 persons.

During the battle the church was the scene of vigorous action. In the loft, Christopher Sauer had stored a number of sheets of the third edition of the Sauer Bible. British soldiers seized the sheets and used them as musket wadding. Sauer, however, collected enough unspoiled sheets to make complete Bibles for each of his children. A tablet within the church honors the memory of this pioneer scriptural printer, who became a bishop in 1753.

At Phil-Ellena Street, on the northeast corner, stands ST. MICHAEL'S LUTHERAN CHURCH (32). Set far back from the street, with a graveyard at both the front and back, St. Michael's Church holds much historic interest. Here for a time Rev. Henry Melchior Muhlenberg, the noted cleric-soldier, served as pastor. The present church is the third on the site. The Colonial structure was looted by British soldiers who dismantled the organ and ran through the streets blowing on the pipes. The first church was built in 1730, and the graveyard contains many stones with curious Colonial inscriptions.

The small, stone building bordering the sidewalk was erected before 1740 and through its early history served as a schoolhouse, the first in Germantown.

The LUTHERAN ORPHANAGE (33), is the only Lutheran children's asylum in the city. It was established in 1859.

The LOVETT MEMORIAL LIBRARY (34), 6945 Germantown Avenue, diagonally above the orphanage, is a branch of the Free Library of Philadelphia.

The library was founded in 1885 and the one-story-and-attic building was erected year later. It has a one-story wing, used as the children's department. The building is constructed of stone with a shingled gable at each side of the entrance.

In a deep hollow just over the crest of a rise beyond the library, lies the business section of Sedgwick, a compact double strip of small stores compressed within a half-block. Victorian type residences of heavy stone rim the bowl of neighborhood commerce, presenting a sharp contrast between past and present.

On the right, north of Allen's Lane, is the LUTHERAN THEOLOGICAL SEMINARY (35), with a splendid memorial to Rev. Henry Muhlenberg on the front lawn.

The PENNSYLVANIA SCHOOL FOR THE DEAF (36), 7500 Germantown Avenue, is distinguished by its acres of green lawn, and its great, gray buildings set on gentle slopes, far back from the avenue. "P. S. D.," as the school is known throughout Germantown, is the largest oral school for the deaf in the United States.

The institution had its beginning in a small shop. David Seixas, proprietor of a grocery store on Market Street near Seventeenth, gathered together a few deaf and dumb waifs who had been left to roam the streets uncared for. In his small shop he opened a school, taught the children what he could, and clothed and fed them. That was in 1819. One year later a town meeting was called by a group of public-spirited citizens whose attention had been drawn to Seixas' efforts, and the school was founded.

Through the years it has been enlarged and improved. Its 535 boys and girls, from 6 to 21 years old, receive a thorough vocational and academic training. All the pupils are instructed orally by the lip-reading method and are taught to use speech. State appropriations, endowments, and the tuitions of paying pupils support the institution.

Germantown Avenue passes over Chestnut Hill and merges with Germantown Pike.

R. from Germantown Pike on City Line Ave.

The MORRIS ARBORETUM (37), on City Line Avenue *(open Wed., Thur., Sat., and Sun. 1 to 5 ; adm. free)* is one of the best-known gardens of its kind in America ; its 176 acres contain many rare and exotic trees, flowers, and shrubs gathered from every part of the world. Bequeathed to the University of Pennsylvania by the late Lydia Thompson Morris, it was opened to the public on June 2, 1933.

Although the arboretum has come to be identified as a place of public interest, it is still utilized by the university as a practical illustration for lectures and classes on horticultural and botanical subjects. Here each year women of the university hold their May Day frolic, marked by the crowning of a May Queen and the presentation of a play.

As its educational influence and prestige expanded, it became necessary to provide for the arboretum's future growth by developing young plants for later use in botanical groupings. A nursery was built on the farm to receive the young stocks. Another nursery was added near the green houses on land having a higher acid content.

A working arrangement has been entered into with the important botanical gardens of Europe and Asia, which makes it possible for the arboretum to obtain plants and seedlings.

The Morris mansion on the grounds, a medieval-looking, gray stone structure, formerly the home of John and Lydia Morris, has been adapted to provide office and laboratory space and to house the herbarium. A growing library for the use of students and a laboratory for forest pathology, adequately equipped for research, are attached to the mansion. Within the grounds, but across the Montgomery County line, is a farm group which includes an old mill and a stone blacksmith shop. Of two old farmhouses in the group, one, dated 1834, has walls, made of large, long, thin stones.

Retrace on City Line Ave.; L. on Germantown Turnpike; R. on Mt. Pleasant Ave.; L. on Lincoln Drive.

GERMANTOWN UNITARIAN CHURCH (38), at 6511 Lincoln Drive, erected in 1928 and designed by Edmund B. Gilchrist, presents stained glass windows and mosaic work in the finest tradition of church decoration. The memorial window in the chancel, of antique glass, was designed to harmonize with the Colonial Georgian style of the architecture.

L. from Lincoln Drive on Wayne Ave.; R. on School House Lane.

The WILLIAM PENN CHARTER SCHOOL (39), on School House Lane, is a direct outgrowth of the first school established in Philadelphia.

L. from School House Lane on Henry Ave.; R. on Midvale Ave.; L. on East River Drive, which leads to the Parkway and City Hall.

WEST PHILADELPHIA

METROPOLITAN subdivisions, like cities themselves, have a definite character. West Philadelphia's is uniformity. Looking across West Philadelphia from the Market Street Elevated Railway or from any other vantage point, the eye travels miles over low flat roofs toward a horizon broken only by chimneys, a tangle of radio aerials, and occasional church spires.

Row houses are West Philadelphia's characteristic. Row upon row, each house differs from the others only in its window shades and curtains, in its porch furniture, or the flowers on tiny front lawns.

The reason for this uniformity lies in the sudden growth of the section. West Philadelphia was a plain of grass before Philadelphia leaped the Schuylkill and surged westward a half century ago. Homes were built rapidly to provide cheap housing, and the architects who designed them held expenses down by adhering to a pattern. South of Market Street hundreds of apartment houses, duplexes, or single homes relieve the monotony of row houses.

Running along Market Street, the backbone of the community, is the elevated, its platform throwing the street into perpetual semi-gloom. Business houses line both sides of this double-tracked thoroughfare.

491

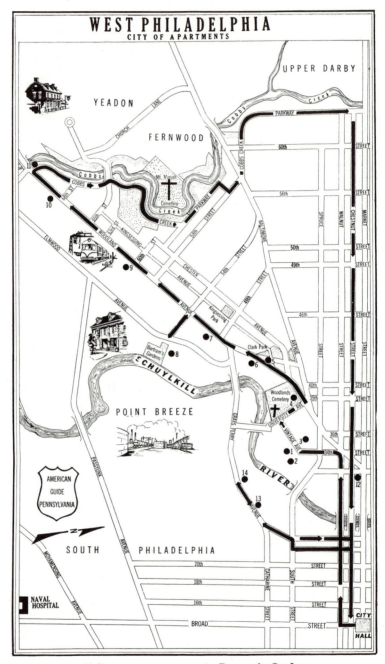

WEST PHILADELPHIA
CITY OF APARTMENTS

1. Convention Hall
2. Commercial Museum
3. Philadelphia General Hospital
4. Woodland Cemetery
5. Philadelphia College of Pharmacy
6. Breyer Ice Cream Company
7. The Mercy Hospital
8. Bartram's Gardens
9. Brill Car Works
10. St. James' Church
11. Blue Bell Tavern
12. Drexel Institute
13. Naval Home
14. Schuylkill Arsenal

Tour A- City of Apartments
City Tour 7

S. on Broad St. from City Hall; R. on Walnut; L. on 34th.

After passing through prosaic business sections and over the muddy Schuylkill, the route enters a neighborhood of quiet dignity as it turns left on Thirty-fourth Street and crosses the campus of the University of Pennsylvania *(see City Tour 14).*

At the junction of Thirty-fourth Street and Vintage Avenue are two massive buildings. CONVENTION HALL (1) faces on Vintage Avenue, while the COMMERCIAL MUSEUM (2), now an adjunct to Convention Hall, is reached by a short driveway to the right of the hall.

Convention Hall presents a sharp contrast, architecturally, to City Hall. Designed by Philip Johnson in the style of the Italian Renaissance, it is constructed of marble, limestone, and steel and has succeeded conspicuously in meeting the various needs for which it was built.

It has been the scene of diverse events from the athletic to the esthetic ; from the spectacular to the commonplace. Its greatest moment to date came in June 1936, when the Democratic National Convention nominated President Franklin D. Roosevelt here for a second term. Basking for a week in the white glare of international publicity and drawing to the city throngs of visitors, including the Nation's executives, Convention Hall more than fulfilled the hopes of its sponsors.

The building, begun in 1929 and opened with ceremony on September 17, 1931, by Mayor Harry A. Mackey, cost $5,350,000. It covers a ground space of 96,288 square feet.

The main hall, seating 13,500, is 300 feet long and 226 feet wide, with an arched ceiling rising 88 feet above the floor. Built with hanging balconies, its roof supported by 12 giant trusses, the hall has no pillars to obstruct the view. The great stage, which can seat an additional 1,500 persons, is 116 feet wide and 56 feet deep, with dressing rooms and other accommodations in the wings. The equipment includes an amplifying system, capable of carrying a whisper to any part of the hall, and a giant asbestos curtain weighing 42 tons. In the building are 23 smaller meeting rooms, which range in seating capacity from 500 to 1,800. The second-floor ballroom has a complete stage equipment of its own.

Convention Hall is used for exhibition purposes as well as for conventions. With its 80,000 square feet and the 150,000 square feet in the adjacent Commercial Museum, enough floor space can be provided jointly to house the largest of trade shows.

One of the features is a beautiful restaurant, with a modern hotel kitchen and a seating capacity of 884 persons.

In the first three and a half months following completion of the hall, 22 different types of events were held, attracting a total of 415,000 persons. Yearly more than 2,000,000 persons, exceeding Philadelphia's entire population, have witnessed the dances, contests, luncheons, graduations, tennis matches, automobile shows, political rallies, concerts, dog shows, boxing and wrestling bouts, and folk pageants flowing endlessly through this great coliseum of the twentieth century.

R. from 34th St. on Vintage Ave.

Opposite Convention Hall is the PHILADELPHIA GENERAL HOSPITAL (3). This institution, organized in 1732 as an almshouse, is one of the largest municipal hospitals in the country.

R. from Vintage Ave. on University Ave.

WOODLAND CEMETERY (4), on the left, was laid out in 1839 when Thomas Mitchell established Woodland on his own property. Rare and exotic plants and hundreds of trees are in the grounds.

L. from University Ave. on Woodland Ave.

The oldest American collegiate institute for the training of pharmacists, the PHILADELPHIA COLLEGE OF PHARMACY (5), is at Forty-third Street. Since its establishment in 1821 in Carpenters' Hall as the Philadelphia School of Apothecaries, it has progressively broadened its activities.

L. on 43d St.

The plant of the BREYER ICE CREAM COMPANY (6) is on Forty-third Street near Woodland Avenue *(open to visitors between*

Convention Hall
"Today a boxing match—tomorrow a political conclave"

CITY OF APARTMENTS (CITY TOUR 7)

Sept. 1 and June 1 only; daily tours at 10:30 and 1, except Sat. and Sun. ; arrangements for visit must be made in advance).

The finished product of this plant is the result of five manufacturing processes. A properly proportioned "mix" of cream and granulated sugar is heated sufficiently to melt the sugar. The "mix" is then clarified and pasteurized at a temperature of 150 degrees Fahrenheit. Under high pressure it is forced through a viscolizer, which makes the product smoother and more digestible. After cooling, the "mix" is placed in a freezer where fresh fruit and pure extracts are added for flavoring. From this freezer it flows into containers which are stored in a refrigerator until frozen. The ice cream is then ready for shipment in the refrigerated delivery trucks.

The Breyer plant is said to be the largest modern ice cream manufacturing unit in the world. A fully equipped laboratory and a staff of chemists are maintained to test the finished product and the ingredients that go into it.

Retrace on 43d St. to Woodland Ave.

The MERCY HOSPITAL (7), at Fiftieth Street, is maintained for and by Negroes. The hospital conducts a nurses' training school. The hospital proper is housed in the buildings formerly occupied by the Philadelphia Divinity School.

L. from Woodland Ave. on 54th St.

BARTRAM'S GARDENS (8), Fifty-fourth Street and Eastwick Avenue *(open daily 8:30 to 5; adm. free)*, the first botanical gardens in the American Colonies, were established in 1728 by John Bartram, America's first scientific botanist of eminence.

Healthy specimens of pine, fir, and English oak trees, and two fine boxwoods, sent to Bartram 150 years ago by the Earl of Bute, line both sides of a gravel walk leading to the eastern doorway of the house. Along the adjoining walks a canopy of acacias, magnolias, Norwegian pines, balsams, and cypress trees whispers in the breeze.

Until 20 years ago there stood in these gardens, reaching its mighty limbs into the sky, one of the largest cypress trees in the country. It dated from a time when Bartram was journeying through the Georgia swamps on horseback. He lost his whip and while searching for a switch discovered a twig of a rare specimen of the cypress. He brought it home and planted it, predicting that some day it would grow to a great height. It eventually towered to 175 feet, and had a circumference of 27½ feet at its base.

Throughout the grounds unusual and exotic plants and herbs were once abundant —— botanical oddities gathered by Bartram from the four corners of the globe.

Bartram built with his own hands an 18-room house of hewn stone, completed about 1731. A stone in one of the gables bears a Greek inscription which may be translated, "May God save," followed in

495

Bartram House, Close-up View
"It is God alone Almyty Lord
The Holy One by me ador'd"

English by "John and Ann Bartram, 1731." It is probable that important additions and changes were made later, when a stone bearing the following inscription was placed over the study window:

IT IS GOD ALONE ALMYTY LORD
THE HOLY ONE BY ME ADOR'D
JOHN BARTRAM 1770

Successive additions and alterations have changed the interior more than the exterior.

The Bartram house is a simple two-and-a-half story gable-roof structure of large, rough-hewn stone. The east facade has a characteristic trellis-shaded doorway with quaint Dutch seats at each side. The western facade has an odd, recessed porch between rude Ionic columns of native stone. Crudely carved, elaborately ornamented window casings, lintels, and sills form a curious feature of this facade. The carved stone designs around the windows are unlike anything in any other American house of the period. Clinging ivy and climbing roses give the house a rustic appearance.

Virtually none of the exterior woodwork is original. The three dormer windows, probably restorations, show unmistakable signs of comparatively recent work.

In the hallway is one of the earliest Franklin stoves, presented to Bartram by his friend, Benjamin Franklin. In the kitchen is one of the oldest fireplaces in the city, complete with brick hearth, crane, and Dutch oven ; and in one of the rooms above are two small closets over the mantel, where soapstones were heated for warming beds. An ancient loom, a spinning wheel, and other equipment are also stored in the old workroom. Pieces of furniture arranged throughout the house are contemporary with those used in Bartram's time. Another curio still remaining is an old cider press drilled out of solid rock.

Bartram was born near Darby, Pennsylvania, March 23, 1699. From childhood he manifested a love for everything that sprang from the earth. When old enough to strike out for himself, he set forth on a long journey, searching for a spot suitable for a garden where he might study trees and plants.

In 1731 he came upon the present site of the gardens and purchased it at sheriff's auction. The property, edged by the winding Schuylkill River, was originally a wilderness in a section which the Indians called Chinsessing (Kingsessing) after a tribe living in that vicinity.

Some time after Bartram had established his home, he found himself financially distressed, and in 1742 a subscription was started to enable him to travel in search of botanical specimens.

Franklin, introducing Bartram to Jared Eliot in 1775, wrote : "I believe you will find him to be at least 20 folio pages, large paper, well filled, on the subject of botany, fossils, husbandry, and the first creation." The great Linnaeus, with whom Bartram regularly corresponded, referred to him as "the greatest natural botanist in the world."

His talents were recognized when he was appointed "American Botanist to King George III." He was the author of the book *Observations Made in Travels from Pennsylvania to Onondaga, Oswego and Lake Ontario*, published in London in 1751, and many other treatises of a similar nature.

After Bartram's death on September 22, 1777, his son William, also an eminent botanist, carried on the work. Later his son-in-law, Colonel Carr, did likewise until the place became one of the most interesting botanical gardens in the country.

In 1851 the estate was purchased by Andrew Eastwick, who erected a large residence in another part of the grounds. In 1893 the city bought Bartram House and its immediate grounds and in 1897 acquired the remainder of the estate. The old house was then furnished and put in good condition by descendants of the Bartram family, and the entire estate was converted into a public park. Today the gardens are under the supervision of the Fairmount Park Commission.

Retrace on 54th St.; L. on Woodland Ave.

The BRILL CAR WORKS (9), home of America's largest manufacturer of urban and interurban high speed traction equipment, extends from Fifty-eighth Street to Sixty-second Street on the left side of Woodland Avenue.

Since 1868 the J. G. Brill Company has been identified with every step of the industry — from horsecars through cable and electric cars to the latest self-propelled types; from flimsy contraptions of wood to streamlined conveyances of stainless steel.

The history of the Brill Company provides a classic example of the concentration and centralization of industry and its fusion with the financial structure. The plant that John G. Brill and his son, G. Martin Brill, employed when they entered business on their own, would be lost in a single department of the modern structure, which occupies 30 acres of ground and contains 725,000 square feet of floor area.

The firm passed through various stages. In 1906 the capitalization was increased to $10,000,000. In 1926 the Brill Corporation was organized as a holding company controlling three enterprises — J. G. Brill Company, the American Car and Foundry Motors Company, and the Hall-Scott Motor Company. The Brill Automotive Car Division was set up in 1923 for the production of gasoline-driven rail cars.

The principal outlet for Brill products is, of course, the transit industry, for which three types of vehicles are made — streetcars,

Bartram House, full view
"Built by the hands of America's first botanist"

Bartram House, Interior
"Here Bartram and Franklin exchanged pleasantries and ideas"

trackless trolley cars, and motor coaches. The concentration under single control of the Hall-Scott engine, the A. C. F. design features, and Brill experience, virtually assures this company a monopoly in these spheres. Brill has furnished two-thirds of all trackless trolleys in operation since 1931.

The problem of greater seating capacity was solved with the invention by John A. Brill, youngest son of the founder, of the double-truck or eight-wheeled car, now in general use. This necessitated a new process, also devised by the Brill Company, of solid-forging the truck side frames for strength and durability. All-steel car construction originated with the Brills, as did innumerable less-well-known developments.

ST. JAMES CHURCH (10), at Sixty-eighth Street, was established in 1760 as St. James of Kingsessing, a "Swedish church to be officiated and served in the English tongue by the Swedish ministers at Wicaco near the city of Philadelphia forever." Wicaco was the name of the original Swedish settlement on the Delaware.

Tall ash and maple trees shade the entrance to the Georgian Colonial church, rectory, and parish house, which are constructed of local gray stone. The original double row of oblong windows of the church has been replaced by long, narrow windows with arched tops and white shutters. On the exterior, S-irons clamp the interior beam ends to the outside walls. The wide mortar lines are studded with small pieces of the same stone, in the odd "plum pudding" style.

The main door has a massive hand-wrought latch and lock with heavy key. The interior walls were originally bluish gray, with the plaster laid directly on the stone. They were later furred and colored a pale buff. Their timbers are pegged with wooden pins. The chancel, altar, and pulpit are of oak, and new doors have been put on the white-lined oak pews.

Over Woodland Avenue, variously known in former times as Darby Road, Chester Pike, or King's Highway, Washington marched his army after the defeat at Brandywine. Later he stopped frequently at the BLUE BELL TAVERN (11), at Seventy-third Street, and it was there that the first welcome was tendered him when he came from Mount Vernon to Philadelphia. The picket guard of the Revolutionary Army was stationed there in 1777. The tavern consists of two buildings, both of plain rough stone. The older of the two is two stories high, the later building three stories with attic and hipped roof.

R. from Woodland Ave. on Cobbs Creek Parkway; L. on 59th St. to a junction with 58th; L. on 58th to Cobb's Creek Parkway; R. on Chestnut St.

On the northeast corner of Chestnut and Thirty-second Streets is the DREXEL INSTITUTE (12), offering comprehensive courses in the branches of engineering and technical business training. The cooperative college system is in practice here. After the freshman year, the student spends half his time in college and the other half in a carefully selected position with some business or industrial firm — alternating in three-month periods between the college and his outside position.

The main building is constructed of light buff brick with terra cotta ornamentation and stained glass. The Chestnut Street facade is Renaissance, richly ornamented. The architects were Wilson Brothers & Co., and the building was completed in 1891.

The LIBRARY AND GALLERY *(open weekdays 10 to 4, Sat. 10 to 12; adm. free)* contain priceless collections of manuscripts and paintings.

The rotating exhibit in the picture gallery on the third floor includes works gathered by Anthony J. Drexel, John D. Lankenau, and Lillie Belle Randell. The collection affords an opportunity to study representative works of nineteenth century German artists and of French painters of the Barbizon school which flourished at the beginning of the nineteenth century.

The collection of manuscripts includes two highly prized originals, Charles Dickens' *Our Mutual Friend* and Edgar Allan Poe's *Murders in the Rue Morgue.* Many other valuable manuscripts, Japanese prints, and William Hogarth engravings enhance the collection. Some are too valuable to be left on display and may be seen only with special permission.

Among the curios in the museum are a chess table used by Napoleon Bonaparte during his exile on the Island of St. Helena ; the desk on which Lord Byron wrote *Don Juan* ; and a harp once owned by the Irish poet, Thomas Moore. A clock made by David Rittenhouse after the style of Chippendale, with a very accurate orrery above the dial, is also displayed.

Museum features include the collection of old ivory assembled by George W. Childs ; an exhibit of rare works in bronze, brass, copper, pewter, and silver ; old coins, laces, ceramics, sculpture, jewelry, and furniture ; some very fine examples of Flemish, Old English (Mortlake), and French tapestries ; Indian pottery and baskets, and shoes of all nations.

In the process of collection, some of the pieces in the museum have acquired interest second only to their value as art. Moore's harp, green and adorned with gilt shamrocks, was at first an enigma to the museum authorities, who did not know whence it had come. After a lapse of two years they learned that it had been purchased from the poet's family by George W. Childs and had been presented to the museum by Mrs. Childs. Museum officials since have discovered that the harp was the model for the improved American harp. It was made by John Egan, noted Dublin harpmaker (about 1800).

R. from Chestnut St. on 22d; R. on South; L. on Gray's Ferry Ave.

The NAVAL HOME (13), (R), Gray's Ferry Avenue and Bainbridge Street, provides an honorable and comfortable harbor of refuge for old, disabled, and retired officers and men of the Navy and the Marine Corps who are entitled by law to the benefits of the institution. It is under the direction and supervision of the Bureau of Navigation, subject to the control of the Secretary of the Navy.

Before the Revolution the site of the Naval Home, was known as the Pemberton Plantation. In 1799 an act of Congress provided a hospital fund to which all persons in the Navy were required to contribute 20 cents monthly out of their pay. This practice is still carried on. From funds thus secured from the personnel of the Navy the Old Pemberton Plantation was purchased in 1826 from Timothy Abbott.

Construction was begun in 1830, and the home was opened in 1831 with four regular inmates. Lieut. J. B. Cooper, a veteran of the War of 1812, was the first superintendent. The first governor was Commodore James Biddle, a noted Philadelphia naval officer, who served from 1838 to 1842.

For 50 years the institution was called the Naval Asylum, then the name was changed to the Naval Home. As late as the 1880's sailors spoke of it as the "White House."

U. S. Naval Home
". . . and the sailor home from the sea"

The home consists of four structures, separated from one another, yet forming one entire plant : the main building ; the residence of the governor, executive officer, and the surgeon ; executive offices ; and an annex in the rear of the main building. There are also numerous small outbuildings on the grounds.

The main building is three stories high, built of Pennsylvania marble, and is embellished with a handsome portico of eight Ionic columns. The wings contain verandas on each story.

Fine walks, flowers and trees adorn the grounds. A ship's bell from the cruiser *Philadelphia* strikes ship's time from its place on the lawn. Here, too, are brass howitzers from the Civil War period and a 12,000-pound wood-stock anchor. These — reminders of the "Old Navy" — serve to impart a certain shipboard atmosphere to the place. There are also a number of brass cannon from the Brandywine battlefield and carronades captured by Commodore Charles Stewart, the last of the old "sea lions," from the British sloops *Cyane* and *Levant*.

In the portico are two colossal stone balls brought from the Dardanelles in the *Constitution* in 1838 and presented by Commodore J. D. Elliott.

The figurehead of the old frigate *Franklin* of 1815 was obtained in 1929 from the Naval Academy and is on the grounds. It is a bust of Franklin, of fine workmanship, by Gerrish.

Rifles, boarders' pikes, cutlasses, and ship models adorn the walls of the assembly hall. There is also a tablet of the governors hung in the hall and inscribed with their names. On this list are names famous in the War of 1812, the Civil War, the Spanish-American War, and the World War.

In the winter of 1836-37 many old trees on the grounds were cut down and used for fuel. The larger trees that stand today were for the most part planted by Captain Biddle in 1838-40.

It was also in his time that the midshipmen who were under instruction on board receiving ships at Boston, New York, and Norfolk were brought to Philadelphia, and a naval school was established at the asylum. The scheme was not altogether a success, and in 1845 the school was transferred to Annapolis, Md., becoming the United States Naval Academy.

The home is planned with a spacious mess hall, where all meals, except those for the aged and infirm, are served. Two poolrooms are in operation, and at each end of the wings on all floors are sitting rooms where newspapers and periodicals are provided. Sound motion-picture equipment is installed, and two programs are shown each week. The library, under the supervision of the chaplain, contains 5,000 volumes of reference, history, and fiction. The care of the inmates extends to every need.

503

A typical room is about 9 feet wide and 12 feet long, with a window opening on a veranda. It is furnished simply with a bed, mattress, linens, blankets, pillows and coverlets, chair, small table, mirror and clothes locker, and such other personal furniture and decorations as a radio, pictures, and the like.

The average age of the home's beneficiaries is 61. The youngest inmate was 27 years ; the oldest was 91. Among the disabled are those who have served less than five years in the Navy or with the Marines ; among the infirm are aged men who have served more than 30 years. The governor (1937) of the home is Rear Admiral Harris Laning, retired. Lieut. Richard G. Ganahl is the executive officer.

The SCHUYLKILL ARSENAL (14), Gray's Ferry Avenue and Washington Avenue, though designated by the War Department as an arsenal, does not fabricate arms and explosives. After the War of 1812 it ceased storing arms and began fabricating clothing, blankets, bedding and tentage for the soldier. It is now used as a school to instruct commissioned officers of the Army in the duties and functions of the Quartermaster Corps.

Its record dates back to 1781. In 1799 the War Department, without awaiting Federal appropriation, purchased the 8-acre site on the Schuylkill. Four large three-story brick storehouses, forming a hollow square, composed this early military unit. It was completed in 1806 at a cost which had been announced in Congress, four years earlier, as $152,607.02. The commanding officer's residence, a powder magazine, and several miscellaneous structures supplanted the earlier temporary buildings.

The powder magazine, or "pill box," constructed about 1799, is a two-story-and-attic structure with lower walls of stone five feet thick and upper section of brick. The roof of brick-groined arches is supported on four stone columns. At a later date, a brick superstructure, with lock-jointed oak beams in the roof, was added. The magazine is surrounded by a 10-foot moat and has a bridge to a second-story entrance.

The enlisted men's barracks, or the Ludington Building, erected in 1800, is a two-story-and-attic, rectanguler structure with walls of Flemish bond brick and dormer windows. The timber work is of oak, held together by wooden pegs. At each end of the house, a circular staircase extends from basement to roof. The brick vaulting of the basement is noteworthy.

During the Civil War disbursements at the arsenal were valued at $20,000,000 to $35,000,000 a year ; during the World War, when more than 850 persons were employed, the disbursements increased tremendously.

In 1803 the Schuylkill Arsenal cooperated in equipping the famous Lewis and Clark expedition to the Pacific Northwest. The explorations of Lewis and Clark resulted in the annexation of this northwest territory. The total outlay for the expedition was $2,160.40 — far less costly, proportionately, than the traditionally sharp bargain driven by the Dutch in their purchase of Manhattan Island from the Indians. The arsenal participated also in sending tribute to the Barbary pirates as insurance for United States shipping. In February 1792 the Senate voted to pay $100,000 annually for immunity from piracy and $40,000 for ransom of captives. This, shipped under direction of the Purveyor of Public Supplies and partly in the form of merchandise, was sent from Philadelphia.

Retrace on Gray's Ferry Ave. to 23d St.; Continue on 23d St. to Chestnut; R. on Chestnut to Broad St.

Tour B—Toward The Suburbs

City Tour 8

LEAVING City Hall, the route leads out Market Street and crosses the Schuylkill River on the Market Street Bridge. At Thirtieth and Market Streets, on the right is the PENNSYLVANIA RAILROAD STATION (1), opened in 1933. Its erection contributed to the city's significant westward movement. This enormous building is part of a plan which contemplates demolition of the old Broad Street Station and of the "Chinese Wall," a long, high, track bed preventing commercial development on the north side of Market Street between Fifteenth and Eighteenth Streets.

Of monumental proportions, the design of the station is based upon the classic Roman style. The exterior is of Alabama limestone with base and trim of granite; the interior is lined with Italian travertine. The station proper is 328 by 638 feet. The architects were Graham, Anderson, Probst & White.

East and west covered porticos, with huge fluted Corinthian columns, provide access to the great concourse, 134 feet wide, 295 feet long, and 94 feet high. Ten octagonal chandeliers, approximately 18 feet long and 5 feet in diameter, hang from the red and gold coffered ceiling.

In the west end of the main waiting room is Karl Bitter's mammoth plaque, *Spirit of Transportation*, transferred from Broad Street Station, where it had hung since 1894.

On the main floor are ticket offices, parcel and baggage checking rooms, telegraph offices, telephone rooms, dining facilities, and other features.

An interlocking tower known as "Penn Tower" on the fourth floor, by means of an electro-pneumatic system combining the use of electricity and compressed air, controls all trains operating through the

505

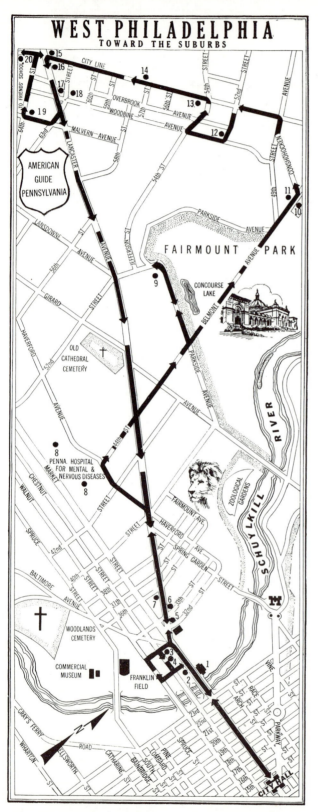

WEST PHILADELPHIA
TOWARD THE SUBURBS

AMERICAN GUIDE PENNSYLVANIA

FAIRMOUNT PARK

1. Pennsylvania Railroad Station

2. Philadelphia General Post O

3. Drexel Institute

4. Abbott Dairies

5. Cavalry Armory

6. Rush Hospital

7. Pennsylvania Working Home
   Blind Men

8. Pennsylvania Hospital for Me
   and Nervous Diseases

9. Edwin Forrest Home for Act

10. Belmont Filtration Plant
    Reservoir

11. Philadelphia Home for Incura

12. Wynnestay

13. St. Joseph's College

14. Episcopal Academy for Boys

15. St. Charles Borromeo Semina

16. Overbrook Presbyterian

17. St. Paul's Memorial (Episcop

18. Our Lady of Lourdes (Ro
    Catholic)

19. Pennsylvania Institution for
    Instruction of the Blind

20. Friends Central School.

station. Here, also, are automatic and manual telephone exchanges for the entire railroad network in the Philadelphia area.

Ten of the station's 14 tracks are level with the river.

To the left, across Market Street, is the PHILADELPHIA GEN-ERAL POST OFFICE (2), completed in 1935 at a cost of $4,500,000. Huge and imposing, it faces the Schuylkill River and is accessible by road, rail, water, and air.

The exterior, a simplified modernized classic treatment of Indiana limestone and Deer Island granite, is notable for its rhythmic arrangement of huge piers, window bays, and smaller windows above. The window frames along the driveway are of stainless steel, the exterior doors of bronze, and the workroom walls of buff-colored tile. Rankin and Kellogg were the architects, the firm of Tilden, Register & Pepper their associates.

Identical entrance rotundas at Market and Chestnut Streets are roofed with domes of green and blue mosaics. Above each entrance is an American eagle flanked on either side by carrier pigeons, symbolizing one of the earliest means of communication. Between the entrances runs the long corridor used for public mail transactions. Of marble trimmed with nickel silver, its long tables and many windows give it the appearance of a large banking room.

Steel chutes and belt conveyors facilitate rapid handling of approximately 1,125,000 pieces of mail daily. Robot "selectoveyors" automatically load and unload trays of mail destined for various places. A changing of air, electric dryers for letter carriers' clothes, and a heating system that keeps the roof free of snow and ice are other innovations. The spacious roof has been laid out as a landing place for autogyros. The loading platform has room for 100 trucks.

Like many other Philadelphia institutions the Post Office has its historic memento. A cannon, believed to have been spiked and abandoned by Washington after the Battle of the Brandywine, rests at the east Market Street entrance. This cannon was unearthed during excavations for the Market Street Subway.

L. from Market St. on 30th; R. on Walnut; R. on 32nd.

On the northeast corner of Thirty-second and Chestnut Streets is the DREXEL INSTITUTE (3) *(see City Tour 7)*.

R. from 32nd St. on Chestnut.

At 3043 Chestnut Street, on the left, is the modern plant of the ABBOTT DAIRIES (4). *(Conducted tours at 9 a. m. and 1 p. m. on weekdays, by arrangement)*.

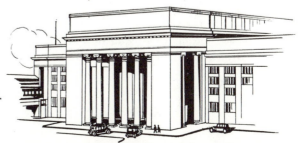

Thirtieth Street Station, P. R. R.

The milk prepared at this dairy is brought from three States—Pennsylvania, Maryland, and New Jersey. The farmers deliver the milk to country receiving stations, scattered throughout these States. There it is cooled, pumped into sanitary, glass-lined trucks and brought to the city plant. Dairymen close to Philadelphia make delivery to the plant.

Upon arrival the milk is tested for richness and purity. Pasteurization — heating to and maintaining a temperature of 143 to 145 degrees for 30 minutes — follows. After pasteurization the milk is cooled to 38 degrees in preparation for bottling. Conveyors feed freshly sterilized bottles to six automatic filling machines. Each of these is capable of filling, capping, and sealing 50 bottles a minute. The bottles are placed in wooden cases and conveyed to a large refrigeration room, where they await delivery to the consumer.

The Abbott plant consists of three floors. A power plant, a large repair shop, and a fully-equipped laboratory are maintained. Laboratory facilities are also maintained at the rural receiving stations.

L. from Chestnut St. on 30th ; L. on Market ; R. on Lancaster Ave.

The 103d CAVALRY ARMORY (5), built in 1916, is on the right at Thirty-second Street and Lancaster Avenue. The avenue, swinging to the northwest, begins at this point. The castle-like armory houses the famous old Second Light Horse (B) Troop.

On the northwest corner at Thirty-third Street is the RUSH HOSPITAL (6), which specializes in the treatment of pulmonary, bone, and laryngeal tuberculosis. It cares for about 550 patients each year. Chartered on September 16, 1890, the hospital opened on June 4, 1891, as a dispensary. The institution was then at Twenty-second and Pine Streets. It was moved to its present site in 1895.

At 3518 Lancaster Avenue, to the left, is the PENNSYLVANIA WORKING HOME FOR BLIND MEN (7) *(open 9 to 5, Mon. to Fri. ; adm. free)*, a complete community serving all the needs of blind men, and to some extent compensating them for their luckless plight. In the industrial department inmates are taught chair caning, rag rug weaving, and broom and brush making. These articles are sold at a profit, the funds thus realized being used for maintenance of the institution and to pay small salaries to the workers. The men have living quarters in the lawn-fronted dormitories.

L. from Lancaster Ave. on Haverford Ave. at 40th St.

On the left, extending from Forty-second Street to Forty-ninth, is the PENNSYLVANIA HOSPITAL FOR MENTAL AND NERVOUS DISEASES (8), opened in 1841 as a department of the old Pennsylvania Hospital, when the many incoming mental and nervous cases necessitated larger quarters and better facilities *(see City Tour 2)*. Dr. Thomas S. Kirkbride, from whom the institution takes its popular name, "Kirkbride's," was the first chief physician and superintendent of the institution.

The spacious administration building is capped by a round dome, which is surmounted by a small lantern cupola. A short flight of stone steps leads up to the simple pedimented doorway, flanked by fluted Doric columns of sandstone. The left and right wings have porches with fluted Doric columns. Each wing is surmounted by a hexagonal dome. It is constructed of Pennsylvania stone, stuccoed, with wood trim painted white.

R. from Haverford Ave. on 44th St. (which becomes Belmont Ave. above Lancaster Ave.); L. on Parkside Ave.

At 4849 is the EDWIN FORREST HOME FOR ACTORS (9). Established through the will of Edwin Forrest, noted Shakespearean actor, it serves as a sanctuary for disabled and infirm actors past 60 years of age.

Retrace on Parkside Ave.; L. on Belmont.

On the right at Conshohocken and Belmont Avenues is the BELMONT FILTRATION PLANT AND RESERVOIR (10), a series of low, buff brick buildings with blue slate roofs, built in 1903. Beyond, on the left, is the PHILADELPHIA HOME FOR INCURABLES (11). Early in 1877 Annie G. Ingles, a child crippled from infancy, gave a gold dollar to her mother, requesting her to "please use this in some way to start a place to take care of poor, sick, suffering children." Thus began a movement which in a short time resulted in the collection of almost $1,000,000 and the founding of the home. The gold dollar given by the child is displayed on the door of the Gold Room.

Wynnestay
Home of Penn's Physician

The buildings, a modern adaptation of Gothic architecture, form a U-shaped composition. In the loop of the U is a garden used for recreation and exercise. One wing of the main building is for children, another for cancer patients. There is no age restriction.

L. from Belmont Ave. on Conshohocken ; L. on City Line ; L. on 52nd St.

At Woodbine Avenue is WYNNESTAY (12), construction of which was begun in 1690 as a residence for Dr. Thomas Wynne, physician and personal friend of William Penn. In 1872 it passed from the Wynne family, immortalized in S. Weir Mitchell's novel *Hugh Wynne*, to the Smedleys, then its occupants.

Although Revolutionary cannon balls and bullets have left their marks upon it, the structure is in an excellent state of preservation and exemplifies Pennsylvania's Welsh Colonial architecture. The heavy walls of local gray field stone are set in rubble style with white mortar, and doors and windows are wide and low. The cornice is bold and, at the gable, frames a pediment in which is a small central circular window.

R. from 52nd St. on Woodbine Ave.; R. on 54th St.; L. on City Line Ave.

ST. JOSEPH'S COLLEGE (13), on the left, covering the area between Fifty-fourth and Fifty-sixth Streets, stands on one of the highest elevations within the city. The college first opened its doors in Willing's Alley in 1851.

The rapidly increasing enrollment forced the officials to move into a three-story building at Filbert and Juniper Streets, the present site of the *Evening Bulletin*. The college was later returned to Willing's Alley. Then, a northern trend continuing, a tract of land, bounded by Stiles, Thompson, Seventeenth, and Eighteenth Streets, was purchased for the erection of a chapel, additional buildings for student work, and the Church of the Gesu. The first classes were held there on September 1, 1889. Classes were transferred from the old college to the present 23-acre site in 1927. The new buildings, collegiate Gothic in design, are constructed of local gray field stone, with white sandstone trim and a steep slate-covered roof. A crenellated central tower, dormer windows, and lancet arches add to its charm. The stadium, built in the form of a horseshoe in a natural hollow, has a seating capacity of 8,000.

On the northeast corner of Berwick Road and City Line Avenue is the EPISCOPAL ACADEMY FOR BOYS (14). Established in 1785, it is one of the oldest schools in Philadelphia, and moved from the center of the city to its present quarters in 1921.

The school is a gray stone Victorian building with an ornate, square central tower and a large, white Doric portico. The gymnasium, to the left, is a large building of Tudor Gothic design, constructed of

St. Joseph's College
"Steeped in rich cultural traditions"

Seminary of St. Charles Borromeo
"Going, teach all nations"

gray stone with a high, red slate roof. The school is surrounded by spacious lawns and shade trees.

The northeast corner of City Line and Lancaster Avenues forms the southwest corner of the grounds of ST. CHARLES BORROMEO SEMINARY (15), where young men are trained for the Catholic priesthood.

An atmosphere of peace and quiet surrounds the three principal seminary buildings.

The Major Seminary, erected in 1866, is a large, rough gray stone Victorian building. The central unit is surmounted by a high domed lantern and the end wings by smaller domed lanterns. Samuel S. Sloan and Addison Hutton were the architects. Later additions are of Italian Renaissance design.

The huge Minor Seminary is a low, three-story, Italian Renaissance structure of limestone and gray granite. Above the central portico, with large Roman Doric columns, rises a square tower and a tall domed lantern. Huge wings extend to the rear.

St. Martin's Chapel, also of limestone and gray granite, is designed in the Spanish Renaissance style, with a large semi-circular Roman Doric portico. At the left of the chapel is a beautiful, tall campanile, also Spanish Renaissance in design, of light limestone and gray granite.

Between the chapel and the eastern end of the Minor Seminary is a beautiful cloister with delicate, Ionic columns and gray plastered walls and vaulting.

The new seminary group, consisting of the main building, church, campanile, cloister, and infirmary, was designed by Paul Monaghan and erected in 1928.

L. from City Line Ave. on Lancaster.

Three churches are grouped here in a small area, the OVER-BROOK PRESBYTERIAN (16), on the northwest corner at City Line Avenue; ST. PAUL'S MEMORIAL (Episcopal) (17), on the south-west corner at Sherwood Road; and OUR LADY OF LOURDES (Roman Catholic) (18), on the southwest corner at Sixty-third Street.

R. from Lancaster Ave. on 63rd St.; R. on Malvern Ave.

The Overbrook School for the Blind — PENNSYLVANIA INSTITUTION FOR THE INSTRUCTION OF THE BLIND (19), extends west to Wynnewood Road from the northwest corner at Sixty-fourth Street. Started in 1889 and completed in 1900, it is an attractive two-story building in the Spanish Mission style of stone and brick covered with white plaster wash stucco.

The upper facade with its flanking towers is embellished with huge scrolls. Above the rotunda of the main building is a low, broad, octagonal lantern. The roof is of reddish brown, glazed, mission tile. Each of the wings encloses a cloistered patio or quadrangle around a garden. Architects were Cope & Stewardson.

Founded in 1833 at Third and Race Streets by Julius R. Friedlander, the school is liberally endowed under the will of William Young Birch, former superintendent. The curriculum includes studies from kindergarten to high school and both academic and manual training subjects. Athletics are an important feature, and Overbrook's wrestling teams have brought fame to the school.

R. from Malvern Ave. on 64th St.; L. on City Line Ave.

FRIENDS CENTRAL SCHOOL (20), is on the right at Sixty-eighth Street and City Line Avenue. Previously on the old Quaker Meeting plot at Fifteenth and Race Streets, the school was moved to its present location, formerly a private home, in 1925. Of Tudor design, the structure is of rough stone with red tiled roofs. A small gymnasium, shop buildings, and the "lower" school, a low, simple, Tudor building constructed of gray stone, are to the north. The school offers general courses, with special emphasis on college training through its affiliation with Swarthmore College. Friends Central is also affiliated with Friends West Philadelphia and Friends Germantown Schools.

Retrace on City Line Ave.; R. on Lancaster Ave.; L. on Market St. to City Hall.

THROUGH INDUSTRIAL PHILADELPHIA
City Tour 9
Typical Philadelphia Activities

DESPITE its historic past, its scientific, educational, and artistic importance, Philadelphia is primarily an industrial city. The transition from the little Colonial metropolis is complete. Today, the only forests are factory chimneys of steel, brick, and cement, and the gloom of smoky streets replaces the dim wilderness trail. Most of the city's vast industry is concentrated in Frankford and Kensington, although no section of Philadelphia is without its variety of industrial establishments, sprouting up in the midst of residential or mercantile areas.

The names Frankford and Kensington persist merely as sentimental recollections of the time prior to January 31, 1854, when they were independent municipalities, already industrialized and thriving. There lingers still an occasional weed-infested field where the hum of crickets provides an obbligato to the blatancy of neighboring factories, but these are being slowly and surely eliminated.

Frankford is generally considered to lie to the north of Kensington, although of late years the names have tended to become interchangeable, designating a single area which is part of Philadelphia's great

513

INDUSTRIAL TOUR

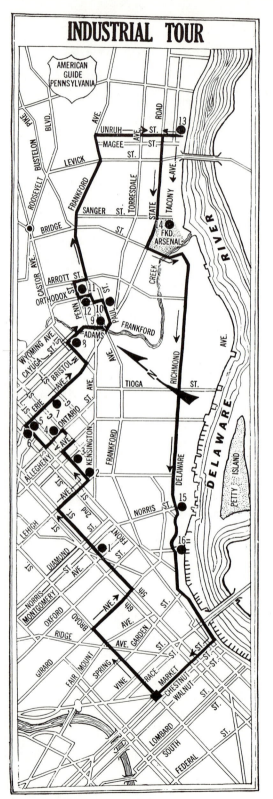

1. John B. Stetson Plant

2. Mill of John Bromley & Sons, Inc.

3. H. C. Aberle & Co. Hosiery Plant

4. Philco Radio and Television Corporation

5. S. K. F. Plant

6. Sloane-Blabon Corporation

7. Cuneo Eastern Press. Inc.

8. Carl Mackley Houses

9. Home of First Building and Loan Association in the United States

10. La France Art Institute

11. Frankford Historical Society

12. Orthodox Friends' Meeting House

13. Henry Disston & Sons, Inc., Plant

14. Frankford Arsenal

15. Cramp Ship and Engine Building Company

16. Plant of the Pennsylvania Sugar Company

Northeast. The area may be loosely defined, rather than bounded, by Front Street, the Delaware River, Bridge Street, and Kensington and Frankford Avenues.

Textiles, employing about one fourth of Philadelphia's industrial workers, are the foundation of all local industries. They are concentrated in Frankford and Kensington, where textile mills predating the city's amalgamation still exist. Variety is the distinctive feature of the other products, which range from magazines to ball bearings and from sugar to radios.

N. on Broad St. from City Hall; R. on Girard Ave.; L. on 5th St.

Fifth Street, a much-used northbound artery, formerly a select residential street, is lined with worn brick houses, minor shops, and factories of all sorts. At Montgomery Avenue, on the right, are the several brick buildings of the JOHN B. STETSON PLANT (1). *(Open Mon. to Fri. for group visits only. Arrangements must be made in advance.)*

John B. Stetson made a better hat, and the world beat a path to his door. Even Emerson, however, might have agreed that some promotion was necessary. Stetson made of his work a business, a profession, a science, and an art. He was an economist, an organizer, and a humanitarian — and became, incidentally, a rich man. Stetson wearers may be found in all parts of the world, whether it be in a German hamlet, on a Japanese street, or on an Argentine ranch.

Stetson was born in Orange, N. J., in 1830. His first hat was made when he demonstrated to skeptical friends how cloth or felt could be made without a loom by the ancient process of felting. Hats in those rough days were something of a luxury. Stetson's first hat attracted considerable attention. It was big and picturesque, and it was bought for $5 by a bullwhacker. This transaction may be said to have been the start of a giant industry.

He came to Philadelphia in 1865 with $100 and the determination to enter the hat business. With his small capital he bought tools and $10 worth of furs and rented a room at Seventh and Callowhill Streets. At first his efforts to create a style market failed. He was told derisively that fashions came from across the sea — words which have a familiar ring even today. Undismayed, he made a two-ounce hat, donned it rakishly and, simulating the swagger of a town blade, created a vogue single-handed.

However, profits were small until Stetson heeded the call of his guiding star and first customer, the bullwhacker. He evolved the "Boss of the Plains," a lush, 10-gallon affair in qualities selling from $5 to $30. Its success was immediate — westerners apparently took their headgear seriously. In 1865 Stetson discarded his local trade and viewpoint, purchased land at Fourth Street and Montgomery Avenue, then a suburb, and erected a three-story building covering an area

515

Stetson Hat Company
"Covering the heads of the world"

"Sattidy Evenin' Post—Just out"
Curtis Publishing Company

100 by 30 feet. Expanded greatly, this location today is one of the world's largest hat-producing factories, with an annual output of more than three million hats. The largest foreign markets are in Mexico, Argentina, Canada, South Africa, and Europe.

Stetson preferred to manufacture everything that went into his hats as well as the hats themselves. He controlled his raw supplies, made his own blocks, ribbons, and boxes. His name stands for hat, and if imitation is flattery, he must have been surfeited with praise when he died in 1906.

The Stetson plants extend over six acres of land and contain 30 acres of floor space. In busy times employees number 2,500 men and 1,000 women.

The hats are made of fur—United States and Canadian beaver and muskrat, Argentinian nutria, and rabbit from England, Scotland, and Continental Europe. Fifteen million fur skins are used annually.

The first process applied to the skins is that technically known as "carroting," which consists of applying a solution of nitrate of mercury with a coarse brush. This process adds to the felting properties of the fur fibers and causes them to mat more readily. Under the microscope these fibers appear to be a barbed wire shaft covered with scales. Carroting causes these scales to open so that they will interlock when the fibers are shrunk in hot water. Millions of the carroted fibers are stored in fur cellars, sometimes for months, before they are taken to the fur-cutting department, where they are brushed by machinery. A machine then cuts the hide into shreds, and the fur emerges on an endless belt.

The most desirable fur of water animals is from the belly, while from the rabbit the best is taken from the back. Graded, the fur is placed in five-pound paper bags and sent to storerooms.

Activity starts anew in the blowing rooms where the fur is automatically fed into large machines, the revolving cylinders of which, equipped with thousands of steel teeth, tear the fibers apart. The fur rises, passing through the several compartments of the machine, and the heavier hair falls to the bottom, whence it is eliminated along with foreign matter. Other machines blend the fur in the proper proportions to produce various qualities.

The forming machine shapes the body of the hat. At one end a quantity of blended fur is weighed, and upon being fed into the machine, is projected into a chamber containing a minutely perforated copper cone about three feet high. The cone revolves; thousands of mistlike particles are drawn by suction to its damp outer side, forming a thin covering of felt depending on the character of the hat to be made. The cone and felt, protected by flannel wrappings and a metal covering, are placed in hot water until thoroughly soaked, after which the formed body is removed. A most important

517

step in the manufacture is sizing. The task here is to arrange so that the shrinkage shall leave the hat lightest at the tip of the crown with a gradually increasing thickness down to the brim.

In the coloring department the bodies are placed in dye baths. Stiff hats are immersed for more than two hours, soft hats for three. When thoroughly rinsed and dried, they are ready for the stiffening department. Here the body which is to become a soft hat has the future brim dipped in a preparation of shellac dissolved in alcohol, water, and other ingredients, and the set bodies are steamed to soften the shellac.

In the blocking department the hat body, after being worked in hot water on a wooden block, becomes recognizable. The hat is pulled off the proper block, steamed, sponged, and ironed. The brim is ironed perfectly flat and cut to the desired width. Next, the brim is curled, and operations in the trimming department prepare the hat for packing.

R. from 5th St. on Lehigh Ave.

This is a double-track thoroughfare, nine squares north of the Stetson plant, cutting through the heart of Kensington. At A Street and extending to B, on the left, is one of the largest centers for the manufacture of rugs, lace, and lace curtains in the country — the MILL OF JOHN BROMLEY & SONS, INC. (2) *(may be visited by appointment)*. Founded in 1863, it now covers an entire city block and rises to a height of five stories. The administrative and business offices are at the mill. The present quarters were first occupied in 1899, when the company removed in units from its former plant at Front and York Streets.

Seventy-five looms are used in the manufacture of lace and lace curtains. Artists make all the designs, creating various patterns for this department. Products are graded according to weave, the quality of the materials being the same.

The weaving of rugs and carpets is done on 30 broad looms and 20 narrow looms. The wool used is purchased in the chief wool-raising centers of the world. The cleaning, mixing, and combing of the wool, and its transformation into yarn are all done in the mill. There are facilities for dyeing the yarns, and artists make all the designs and number the various yarn colors that are to be used. The rugs and carpets produced here are of many dimensions, but of only two types ; Axminster and broadloom.

When finished, rugs are rolled on bamboo poles and wrapped in burlap or paper ready to be placed on sale. The lace and curtains are packed in cartons. A thorough inspection is made before an item is certified. The plant employs approximately 800 workers.

Actual process of rug and carpetmaking begins with the selection of materials ; there are 400 types of carpet wools. (North America, a great wool center, yields no grades suitable for carpets.) Of chief importance to the buyer of wool are length, strength, resilience, loft or curl, color, and sheen of the staple. Above all, the wool must be lively, so that it will spring back after being stepped on.

Raw wool is introduced into the mixing bowl, where the blender, thinking in terms of the final tuft, combines different varieties into the proper proportions to meet the requirements of certain grades. The scouring machine receives the wool, after the opener has beaten out some of the dirt, and removes 10 to 40 percent of the original mass. The scouring temperature must be watched carefully to prevent too great or too little elimination of the natural animal grease.

The wool is then dried. From the driers it is blown through air conveyors to the blending bins, while switches control the destination of any particular batch. In the bins it is stacked in piles. The picker untangles the wool and mixes it, and it is ready for the carding machinery, which completes the mix, combs it out, and interlocks the separate fibers into a soft web. It then separates the wide web into small strands and rubs them into the roving.

Spinning produces finished yarn from the roving by simultaneously drawing it down to the proper weight and twisting it. The spun strand of yarn is rather small. In order to make a bulkier thread — and also to obtain particular textural effects in the finished rug — multiple strands are combined to make two, three, or four-ply yarn. Worsted yarn uses only the long wool fibers, laid parallel, while in woolen yarn all the fibers are used, and the textile strength is due to interlocking. Worsted yarn is a very fine thread, and this must be built up before it can be used in a rug.

After the yarn is made, it is dyed, dried, bundled, and stored to await spooling and setting. Samples of each color are placed on a large rack, which the colorist consults when he receives a new pattern from the designers, to see if the indicated colors are in stock in the needed amounts.

When it comes from the loom the pile of the rug is slightly uneven and must be sheared. Long chains of rugs are sewn together and fed into a machine, which, like a gigantic lawn mower, shears the pile to the correct height. Three shearings are necessary to produce the smooth, velvety appearance of the finished article.

Completed rugs are inspected for missing tufts. The rugs are laid over glass-topped tables with underneath illumination, enabling the "pickers" to see the tiniest hole. The holes are marked with white thread, and tufts are sewn in by hand in the proper color, after which the corrected fabric is again scrutinized for flaws by another group of inspectors.

The trimming of a rug varies according to type and quality. Some rugs are made with a self-fringe, which is formed by a continuation of the warp threads. Others are hemmed, with no fringe, and still others are furnished with a sewn-on fringe.

L. from Lehigh Ave. on A St.

At Lippincott Street is the H. C. ABERLE & CO. HOSIERY PLANT (3) *(open Mon. to Fri. for group visits only. Arrangements must be made in advance).*

Beginning with the knitters who settled in Germantown before the arrival of William Penn, the hosiery industry has continuously flourished, until today Philadelphia is one of the world's leading hosiery producers. Kensington's activity centers around this industry.

Because of the demand for finer texture (among other factors), numerous changes have been made in the delicately machined and finely adjusted hosiery manufacturing equipment. Gauges have risen to the point where today the knitting machines producing some of the finer stockings require the use of 40 needles to the linear inch.

In contrast to plain stockings, which are knit straight and then stretched to shape, the hose produced by full-fashioned knitting machines is actually knit to proportion. When the stocking is completely knitted, it is stitched up the back on a sewing machine.

The first operation after seaming is degumming and dyeing. These two processes are usually done at one time to save the silk from too much processing. These stockings are then taken to the boarding room, where they are boarded on aluminum forms. Their next stop is in the inspection department, where they are graded for quality and separated into sizes. They are then folded, boxed, and are ready for shipping.

The intersection of A and Lippincott Streets is typical of Frankford and Kensington. The massive factory here dwarfs the rows of workers' homes, which are tiny, in need of repair, and unrelieved by any sign of vegetation. Most of them were built during the industrial boom in the early part of the present century, but construction improvements during recent years have left their dreariness unaltered.

R. from A St. on Allegheny Ave.; L. on C St. to Ontario.

The PHILCO RADIO AND TELEVISION CORP. PLANT (4) at C Street *(may be visited by appointment)*, are distributors of approximately 30 percent of all radios produced in the United States. The manufacturing company, the Philadelphia Storage Battery Company, began its phenomenal industrial career in 1906 as a manufacturer of storage batteries.

Launched with a capital of $50,000, equally contributed by five founders, the battery company has survived serious vicissitudes to become one of the giants of the radio industry.

By 1929 Philco had inaugurated intensive methods of mass production — from the arrival of the raw material·in the form of metal sheets, wire, and wood to shipment of the packaged product. The various parts of the radio set, manufactured in separate departments, flow together to the final assembly lines. One fifth of Philco's workers are inspectors. The plant maintains no storage room ; the completed radio sets go from assembly lines and packers to the trucks and freight cars. There is at the plant a private railroad siding with nearly a half mile of track. Packaging is a careful process, especially for the automobile set, which is tested for loose parts by being slammed on a one-inch-thick lead plate, pounded with a heavy, rubber mallet, and shaken in imitation of road conditions. The final package is thrown against the floor.

Successive improvements have emerged from Philco's research and engineering department — automatic volume control, tone control, 6.3-volt tubes of universal application, shadow tuning, inclined sounding board, short-wave reception, all-wave aerial, automatic aerial selector, acoustic clarifiers on high fidelity models, precision radio dial, automatic tuning, magnetic tuning, cone centric tuning, spread band dial, and music interpretation controls. In special laboratories extreme climatic conditions are reproduced. Another testing room is the "padded cell," soundproofed, where each new speaker is tested so that it "hurts" the ear, to assure the reproduction of sound for the entire range of the human ear, including many vibration frequencies audible to but few persons and also some only to insects.

Television has been pioneered in the local factories, and a television broadcasting station sends regular programs, received at many suburban test stations.

L. from Ontario St.; R. on Front.

At Erie Avenue, on the right, is the S.K.F. PLANT (5) *(visitors not admitted)*, a low, modern structure fenced in and surrounded by a lawn. Ball bearings are manufactured here. The plant was built in 1912 and designed by Dodge Day Zimmerman.

The official name of this establishment is S.K.F. Industries, Inc. S.K.F. was derived from the name "Aktiebolaget Svenska Kullager Fabriken" (Swedish Ball Bearing Co.).

In the manufacture of ball bearings, Swedish and American steel are used — metal of extreme hardness and toughness, free from defects and chemically pure. The pressure between the balls and the raceways at the point of contact is about 150 pounds per square inch. Ball and roller bearings have their loads concentrated in a comparatively limited space. Of paramount importance are accuracy of dimensions, surface finish, and strength.

At the beginning of the manufacturing process, the material used is in the form of bars, tubes, and forgings. These must be annealed

J. B. Brill Co. Plant
Steel giants press more steel into cars

to permit turning on automatic lathes, screw machines, and a special chamfering machine. During these operations a small amount of material is left over in the ball to permit grinding after the parts are hardened. In the turnings tolerances are as high as a few thousandths of an inch, while the grinding operations restrict tolerances to a few ten-thousandths. The standard tolerance for balls and rolls is .0005 of an inch. Such accuracy is necessary to insure uniform loadings, as overloading on any single bearing in a series would result in its early failing.

R. from Front St. on Erie Ave.

At Erie Avenue, left, is the vast PLANT OF THE SLOANE- BLA- BON CORPORATION (6), manufacturers of linoleum, both inlaid and printed.

The CUNEO EASTERN PRESS PLANT (7), at F Street *(may be visited by appointment, singly or in groups)*, a red brick, three-story structure, with overhead ventilation and 350,000 square feet of floor space, is one of eight plants controlled by the Cuneo Press, Inc. It contains 70 presses, from the tiny job press to the towering four-color rotary press, and has a capacity of more than 250 tons of printed material daily. Its chief products include such well-known magazines of national distribution as *Aero Digest, American Homes, American Legion, Cosmopolitan, Delineator, Good Housekeeping, House Beautiful, Liberty, Motor, Screenland, Silver Screen,* and many others.

To copy coming in is assigned one of the many type faces, and type size and paper texture are determined in order to estimate the size and volume the printed matter will occupy. Type faces, illustrations, and paper are harmonized, since a delicate type design would be lost on rough paper.

The old method of hand composition, used for small jobs and special work, entails setting the type in lines in a device called a "stick," open on one side, and one end of which is adjustable to the width of the line desired. When set in the stick the type is upside down. Sentences are "justified," or made even, by inserting or removing spaces, which are measured on the point and pica basis, to insure an accurate fit when used in combination.

The filled stick of type is then transferred to a galley — a long, shallow, metal tray which holds the type firm for inking. The impression taken from the galley-held type by pressure from a roller is a galley proof, used for proofreading.

The two machines used for composing are the linotype and the monotype. The linotype assembles brass molds or matrices in a line, each bearing a letter or character which has been stored in a magazine in the machine. Molten metal enters the assembled brass moulds and a metal line or "slug" of type is cast by the action. The cast line

523

is ejected by the machine and the brass moulds automatically redistributed. No correction can be made without recasting the entire line, called a "slug." When the printing job has been completed, the "slugs" are remelted into fresh type metal. The linotype is used in all grades of magazine and pamphlet printing.

The monotype consists of two distinct parts, a composing machine with keyboard, and a caster. The keyboard perforates a paper roll, and can be operated at any speed regardless of the limitations of the casting part of the operation. The perforated paper roll is then transferred to the caster where compressed air passes through the perforations, forcing a jet of molten type metal into a mold corresponding to the letter whose pressure created the perforation. The connection with the actual physical production of the type metal is thus relaxed, and this constitutes the principal advantage of the monotype machine, conceived in 1890 by Lanston and manufactured at the present time at Twenty-fourth and Locust Streets, Philadelphia.

After the galley proof has been pulled, it is corrected in the plant to eliminate compositor's errors. This copy is sent back to the compositor, who makes indicated corrections. A revised proof is then submitted to the author and is returned by him with further corrections or approval.

After the type has been set in galleys and the galley proofs corrected, it is divided into page lengths ; running heads and page numbers are added, and the mass of type is tied up in page units. Title pages, illustrations, and other matter also are set up in blocks of page size, the unused areas being filled in with metal or wooden strips of varying width. "Imposition" is the arrangement of page blocks on a metal slab, called the stone, in such position that they will emerge in proper order when the sheet is printed and folded. Strips of wood or metal called "furniture" are placed between the page blocks to form the margins of the printed pages. A metal frame called a chase is put around the pages so arranged on the stone. The vacant space in the chase is built into a firm mass of type pages and furniture, tightened by expanding keys called quoins. This locked-up mass of metal, furniture, and chase is called the form. Ordinarily the printing is done from the surface of this form. When a form is locked for the press, it is called the press lock-up. If single pages or small units are locked for the stereotyper or electrotyper they are called "foundry lock-ups." If the edition is large the form itself is not used directly, but the printing is done from either stereotyped or electrotyped plates.

In stereotyping, a matrix ("mat"), composed of several sheets of absorbent paper pasted together in a mass, is moistened and pressed into every part of the surface of the form. The mat is dried, type

524

metal poured into it, and a negative plate or cast, an exact reproduction of the original form, results. This cast or stereotype is mounted on a block and used as a form. The mat can be used for making additional casts, if needed. Ordinary stereotypes will not reproduce fine screen illustrations well.

In electrotyping, the form is pressed into a sheet of metal heavily surfaced with wax and coated with fine graphite. The wax surface takes a positive mold of the form, as in the case of the stereotyped mat. That part of the mold which is to be plated is again dusted or washed with graphite and placed in a bath of copper sulphate through which an electric current is passed. The selected part of the wax mold is thereby plated with a thin shell of copper which is an exact duplicate of the original form. When a shell of sufficient thickness has been deposited, it is peeled from the wax, trimmed, backed up with type metal, mounted on wood or metal base, and used in place of the original form. Electrotyping, slower and more expensive than stereotyping, is used for fine printing. After the forms have served their purpose they are broken up and used for type metal.

The cuts, stereotype or electrotype plates, may now be attached in their proper sequence on the press, an intricate mechanical task on the large presses.

Small job presses and great color machines, with their rows of cylinders, fit into the pressroom. Presses here are operated day and night.

Good register — the exact meeting of lines on both sides of a sheet — is the concern of stoneman and pressman. The former determines the margins and the position of the pages ; the latter sees that the paper goes on the press accurately. In color work, in which several impressions may be printed over each other, exactness is particularly important.

In the bindery, thousands upon thousands of sheets from the presses are put through folding, gathering, stitching, covering, and trimming machines. The conveyor system in use runs 24 hours a day.

The addressing and mailing department releases the flood of printed matter to every corner of the world. "The Cuneo" has one press among its great battery, capable of printing 10,000 books in each of the 17 hours it runs daily. With such Niagaras of the printed word in action, it is easy to understand why, in the year 1936, the shipping department was called upon to handle 31,200,000 shipments, totaling 125,000,000 pounds.

L. from Erie Ave. on M St.

At Bristol Street are the CARL MACKLEY HOUSES (8) (named for a hosiery worker who was killed during a strike on March 6, 1930), constituting one of the first low-rent housing developments established in the United States with the aid of the Federal Government. The group of four multi-family apartment houses, situated across from the onetime farm of Stephen Decatur, Jr., occupies a city block and was erected in 1934 by the Hosiery Workers Union through the Juniata Park Housing Corporation. The strikingly modern design of these buildings is warmed by the use on the exterior of buff and yellow glazed terra-cotta tiles. The units are three and three-and-a-half-stories high, built of reinforced concrete, and are without ornamentation, except for plaster surfaces around exterior doors. The project was sponsored by the American Federation of Hosiery Workers and erected with the proceeds of a $1,039,000 loan from the Public Works Administration, to be repaid over a 35-year period, with interest of 4 percent and annual amortization charges starting at 1.51 percent. The group of buildings was designed by Kastner & Stonorov and William Pope Barney. The cost of the plot was $115,000. Work began in January 1934, and the first tenants were received in January 1935. All but seven of the 284 apartments had been rented by November of that year.

Included in the rental prices are steam heat, electric light, power for refrigeration and stoves, the use of electric washing machines, and laundry driers in rainy weather. The construction, two rooms deep, eliminates corridors, provides cross ventilation, and admits a maximum of sunlight.

Most of the apartments have porch balconies, and the roofs of the units have been utilized as terraces for work and recreation. A swimming pool ; a wading pool for small children ; a nursery school ; an auditorium ; a free library ; recreation rooms ; art, modeling, and woodworking classes ; and work shops are available to tenants.

Although the group was established primarily to solve an acute housing problem for members of the American Federation of Hosiery Workers, tenancy is not restricted to members. Approximately 60 percent of the residents are members of some union, the remainder being made up largely of industrial and clerical workers.

The relationship of management to residents is mildly paternalistic, and the "human element" is carefully considered. There is no suggestion of the "take it or leave it" attitude. Reasonable complaints are considered ; no pressure to obtain immediate payment of rent is exerted on tenants whom illness or unemployment has placed in financial extremity. Despite this lenient policy, rent arrears are negligible. Cooperating with the management is a steering committee of tenants, whose nine members debate any questions or grievances that may arise. The residents operate a credit union and a cooperative market.

The auditorium is available free, but only for those functions in which all residents may have a part. No dues may be charged by any of the clubs using the buildings' facilities.

Three acres of the block containing the houses is open area, largely lawns and gardens ; and care was taken in the initial design to provide light, air, and space, along with safety for the children. There is but one street on the entire block, Juniata Park and Juniata Public Golf Course bordering the community on the north.

R. from M St. on Cayuga ; L. on Adams Ave. to Frankford Ave.

This leads to a point a little to the right of where Kensington Avenue merges into Frankford Avenue. Overhead are the Frankford "El" tracks, main connecting link with the central shopping district and with West Philadelphia.

At 4217-21 Frankford Avenue, a short distance to the right of the Hunting Park Avenue intersection, is the HOME OF THE FIRST BUILDING AND LOAN ASSOCIATION IN THE UNITED STATES (9).

On January 3, 1831, a meeting was held in the public house of Thomas Sidebotham (Side-both-am's Inn) for the purpose of "forming an association to enable contributors thereof to build or purchase dwelling houses." The organization name selected was the Oxford Provident Building Association of Philadelphia County. The association matured in 10 years, the first payment being made January 17, 1831 ; the last, January 11, 1841. It is said the first loan was made to a lamplighter, Comly Rich, who borrowed $500 to buy his little two-and-a-half-story frame house in Orchard Street. This house is still standing. The Oxford association had been patterned after the plan of the Earl of Selkirk's association, instituted in Scotland in 1815, and the founders of the Philadelphia organization learned of it through correspondence with relatives and friends in that country. It was a terminating association and unincorporated, but in the main its features have been the basis of all the building and loan associations in the United States, one seventh of which are in Philadelphia.

On August 11, 1931, a boulder, to which was attached a bronze plate commemorating the construction of 8,000,000 houses, through the agency of American building and loan associations, was dedicated in Womrath Park, Frankford, a tiny square opposite the former inn.

L. from Frankford Ave. on Church St. ; L. on Paul.

The LA FRANCE ART INSTITUTE (10), 4420 Paul Street *(open 9 to 4 daily, except Sat. and Sun. ; adm. free)*, was founded in 1920 as an affiliate of the La France Industries, weavers of upholstery fabrics. The institution has greatly expanded its scope, and is now an important factor in the art education of Philadelphia.

The La France museum contains collections of contemporary painting and sculpture, wood carving, posters and other objects. There are two large exhibition galleries and six small rooms displaying etchings,

527

water colors and gouaches. Recently the works of American painters, especially Philadelphians, have been added. The school is strongly influenced by L'Ecole des Beaux Arts, Paris.

Continue on Paul St. to Sellers ; R. from Paul on Sellers ; R. on Frankford Ave. ; L. on Orthodox St.

The building at 1507 Orthodox Street houses the FRANKFORD HISTORICAL SOCIETY (11) *(open Tues. 8 to 10 p. m., Thurs. 2 to 4 p. m. ; adm. free)*, founded in 1905 to preserve the records and history of Frankford. Built in Georgian Colonial style, of red brick with limestone trim, it houses an interesting collection of relics, manuscripts, and pictures dealing with historic Frankford.

Directly opposite is the ORTHODOX FRIENDS' MEETING HOUSE (12), built in 1831. It is a frame structure, with a carriage shed attached.

R. from Orthodox St. to Penn ; Continue on Penn to Arrott ; R. from Arrott to Frankford Ave. ; R. on Frankford to Meadow ; L. on Meadow to Paul to Frankford ; R. on Frankford to Unruh ; R. on Unruh.

At Milnor Street is HENRY DISSTON & SONS, INC., PLANT (13) *(open weekdays from 9 to 4).*

The life story of Henry Disston, founder of a vast industrial plant, recapitulates in minature the history of American industry during its period of ascension.

He came to Philadelphia from Tewkesbury, England, in May 1833, at the age of 14. The same year he apprenticed himself to a saw-maker, who later failed in business, leaving in lieu of wages a few unfinished saws. Henry completed and sold them, thus obtaining the small capital with which he started his own venture in a room and basement near Second and Arch Streets.

In 1846 Disston took larger quarters. When the new plant was destroyed by fire in 1849, he rapidly erected a four-story factory, 50 by 100 feet, on an adjoining site.

Disston evidenced skill, persistence, and an eagerness to try new methods and devices. He was always ready to experiment with a new machine or a new labor saving device which would lower the cost of production. He never lost a market once gained. Through his efforts, this country became independent of English producers of saws, files, and other tools.

During the Civil War, Disston equipped an enlisted company of his workmen at his own expense, and one of his sons marched as a private in its ranks. He discovered that it paid to encourage harmony among his workers. He gave them an excursion up the Delaware at a time when company outings were a rarity ; when the Centennial Exhibition revealed his display of steel tools as among the finest ever seen in the country, he spent $500 to pay admissions for his workers.

528

Today the plant is the largest saw works in the world, employing 2,600 workers in 68 buildings that cover 65 acres.

The simple handsaw involves more than 80 progressive operations. Steel is made in the company's steel mill using the latest electric furnaces, steam hammers, and rolling mills ; there are also pyrometers that control furnace heat, testing apparatus, chemical and physical laboratories.

Cast, the steel ingot is rolled into a plate and then trimmed. The transformation actually commences in the handsaw department. Massive power shears cut the sheet to form and size. These machines are hand fed, and the speed and precision of the operators seem almost automatic. Each blade is stamped with a figure indicating the number of points to the inch it will have, and an automatic toothing machine tooths the saw blade.

The blade here is soft and unfit for sawing. It goes now to the hardening shop, where special oil-burning furnaces heat it to the desired temperature. It is then plunged edge first into a special hardening bath, where it becomes so hard and brittle that care must be used in handling it until after the blade is tempered. This delicate operation, which dictates to a considerable extent the durability and cutting qualities of the saw, consists of drawing or reducing the extreme hardness imparted during the previous operation, thus relaxing the molecular rigidity and imparting life and elasticity to the saw blade.

"Smithing-in-the-black" — the skillful hammering of the saw blade to straighten and flatten it — is the next operation before sending the blade to grinding machines. "Smithing" requires the highest development of the saw maker's skill. In a room 430 feet long, where the operation is performed, the line of men fades away in the distance, while the rhythmical tapping of their hammers sounds like the regular vibrations of some gigantic machine. A man lifts a blade, sights along it toward the light to learn from the shadows on the blade just where the hammer should fall. The wavering nature of artificial light makes daylight essential for this kind of work.

Across the same room are the grinding machines, extending in an uninterrupted line the entire length of the building.

In these, the blade is ground to the proper gauge or thickness, and taper-ground towards the back. The handsaw blade is ground so that it tapers in thickness from the tooth edge to the back and from the handle to the point. The tooth edge is of even thickness from end to end.

Tension, the next step, is a process of hammering. It requires considerable skill and experience, for in it the blade is given the proper amount of tension, spring, or character. In a "fast" blade the metal is too long on the edge, and needs expanding from the center. In a "loose" blade the metal must be stretched on the edge. A saw not properly tensioned will not cut straight. Without tensioning, the blade would buckle in the wood.

The blade is then ground a second time. This is the final, or "draw" grinding, which prepares the blade for a higher polish. Glazing or buffing is necessary to give polish to the finished blade.

The next operation, "blocking," done by highly experienced workers, consists of tensioning and correcting any slight irregularities which may have developed during the "draw" grinding or glazing.

In addition to the anvil, these men use also a lignum vitae block, whence the name of the operation — blocking. While affording a base sufficiently hard for the work, this wood prevents hammer marks from appearing on the finished blade. After blocking, the blade is polished and stiffened to restore the spring of the steel, which is more or less affected by the previous operations.

After stiffening, the blade is passed into the etching room, where the mark of quality is placed on it, and it is now ready for the setting of the teeth. A skilled workman lays the blade on the setting block or stake, and beginning with the first tooth at the butt end sets each alternate tooth. Then the blade is reversed, and beginning with the first unset tooth at the point, each alternate tooth is set. A hammer with a long, tapering head is used. A tap of the hammer sets each tooth half the thickness of the blade, making the cutting edge about twice as thick as the blade. This prevents binding.

Sharpening follows setting. With the saw fastened in a special vise, and the file held in both hands, the sharpener moves swiftly from tooth to tooth, giving each the proper bevel and a keen edge. To the amateur, with whom saw filing is a slow and laborious process, the speed attained by these experts is astonishing. The file seems to leap from tooth to tooth, and yet every stroke has the sureness gained from long experience and practice.

Retrace on Unruh St.; L. on State Rd. to Bridge St.

This street crosses the approach to the Tacony-Palmyra Bridge, which spans the Delaware here. Designed by Ralph Modjeski, Frank M. Masters, and Clement E. Case, and begun in 1928, the main span measures 2,324 feet. Extensive factory grounds line State Road on the right.

The FRANKFORD ARSENAL (14), one boundary of which is the left side of State Road (also Tacony Avenue) *(open 10 to 4 except Sat. and Sun.; adm. free)*, is used by the Federal Government for the manufacture of small arms, ammunition components, and fire control instruments. The arsenal stands on the point of land formed by the confluence of Frankford Creek and the Delaware River, extending along the northern boundary of the creek to Bridge Street.

The arsenal's 282 buildings and grounds cover an area of 94 acres and include shops, storehouses, and barracks. It is one of the oldest institutions of its kind in the country. It was provided for in an act of Congress on February 8, 1815, and the construction of buildings was begun in 1816.

Those that are of interest in point of both age and architecture are, in chronological order : Nos. 2 and 3, of brick with oak beams, evidently purchased with the original tract ; No. 6 and the west storehouse, of stone and timber, dating from 1817 ; Nos. 4 and 5, of stone and timber, built in 1820 ; and the house of the commandant, which is of stone faced with brick. No. 1, the most recent of the old houses, is of stone and was built in 1823.

All these buildings are painted yellow with a black trim. The roofs of some are of slate ; others of tin. The architectural style is very simple, exhibiting the influence of the Greek Revival. The timber framework is of oak, joined by wooden pegs.

The first purchase of land for the arsenal, approximately 21 acres on Frankford Creek, was made from Frederick Fraley and his wife at a price of $7,680.75.

Originally, the arsenal, besides being a storage depot, was used for the repair and cleaning of small arms and harness, the manufacture of percussion caps, friction primers, brushers, and musket balls, and for the proving and inspection of gunpowder. In 1851 there was introduced the manufacture of small arms, fixed ammunition, and cavalry, artillery, and infantry equipment. Standard gauges, scales, weights, calipers, and measures of proportion are made here for use in Government shops elsewhere. A large part of the small-arms ammunition for use by the Federal forces is manufactured at the arsenal.

The arsenal has had a placid history, with the exception of the Civil War period. Capt. Josiah Gorgas, a native Pennsylvanian who commanded the arsenal at that time, resigned April 3, 1861, just before the first guns were fired upon Fort Sumter, and cast his lot with the South.

L. on Bridge St. ; R. on Richmond St.

At the foot of Norris Street are the buildings of what was formerly the PLANT OF THE WM. CRAMP & SONS SHIP AND ENGINE BUILDING CO. (15), later occupied by the I. P. Morris Iron Works a company which passed into the control of Cramps in 1891.

From 1830 until 1927 this plant constructed vessels for peace and war. William Cramp, the founder, contributed greatly to the perfection of the modern warship. In 1830, with a capital saved from his earnings as a journeyman ship carpenter, he began as a shipbuilder at the foot of Otis Street, now East Susquehanna Avenue. In 1872 the William Cramp & Sons Ship and Engine Building Company was incorporated with a capital of $500,000. Subsequent growth

531

was rapid. The main works, fronting 1,000 feet on the Delaware River, and the adjacent Port Richmond Iron Works, owned by the subsidiary, the I. P. Morris Company, made this one of the largest shipbuilding plants in the world.

A slump in naval construction following the Washington Naval Limitation Treaty of 1921, intensified by increasing competition, forced the Cramp organization to suspend activities in 1927.

At Delaware Avenue (into which Richmond Street merges) and Shackamaxon Street, left, the PLANT OF THE PENNSYLVANIA SUGAR COMPANY (16) *(visiting hours 8 to 5, except Sat. and Sun. ; report to engineer's office)* rises in a strangely shaped geometrical brick mass, from which protrude at fantastic angles a variety of tanks and metal pipes.

This huge refinery imports its raw material from Cuba, Puerto Rico, the Philippines, and Hawaii. The dark brown raw sugar, in 325-pound bags, is transferred from the docks to a long conveyor, at the end of which workmen open the bags for mechanical emptying into a hopper. The raw mass is raised to a bin of 1,000-ton capacity on the roof of the melter house or into the warehouse from which it is reclaimed by a system of conveyors. The residue in the bags, amounting to five tons a day, is conserved by a laundering process.

From the minglers where the crystals are puddled with saturated syrup, they pass through rapid centrifugals, similar to laundry driers, which wash the now fluid mass free of impurities and of molasses, leaving it ivory colored. In the melters, water converts it into a thick syrup. The melters are a maze of piping and tanks.

Passage through a corridor of mechanical filters, consisting of filter leaves covered with minutely perforated monel metal cloth, is the next step. These cloths are covered with a spongy mass of diatomous silica, composed of myriads of capillary tubes, and by the time the syrup has passed through it is amber in color. It is then pumped through bright copper piping to the char house, a 12-story building filled with an array of pumps, piping, batteries of filters 10 feet in diameter by 25 feet deep, and oil-burning kilns for revivifying the char. The filters are charged with 5,000 tons of hard, granulated, porous charcoal which decolorizes the amber syrup. An operator watches the liquid to detect a slackening of the decolorizing power of the char, in which case he drains the sugar syrup, washes the char with hot water, and sends it through the tight retorts in a red-hot furnace for restoration.

The colorless syrup proceeds to the storage tanks in the top of the pan house to await its turn to be drawn into the vacuum pans — large tanks built of heavy copper plates and fitted with steam coils, a condenser, and a vacuum pump. The pump lowers the temperature of the boiling liquid to about 130 to 170 degrees, and prevents scorching. In the pans, crystals of any size are produced from the fine caster sugar to "Sparkling A," or even as large as $\frac{1}{4}$-inch rock candy. The crystals form slowly and float in the "mother syrup." Centrifugals (bronze baskets 40 inches in diameter, with finely perforated screen perimeters) spin toplike at a speed of 1,000 revolutions per minute, ejecting the syrup while the crystals remain on the screen to be washed. The wet sugar is delivered to the revolving dryers for drying and separation into various sizes.

In the packing house a great variety of automatic weighing and packing machinery fills bags and cartons of all sizes from two pounds to 100, all within an accuracy of a fraction of an ounce. For special trade, kosher sugar is furnished. Some customers require their sugar packed in wooden barrels containing 350 pounds. Some export buyers demand moisture-proof bags, and the southern housewife has a predilection for cotton bags which make good dishcloths.

Cubes and tablets of various sizes and shapes are made in cylindrical presses fitted with automatic packers. Powdered sugar is produced in large pulverizers from standard sugar and is packed immediately.

Final product of the refining process is black strap molasses, containing sugar, glucose, potash, and various chemicals. This is sometimes refined into table syrup, but in the Pennsylvania refinery it is sent to the byproducts plant. Here it is used for alcohol production, being mixed with yeast which breaks up the glucose into alcohol and carbonic acid gas. The latter bubbles through the mash and is recovered.

The mash, containing about 8 percent of alcohol, is pumped into a continuously operating still, where the alcohol is boiled off and then packed for such uses, as an antifreeze, a flavoring, and a solvent.

The final processing of the distillery slop completes the cycle, delivering fertilizer for the production of sugar cane.

R. from Delaware Ave. on Market St. to City Hall.

ALONG THE WATER FRONT

City Tour 10

Route: Take Market St. subway train marked Frankford, east bound, from City Hall Station to Fairmount Ave. Returning: north on Broad St. to City Hall.

THERE was a time when the bowsprits of schooner, brig, and barque cast their shadows upon Delaware Avenue ; a time when long jib booms thrust their tips into the upper windows of buildings across the then narrow thoroughfare. There was a time,

533

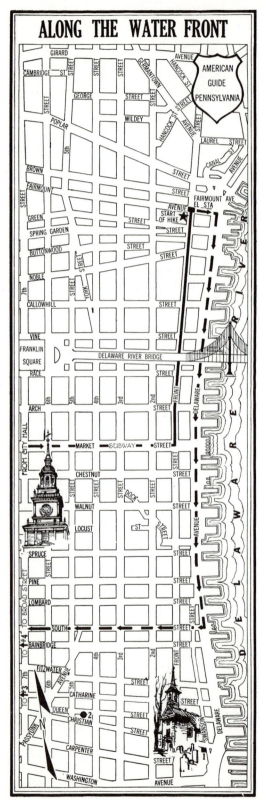

ALONG THE WATER FRONT

1. Church of Gloria Dei
2. Settlement Music School
3. Graphic Sketch Club
4. Arthur House

moreover, when Delaware Avenue did not exist ; what is now Water Street — one half block westward from the avenue — actually fronted on the river at Market Street.

When the eyes of white men first beheld what is now Philadelphia's busy water front, the woods on the embankment almost reached the water's edge. Near the present Market Street a steep hill rose inland ; into the slope of this hill were dug the caves which for a time sheltered some of the settlers who had preceded Penn. The hill, its grade especially noticeable where today's Market Street dips downward to Delaware Avenue, is responsible for Market Street's original name — High Street.

Water Street still exists behind its barricade of brick-walled structures, but the tall ships live only in memory. Gone are the square-riggers and schooners, gone also, the fast clippers which in the latter days of sail tried desperately to match canvas and wood against steam and steel.

Nowadays, the water front is the home of a great industry with its particular job to do. Its business is the transshipment of commodities, and it is geared to do that job with the least possible delay and the greatest possible profit. The sail lofts of an earlier day have been replaced by factories and warehouses. Along Delaware Avenue, once a strip of gluey mud, locomotives now crawl, hauling clanking box-cars ; while overhead, from Arch to South Street, the "El" rumbles and quakes to the passage of electric trains. Where once only horses strained against the traces of high-piled drays, trucks now too dart between the supports of the "El" structure. Along the avenue are refineries that produce a major portion of the Nation's sugar supply ; distilleries that turn out a vast amount of alcohol and whiskey ; and great factories with a dozen other products.

The old taverns with their aroma of ale and rum have long since disappeared, and their places have been taken by tawdry taprooms, where the sailor home from a voyage may seek relaxation in cheap whiskey and cheaper women. And home to the Delaware the voyagers do come, from all over the world. The water front is almost a hundred miles from the sea, yet along its piers are tied vessels from the banana republics to the south of us, ships with cargoes of jute and tea from India, copra from the South Seas, manganese and copper from Africa, or wares from the Orient. Rising and falling on the quiet Delaware, these ships, with their businesslike, bluff bows and neat deck-houses, in no way suggest the perils and adventure of the sea.

R. from Elevated Station at Fairmount Ave. ; R. on Delaware Ave.

Walking along the river side of Delaware Avenue, where wavelets slap against bulkheads that prevent the street from sliding into the water, gazing at ships whose names recall far places, even a landsman may feel the urge that has moved men immemorially to go down to the sea in ships. Walking there, few may escape a wish to take part in that moving world.

On summer nights when warm breezes crisp the water and the moon rides high, the river is gay with brightly lighted excursion boats plying between Philadelphia and Wilmington. The music of jazz bands floats across the water — now soft and low, now swift and blaring. The boat decks are a favorite rendezvous for lovers.

By day, these same boats are converted into a floating picnic ground for hundreds of women who, with their children, sail leisurely up

Delaware River Bridge
"A poem of stone and steel"

stream and down, munching sandwiches and commenting upon the sights — and smells — of the Delaware.

From Fairmount Avenue to South Street, many piers, some large and some small, line the riverbank, and through the doors of each passes a never-ending stream of commodities. The banana boats unload their cargoes at Pier 9, North. The size of the cargo varies with the season. One boat arrives each week during the winter ; in summer the shipments are doubled. About 30,000 bunches of bananas are imported in each boat.

A common sight is the long queue of teams lined up in the middle of the avenue near Pier 9. These, the banana wagons awaiting their turn to drive into the warehouse, sometimes extend for blocks on the busy streets, and so closely are they drawn up that the horses of one wagon may nuzzle the tailboard of the wagon in front.

A stroll southward from Fairmount Avenue is as hard upon the feet as it is interesting to the eye. The jaunt is likewise, for the unwary, attended with a certain amount of hazard. To view all the phases of activity, the wayfarer must weave in and out of narrow lanes between railroad cars, dodge hurrying trucks and drays rumbling from warehouses, and generally risk injury a dozen times within a block.

On the right are factories and warehouses, constructed with a view to efficiency rather than to architectural beauty, and typical of a progress indifferent to everything but the efficient movement of its machine. Crowded, almost stifled, by these grimy and ugly monuments to the speeding-up of commerce are the few small shops that still retain the old-time flavor of the sea — among them are the pipe shops, catering to seafaring men and carrying in stock tobaccos from all parts of the world.

Impressive in its graceful sweep is the Delaware River Bridge, arching over the river from a point between Vine and Race Streets. One of the longest single-span suspension bridges in the world, it has eased the traffic jams and tie-ups that were so frequent on Delaware Avenue when ferries provided the only means of transportation across the river.

The bridge, designed by Ralph Modjeski and completed in 1926 at a cost of more than $37,000,000, has a length of 1.81 miles and an over-all width of 125 feet, 6 inches. A 57-foot roadway provides space for six traffic lanes. On each side of the way is a trolley track and a high-speed track, with a 10-foot pedestrian walk suspended above the tracks on either side. The high-speed line began operation in June 1936.

As for the construction details, the span has two main cables 30 inches in diameter, each consisting of 18,360 wires strung on what is called a traveling spider. More than 22,000 miles of wire, weighing

537

6,100 tons, was used ; the steel has an ultimate tensile strength of 229,500 pounds per square inch.

The height of the main span is 135 feet above mean high water ; the Delaware River itself is, and was from early days, quite deep in the vicinity of the Race and Vine Street fronts. It is recorded that when the ship *John Trux* was sunk by crushing ice floes off Race Street in the winter of 1863, her topsail yards were not visible above water.

Market Street, two blocks south of Race, had for its terminus as late as 1800 a wood wharf and a fish market. The hill here was used in winter as a race course for sleds, which sped from the summit to the water's edge. Here, during early years of the nineteenth century, a portion of the wharf acquired the name Crooked Billet (because it was made of crooked and twisted lumber) and won for itself the sinister reputation of a mantrap. History preserves the name of one victim, Isaac Jones, who at the age of 64 slipped off the icy wharf to his death in the Delaware.

From the first wharf below the Crooked Billet (this name is perpetuated in a small bystreet south of Market), a line of fast packets in 1805 forged a commercial link with New York. Other lines nearby made contact with the South, bringing in cargoes of watermelons that sold at the dock for a penny apiece ; and peaches for six pence a half-peck. Old-fashioned shallops brought hickory, pine, oak, maple, and gum. By the time of Stephen Girard commerce had so increased as to make imperative better wharfage facilities and an improved thoroughfare along the river.

Girard had dreamed of some day building a tree-lined boulevard along the water front. He died before he could realize his dream, but in his will he made a $500,000 bequest for the laying out of Delaware Avenue. In the vicinity of Market Street the land required for the avenue had to be reclaimed from the river. But no trees were planted ; rapidly encroaching warehouses and other structures doomed forever the hope of a tree-canopied boulevard. Thus Girard's wishes were only partly fulfilled.

Probably the most interesting section of the water front historically, as well as the most important commercially, is that part just south of Market. Here, under the frowning canopy of the "El," where rail-

Delaware Avenue at Noon

Claimed from the river by Stephen Girard

road beltline, ferry traffic, taxicabs, and freight trailers contribute their individual discords to the general dissonance, can be found occasional mementos of a day when river grass grew where hard-packed granite blocks now lie.

For example, at the northwest corner of Delaware Avenue and Walnut Street, on the Merchants Warehouse — a building occupying an entire block from Chestnut Street to Walnut, and from Delaware Avenue to Water Street — hangs a bronze plaque bearing this inscription :

EXILES
FOR CONSCIENCE SAKE
To the memory of the followers of
CASPAR von SCHWENCKFELD
who fled from Silesia and found
in Pennsylvania a haven of
religious toleration
They landed near this spot 1731-37
Erected by the Society of the Descendants of
The Schwenkfeldian Exiles September 22, 1934

In the rear of the same building, and about midway between Chestnut and Walnut on Water Street, are two more plaques. One, over the garage entrance, reads :

THIS TABLET MARKS
THE SITE OF TUN TAVERN
THE BIRTHPLACE OF THE
UNITED STATES MARINE CORPS.
HERE IN 1775 CAPTAIN SAMUEL
NICHOLAS, THE FIRST MARINE
OFFICER, OPENED A RECRUITING
RENDEZVOUS FOR THE MARINE
BATTALIONS AUTHORIZED BY
RESOLUTION OF THE
CONTINENTAL CONGRESS
NOVEMBER 10, 1775.

The other, to the left of the garage entrance, reads :

ON THIS SITE STOOD THE TUN
TAVERN, WHERE, ON ST. JOHN'S
DAY JUNE 24th, 1732, A GRAND
LODGE OF THE ANCIENT AND
HONORABLE SOCIETY OF
FREE AND ACCEPTED MASONS
WAS HELD.
IN COMMEMORATION, THIS TABLET
IS ERECTED BY THE PHILAD'A.
CHAPTER # 16, SOJOURNERS
CLUB, JUNE 2d, 1926.

Dock Street, the city's market basket, winding from Delaware Avenue below Walnut to Third Street near Chestnut, is a teeming community, alive with trucks and piled high with foodstuffs during

540

Old Swedes' Church
"Across the meadows were
wafted sounds of psalms"

Old Swedes' Church
Graveyard
"Eternal rest in Gloria Dei"

the gray hours preceding dawn. Activity slows to a whisper during the day *(see City Tour 2)*.

R. from Delaware Ave., on South.

South Street, the "bargain basement" of Philadelphia, is lined on both sides, from 4th Street to 15th Street, with shops that cater to the apparel needs of the city's slim-pursed element.

Barkers, who solicit trade for the stores, employ both physical force and oral persuasion in their efforts to ensnare a prospective purchaser. To the uninitiated visitor, this practice may be both alarming and embarrassing.

Saturday night transforms the street to a garish scene of neon signs ; brilliantly lighted windows arrayed with tawdry finery and cheap jewelry to attract the dollars of the milling shoppers.

R. from South St., on Broad to City Hall.

Alternate route from Delaware Ave. and South St. to Broad, traverses the older section of the city.

R. from Delaware Ave. on Christian St. ; R. on Swanson.

In the midst of the teeming water-front slums of Philadelphia stands the small, ivy-covered, red brick CHURCH OF GLORIA DEI (1) *(open daily 9 to 5)*. As lavish in historical tradition as it is simple in design, is Old Swedes', the oldest church still standing in this city and one of the oldest in the country.

The congregation of Gloria Dei had its beginning in a small structure on Tinicum Island, possibly as early as the middle of the seventeenth century. When Swedish colonization moved farther north on the Delaware, a blockhouse at Wicaco was utilized for religious gatherings. Wicaco was a settlement in what is now a part of southeastern Philadelphia, extending possibly as far north as the present line of South Street and as far west as Seventeenth. Divine services were held in the blockhouse from about 1666 to 1671, with Pastor Lars Lock paddling upriver from Chester each Sunday to preside.

The first resident ordained clergyman to preach to the Wicaco settlers was Rev. Jacobus Fabritius, a Dutchman, who took charge in 1677. As the congregation grew in size, it became increasingly imperative that a more churchlike edifice be erected. Thus, in May 1698, work was begun on a structure to occupy the site of the old blockhouse, and in 1700 Gloria Dei was completed and opened. Rev. Eric Tobias Biork pastor of the New Church at Christina, delivered the dedication sermon on July 2 of that year.

In 1846, narrow galleries were added. The fine pipe organ was imported from Germany and installed in this church. The comparative modernity of the galleries is attested by their small iron supporting columns. The present-day pews were added in 1902. A visit to the church is interesting from both the historic and the architectural point of view. The compactness of the structure is striking.

The exterior of red brick with white wood trim is unusual because of the large size of its front and side bays, compared to the size of the structure. The brick is laid in both Flemish and common bond. About the only touches of Swedish architecture are the steep peaked gables over the main entrance, and possibly the squareness of the

542

fine little bell tower. Entrance wings, similar in design to the main entrance, were added on either side in 1703 to strengthen the walls. The detail work, especially the doors and the square, many-paned windows, shows a decided English influence.

The interior walls, ceiling, and wainscoting are original, and the building has a certain mellowness of character. From the front door to the rear wall behind the pulpit, the church is not much more than 50 feet long. The ceiling of the interior does not follow the slope of the roof, but is almost a barrel vault in form, following the Swedish style.

In the center aisle are three stones, marking the graves of early pastors. The first stone between the door and pulpit is that over the grave of Olavius Parlin, a missionary sent from the mother church in Sweden, who died in 1757. Next is the grave of John Dylander, pastor of the church for four years, who died in 1741. The grave nearest the pulpit is that of Rev. Andrew Rudman, who died in 1708.

On the side walls are plaques commemorating the long service of Nicholas Collin, last missionary sent here from Sweden ; John Curtis Clay, first Episcopal rector ; and Snyder Binn Simes. The pastorates of these three covered a period of 124 years. The first died in 1831 and the last in 1915. To the right of the pulpit is a stone baptismal font, brought from Sweden by early colonists. It dates from about 1550. One of the pews is marked with the name plate of Justus Faulkner, who occupied the original. It was at Faulkner's ordination that the first concert held in Philadelphia was given by members of the Hermits of the Wissahickon, a mystic religious order.

Hanging below the organ loft is a figurehead showing two gilded angels above an open Bible. It was a decoration on the prow of one of the ships that brought the settlers from Sweden.

A narrow door leads into the vestry, which contains many interesting relics. In a frame on the wall is a parchment, yellowed by age. It is the naturalization certificate of Rev. Mr. Rudman, signed by William Penn, and dated "Three and Twentieth day of the fifth month in the Thirteenth Year of the Reign of William the Third over England." In a case below the parchment are a number of books, including a Book of Common Prayer, printed in London in 1716 ; a Psalm Book printed in 1762 ; a Charles XII Bible, published in Stockholm in 1707, the flyleaf bearing a Swedish inscription written by Dr. Nicholas Collin in 1796 ; and a catechism in the dialect of the Lenape Indians.

On another wall are photostatic copies of early marriage records. Included are references to the wedding on June 15, 1777, of Joseph Ashbourne and Elizabeth (Betsy) Ross. The wedding in Old Swedes was her second. An autographed letter by Jenny Lind, who sang in the church, is on still another wall, as is a letter in Swedish from Gustavus Adolphus, King of Sweden, dated 1618.

In the churchyard are a number of old tombstones, the oldest marking the grave of "Peter, son of Andreas Sandel, minister of the church, died 1708." A number of others are nearly as old, but virtually undecipherable. One slab, marking a grave dating from 1763, has sagged in the middle like a warped board, although no crack is apparent in its surface. Alexander Wilson, father of American ornithology, is buried here.

543

Old sailing vessels doomed by man's desire for faster travel

ALONG THE WATER FRONT (CITY TOUR 10)

The congregation of Old Swedes' Church was united with the Protestant Episcopal Church at the Episcopal Convention of 1845, largely because of the curtailment of financial support from Sweden and the gradual adoption of the English tongue following the Revolution.

From this historic spot some might wish to continue southward to the "Ship Graveyard," where three wooden sailing vessels lie rotting in the mud of the Delaware River off McKean Street. These four-masted topsail schooners in various stages of decay are the *Albert D. Cummins*, the *Francis J. McDonald*, and the *Marie C. Cummins*. Together with an iron barque, the *Severn*, which was scrapped two years ago, they belonged to Francis J. McDonald and Albert D. Cummins. They were laid up in Philadelphia shortly after the World War, and eventually were stripped of gear and fittings. Now only the schooners remain. They lie in the squat shadows of the Cities Service plant, their keels imbedded in mud and their main decks awash. All their masts are apparently intact ; and of the forward spars, only the jib boom of the *Francis J. McDonald* is gone, leaving the blunted tip of the bowsprit pointing obliquely skyward.

Retrace on Swanson St. ; R. from Christian ; R. from Christian on Fourth ; L. on Queen.

SETTLEMENT MUSIC SCHOOL (2), 416 Queen Street (*open daily, 9:30 to 6 and 7 to 10; adm. free*), has for its major objective the promotion of music on a community basis. Conceived in 1908, it had its birth in a few rooms donated by the College Settlement which it now adjoins. Not only the residents of this densely populated section, but also those of modest means throughout the city, may study music or other cultural subjects here.

The school is now housed in a four-story red brick building of modified Colonial Georgian design. The gray marble base, the trim and the pediment above the recessed central section, together with the free-standing entrance piers of its doorways, set this building apart.

Mrs. Mary Louise Curtis Bok made provision for the erection of the present building in 1917 as a memorial to her mother, Mrs. Louisa Knapp Curtis, first wife of Cyrus H. K. Curtis, publisher and philanthropist. Mrs. Bok has also established an endowment for the maintenance of the building and personnel. Part of the United Campaign fund is allotted to the school.

Activities for adult groups include classes in modeling, sketching dramatics, dancing, and adult and child psychology; round table discussions; an Italian women's club; monthly socials for parents and neighbors; personnel service; vocational guidance; and various forms of social recreation. For children, in addition to instruction in various branches of music, there are folk and rhythmic dancing classes, modeling and sketching classes, dramatic clubs, a creative English class, and general social clubs. A number of concerts and students recitals are sponsored, and each spring an art exhibition of students' work is held.

During the winter, when attendance is greatest, the faculty consists of eight staff workers, assisted by 30 part-time instructors and several WPA workers. The enrollment is more than 1,100.

In 1922 a conservatory department was established. The supply of native talent in this section was so plentiful that the school's facilities were overtaxed. The success of the conservatory gave impetus to the

R. From Queen St. on 5th to Catherine; L. on Catherine.

545

idea for the Curtis Institute of Music, which was established in 1924
Branch settlements have been opened throughout the city. Two
of these—the Lighthouse Settlement and the Reed Street House—
have become independent.

R. from Queen St. on 5th ; L. on Catharine.

The GRAPHIC SKETCH CLUB (3), at 711-19 Catharine Street
*(open Oct. 1 to May 1, Mon. to Fri., 9 a. m. to 10 p. m., Sat., 9 to 5 ;
Sun., 1 to 5; other months, Mon. to Fri. only, 9 to 5),* was founded
by Samuel S. Fleisher in 1899. Its objectives were and are to foster
study and appreciation of the fine arts and to provide opportunities
for self-expression and development of latent talent along cultural
lines for all classes of people, without limitation as to religion, race,
or economic status.

In pursuance of these ideals, tuition in the various classes is free
and attendance voluntary. The school has a registration of 2800
students, ranging in ages from children of four to men and women
well in the seventies.

The curriculum includes courses in charcoal drawing, oil painting,
water-color painting, clay modeling, etching, fashion design and
illustration, and rhythmic expression in the dance. Twelve competent
instructors are in charge of these classes.

Albin Polasick's beautiful statue of a man chiseling himself out
of a block of rock represents the club's motto, "Man chisels his own
destiny."

The club, which had its beginning at the Neighborhood Center,
428 Bainbridge Street, moved into its present location during the
year 1914, when Mr. Fleisher acquired the buildings of St. Martin's
College, an Episcopal training school for boys, extending from 715
to 719 Catharine Street.

The growth of the institution, spirited from the start, demanded
further expansion in 1922, and in that year the beautiful sanctuary
of the Church of the Evangelists, together with the church house,
711 to 713 Catharine Street, adjoining the college, were annexed.
Alterations were made to permit communication between the three
units, so that they now constitute a single building, with entrance
at 715 and 719.

The museum, has a permanent exhibition of art pieces from all
corners of the world. The exhibit includes carved ivories and other
old Japanese art, pottery, brocades, ancient Greek, Roman, and Venetian glass, and beautiful rugs.

The Sanctuary, formerly the Church of the Evangelists, houses a
museum of religious works of art bearing upon the Old and New
Testaments. A portion of this building is more than one hundred
years old.

Lining the side aisles are colored frescoes of Biblical scenes, the
work of Robert Henri, Nicola D'Ascenzo, and other outstanding
artists. The altarpiece, by Miss Violet Oakley of Philadelphia,
represents the daughter of Pharaoh holding the infant Moses, and
surrounding this, in a beautiful frame, are scenes depicting outstanding events in the life of Moses. It is a memorial to Mrs. Celia H.
Fleisher, mother of the founder. On the door of the Sanctuary,
which adjoins the main gallery, is this invitation, "To patrons of
the busy streets of Philadelphia—Enter this Sanctuary for rest, medi-

546

tation and prayer. May the beauty within speak of the past and ever-continuing ways of God."

No sermons of any kind are preached during the entire year, but everyone is welcome to enter for the sole purpose of meditation. Organ recitals are held in the Sanctuary every afternoon, and people of all faiths come here for silent meditation and prayer.

The art teachers' reference library on the third floor of the church house, presented to Graphic Sketch Club by the Carnegie Foundation, contains four hundred text books and more than two thousand colored and other prints of outstanding paintings, architectural photographs, textiles, sculptures.

R. from Catherine St. on 10th.

The ARTHUR HOUSE (4), 721 S. Tenth Street *(private)*, was for many years the home of Timothy Shay Arthur, a prolific writer of temperance tracts, who was the author of *Ten Nights In a Barroom and What I Saw There.*

Arthur, who had embarked on a literary career in Baltimore, joined a temperance society in 1830 when he was 21. He devoted his talents to producing tracts on temperance, and in 1841 he left Baltimore and settled in Philadelphia.

While living in this three-story, red-brick house, he turned out dozens of pamphlets on the evils of intemperance. In 1854 he completed his most famous work. As a novel, *Ten Nights in a Barroom* has run *Uncle Tom's Cabin* a close second in sales and circulation. Arthur died on March 6, 1885.

Retrace on 10th St., to South ; L. on South to Broad ; R. on Broad to City Hall.

FAIRMOUNT PARK

The sections of Fairmount Park through which these tours pass constitute a vast outdoor museum, with man's artistic efforts, in the form of statuary, consigned to a secondary place by the surpassing creations of the master artist— Nature. Statues, solitary and in groups, are scattered along the drives.

Mansions that hark back to the Colonial era of Philadelphia are numerous in the park, many of them restored and open to public inspection. In many instances these houses, of Georgian design, have been placed in settings that closely approximate the quiet charm and dignity of an English countryside.

East Park
City Tour 11

This route passes through the part of Fairmount Park which lies east of the Schuylkill, where the natural scenic splendors are typical of the park as a whole. It winds through rolling, tree-dotted hills, follows for a long stretch the serene Schuylkill River, and passes between high cliffs.

N. W. from City Hall on Parkway ; R. around Pennsylvania Museum of Art into East River Drive.

To the right of the drive is the statue, SILENUS AND THE IN-FANT BACCHUS (1), which was reproduced by the Barbedienne

547

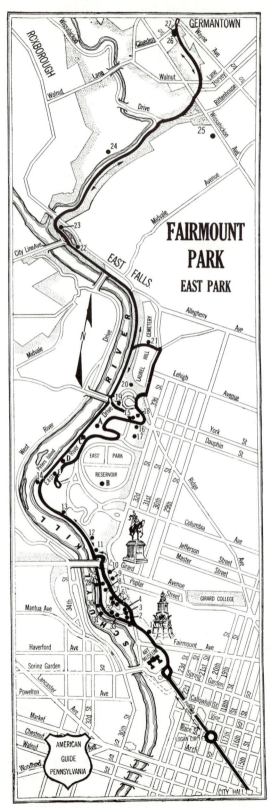

1. Silenus and the Infant Bacchus

2. Lincoln Monument

3. Lioness Carrying a Wild Boar to Her Young

4. Seaweed Fountain

5. The Wrestlers

6. Site of the Lemon Hill Pavilion

7. Statue of Morton Mc-Michael

8. Grant's Cabin

9. Humboldt Monument

10. Jeanne D'Arc

11. Tunnel

12. The Cowboy

13. Statue of Gen. U. S. Grant

14. A Pavilion

15. Statue of the Indian Medicine Man

16. Grand Fountain

17. Woodford Tennis Courts

18. Woodford Mansion

19. Strawberry Mansion

20. Robin Hood Dell

21. East Laurel Hill Cemetery

22. Queen Lane Pumping Station

23. Gustine Lake

24. Wissahickon Valley

25. Kenilworth

26. Mayfair House

27. Home of Connie Mack

28. Stone Plaza

29. Garfield Memorial

30. Statue of the Viking

31. Boathouse Row

32. The Puritan

33. Tam O'Shanter Group

Foundry of Paris from Praxiteles' original in the Louvre. Silenus, oldest of the satyrs, holds the infant Bacchus in his arms.

A short distance ahead, in the center of the intersection of East River and Sedgley Drives, is the LINCOLN MONUMENT (2), a huge seated figure of the Civil War President holding a copy of the Emancipation Proclamation. This vigorous work, created by Randolph Rogers, was erected in 1871, a gift of the Lincoln Monument Association.

R. from East River Drive on Sedgley Drive.

At the foot of the hill to the left stands a BRONZE GROUP, *Lioness Carrying a Wild Boar to Her Young* (3), an arresting animal study in bronze by August Cain, placed here in 1888.

A few feet ahead is the SEAWEED FOUNTAIN (4), a charming creation by Beatrice Fenton. Roughhewn rocks form the pedestal for this fountain, and in the center of the pool is a large sculptured tortoise with the figure of a child perched daintily on its back. Water trickles from the seaweed that trails from the outstretched finger tips of the child. Presented by Edwin F. Keen, it was placed here in 1922.

The STATUE entitled *The Wrestlers* (5), on the left, reproduced in bronze by Barbedienne from the original in the Royal Gallery at Florence, Italy, is a striking study in muscular development. Presented by A. J. Drexel, it was placed in November 1885.

To the left, several hundred feet off the road, on top of a hill, is the SITE OF THE LEMON HILL PAVILION (6). Summer symphony concerts were once presented in the pavilion. The old mansion still stands, calm behind its neat white fence. Lemon Hill, the broad area surrounding the mansion, was at one time the country seat of Robert Morris, financier of the American Revolution.

The STATUE OF MORTON McMICHAEL (7), onetime president of the Fairmount Park Commission and editor of the Philadelphia *North American*, is a sculptural work of J. H. Mahoney. Surmounting a grassy rise a short distance ahead, this statue, the gift of McMichael associates, was placed in 1882.

To the left, at the far side of the road entering the drive, is GRANT'S CABIN (8), used by the general at City Point, Virginia, during the siege of Richmond, and transported to its present site in 1868. Set in a scene of serenity, the small, unassuming cabin gives no hint of the turbulent activity that throbbed within its walls during the siege. It is surrounded by a memorial oak grove.

On the right is the HUMBOLDT MONUMENT (9), gift of the German Society of Philadelphia in memory of Alexander von Humboldt, naturalist and statesman. The work of Frederick Drake, of Berlin, it was dedicated in 1876. On the near right at the Girard Avenue intersection is the bronze JEANNE D'ARC MONUMENT (10), the work of Emmanuel Fremiet, erected in 1890.

549

R. from Main Drive across Girard Ave. into loop, circling L. and down to East River Drive.

A short distance ahead is a TUNNEL (11), hollowed out of a huge solid rock, the steep side of which reaches down to the water's edge. In 1935 the Park Commission, with the financial assistance of the Federal Works Program and Col. Robert Glendinning and his friends, transformed the roof of the tunnel and the area to the right into a rock garden with brilliant-hued bushes and flowers set among varicolored stones, with a small pond in one of its corners.

Immediately beyond the tunnel, to the right, surmounting a natural rock formation, is Frederic Remington's lusty FIGURE of *The Cowboy* (12), erected in June 1908.

Centering the intersection of Fountain Green Drive is a bronze equestrian STATUE OF GEN. U. S. GRANT (13), by Daniel Chester French and Richard C. Potter, erected in 1899.

A PAVILION (14), on the left, beyond the concrete Columbia Bridge of the Reading Railroad, marks the finish line of the Schuylkill Regatta course. Local, national, and international rowing events

Indian Medicine Man
"Keeps lonely vigil o'er his people's hills."

and motorboat races held here during the summer and fall months attract thousands of spectators.

About a mile north, the steel span of the Dauphin Street Bridge, completed in 1897, throws a wide-arched silhouette against the sky.

R. around hairpin turn just beyond Dauphin St. Bridge.

The road follows an S curve uphill and passes through picnic grounds to the bronze equestrian STATUE of *The Indian Medicine Man* (15), left, by Cyrus E. Dallin, erected in December 1903.

At the Statue is a junction with a winding road.

Right on this road, beyond a curve, stands the RANDOLPH MANSION (a). This fine old residence was once the home of Dr. Philip Syng Physick, noted Philadelphia surgeon, who was known as the "Father of American Surgery." It became the Randolph mansion in 1828, when Dr. Physick presented it to his daughter, Mrs. Randolph. Earlier it was known as Laurel Hill.

Built in 1748 by Joseph Shute, it is interesting both architecturally and historically, and is unusual for its asymmetrical plan. Its central portion is a two-story-and-attic Georgian Colonial mansion. On one end is a transverse wing housing an octagonal ballroom, and on the other end is a one-story kitchen. The structure is of brick, painted yellow with white wood trim. The pediment of its simple classic doorway is emphasized by another above the cornice line. The windows are of the flat arch type throughout the central portion, and the interior woodwork is exceptionally fine.

Samuel Shoemaker, early Philadelphia mayor, lived in the house during the British occupation of the city. When the Revolutionists recaptured Philadelphia, Shoemaker fled to New York, and the house was searched by the soldiers and later stoned by Revolutionary sympathizers. The mansion came into possession of the city in 1868.

Sharp R. at next intersection.

On the left is the EAST PARK RESERVOIR (b), and on the right, the ORMISTON MANSION (c), built in 1798 on the estate of Joseph Galloway, a Tory whose land was confiscated during the Revolution. The residence later came into the possession of Edward Burd, son-in-law of Chief Justice Shippen, who named it Ormiston after his father's estate in Scotland.

Set on the edge of a deep glen, Ormiston is a square, two-story, rough stucco building with a hip roof and wide porches on the river and land facades.

R. at fork of road.

ROCKLAND MANSION (d), on the right beyond the fork, was built in 1810 by George Thompson on an estate once owned by John Lawrence, Colonial mayor of Philadelphia.

A two-story-and-attic dwelling of cubelike proportions, it is of stucco-covered stone. On the roof is a "captain's walk." The doorway is deeply recessed, arched, and paneled, with a fine fanlight. The portico is notable for its finely fluted Doric columns and pilasters.

Farther along on the right is MOUNT PLEASANT MANSION (e) *(open weekdays 10 to 5 ; Sun. 1 to 5; adm. adults 25¢, children 10¢)*, historically the most important of the four mansions.

Mount Pleasant dominates a picturesque group of barns and other outbuildings suggestive of the manorial settings of old Virginia mansions along the James River, and has been completely refurnished in harmony with its period by the Pennsylvania Museum of Art.

Mount Pleasant Mansion rises two-and-a-half stories above a high foundation of hewn stone, with iron-barred basement windows set in stone frames. It is of massive rubblestone masonry, covered with buff, roughcast stucco. There is a horizontal belt course at the second floor level and the heavy quoined corners are of red brick. The keyed lintels of the large ranging windows are of faced stone.

The interior wood trim is exceedingly fine. Beautiful tooled cornices, graceful pilasters, nicely molded doors and window casings and heavy pedimented doorheads are all of excellent design and more carefully wrought than most Georgian Colonial work. The most elaborate room is a chamber on the second floor overlooking the river, and probably the boudoir of the mistress of Mount Pleasant. The architectural treatment of the fireplace end of this room, with exquisite carving above the overmantel panel and above the closet doors, is excellent.

The erection of Mount Pleasant was begun in 1761 by John MacPherson, a sea captain of Clunie, Scotland, who amassed a fortune in the adventurous practice of privateering. He lived in manorial splendor, entertaining the most eminent personages of the day with prodigal hospitality.

In the spring of 1779 MacPherson sold Mount Pleasant to Gen. Benedict Arnold. Following the discovery of Arnold's betrayal of his country, his property was confiscated and Mount Pleasant was leased for a short period to Baron von Steuben. Thereafter, it passed through several hands and finally to Gen. Jonathan Williams, of Boston, in whose family it remained until the middle of the nineteenth century, when it was acquired by the city as a part of Fairmount Park.

Retrace to Medicine Man statue at intersection.

The GRAND FOUNTAIN (16), on the right, in the center of a circular basin, is surrounded by a brown sand walk and a profusion of flowers. Of bronzed iron, about 25 feet high, it is mounted upon a concrete foundation. The circular base consists of five winged cherubs seated on rocks, holding frogs which discharge streams of water into the basin. Interspaced are lions' heads also emitting water. Standing around the massive pillar in the center are three tall and beautiful maidens, heads lowered and arms upraised, holding a huge round tray, edged by small lions' heads and three cherubs, holding vases and wands. A long, narrow, decorated vase surmounts the fountain. Sunlight on the flowing water causes a beautiful and dazzling effect. The fountain was erected in 1879 and presented to the city by the Fairmount Park Art Association. Behind the fountain are

Exterior of Mt. Pleasant

Interior of Mt. Pleasant
Memories of lovely Peggy Shippen

the WOODFORD TENNIS COURTS (17). *(A varying fee is charged for use of courts.)* During the summer months the 32 courts are in constant use.

L. just inside Dauphin St. entrance to Park.

A short distance along the drive is the WOODFORD MANSION (18), an excellent example of Georgian architecture.

Woodford's stateliness is due, in great measure, to its peculiar design and coloring. It was erected some time before 1730 as a one-story building. Judge William Coleman, in 1756, added a story and a wing, and a cornice was run around three sides at the first floor level. At the second floor is a heavier cornice, above which rise a hip-roofed attic and a "captain's walk." A heavy pediment above the first floor cornice adds an impressive weightiness to the facade. A buff wash applied over the Flemish bond brickwork gives the mansion a soft, tawny color.

The fine doorway is flanked by Doric columns and surmounted by a beautiful Palladian window and a pediment. The two rooms of the original first floor contain a wealth of interesting architectural detail. The oak floors, an inch and a half thick and doweled, and the stairway balustrade with its luxurious ramps and easings, are well preserved.

The mansion was used in later years as a park guard station, but after restoration in 1928 was opened to the public. It houses the collection of Colonial furniture belonging to the estate of Naomi Wood.

R. at fork of road ; bear L. on circular driveway.

STRAWBERRY MANSION (19), on the left *(open daily 11 a. m. to 5 p. m. ; adm. 25¢)*, once was the home of United States District Court Judge William Lewis, a friend of George Washington. The central unit, a two-and-a-half story structure, built by Judge Lewis in 1798, is in the Georgian Colonial style with gabled roof and dormers and Doric columns supporting the pedimented hood over the paneled doorway. The three-story wings, added about 1825 by Judge Hemphill, a friend of Thomas Jefferson, belong to the period of the Greek Revival, as evidenced by the design of their cornice and heavy scroll at the top. The central hall runs through to the rear, and has delicate arched niches and fluted Doric pilasters. The music room, to the left, shows the Greek Revival influence, notably in the windows, wide doorway, and fretted central ceiling panel. Especially fine in its delicate plaster work is the fireplace mantel in the parlor. The old kitchen, called the Indian Queen Room, is of plain plaster, and contains a huge fireplace, with a swinging crane, and antique furnishings. A hall runs along the entire rear of the second floor, and end wings rise four steps above the central section. The house is furnished throughout with fine old period pieces.

In 1835 the place was abandoned as a summer home, and the grounds became a picnic spot. When the park was opened, the house was utilized as a restaurant. It was restored by the Women's Committee of 1926.

Beyond a parking space in the crotch of the next fork in the road, lies ROBIN HOOD DELL (20) *(open every evening except Wed. from mid-June to mid-August ; adm. 50¢ upward).*

There was a time when the Philadelphia musical season closed with the coming of spring. Today, however, excellent music is available throughout the summer. In Robin Hood Dell, a beautiful natural auditorium, walled by wooded slopes and open to the sky, world-renowned artists present concert, ballet, and opera through eight weeks each summer. The regular orchestra, composed chiefly of members of the Philadelphia Orchestra, is a cooperative organization in which the members share the profits. Conductors of the first rank and soloists whose names are familiar throughout the world are engaged to bring the music of the masters to thousands who cannot afford seats for the regular concert season.

Audiences that often overflow the dell's 6,000 seats relax on summer nights in the cool comfort of out of doors to enjoy the immortal melodies of the world's greatest composers or, on occasion, lighter music of the popular concert variety.

Many nonpaying listeners who nightly sit or lie on newspapers along the grassy rim of the auditorium are joined for weekend or special programs by the hundreds unable to obtain tickets.

The dell was known in the nineteenth century as Robin Hood Glen and was occupied by a hotel which gained wide popularity because of its enchanting surroundings. Time leveled the hostelry.

The summer concert series was planned in response to popular demand, and Robin Hood Dell was selected as the auditorium. It was developed through the joint efforts of patrons of music and the Fairmount Park Commission. The finely proportioned but unadorned orchestra shell and the layout of the auditorium were designed by Walter Thomas.

Wooden benches rise in terraces on the sloping floor of the valley. A barbed wire fence, woven through dense vegetation, prevents entrance to the seating area except through gates at the heads of rustic stairways.

The shell is equipped to provide the necessary scenic and lighting effects for operas and ballets, and amplifiers carry the music to the outer fringe of the audience.

Well-policed parking areas are adjacent to the dell.

555

Schuylkill River from West Drive
Nature comes close to the heart
of a city

EAST FAIRMOUNT PARK (CITY TOUR 11)

L. on Ridge Ave., skirting park to R. of parking area; L. on Nice-town Lane.

Nicetown Lane cuts through the heart of EAST LAUREL HILL CEMETERY (21), where many old Philadelphia families maintain burial lots.

R. from Nicetown Lane on East River Drive.

Beyond the Falls Bridge and opposite the point where City Line Avenue enters the drive at an angle from the left, is the QUEEN LANE PUMPING STATION (22) and GUSTINE LAKE (23), an artificial pool on which children sail boats and wade in summer and skate in winter.

East River Drive becomes Wissahickon Drive across Ridge Ave. (double car tracks).

This drive follows the Wissahickon Creek, twisting along the east bank of the stream, with sheer cliffs rising from the roadway on the right. Unfortunately the most attractive features of the WISSA-HICKON VALLEY (24) cannot be seen from the drive *(see City Tours 15, 16, and 17)*. The undulating hills, the glens, and the tiny streams that trickle down the ravines are hidden from the motorist. Nevertheless, the landscape is lovely enough to warrant a drive along its length, to Paper Mill Road, where Lincoln Drive begins.

At intervals along the upper section of the drive, the great masses of apartment houses that crowd the fashionable Germantown section can be seen, bordering upon the park, their roofs just topping the tall trees on the crest of the hills.

KENILWORTH (25) is one of Philadelphia's most exclusive apartment structures. Four giant buildings form the manor, with a private golf course, tennis courts, swimming pools, and a theatre, making it almost self-sufficient in the realm of recreation.

Farther on, just before the drive crosses Wayne Avenue (double car tracks) is the MAYFAIR HOUSE (26), on the left, another fashionable apartment dwelling. In the rear of the Mayfair House is the HOME OF CONNIE MACK (27), patriarch of baseball and manager of the Philadelphia Athletics.

Retrace on Wissahickon and East River Drives to Girard Ave. Bridge, passing this time under the bridge.

Below the bridge a STONE PLAZA (28) has been built along the riverbank. In 1936 plans were under way for statues by Gaston Lachaise and Robert Laurent, presenting allegorically the history of America, to be erected along the plaza. Economic stress altered the plan.

GARFIELD MEMORIAL (29), a portrait bust of the martyred President, stands on the opposite side of the road. By a bend in the river is a STATUE of *The Viking* (30), (R). Thorfinn Karlsefni, whom it honors, is said to have been the first European to attempt colonization of the American Continent. The statue is the work of Einar Joneson, noted Icelandic sculptor.

Beyond, on the right, is BOATHOUSE ROW (31), home of the Schuylkill Navy.

From the rivers, lakes, and canals of Europe and Canada; from almost every watercourse in America, brawny oarsmen have come to test the mettle of the Schuylkill's sons. During the last eight decades many symbols of international supremacy have graced the cup-room of one or another of these sturdy clubhouses.

Eleven rowing clubs, the Philadelphia Canoe Club, and the Philadelphia Skating Club are housed in as many vine-covered buildings. Built during the nineteenth and early part of the twentieth centuries, these structures of wood, stone, stucco, and brick against a background of old shrubbery represent the varying tastes of that period.

Dawn finds ambitious young oarsmen, and perhaps a few oldsters who have retired from competition, carrying fragile shells or sturdier work boats down the slips to launch them for a sunrise spin on the river. Rowlocks creak...coxswains chant in raucous rhythm... coaches' megaphones bellow...trainers clump down the gangplanks for a look at their protégés ... Philadelphia's youth is lacing the river with tangled skeins of foam, intent on holding for the Quaker City the renown it has won as a rowing center.

This claim to fame has been ably defended since 9 rowing organizations first combined, on October 5, 1858, to form the Schuylkill Navy, the history of which is inseparable from that of Boathouse Row.

The Fairmount Rowing Club, organized in 1883, and the Quaker

Boathouse Row
Home port of the Schuylkill Navy

EAST FAIRMOUNT PARK (CITY TOUR 11)

City Barge Club, organized in 1858, now inactive in competition, have their quarters in the first of the twin structures. Next is the double building in which are the Pennsylvania Barge Club, the history of which dates back to 1861, and the Crescent Boat Club, founded in 1867.

The Bachelors Barge Club, which had its inception on July 4, 1853, occupies a single building. Next to it a twin structure quarters the University Barge Club, organized in 1854, with which the Philadelphia Barge Club has been merged, the combined club now using the entire building.

The Malta Boat Club and the Vesper Boat Club, the former organized February 22, 1860, and the latter five years later to the day, occupy the next twin structure. Beyond these is the clubhouse of the University of Pennsylvania Rowing Association, the members of which compete in interclub events under the name of the College Boat Club, active on the river since 1872.

The most recent addition to the fleet of the Schuylkill Navy, the Penn Athletic Club Rowing Association, which was organized in 1925, occupies the former building of the West Philadelphia Barge Club, which was a member of the navy from 1873 to 1925.

The Undine Barge Club, an outstanding factor in rowing activities since May 9, 1856, and a leading contender in the athletic activities of the navy, occupies the last of the clubhouses in the row, next to the Philadelphia Canoe Club.

The Vesper eight-oared shell swept to the row's first Olympic triumph at Paris in 1900, repeating its victory at St. Louis in 1904. John B. (Jack) Kelly was the first American oarsman to win the Olympic single sculls, a feat which he accomplished at Antwerp, Belgium, in 1920. In the Olympics of 1920, and again in 1924, at Paris, France, Kelly paired with Paul Costello to win for America the double sculls championship. On Kelly's retirement, Costello teamed with Charles J. McIlvaine to win in double sculls at Amsterdam in 1928, and thus establish the remarkable record of being the only athlete to win in the same event in three consecutive Olympics. Five crews from Boathouse Row wore the American insignia in the 1928 Olympic games.

W. E. Garrett Gilmore and Kenneth Meyers, also from Boathouse Row, captured the double sculls race in the Olympics at Long Beach, Calif., in 1932. The row won the honor of representing the United States in four of the seven events in this meeting, in which America for the first time captured the pair-oared race with coxswains. The winners of this event were Charles Keiffer, Joseph Schauers, and Edward Jennings.

The long list of international victories won by Schuylkill Navy oarsmen includes such achievements as Walter Hoover's winning of

559

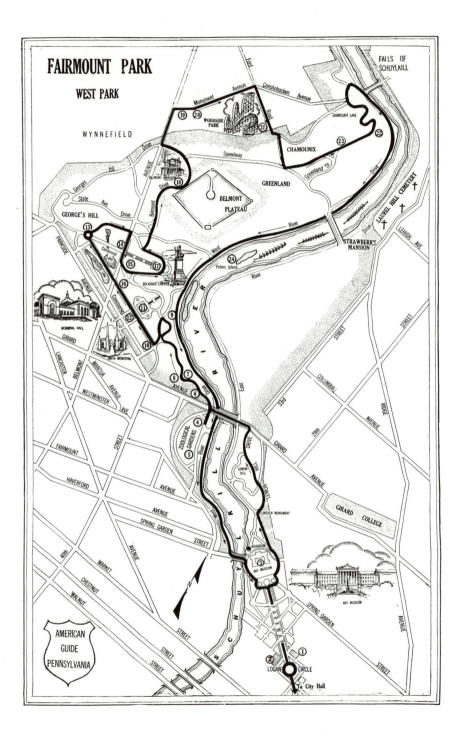

FAIRMOUNT PARK

WEST PARK

FALLS OF
SCHUYLKILL

WYNNEFIELD

WOODSIDE
PARK

CHAMOUNIX LAKE

CHAMOUNIX

GREENLAND

BELMONT
PLATEAU

GEORGE'S HILL

LAUREL HILL CEMETERY

STRAWBERRY
MANSION

Peters Island

West River

MEMORIAL HALL

SMITH MEMORIAL

RELIGIOUS LIBERTY

ZOOLOGICAL GARDENS

LEMON
HILL

GIRARD COLLEGE

LINCOLN MONUMENT

AQUARIUM

ART MUSEUM

LOGAN CIRCLE

To City Hall

GIRARD

LANCASTER

BELMONT

MANTUA

WESTMINSTER

FAIRMOUNT

HAVERFORD

AVENUE

SPRING GARDEN

MARKET

CHESTNUT

WALNUT

COLUMBIA

RIDGE AVENUE

33rd

29th

AMERICAN
GUIDE
PENNSYLVANIA

the Diamond Sculls, famed English trophy, in 1922, and the Penn Athletic Club's annexation of a world championship in the international eight-oared race at Liege, Belgium, in 1930.

The Philadelphia Gold Challenge Cup, offered by the Schuylkill Navy in 1920 as a suitable memorial for the achievement of Jack Kelly, goes automatically to the single sculls winner in each Olympic meeting, and must be defended by its holder, on proper challenge during the interval between Olympic games. This solid gold cup, 18 inches high, has been taken to the farthest parts of the world by triumphant oarsmen.

Canoes and rowboats may be hired by the hour or day at the public boathouse. Here individual owners of rowboats or canoes also rent space for housing their craft.

Opposite Boathouse Row is one of the most widely known works of Saint-Gaudens, the STATUE OF THE PURITAN (32). Nearby is the TAM O'SHANTER GROUP (33), by James Thom. In this work four stone figures represent characters in the poem of Robert Burns. A rustic wooden shelter protects it.

L. on Parkway to City Hall.

WEST PARK

City Tour 12

FROM City Hall's seething traffic circle, the wide Parkway leads past the LOGAN LIBRARY (1), on the right, and FRANKLIN INSTITUTE (2), on the left at Twentieth Street, terminating at the ART MUSEUM (3), which crowns the entrance to the sylvan beauty of Fairmount Park *(see Points of Interest for 1, 2, and 3).*

R. around Museum into E. River Drive; R. at Lincoln Monument on Main Drive; L. on Girard Ave. and across bridge.

On the left immediately beyond the bridge are the PHILADELPHIA ZOOLOGICAL GARDENS (4) *(open daily 9 to 5 in winter, 9 to 6 in summer; adm., adults, 25¢; children, 5 to 12 yrs., 15¢; under 5 yrs., free).*

---

1. Logan Library
2. Franklin Institute
3. Art Museum
4. Philadelphia Zoological Gardens
5. Solitude
6. Letitia Street House
7. Sweetbriar Mansion
8. Bronze Group
9. Cedar Grove Mansion
10. Smith Memorial Arch
11. Memorial Hall
12. Welsh Memorial Fountain and Garden
13. Roman Catholic Centennial Fountain
14. Statue of Christopher Columbus
15. Statue of Anthony Drexel
16. The Japanese Gardens and Pagoda
17. Horticultural Hall
18. Belmont Mansion
19. Methodist Episcopal Home for the Aged
20. Methodist Episcopal Orphanage
21. Woodside Park
22. Plumstead Estate
23. Chamounix Lake
24. Peters Island

One of the most diversified animal collections in the world and an exceptional record of pioneering in important scientific research distinguish the Zoological Gardens, first "zoo" to be established in the United States.

The Philadelphia Zoo was incorporated in 1859. Today it contains 2,700 specimens, including 600 mammals, 1,000 birds, 1,000 reptiles, and 100 amphibians.

The Penrose Research Laboratory, named for its donor, Dr. Charles B. Penrose, was established in 1901 as the first zoological laboratory in the country in a zoological garden. Dr. Penrose, who died in 1925, maintained his intense interest in all phases of zoological activity throughout his life. The laboratory's research into animal diet has won for it the acclaim of scientists and interested laymen everywhere. Its work in the prevention and control of tuberculosis among apes and monkeys is outstanding.

Since the Penrose laboratory has been engaged in dietary research and diagnoses and autopsies, malnutrition as a cause of death has been lowered by 80 percent. This work has also helped immeasurably to preserve the natural color and texture of animal coats. In the primate groups, a substitution of food rich in vitamin E (incidentally, more costly than that formerly used) has helped to increase reproduction.

A laboratory of comparative pathology is also maintained. It contained 3,419 exhibits in 1933, and improvements in its buildings and collections are constantly being made.

About 45 varieties of simians are housed in the buildings devoted to primate groups. These include a number of animals born in the garden, a gibbon maintained in captivity for 31 years, and "Bamboo," the largest gorilla in captivity. "Bamboo" weighs 350 pounds and has spent ten years in the Philadelphia Zoo, a period longer than the previous life span of captive gorillas.

The reptile house is the home of one of the largest collection of snakes in the United States, the finest crocodile group in the country, and an excellent turtle collection. Plants, rocks, and pebbles simulating the native habitats of the various reptiles form the settings within glass-enclosed pens.

In the bird collection are such odd varieties of bird life as the rare hornbill, spoonbill, and cock-of-the-rock. An aged griffon vulture, an inhabitant of the zoo for 36 years, is the oldest bird in the garden. The cassowary group, related to the ostrich, is regarded as one of the best in the country.

The great mammal collection includes a rare Indian rhinoceros, a forest elephant, and an immense Siberian tiger. Among the smaller mammals are badgers, lemurs, ocelots, civet cats, and grisons.

Two thousand meals are prepared daily for the zoo's beasts, birds,

562

and reptiles. The enormous food stocks required annually include approximately 550,000 pounds of hay, 868 dozen eggs, 60,000 pounds of fish, 130 horses averaging 1,000 pounds each, more than 150 gallons of cod-liver oil, and 180,000 pounds of grain.

An additional feature of the Zoological Gardens is the collection of trees and plants. An effort has been made to maintain as complete a collection of plants as it is possible to grow in this climate. The tree groups include the flowering Japanese cherry, dogwood, poplar, and horse chestnut. Among the less commonly known trees are the yellowwood, codralla, Kentucky coffee tree, gingko, and sophora. In

Old Solitude

the shrub groups are azalea, rhododendron, holly, and hydrangea. Beautifully patterned beds of tulips, hyacinths, and crocuses are also seen in season, as are the blooms of roses, delphiniums, hollyhocks, peonies, and irises.

Estimated attendance at the zoo during 1935 was 250,000. It is the belief of the Zoological Society of Philadelphia that attendance could be greatly increased and the educational as well as recreational benefits extended by modernizing the zoo and abolishing admission fees. Accordingly, in 1936 it established a few free days and provided Philadelphians with the opportunity of studying a scale model of a modern cageless zoo the first unit of which was constructed in 1937.

High cliffs, barriers, lush growths of plants and foliage, plateaus, and other natural formations will be built in accordance with this plan, with each animal group confined to its appointed province by a moat instead of iron bars. The moats, designed to give adequate protection to the visitor, will nevertheless be invisible in a broad view of the gardens and will create the illusion that the animals are being viewed in their natural habitats.

Venerable old SOLITUDE (5), the mansion built in 1784 by John Penn, grandson of William Penn, is today within the natural limits of the Zoological Gardens. It was occupied by one of Penn's descendants during a stay in Philadelphia in the early 1850's. The grounds were sold a short time thereafter. This was the last bit of land owned by the Penns in the State. It became part of Fairmount Park in 1867. At present it is used as an administration building. The mansion today is an ivy-clad cubical structure, with tall and severely plain windows. A simple cornice overhangs the four plastered sides, and a double belt of brick extends along the second-story line. The pedimented doorway, flanked by Ionic columns, lends an air of calm and stateliness to the entire building.

The interior is rich and delicate in detail. The parlor, facing the river, contains an excellent ceiling with classical motives of medallions, garlands, and candelabra in the Adam style. Three other rooms in the house have equally fine ceilings. A large hall extends across the entire western front of the mansion. From the southwest corner a stairway with hand-wrought iron railing ascends to the second floor. On this floor are two small bedrooms and a library containing John Penn's Sheraton bookcase. The third floor contains several bedrooms. There is an underground passage.

R. from Girard Ave. (under railroad bridge) on Lansdowne Drive.

The LETITIA STREET HOUSE (6) *(open weekdays 10 to 5; Sun. 1 to 5; adm. adults, 25¢; children, 10¢)*, formerly known as the William Penn house, is on the left of Lansdowne Drive, which parallels the Schuylkill River. This early Georgian Colonial town house, furnished in Queen Anne style, stands upon a wooded knoll and commands a fine view of the river which curves from sight a short distance above.

The plain two-and-a-half-story dwelling originally fronted on Letitia Street. It occupied the Governor's lot, which ran along Market Street from Front to Second and extended back halfway to Chestnut Street. It was removed to the park in 1883 when the city's commercial growth threatened the dwelling's destruction. It was long supposed to have been built and occupied by William Penn, but it is now

Interior of Letitia Street House

known to have been erected between 1703 and 1715. For many years it served as a tavern. Carefully taken down and re-erected in the park as an outcome of the historical interest enkindled by the celebration of the bicentennial of the founding of Pennsylvania, it has been restored and refurnished by the Pennsylvania Museum.

The house, a fine example of an eighteenth century town house, is a small building with a steep gable roof. The broad doorway has a beautifully wrought hood of unusual design. Bricks are laid in Flemish bond with heavily vitrified headers. Joined boards form a cove cornice which extends around the house above the second-story windows. The windows are of simple design, those on the first floor having shutters and brick arches.

In the entrance hall is a large walnut gate-leg table and chairs of turned and spiraled members, characteristic of the style of the early eighteenth century. One side chair, with spiraled legs and stretchers, was used originally in Penn's manor house on the Delaware River. On the mantel shelves in the hall and kitchen are plates of fine Delftware.

The interior woodwork bespeaks the good taste and competent workmanship which prevailed at that time. A simple staircase leads from the hall to the upper floor, where three large chambers are furnished with rare pieces made in Philadelphia. Noteworthy are a walnut chest of drawers with ball feet, a hutch table, and a corner washstand.

On the right, 300 yards along Lansdowne Drive after a sharp, up-hill bend, is SWEETBRIAR MANSION (7) *(open daily, except Sun. 10 to 5 ; adm. 25¢)*, a two-and-a-half-story stone house set in what was once a beautiful, sloping lawn terminating at the river. It was built by Judge Samuel Breck in 1797 and was his family residence until 1836. Sweetbriar was restored in 1927 to its original appearance. It was furnished with authentic pieces of Colonial days by the Junior League of Philadelphia, in whose charge, under the jurisdiction of the Fairmount Park Commission, the mansion now is.

The simplicity of the architecture and the delicacy of the woodwork are impressive. A charming mansion in late Georgian Colonial style of cream-colored plastered stone, the building has a dignified symmetrical facade with quoined corners. Above the tall Doric entrance with simple fanlight is a roundheaded window with crownlike design. Two arched dormer windows rise above the cornice of the second floor.

The lower floor consists of a hallway, living room, reception room, and small office. At the head of the stairway leading to the second floor is a balcony believed to have been built for the use of musicians at social functions. The second floor consists of five bedrooms. The

566

Sweet Briar

walls and woodwork are decorated in Adam style, painted gray, salmon, buff, and blue. The reception room contains carved Hepplewhite side chairs, a pair of mahogany card tables, and a Hepplewhite sofa. Wedgwood vases, gilded torcheres, and a large Oriental rug are imported furnishings which the room might have exhibited in its original state, while from the walls hangs a rare and complete set of William Birch's views of Philadelphia.

Directly opposite Sweetbriar is a BRONZE GROUP, *Stone Age in America*, (8), the work of John J. Boyle. The statue depicts a mother poised to protect her baby from a threatened attack by wild beasts.

567

CEDAR GROVE MANSION (9), beyond Sweetbriar on the right fork *(open weekdays 10 to 5; Sun. 1 to 5; adm. 25¢)*, is a true example of Georgian Colonial architecture. Within its walls are the original furnishings, ranging from the simplicity in style of the William and Mary period to elegant examples of Hepplewhite, Sheraton, and Chippendale. The house is a plain, gray stone dwelling of two stories with picturesque gambrel roof punctuated by tall brick chimneys and dormer windows.

Built in 1721 on Kensington Avenue near Harrowgate Station, and at one time the home of the Isaac Wistar Morris family, it was enlarged in 1795 without marring its architectural integrity. In 1927 it was removed to its present location, high above the river, when Miss Lydia Thompson Morris supplied furnishings appropriate to the date and simple character of the house and presented it to the city. Most of the furnishings date from 1700 to 1770, but some are later, in keeping with the remodeling of the house in 1795.

The entrance leads directly into the living room. A Chippendale sofa upholstered in yellow brocade, a pie-crust table, and six ball and clawfoot chairs are in contrast with the earlier William and Mary highboy and lowboy in the room.

In the dining room the majority of pieces are in the formal Hepplewhite style, but the kitchen remains in a simple state, its large fireplace adequately supplied with cranes and pots. Upstairs there are several rooms furnished mainly in Hepplewhite style.

Bear L. on Lansdowne Drive; R. on North Concourse Drive.

On the left fork of Lansdowne Drive is SMITH MEMORIAL ARCH (10). On the far side of the monument with its two tall pillars surmounted by statues of General Meade, by Daniel Chester French, and General Reynolds, by Charles Grafly, is North Concourse Drive. During the Centennial Exhibition in 1876 this wide straight roadway, lined with tall and stately trees, was the main entrance to the grounds.

At the base of the Reynolds column is the figure of Richard Smith, the donor, modeled by Herbert Adams. The equestrian statue of Gen. Winfield Scott Hancock, and that of Gen. George Brinton McClellan are the works of Messrs. French and Potter. The two granite abutments surmounted by eagles are the work of J. Massey Rhind. The arches between niches contain the busts of Admiral Porter and John B. Gest, by Charles Grafly; Major General Hartranft, by A. Sterling Calder; Admiral Dahlgren, by George E. Bissel; James H. Windrim, by Samuel Murray; Maj. Gen. S. W. Crawford, by Bessie O. Potter; Governor Curtin, by Moses Ezekiel, and Gen. James A. Beaver, by Catherine M. Cohen.

MEMORIAL HALL (11), on the right *(open daily 10:30 to 5; adm. free)*, is built on a terraced elevation commanding a view of the

Exterior of Letitia St. House

Interior of Cedar Grove Mansion

Schuylkill River. It was erected in 1876 for the Centennial Exhibition and as a permanent repository for the city's art treasures. Of modified classic design, the building is faced with granite. A triple-arched entranceway is the main feature of the huge central unit from which arched arcades connect with the massive square-corner pavilions. Above the building is a square Bishop's dome of iron and glass over which rises a figure of Columbia. At each corner of the dome are figures symbolizing the four quarters of the globe. The 52-foot high entrance hall is Renaissance in style. The building was designed by Herman J. Schwarzmann.

In this permanent memorial is a complete model of the grounds and buildings of the Centennial City. Here is the Pennsylvania Museum of the School of Industrial Art, a collection of ceramics, medals, metals, furniture, and textiles. Housed here also is the Wilstach collection of paintings, founded in 1892 as the nucleus of a municipal art gallery.

Directly across the drive is the WELSH MEMORIAL FOUNTAIN AND GARDEN (12), built to honor John Welsh, who was responsible in a large measure for the success of the Centennial Exhibition.

The drive courses westward past Centennial Lake, on the right, and Concourse Lake, on the left, before coming to its end at the ROMAN CATHOLIC CENTENNIAL FOUNTAIN (13). This group of statuary by Herman Kirn includes a figure of Moses, encircled by monuments to Bishop John Carroll, of Baltimore ; Commodore John Barry, preeminent figure in our early Navy ; Father Theobald Mathew, champion of temperance ; and Charles Carroll, signer of the Declaration of Independence.

The figure of Moses looks across to a picturesque little arbor, at the farther end of which is a STATUE of *Christopher Columbus* (14), dedicated in 1876 by the Italian citizens of Philadelphia.

Retrace to Belmont Ave ; L. on Belmont Ave. ; R. on Lansdowne Drive.

On this drive, a few yards beyond Belmont Avenue, right, is a STATUE of *Anthony Drexel* (15), head of a prominent Philadelphia family and founder of Drexel Institute. The statue was executed by Moses Ezekiel.

THE JAPANESE GARDENS AND PAGODA (16) are on the right. The gardens were installed during the Centennial Exhibition. The Nio-mon, a temple gateway which is commonly called the Japanese Pagoda, was brought from Japan and reassembled at the St. Louis Exposition in 1904. It was later purchased by John H. Converse and Samuel M. Vauclain, who presented it to Memorial Hall.

The gate measures 45 feet in height, 30 feet in length and 18 feet in depth. It has a balcony supported by 12 round wooden columns, two of which are interior supports. The tiled roof has an overhanging denticulated cornice.

The interior contains two large wooden figures about eight feet in height, representing guards. These are attributed to Fuyii Chuyiu, a celebrated sculptor. The painting on the ceiling was executed by Kano Tokinobu. There is also a bronze temple bell suspended from one corner of the roof. The original wood carvings and metal work have been removed to Memorial Hall for safekeeping. The gardens are fringed with delightful plots of shrubbery, which are spaced in season by colorful flower beds.

A short distance beyond the gardens is HORTICULTURAL HALL (17) *(open daily 9 to 5 ; adm. free).*

Gray, friendly ghost of a fading age, quickened by wild, exotic plant life from far corners of the world, Horticultural Hall is host not only to the most beautiful and the most bizarre of Nature's handiwork, but to glamorous memories of the Centennial Exhibition.

The Crystal Palace erected in London in 1850 and the Crystal Palace built in New York in 1853 suggested the style which the architect, Hermann J. Schwarzmann, followed in his design for the building. The structure, a Moorish interpretation, of glass and iron, was a forerunner of modern construction methods.

Standing today as one of the few surviving monuments to the Centennial, this great conservatory, built at a cost approximating $300,000, is the permanent home of a horticultural collection which had its nucleus in a hall adjoining the Academy of Music, at Broad and Locust Streets, whence it was removed to the exhibition grounds in 1876.

The hall's physical aspects are subordinated to the beauty of its exhibits. Confusing draperies of creepers mount the branchless trunks of palms. Near them in the glass-enclosed conservatory, bamboo trees and tropical evergreens reach their heads into the filtered sunlight.

Two tropical houses, two fern houses, and a cactus house connect with the palm house, which is the central building. Coconut, oil, and date palms feature the 32 varieties of palms — representing virtually every country in the tropics. A turn to the right or left reveals a jungle vista — banana and other tropical trees rising from a carpet of tender ferns in which trail long tentacles of aerial roots shot down by giant growths.

A dozen paces from this heterogeneous blend of jungle flora, a cactus collection including specimens from Madagascar, the West Indies, Brazil, and Western United States, breathes the spirit of arid deserts.

Within glass cases in another quarter grow willowy embroideries of fern, nurtured in a moisture comparable to that of the Irish coast or the tropic valleys in which they abound.

Sunken gardens stretching from Belmont Avenue to the main entrance of the hall provide a delightful foretaste of the kingdom within. Rectangular pools, their placid waters dotted by lilies, leafy water flowers, and grasses, run down the center of a concrete plaza, flanked by flower-blanketed and shrub-fringed terraces.

Enshrined among the works of nature in the conservatory grounds stand splendid examples of the works of man — a bronze figure of Goethe, by James Thom ; a bronze of Schiller, by Thom ; a bust of Verdi ; a bronze of John Witherspoon, by J. A. Bailey, erected by Presbyterian churchmen ; the allegorical group, *Religious Liberty*, centered by a female figure in armor and erected by the Jewish society, B'nai Brith, opposite the eastern front.

Circle Horticultural Hall ; R. on Belmont Drive.

On the right are the West Park municipal athletic fields on Belmont Plateau, and above is BELMONT MANSION (18), erected about 1743. Originally the mansion of an early Colonial plantation and the home of a staunch patriot in Revolutionary days, Belmont Mansion is rich in memories of Judge Richard Peters, who entertained Washington and many other distinguished guests here. This huge, three-story building, surrounded by a colonnade, with its beautiful Colonial interior was remodeled to its present form in 1927. The eminence on which it stands affords a fine view of the city.

R. from Belmont Drive, on Belmont Ave.

At Monument Avenue on the right is the METHODIST EPISCO-PAL HOME FOR THE AGED (19). The building, erected in 1865, is a gray stone, Tudor Gothic structure, four stories in height, with a steep gray slate roof. Farther on (R) is the METHODIST EPISCO-PAL ORPHANAGE (20). From Belmont Avenue, Ford Road extends to the right, passing WOODSIDE PARK (21). This is the largest amusement park within the city limits. The next intersection is Chamounix Drive on the left. Here, to the right, the midcity skyscrapers are clearly visible, and the view from this point is one of the finest around Philadelphia.

L. from Belmont Ave. on Chamounix Drive.

Chamounix Drive continues over the crest of Mt. Prospect, an elevation of 210 feet, which affords a widening panorama of the mid-city to the right. This drive has an abrupt terminus at the site of the PLUMSTEAD ESTATE (22), which formerly was the property of a prominent mill owner. On the estate remain a coachman's frame cottage, a barn, and the Plumstead mansion, a plain structure set upon a bluff overlooking the river.

The mansion, built in 1802, is also known as the Chamounix mansion. The two-story building is of late Georgian Colonial design with cream-colored plaster exterior. The first floor windows drop to floor level, and on the right side is a circular bay window.

A dirt roadway passes the house, winds downhill through a heavily wooded area and crosses a bridge. A few feet above the bridge is a pathway leading past a spring to CHAMOUNIX LAKE (23). This small lake once was the site of Simpson's mill, for which it provided the water power.

The driveway then winds up hill to Falls Road, a WPA project, where a right turn leads on to Neill Drive. Neill Drive becomes West River Drive just a few yards above the Falls of Schuylkill Bridge, across the river from the section known as East Falls.

R. into West River Drive.

Along the drive the river's banks are covered with riotous verdure. Just above Nicetown Lane is the starting point for Philadelphia's numerous rowing regattas, and a mile and a quarter beyond is the finish, near which, in mid-river, stands PETERS ISLAND (24). This woodland in the river was once part of the 220-acre Peters estate.

The drive bends and twists with each curve of the river, allowing a view of the rear of Memorial Hall, visible upon a hill to the right, before passing under Girard Avenue Bridge, and ending at Spring Garden Street.

L. from West River Drive on Spring Garden St. Bridge ; R. around Art Museum into Parkway, which leads to City Hall.

Horticultural Hall
Giant greenhouse of a world's fair

BENJAMIN FRANKLIN

PARKWAY

ITALIAN SEA HORSE
FOUNTAIN 13

FIDELITY MUTUAL LIFE
INSURANCE CO 12

AQUARIUM 14

PENNSYLVANIA
MUSEUM OF ART 11

10

WASHINGTON
MONUMENT
9

FAIRMOUNT AVE
GREEN
SPRING GARDEN
HAMILTON ST
RODIN MUSEE 8
CALLOWHILL ST.

15
BOY SCOUTS
BUILDING

BOARD OF PUBLIC
EDUCATION 16

17 FRANKLIN INSTITUTE

ARMY &
NAVY
PYLONS 7

MAIN PUBLIC
LIBRARY 6

VINE ST.

SHAKESPEARE
MEMORIAL

5

ACADEMY OF
NATURAL SCIENCES
18

LOGAN CIRCLE
FOUNTAIN
4

CATHEDRAL OF
SS. PETER & PAUL 3

RACE ST.

EIGHTEENTH ST.

CHERRY ST.

FRIENDS
SELECT SCHOOL 2

CHERRY ST.

SEVENTEENTH ST.

ARCH ST.

AMERICAN
GUIDE
PENNSYLVANIA

N

19
PENNSYLVANIA
SUBURBAN
STATION

PENNSYLVANIA
BOULEVARD

SIXTEENTH ST.

To BROAD ST.
STATION

To BROAD ST.
SUBWAY

1
CITY HALL

THE TREE-LINED PARKWAY

City Tour 13 — 2 m.

THE BENJAMIN FRANKLIN PARKWAY, linking Fairmount Park and its East and West River Drives with the heart of Philadelphia, is a one-mile stretch of wide, tree-lined boulevard. Splendid examples of architectural achievement, housing art and educational collections and exhibits, border its length.

The several imposing structures which may be noted across the Parkway from those described in the first half of the tour are included in the second half on the way back to City Hall. This eliminates crossing and recrossing the broad thoroughfare in the course of the tour.

The Parkway begins at the northwest corner of City Hall. On the right is REYBURN PLAZA (1), a large, gravel-covered city common that has been the scene of varied events, from concerts by the Philadelphia Orchestra to displays of war machines and May Day battles between police and radical demonstrators.

The bandstand in the middle of the Arch Street side is flanked by a statue, right, of Stephen Girard, whose seat of financial empire was in Philadelphia and whose philanthropic gifts were the foundations of many present-day institutions; and another statue, left, of Maj. Gen. Peter Muhlenberg. This figure shows Muhlenberg pulling aside his clerical vestments to reveal the uniform of a Continental Army officer. One of the founders of the Lutheran Church in America, he declared at the outbreak of the Revolution : "There is * * * a time to preach and a time to fight, and now is the time to fight." The statue of Girard was sculptured by J. Massey Rhind in 1897; that of Muhlenberg, by Otto Schweizer in 1910.

Surrounded by a high, red brick wall, the FRIENDS SELECT SCHOOL (2), on the right at Seventeenth Street, has maintained its excellence as an educational institution throughout the years. Under the supervision of the Friends Meeting, it is a direct outgrowth of the first school in Philadelphia. Courses of study range from kindergarten to college preparatory and include religious instruction.

1. Reyburn Plaza
2. Friends Select School
3. Cathedral of SS. Peter and Paul
4. Logan Circle
5. Shakespeare Memorial
6. Free Library of Philadelphia
7. Army and Navy Pylons
8. Rodin Museum
9. Washington Monument
10. Ericsson Fountain
11. Pennsylvania Museum of Art
12. Fidelity Mutual Life Insurance Company
13. Italian Sea Horse Fountain
14. Fairmount Park Aquarium
15. Philadelphia Council Headquarters, Boy Scouts of America
16. Board of Education Building
17. Franklin Insitute
18. Academy of Natural Sciences
19. Pennsylvania Suburban Station

The grounds occupy the complete block bounded by the Parkway, Sixteenth and Seventeenth, Race and Cherry Streets. The five buildings consist of the school, gymnasium, elementary building, library, and play shed. The school, the main and original building, is a two-story Flemish bond brick structure with a peaked, slate roof. It was built in 1885 from plans of Addison Hutton. A Colonial doorway designed by Walter F. Price was added in 1922. The architect also planned the alterations in the new buildings, placing white keystones over the windows in the Georgian Colonial manner. Within the wall, at the corner of Sixteenth and Race Streets, stands a pre-Revolutionary log cabin, a lone relic of a farm that once covered the site.

The CATHEDRAL OF SS. PETER AND PAUL (3), right, at Eighteenth Street, is the seat of the Roman Catholic archdiocese of Philadelphia. The brownstone building is of Italian High Renaissance design. Four Corinthian columns support the portico. The dim austerity of the interior is relieved by objects of beauty and veneration. The main altar and the painting of the *Crucifixion* by Constantino Brumidi are notable.

In the crypt lie the remains of Bishops Egan, Kenrick, and Connell; and of Archbishops Wood, Ryan, and Prendergast, who served in turn as heads of the See.

Cross 18th St.

Facing the Cathedral is LOGAN CIRCLE (4), one of the five parks included in William Penn's original plan of Philadelphia.

In the center of the circle is a large fountain, surrounded by three heroic bronze figures, each representing one of the waterways of Philadelphia — the Delaware, the Schuylkill, and the Wissahickon. Alexander Sterling Calder was the sculptor, and Wilson Eyre & McIlvaine the architects.

West of Nineteenth Street, in a plot that divides Vine Street and the Parkway, is a MONUMENT (5), erected in joint honor of William Shakespeare and Philadelphia actors and actresses who achieved fame. The controversy that has long existed over the correct spelling of Shakespeare's name is reflected in the inscription on the monument. The words "Shakespeare Memorial" are followed by the information that the group which aided in erecting the shaft is the "Shakespere Society." The latter spelling is that used by the bard when he last wrote his name. The monument, designed by Wilson Eyre & McIlvaine and sculptured by Alexander Sterling Calder, was erected in 1928.

On the right, directly across Vine Street from the monument, is the imposing FREE LIBRARY OF PHILADELPHIA (6), occupying the entire block from Nineteenth to Twentieth Streets along Vine *(see Points of Interest)*.

Continue on Vine St.; to 20th.

576

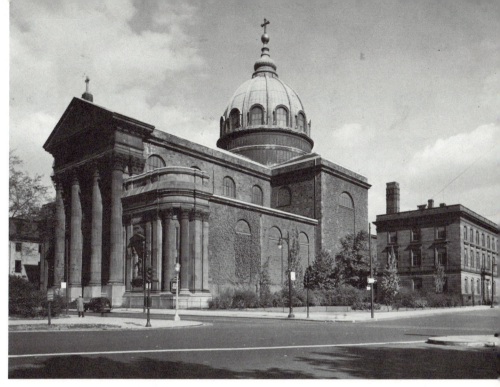

Cathedral of SS. Peter and Paul

Entrance Gate of Rodin Museum

At Twentieth Street and Vine Street, the Parkway broadens into a two-way, four-lane central highway with a one-way two-lane roadway on each side. Grass plots separate the main highway from the auxiliary lanes, with more park land bordering the latter. At this point are the ARMY AND NAVY PYLONS (7), completed in 1927 in honor of the Civil War dead.

On the right at Twenty-second Street is the RODIN MUSEUM (8) *(open daily 10:30 to 5; adm. free)*, a reproduction of the famous Musée Rodin at Meudon, France.

The rugged art of Auguste Rodin, imbued with the rude strength of his peasant origin, but polished and mellowed by communion with cultivated minds of his own and earlier times, found a home in Philadelphia through a casual incident. Jules E. Mastbaum, a pioneer motion picture exhibitor, visited the Hotel Biron (now the Musée Rodin) in Paris in 1924. So impressed was he by the sculptor's work that he persuaded the curator to sell him a small bronze, which he carried home in his pocket. The seed of interest thus sown developed through further acquisitions until the plan of a museum devoted to Rodin's work took shape.

Mastbaum died before the museum was built, but his wife and daughters faithfully completed the project which he had formulated.

The museum building embodies the style of architecture chosen by Rodin — the French Renaissance of the periods of Louis XIV and Louis XVI. It was designed by Paul Philippe Cret and Jacques Greber and was erected in 1929. The entrance is a reproduction of a part of the facade of the old Chateau d'Issy at Meudon, France, the original of which was reconstructed by Rodin from fragments. In front of this gateway, on a stone pedestal, sits *The Thinker*, characteristic of Rodin and probably his best-known work. This is a replica in bronze.

Beyond the gateway is a rectangular reflecting pool and garden wherein some of the artist's larger and more notable works are grouped. On a terrace at the far side of the pool is the museum, constructed of Indiana limestone. Fluted Doric columns are at the front of the entrance loggia, which leads to the famous bronze *Gates of Hell*. In the walls on each side of the loggia are niches containing reproductions of the sculptor's work. The museum consists of a main gallery and three exhibition rooms, a library, and administrative offices. The main gallery is finished in tints of gold and gray. The terrazzo floor is inlaid with marble. In the vaulted ceiling is a large skylight.

Over the east and west walls of the library are two appropriate allegorical groups representing Keats' *Ode to a Grecian Urn* and the *Past, Present and Future* by the Philadelphia artist, Franklin C. Watkins, who was winner of the first prize at the Carnegie Institute International Exhibition in 1931.

The library is devoted entirely to the collection of publications dealing with Rodin and his works. It lacks only a few of the important writings touching upon the sculptor.

The museum proper houses the Mastbaum collection of Rodin's works, and a collection of more than 100 original drawings, water colors, tempera paintings, and studies in plaster by the French master. Many of these drawings and paintings will command the interest of the art lover; they represent the fluid, emotionalized perceptions of the artist in the ardor of conception.

Reproductions of his works exhibited outdoors include *The Thinker* and the arresting *Burghers of Calais*. The latter represents the burghers of the city in the hour of their abasement and in the glory of self-abnegation when they came out to give themselves as hostages to the English after the siege by the troops of the Black Prince. Rodin did not attempt to conventionalize the strong drama of that moment, but presented it without artistic subterfuge. The figures of the burghers, bareheaded and their feet bare, halters about their necks, and in their hands the keys of their city, evoked enthusiastic approval when first shown in Paris. It is characteristic of the artist that, although the city of Calais had commissioned him to do but one figure, so strongly moved was he by his own conception that he did six and charged only the commission which had been promised him for one.

Interesting not alone for its artistic perfection, but for its effect upon Rodin's future work as well, is the *Age of Bronze*. When this work was shown, Rodin was accused of having made his casts directly from the human figure. The controversy raged for three years before the artist was vindicated, and the piece was placed in the salon.

Determined to prove that he did not employ, indeed, had no need to employ, any cheap tricks to create great art, Rodin decided to produce a profusion of figures in bas-relief on a small scale. He did this in the *Gates of Hell*, which was commissioned for a doorway at the Palace of the Decorative Arts in Paris. He took his conceptions from Dante, but the hell he depicted is one of supplication and atonement rather than an inferno of agony and terror.

Intended originally as a part of the *Gates of Hell* is *The Kiss*, generally regarded as one of the most important of the artist's works. It portrays the love of Paolo and Francesca, of Dante's epic. The piece in the museum, a reproduction in Carrara marble, was made by Henry Greber, of Paris.

In the minor works of the collection, the progress of Rodin's art can be studied. In his lifetime, Rodin was the object of extremes of praise and scathing criticism. As a youth he failed of admission to the École des Beaux Arts because he could not satisfy the academic standards. In his later years he worked in the spotlight of the world's esteem. The contrast might have stultified a weaker man, but he retained his deep preoccupation with the reality of common things.

Rodin formed many friendships in the world of politics and belles lettres. His studio at Meudon became a cosmopolitan salon in the true sense. His wide interests are reflected in the many busts he created. Among those in the museums are studies of Clemenceau, George Bernard Shaw, and Balzac.

On the left at Twenty-fifth Street is the WASHINGTON MONU-MENT (9), standing in the center of a traffic island. The equestrian figure of Washington, the work of Rudolph Siemering, was erected in 1896 by the State Society of the Cincinnati of Pennsylvania.

To the right, in the center of another traffic circle, is the ERICSSON FOUNTAIN (10), dedicated to the memory of Capt. John Ericsson, Swedish designer of the *Monitor*, which met the Confederate *Merrimac* in the first engagement of ironclads, at Hampton Roads, during the Civil War. The fountain was designed by Horace Trumbauer, Charles L. Borie, Jr., and Clarence Zantzinger and erected on March 2, 1933.

On the hill overlooking the rushing traffic of the Parkway is the PENNSYLVANIA MUSEUM OF ART (11), a fine interpretation of Grecian architecture and one of the most imposing buildings in Philadelphia. Here are housed extensive collections of art, art objects, and antiques arranged in period rooms *(see Points of Interest)*.

On Pennsylvania Avenue, to the right, is the broad four-story building of the FIDELITY MUTUAL LIFE INSURANCE COMPANY (12), a modern adaptation of classic architecture. The two entrance pavilions have high arches, and the bronze entrance grilles are set in the marble frames of the main doorways. The friezes above the doorways, designed by Lee Lawrie, are symbolic of the seven ages of man.

Continue on Driveway L. around the Art Museum.

The ITALIAN SEA HORSE FOUNTAIN (13), on the right, was presented to the city on June 6, 1928, by the Italian Government in commemoration of the signing of the Declaration of Independence. It was designed by Signor di Fausto, architect of the foreign office in Rome.

Farther along and on the right is the FAIRMOUNT PARK AQUARIUM (14) *(open weekdays 8:30 to 4:30; Sun. 9 to 5; adm. free).*

The aquarium, lodged in a structure set in a great rock which rises from the Schuylkill River, contains a large collection of salt-water fishes and scores of fresh-water varieties.

The rock into which the aquarium's galleries have been placed forms the base for three miniature Greek temples and an ancient

580

mansion, once units of the historic Faire Mount Water Works.

Gaudy types of marine life, yielded by lake and stream and the seven seas, incessantly rise and dive in the glass-fronted illuminated tanks that line the walls of the aquarium. The soft green of the sea and the sparkling silver of rivers tint backgrounds broken by white pebbles, shells, and water plants.

Oddities imagined only by Jules Verne in his prophetic *Twenty Thousand Leagues Under the Sea* are living realities in this thumbnail submarine world.

Inflated balloon fish float belly upward, out of harm's way, on the water's surface, not far from where the sergeant-major fish swiftly don one or another color disguise to conceal themselves against momentary backgrounds. Large porcupine fish from the Caribbean, so named for the spines projecting from their backs, vie for attention with blue and green parrot fish, with curved mouths strongly resembling the beaks of the bright-feathered birds. "King crabs," which are not crabs, but members of the spider family, make futile efforts to scale the rocky sides of their tanks.

Red toadfish, from the West Indies ; saucer-eyed red squirrel-fish, from the waters off Key West ; the vicious green moray, resembling a monster eel ; the queen triggerfish, whose dorsal fin drops into a slot in its back ; and the old maid fish, with wings larger than those of the flying fish, add their respective eccentricities of conduct or appearance.

More than 2,000 specimens in all, representing nearly 500 species of fishes, amphibians, invertebrates, and reptiles, disport themselves in the aquarium's 112 fresh-water tanks and 75 salt-water tanks. One salt-water tank has a capacity of 25,000 gallons. The tanks have a circulation of 150,000 gallons. Salt water is transported from the Caribbean Sea.

The annual visitation by nearly 75,000 pupils from schools all over the country, and teachers of science from Germany, England, and other countries of Europe indicates the institution's educational value.

Classified, the collection includes 389 species of fishes (1,866 specimens) ; 12 species of amphibians (130 specimens) ; and three species of invertebrates (155 specimens). These do not include numerous small fishes and invertebrates bred and maintained as food for larger species and for use as study material in the public schools.

A laboratory is maintained for the study of maladies and parasites to which the finny tribe is subject and for checking the alkalinity or acidity of the water. The water in the various tanks is kept at temperatures prevailing in the native waters of each species.

Proposed by the late Mayor Reyburn as a practical use for the abandoned water purifying and pumping station in the city, the

Facade of Rodin Museum
Replica of the Musee Rodin, at Meudon, France

aquarium was founded in 1911. During 1912 the number of visitors to the new institution exceeded 40,000.

The Graff Mansion, in which the aquarium first was installed, with 19 tanks containing 22 species from Pennsylvania waters, is the largest of the four structures rising from the rock base in which the collection now is housed. It is a domestic-looking structure of plastered stone with gable roof and massive chimneys. The other buildings in the group follow classic Greek temple lines, with wooden Doric columns, and rise in majestic simplicity against tree-fringed Old Faire Mount, the rocky promontory for which the park was named, now crowned by the imposing art museum.

Continue to S. side of Parkway ; R. on 22d St.; L. on Winter.

The PHILADELPHIA COUNCIL HEADQUARTERS, Boy Scouts of America (15) is at the southeast corner of Twenty-second and Winter Streets. This structure of Italian Renaissance design was completed in October 1930. It stands near the Board of Education Building. The style of the period has been sustained in the interior, from the hexagonal red-tile flooring of the covered court with its skylighting, to the ornamented, timbered ceilings of the library, and the council chamber.

On the southwest corner of Winter and Twenty-first Streets is the BOARD OF EDUCATION BUILDING (16), which houses the administrative offices of Philadelphia's public school system and contains a comprehensive pedagogical library.

The building, a large gray limestone edifice, rises 11 stories in its central section. The lower stories, of Italian Renaissance design with two-story wings, extend forward to flank a central court and reflecting pool. The court is enclosed on the four sides by a large wall rising to the height of the second story and pierced by five tall openings on the keystones of whose arches are large scrolls. Similar keystones lock the arches above the windows of the first floor. The upper stories of the building depart from the Italian Renaissance, having between the windows long columnettes terminating in carved busts of eminent men of letters.

At the southwest corner of Twentieth Street is the FRANKLIN INSTITUTE (17), a veritable theatre staging the drama of science. Within the building is the famous Fels Planetarium *(see Points of Interest)*.

R. from Winter St. on 20th; L. on Race.

On the southwest corner of Nineteenth and Race Streets stands the ACADEMY OF NATURAL SCIENCES (18) *(open weekdays 9 to 5; during July and Aug., 9 to 4; Sun. 1 to 5; closed May 30, July 4, December 25, and Labor Day; adm. free).*

The academy, oldest institution of its kind in the United States, had its origin in 1812 as an outgrowth of the activities of John Speakman, a druggist, and a group of his friends. Their interest in natural phenomena led them to delve into the meanings and mysteries of the earth's elements, its vegetation, and its living creatures.

Informal discussions in natural history were begun by the group in 1812 in a small coffeehouse on High (now Market) Street. In 1826 Speakman and his associates purchased the Swedenborgian Church, Twelfth and Sansom Streets, for meeting and for exhibition of their growing collection of specimens. The society grew rapidly and moved its collections to the present site in 1876. The present home of the academy, whose exterior was remodeled in 1905, 1907, and finally in 1910, is an undistinguished classical structure of red brick with limestone trim.

From its humble beginning the academy has risen throughout the years to a position of high prominence, its development guided and molded by men outstanding in the natural sciences. Numerous expeditions have scoured the world for specimens now exhibited in the museum. During 1935 alone 48 field trips to 19 foreign countries were undertaken by members of the academy and their friends.

Exhibited in the hall to the right of the entrance is the skeleton of a great hadrosaurus unearthed in Haddonfield, N. J., about 1869. The animal lived about 100,000,000 years ago, when the eastern part of the continent was a vast marsh.

In Mineral Hall on the gallery is one of the most fascinating exhibits in the academy — at first glance merely a number of colorless stones and mineral ores in a plain glass case. When the touch of a switch replaces ordinary light with violet rays, however, radiant hues leap forth from the fluorescent minerals. The stones and ores glow in a weird aura of light. Then another ray, releasing still more dazzling hues, brings out on the largest rock a handwritten inscription explaining the principles involved in the demonstration.

The extensive mineralogical collection includes a relief map of Philadelphia showing the various strata of rock. Another exhibit portrays the composition of the earth in cross sections from outer crust to core. There are brilliant representations of the largest gold nugget ever unearthed and of the world's most famous diamonds, and specimens of almost all the known minerals.

A large collection of mounted birds occupies the room at the top of the stairway which is opposite the entrance. Beyond this room are the academy's newest exhibits, the natural habitat groups. The displays, assembled with much effort and at great expense, are faced with plate-glass windows through which the spectator sees groups of lifelike animals mounted in surroundings representing their natural homes. Expeditions were sent far and wide to collect these groups, members of the parties gathering grass, moss, stones, rocks, and shrubbery at the scenes of the trapping and shooting. They also made

584

sketches of the different localities as a help in reassembling the groups, and the resultant displays have a remarkably natural appearance.

Among the rarer animals in these groups are the giant panda and the takin from western China, and the giant sable antelope from East Africa. The larger habitat groups include the Alaskan brown bear, Greenland musk ox, American bison, African lion, whistling swan, American eagle, and caribou.

An entomological collection illustrates the life histories of some of the more common insects, particularly those having significance in the economic world. In the same section is the extensive collection of butterflies gathered by Titian Ramsey Peale, the artist.

The Samuel George Morton collection of human skulls traces the development of man from prehistoric days to the present.

In the western end of the academy's north building is lodged the institution's herbarium, with its 700,000 specimens of flowering plants, ferns, mosses, lichens, algae, and fungi, arranged in classified sections. The herbarium boasts an international reputation for its work on the classification and distribution of plants.

Beside the entrance to the academy stands the statue of Joseph Leidy, eminent physician-scientist at one time associated with the University of Pennsylvania, whose achievements in the field of natural history are widely recognized. The monument, designed by Samuel Murray in 1907, once stood on the west plaza of City Hall and was moved to its present site in 1930.

The academy has a natural history library of more than 116,000 volumes. Visitors may consult the books in the reading room. Numerous scientific lectures are held in the auditorium.

Eight natural history organizations are affiliated with the academy, among them the Delaware Valley Ornithological Club, the Philadelphia Mineralogical Society, and the American Entomological Society.

R. from Race St. on Parkway; R. on 16th St.; L. on Pennsylvania Blvd.

At the northwest corner of Sixteenth Street and Pennsylvania Boulevard is the PENNSYLVANIA RAILROAD SUBURBAN STATION (19), a vast underground railroad station over which looms a massive modern building containing public offices and the private offices of the Pennsylvania Railroad Company.

Proceed on Pennsylvania Blvd. to City Hall.

AROUND PENN'S CAMPUS

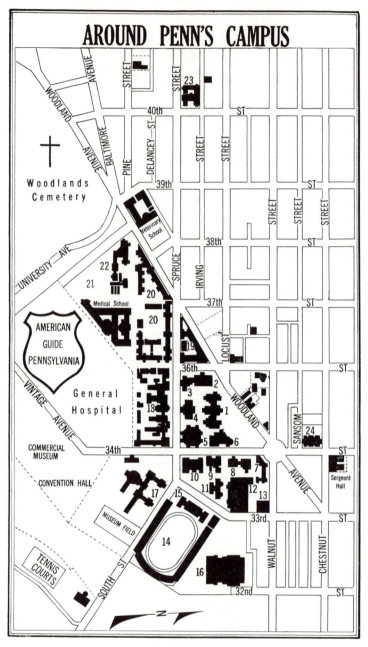

1. College Hall
2. Logan Hall
3. Robert Hare Chemical Laboratory
4. Houston Hall
5. Irvine Auditorium
6. Library
7. Bennett Hall
8. Randal Morgan Laboratory of Physics
9. Hygiene Laboratory
10. John Harrison Laboratory of Chemistry
11. Fine Arts Building
12. Engineering Building
13. Moore School of Electrical Engineering
14. Franklin Field
15. Weightman Hall
16. Hutchinson Gymnasium
17. University Museum
18. University Hospital
19. Wistar Institute of Anatomy and Biology
20. Men's Dormitories
21. Botanical Gardens
22. Vivarium
23. Thomas W. Evans Institute
24. Law School

Around Penn's Campus

City Tour 14 — 3.8m.

"**O**LD PENN," or as the *Pennsylvanian,* student daily newspaper, would prefer, "the University," retains within its seething academic body the pride of high ancestry.

Rivaling in this respect such aged institutions as Harvard, Yale, and Princeton, the University of Pennsylvania struggles against the fate which has imprisoned it within the confines of a great urban center. To attempt to maintain the serene spirit of learning, the quiet charm of academic thought, under such circumstances, is in the nature of a contradiction.

It is true the surroundings of the university lack some of the beauty and repose which are evident in other equally famous institutions. Hemmed in by telegraph wires, screeching streetcars, honking automobiles—the vast discordant, formless blare of a great city—it is with the utmost difficulty that the university manages to retain a fitting character. To a certain degree it succeeds in doing so. The older ivy-clad buildings, the green expanse of the campus, the various college walks, the freshmen with their blobs of caps, the members of secret societies sporting queer hats, and the upper classmen with their colorful blazers—all reveal glimpses of many-sided university life. Patterns woven by the feet of many student generations crisscross on the greensward. On the outskirts of the clustered college buildings are the homes of Greek letter societies and fraternities, boarding houses (under the approval of special college authorities), a fringe of restaurants, cafeterias, and beaneries, the haberdasheries and bookshops, which have achieved the status of institutions. The general picture is one that is repeated in many a large city where a university exists, where the stream of university life, like a great river, has carved from the surrounding refractory mass a recognizable path, under the constant threat, however, of having its banks crumble in upon it. The busy streets and the city's residents proceeding about their non-academic pursuits have been the tolerant witnesses of innumerable student upheavals ; freshman-sophomore pants fights, when unfortunate members of either class have been placed on crowded street cars, clad only in underwear ; the uproarious "Rowbottoms," beginning usually in the dormitories but often spreading to harass the general public ; the marches and snake dances celebrating football victories, the disconnection of trolley poles ; the baiting of police stationed near the campus, and other extra-curricular exercises. The student life is a wine which loses none of its headiness because its partakers are forever under the eyes of somber and disapproving spectators.

The intellectual life of the university will bear comparison with that of any similar institution in the world. Here its urban setting is an advantage ; for the large number of its students who live in the city, close to normal adult life, imbue it with a sense of actuality, bring to it real and pressing outlooks, and are a living barrier to the growth of that academic insularity evident in so many college towns. Its great size, wealth, and scope have attracted outstanding teachers and made possible the installation of modern facilities in all departments.

The university began as a charity school in 1740. Benjamin Franklin was the foremost of a body of men whose idea it was to establish a free school for the instruction of young men in modern languages and the professions. Among this group were 10 of the signers of the Declaration of Independence, seven signers of the Constitution, and 21 members of the Continental Congress. A number of others later held high rank in the Continental Army. Franklin for years had been pointing out the necessity for organizing such an institution. He issued a pamphlet expressing these sentiments, and in 1749 his cherished "Academy" was established in the old buildings of the charity school, Fourth and Arch Streets. Franklin became the first president of the board of trustees and served from 1749 to 1756 and from 1789 to 1790.

These buildings were the scene of several stirring events during the six decades they served as the home of the growing school. During a period of 15 months in 1777 and 1778 they were occupied by British troops and the College was closed. At another time they were used by soldiers of the Continental Army. In 1778 Congress met in the Old College Hall, and members of the Congress, George Washington and others prominent in the early history of the country attended the public functions and commencement exercises.

The Presidential Mansion at Ninth and Chestnut Streets, built for the occupancy of the President of the United States when Philadelphia was the Nation's Capital, was occupied by the university in 1802. The ground was cleared in 1829, and two new structures built on this site housed the university until 1872, when pressing need for more spacious quarters resulted in its removal to its present situation. College Hall, Logan Hall, and the main building of the University Hospital were constructed in the years immediately following the purchase of the site.

The school, nonsectarian, prospered under its first provost, Dr. William Smith. In 1755 the academy became a college, and in 1765, under Dr. John Morgan, added one of the first medical schools in America. Lectures were given in Anatomical Hall, on Fifth Street above Walnut. This school grew rapidly and attained a prominence which later made it the foremost institution of its kind. In 1790

James Wilson, one of the Associate Justices of the United States Supreme Court and one of the most important framers of the Constitution of the United States, was elected to a newly established professorship of law, and in the following year a charter was granted to "The University of Pennsylvania." Thus, the institution became one of the first and eventually one of the leading universities. A formal School of Law was opened in 1850.

Of particular interest is the university's record of leadership in the pursuit of new ventures in education. Not only did it establish an early school of medicine in North America, but the first department of botany in this country also had its origin there, in 1768, and the first teaching hospital in 1874. The Wharton School of Finance and Commerce, established in 1881, was the first university school of business, and in 1896 one of the world's pioneer psychological clinics was established at the university. In 1910 the first department of research medicine was started in connection with the university's School of Medicine, and in 1916 the first comprehensive Graduate School of Medicine was established. In addition the university is credited with having participated in the first intercollegiate match in any branch of sport — a cricket match with Haverford in 1864.

Today, its buildings — 164 in all — ivy-covered and of cloistered aspect — are scattered over 106 acres along the west bank of the Schuylkill River. About 26 buildings elsewhere complete the university community. The total property value is $53,000,000. The undergraduate student enrollment for degrees is approximately 4,400, while the full-time enrollment of candidates for degrees in the professional schools and the Graduate School totals nearly 2,000. In recent years the enrollment including full and part time, and evening and summer school students, has been approximately 16,000. Virtually every State in the United States and many foreign countries contribute to this number. The faculty numbers 1,428 professors and instructors, and the school's endowment is more than $20,000,000.

S. on Broad St. from City Hall ; R. on Walnut ; diagonally L. on Woodland Ave.

Largest of the main campus buildings is COLLEGE HALL (1), built in 1871, fronting Woodland Avenue and about midway between Thirty-fourth and Thirty-sixth Streets. It is easily recognizable in the center of the group which includes Logan Hall, Houston Hall, the Irvine Auditorium, the Library, and the Hare Laboratory. Dominating the group, which in turn dominates the Woodland Avenue view of the institution, College Hall is the center of the College of Arts and Science. Constructed of green serpentine stone, the building is designed in the Victorian Gothic style. Thomas W. Richards was the architect. Within are the offices of the president, the provost, and the vice-president in charge of the undergraduate schools. A geology collection is on public exhibition *(open weekdays, 9 to 1 and 2 to 5 ; Sat. 9 to 12)*. College Hall is virtually covered by vines of ivy which, as custom dictates, are planted by each graduating class, with a tablet to mark the occasion.

To the right of College Hall is LOGAN HALL (2), built in 1874 for the use of the Medical School. Victorian Gothic in style, of green serpentine stone, highly popular at that time, the building was also designed by Richards. Known as Medical Hall, in 1904 it became the Wharton School, among the leading schools of business administration in the country. The offices of the evening and extension schools are housed in this building.

L. from Woodland Ave. on 36th St.

A short distance from the corner of Thirty-sixth and Spruce Streets is the ROBERT HARE CHEMICAL LABORATORY (3), also of green serpentine.

L. from 36th St. on Spruce.

On the left side beyond Thirty-sixth Street and immediately back of College Hall is one of the main centers of undergraduate activities, HOUSTON HALL (4). A pleasing three-story Tudor Gothic building of gray stone, it was the gift of Henry Howard Houston, in memory of his son, and was opened in 1896. Frank Miles Day was the architect. There are quiet reading and lounging rooms which the students use in off periods ; big open fireplaces that throw off a cheering warmth in winter, reminding one of scenes which have been described in a thousand books on college life ; offices of the student council and other undergraduate organizations ; a large auditorium where prominent persons from various walks of life have addressed the students ; and the much used billiard rooms. The university store, cafeteria, post office, and barber shop are also in Houston Hall.

The IRVINE AUDITORIUM (5), the large building on the northwest corner of Thirty-fourth and Spruce Streets, seats 2,127 persons. Designed by Horace Trumbauer and erected in 1926, it houses, besides the spacious auditorium, the general alumni offices, certain administrative offices, and the Department of Music. The auditorium contains a large modern organ, the gift of the late Cyrus H. K. Curtis. The building is of red brick and limestone, a Normandy Gothic adaptation somewhat like a massive pyramid, culminating in a central tower with a slate roof, over which rises a small spire. The walls of the interior are vividly decorated with colored Gothic designs.

L. from Spruce St. on 34th.

The LIBRARY (6), erected in 1889, a Gothic structure of red brick and terra cotta, is on the left, midway between Spruce and Walnut Streets. *(Open Mon. and Fri. 8:15 a. m. to 10 p. m. ; Tues., Wed. and Thurs. 8:15 a. m. to 8 p. m. ; and on Sat. 8:15 a. m. to 6 p. m. ; closed Sun.)* It was designed by Furness & Evans. The rooms and

590

Irvine Auditorium   Entrance to U. of P. Quadrangle

stacks accommodate approximately 850,000 volumes. The library occasionally displays incunabula, and there is a permanent exhibition of Frankliniana. Unofficially, it is a student rendezvous.

The late Henry V. Massey started the collection of Franklin imprints in 1896. In eight years he amassed one of the largest single collections of Frankliniana, consisting of 1,740 separate items, exclusive of a long run of the Pennsylvania *Gazette*.

In 1908 the collection was purchased by John Gribbel, who added considerably to it and transferred it to Cyrus H. K. Curtis, then publisher of the *Saturday Evening Post*. The collection contains the first publication on which Franklin's name appeared as publisher ; the first book on which he worked while in London ; the first book on which he worked when he and Meredith set up in business for themselves ; the first book to bear his imprint alone after Meredith left him ; the last book to bear his name, issued from his Philadelphia press ; and specimens from the press that he set up at Passy, for his own amusement, while he was envoy to France.

Of special interest is the remarkable collection of the *Poor Richard's Almanac*, probably the finest in existence. It lacks only four of the 34 issues that Franklin printed.

Of the 14 Indian treaties that he printed, 12 are in the collection, including the first and rarest of them all, and four of them have copious manuscript annotations in Franklin's handwriting. These four he annotated for and presented to Lord Shelburne, who later became prime minister of Great Britain. Among other books that are of interest because of their rarity, some being unique, are *Mystische und sehr Geheyme Sprueche*, 1730 ; *Evans' Minister of Christ*, 1732 ; blank form for a deed, 1733 (or earlier) ; Brady and Tate *Psalms*, 1733 ; Cato's *Moral Distichs*, 1735 ; Fox's *Instructions for Right Spelling*, 1737 ; Rowe's *History of Joseph*, 1739 ; *My Dear Fellow Traveller*, 1740 ; *The Querists*, Part III, 1741 ; *Catalogue of Books*, 1744 ; both the first and second impressions of *Cato Major*, 1744 ; and More's *American Country Almanack* for 1752, 1754, and 1757.

On the southeast corner of Thirty-fourth and Walnut Streets is BENNETT HALL (7). Designed by Stewardson & Page and erected in 1924, it follows the traditional Tudor collegiate architecture modified to meet modern requirements. It contains a gymnasium for women students, and houses the School of Education, the Graduate School, the College of Liberal Arts for Women, the summer school, and the Maria Hosmer Penniman Memorial Library, consisting mainly of books on education. James H. Penniman, brother of the Provost Josiah H. Penniman, endowed this library as a memorial to his mother.

Retrace on 34th St.

On the left, and between Walnut and Spruce Streets, is the RAN-

DAL MORGAN LABORATORY OF PHYSICS (8), particularly well equipped for research work in heat radiation, and electromagnetic phenomena. Built in 1873, it is a three-story, red brick building in the Italian Renaissance style. General laboratories occupy the first floor, lecture and classrooms the second, and research rooms the third. The museum contains a large collection of relics associated with the early development of the telephone and other modern inventions.

Next door, toward Spruce Street, is the HYGIENE LABORATORY (9), in which courses in bacteriology and public health are given and which also houses laboratories of the Pennsylvania Department of Public Health.

A few steps farther on is the JOHN HARRISON LABORATORY OF CHEMISTRY (10), at the corner of Thirty-fourth and Spruce Streets. It was added to the university group in 1894. This is a three-story brick dwelling designed in the Italian Renaissance style, and contains modern equipment for research in chemistry and the Edgar F. Smith Memorial Library *(open weekdays 9 a. m. to 5 p. m. ; Sat. 9 a. m. to 1 p. m.)*.

L. from 34th St. on Spruce ; L. on 33d.

Many important campus buildings are concentrated within this small irregular area. At the rear of the Hygiene Laboratory, and opposite the Franklin Field Stadium, is the FINE ARTS BUILDING (11), housing the School of Fine Arts. It contains a library of 8,000 volumes, a collection of 170,000 photographs, plates, and illustrations, and 29,000 lantern slides. Fifty foreign and American periodicals are subscribed to for the library files.

The large building on the left next toward Walnut Street is the ENGINEERING BUILDING (12), which houses the Towne Scientific School, with its departments of Civil, Mechanical and Chemical Engineering. The school was founded in 1875 by John Henry Towne, a trustee of the university who bequeathed a large sum of money for this purpose. It is a broad, three-story Georgian structure of red brick and limestone. The Roman Doric motif is employed on the entrance at either end with fluted Ionic pilasters rising above the first story.

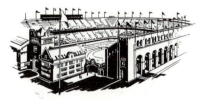

Franklin Field
"Fight on, Pennsylvania"

On the southwest corner of Thirty-third and Walnut Streets is an unpretentious brick building housing the MOORE SCHOOL OF ELECTRICAL ENGINEERING (13).

Retrace on 33d St.

On the left and extending from a point about opposite the Fine Arts Building to the intersection of South Street is FRANKLIN FIELD (14), fronted by WEIGHTMAN HALL (15). The building contains a gymnasium, offices, and a swimming pool 100 feet long. A broad, red brick Tudor structure with square towers rising above the entrances at the ends, it was built in 1903 by Day & Klauder, architects for Franklin Field, constructed the same year.

The huge stadium (seating capacity, 78,000), immediately back of it, is the prodigal offspring of gridiron popularity. Horseshoe shaped and double decked, of steel and concrete construction, its exterior is faced with red brick trimmed with limestone. A huge arcade lines the outside beneath the upper stands. The famous Penn Relays — track and field events — are held here annually. In Franklin Field, on June 27, 1936, President Roosevelt delivered his speech accepting the Democratic nomination for the Presidency.

When some athletic or political spectacle draws great crowds to Franklin Field, other sections of the city feel the impact of mass movement. At the end of a game or rally, currents of humanity stream from the stadium's gates into already congested streets. Every thoroughfare near Franklin Field bears a tide of humanity surging homeward or, in many cases, towards the bright gaiety of the central city. Staid Chestnut Street assumes a festive air, while Philadelphians going about more prosaic affairs become that curious anomaly — spectators of spectators.

On the irregular plot of ground across Lombard Street from Franklin Field stands HUTCHINSON GYMNASIUM (16) designed by Day & Klauder and built in 1926-27. It contains the Palestra, or basketball court. Basketball games attract crowds of 10,000 persons. The gymnasium is modern and completely equipped, with a 75-foot swimming pool, a beginners' pool 35 feet in length, and steam rooms.

Opposite the stadium, on South Street (South Street links with Spruce Street west of Thirty-third), is the UNIVERSITY MUSEUM (17) *(open weekdays except Mon. 10 a. m. to 5 p. m.; Sun. 1 to 5 p. m. adm. free)*. The museum exhibits important archeological and ethnological collections and maintains a large field research section which has annually contributed to man's knowledge of his unrecorded past. Relics of early civilizations in Asia Minor, Africa, the South Seas, Yucatan, and Peru are on view. On the lower floor is the Coxe Egyptian wing, holding evidence of hard and fruitful work at Memphis on the upper Nile. On the upper floor are specimens of wrought gold from Colombia ; rugs, pottery, buffalo robes, and feather baskets

594

U. of P. Dormitories
"Fond memories for Old Grads"

from the American Southwest; and canoes and utensils of Eskimo origin. There are galleries in the museum which contain discoveries made during expeditions to places with such exotic names as Nippur, Ur, Tell Billa, and Tepe Hissar, in the Near East. The main hall of the Sharpe wing is given over to Greek vases, Greco-Roman sculpture, and unrivaled collections of still earlier pottery and burial furnishings from Crete, Cyprus, and Etruria.

There is an auditorium with excellent acoustics, and classrooms and studios where the city's school children are initiated into the realms of history, archeology, and esthetics.

The building is an example of twelfth century Romanesque style of architecture. The circular front of the auditorium affects the exterior design of the structure. Gates, walls, flower beds, and the reflecting pool in the courtyard harmonize with the building; white and colored marble ornamentation are utilized skillfully in the general scheme, particularly in the arches beneath the cornices. Work on the museum was started in 1897 with Wilson Eyre, Jr., Cope & Stewardson, and Frank Miles Day & Bro. cooperating on its design and execution. Chief credit for the design belongs to Mr. Eyre.

Continue W. on Spruce St.

On the left, directly across from the main campus, is the group of hospital buildings including the Nurses' Home, the UNIVERSITY HOSPITAL (18), the Martin Maloney Clinic Building, and the Agnew Memorial Pavilion. These extend from Thirty-fourth to Thirty-sixth Streets.

On the right and forming a triangle bounded by Woodland Avenue, Spruce Street, and Thirty-sixth Street is the group of buildings composing the WISTAR INSTITUTE OF ANATOMY AND BIOLOGY (19), which contains human embryos, brain and skull collections, and many other important permanent exhibits. This is the oldest biological institute in the country. It was named for Dr. Caspar Wistar, professor of anatomy at the university in the first decade of the nineteenth century, whose extensive collection of brain dissections was turned over to the university upon his death. The institute, founded by Isaac J. Wistar in 1892, is a center for biological and anatomical research. Six journals of international importance in these fields are published here. The institute's colony of white rats bred for experimental purposes, is a source of material for many laboratories.

The intersection of Thirty-sixth and Spruce Streets is near the geographical center of the university. Here are the MEN'S DORMITORIES (20), stretching from Thirty-sixth Street to Woodland Avenue between Spruce Street and Hamilton Walk.

The main entrance is at the intersection of Spruce Street, Thirty-seventh Street, and Woodland Avenue. The quadrangle of Men's Dormitories has the appearance of a rectangle ("Big Quad"), with a right

596

triangle ("Little Quad") extending along Woodland Avenue. The 30 buildings included in the dormitory group are among the most attractive on the campus. The stately towers, charming entrances and archways, the arcaded terrace, and landscaped courtyards convey a spirit of restfulness and quiet repose befitting their purpose. The buildings are constructed of red brick trimmed with white sandstone and are designed in the Jacobean style.

Hundreds of students living under such favorable circumstances naturally generate a form of electricity. There are times, during examination weeks, when the atmosphere of tense effort fairly crackles. "Rowbottoms" usually occur at the close of such periods. Rowbottom, legend has it, was the roommate of a student given to wassail and late hours. Moreover, the scapegrace usually forgot his key. When he returned to the dormitory after an especially strenuous evening he would stand below his window yelling:

"Yea, Rowbottom, it's me : throw it down !" (meaning the key).

Today, and of recent years, when the resounding cry shortened to "Rowbottom" is heard, it is the signal for wild alarms and spontaneous, if destructive, activity. A miscellany of objects which have comforted the student during the long academic year, bureau drawers, footstools, wastebaskets, electric bulbs, bathroom appliances come flying in a hail from a hundred windows, to the accompaniment of uncontrollable excitement. Soon all the dormitory students are engaged in relieving their pent-up feelings.

Most of the student activity of the sort which popular belief attributes to collective life, arises (not always only in the form popularly credited) in the dormitories. This is natural, since these are the young men upon whom beat the concentrated rays of student life, which though rich and interesting is still one-sided enough to become monotonous. Thus, the "Big Quad" is the focal point of student rallies prefacing important football games, the scene of victory celebrations, and many other functions, regular or irregular, which crop up during the college year.

L. from Spruce St. on 36th ; R. on Hamilton Walk.

Hamilton Walk, one of the most popular campus lanes, begins at the Thirty-fourth and Spruce Streets intersection and parallels Spruce Street to Woodland Avenue. Near its terminus at Woodland Avenue are the Botanical Gardens, and along its length are the Medical School buildings, Macfarlane Hall (botany), greenhouses, Vivarium, and Zoological Laboratories.

The BOTANICAL GARDENS (21), on the left, are used for practical studies in botany. The gardens center around a pond surrounded by an artistic arrangement of flowers and rocks. The pond holds small aquatic life. Only art could convey the full beauty of the gardens on the sunny days of late spring when they exhale scents quite different from the odors of steam-heated classrooms. The traditional function of gardens the world over — to inspire poetry and romance — is fulfilled here, unimpeded by abstruse purposes or scientific exactitude.

The greenhouses contain a collection of plant life representative of flora in all parts of the world. Students of the physiology or morphology of plants have at their disposal the experimental or "stove" house, so-called because of its constant high temperature. This house contains a collection of tropical plants. There is an aquatic house, containing a tank with a fine collection of water plants, and the central unit houses an exhibit of rare orchids. These gardens are now supplementary to the much more important botanical facilities of the University at the Morris Arboretum in Chestnut Hill.

The VIVARIUM (22), west of the Botanical Gardens along Hamilton Walk and between Macfarlane Hall and the Zoological Laboratories, is used for practical instruction in biology.

Important units of the university are at some small distance from, but still convenient to, the major part of the campus. The school of dentistry in the THOMAS W. EVANS INSTITUTE (23) is at the corner of Fortieth and Spruce Streets. The building is of French Gothic design, three stories high, of red brick trimmed with white sandstone, and dates from 1914. It maintains a clinic with 132 chairs, a large section for graduate instruction, and laboratories of bacteriology, histology, and pharmacology, and the Thomas W. Evans Museum *(open weekdays 9 a. m. to 5 p. m. ; Sat. 9 to 12 noon).*

The LAW SCHOOL (24), on the corner of Thirty-fourth and Chestnut Streets, is also of red brick and white sandstone. It contains executive offices, a mock courtroom, student club rooms, a library, classrooms, and a reading room. Tennis courts are on the adjoining plot.

Continue on Chestnut St. to Broad ; L. on Broad to City Hall.

Statue of Benjamin Franklin
"A college founder— among many things."

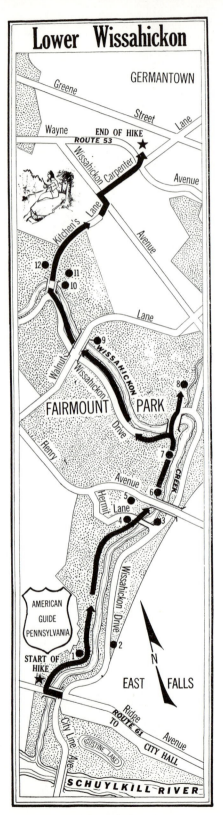

Lower Wissahickon

GERMANTOWN

1. Canoe House
2. Wissahickon Hall
3. Hermit Lane Bridge
4. Hermitage Estate
5. Hermit Lane Nursery
6. Henry Avenue Bridge
7. Lover's Leap
8. Rittenhouse Home
9. Walnut Lane Bridge
10. Kitchen's Lane Bridge
11. Mom Rinker's Rock
12. Monastery

THE LOWER WISSAHICKON

City Tour 15

Route: Take Route 61 trolley marked
Manayunk, northbound at 9th and Market
Sts., to entrance of Wissahickon gorge at
Ridge Ave. and Wissahickon Drive. Enter
path to the left of the falls and proceed
along creek. Returning, leave park at Kitchen's Lane and walk right to Wissahickon
Ave. Turn left on Carpenter Lane, and at
Wayne Ave. take Route 53 trolley southbound to Broad St. and Erie Ave., then
subway, southbound to City Hall. Length of
hike—4 m.
Motor Route: From City Hall on Parkway
and East River Drive to Ridge Ave.

THE Wissahickon Valley extends seven miles from Ridge Avenue
on the south to City Line on the north, with Wissahickon and
Roxborough on the west, Germantown and Mount Airy on the
east, and its northern extremity cutting through Chestnut Hill.

Centuries of constant erosion created the rugged gash called the
Wissahickon Valley, and its chief artisan was the sparkling creek it
cradles. In autumn the foliage blazes with arresting colors, while in
winter the ice-covered shrubs and whitened boughs of the firs convey
a picture of vigorous beauty.

The park is dedicated to the people of Philadelphia as a sanctuary
from the excitement and confusion of metropolitan life. Bridle paths
and foot trails abound. Wooden bridges and stone bridges, high
bridges and low bridges, ancient and modern, span the stream at intervals along its winding course.

Except for a mile on Wissahickon Drive, where it parallels the
creek north of Ridge Avenue, automobiles are barred from the valley,
but park guards are inclined to be lenient with visiting motorists un-
aware of this restriction. Motorists who come to the Wissahickon are
permitted to park in the valley, near points of entrance ; but only
horses, carriages, and pedestrians are allowed to traverse the drives
along the stream.

To the right of the Ridge Avenue entrance is a waterfall. The cas-
cading water forms a thin sheet of silver, and then reluctantly flows
on to the nearby Schuylkill. Here the path to the left leads along the
creek, where great overhanging rocks border the trail. Wooded cliffs

601

loom high over the valley on the left, while on the opposite side of the creek winds Wissahickon Drive with its burden of traffic.

Behind the falls, like an ancient Roman viaduct, the Reading Railroad bridge rears its stone bulk over creek and drive. A short distance beyond the bridge, the creek's flow is interrupted by another smaller waterfall. On the left, a few hundred feet farther up, is a CANOE HOUSE (1) *(open from the beginning of April to late autumn ; canoes, 75 cents an hour ; $1.25 for two hours, $1.50 for three hours ; rowboats, 50 cents an hour ; available daily from 11 a. m. to 4 p. m.).*

A cable ferry crosses to the drive in front of the old WISSAHICKON HALL (2). This building, formerly one of the numerous taverns and inns in the valley and a rendezvous for gay sleighing and carriage parties from the city, now is a barracks for park guards. Like other inns and taverns along the Wissahickon, it specialized in catfish and waffle dinners. Old-timers, passing by, still sniff reminiscently.

Wissahickon Hall was built in 1849. It is set snugly in a recess at the bottom of a towering rock formation at the point where Gypsy Lane meets Wissahickon Drive. It is a three-story, stucco-covered stone and frame building, with first and second floor porches extending along the front and both sides.

The cable ferry consists of a small, flat-bottomed boat fastened to a cable stretching from landing to landing. The craft is operated by hand, and accommodates as many as 10 passengers at a time. Those wishing to cross from the drive for canoeing are carried free. To others the fee is five cents a trip. This primitive method of transportation, anachronistic in our modern age, lingers here on the Wissahickon almost in the shadow of gigantic bridges.

High in the air above the placid stream occasionally drone airplanes ; giant industries not far distant exhale their black breath against the sky ; trains roar along steel highways beyond the park, and in the busy Delaware ply great cargo ships ; but at this spot on the Wissahickon Creek the cable ferryboat still reigns.

In the early days the Wissahickon abounded with catfish, but trout are now the angler's chief quarry there. In winter, skaters by the hundreds glide up and down the creek from the Henry Avenue Bridge almost to the falls.

North of the canoe house, the path follows the gentle slopes of the ridge before descending to HERMIT LANE BRIDGE (3), a small arch of stone spanning the stream. The trail swings to the left at the bridge and leads up to the HERMITAGE ESTATE (4) on the hill's crest. The Hermitage estate, last owned by the Powelton family, comprises about 66 acres of rolling green hills, shaded with a variety of trees, along the banks of Wissahickon Creek. The history of the place began with Johann Kelpius and his followers who organized the Hermits of the Mystic Brotherhood. The only visual evidence of this now extinct sect is the remains of a cabin which is believed to have been part of the tabernacle used by the brotherhood. The only building on the land is an ordinary stone house of two stories, which was built about 1848 and is occupied by Thomas S. Martin, secretary of the Fairmount Park Commission. The commission acquired the property in 1868. The HERMIT LANE NURSERY (5) stands opposite the estate on the right side of Hermit's Lane. The lane meets Henry Avenue at the top of the hill, and the way turns left on Henry Avenue. After a few yards, a narrow, obscure path to the left leads downward about a hundred feet to a cave where, according to legend, Johann Kelpius lived. This "cave" is nothing more than a spring house. A spring bubbles from the rocks close by.

Kelpius and his Pietist followers here founded the Society of the Woman of the Wilderness. Popularly, the group was called the Hermits of the Ridge. A mystic of Seibenburgen, Germany, Kelpius came to America in 1694 to await the millennium. He believed it would arrive around 1700. Gathering a group of devotees from Germantown, he founded a colony on the Wissahickon. Members of the group practiced and taught magic, divining, healing, and the casting of horoscopes. Kelpius developed the first garden in America for the growing of medicinal plants for use and study. While the garden was the first of its kind to be planned according to the botanical arrangement of plants, it was not actually the first botanical garden in this country because of its limited scope. Broadly speaking, the first botanical garden in America was started by John Bartram, renowned botanist, in 1728.

Dr. Christopher Witt, a follower of Kelpius, established the second medicinal botanic garden in 1711 shortly after the death of Kelpius.

Kelpius established free education in the schools of his colony, and his reputation as saint and sage spread through the length and breadth of the Delaware Valley. On the site of the present mansion he and his companions constructed the Tabernacle of the Mystic Brotherhood. Their piety, however, was touched with paganism. On St. John's Eve it was their custom to ignite a pile of leaves and pine knots on the wooded hillside. As the embers glowed, they flung the flaming brands into the valley to signify the end of the sun's power.

The long-awaited millennium did not materialize, but the colony of hermits thrived. In 1708, his slender strength sapped by the austerities of asceticism, Kelpius succumbed to tuberculosis. He then was 35 but, despite his youth, his had been the will which bound the forest sect together. After his death the community disintegrated. Most of his followers returned to normal pursuits in Germantown. The others lingered for a while in their old haunts, and then migrated to Ephrata.

Kelpius was buried somewhere in the lower Wissahickon ; precisely where, none living knows. Should his grave be found, these lines from Whittier might well serve as an epitaph:

> Painful Kelpius from his hermit den
> By Wissahickon, maddest of good men,
> Deep in the woods, where the small river slid
> Snakelike in shade, the Helmstedt Mystic hid,
> Weird as a wizard, over arts forbid.

Most of the caves used by the hermits have disappeared, although determined searchers now and then find traces of them in places hardly accessible to the casual follower of the trail.

Retracing the way to Hermit Lane and the bridle path on the left, the trail leads under the HENRY AVENUE BRIDGE (6), opened in 1932. This bridge acclaimed for its architectural beauty, was designed by Ralph Modjeski and is constructed of concrete and field stone with a light trim of limestone, and forms a sweeping arc almost directly over Hermit Lane Bridge. Two parallel spans support the roadbed. The bridle path continues past LOVER'S LEAP (7), a rocky precijice jutting into space above the creek, on the right. This is the summit of a mess of rocks overhanging the stream. According to legend, an Indian maiden and her lover jumped to their deaths from this rock when their wedding was frustrated by an older, wilier suitor. There are those who like to believe that George Lippard, romancer of the Wissahickon, sought to defy the rock's grim spell when, on a moonlit night in 1847, he stood there with his frail young sweetheart and was married to her by Indian rites. Kelpius used this eminence as a place of meditation and for studying the heavens.

After leaving Lover's Leap, the trail descends gradually to an open field upon which a public golf course is being constructed. Here it meets Shur's Lane and Shur's Lane Bridge, commonly known as the Blue Stone Bridge, which replaced an old covered bridge that once occupied the site. From the center of this span the camera can capture much of the beauty of the Wissahickon.

Shur's Lane meets Lincoln Drive at a sharp turn in the creek. Just inside the park from the drive on the left side of the lane is a bronze tablet commemorating a Revolutionary skirmish in 1777 between Continental soldiers and a detachment of Hessians. The latter, acting as an outpost for the British encamped in Philadelphia, occupied the high ground on the right of the creek. Pennsylvania militia, under command of Gen. John Armstrong, failed to dislodge them. A brief account of the maneuver is given on the tablet :

> On the Morning of the Battle of Germantown
> October 4, 1777
> The Pennsylvania Militia under Gen'l
> John Armstrong

604

THE LOWER WISSAHICKON (CITY TOUR 15)

Occupying the high ground of the west side
Of the creek opposite this point engaged in a
Skirmish the left wing of the British Forces
In command of Lieut-Gen'l Knyphausen,
Who occupied the high ground on the
East drive along School House Lane
Erected by the Pennsylvania Society of Sons
of the Revolution, 1907.

On the drive to the left is the RITTENHOUSE HOME (8), where lived the famous astronomer, statesman, and clockmaker, David Rittenhouse. The structure, built in 1707 of stone, has well withstood the ravages of time. The house is a two-and-a-half-story whitewashed rubblestone building with green shutters, harmonizing with the rare natural beauty of the spot where it was erected. The little house is simplicity itself ; without any semblance of symmetry, it exemplifies a type of Pennsylvania Colonial architecture now virtually forgotten. A stone chimney rises in the center of the building, and a broken roof line is formed on either side by gable roofs of different pitches. The junction between the gable and the roof is formed by large, plain boards, and each gable has a window. The building is interesting for its varied fenestration and for the projection of its joists through the wall on the stream side. A tiny brook, called Paper Mill Run, tumbles through a moss-covered spillway along one side of the house, which marks the site of Rittenhouse's mill, one of the first paper mills in the Colonies.

WALNUT LANE BRIDGE (9), popularly called Suicide Bridge, is a span almost as high as, and of similar construction to, the Henry Avenue Bridge. It is 148 feet high, one of the highest single-span concrete arches in the world. It rises in a smooth, superb crescent of beauty, its white flanks gleaming in reflected sunlight. The bridge was opened in 1907. George S. Webster was chief engineer, with Henry H. Quimby as his assistant. In recent years a number of persons have leaped from the railings of the bridge to death on the rocks of the valley.

Beyond Walnut Lane Bridge the left fork of the trail parallels the creek, following a pathway cut into a high rampart of cliffs standing guard over the valley. A short distance farther on the cliffs converge to form a narrow gorge. Oaks and beeches blend with hemlocks to adorn the hillsides with shade and beauty. The route continues on Kitchen's Lane, just beyond.

KITCHEN'S LANE BRIDGE (10) is a picturesque span of trellised wood which catches the slanting sun rays and embroiders them into a pattern of shadows upon the floor. Not far away, towering atop a rocky cliff above the stream, stands a STATUE OF WILLIAM PENN, erected in 1883 by John Welsh, onetime American Minister to Eng-

605

land. The heroic image, bearing the simple inscription "Tolerance," occupies an eminence on MOM RINKER'S ROCK (11), a massive shoulder of stone that basks in sunlight long after the valley is clothed in deepening shadow. It owes its name to one of many Revolutionary legends. The original Mom Rinker, so goes the story, was a shrewd old woman who would sit for hours upon the rock, placidly knitting a piece of handiwork that she never seemed to finish. Because of her innocent appearance, she did not excite the suspicion of British patrols guarding the army encamped in Philadelphia.

But, continues legend, while Mom Rinker appeared only to be knitting, she actually was biding her opportunity to drop a ball of yarn, containing information on British activities, down the rocky ledges to an American patriot waiting below. The Colonial, hidden from patrols by trees and shrubbery, would carry the message to Washington's headquarters.

The trail continues to the right up Kitchen's Lane. High on the cliff to the left is the MONASTERY (12), erected in the middle of the eighteenth century by Joseph Gorgas, a Dunkard, on the site of a cabin built in 1737. This old stone structure, greatly in need of repair, is of particular interest for its double pent roof, one running around the building above the first floor and the other above the second floor. Gorgas established here a Seventh Day Baptist community as a branch of one in Ephrata. This second hermit colony was founded about 20 years after the decline of Kelpius' community. It observed fasts and practiced a modified form of mysticism.

Converts were inducted into the order by baptism, the ceremony being performed in a pool along the creek. The community lasted only a few years, most of the members going to Ephrata Cloisters. The Monastery, built of wood and stone, now is used as a guardhouse.

A half mile up the hill the trail turns left on Wissahickon Avenue to Carpenter Lane. Right, on Carpenter Lane, along the edge of the woods, it leads to the terminal of Route 53 trolley, and the end of a brief vacation in the valley. Once again the visitor to the Wissahickon feels the impact of commerce and industry and the tension of a fast-moving civilization.

ALONG CRESHEIM CREEK

City Tour 16

*Route: 23 trolley marked Bethlehem Pike or Mer-
maid Lane at 11th and Market Sts., to Cresheim
Drive. Walk (L) through Cresheim Valley to
Wissahickon Creek and follow the stream to Kit-
chen's Lane and Bridge, turn (L) on Kitchen's
Lane to Wissahickon Ave., then (L) to Carpenter's
Lane and (R) to Wayne Ave. 53 trolley south-
bound to Broad St. and Erie Ave., then Broad St.
Subway to City Hall. Length of hike—3 m.*

*Motor route: North on Broad St., L. on Butler St.,
R. on Germantown Ave. to Cresheim Drive.*

CRESHEIM VALLEY is the age-long work of Cresheim Creek,
a tributary of the Wissahickon. It is much smaller and more
peaceful than the Wissahickon Valley, and its slender stream,
where the sun catches it, sparkles like silver.

Except for a hundred yards of paved roadway on Cresheim Drive
from Germantown Avenue westward, the valley has never been landscaped, thus preserving the impression of nature in the rough—
rambling and wooded. And there is added charm in the contrast between the wildness of the valley and its urban surroundings.

At the entrance to the drive stands an OLD STONE FOUNTAIN
(1), which bears the date, October 4, 1774, erected in memory of the
Germans who settled the valley and named it Krisheim after their
native village. An arbor forms a background for the fountain, and
the outspread branches of a towering beech shade it constantly.

About 50 feet to the left of the fountain, beginning at Germantown
Avenue, a narrow footpath, parallel with creek and driveway, leads
beneath a bower of trees. Through occasional openings in the sloping
woods to the left loom the turrets of the Pennsylvania School for
the Deaf.

Not far behind the fountain a small park guardhouse stands in
the fork of Cresheim Drive, and another thoroughfare leads, right,
to Lincoln Drive. At the left of the guardhouse the foot trail passes
under a stand of hemlocks and turns into Cresheim Drive. Here the
creek also swerves and flows unseen, but not unheard, beneath a
bridge, to reappear on the right of the roadway.

The trail continues along Cresheim Drive, where tall beeches and
hemlocks cover the slopes on the left, and the creek, now far to the
right and down in the valley, can be faintly heard. Gradually the
drive descends, finally leveling out and passing under a high railroad
trestle. Lincoln Drive leads right, but the route follows Cresheim
Drive, which merges with Emlen Street, an unpaved road.

607

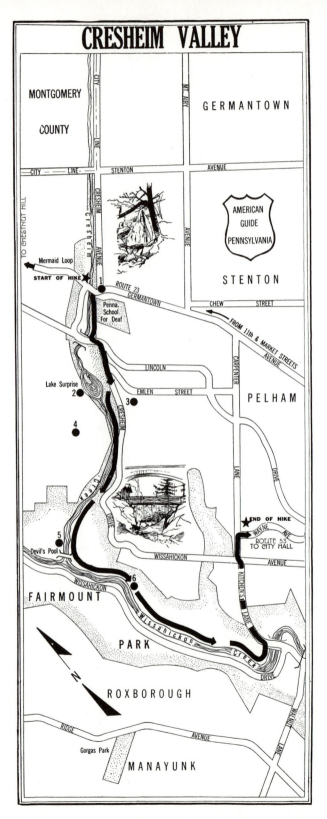

CRESHEIM VALLEY

1. Old Stone Fountain
2. Lake Surprise
3. Buttercup Cottage
4. Woodward Estate
5. Devil's Pool
6. Valley Green Canoe Club

Along Cresheim Creek (City Tour 16)

As though weary of being cramped in narrow gorges, the valley spreads into a wide meadow of thick grass, daisies, and black-eyed susans, through which the creek meanders between retaining walls of field stone. In the meadow are irregular clumps of weeping willows, their drooping boughs interlaced in an unbroken canopy of green. Though squirrels abound in the park, this meadow is their favorite playground. Here their chatter mingles with the song of the wood thrush and the Kentucky warbler.

The creek suddenly widens into LAKE SURPRISE (2), fringed with water birches and clumps of tiger grass. Not far from the inlet a tiny island clustered with willow breaks the surface of the lake. At the spillway water pours over a stone breastwork and flows down the valley.

On Emlen Street, past a small park of hemlocks, the way leads to BUTTERCUP COTTAGE (3), shielded by a vine-choked picket fence, at the head of Buttercup Lane. Built about 1812 for exclusive use as a farmhouse, it consisted of six rooms and an adjacent barn. The buildings were designed in the Georgian Colonial style. An open porch extends on three sides of the house and ivy covers the northeast wall.

True to its floral appellation, the rooms bear the names of various flowers such as buttercup, forget-me-not, and pansy. Each room is reminiscent of the days when the guests retired by candlelight, and a shelf above each bed holds a candlestick of hand painted china bearing the flower for which the room is named.

About 1887 the Houston estate established the house as a vacation home for working girls, the first of its kind in Philadelphia. The building was enlarged to 25 rooms, and many other improvements were made. The white, wooden fence which surrounds the building was purchased from the Sesqui-Centennial in 1926.

The cottage is closed during the winter due to lack of heating facilities for the entire house, but is open from June to October of each year.

Near the junction of Emlen Street and Cresheim Road the trail shifts sharply right into a bridle path. Behind Buttercup Cottage lies another meadow where buttercups and wild strawberries grow in abundance in season.

Excursions in the meadow may be made at random, but a convenient weed-grown trail skirts the creek and eventually climbs to the bridle path from Buttercup Cottage. The bridle path clings to a slope, wooded with maple, oak, hemlock, and beech, growing so densely that even at high noon the way is a darkened corridor.

After a short distance the trail descends to a lower level, where a road entering the valley from the right joins the bridle path at the tunnel bridge. The bridle path turns left ; the tour follows a footpath

609

leading to the valley floor. The trail is rough, littered with upthrusts of rock and exposed roots. Not much farther on, the trail rejoins the bridle path under an iron highway bridge. Here the path drops sharply, and the creek, on the right, tumbles over a 10-foot declivity into a dark pool, the blackness of which is intensified by overhanging beeches.

Below the falls, where the stone-guarded spring flows from the cliff, the bridle path turns, right, over a bridge. Beside the spring to the left, a narrow footpath crosses a split-log bridge over a gulch and for some distance follows the wooded hillside.

Beyond the bridge the bridle path skirts the creek. On the right a private road, with a "No Dogs Allowed" sign at the entrance, leads a few hundred yards uphill to the gardens of the WOODWARD ESTATE (4) *(admission free to visitors during daylight hours)*.

Upon the hillside sloping down to the creek, the expertly tended flowers mass in deep contrast, each spring and summer, their color-ful and fragrant blooms. The wild and the cultivated — pink dogwood and tulips, violets and arbutus — grow side by side among the quiet terraced pools from which, level by level, clear waters cascade to the Cresheim. The route descends through the gardens and rejoins the bridle path where it fords the creek.

Past the entrance of the Woodward estate the bridle path pene-trates a belt of woodland, where an immense stone chimney rises amid the trees. This shaft of field rock is all that remains of an old settle-ment. Emerging from the woods into an open meadow, opposite a hillside thick with evergreens, the path splits; one branch, swinging sharply left, fords the creek and leads to Kitchen's Lane. A foot trail also crosses the creek and skirts the left bank. The route, how-ever, follows the right branch of the bridle path away from the creek and over a hill.

After a short distance the bridle path descends to the creek, where a wooden bridge crosses the stream. Here several bridle and foot paths meet. The route follows a path on the left of the creek which is accessible only to pedestrians. Though it follows the precipitous slopes, the path has been beaten into a safe aisle by countless human feet.

The creek plunges on through the valley, now narrowing into a gorge, now widening into a glen. The path swerves toward and then away from the stream, following the gentler slopes to a small open space, long used as a picnic ground. Though tables and benches are available, fires of any kind are prohibited by the Park Commission. From the picnic ground the trail ascends toward DEVIL'S POOL (5), which the credulous believe bottomless. That, however, does not deter the neighborhood youngsters from using it as a swimming hole on hot summer days.

Devil's Pool

A wooden bridge shadowed by tall trees spans the creek at the pool. Its rails are covered with a design of hearts, monograms, and initials carved by lovers who frequent this secluded spot. On the side stands a rustic pavilion, and high above is a stone bridge which carries a pipe line over the narrow valley. Cresheim joins the Wissahickon a few feet beyond.

The trail continues along the left bank of the Wissahickon, hugging slopes sheltered by tall hemlocks and beeches and flanked by moss-coated rocks. Soon it reaches the VALLEY GREEN CANOE CLUB (6), housed in a structure built in 1696 and enlarged in 1747, and known variously as the old Livezey House and Glen Fern. The house consists of three increasingly larger but similar units, the smallest having been built first and the subsequent units added as the owner prospered. Each roof has a small flat-roofed dormer window. Within the first section is a huge fireplace with windowed "courting nook." The fine paneling, fireplace, and staircase are well executed. This ancient building was the home of Thomas Livezey III, miller, poet, and statesman, who purchased it in 1747. His descendants retained possession of the dwelling until the valley was dedicated to public use.

In 1909 the Livezey family founded the canoe club now occupying the building. The club membership numbers about 50 business and professional men. The creek has been deepened and widened in the vicinity to improve canoeing facilities.

Just off the creek, below the famous house, lie the ruins of the old Livezey mill — long famed as the largest gristmill in the Colonies. Farther downstream, on the far side of the creek, stands a lone pier, the only visible remains of a bridge which 150 years ago carried farm wagons over the creek to the mill.

A flight of stone steps ascends sharply to where the trail again levels out on a higher plane, crossing a wooden bridge over a narrow gulch. In some places the trail is flanked by towering trees, and at other points gigantic rocks overhang the pathway.

Again the trail descends to the creek. It leads to ALLEN'S LANE BRIDGE, which must be crossed to reach a group of old caves in the cliffs above Gorgas Lane, to the right. The largest of the caves recalls the "gold rush" of more than a century ago, when a local "explorer" wandering through the glens of the Wissahickon came upon a glittering fragment of rock near the bridge. As a result hundreds of Philadelphians rushed to the valley and staked claims, expecting to carve their fortunes from the hills. Analysis of the metal hewn from the rocks showed it to be iron pyrites, or "fool's gold," a worthless substance found in abundance in many places.

The trail continues on the right bank of the Wissahickon along the drive to Kitchen's Lane Bridge, thence across the bridge and up the hill to Wissahickon Avenue. A half block left of Carpenter Lane, then right to Wayne Avenue, brings one to the end of the hike.

Indian Statue
Lenape council fires burn here no more

Upper Wissahickon

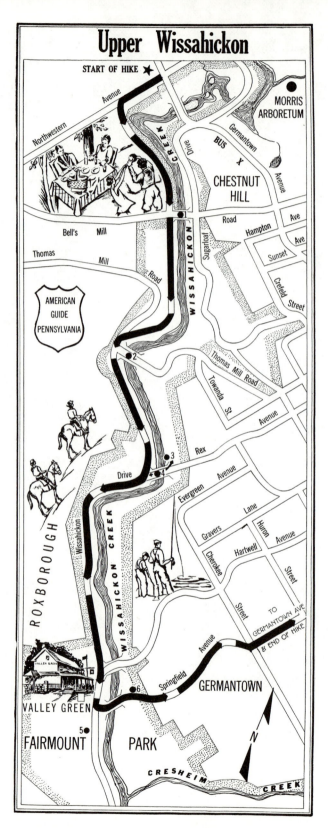

1. Bell's Mill Road Bridge
2. Old Covered Bridge
3. Rex Avenue (Indian Rock) Bridge
4. Indian Rock
5. Valley Green
6. Wayside Shrine

AROUND VALLEY GREEN
City Tour 17

*Route: Take northbound 23 trolley marked
Bethlehem Pike at 11th and Market Sts.
At end of line transfer to Bus. Leave bus at
City Line Ave. and Germantown Pike and
walk left to park entrance. Proceed down
creek drive through park to Valley Green to
Germantown Ave. Take southbound trolley
23 to City Hall. Length of hike—3½ m.
Motor route: North on Broad St. L. on
Butler St., R. on Germantown Ave., to City
Line ; L. on City Line to Wissahickon Creek.*

AT THE park's entrance is a 20-acre tract known as HARPER
MEADOW, which was filled in and landscaped by WPA under
sponsorship of the Friends of the Wissahickon, to serve as a
picnic ground and a recreation spot. The plot which is named in honor
of William Warner Harper, of Andorra, "a lover of nature in all its
forms," was formally dedicated in the spring of 1937.

A dirt road, left, from City Line into the park, skirts the meadow
and slopes almost imperceptibly to the creek under oak and maple
trees. Where the road meets the creek at a sharp bend stands the
shelter in which a memorial tablet was placed during the dedication
exercises.

A quarter mile down the valley looms the first of the tree-cloaked
Wissahickon Hills. A few hundred yards farther on, BELL'S MILL
ROAD BRIDGE (1), a low stone span, must be crossed to reach a
wide bridle path shaded in season by walnut, oak, hemlock, beech,
and tulip trees. Sheer cliffs rise above the roadway for a half mile ;
across the creek the hills slope gently upward. In early summer the
air is fragrant with the scent of flowers. Farther on the OLD COV-
ERED BRIDGE (2), known also as Thomas Mill Road Bridge —
relic of a day when the valley was the industrial center of Philadelphia — leans uncertainly over the water. Its dim recesses, lighted here
and there by sunlight sifting through openings near the roof, conjure
up the shades of long-departed pioneers.

Through the bridge and down the drive to REX AVENUE (or
INDIAN ROCK) BRIDGE (3). To the left on Rex Avenue Bridge
to INDIAN ROCK (4), and statue of Tedyuscung.

The rock is reached by a short flight of stone steps leading to a
winding path. According to legend, some of the early Lenni Lenape
(named Delawares by the English) held tribal councils near this
rock. Atop this massive formation crouches the stone figure of an
Indian, tomahawk on bent arm and gaze fixed across the valley. The
statue, that of Tedyuscung, famed pre-Revolutionary chieftain of the
Delawares, is the work of Massey Rhind. It was erected in 1902 by
Mr. and Mrs. Charles W. Henry to replace a crude wooden figure
which previously occupied the site.

Old Covered Bridge
Another vanishing American

Livezey House
Mellowed by more than two centuries

In late afternoon, when the sun's rays project a belt of brilliance upon the forested heights, the arresting image of that sagacious but intemperate chieftain stands in white relief against rock and trees. Below the stone figure nestles a small cave, frequented by children "playing Indian" in the very shadow of the Lenni Lenape's last great representative.

From the bottom of the steps the trail leads across Indian Rock or Rex Avenue Bridge, and then, left, on the drive to one of the first drinking fountains erected in Philadelphia. The fountain, moss-covered and weathered, bears the inscription :

"Pro Bono Publico A. D. 1854 Esto Perpetua."

Some distance below the fountain stands a slate-roofed park guardhouse. Originally it served as an office for the last of the Wissahickon paper mills and now remains a link between the present and the time when the valley hummed to the rhythm of a half hundred water wheels.

As early as 1690 the Wissahickon Valley became an industrial center, growing with the years. For almost a century and a half, while laden wagons and straining horses blazed the highways of commerce to the valley, the gentle stream turned the wheels of mill after mill, grinding corn into meal, pressing linseed into oil, and changing wheat into flour.

Such names as Paper Mill Run, Wise Mill Dam, Bell's Mill Road, Thorp's Lane, Levering Mill Lane, Livezey Lane, Righter's Ferry Road, and a score of others perpetuate the memory of the Wissahickon's busy life in the days when 60 thriving industries drew power from the crystal water. The last of the Wissahickon's mills was the Megargee Paper Mill, removed by the Park Commission in 1884. With the departure of this rear guard of a retreating industry, the creek settled back to the quiet of former years and was given over to the service of those who come to dream and to delight in its manifold beauties.

From the fountain it is an easy stroll down the drive past Hartwell and Springfield Avenue Bridges to VALLEY GREEN (5), an ancient tavern where light refreshments can be purchased. Though little remains of its original interior, the century-old structure retains in outward aspect a strong flavor of Colonial architecture. Its green, steep-gabled roof and green shutters contrast sharply with the white plaster of its facade.

Here the stream serves as a feeding ground for a mixed colony of wild and domesticated ducks. On almost any summer day visitors line the fence along the stream, watching delightedly as the ducks clamor and fight for crusts thrown into the water.

On the other side of the drive the slopes rise sharply, though not

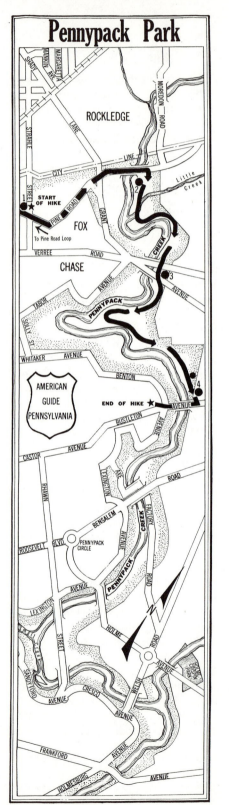

PENNYPACK NO. 1

1. Pine Road Loop

2. Stone Bridge

3. Verree Road

4. Bustleton Avenue Bridge

too steeply for climbing. Giant hemlocks, clinging to the hillsides, shadow the inn and the creek, even at midday.

Valley Green has long been a rendezvous for horsemen. Automobiles are allowed to cross Springfield Avenue Bridge to park at the tavern. Trips up and down the drive, however, must be made by horseback, carriage, bicycle, afoot, or, in winter, by sleigh. When snow cloaks the valley the inn becomes a gathering place for sleighing parties and devotees of snowshoe, ski, or sled.

In nearby reaches of the creek trout fishing is popular. During the season scores of fishermen in hip boots wade the stream, casting for the elusive trout in water once teeming with catfish. To improve trout breeding a number of retards of twigs and stone have been installed by the WPA, with runways or deflectors, which quicken the flow of water in sluggish places. These devices not only serve to aerate the water, but provide shelter in times of flood. The stream is stocked annually, and fishing is permitted every Wednesday, Saturday, and Sunday during the trout season (April 15 to July 31).

Springfield Avenue Bridge is a stone span about 100 yards north of Valley Green Inn. After crossing this bridge the hike winds up Springfield Avenue through wooded slopes. Some distance beyond the bridge, to the left of the roadway, stands the WAYSIDE SHRINE (6), erected March 11, 1920, tribute of Mrs. Samuel F. Houston to the memory of World War dead. It is a tiny shelter perched on a narrow shaft. Under the pedestal's sharp-gabled roof a diminutive soldier once offered a crown of laurel to a thorn-crowned Christ. On January 15, 1937, the bronze soldier was ripped out and carried away by vandals.

Springfield Avenue leads uphill approximately a mile to Germantown Avenue.

ALONG THE PENNYPACK
By the "Ol' Swimming Hole"
City Tour 18

Route: From City Hall N. on Broad St. Subway. At Olney Ave. transfer to trolley eastbound, marked Fox Chase. Ride to Pine Road loop, then walk R. to the Pennypack. Follow the creek through the park to Bustleton Pike. To return, board trolley southbound and transfer to Frankford Elevated southbound. Length of hike—5 m.

Motor route: From City Hall N. on Broad St., to Roosevelt Blvd.; R. on Roosevelt Blvd., to Rising Sun Ave.; L. on Rising Sun Ave., to Pine Rd.; Continue on Pine Rd., to Pennypack Creek.

619

THERE is something curiously exciting and unexpected about this region of rich woods, checkered with open fields, which climaxes just a brief ride from the strident, mechanized center of the city. A walk through the stretches of Pennypack Park is hal-

Concrete Bridge over Pennypack Creek
God's work and man's—in harmony

lowed by a silence broken only by the muted murmur of the creek and the caroling of birds.

From the PINE ROAD LOOP (1) (Pine Road at the end of the 26 car line is the most convenient entrance to the park) the path winds through columns of sycamores, poplars, and silver maples, past Susquehanna Road and over a STONE BRIDGE (2), spanning Pennypack Creek.

A turn, right, across the fields leads downhill to Pennypack Creek, where the winding trail now weaves close to the water's edge and then rises high on the rocky cliffs. After a mile, the path merges at VERREE ROAD (3) and turns left 50 feet on Verree Road, then right on a bridle path. Traversing a picnic ground and a strip of dense woodland, the way cuts through a wilderness of trees and over grassy plots and banks.

From the woods, the bridle path passes through farm land bordered with gleaming white farm buildings and fences. Dipping down hill, the trail returns to the creek and passes beneath a railroad trestle. The route climbs up the embankment and follows the road a short distance, right, returning to Pennypack Creek 50 yards north.

The creek swings northward into wild country, heavily wooded, the ground beneath the trees fretted with a tangled maze of weeds and underbrush. The path pierces this section to BUSTLETON AVENUE BRIDGE (4), then an ascent of the embankment leads to the street and to the old Pennypack Baptist Church — a short walk to the left. The burial ground surrounding the church, which antedates the Revolutionary War, contains tombstones more than 150 years old.

Rendezvous for Izaak Waltons
City Tour 19

Route: Frankford Elevated to Margaret St. Station. Transfer to northbound 59 trolley to Bustleton Ave. Bridge. Walk R. along creek to Frankford Ave. Returning, take 66 trolley southbound and transfer at Bridge St. to Frankford Elevated to central city district. Length of hike—5½ m.
Motor route: N. from City Hall on Broad St., to Roosevelt Blvd.; R. on Roosevelt Blvd., to Lexington Ave.; L. on Lexington Ave., to Bustleton Ave.; Continue on Bustleton Ave. to Creek.

FROM Bustleton Avenue Bridge, Pennypack Creek stretches eastward through a maze of woodland, swamp, and grassland.

A narrow footpath follows the creek for several hundred yards before it encounters an almost impenetrable wall of matted vines, interwoven with weeds and shrubbery. The path skirts the creek as

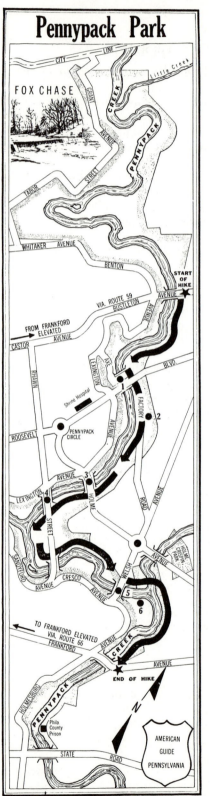

PENNYPACK NO. 2

1. Pennypack Bridge
2. Axe Factory Road
3. Holmes Avenue Bridge
4. Rhawn Street Bridge
5. Welsh Avenue Bridge
6. Waterfall

it turns southward through high banks dense with foliage. Great weeping willows fringing the stream dip their long fingers into the cooling water. Sumach, sycamore, and silver maple trees rise on either side.

A short distance along the trail there is a turn into a bridle path, edged with hemlocks and catalpas. Just a few yards from PENNY-PACK BRIDGE (1), sometimes called the Bensalem Avenue Bridge, on the Roosevelt Boulevard, the trail strikes a pool where fishing is permitted on Wednesdays, Saturdays, and Sundays in season. The stream is patrolled and stocked by the Philadelphia Chapter of the Izaak Walton League.

The trail proceeds along AXE FACTORY ROAD (2), parallel with the creek, intersects a bridle path and turns, right, on the path. The dense woods on the left make progress difficult.

The bridle path leads to HOLME AVENUE BRIDGE (3), beyond which lies the least frequented section of the park. The way passes under RHAWN STREET BRIDGE (4) and through forest land, carpeted to the water's edge with waist-deep ferns. The path, dotted with sharp-scented mint beds, ascends a hill, drops again into the valley in the heart of a violet-strewn glen, and then passes under WELSH AVENUE BRIDGE (5).

Just beyond, a WATERFALL (6) breaks the flow, the stream rushing over the declivity with a roar.

The creek again takes a horseshoe bend, then flows past palisades that rise on the right bank. Beyond the cliffs the trail leads under a railroad trestle and follows the path through a wooded area to Frankford Avenue.

Pennypack Baptist Church—Piety and simplicity blend

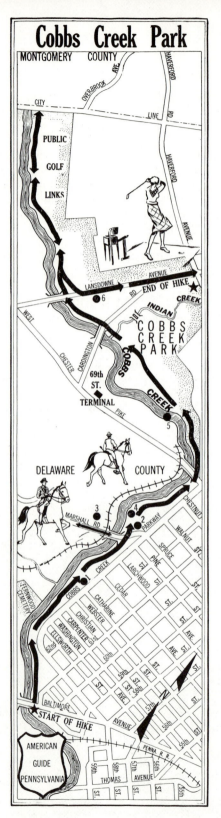

Cobbs Creek Park

MONTGOMERY COUNTY

OVERBROOK AVE.

HAVERFORD RD.

CITY LINE

PUBLIC

GOLF

LINKS

HAVERFORD AVENUE

LANSDOWNE AVENUE

END OF HIKE

6

WEST

INDIAN CREEK

COBBS CREEK PARK

CHESTER

CARDINGTON

COBBS CREEK

69th ST. TERMINAL

PIKE

5

DELAWARE COUNTY

MARSHALL RD.

3

4

2

PARKWAY

CHESTNUT ST.

WALNUT ST.

SPRUCE ST.

PINE ST.

CREEK

LARCHWOOD ST.

FERNWOOD CEMETERY

COBBS

CEDAR AVE.

CATHARINE ST.

WEBSTER ST.

CHRISTIAN ST.

CARPENTER ST.

WASHINGTON AVE.

ELLSWORTH ST.

60th ST.

59th ST.

58th ST.

57th AVE. ST.

BALTIMORE

START OF HIKE

AVENUE

56th ST.

55th ST.

AMERICAN GUIDE PENNSYLVANIA

PENNA. R.R.

59th ST.

58th ST.

57th AVENUE ST.

THOMAS

56th ST.

55th ST.

1. New Guardhouse

2. Old Cobbs Creek Guardhouse

3. Cardington

4. Hollows

5. Cobbs Creek Falls

6. Cobbs Creek Golf Club

By Placid Cobbs Creek

City Tour 20

Route: Take 34 subway-surface trolley car westbound from City Hall concourse to park entrance, 61st St. and Baltimore Ave. Returning, route 10 trolley car eastbound on Lansdowne Ave. to 15th St. subway-surface station. Length of hike—4 m.
Motor route: From City Hall S. on Broad St., to Walnut St.; R. on Walnut St.. to Baltimore Ave.; L. on Baltimore Ave., to 61st St. and Cobbs Creek.

COBBS CREEK PARK in West Philadelphia, although not so heavily wooded as other park areas in the city, offers an excellent hiking route, with a wide variety of scenic and trail attractions.

The hike extends north from Baltimore Avenue and Sixty-first Street, the latter street running parallel to the creek. A red clay bank rises about 12 feet on the right, completely blotting from view the landscape on that side.

Impressive rows of soldier-like Lombardy poplars line both sides of the stream. On the side opposite the clay bank the trees partly screen a heavily wooded section.

NEW GUARDHOUSE (1), opposite Catharine Street, was built by WPA workmen. The new building is Georgian Colonial in design and constructed of gray stone with dark blue slate roof. The stone used in the building was taken from an old mill demolished by WPA labor. Herman Miller, WPA architect, designed the building.

On the first floor, the center hall is the roll room off which is an ante-room used by the Fairmount Park guards as a private office for the sergeant. The north wing is used by the park maintenance foreman as a tool shop and blacksmith forge. The south wing houses the stable for guard horses. The second floor is used for storage.

The OLD COBBS CREEK GUARDHOUSE (2), standing athwart the path, is just south of Marshall Road Bridge. This structure, built more than 100 years ago, at one time housed the offices of the Henry mill, an old paper mill that used the stream for water power.

Directly across the creek in Delaware County is CARDINGTON (3), a community of quaint homes, in groups of two-story row houses of rough stone covered by buff plaster. A busy little town a century ago, today its mills stand idle, relics left by an advancing industry that has no use for outmoded machines.

Across Marshall Road the route proceeds along a narrow trail that cuts through a group of shrubs and trees. A short distance farther

625

on, the path emerges upon the HOLLOWS (4), a community athletic field.

Passing under the Market Street Elevated tracks the creek turns to the left. At this point the stream is dotted with rocks and boulders, the water swirling over and around them.

The creek is banked on the right by a stretch of high rocks that afford an opportunity for climbing. Beyond the rocks is COBBS CREEK FALLS (5), about six feet high, over which the water runs so smoothly that it has the appearance of a transparent film stretched over a concrete wall.

The path leaves the creek at the falls and turns right. It continues past the clubhouse of the COBBS CREEK GOLF CLUB (6), the first of the municipal links of Philadelphia, and on to Lansdowne Avenue. The way turns, right, on Lansdowne Avenue a short distance, returning then to the park, and turning, left, up the left bank of the creek. This, the last part of the hike, is the most beautiful. A wood, dense with oak, beech, and maple trees, lines the right bank. On the left are a number of abandoned quarries.

At a stone crossing just short of the wood's end, the route crosses the creek to the other bank and returns down stream to Lansdowne Avenue.

Long trod by moccasined feet—Cobbs Creek Park Trail

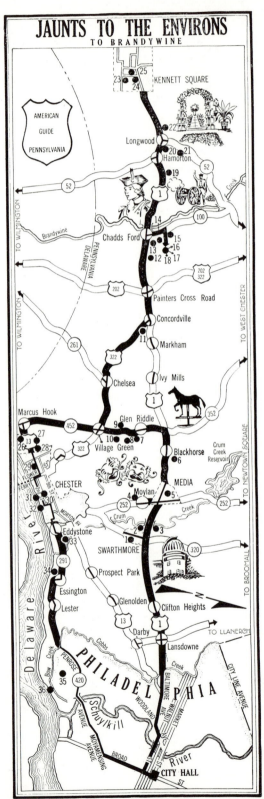

JAUNTS TO THE ENVIRONS
TO BRANDYWINE

1. Swarthmore College
2. Victoria Plush Mills
3. Delaware County War Memorial Bridge
4. Hedgerow Theatre
5. Delaware County Courthouse
6. Black Horse Tavern
7. Samuel Riddle House
8. Glen Riddle Farm
9. Riddle Mills
10. Riddle Mills
11. Concord Meetinghouse
12. Brandywine Baptist Church
13. Chadds Ford Inn
14. Chadds House
15. Marker
16. Lafayette Cemetery
17. Birmingham Meetinghouse
18. Octagonal Schoolhouse
19. Kennett Meetinghouse
20. Anvil Tavern
21. Longwood Gardens
22. Longwood Meetinghouse
23. Shipping Platforms
24. Bayard Taylor Memorial Library
25. Site of Taylor's Birthplace
26. Plant of the Viscose Company
27. Congoleum-Nairn, Inc.
28. Plant of the General Steel Castings Co.
29. Mills of the Scott Paper Co.
30. Ford Motor Co.
31. Yards of the Sun Shipbuilding & Dry Dock Co.
32. Aberfoyle Manufacturing Co.
33. Baldwin Locomotive Works
34. Lazaretto
35. Model Farm
36. Fort Mifflin

TO BRANDYWINE BATTLEFIELD
Environs Tour 1

*Note: For visit to Fort Mifflin permission
must be obtained from U. S. Engineer
Corps, Custom House, Second and Chestnut Streets.*

Philadelphia—Lansdowne—Clifton Heights—Swarthmore—Media—
Concordville—Chadds Ford—Kennett Square—Marcus Hook— Chester—Eddystone—Essington—Philadelphia. *85.2 m.*
The Pennsylvania R. R. parallels the route at intervals on the outward
trip.
Concrete and macadamized roadbed except between Chester and Philadelphia. Poor roads on latter portion.

PEACE now reigns on the Brandywine, as it flows sluggishly amid its low ring of hills ; yet along its banks there lingers, for an ear attuned to history, the rolling echo of gunfire. And, if the ear were very delicately attuned, it might catch above the low lisp of purling waters the startled accents of a British baronet. For it was here that Sir William Howe discovered to his astonishment that he was fighting, not a rebellious mob, but an army of determined men who might be checked, but could not be beaten. Here occurred an American defeat, which was the beginning of American victory. After this engagement it was mainly by means of quick thrusts and cal-culated retreats that Washington wore down the foe, and at last brought him to bay at Yorktown.

The route to the battlefield was once the King's high road to the South ; it is still an important motorway.

South from City Hall on Broad St.; R. on Walnut St.; L. on Wood-land Ave. at 34th St. ; R. on Baltimore Ave. at 39th St. (US 1)

South of the Philadelphia city line, Baltimore Avenue becomes Baltimore Pike, a portion of US 1. At *4.6 m.* it passes through the northern tip of suburban YEADON (115 alt. ; 5,430 pop.) The town's name is derived from Yeadon Manor, the homestead of William Bullock, an early settler. To the left is FERNWOOD (90 alt. ; 700 pop.), a thickly settled comunity of middle-class homes. On the right is East Lansdowne (108 alt. ; 3,212 pop.), a residential section.

At *6.4 m.* the route enters LANSDOWNE (120 alt.; 9,542 pop.), a suburb of well-kept homes set in spacious lawns along shaded streets. Many of Lansdowne's homes bristle with the turrets, towers, and decorations of the architectural mélange characteristic of the nine-teenth century.

At *7 m.* is CLIFTON HEIGHTS (160 alt.; 5,057 pop.), a borough named for Clifton Hall, the home of Henry Lewis, a Welsh Quaker who settled here. The borough's houses, many of them needing repair, rise against a background of wooded hills. Most of its workers are engaged in the manufacture of cotton and woolen goods. The town

629

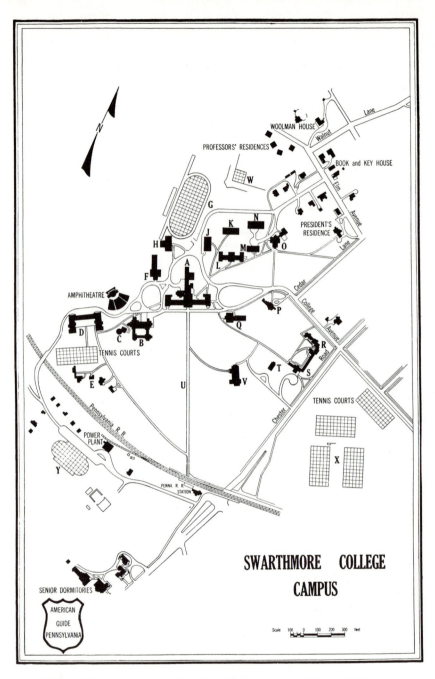

SWARTHMORE COLLEGE
CAMPUS

a. Parish Hall
b. Isaac H. Clothier
   Memorial
c. Sproul Astronomical
   Observatory
d. Wharton Hall
e. The Cloisters
f. Hall Gymnasium
g. Swarthmore Field
h. Edward Martin Bio-
   logical Laboratory

j. Beardsley Hall
k. Hicks Hall
l. Science Hall
m. Hall of Chemistry
n. Bartol Foundation
   Laboratory
o. Meetinghouse
p. Students' Astronom-
   ical Observatory
q. Somerville Hall

r. Worth Hall
s. Bond Memorial
t. Benjamin West
   House
u. Magill Walk
v. Library
w. Alumni Field
x. Cunningham Field
y. Field House for Men

gradually loses its identity in a fertile countryside of well-kept farms and estates.

At *10.7 m.* the highway cuts across the northwestern corner of SWARTHMORE (115 alt.; 3,405 pop.), center for intellectuals from all parts of the country, home of Swarthmore College, and a residential borough of considerable wealth. The college was established by the Society of Friends in 1864 and is named for Swarthmore Hall, home of George Fox, founder of the society. The persistent dignity of the Quaker makes itself evident in the restrained Colonial architecture of Swarthmore's homes and the quiet aspect of its tree-shaded streets.

At *10.8 m.* is a junction with Chester Road (State 320).

Left on this road *0.7 m.* to SWARTHMORE COLLEGE (1), founded in 1864 through the efforts of members of the Society of Friends. At the top of a broad campus, with lawns rising gently uphill from the railroad station, is PARRISH HALL (a), the administration building. This, the oldest of the group, is a three-story Victorian structure of gray stone with Roman Doric porches of wood, painted white. The central section is surmounted by a large, slate-covered dome with wood-railed platform on top. On the ground floor are the administrative offices, classrooms, reception rooms and dining hall. In the main section the upper floors contain a social hall, classrooms, and offices. In the wings are an infirmary and dormitory rooms for freshman, sophomore and junior women.

To the right of Parrish Hall is the ISAAC H. CLOTHIER MEMORIAL (b), designed by Walter T. Karcher and Livingston Smith, started in 1929 and completed in 1931. The memorial consists of a quadrangle of buildings, including a bell tower connected by cloisters with a suite of seminar rooms, the managers' room, and a hall seating 1,000. They are designed in collegiate Tudor Gothic style of local gray field stone with gray granite trim. Massive towers flank the central entrance. To the left is the cloister which connects the lofty Clothier Memorial Tower to the main body of the memorial. Large hammerbeam trusses span the simple auditorium.

Behind the Clothier Memorial rises the green dome of the SPROUL ASTRONOMICAL OBSERVATORY (c), equipped for advanced research. In another part of the campus is a Students' Astronomical Observatory.

Behind this is the men's main dormitory, WHARTON HALL (d), a long, gray stone building with limestone trim, of collegiate Tudor Gothic design. Directly below this are several tennis courts and four fraternity lodges, known as THE CLOISTERS (e), used solely as social gathering places for men.

Return to Parrish Hall. Just to the rear of the building is HALL GYMNASIUM (f) and the swimming pool.

Near SWARTHMORE FIELD (g), is one of the recent additions, the EDWARD MARTIN BIOLOGICAL LABORATORY (h) for undergraduate instruction and for research. This is a gray stone building of three stories, with limestone trim and aluminum window spandrels. The architects were Karcher and Smith, with Cram and Ferguson as consultants.

On the other side of the Parrish Hall rear extension are BEARDSLEY HALL (j), the engineering shop building with forge, foundry, machine shop, and wood working equipment; HICKS HALL (k), the headquarters of the Engineering Department with civil, electrical, and mechanical laboratories, library, etc.; SCIENCE HALL (l), containing laboratories for the physics and economics departments; and the HALL OF CHEMISTRY (m), which contains laboratories, a lecture amphitheatre, and a research library.

At the far end of this group is the BARTOL FOUNDATION LABORATORY (n), erected in 1928 by the Franklin Institute for research in physics. This is used by a group of research physicists, entirely independent of the college. John T. Windrim planned this plain, two-story, light stone structure of Greek design, with four massive piers supporting a broad entablature to form the central unit of the facade. It was erected in 1928. The central front motif is repeated in the rear of the building. On the very broad frieze of both the front and rear entablatures is carved the following inscription :

> Henry W. Bartol Foundation of the Franklin Institute for the conduct of researches in the physical sciences and for the investigation of problems of a scientific nature arising in the industries.

> 1824 In Memory of Henry W. Bartol 1928.

On the way back to the administration building is the MEETING-HOUSE (o) of the Swarthmore Society of Friends and the college, also the STUDENTS' ASTRONOMICAL OBSERVATORY (p).

To the east of Parrish Hall is SOMERVILLE HALL (q), the women's gymnasium and swimming pool.

A footpath leads to WORTH HALL (r), the senior women's dormitory. This is a charming group of six low, connected Tudor structures of gray and rust-colored stone with variegated slate roofs, and stone chimneys. The buildings are contiguous, but each has its own entrance and staircase. Forming a quadrangle with Worth Hall are the women's activities' lodges and BOND MEMORIAL (s), social center for all women students. Worth Hall was erected in 1924 and Bond Memorial Hall in 1927. Walter T. Karcher and Livingston Smith were the architects.

Close by is the BENJAMIN WEST HOUSE (t), a quaint two-story structure with gambrel-roof attic, containing two dormers on each side. The exterior is of a gray stone, buff stuccoed on the north side. Above the first story is a shingled Germantown hood, completely surrounding the house. A similar but smaller hood above the second story continues the cornice of front and back. It was built 1724; restored, 1875.

On the path leading to oak lined MAGILL WALK (u), which runs

To Brandywine Battlefield (Environs Tour 1)

from the railroad station to the administration building, is the LIBRARY (v), a two-story Tudor Gothic building of blue-gray granite and light limestone trim, with a heavy clock tower above the low entrance. The library, in part the gift of Andrew Carnegie, contains a collection of 100,000 volumes. A recent addition provides a storeroom for 150,000 volumes. The Library houses the Friends Historical Library collection of books, also a museum of old furniture and costumes of Quaker interest. The Friends Historical Library, founded in 1870 by Anson Lapham, contains a valuable and growing collection of Friends' records, books, tracts, and early writings (many very rare), portraits of representative Friends, pictures of old meetinghouses, objects and relics of personal and historic interest, and manuscripts relating to the society and its history.

Parrish Hall surmounts the rolling campus
Swarthmore College

There are three athletic fields: Swarthmore Field, ALUMNI FIELD (w) for men and CUNNINGHAM FIELD (x) for women.

On the south side of the railroad tracks is the FIELD HOUSE FOR MEN (y), a low, modern, concrete building designed along broad, horizontal lines. This building, recently completed, was designed by Robert E. Lamb, of the board of managers. It includes two basketball floors and a clay floor large enough for baseball, football, soccer, and other out-of-door games; also a cinder track and tennis court.

From Swarthmore the road dips into the valley of Crum Creek (a corruption of the Swedish Cromkill, or "Crooked Creek") and passes the picturesque cluster of the VICTORIA PLUSH MILLS (2), *12.1 m.*, in a deep hollow on the left. The site originally was owned by ancestors of Albert Lewis, who had a gristmill on the bank of the stream during the Revolution. Washington and his men at one time camped nearby and were fed at the mill. Lewis later transformed the gristmill into a cotton mill and built for himself the house on the pike now occupied by John Turner, head of the Victoria concern. One section of the house was built in 1763, the other in 1789. The present owners took over the site and built additional mills in 1897.

A monumental Doric arch towers above the roadway at the DELAWARE COUNTY WAR MEMORIAL BRIDGE (3), which crosses Crum Creek at *12.2 m.* Both bridge and arch are of concrete, and the latter is inscribed : "Erected to those from Delaware County who served in the Great World War."

Bordered by young trees and flanked by gentle slopes, the road rises toward Media.

At *13.5 m.* is a junction with State 252. Just within borough limits of Media.

> Left on State 252, sharp R. on Possum Hollow Road after crossing railroad bridge; R. on Rose Valley Road at bottom of valley, to HEDGEROW THEATRE (4), *1.8 m.*
>
> At the junction of Possum Hollow Road and Rose Valley Road a row of buff-plastered houses stands close to the road. They were built as the homes of workers in the days when the building now housing the theatre was operated as a mill.
>
> Hedgerow Theatre, in a grove of sycamore trees (R). was founded on April 21, 1923. It is one of America's first summer playhouses and one of its most unusual. Two black, modern figures of horses. carved from wood by a resident of the valley, guard the entrance. Parking space is provided on the near side of the theatre.
>
> The building, originally a snuff mill, was erected in 1807 and later remodeled as a hand-weaving mill. It is of local field stone, buff plastered. An arched entrance way of more recent date gives a Spanish character to the otherwise early American mill structure. The fish pond between the parking space and the theatre originally was a millrace. Residents of the valley, many of them artists, formed the Rose Valley Association in 1900 and started a handicraft venture

Glen Riddle Homes
"Home" to generations of millworkers

Concord Meetinghouse
Once a shelter for wounded Redcoats

in the old mill. This enterprise was not very successful, however, and the building later became a community center. A stage was built for amateur theatricals, and the players' group, now nationally famous, thus was organized as a community activity. The auditorium seats only 168 persons.

Here, under the leadership of Jasper Deeter, 21 actors and actresses live and work. They live by their own hands — all the work in and about the theatre and garden is done by the members — and aim constantly to improve their art.

Cooperation is the keynote of the group, cooperation that goes beyond the footlights and includes the audience. A memorable pamphlet was distributed at the door one evening, addressed to the audience. "We spend from $15,000 to $20,000 a year," it read. "What do you sell? Where is your place of business?" It proposed that Hedgerow buy its necessities from its customers through a plan that may develop into something revolutionary in the history of the American theatre. The director of this company, Jasper Deeter, is a onetime news-paperman who left a job on a Harrisburg newspaper to turn his attention to the Provincetown Players of New York, a group that included Eugene O'Neill, Maxwell Bodenheim, Edna St. Vincent Millay, and other writers and actors now famous.

From there, in 1923, he journeyed to Hedgerow and began his experi-ment in the theatre. Young and aspiring persons coming to the theatre—and there is usually a waiting list including hundreds of names—agree to act and work about the old mill, the renovated chicken coops that serve as bunkhouses, and the garden that supplies food, in return for Deeter's training, and $5 a week spending money. Best known of Deeter's pupils is Ann Harding, motion picture star. Miss Harding returns to Hedgerow occasionally and takes a part in the current play.

MEDIA *13.6 m.* (210 alt. ; 5,375 pop.), seat of Delaware County and named for its geographical position in the center of the county, is situated on a hill and surrounded by quiet groves and woodlands. Founded by Quakers in 1848, and originally known as Providence, the town blends an air of pastoral dignity with the bustling activity incident to its county offices. It was incorporated as a borough in 1850 under an act of the State Legislature forbidding the sale of "vinous, spirituous or other intoxicating liquors within the limits of said borough, except for medicinal purposes or for use in the arts." Becoming thus the only Pennsylvania town for which direct legis-lation of this kind was enacted, it remained, until passage of the Pennsylvania Liquor Control Act, a battleground of "dry" and anti-prohibition forces.

The DELAWARE COUNTY COURTHOUSE (5), South Avenue at Fifth Street, is a handsome white marble building with Ionic en-trance portico and with Ionic columns at the sides. The grounds cover a full city square. At the east end of the courthouse stands a soldiers' and sailors' monument erected in memory of those from the borough who fell in the Civil War.

West of Media the highway climbs through rolling uplands, and at *16.1 m.* passes (R) the BLACK HORSE TAVERN (6). Erected in 1739, this was an important hostelry on the southern stage route in Colonial days. It is now a Pennsylvania State Highway Patrol station, as well as a hotel.

Beyond the inn the road dips into a narrow valley, crosses the east branch of Chester Creek, and climbs a steep grade. From the summit there is a fine view of the Chester Creek valley to the left.

Chester Creek is a source of water power for numerous mills. Once it was naviagable by large vessels for two miles from its mouth at ˙Upland (now Chester), but its volume has diminished since numerous communities began to draw upon it for their water supply. Along the creek and along the highway on either side of the crossing there is a stand of young pine and oak trees planted by the State as part of a reforestation program.

At *17 m.* is the junction with State 452. Here, the route leaves US 1, turning R. on State 452.

Pitching down a steep grade, the road passes through the picturesque Colonial mill town of GLEN RIDDLE *18.2 m.* (160 alt. ; 339 pop.), founded in 1850 and named by Samuel Riddle for a town of the same name in Scotland. Clinging to the hillside are wooden houses, built for workers in a bygone day when the hum of the white-stuccoed mills in the valley drowned the babbling of the creek.

On the far left corner of the crossroads, near the bottom of the grade, stands the white-stuccoed SAMUEL RIDDLE HOUSE (7) in which Riddle lived. It was built in 1823, and is now occupied by the original owner's youngest son, L. W. Riddle. High on the hill behind it lies GLEN RIDDLE FARM (8), estate of Samuel Doyle Riddle, also a son of the founder and noted as a breeder of race horses and hunters. The rambling white house is visible from the route. Man o' War, who made racetrack history in 1919 and 1920, was a Riddle thoroughbred. Man o' War sired War Admiral, winner of the Kentucky Derby, the Preakness, and the Belmont in 1937. Several of Man o' War's colts are stabled on the estate, and may occasionally be glimpsed in the pasture near the crest of the hill.

All but two of the old RIDDLE MILLS (9) and (10), originally engaged in the manufacture of cotton textiles, are now idle. One uphill (R) at *18.3 m.* is operated today as a towel mill, while another, at *18.5 m.* (L) now functions in the production of tapestries.

At *21.5 m.* US 322 swings right, to a junction with US 1 at Concordville. The route follows US 1 westward.

CONCORDVILLE, *24.8 m.*, (422 alt. ; 438 pop.) is a community of old houses that lies deep in a wood along a high ridge.

Concordville derives its name from Concord Township, which was so called by its Quaker settlers in token of the harmonious relations among them. Such relations, however, did not exist between the settlers and their Indian neighbors, for in 1685 the Penn government was petitioned to punish the Indians for "ye Rapine and Destruction of Hoggs." There are large nurseries on the outskirts of the village, and in the vicinity is a feldspar quarry.

On the right of US 322 near its junction with US 1, overlooking the Brandywine Valley, is the CONCORD MEETINGHOUSE (11), built in 1694 on land leased to the meeting by John Mendenhall for "one peppercorn yearly." It was used as a hospital by the British after the Battle of the Brandywine.

From Concordville the road descends through gently rolling hills which rise on the left (Brandywine Summit), set against a backdrop of a sparse growth of young trees. It crosses Harvey Run at *26.2 m.* and follows the valley worn by the stream. At *27.8 m.* the road passes (R) the BRANDYWINE BAPTIST CHURCH (12), a simple gray stone structure with white trim. The building, erected in 1713, was the third Baptist edifice in Pennsylvania. In the churchyard are a number of moss-grown tombstones, some of which mark the graves of Revolutionary soldiers.

The road descends rather steeply to CHADDS FORD, *29.6 m.* (168 alt. ; 200 pop.), a quiet rural community on the east bank of the Brandywine Creek and at the eastern edge of the Brandywine Battlefield. At the ford is the old CHADDS FORD INN (13), a modernized wooden structure built in 1737 ; a post office and a few homes.

One hundred yards beyond the inn is a junction with Brandywine Creek Road, which this route follows, R.

This macadam road leads to the scene of action in the Battle of the Brandywine. Here the route winds along the creek, through the narrow valleys and over the low knolls where the soldiers of a young republic faced British guns.

This tranquil rustic setting holds no suggestion of the roar of cannon, the sharp crackle of musketry, yet, here the ragged Continental Army suffered perhaps its most decisive defeat of the war — a reverse that left Philadelphia open to British occupation in the fall of 1777.

The Baltimore Pike, a direct route to Philadelphia from his landing place on Chesapeake Bay, was the objective of General Howe and his army of 18,000. On September 3, 1777, he began his march from the mouth of the Elk River northward through a countryside teeming with Tories. One of his two columns was commanded by Lord Cornwallis, the other by the Hessian, General Knyphausen.

The Supreme Executive Council of Pennsylvania, upon learning that the State was being invaded, had issued a proclamation calling upon all able-bodied men to help resist "the only British army that remained formidable in the world." Despite the council's eloquent plea for reprisal against the "wanton ravages and brutal butcheries perpetrated in New Jersey and New York," Washington set out to meet the enemy with less than 11,000 men.

The American Army took position behind Red Clay Creek, near Kennett Square, and General Maxwell's light infantry was sent across the creek to prepare an ambuscade. Maxwell's skirmishers engaged the British, and Howe's troops were checked temporarily, but by September 8 they were moving forward to attack Washington himself and to turn his flank.

By a dexterous movement on the night of September 9, Washington fell fack to Chadds Ford on the Brandywine, established strong positions on the hills that border the eastern bank of the stream, and there awaited the enemy. The next morning the British at Red Clay Creek were greatly astonished to find that Washington had moved and entrenched himself at the Brandywine. Howe's two columns separated at Kennett Square. The one under Cornwallis moved up Lancaster Road toward the forks of the Brandywine early the next day, September 11. The other column, mainly Hessians, advanced to Chadds Ford. A thick fog blanketed the entire countryside, and it was extremely difficult to recognize friend or enemy even at a distance of several feet.

General Greene's division, composed of the brigades of Muhlenberg and Weedon, made up a part of Washington's left wing. Greene's division was held in reserve and Anthony Wayne commanded the main left division. Proctor's artillery, of Wayne's division, completed it. This wing occupied the hills east of Chadds Ford. Composing the right wing were the brigades of Sullivan, Stirling, and Stephen, extending along the Brandywine to a point above the forks. General Armstrong and 1,000 Pennsylvania militia held Pyle's Ford, two miles below the main crossing.

The light troops of General Maxwell, which had taken part in the preliminary skirmish, were stationed west of the creek to meet the approaching Hessians under Knyphausen. When the latter attacked, Maxwell, skirmishing every inch of the way, was pushed to the Brandywine's banks, where he was joined by reinforcements. With this assistance he turned upon his pursuers and drove them back upon the main body of their troops. Then, foreseeing the possibility of being flanked, Maxwell turned back across the stream and left the west bank in the enemy's possession.

This gave Knyphausen the opportunity to set his artillery in position, and the bombardment of the Americans began. The main object of this maneuver was to divert the attention of Washington and

639

thereby permit the unmolested advance of Cornwallis and his troops, now approaching the scene of action from the forks of the creek. The American commander-in-chief, quickly sensing the significance of this strategy, detailed Sullivan to cross the Brandywine from above and check Cornwallis first, while Washington and Greene would move forward simultaneously and attack Knyphausen.

But Sullivan failed! Cornwallis came down upon the Americans and had almost surrounded Sullivan before that general was aware of peril. In this skirmish Lafayette was wounded, but he continued to fight until the Continentals retreated.

Greene, whose advance guard had crossed at Chadds Ford, in keeping with Washington's plan, was recalled. Taking advantage of the fog, Greene began one of his famous strategic retreats, pulling the enemy after him and allowing the beleaguered Americans a breathing spell. Knyphausen, is spite of Proctor's artillery, crossed directly at Chadds Ford to follow Greene. The American forces under Wayne fought desperately against the superior enemy until compelled to retire. This they did in good order, as soon as darkness fell, and the British advance ceased.

Washington led his rallied troops in a rapid march for four miles from the scene and prevented the actual surrounding of his army by the opposing forces. Maxwell's light troops lay in ambush to cover the retreat, and as the twilight faded, a slight skirmish took place between them and a body of British grenadiers. This action, however, was but an anti-climax to the defeat of the Continental Army.

The estimated loss to the Americans in the Battle of the Brandywine was about 1,200 killed, wounded, and prisoners ; to the British, about 800.

Right on Brandywine Creek Road is CHADDS HOUSE (R) (14), an old stone structure.

At *32.8 m.* is the junction with Dilworthtown Road ; R. on this road.

At *34.2 m.* (R) at a crossroad is a MARKER (15) that records that the British attack upon the American right wing under Sullivan began here.

Here the route turns R. to the LAFAYETTE CEMETERY (16), *34.5 m.* where stands a stone obelisk to Lafayette, and another to Brig. Gen. Casimir Pulaski. Both were erected by the grandson of a soldier who served under Wayne in the fight at this spot. A stone stile (R) leads into the wooded grounds of the BIRMINGHAM MEETINGHOUSE (17), *34.5 m.* Built in 1763, it was used as a hospital after the battle.

The route continues past the meetinghouse.

The OCTAGONAL SCHOOLHOUSE (18), *34.5 m.* was established in 1753 under John Forsythe, who became the first headmaster of Westtown Boarding School (1799). The Octagonal School, scene

To Brandywine Battlefield (Environs Tour 1)

of the bloodiest fighting on the Brandywine, changed hands 11 times in 45 minutes.

At the schoolhouse, retrace on Dilworth town Road ; at *36.8 m.* the route turns left on Brandywine Creek Road, at *39.4 m.* is a junction with US 1. The route turns right and continues westward, on US 1 entering Kennett Township at *40.1 m.*

The township was erected in 1705 from part of a 30,000-acre tract ceded by William Penn to Sir John Fagg. The township has been immortalized in *The Story of Kennett* by Bayard Taylor, distinguished poet, chronicler of Pennsylvania, and traveler, who was appointed United States Minister to Germany shortly before his death in 1878.

The KENNETT MEETINGHOUSE (19), at *40.1 m.* (R), was erected in 1707. It stands in a grove of old trees, with characteristic carriage sheds in the background.

Right, at *41.2 m.*, stands the ANVIL TAVERN (20), now a private dwelling, at which General Knyphausen's forces encamped on September 10, 1777.

At the Anvil Tavern is the junction with an unmarked road.

Right, on this road and R. at second fork *.8 m.* is LONGWOOD GARDENS (21), the estate of Pierre S. duPont. (*Open weekdays 11 to 5; admission free; first and third Sun. of each month, admission 50¢*).

Among its attractions is a $1,500,000 conservatory housing a magnificent display of plants and flowers. Approximately 108,000 square feet of earth is under glass.

Longwood, known originally as Pierce's Park, was conveyed by a grant from William Penn to George Pierce in 1701. The permanent home of the Pierce family was built there in 1730 with bricks brought from England. The original structure, which now forms the southern front of the duPont home, contains hand-hewn roof timbers and floor joists which have withstood the elements for more than two centuries.

The estate includes more than 1,000 acres, of which 800 are under cultivation. About 50 acres have been made into a nine-hole golf course ; 15 more acres are devoted to flower gardens and lawns, while many more are covered with trees, among them pines planted by the Pierce family as early as 1800. There are also hemlocks more than 100 years old, a cucumber magnolia nearly four feet in diameter, and a number of bald cypresses brought from the Dismal Swamp of Virginia many years ago.

The Pierce homestead was started in 1725. Since passing into duPont possession, each generation has added to and improved the gardens. The most distinctive and noticeable object in the gardens is the circular Clock Tower, flanked by pine trees, with a lake in front and a rocky eminence to the left.

Every 15 minutes the clock chimes melodiously. At 2 p. m. each day in clement weather the fountains are set into play, sending cascades of water over the rocks. Numerous small fountains throw jets of water into the air—jets which, caught by the wind, fall in spray into a blue channel.

Octagonal Schoolhouse
Classes . . . on the scene of a bloody battle

Sproul Observatory
For mental scions of the old Chaldeans

The Conservatory is a kaleidoscope of beauty. New and startling blends of color and form unfold at every turn in the aisles. Vine-sheathed pillars rise to the lofty glass ceiling, from which wide shafts of sunlight slant downward on clear days to bathe thousands of blooms in warmer color and transform the graceful jets of fountains into showers of brilliants. Subtle perfumes mingle in the warm, still air, and the profusion and perfection of nature, enriched by the skill of man, are everywhere evident.

In one wing of the Conservatory peaches and nectarines are seen apparently growing on vines, the trees having been trained and pruned so that all of their branches, laden with fruit in season, spread fanwise on coarse wire trellises.

Chairs on a stone terrace overlooking the sunken, formal garden invite leisurely absorption of its splendor.

Next in interest, during those seasons when the species it contains are blooming, is the adjoining Azalea House, where in addition to many varieties of azalea, ranging from pure white through salmon and many shades of pink to crimson, are displayed huge rhododendrons and a comprehensive collection of acacias.

Below the broad stone terrace in front of the greenhouses is the Electric Fountain, placed in operation after nearly every evening performance at the Open-Air Theatre, about 1,000 feet to the left. This fountain is installed in a beautiful lawn about the size of a city square, spotted with huge clumps of boxwood and bordered front and back with boxwood hedges and on the sides with double rows of maple trees. Spray nozzles are arranged in pairs in the sides of a wide canal behind the hedges, and around each pair are grouped 10 waterproof flood lamps—two each of red, blue, green, amber, and white. Water from the canal overflows down a flight of stone steps and divides to encircle a single boxwood bush 35 feet in diameter and 12 feet high. This boxwood, more than two centuries old and valued at $2,000, is one of the largest in the United States.

The Open-Air Theatre, which occupies the site of the old Pierce barn, with the former barnyard for its auditorium, employs a vine-covered stone wall for a backdrop; growing hemlocks, trimmed flat on two sides, for its wings; and a line of closely spaced small jets of water, rising six feet and rendered opaque by strong white light from the wings, for a curtain. The auditorium will seat 2,200 persons. The Water Garden, some distance beyond the theatre, was laid out by Pierre duPont after the pattern of the garden at the Villa Gamberaia, near Florence, Italy, following his visit to the villa in 1925. It consists of six pools in a rectangular plot of lawn, bordered by fountains and trees, with an observation platform occupying the place where the villa is situated in the original gardens.

Four of the pools are nearly rectangular in form, with the inner corners cut to the curve of a circular pool in the center. The sixth pool lies at the farther end of the garden. A fountain plays in the center of each pool. The output of these fountains when all are in operation is about 4,500 gallons of water a minute.

The estate is a sizeable village in itself. Workers' families occupy 80 tenant houses on or near the grounds, and single employees are quartered in dormitories adjoining the greenhouses. In one month

Longwood consumes about 30,000 kilowatt hours of electric current—
enough to supply an average family for 40 years; 150,000 cubic feet
of gas, which would cook the meals of one family for 5 years, and
more than 1,000,000 gallons of water—a 10-year supply for the usual
household.

Employees have a volunteer fire department, a gun club, and baseball team, and are permitted the use of the golf course and tennis
court.

Longwood received its present name from the "Long Woods," as the
section was known just prior to the Civil War, when it sheltered
groups of Negro slaves fleeing from southern plantations. This station
on the "Underground Railroad" was fostered by a group of Quaker
abolitionists from Kennett Square, Hamorton, and Wilmington, Del.

In the cemetery adjoining the historic LONGWOOD MEETING-
HOUSE (22), on the right at *41.3 m.* on US 1, is a cylindrical stone
marking the grave of Bayard Taylor. Here the road enters the village
of Longwood.

The road passes over Toughkennamon Hill, affording a fine view
of the rolling hills and mica schist country of southern Chester
County, and, just before entering Kennett Square, traverses the mushroom district where a great part of the Nation's supply of mushrooms
is grown. Many nurseries of this edible fungus lie within sight of
the road.

KENNETT SQUARE (380 alt.; 3,091 pop.), center of the mushroom industry, is reached at *44 m.*

In the environs of Kennett Square are situated the SHIPPING
PLATFORMS (23), at *44.2 m.*, where mushrooms destined to glorify
steaks from Maine to California begin their journeys. Here, in the
late afternoon of every weekday, hundreds of crates of these delicate
morsels are loaded on trucks. The growing of mushrooms in the
borough was condemned as a nuisance some years ago because of the
stench caused by wetting down and stirring of carloads of horse
manure used in the production of ammonia, which is essential to the
cultivation of this crop. The nurseries and greenhouses are now confined to the environs of the borough.

On South Broad Street stands the BAYARD TAYLOR MEMORIAL
LIBRARY (24), at *44.4 m.*, where many of the books, paintings, and
drawings of the author are displayed, and a tablet at Station and
Union Streets marks the SITE OF TAYLOR'S BIRTHPLACE (25),
at *44.5 m.* He was born here in 1825. While still in his teens, Taylor
made his way to Europe, virtually without funds. His *Views Afoot,*
or *Europe Seen with a Knapsack and Staff*, was a best seller before
he attained his majority. At 21 he was publishing a newspaper at
Phoenixville, and at 22 he joined the staff of the New York *Tribune.*
His later residence, "Cedar-Croft," is one mile south of Kennett
Square.

644

To Brandywine Battlefield (Environs Tour 1)

Retrace on US 1 to Concordville; R. from Concordville on US 322 to Village Green; R. on State 452 to Marcus Hook; L. on US 13.

Here the tempo changes, and the whisper of history is lost in the roar of industry.

MARCUS HOOK, *64.8 m.* (20 alt.; 4,867 pop.), lying close to the edge of the Delaware River and once a quiet boatbuilding community, is today steeped in the smelly lifeblood of the automotive age — gasoline and oil. Refineries and huge storage tanks of the Sun Oil Co., the Pure Oil Co., and the Sinclair Refining Co. line both sides of the route. The odor of oil is heavy on the air, and oily vapors cling at times to the windshields and windows of passing automobiles. Flame-belching stacks and ponderous, complicated refinery equipment loom against the sky.

Land in what is now Marcus Hook was granted by Queen Christina of Sweden to Capt. Hans Amundson Besk on August 20, 1653. Although Besk never took up the grant, the region was settled in the ensuing years by Swedes and Finns.

In a later patent to a tract of 1,000 acres on the same site, dated 1675 and signed by Sir Edmund Andros, governor of the Duke of York's colony, the name of the settlement appeared as "Marreties Hoeck." The first half of the name, sometimes appearing as "Marretie's Hoeck," or "Maarte's Hoeck," in the possessive form, was believed by historians to refer to an Indian chief residing in the place. "Hoeck," from the Dutch, signified "a corner, point, or spit of land." The combination eventually was corrupted into Marcus Hook.

The English, on their arrival in 1682, changed the name by legal process to Chichester. The older name had taken root, however, and clung to the town in defiance of their legislation. As its shipbuilding industry sprang up and flourished, Marcus Hook threatened to rival Chester, yielding only in the latter part of the nineteenth century, when the evolution of larger, ocean-going vessels found its facilities inadequate, and the industry moved to the neighboring city.

According to tradition, Marcus Hook in the late seventeenth and early eighteenth centuries was a popular rendezvous for Blackbeard and other notorious pirates, who left the memory of their noisy brawls in the name of Discord Lane.

Beyond the refineries, (R) stands the huge PLANT OF THE VISCOSE COMPANY (26), one of the largest producers of rayon yarns, occupying one and a quarter million square feet of floor space. An experimental laboratory is maintained here, and from this oldest of the company's six plants the activities of its 20,000 employees are directed.

Another great industrial company in Marcus Hook is CONGO-LEUM-NAIRN, INC. (27), at Ridge Road and Congoleum Avenue.

The plant, occupying 52 acres, consists of 42 brick and steel buildings and is engaged in the manufacture of felt-base floor coverings and linoleum.

A short distance beyond the Viscose plant, the route enters CHESTER, *67.8 m.* (22 alt. ; 59,164 pop.), formerly called Upland. This, the place where Penn first trod Pennsylvania soil, is today one of the leading industrial cities of the Commonwealth.

In Chester, the route passes by or near great factories and foundries manufacturing a wide variety of products. On Highland Avenue, at Sixth Street, is a PLANT OF THE GENERAL STEEL CASTINGS CO. (28). This company also operates plants at Delaware Avenue and Jeffrey Street, Chester, and at Essington.

At the foot of Market Street, a few blocks to the right of the route, are the MILLS OF THE SCOTT PAPER CO. (29). The large assembly plant of the FORD MOTOR CO. (30) is situated on West Front Street. At the foot of Morton Avenue are the YARDS OF THE SUN SHIPBUILDING & DRY DOCK CO. (31). The plant of the ABERFOYLE MANUFACTURING CO. (32), makers of yarns and textiles, stands at Third Street and Morton Avenue.

Leaving Chester on State 291 the route enters EDDYSTONE, *71.6 m.* (19 alt. ; 2,414 pop.), passing (L) the BALDWIN LOCOMOTIVE WORKS (33).

From Eddystone the route enters ESSINGTON, *73.9 m.* (20 alt. ; 400 pop.), and turns left on State 420. The LAZARETTO stands (R) (34) on a site now occupied by the New Essington School of Aviation. The Lazaretto is a simple, red brick structure of late American Georgian design. The square central section, three stories in height, is topped by a domed cupola surmounted by a ball and weather vane. The two side wings are of two stories with dormers in the attic. Flemish bond finishes the front of the building, and an open porch with Doric columns and jig-saw supporting brackets extends along the front.

The Lazaretto was devoted to use as a quarantine station for the State of Pennsylvania from 1799 to 1895. Ships coming up the Delaware were met by the quarantine officers, and those passengers suffering from contagious diseases were removed.

Title to the Lazaretto passed to the Board of Health of Philadelphia after 1895, and during the World War it was used as a training school for aviators by the Government. After the war it was leased by the city to a group who ran an aviation school, and its subsequent history has been closely allied with the development of aeronautics.

From Essington the road follows along the Delaware River, passing through Bow Creek and Point Breeze, with its Goldbergian maze of oil storage tanks and pipes.

At Penrose Ferry Avenue and Island Road, *79.1 m.*, is the

646

Fort Mifflin
Strategic stumblingblock to the British

Basking in an Olden Glory
Now garrisoned by caretakers

MODEL FARM (35) of the city of Philadelphia. Upon the 200 acres of the Model Farm, under the jurisdiction of the bureau of city property, the superannuated horses of the police department and the draught horses of the department of public works disport themselves in equine Elysian Fields.

At 80 m. bear R. on Magazine Lane, marked with a sign to Fort Mifflin 80.6 m.

FORT MIFFLIN (36) *(permission to visit must be obtained from U. S. Engineer Department, Custom House.)* The upper half of the Old Fort Mifflin reservation is now used as an Army Engineer storehouse, supply depot, repair yard, and docking base for floating plant, and the lower half is used as a naval ammunition depot. The fortified section of the fort is located on the northern half of the reservation, and is important as the scene of a strategic engagement in the Revolutionary War. The fort during that period guarded the waterways which give access to Philadelphia from the south. In the autumn of 1777, when British forces, advancing by land and sea, menaced the flickering life of the newborn republic, General Washington sent to the garrison's handful of valiant men this message :

"The post with which you are now entrusted is of the utmost importance to America, and demands every exertion of which you are capable for its security and defense."

Washington's reverse at Brandywine on September 11 had opened for the British an unobstructed path to Philadelphia from the west. The invading troops, commanded by Gen. Sir William Howe, marched into the city on September 26. Denied support by a hostile population, however, Howe found his position untenable without the war materials and food that could be supplied only by the British fleet, whose sole means of access to the city lay under the muzzles of Fort Mifflin's guns.

This key stronghold, known then as Mud Fort, occupied the southwestern extremity of Mud Island, one of several islands formed by alluvial deposits at the junction of the Delaware and Schuylkill Rivers, approximately seven miles from Philadelphia's central section. Fort Mifflin had a garrison of about 300 men and 20 cannon. Eight of the guns commanded the back channel between the island and the Pennsylvania shore.

The British, rather than subject their ships to the fire of 17 cannon, erected batteries on Province Island, 400 yards from Mud Island and somewhat to the north, where artillery could be trained upon the weakest side of the fort. Construction of these batteries began about October 12, and before their completion a raiding party from the fort attempted to take them. The attack failed because of the swampy land.

648

To Brandywine Battlefield (Environs Tour 1)

On November 10 the British guns opened a final assault on Fort Mifflin. Cannon on floating emplacements subjected the fort and its defenders to a withering hail of shot—a savage cross-fire from 250 artillery pieces. For six days and nights the diminishing garrison held out, with earthworks riddled, guns torn from their mountings, parapets leveled, and enemy ships so close in the back channel that hand grenades tossed from their topmasts fell at the feet of Fort Mifflin's gun crews. Not until then did the intrepid defenders abandon their posts, escaping in small boats to Red Bank on the New Jersey side of the river.

Fort Mifflin as a military safeguard for Philadelphia was first conceived by the British Colonial Administration in 1762. Ten years later the task of drawing up plans for the fort was begun. The Revolutionary War broke out while the fort was still under construction, and it was hastily completed in 1777 by the Committee of Safety, aided by the Continental Congress.

As originally constructed, the fort had vertical timber palisades and a blockhouse at each of the three corners. Only the moat which surrounded the fort remained undamaged by British fire. Capt. John Montressor of the Royal Engineers participated in the attack which almost demolished the structure.

Fort Mifflin survives. Its battle scars healed by restoration, it remains a monument to the courage of its nameless heroes, but its armaments are gone, and now its "garrison" consists of a few civilians from a neighboring depot.

The fort has been frequently reconstructed. The Pennsylvania Assembly appropriated $5,000 for that purpose as early as 1793. Two years later the State ceded it to the Federal Government, and it was renamed Fort Mifflin in honor of Governor Mifflin, who had served as Washington's aide-de-camp. In 1798 the fort was rebuilt of stone after the plans of Major Pierre Charles L'Enfant, planner of Washington, D. C., and work was carried on under the direction of Col. Louis de Toussard, a skilled military engineer, who had served with Lafayette.

Behind the irregular walls, with their barbed or pointed projections, extending 600 feet north to south, and 475 feet east to west, was built a simple but interesting group of structures. The commander's headquarters in the center of the group are in a one-story-and-attic building of simple classic design, with regularly spaced Doric pilasters on all sides and a lookout cupola on the roof. The barracks nearby, also one-story-and-attic in height, has a colonnaded porch along its entire front. The officers' quarters are two stories high, a full length two-story colonnade supporting a second-story balcony which has a wrought iron railing.

The hospital, a two-story structure with Ionic columns, outside

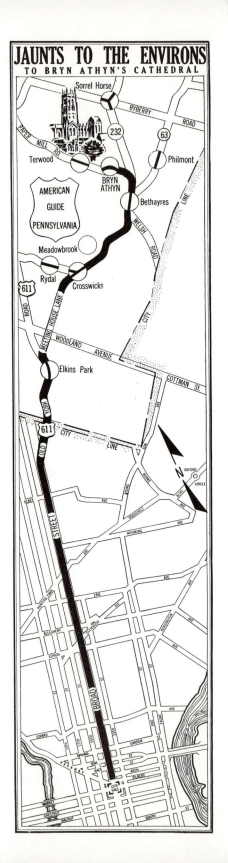

JAUNTS TO THE ENVIRONS
TO BRYN ATHYN'S CATHEDRAL

Sorrel Horse

BYBERRY ROAD

PAPER MILL RD.

232

63

Terwood

Philmont

BRYN ATHYN

AMERICAN GUIDE PENNSYLVANIA

Bethayres

WELSH ROAD

LINE

Meadowbrook

Rydal

611

Crosswicks

MEETING HOUSE LANE

CITY

WOODLAND AVENUE

Elkins Park

COTTMAN St.

OLD YORK ROAD

611

CITY LINE

N

OXFORD CIRCLE

OLNEY

AVE.

ROOSEVELT AVE.

WYOMING

STREET

ERIE

HUNTING PARK

ALLEGHENY

LEHIGH

BROAD

GIRARD

CARDEN

SPRING

VINE

ARCH

FILBERT

CITY HALL

MARKET

CHESTNUT

WALNUT

SOUTH

the walls (so that it would not be in the line of fire during bombardment), was built in 1812. The arsenal was added in 1816, and at the outbreak of the Civil War the present brick facings of the ramparts were installed, replacing the old wooden ones. The white of the corner quoins and trim of the gates contrasts with the red brickwork. The artillery shed, commissary building, and blacksmith shop were constructed during the Rebellion, and the main magazine in 1867.

Captured Confederates were imprisoned in various forts along the Delaware. Some of Moseby's celebrated guerrillas languished for a time in Fort Mifflin's five dungeons. These subterranean vaults of brick masonry — cold, damp sepulchres penetrated only now and then by vagrant rays of sunlight — still contain the double-tier planks that served as cots. The bakery, 15 ft. by 80 ft. in size, adjoins the dungeons. It still has the two ancient brick ovens in which bread was baked in times of siege or attack.

In 1904 the fort was dismantled and every gun removed. It fell into partial decay, being used as a storehouse by the Army's engineering department, which at that time was engaged in improving the Delaware River and its tributaries. In 1915, an Executive order declared the fort a national monument and placed it under the care of the United States Engineering Department-at-large.

Final and thorough restoration was authorized in 1930 by the War Department. Col. Earl I. Brown, District Engineer of the United States Army Engineers, renovated all the buildings both inside and out. The grounds were cleared of debris, the walls repaired, and the entire structure restored, so that today the fort closely resembles that rebuilt by de Toussard.

Retrace on Magazine Lane ; R. on Penrose Ferry Ave., which becomes Moyamensing Ave. ; L. on Broad St. to City Hall.

City Hall to Bryn Athyn Cathedral

Environs Tours 2

Route: N. on Broad St.. R. on Old York Rd. at *66th Ave. Continue on Old York Rd. bearing* R. at Meeting House Lane (just *beyond Elkins Park). Continue on Meeting House Lane (State 232) to Huntingdon Valley.* Left on Paper Mill Rd. to Bryn Athyn. *Round trip—28.8 m.*

THIS tour traverses fertile farming country and fine residential communities, passes quaint homes reminiscent of old Quaker settlement, and terminates at Bryn Athyn (Welsh, *hill of cohesiveness*), center of Swedenborgianism in the United States.

Elkins Park, on the route, contains many luxurious homes. Beyond this town can be seen clean, whitewashed farmhouses, alternate low

At the Swedenborgian Cathedral
Divinely inspired, it grows from day to day

hills and flat country, and a terrain drained by occasional brooks.

The beautiful cathedral stands on a promontory that overlooks a widespread checkerboard of variegated farm land. For 21 years this edifice has been under construction, and although today it is not complete, it stands out as an architectural landmark.

This shrine is the realization of a dream long cherished by members of the General Church of the New Jerusalem, or Swedenborgians, of whose faith it is to be an architectural symbol.

Followers of Emanuel Swedenborg, Swedish doctor of philosophy who turned to religion in 1743 as the apostle of a new dispensation, call themselves New Jerusalem churchmen. Their doctrines teach that the spiritual world being the real one, the Sacred Scriptures reveal it ; the important service of Swedenborg is in the disclosures concerning the Word.

The symbolism of the Swedenborgian church differs widely from that traditionally used in Christian churches. Instead of using symbols and emblems to represent the various phases of dogmatic theology or to depict sacred personages, the General Church of the New Jerusalem had developed a symbolism which is applied to the "Science of Correspondences," in the writings of Emanuel Swedenborg.

The Bryn Athyn Cathedral, in consonance with this new symbolism, represents the "inward form," that is, the mind of man rather than the external form represented by the shape of man's body. The major divisions of the cathedral, in turn, are symbolic of the degrees of life in man. The inmost mind is represented by the sanctuary ; the internal mind by the chancel ; and the external mind by the nave.

Plans for the cathedral were discussed shortly before the turn of the century. The dream of erecting it moved a step nearer realization in 1908, when John Pitcairn donated $30,000 to the building fund. The cornerstone was laid in 1914.

By the will of John Pitcairn, the project received a bequest of an additional large sum of money, thus permitting completion of the main church building, dedicated in 1919. Following Pitcairn's death, his son, Raymond, directed the construction of the edifice, whose main body is fourteenth century English Gothic and the choir chapel twelfth century Romanesque. Raymond Pitcairn has spared neither time nor money in the work of erecting the cathedral, which, it is estimated, may not be completed for another 50 years.

Methods used in the building of this structure differ from the accepted, modern procedure. Some parts of the buildings and all decorative pieces are finished by hand. Models are made on the scene by designers and craftsmen in stone, metal, glass, and wood. Each process and individual part is carefully inspected at each step. Granite used

653

in its construction comes from a nearby quarry, and its timber from adjacent woodlands.

At present, the group of buildings, in harmonious design, consists of three sections — the church, the council, and the choir rooms. A handsome, square-pinnacled tower, rising to a height of 150 feet above the crossing, dominates the group. Cram, Goodhue & Ferguson, architects of the Cathedral of St. John the Divine in New York City, designed Bryn Athyn Cathedral.

The building is of granite with yellow, red, green, and gray tints, giving the exterior a tone of warmth. The trim is of white Kentucky limestone. The use of these materials in both the Gothic and Romanesque parts helps to unify the structure.

The west or main facade consists of a porch of three bays between buttresses, with a lofty window above. Within the main (but temporary) door, with exquisite monel metal hinges, is the narthex, also with three bays, and three arches supporting the balcony above. The nave, five bays in length, is lighted by the great west window, by the five clerestory windows on each side and, below, by the light from the side aisles.

Above the arches of the tower, doubled on the transept sides, are small colored lancet windows, two on each side. The ceiling of the tower is 70 feet from the floor.

The chancel is divided into three sections, each receding section rising three steps. The third section, the sanctuary, has lofty windows on three sides, below which are 21 stone arches. The ceiling of the sanctuary is of stone supported by stone ribs. A temporary altar overlaid with gold is surrounded by seven tall, gilded candelabra. A monel metal screen between four arches separates the south transept from the chapel. The windows, warm in color, except for the predominant blue of the sanctuary, are exceptionally fine.

An aisle leads from the south transept through the fine Ezekiel tower room, with its two rose windows, into the council building, both the building and the tower being of simple twelfth century design. The council hall, with its high, steep, oak-beamed ceiling, a rose window in the west wall and triple lancet windows that light the east wall, is notable for its stone carvings. A winding staircase with a metal railing leads to the undercroft. The lancet windows of the stairs are an interesting feature of the exterior of the building.

Broad, white-plastered surfaces, heavy stone trim and huge oak beams of the choir hall give it an air of extreme simplicity. The delightful irregularity of line and planes is probably best illustrated in the shape of this room and the completed portion of the cloister on the outside of its western wall.

Among contemplated future additions to the cathedral are the extension of the western facade, with the addition of two towers ; the

To Bryn Athyn Cathedral (Environs Tour 2)

heightening of the tower at the crossing; the completion of the choir building and the cloister; and the placing of mosaics in the arches and vaulting of the tower room.

The Academy of the New Church is near the cathedral. The president of the academy is also bishop of the General Church of the New Jerusalem. The institution consists of four schools, a library, and a publication office.

A Vaulted Portico of the Swedenborgian Cathedral,
From surrounding hills the stones were hewn

1. Latham Park
2. Melrose Academy
3. A Bronze Tablet
4. Old York Road Country Club
5. Abington Library
6. Baederwood Golf Course
7. Abington Presbyterian Church
8. Abington Presbyterian Cemetery
9. Abington Memorial Hospital
10. Old Forge Inn
11. Fountain Hotel
12. Willow Grove Park
13. Mineral Springs Hotel
14. Horsham Friends Meetinghouse
15. Pitcairn Autogiro Company
16. Graeme Park
17. Union Library
18. Crooked Billet Tavern
19. Crooked Billet Monument
20. Site of Log College
21. Presbyterian Church of Neshaminy
22. Robbins House
23 Museum of the Bucks County Historical Society
24. Fountain House
25. Fonthill
26. General Greene Inn
27. Buckingham Meetinghouse
28. Buttonwood Inn
29. Catalpa Inn
30. Solebury Baptist Church
31. Union Paper Mill
32. Thompson-Neely House

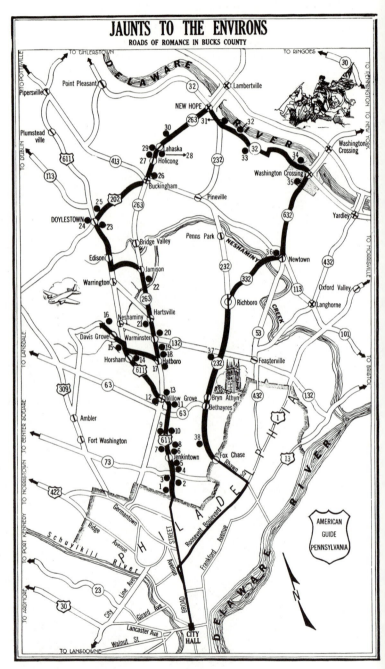

JAUNTS TO THE ENVIRONS
ROADS OF ROMANCE IN BUCKS COUNTY

AMERICAN GUIDE PENNSYLVANIA

33. Bowman's Hill Observation Tower
34. Washington Crossing State Park
35. Washington Crossing Inn
36. Old Newtown Presbyterian Church
37. Southampton Baptist Meetingho[use]
38. Rydal Country Club

To New Hope

And Washington Crossing

Environs Tour 3

Philadelphia — Jenkintown — Abington — Willow Grove — Hatboro — Doylestown — New Hope — Washington Crossing — Newtown — Bryn Athyn — Philadelphia. 84.8 *m.* USS 611 ; State 233 263, 202, 32, 632, 332, and 232. Round trip 84.8 m.

The Reading and Pennsylvania Railroads parallel the route at intervals.

Roadway paved throughout.

THE route traverses a region rich in productive soil, historical associations, scenic beauty, and picturesque hamlets. Across the Philadelphia County Line the highway enters Montgomery County, and, following roads laid over the course of old Indian trails, describes a rough circle, through Bucks County to the artists' colony at New Hope and back to Philadelphia.

North from City Hall on Broad St. ; R. on Old York Rd. (US 611) just beyond Sixty-sixth Ave.

Crossing CITY LINE at *7.9 m.*, the route enters an area, the rural aspects of which are steadily being transformed by real estate developments. Tracks of the P. R. T. trolley system follow the highway as far as Willow Grove.

At *8.2 m.* an elaborately designed iron gateway (L) frames the entrance to LATHAM PARK (1) *(open).* Fine homes line the wide parkway which cuts through the center of this skillfully landscaped development. Just beyond the west end of the park is a settlement known as La Mott, a corruption of the name of Lucretia Mott, famous abolitionist and advocate of women's rights, who lived in this vicinity.

MELROSE ACADEMY (2), a large brownstone building housing a school for girls, surmounts a low hill at *8.4 m.* (R).

ELKINS PARK, 9 m. (175 alt., 314 pop.), is one of the suburban developments which sprang up in 1927. A number of fine homes set in wide, tree-shaded lawns line the route as it approaches the compact business section. The original name, Shoemakertown, was changed to Ogontz by Jay Cooke, who laid out a large estate here. Although officially Elkins Park, the name Ogontz is quite commonly used.

A BRONZE TABLET (3), set in stone on a lawn (L) at *9.3 m.*, marks the site of the first religious meeting "hereabout." What is now known as the Abington Meeting of the Society of Friends was held here in 1683.

Beyond Elkins Park the highway is flanked by large walled and

657

hedged estates, among them Lindenhurst, the old Wanamaker property. This 102-acre estate, now owned by Henry W. Breyer, ice cream manufacturer, was once a show place, but the mansion is unoccupied and the grounds show signs of neglect.

At *10.2 m.* the route enters JENKINTOWN (211 alt. ; 4,797 pop.), named for Stephen Jenkins, an early Welsh settler. A few hundred yards farther (R) is the OLD YORK ROAD COUNTRY CLUB (4) *(private)*. Much of the acreage of this 18-hole course is hidden by a high, thick hedge which parallels the highway. At *10.5 m.* is the business section of this community.

At *10.8 m.* (within the Jenkintown limits), is the ABINGTON LIBRARY (R) (5), housed partly in the original building of the Jenkins Town Lyceum. The lyceum was built in 1839, the same year the society was founded for the purpose of holding debates and giving lectures. The Abington Library Company, organized in 1803, moved into the lyceum building in 1910. A fine collection of Pennsylvaniana is included among the 25,000 volumes contained in the library.

When the library company purchased the building, two wings, in the Classic Revival style of the original, were added. A rear arm was erected in 1913. The structure is of white, stuccoed local stone set back in a maple-studded lawn. The front pediment of Roman Doric design, is supported by four unfluted white columns.

At *11.2 m.* the highway crosses a bridge over the Reading Railroad tracks. At *11.3 m.* a dense hedge (R) borders the Old York Road side of the 18-hole BAEDERWOOD GOLF COURSE (6). This is a public daily-fee course.

A real estate development is passed at *11.7 m.* just before entering ABINGTON *11.9 m.* (340 alt. ; 2,000 pop.). The lawn-flanked dwellings of Abington (founded in 1714 and named for the Abington Friends Meeting in England) are, in general, typical of the prosperous suburb.

At *12 m.* are the ABINGTON PRESBYTERIAN CHURCH (7) (L) and (R) the ABINGTON PRESBYTERIAN CEMETERY (8). The congregation was organized in 1714, and in 1719 a log church was built. This was replaced by a more substantial structure in 1793. The present ivy-covered stone edifice was erected in 1863. It has a spire which rises from the ground.

Within a low stone wall on the opposite side of the road is the cemetery. A number of the graves date from the 1720's, but time and the elements have rendered many of the inscriptions illegible. A huge tulip tree graces the front of the graveyard.

The ABINGTON MEMORIAL HOSPITAL (9) (L), at *12.2 m.* is a modern adaptation of Georgian Colonial architecture, this group of connected units of red brick laid in Flemish bond is set back in a

Robbins House
"*A young French soldier came to aid — — —.*"

Old Forge Inn
Welcome after a weary trip by stage

wide, carefully tended lawn. The central unit is dominated by a portico of four piers of marble. A delicate cupola rises above the roof. Incorporated in 1913, the first buildings were erected in 1914 ; additions were made in 1919 and in 1929. There are 234 beds.

OLD FORGE INN (10), built in 1803, is at *12.5 m.* (R). The white-plastered stone walls of this two-story-and-attic building are emphasized by green shutters. The porches fronting the first and second stories are recent additions.

Just beyond the inn a wide pasture spreads away to the right with a small wood in the distance.

The route tops a rise at *13 m.* and descends a gentle slope, passing a number of small, neat homes to the right and left and affording a fine vista straight ahead.

A number of inns were established in the early eighteenth century as stopping points for coaches on the stage routes which converged here in their course between Philadelphia and northern points. One of these, FOUNTAIN HOTEL (11), also known as the McAvoy House (R), where the road enters the business section, has been altered but little since its erection in 1717. This two-story-and-attic structure with white-plastered stone walls stands at the edge of the roadway. Stage passengers, no doubt, were able to step from the coach to the first-floor porch. At about roof level of the old four-wheelers is a second-floor veranda.

WILLOW GROVE *14.2 m.* (284 alt. ; 2,065 pop.) settled in 1719, is a community of frame, bungalow-type dwellings built around WILLOW GROVE PARK (12), one of Pennsylvania's largest amusement parks.

At one time this community was known as Red Lion after an earlier inn of that name. The present name was taken from the willow trees which abound in and about the park.

MINERAL SPRING HOTEL (13) (R), at *14.4 m.*, the junction of US 611 and State 263, is a yellow-painted structure of stuccoed stone. This inn, established in 1803, depended for its patronage largely on those attracted by the mineral waters of its excellent spring.

Opposite the hotel is the entrance to WILLOW GROVE PARK (L) *(season runs from Decoration Day to Labor Day)*. Opened in 1896, the park offered band concerts in addition to the standard amusement park activities. The concerts rapidly increased the popularity of the park, and it was not long before famous bands and symphony orchestras were being presented in the open-air concert shell. Among the bands and orchestras which appeared here year after year were those of such notable directors as Sousa, Damrosch,

Creatore, Pryor, and Herbert. Since the latter part of the 1920's the stage of the pavilion has been devoted to a variety of purposes.

The 100-acre grounds contain all the usual amusements found in such parks. Boats are rented for use on the large artificial lake. One of the attractions is the John Philip Sousa Memorial Fountain in the center of the lake. The fountain is turned on nightly during the season.

Left at fork on US 611. The route traverses a productive farming area.

HORSHAM, *18.4 m.* (250 alt. ; 800 pop.), is a farming community with unpainted frame dwellings clustering around a crossroad. Here (R) is the HORSHAM FRIENDS MEETINGHOUSE (14), built in 1803 to house a meeting founded in 1716. The house is of brown local stone ; the doors and shutters are painted white. It consists of two stories and attic and is flanked on three sides by a wide, covered walk, paved with flagstones. A low wall on the opposite side of the road encloses the burial ground.

The white-painted hangar and the spacious landing field of the PITCAIRN AUTOGIRO COMPANY (15) are (L) at *19.1 m.* The late Juan de la Cierva, inventor of the autogiro, conducted much of his experimental work here.

At *19.5 m.* is a junction with a macadam road.

Left on this road is DAVIS GROVE, *0.8 m.*, a delightful nineteenth century crossroads village. On the far right corner of the cross-roads is the home of Morris Penrose, member of the family that occupied Graeme Park from 1801 to 1920. Proceed straight through Davis Grove to GRAEME PARK (16), *1.8 m.*, onetime estate of Sir Walter Keith, Governor of Pennsylvania from 1717 to 1726.

A tract of 1,200 acres was purchased by Sir William Keith in 1718 for £500. Here in the woods the governor built a stately stone manor house of three stories, surmounted by a gambrel roof with dormer windows. Its walls, two feet thick, are constructed of brown field stone. The extreme narrowness of the windows and doors is a notable feature. The house, unoccupied and virtually unfurnished, offers a well-preserved example of Georgian Colonial architecture.

The interior, with its paneled walls, massive fireplaces, and high ceilings is sophisticated for so early a country residence in this region. In Spring, windows opening on the back lawn frame gay masses of golden daffodils.

Within this now deserted mansion Governor Keith entertained royally. In front of the house is Sir William's "lifting-stone," a large mush-room-shaped boulder which he used to test the strength of slaves before purchasing them. A portion of the wall of the old slave quarters still stands near the house.

The road from Horsham Meeting to Willow Grove, now part of the Doylestown Pike, was built by the Province for Sir William's use.

In 1726 Sir William fell at odds with the Proprietary Government and was removed from office. He retired to his estate, and in the

Friends' Meeting House at Horsham
Sunday worship once filled the shed with carriages

Keith House at Graeme Park
Memories of Eighteenth Century splendor

following year returned to England. The expense of maintaining his Pennsylvania estate and his many charities soon exceeded his income, and he was twice imprisoned for debt, dying in the Old Bailey in 1749.

Graeme Park and the Keith House were conveyed in 1737 to Dr. Thomas Graeme, who had married Sir William's stepdaughter; and during the period that followed, Benjamin Franklin and John and Thomas Penn were among the many leaders of the Colony to be entertained there. Dr. Graeme bequeathed the property to his daughter, Elizabeth Graeme Fergusson, who was its occupant during the Revolution.

In October 1777, when his forces encamped nearby, Washington was graciously welcomed to the house of Mistress Fergusson, in spite of the fact that her husband had enlisted under British colors.

Retrace on US 611 to road just above Horsham. Continue on this road to Hatboro.

At HATBORO (239 alt.; 2,651 pop.), ancient, frame houses flank the broad, modern highway which the route now traverses. The name is derived from the fact that one of the early industries was the manufacture of hats.

UNION LIBRARY (17), 243 S. York Road *(open daily 10 to 12 and 2 to 5:30; Sat. 10 to 5:30; Tues. and Fri. evenings, 7 to 9)*, founded in 1755, is the third oldest in Pennsylvania. Built in 1849, the one-story structure, of white-stuccoed local stone, is in the Greek Revival style.

At the northern end of the town is the old CROOKED BILLET TAVERN (18) (R), now a private dwelling. The CROOKED BILLET MONUMENT (19), at *22.1 m.* (R), was erected to commemorate the Revolutionary skirmish near here in which 30 American soldiers were slain.

The monument, of white marble on a base of gray granite, stands in a small, square grass plot above the level of the roadway. A red sandstone wall supports the front of the embankment, and steps lead up to the monument.

With a detachment of 50 men, Gen. John Lacey had been detailed to protect American and harass British supply trains in this region. Seriously hampered by Lacey's activities, the British dispatched a force of 700 infantry and cavalry to the section. On May 1, 1778, the British surrounded and attacked Lacey's men. Seventeen were wounded in addition to those killed.

Beyond the monument, dwellings are few. At *22.7 m.* a white board marker (L) indicates the way to the actual scene of the Crooked Billet massacre.

At the intersection with State 132 in WARMINSTER, *24.2 m.* (300 alt.; 131 pop.), is a stone tablet (L) marking the spot where John Fitch is reputed to have "conceived the idea of the first steamboat." Part of the inscription reads : "He (Fitch) ran a boat with side wheels by steam on a pond below Davisville, in 1785." The marker is placed in front of a gasoline station.

A monument at 24.6 m. (R), consisting of three bronze tablets mounted on a granite stone, marks the SITE OF LOG COLLEGE (20). In October 1727 Rev. William Tennent, a Presbyterian clergyman, built the log cabin which became known as Log College. The college was discontinued 20 years later, when members of the Presbyterian synod united in the organization of the "College of New Jersey at Elizabeth Town." The latter is the present day Princeton University.

The middle panel of the monument bears a bas-relief of Log College and an inscription. The panels on either side list the names of the 63 colleges of which Log College is said to be the progenitor. Among them, in addition to Princeton, are Washington and Jefferson, Illinois, and Lafayette.

At 25.5 m. (L) is the PRESBYTERIAN CHURCH OF NESHAMINY (21), erected in 1842 for a congregation founded in 1710. The building, set back in a spacious lawn, is of red sandstone stucco covered. Four Tuscan columns which rise from a sandstone base support a wooden pediment. A double doorway opens from a wide portico. On either side are four long windows each containing three sashes.

Splendid vistas on either side are afforded at several points between HARTSVILLE, 25.6 m. (250 alt. ; 300 pop.), and the ROBBINS HOUSE (22) (known also as the Moland house and the Bothwell house, for its various owners). This two-story-and-attic stuccoed stone dwelling, (R) at 26.2 m., which was used as a headquarters by Washington from August 10 to August 23, 1777, was built in 1763. On the side of the house facing the road is a marker commemorating Washington's occupancy and relating that "here the Marquis De Lafayette first joined the Army." The grounds around the house are graced by a number of huge silver and Norway maples.

As the route passes through a slight cut at 26.6 m. several veins of sandstone (R) are noticeable. This outcropping is an indication of the reason for the prevalence of sandstone structures in this region. The sandstone in most places is but a few feet beneath the surface.

At JAMISON, 27.6 m. (1,071 alt. ; 93 pop.), a settlement on a high ridge, is a junction with State 152. Left on this, State 152. The highway cuts through fertile farm land to US 611. Right on US 611, which follows a winding course.

DOYLESTOWN, 32.8 m. (355 alt. ; 4,577 pop.), is the seat of Bucks County, one of the three original counties into which Penn divided his Province. The town, originally settled simultaneously by various national groups, is the center of a rich dairying and farming area. The name is derived from the Doyle tavern, which was a stopping place for the Philadelphia-Easton stagecoach.

Numerous old but well-preserved frame houses, guarded by paling fences and surrounded by aged trees, lend an air of old-fashioned charm to the town's side streets.

Visible through the trees, (R) before reaching the business center, is the MUSEUM OF THE BUCKS COUNTY HISTORICAL SOCIETY (23) *(open weekdays 8 to 5, and from April 1 to Nov. 1 on Sun. 1 to 5 ; adm. free)*. The entrance to the building is on Pine Street. The museum is a large reinforced concrete structure connected by a passage to the Colonial red brick building of the society. The lofty museum was constructed in 1914-16 under the personal supervision of the late Dr. Henry Mercer, a manufacturer of pottery and tile, and curator of American and prehistoric archeology at the University of Pennsylvania. Its many gables, chimneys, turrets, and dormers give it a restless effect.

The building contains a collection of approximately 25,000 ancient tools and utensils used in the United States until about 1820 ; some imported by colonists, others copied here from European types. In addition, there is a library of 8,000 volumes and a few relics of Indian handiwork. The interior court of the museum is surrounded by three galleries, with 33 fireproof rooms and 36 alcoves.

Among the exhibits are : a wooden food chopper, a wooden sausage stuffer, a spice grinder, old china and willowware, an early printing press, a large cider press, a fire pumper, Conestoga wagons, a Dearborn wagon, a log sled, a whaleboat and equipment, a cod fisherman's boat and equipment, dugout canoes, several types of mills, and tobacconist and tavern signs.

A glass showcase on the first balcony contains an inkwell and sandbox that belonged to Edgar Allan Poe ; a sword that belonged to Gen. Daniel Morgan ; the claymore or Scottish broadsword worn by Edwin Forrest in *Macbeth* ; a wampum belt presented to Henry Clay by an Indian chief ; and the rifle and account book of Edward Marshall, a participant in the famous "Walking Purchase."

On the Historical Society grounds near the museum is a log cabin, which, according to a concrete marker, is : "Log house of Colonial pattern built by John Byerly or Thos. Roberts between 1799-1812." Huge, square logs, notched at the corners and recently patched with concrete, make up the construction of this one-story-and-attic cabin.

FOUNTAIN HOUSE (24) NW. corner of Main and State Streets, licensed in 1717, was a stopping place on the old stage lines. The present structure, the oldest section of which is said to have been erected in 1748, is a two-story-and-attic building with a broad gambrel roof. It is of white-plastered stone with porches running along the front of the first and second stories. The remains of a cobbled court-yard fronts the hotel. The inn derived its name from a fountain which once flowed in this courtyard.

> On East Court Street, is FRONTHILL (25) *(private)*, the chateau-like former residence of Dr. Mercer. The building is an unusual structure of concrete and stone with a red tile roof. The interior rooms, decorated with a variety of colorful tiles, are on many different levels.
>
> On the right of the building a road leads to the U-shaped pottery works. The design of the pottery works shows most forcibly the effects of Dr. Mercer's archeological vists to Yucatan. A gray, rough concrete building, it is Spanish in style. The restrained use of decorative tiles brightens the drab concrete.

At *32.8 m.* is East State Street. (US 202) right on US 202, which rolls over hills and through farming and woodland stretches, bridging several streams and passing a number of red barns. At *35.7* (R) is a splendid view with distant haze-shrouded hills forming a background for farming and grazing lands.

BUCKINGHAM, *36.8 m.* (217 alt. ; 200 pop.), consists largely of rustic, well-kept dwellings. The surrounding country, its fertile soil well-watered by four creeks, is excellent farming land. There are also several fine limestone quarries in the vicinity. At the crossroads on the northeast corner is the GENERAL GREENE INN (26), a hostelry that has retained its Colonial dignity. Inside is the General's "den," containing antique furniture, muskets, and other mementos.

Left at dead end, *37 m.* on US 202. The route traverses pine-dotted farm land with an excellent view (R) at *37.9 m.*

HOLICONG, *38.2 m.* (240 alt., 250 pop.), is a farming community of the staid appearance appropriate to its centuries of existence.

On the summit of a hill (L), at *39 m.* is the BUCKINGHAM MEETINGHOUSE (27), a two-story-and-attic structure of native stone set in sloping ground. The pedimented hoods protecting the simple doorways, the white shutters of all the windows, and the simple coved cornice which surrounds the building are the principal exterior features. Within, the paneled woodwork remains unpainted in contrast to the white-plastered walls.

The meeting was founded in 1720, and the present building was erected in 1763.

From the highway at this point, is a widespread view (R), into a shallow valley of fields dotted with small groves and larger woods.

LAHASKA, *39.2 m.* (300 alt. ; 218 pop.), is the site of two old inns. Either side of the road here is flanked by white-painted, green-shuttered houses. BUTTONWOOD INN (28) (R), built in 1760, faces CATALPA INN (29) (L), said to have been built before the Revolution.

To Artistic New Hope (Environs Tour 3)

At *40.3 m.* is (L) the SOLEBURY BAPTIST CHURCH (30). Set back from the road with a graveyard adjoining, this one-story building of stucco over local stone was rebuilt in 1851. There are three windows on each of the two sides and a small belfry near the front of the sloping roof. Large coal oil lamps are suspended from the ceiling of the stuccoed interior.

Several excellent views are afforded on both sides from the church to AQUETONG, *41.1 m.* (240 alt. ; 75 pop.), a crossroads hamlet consisting of a sprinkling of tottering old houses.

Ingham Spring Creek has its source, Ingham's Spring, near here in a ledge of red shale and limestone. The spring is the largest between Maine and Florida, having a flow of hundreds of thousands of gallons daily. Indian legend has it that the spring was caused by the tears of a young Indian who pursued a deer into the crevice and became wedged there.

At *41.6 m.* is a small lake (R) formed by the damming of Ingham Spring Creek for the benefit of a number of mills. The builder of one of these mills was Samuel D. Ingham, for whom the spring and creek are named. The important process of making paper from old rope and bagging was developed in Ingham's mill, which was in use until it was burned in 1867.

From Aquetong the road skirts woodland stretches, passing an occasional weather-beaten mill or inn. Low hills open on vistas of geometrically patterned farm land.

NEW HOPE (86 alt. ; 1,113 pop.), is entered at *43.1 m.* Small homes line the highway as it swerves right, drops down a slight hill, crosses railroad tracks, and bridges the New Hope canal.

One of the few permanent artist's colonies in the east, New Hope lies along the Delaware River. The old canal of the Lehigh Coal Navigation Company runs through the town. Rustic and modern dwellings, an occasional inn, or abandoned mill, where once the water wheel sang a song of power, provide a natural setting for the colony.

Once known as Coryell's Ferry, the community acquired the name of Hope Mills after the erection of several mills here. When a fire destroyed these mills, other buildings were erected in their places, and the name New Hope Mills, later shortened to New Hope, was adopted.

The art colony was established during the summer of 1900 by William Lathrop. His home is near the canal's edge. The landscapes which attracted Lathrop soon drew not only painters, but also representatives of virtually every other field of art to this town. During spring, summer, and fall art exhibits are conducted on random dates in the village and environs.

In addition to Lathrop, such distinguished wielders of the brush as Redfield, Garber, and Follansbee are leading members of the

667

colony. What is now known as the "Delaware Valley School" of American art has been developing rapidly in recent years. A favorite setting for many of the paintings are the picturesque locks where unhurried bargemen once eked out a livelihood on the canal.

Pearl S. Buck, author of *The Good Earth* and other novels of Chinese life and customs, has taken up her residence in the vicinity.

Other authors and playwrights who have joined the "back to the farm" movement to this neighborhood are Sam and Bella Spewack, whose farce *Boy Meets Girl* was a Broadway success. They own a 100-acre farm. Edwin Justis Mayer, author of *The Firebrand*, has a farm at Tinicum, a short distance from that of Dorothy Parker. George S. Kaufman, Lester Cohen, and George Anthiel have also joined the movement.

New Hope was the principal town in the line of march taken by Washington in his advance on Trenton. On Malta Island, in the Delaware River, just below New Hope, Washington assembled the Durham boats he used on that memorable Christmas night.

Canal at New Hope
Fit subject for Van Gogh

To Artistic New Hope (Environs Tour 3)

At *44.1 m.* is a junction with State 32. Right on State 32 which lies between the river and the canal. At *44.6 m.* the route crosses a bridge (R) and then turns (L) to parallel the canal on the shore side. Wooded slopes (R) flank the road and at intervals tiny wooden footbridges cross the canal. Rapids in the river are visible along here.

The UNION PAPER MILL (31) (L.), across the canal at *45.1 m.,* is an eighteenth century mill that is still in operation. Dwellings of red brick, frame, or local stone construction, many of them painted white or yellow or whitewashed, are scattered along the highway. In appearance these range from dilapidated to pin-neat.

At *46.4 m.* a tower may be seen ahead to the right rising from tree-cloaked Bowman's Hill.

The Solebury Copper Mine is near here. The activities in this mine cannot be dated with any certainty. An Indian tradition that white men mined copper in a drift near the river was passed on to the early settlers. Not until 1854 was the entrance to the mine discovered. Competent investigation indicated that the tools and drills which had left their marks on the mineral within the shaft had been used at least 200 years before that time. It was suggested that the Mound Builders may have been the mysterious miners, but the Indian tradition was specific in identifying the workers as white men. It is now considered possible that they may have been Swedes, who came to Pennsylvania in 1637, or West India Company employees who were known to have traded with the Indians at the Falls of the Delaware near here.

At *46.7 m.* is (L) the THOMPSON-NEELY HOUSE (32) in the Bowman's Hill section of Washington Crossing State Park. The broad two-story-and-attic farmhouse of rough local stone and wood is set in carefully tended grounds. The house, an excellent example of early Pennsylvania architecture and masonry, was built in three sections. The central section was built in 1702 by John Pidcock, a trader and miller. The west end, nearest the road, was built by Robert Thompson and bears a quaint date stone carrying the initials "H R T" and the date "1757." The east end was probably erected in 1786. The doors and shutters are white, and each unit has a different type of doorway. There are four massive stone chimneys.

The building served as headquarters for General Lord Stirling (William Alexander) and his staff prior to the Battle of Trenton. James Monroe, later President, was a lieutenant attached to Stirling's command.

On the opposite side of the road along Pidcock Creek stands the stuccoed stone and frame Neely gristmill with its huge water wheel ponderously turning around and around. The highway crosses Pidcock Creek on a stone bridge.

At *47.2 m.* is a junction with an asphalt road.

Right, on this road, *1 m.*, is BOWMAN'S HILL OBSERVATION
TOWER (33). The hill was named for Dr. Thomas Bowman, who
lived in a cabin at its base. The tower is a tall, square, stone structure
rising to the height of 110 feet above the top of the hill. It has a
spiral staircase of 100 steps leading to a platform from which an
excellent view of the surrounding country is afforded. An octagonal
turret tops the tower.

The tower, which stands on the site where Colonial troops built a
crude lookout platform prior to the Battle of Trenton, was erected
in 1930 to commemorate the battle.

Beyond this road rolling land spreads away (R) to distant green
hills. At *49 m.* the highway crosses a small whitewashed stone bridge,
and at *49.4 m.* another bridge is crossed and the route is close to and
parallel with the Delaware. Level farming land lies to the right.

WASHINGTON CROSSING, *51.6 m.* (60 alt. ; 175 pop.), is situated
within the confines of the main section of WASHINGTON CROSSING
STATE PARK (34). The village green or common (L) is flanked on
three sides by clean, white-stuccoed houses of late American Georgian
architecture. Overhanging shade trees enhance their quiet charm.

The park, established by the Commonwealth in 1917, is dedicated
to the memory of Washington and the 2,400 soldiers who crossed the
Delaware from this point on Christmas night, 1776, to surprise the
merrymaking Hessian mercenaries and capture Trenton.

In the park a stone gateway gives entrance to Concentration Valley,
where the ragged troops assembled while Washington made preparations for his coup, and a monument marks the point of embarkation,
where the soldiers entered the roomy Durham boats during a blind-
ing snow and sleet storm.

At *51.8 m.* is the junction with State 632. At the intersection (R)
stands WASHINGTON CROSSING INN (35), a large, white-plastered structure with white and green-shutters. It consists of several
units, in the late American Georgian style. What is now the southwestern end of the inn was erected in 1812.

Right, on State 632. Continental troops gathering for the Battle of
Trenton tramped over this road, which was known for many years
as Continental Lane. It is now called Washington Memorial Boulevard.

Dense woods close to the road break the monotony of the flat farm
lands. At several places are wide vistas on either side. Especially noteworthy is the view (R) at *56.1 m.* Here level land near the road
merges with rolling terrain, dotted with red-roofed barns and broken
by small groves. A smoky blue haze partly shrouds the hills in the
distance.

To ARTISTIC NEW HOPE (ENVIRONS TOUR 3)

At *58 m.* (R) is the OLD NEWTOWN PRESBYTERIAN CHURCH (36), a one-story native brownstone structure erected in 1769. Services of this congregation, which was founded prior to 1735, are now held in a modern church in the center of Newtown.

A wide lawn surrounds the old edifice, and a graveyard is in the rear. A white wooden porch fronts the building, and on either side are three long windows flanked by green shutters. A balcony runs around three sides of the interior, and old-fashioned kerosene lamps are suspended from the flat, white-plastered ceiling. During the Revolutionary War Hessian soldiers were quartered here for a time.

At *58.2 m.* the outskirts of NEWTOWN (175 alt. ; 1,824 pop.) are reached. This town, founded by Penn in 1684, was the county seat of Bucks County from 1724 to 1804. There are a number of houses dating from Revolutionary times in and about the community. The route skirts the western edge of the town.

At *58.3 m.* is a junction with State 332. Right on this. The route is now State 332 (Newtown Pike). Along here the highway traverses farming country. At *59.6 m.* the route turns R. into an old but well-preserved covered wooden bridge over the Neshaminy Creek. Left at *62.3 m.* a striking panorama greets the eye.

At *62.6 m.* is a junction with State 232. Around this intersection are the neat homes of the town of RICHBORO (280 alt. ; 310 pop.). Left on State 232.

SOUTHAMPTON, *66.1 m.* (260 alt. ; 800 pop.), with homes set in tree-shaded lawns, presents an especially prosperous appearance. The SOUTHAMPTON BAPTIST MEETINGHOUSE (37) (R) in Southampton, was founded in 1751, rebuilt in 1772 and enlarged in 1840. It is a broad yellow-plastered structure with wood trim painted white. An avenue of shade trees leads to the carriage sheds (R). The cemetery (L) contains gravestones dating from the early nineteenth century. A balcony supported by slim Doric columns runs around three sides of the interior, which is heated by four free-standing stoves. The built-in pews are painted white, and the walls buff.

At *68.8 m.* the route passes the outskirts of BRYN ATHYN (280 alt. ; 736 pop.), site of the Bryn Athyn Cathedral and center of Swendenborgianism in the United States. *(See Environs Tour 2.)*

At *71.8 m.* (R) is the RYDAL COUNTRY CLUB ·(38), a private club with a nine-hole golf course. The Montgomery-Philadelphia County line is crossed at *73.4 m.* At *76.6 m.* is a junction with Roosevelt Boulevard (US 1).

Right on Roosevelt Blvd. to Broad St., L. on Broad St. to City Hall, 84.8 m.

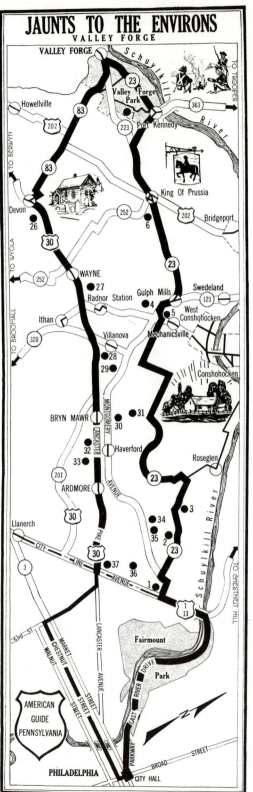

JAUNTS TO THE ENVIRONS
VALLEY FORGE

1. Wisconsin House
2. Chinese Burial Ground
3. G. Brook Roberts Estate
4. Pet Animal Cemetery
5. Overhanging Rock
6. King of Prussia Inn
7. Valley Forge
(Number 8 to 25 refer to description in tour. Locations of these points of interest are shown in map obtainable free at Valley Forge.)
8. Washington Memorial Chapel
9. Washington Memorial National Carillon
10. Valley Forge Museum of American History
11. Grand Parade
12. General Varnum's Headquarters
13. Old Camp Schoolhouse
14. National Memorial Arch
15. Pennsylvania Columns
16. Statue of Gen. Anthony Wayne
17. Site of Scott's Brigade
18. Statue of Baron Von Steuben
19. Fort Washington Redoubt
20. Mount Joy Observatory
21. Site of Maxwell's Brigade
22. Dogwood Grove
23. Washington Inn
24. Washington's Headquarters
25. Headquarters of General Knox
26. St. David's Protestant Episcopal Church
27. Radnor Open Golf Course
28. Villanova College
29. Rosemont College for Women
30. Baldwin School
31. Bryn Mawr College
32. Old Buck Inn
33. Haverford College
34. Old Merion Meetinghouse
35. General Wayne Inn
36. Barnes Foundation
37. Seminary of St. Charles Borromeo

VALLEY FORGE

Environs Tour 4

Philadelphia—Gulph Mills—King of Prussia—Valley Forge—Devon—
Wayne—Bryn Mawr—Haverford—Ardmore—Philadelphia. State 23
and 83, US 30—*51 m.* The route winds back and forth across the
tracks of the Pennsylvania R. R. and Reading R. R. on the outward
trip, and parallels the Pennsylvania R. R. on the return. Round trip
61 m.

Concrete or macadamized roadbed over entire route passable in all
weathers.

FROM City Line Avenue (a boundary of Philadelphia) State 23
winds in a northwesterly direction through some of Philadelphia's wealthiest suburban sections, a picturesque countryside of
extensive, cultivated estates, and wide stretches of meadow and forest.
There are steep-walled valleys, brooks, and thickly wooded settings
which belie the nearness of a metropolitan center.

This region was well settled long before the Revolution, and an
occasional square, stone house, dating back to Colonial times, stands
in sight of the road. Farming is confined chiefly to gardening and
horticulture for pastime rather than livelihood. The route is rich in
historic interest, especially as it nears Valley Forge.

After passing through Valley Forge Park, the route returns over
State 83 to Devon ; thence over US 30, the southernmost of three
national highways crossing Pennsylvania and passes through the
heart of the Main Line, a chain of prosperous suburbs west of Philadelphia.

From City Hall, Philadelphia, follow the Parkway NW. ; R.
around Logan Circle and skirting the Art Museum, into Fairmount
Park ; L. around the Lincoln Monument into East River Drive ;
at *5.7 m.* L. on US 1, which crosses City Line Avenue Bridge.

At *6 m.* (R) WEST LAUREL HILL CEMETERY may be seen. Large
private estates line the right-hand side of City Line Avenue, shut
off from the road by stone fences, over which bloom dogwood, wist-
aria, and flowering shrubs. At *6.7 m.* (L) paralleling the road for
an eighth of a mile, is the walled ATHLETIC FIELD OF THE FRIENDS
SELECT SCHOOL.

At *7.2 m.* is a junction with State 23 ; R. on this. Now the route is
State 23 (Conshohocken State Road).

Standing serenely a short distance beyond the intersection (L) is
the old WISCONSIN HOUSE (1), a square, clapboard structure with
a weathered sign lettered "Wisconsin" on the front of the upper story.
This was the Wisconsin State Building at Philadelphia's Centennial
Exhibition. Purchased by the Simes estate, it was moved here from

673

Fairmount Park, where it had stood between the English and Ohio buildings.

The first contractors engaged to move the building were unable to complete the job and, as a result, it rested for more than a year in the middle of Conshohocken Road near Belmont Avenue. The transfer was completed only when Philadelphia authorities threatened to burn the structure. Phipps and Bair opened the building on its present site as a hotel, calling it the Wisconsin House ; then sold it to Dan Titlow, a local resident, from whom it was purchased by W. H. Doble, father-in-law of the present owner. It was operated as a hotel until 1915.

The cupola, shown in old engravings, is gone, and one of the three porches was removed to permit widening of State 23. Part of Union Avenue, formerly Ford Road, fronting the Wisconsin House, was given to the owners of the hotel at the time of the construction of State 23.

Left of the Wisconsin House is a white-plastered house dating from Revolutionary times. At *7.6 m.* (L) is the SITE OF AN OLD TOLL HOUSE.

At *7.7 m.* is the Bala-Cynwyd station of the Pennsylvania R. R. BALA-CYNWYD (250 alt. ; 3,000 pop.) is a suburban community composed chiefly of large estates.

The highway crosses the railroad tracks and turns R.

At *8.7 m.* (L) is the CHINESE BURIAL GROUND (2), founded in 1888, where most of the Philadelphia Chinese bury their dead with all the ancient ceremonies of the race. Each headstone is engraved in Chinese letters, which give the year, name, and home district of the deceased. The custom of leaving spirituous liquors on the grave to accompany the body on its journey to the Temple of Confucius is observed. The brick ovens in the cemetery are used for burning paper money, paper clothes, and incense in accordance with their funeral traditions. When the family accumulates enough money the body is exhumed and sent to China.

At *10.2 m.* (R) is the G. BROOK ROBERTS ESTATE (3), fenced in by a wistaria-covered stone wall. The main entrance is guarded by a three-inch oak gate bound with wrought-iron strap hinges four feet long, and fitted with a massive latch of the same metal. Just inside the entrance is a sunken circular pool, and directly ahead a mansion of polished brick rises from several levels of terraced stone and brick work. These terraces are adorned with fountains and statuary-filled niches ; curving stone stairways mount the eminence on either side. On the left of the gateway is an ascending rock garden, bright with varicolored flowers ; on the right, huge banks of rhododendron. This was the home of the late G. Brook Roberts, former president of the Pennsylvania Railroad.

Sign at King of Prussia Inn
Purported to be the work of a master

Gulph Mills
Tranquillity and trees

PENN VALLEY is reached at 11.2 m. There is a sheer drop (R), to sparkling Mill Creek. The road descends to the valley floor and crosses Mill Creek, passing two small cascades a little farther on. Again the road winds past vast estates skirted by luxuriant flowers, shrubs, and trees.

At *16 m.* is a junction with Eagle Road.

> Left on Eagle Road. *6 m.* is a PET ANIMAL CEMETERY (4). The cemetery is attached to the Francisvale Home for Smaller Animals, founded by Mrs. George Hare McClellan as a memorial to her pet dog "Francis." In the cemetery are graves of more than 3,500 animals, including dogs, cats, monkeys, canaries, parrots, two horses, and a lion. Many of these were interred in elaborate concrete or steel coffins. Granite monuments, some with pictures of the dead pets under glass, have been erected over many of the graves.

At *16.6 m.* (R) is a large OVERHANGING ROCK (5), under which Washington marched with his army during the retreat from Germantown to Valley Forge. There is a legend that Washington used the rock as a stand to review his troops.

GULPH MILLS, *17 m.* (160 alt. ; 100 pop.) consists of a post office, a store, a gasoline filling station, and a few homes. State 23 swings left at the fork. At *17.4 m.* (R) is the Gulph Mills Golf Course.

At KING OF PRUSSIA, *20.4 m.* (187 aut. ; 129 pop.) stands a great oak tree (R), which dates from the period when only Indians inhabited the land. A short distance beyond (L) is the KING OF PRUSSIA INN (6), erected in 1709. The builder, a native of Prussia, named it for the Brandenburg ruler who, a few years earlier, after transforming Prussia from a dukedom into a kingdom, had become King Frederick I.

A weather-beaten sign showing the king on horseback, supposed to be the work of Gilbert Stuart, still hangs outside. The old kitchen is roofed with great oak beams and contains a fireplace large enough to permit the roasting of an ox. On the second floor, reached by a steep, narrow flight of stairs, worn with use, is the room in which Lafayette joined the Masonic order (in what is now the Norristown Lodge), and where the Mount Joy Society for Recovery of Stolen Horses and Detection of Thieves convened semi-annually.

The original stables and springhouse remain, as do some of the original furnishings, mantels, doors and the old stair rail of the inn. At the door which led from the kitchen to the back yard but now opens on a spacious enclosed porch (the only addition to the inn) is a stone sill hollowed to a depth of several inches by the footsteps of two centuries.

Many famous men, including Washington, patronized the inn, but nothing is said about Washington having slept there, although there are few houses of Colonial or Revolutionary origin in these environs that do not claim that distinction.

676

Valley Forge (Environs Tour 4)

At *22.9 m.* at an intersection, the route turns right on State 23.

Beyond, Mount Joy, surmounted by the observation tower (L.), which is within Valley Forge Park, looms in the distance. State 23 bears left and enters the park at Port Kennedy.

VALLEY FORGE (7), a State park of 1,500 acres, is flanked by natural military advantages — the river and high ground. Washington's army, during its encampment on this site, consisted of 11,000 soldiers, one third of whom were rendered unfit for duty by illness or lack of necessities. The ragged army arrived at Valley Forge on Dec. 19, 1777. Of its desperate plight during that winter, Cyrus T. Brady has written:

"No spot on earth, not the plains of Marathon, nor the passes of Sempach, nor the Place of the Bastille, nor the dykes of Holland, nor the moors of England, is so sacred in the history of the struggle for human liberty as Valley Forge."

(Note: *A detailed map of the park may be obtained free from the uniformed attendants in the park.*)

Within the park State 23 swings left.

Valley Forge Chapel Interior
"Author of liberty, to Thee we sing"

The WASHINGTON MEMORIAL CHAPEL (8) (R), the WASH-
INGTON MEMORIAL NATIONAL CARILLON (9), and the adjoining VALLEY FORGE MUSEUM OF AMERICAN HISTORY (10)
(open 10 to 5 except Sun.; adm. adults 15¢; children 10¢) are within the park limits, but are privately owned.

The chapel's architecture is simplified English Gothic, in granite
with limestone trim. On the facade is a large stained glass window;
many of the structure's details and furnishings are symbolic. The
Porch of the Allies, Patriot's Hall, the five bays named for Lafayette,
Rochambeau, DeKalb, Von Steuben, and Pulaski; the pews, pulpit,
lectern, prayer and litany tables, and the doors, screens and choir
stalls commemorate Revolutionary leaders or events.

The ceiling, composed of 48 panels, each bearing the arms of
a State, pictures early patriotic achievements. The windows, in alle-
gory, tell of the Nation's founding.

The museum contains many interesting relics, including a tent
supposed to have been used by Washington.

Washington's tent or marquee passed to his stepgrandson, George
Washington Parke Custis, and for many years was kept at Mount
Vernon. Custis bequeathed it to his daughter, who married Gen.
Robert E. Lee. During the Civil War, after the Lee home was seized
by the Federal Government, the marquee was taken to Washington
and exhibited in the Library of Congress. Mrs. Lee's protest to President Andrew Johnson was disregarded, and the marquee was placed
in the National Museum. Under McKinley's administration it was
returned to Mary Custis Lee, the general's daughter. It was later purchased by Rev. Dr. W. Herbert Burk, founder of the Washington
Memorial Chapel, and placed in the museum by him.

Behind the chapel is the carillon erected on July 4, 1926, by the
Thirteen Original States in memory of their troops. Directly opposite the chapel stretches a broad unwooded area, the GRAND
PARADE (11), on which field Baron von Steuben, the Army drill
master, trained the undisciplined Revolutionary troops. On May
6, 1778 news of the alliance with France was read to the army
assembled at this place. On the slight slope leading to the parade
ground from State 23 is the Lt. John Waterman Monument, which
marks the only identified resting place of all the 3,000 who died in
the encampment during that terrible winter. Farther along (L) stands
the stone residence that was GENERAL VARNUM'S HEAD-
QUARTERS (12) *(open daily 9 to 5; adm. free)*.

Beyond the parade grounds is the plant of the Ehret Magnesia Co.
It is one of several plots within the park boundaries which (1937)
has not been acquired by the park commission.

Left on Baptist Road. At the intersection with State 223 (Gulph
Road) stands the OLD CAMP SCHOOLHOUSE (13) (R) *(open daily*

9 to 5; adm. free), erected in 1705 by William Penn's second daughter, Letitia. It was used as a hospital during the encampment. It was restored by the park commission in 1907.

> Left on State 223 and L. at the county line marker on a road to the Ehret magnesia plant and quarries. On either side of the road beyond the plant the quarries are filled with water turned turquoise blue by chemical action of the magnesia. Except for occasional scrap heaps and broken frequently by growing trees rooted in their beds and brightened by their contrasting backdrops of white rock, these blue lakes provide a pleasing picture. Retrace to State 223.

Left on 223, up the hill (R) is the NATIONAL MEMORIAL ARCH (14). It marks the site where Washington's Army broke ranks, forming upon the left the Pennsylvania line, marked by the PENNSYLVANIA COLUMNS (15), and on the right a line of troops from other Colonies.

Right, circling the arch, on Outer Line Drive between the Pennsylvania Columns.

Immediately beyond the columns is a reproduction of one of the soldiers' huts. Its "hard pan" floor, uncovered during excavations, is the same that was trodden by soldiers who occupied a similar hut on the site. Down the hill a short distance is a reproduction of a field hospital containing an operating table of rough logs. As a result of primitive conditions and almost primitive methods, four fifths of the patients died. In the nearby woods are two reconstructed bake ovens.

A short distance beyond is the equestrian STATUE of *Gen. Anthony Wayne* (16), facing in the direction of Waynesborough, the town where Wayne was born. He was chosen to lead Washington to the Valley Forge winter quarters, because of his knowledge of the country.

The road passes the SITE OF SCOTT'S BRIGADE (17) (R) and the STATUE of *Baron Von Steuben* (18) (R), erected in 1915 by the National German-American Alliance, and winds past the FORT WASHINGTON REDOUBT (19) L), one of the inner lines of earthworks stretching from the foot toward the crest of Mount Joy, to which the road ascends.

MOUNT JOY OBSERVATORY (20), on the summit, affords a splendid view of pastoral Chester County.

Leaving Mount Joy the road makes a sharp turn L. The curving descent skirts the camp SITE OF MAXWELL'S BRIGADE (21) (L) and affords a glimpse of the Schuylkill glinting through the trees.

Left on Gulph Road.

The DOGWOOD GROVE (22) on either side in spring is a thick mass of pink and white blossoms. The way descends to Valley Road.

At the intersection (R) is the WASHINGTON INN (23), in the

cellar of which the army's bread was baked. One hundred yards to the right on Valley Road, opposite willow-fringed Valley Creek, is WASHINGTON'S HEADQUARTERS (24) *(open 8 to 5 ; adm. free)*, a small two-story farm structure of rough stone with tints of pink, yellow, and gray, built in 1758.

In 1777 this structure was owned by Isaac Potts, a young Quaker preacher, and occupied by a tenant, Deborah Hewes. Though he could have commandeered it, Washington paid £100 for its use for six months. Staff conferences with Lafayette, Knox, Morgan, Wayne, Nathaniel Greene, Alexander Hamilton, Von Steuben, DeKalb, and Muhlenberg were held in it during the encampment. The furnishings duplicate those used by Washington. Adjoining Washington Head-quarters stands the original building which first stabled Washington's

Washington Memorial National Carillon
"The rhyming and the chiming of the bells"

horses and was later used as a hospital. It now houses a museum containing some interesting Valley Forge relics. *(Open daily 10 to 5; adm. free).*

Retrace to Valley Road ; turn right.

In Valley Creek, which winds along Valley Road, were two small dams that in Washington's day formed a partial moat for the camp. Farther south on the creek is the site of the Lower Forge. The original Upper Forge, destroyed by the British in 1777, has been uncovered and is to be restored. The road swings L. past the HEADQUARTERS OF GENERAL KNOX (25) (L), which is outside the confines of the park, and passes through a wooded countryside.

From Valley Forge R. on State 63 ; L. on US 30.

From this point the route follows the Main Line through a continuous chain of prosperous suburbs.

DEVON *31.8 m.* (536 alt. ; 125 pop.), on a gently rising crest, is famous for its annual horse show.

At *40 m.* is a junction with Dorset Road.

Right, on Dorset Road, is ST. DAVID'S PROTESTANT EPISCOPAL CHURCH (26) *1.8 m.,* erected in 1715 by Welsh settlers. It is a small, ivy-clad, native gray stone structure, with white painted wood trim, low arched door, and shuttered windows. St. David's first congregation, dating before 1700, worshipped in a log building on the site of the present church. There was no rector until the fall of 1714 when, on petition of the congregation, Rev. Mr. Clubb was sent by the London Society for the Propagation of the Gospel in Foreign Parts. Clubb has recorded that at a meeting held on Sept. 7, 1714, his people "agreed to build a handsome stone church." The cornerstone was laid on May 9, 1715, and by the first Sunday in September the building was complete except for the stone staircase leading to the gallery from the outside. This was built in 1771. The church has been well preserved, but never enlarged or materially altered.

The building was used as a hospital during the Revolutionary War. Hard pressed for ammunition, Washington's army, while facing Howe's well-equipped troops, used the lead sashes of the church windows to melt into bullets.

In the vestry room are a number of interesting relics, including books sent out in 1714 by the London Society, an ancient pewter communion service and the old base viol used in the choir before the days of organs.

In the churchyard is the Tomb of Gen. Anthony Wayne, who was a vestryman. A monument to his memory was erected here by the Society of the Cincinnati in 1809. It bears on its north face the inscription: "Major General Anthony Wayne was born at Waynesborough, in Chester County, State of Pennsylvania, A. D. 1745. After a life of honor and usefulness he died in December, 1796, at a military post on the shores of Lake Erie. commander-in-chief of the United States Army. His military achievements are consecrated in the history of his country and in the hearts of his countrymen. His remains are here deposited."

Cabin at Valley Forge
"The numerous camp-fires scattered near and far"

On the south face are these words: "In honor of the distinguished military services of Major General Anthony Wayne and as an affectionate tribute to his memory, this stone was erected by his companions in arms. The Pennsylvania State Society of the Cincinnati, July 4, 1809, A. D., 34th anniversary of the Independence of the United States, an event which constitutes the most appropriate eulogium of an American soldier and patriot."

In the churchyard are the graves of "Mad" Anthony's ancestors. The oldest tombstone bears the date of 1715, but there are a number of unmarked graves said to be older. There is also the grave of the Dr. Carter who was surgeon on Lord Nelson's flagship at Trafalgar when Nelson was killed.

During the summer of 1876 while on a visit to the Centennial Exhibition in Philadelphia, Henry Wadsworth Longfellow went to St. David's Church. His charming poem *Old St. David's at Radnor* reveals the impression made upon him.

October of each year sees a revival of a century-old legend that clings to the church and its graveyard as tenaciously as the climbing ivy clings to the church walls. According to this legend, General Wayne rises from his grave, mounts his waiting steed, "Nancy," and rides up and down the highway, brandishing his sword as though he were still leading his military command in combat. So vividly has this legend played on the imagination of inhabitants that police have frequently been called to guard the cemetery. As recently as 1933, highway police spent several nights on duty here.

682

Valley Forge (Environs Tour 4)

WAYNE, *33.8 m.* (494 alt. ; 3,000 pop.) was named for General Wayne.

At *34.8 m.* is the RADNOR OPEN GOLF COURSE (27) on both sides of the road. This was formerly the St. David's Golf Club, the second oldest golf course in the vicinity of Philadelphia and the seventh oldest in the United States. When it opened in 1894 each of the 18 holes had a name, as was the custom in Scotland. In 1927, when St. Davids Golf Club moved to a new course at Aronomink, these links were converted into a public course.

VILLANOVA, *36 m.* 421 alt. ; 1,000 pop.) is the seate of VILLA-NOVA COLLEGE (28) (L), founded in 1842 by Augustinians of the Roman Catholic Church and named after St. Thomas of Villanova, bishop of Valencia. The college has about 2,000 students. A library of 25,000 books in the east wing of Austin Hall contains rare manuscripts of the fourteenth, fifteenth, and sixteenth centuries, on parchment and white vellum, illuminated in colors and gold ; and incunabula or "cradle books," including a Bible and a Latin grammar printed by Anthony Koburger, in 1482.

A century ago a taproom stood near the site of the college. At 11 o'clock each night, when a gong sounded behind the oaken bar, service ceased, and patrons were requested to leave immediately or join the host and hostess in prayer. The latter were ex-slaves, Billy and Mary Moulton, who had been freed by the widow of John Randolph. After the arrival of the Augustinians, the Moultons were converted to Catholicism.

ROSEMONT *36.8 m.* (360 alt. ; 2,600 pop.) is another suburban development.

> Left from Rosemont on County Line Road, R. on Airdale Road under the railroad tracks, and L. on Montgomery Avenue. ROSE-MONT COLLEGE for women (29) (L) was founded and incorporated in 1922 by the nuns of the Society of the Holy Child Jesus. The 40-acre campus, on which are erected the six gray stone buildings of English Gothic design which comprise the college group, contains many rare trees of interest to arboriculturists. Degrees in art, science, and letters are conferred by the college.

BRYN MAWR (Welsh, *great hill*) *37.9 m.* (420 alt. ; 20,200 pop.) is internationally known as the seat of Bryn Mawr College, one of America's great colleges for women.

> Left at traffic light on Bryn Mawr Ave., R. in a half circle under Pennsylvania R. R. tracks at Bryn Mawr station into Morris Ave.
>
> At the intersection of Morris and Montgomery Avenues, on the far right corner, set back on spacious grounds behind a high wrought-iron fence, stands the BALDWIN SCHOOL (30), a girls' preparatory school, founded in 1888. It has an enrollment of 300, and many of its graduates enter Bryn Mawr College. It was among the first

experimental schools chosen by the Progressive Education Commission on the Relation of School and College.

Left from Morris Ave., on Yarrow St., to its junction with Merion Ave. Opposite lies the 52-acre campus of BRYN MAWR COLLEGE (31), its dignified gray stone buildings of Tudor Gothic architecture mellowed by vine-covered walls, old shade trees, and banks and clumps of shrubbery. The college was founded in 1880 by Dr. Joseph W. Taylor, of Burlington, N. J. It was originally affiliated with the Society of Friends, but is now non-sectarian.

The library *(open weekdays 8 a. m. to 10 p. m. ; Sunday 9 a. m. to 10 p. m.)* contains 150,000 bound volumes and 10,000 pamphlets, and was built in 1907 by the gifts of friends, students, and alumni.

It includes the classical library of the late Professor Sauppe of Göttingen, the Semitic library of the late Professor Amiaud of Paris, the mathematical library of the late Prof. Charlotte Angus Scott, the Germanic library of the late Prof. Earl Detlev Jessen, and the geology library of former Prof. Florence Bascon. More than 600 publications and reviews in many languages are received.

Each spring Elizabethan plays are presented. The students' Maypole fete was revived at Bryn Mawr about 20 years ago and continues to attract considerable interest.

The late John D. Rockefeller, Sr., donated money for a power house, and a dormitory.

At Old Buck Lane *45.2 m.* R) is OLD BUCK INN 32). The inn is now used as an apartment house and is partly hidden by a tall hedge. Two of the three simple, gable-roofed units, of fieldstone plastered over, were erected in 1730. After the defeat at Brandywine in September 1777, Washington stopped here for a night, and his army bivouacked nearby.

HAVERFORD, *47.3 m.* (410 alt. ; 4,000 pop.), a Quaker residential community, is the seat of HAVERFORD COLLEGE (33) (R.), founded in 1833 by the Society of Friends. The college consists of several buildings of Colonial Georgian inspiration in gray stone with white trim. Founder's Hall is a three-story building of buff plaster over stone. The student body is restricted to 300. The original campus, 198 acres, cost $17,865. This and an additional 17 acres are now valued at $1,700,000. The income from a $4,000,000 trust fund enables the college to maintain a large faculty and to furnish board and lodging to students at less than cost.

ARDMORE, *48.1 m.* (376 alt. ; 18,000 pop.) is naturally beautiful locality, with close-cropped slopes studded with luxurious estates and a small business section through which the tour passes. It was formerly entirely residential, the well-kept countryside resembling Surrey in England. With the advent of the automobile, Ardmore grudgingly accepted a small amount of commercial enterprise.

684

Left on Ardmore Avenue. At *1 m.* R. on Montgomery Avenue. At *4 m.* on Montgomery Avenue (L) is the OLD MERION MEETING-HOUSE (34), built in 1682. It is a two-storied gabled structure of early Colonial type, with slate roof and brick chimneys and stands on a spacious lot among old shade trees. Its absence of detail befits the austere Quaker faith. It is one of two buildings still standing wherein William Penn preached, and Friends still assemble for service. In the house is the peg on which Penn hung his broad-brimmed hat. One of the founders of the meetinghouse was Dr. Thomas Wynne, Penn's intimate friend and physician, who came over with him on the *Welcome.* Descendants of Wynne still preside at meetings.

Adjoining the Old Merion Meetinghouse is the historic GENERAL WAYNE INN (35), erected in 1704. The hotel was a meeting place for Washington, Lafayette, Wayne, and other famous men. Edgar Allan Poe, when a resident of Philadelphia in the 1840's, was a frequent patron. It is a low structure of plastered stone, fronted by open galleries, with large chimneys at the ends of the low-pitched roof.

At *4.5 m.* bear R. on Old Lancaster Road at its intersection with Montgomery Avenue. Turn R. on City Line Avenue, R. on Lapsley Road to the ART MUSEUM OF THE BARNES FOUNDATION (36) *(Admission by invitation only).*

In 1922, Albert Barnes, of Merion, established an endowment of $10,000,000 for an art museum. A great legal battle was fought in Philadelphia courts over a municipal tax of $756 upon a small office property in that city owned by the foundation.

Meanwhile, the foundation had constructed the Merion museum—a one-story building in Italian Renaissance style, built of light imported stone with tile roof. It houses Egyptian, Greek, and Negro sculpture; Persian, Chinese, Florentine, and Dutch primitives; canvases by Giorgione, Tintoretto, El Greco, Claude Lorrain, Daumier, Delacroix. Courbet, Corot, Renoir, Cezanne, Manet, Degas, and others. The grounds include a 12-acre park and arboretum.

Angered by the municipal tax, Barnes built a wall about the Merion estate, threatened to remove the collection to New York, and limited the exhibition to students personally invited to view it. When the lower courts denied him exemption from the tax, Barnes threatened to convert the property into a national center for Negro education. On January 31, 1934, Barnes won his case, the Supreme Court granting tax exemption on the grounds that the gift was a public charity.

Left on Merion Avenue ; R. on City Line Ave.

At City Line Avenue and Lancaster Avenue (R) is the SEMINARY OF ST. CHARLES BORROMEO (37) *(See City Tour 8).*

Chronology

1609 Henry Hudson discovers Delaware Bay.
1634 Dutch West Indies Company secures claim to all land on both sides of Delaware River.
1642 Swedes establish school at Tinicum Island.
1644 William Penn born in London.
1646 First church in Pennsylvania built on Tinicum Island.
1651 Francis Daniel Pastorius born at Sommerhausen.
1662 Father punishes Penn for Quaker activities.
1664 Dutch and Swedes on the Delaware surrender to Sir Robert Carr.
1672 Penn marries Gulielma Maria Springett.
1677 Lutherans organize congregation at Tinicum.
1681 Charles II grants land in America to Penn's father.
     First shipload of settlers organized by Markham arrives at Upland.
1682 City located and planned by Thomas Holme, Surveyor General.
     Welcome (Penn's ship) sails from England.
     The *Welcome* enters the Delaware Bay.
     Penn signs treaty with Indians.
1683 Population—500 (estimated).
     Penn takes up residence in Philadelphia.
     First German colonists (Crefelders) arrive in Philadelphia.
1684 Population—2,500 (estimated).
1685 William Bradford publishes first book in middle colonies.
1688 First public protest against slavery issued by Society of Friends.
     Baptists organize Old Pennepek Church.
1690 William Rittenhouse builds first paper mill on Wissahickon Creek.
1694 Kelpius, the German mystic, comes to America.
1695 First structure of Christ Church erected.
     Seat of Philadelphia government erected at 2nd and Market Sts.
1699 John Bartram, botanist, born.
1701 City charter granted, with Edward Shippen as first Mayor.
1703 First musical recital in Philadelphia, by Hermits of Wissahickon.
1706 Benjamin Franklin born.
1713 Quakers establish an almshouse.
1718 William Penn dies in England.
1719 Andrew Bradford issues *American Weekly Mercury,* first newspaper published in Philadelphia.
     Francis Daniel Pastorius dies.
1724 Carpenters' Company of Philadelphia founded.
1727 Benjamin Franklin founds American Philosophical Society.
1729 Father Joseph Greaton, S. J., arrives in Philadelphia.
1730 Masons organize first lodge in America.
     Site for State House purchased.
1731 Library Company of Philadelphia founded.
1732 Construction of State House (Independence Hall) begins.
     First insurance company established.
1733 Franklin publishes *Poor Richard's Almanac.*
1736 Union Fire Company organized by Franklin.
1737 "Walking Purchase."
1739 Christopher Sauer issues *High Dutch Historiographer* at Germantown.
1740 University of Pennsylvania founded.
1741 The first magazine in America published by Andrew Bradford.
     Charles Willson Peale, painter, born.
1744 Population—9,750 (estimated).
     "Grumblethorpe" built by John Wister.
1747 Mikveh Israel, Hebrew Congregation, established.
1749 First theatrical performance in Philadelphia.
1750 Stephen Girard born.
1751 Liberty Bell cast by Thomas Lister in London.
     Building erected by Drinker family ; in which was born first white child in Philadelphia.
1752 First patient admitted into Pennsylvania Hospital.
     Liberty Bell arrives in Philadelphia.

1753	Liberty Bell rings for first time and cracks.
1754	First Stock Exchange of Philadelphia founded.
1755	Gilbert Stuart, distinguished painter, born.
1756	Epidemic of small pox strikes city.
1760	Population—18,756 (estimated).
1761	Germantown Academy established.
1762	Site of Fort Mifflin recognized as military safeguard by British.
	First night school in America opened at Germantown Academy.
1764	Germans found society for protection of redemptioners.
1765	Powel House erected.
	Parliament passes Stamp Act.
	Medical School of College of Philadelphia founded.
1767	Mason and Dixon, surveyors, determine the state line.
	James White makes bequest to aid Catholic education in Philadelphia.
	Public meeting held at State House anent tea tax.
1768	North house of Pennsylvania Hospital completed.
	Medical School of College of Philadelphia confers Bachelor of Physics on graduates.
1770	Erection of Carpenters' Hall begins.
1771	John Dunlap issues *Pennsylvania Packet* as tri-weekly.
1772	First movable type made in Germantown.
1773	An inoculation hospital is opened.
1774	Paul Revere arrives from Boston.
	First Continental Congress convenes in Carpenter's Hall.
	Twenty eight Philadelphians organize the First City Troop.
1775	Colony's first woven carpets loomed in Philadelphia.
	Debtor's Prison established at 5th and Walnut Streets.
	Second Continental Congress meets in Independence Hall.
	George Washington given command of Continental Army.
	Thomas Paine's *Common Sense* appears for the first time.
1776	John Hancock and Charles Thompson sign Declaration and John Nixon reads document to crowd in State House yard.
1777	Population—30,000 (estimated).
	First Fourth of July celebrated.
	Washington and troops enter Philadelphia.
	Battle of Chadds Ford.
	British occupy Philadelphia.
	Battle of Germantown.
	Washington and Continental Army encamp at Valley Forge.
	British officers and American Tories present *Meschianza* as a farewell to Sir William Howe.
1778	Howe evacuates Philadelphia ; *Pennsylvania Packet* returns from Lancaster.
	Congress returns to Philadelphia and convenes in Independence Hall.
	Articles of Confederation ratified.
1780	Population—40,000 (estimated).
1783	Thomas Sully, painter, born.
1784	*Pennsylvania Packet* becomes a daily.
1785	Episcopal Academy for Boys established.
1786	Dr. Benjamin Rush opens first medical dispensary.
	John Fitch, Philadelphian, builds steamboat.
1787	Regular mail and stage coach services established with Pittsburgh and Reading.
	Constitutional Convention meets in Independence Hall, and ratifies U. S. Constitution.
1790	Population—54,391 (estimated).
	Franklin dies in Philadelphia at age of eighty-four.
1791	Journeymen Carpenters go on strike.
	First Bank of United States established in Carpenter's Hall.
	First United States Mint established here.
1793	Yellow fever epidemic strikes city.
	Washington inaugurated President.
1794	Chestnut Street Theatre opens.
1796	David Rittenhouse dies.
1798	Robert Morris committed to Debtor's Prison.
	Philadelphia Navy Yard established.

1798 Joseph Hopkinson writes *Hail Columbia* in Philadelphia.
1800 National capital removed from Philadelphia to Washington.
First commercial mention of ice cream in the *Aurora*, a Philadelphia newspaper.
1802 Anthracite first burned in city.
1806 Robert Morris dies.
Edwin Forrest born.
1809 The first steamboat, *Phoenix*, arrives in Philadelphia.
1810 Penn Treaty Elm blown down.
1811 First medical textbooks in America, *A System of Anathomy*, published by Dr. Caspar Wistar.
1812 Stephen Girard aids in financing War of 1812.
1815 Seventy-four gun frigate *Franklin* launched at Navy Yard.
1816 Frankford Arsenal begun.
1820 Thompson Westcott, historian, born.
1821 First issue of *Saturday Evening Post* published.
1822 Lafayette visits Philadelphia.
1824 Historical Society of Pennsylvania formed.
1825 Jefferson Medical College founded.
1827 Charles Willson Peale, painter, dies.
1828 Gilbert Stuart dies.
1830 John Fanning Watson publishes his *Annals*.
1831 Stephen Girard dies.
1832 First locomotive made at Baldwin Locomotive Works.
1834 Ten-hour day movement started in Philadelphia by laborers and coal heavers.
1836 Leary's book store founded.
Public Ledger established by Swain & Abell.
1839 Philadelphia Zoological Institute founded.
1841 Bank of United States fails.
1842 Edgar Allan Poe occupies 530 N. Seventh St.
1847 William Wagner founds Wagner Free Institute of Science.
1848 Girard College for Orphan Boys opens.
Whig Party delegates meet in Philadelphia and nominate Zachory Taylor for presidency.
1850 Population—121,376 (estimated).
Female Medical College of Philadelphia founded.
1853 John Drew (the younger) born in Philadelphia.
1854 Young Men's Christian Association organized in Philadelphia.
1856 Gratz College (Jewish) founded.
1857 Academy of Music opens.
1858 Banks suspend in financial panic.
Steam fire engine introduced.
1860 Population—565,529 (estimated).
Coleman Sellers makes first photographic motion pictures.
Baseball makes its first appearance in city.
Bishop Neumann dies.
German Hospital (Lankenau Hospital) founded.
1861 Lincoln appears in City and raises flag over Independence Hall.
First religious services held in Cathedral of SS. Peter and Paul.
1863 Cornerstone laid for Masonic Temple.
Edward William Bok, philanthropist, born in Holland.
1864 City purchases League Island.
Swarthmore established by The Society of Friends.
George W. Childs buys *Public Ledger.*
1865 John B. Stetson Company, hat manufacturers, established.
Philadelphia Inquirer issues a bulletin announcing the fall of Richmond.
1866 Green's Hotel opens.
1867 Hahnemann Medical Hospital founded.
Commission of Fairmount Park created by act of Assembly.
1869 Jay Cooke and Son Company fails.
1870 Population—673,726 (estimated).
Philadelphia Record appears.
Citizens in referendum, choose present site for City Hall.
1871 Edwin Forrest makes last stage appearance at Walnut Street Theatre.

1871 Isaiah Chase and Prof. Octavius Catto, two prominent Negroes, are slain.
1872 Edwin Forrest dies.
     Federal Building erected upon former site of Presidential Mansion at 9th and Chestnut Sts.
1873 City establishes a national museum in Independence Hall.
1874 Philadelphia Zoo opens.
     Charley Ross kidnapped.
     Cornerstone of City Hall laid.
1875 Successful wireless experiments are carried on by Prof. Elihu Thompson and Edwin J. Houston of Central High School.
1876 John Wanamaker Store and Broad Street Theatre opens.
     Centennial Exhibition opens in Fairmount Park.
1878 Lionel Barrymore born in Philadelphia.
     Thomas E. Cahill bequeathes $1,000,000 for the establishment of Catholic High School for Boys.
1880 Bryn Mawr College founded.
1883 First Free Law Library established.
     Haverford College founded.
1884 Scharf and Westcott publish first standard history of Philadelphia.
1888 Louisa May Alcott dies.
1889 Mask and Wig Club formed.
     Edward Bok becomes editor of the *Ladies Home Journal*.
1891 Anthony J. Drexel founds Drexel Institute.
     Temple College granted rights to confer degrees.
1892 First Electric railways used in Philadelphia.
1894 Central High School erected on southwest corner of Broad and Green Sts.
1896 First public exhibition of motion pictures at Keith's Bijou Theatre.
1897 Commercial Museum officially opened by President McKinley.
1899 First motor car in city appears.
1900 Philadelphia Orchestra organized
1903 The great textile strike occurs.
1905 Passenger service begins in Market Street subway
1906 Poor Richard Club organized.
     University of Pennsylvania confers Doctor of Law degree upon King Edward VII of England.
1907 Temple College becomes Temple University.
1908 Shibe Park opens.
1910 First airplane flight from New York to Philadelphia.
1911 Rudolph Blankenburg elected Mayor of Philadelphia.
1912 Horace Howard Furness, Shakespearian authority, dies.
1916 First appearance of Japanese beetle.
1917 Navy enlists first woman as "yeomanette".
1918 First airport opens in city.
     First ship launched at Hog Island.
1920 Roosevelt Boulevard dedicated.
1921 Edward Bok establishes Philadelphia Award of Merit.
1922 First Bok Award given to Dr. Russell H. Conwell.
1923 Hedgerow Theatre begun.
1924 Curtis Institute of Music established.
1926 Sesqui-Centennial Exhibition begins.
     Delaware River Bridge dedicated.
1928 Pennsylvania Museum of Art opens.
1929 Rodin Museum dedicated.
1930 Population—1,950,961.
     Edward William Bok dies.
1931 Municipal Convention Hall opened.
1932 250th anniversary of landing of William Penn.
1933 Agnes Repplier awarded gold metad by National Institute of Arts and Letters.
1934 Franklin Institute opens for public.
     Philadelphia sees first Sunday baseball game.
1935 Philadelphia sees first Sunday movies.
1936 Democratic National Convention at Convention Hall, renominates President Franklin D. Roosevelt, who delivers acceptance speech before 120,000 persons on Franklin Field.

689

Bibliography

Architecture
Eberlein, H. D. and McClure, Abbot. Practical Book of Early American Arts and Crafts. Philadelphia, Lippincott, 1916.

Drama
Brown, T. Allston. History of the American Stage. New York, Dick & Fitzgerald. 1870.

Hornblow, Arthur. History of the Theatre in America. Philadelphia, Lippincott, 1919.

Education
Broome, Edwin C. Public School System of Philadelphia. Philadelphia, Board of Education, 1935.

Wickersham, James P. A History of Education in Pennsylvania. Lancaster, Inquirer Publishing Co., 1886.

Woody, Thomas. Early Quaker Education in Pennsylvania. New York, Columbia University Press, 1920.

Ethnology
Morais, Henry S. Jews of Philadelphia. Philadelphia, Levytype Co., 1894.

Sachse, J. F. German Pietists of Provincial Pennsylvania. Philadelphia, P. C. Stockhausen, 1895.

Ward, Christopher. Dutch and Swedes on the Delaware. Philadelphia, University of Pennsylvania Press, 1930.

Finance
Holdsworth, John T. Financing an Empire.—A History of Banking in Pennsylvania. Philadelphia, S. J. Clarke Publishing Co., 1928.

Flora and Fauna
Harshberger, John W. Botanists of Philadelphia. Philadelphia, T. C. Davis & Sons, 1899.

Keller, I. A. and Brown, S. Handbook of the Flora of Philadelphia and Vicinity. Philadelphia, Philadelphia Botany Club, 1905.

Stone, Witmer. Birds of Eastern Pennsylvania and New Jersey. Philadelphia, Delaware County Ornithological Club, 1894.

Folkways
Gummere, Amelia M. Witchcraft and Quakerism; a Study in Social History. Philadelphia, Biddle Press, 1908.

Government
Philadelphia's Government, 1932. Philadelphia, Bureau of Municipal Research, 1932.

Highways
Faris, John T. Old Roads Out of Philadelphia, Philadelphia, Lippincott, 1917.

History
Barton, George. Little Journeys Around Old Philadelphia. Philadelphia, Peter Reilly Co., 1925.

Hazard, Samuel. Annals of Pennsylvania, from the Discovery of the Delaware River, 1609—1682. Philadelphia, Hazard, 1850.

Lippincott, Horace Mather. Philadelphia. Philadelphia, Macrae-Smith, 1926.

Oberholtzer, E. P. Philadelphia: A History of the City and Its People. Philadelphia, S. J. Clarke Publishing Co., 1912.

Repplier, Agnes. Philadelphia: The Place and the People. New York, Macmillan, 1925.

690

Scharf and Westcott. History of Philadelphia. Philadelphia, L. H. Everts Co., 1884. 3 vols.

Shackleton, Robert. Book of Philadelphia. Philadelphia, Penn Publishing Co., 1918.

Watson, John Fanning. Annals of Philadelphia and Pennsylvania. Philadelphia, Edwin S. Stuart, 1898.

Indians

Sipe, C. Hale. Indian Chiefs of Pennsylvania. Butler, Ziegler Printing Co., 1927.

Industry

Freedley, Edwin T. Philadelphia and Its Manufactures. Philadelphia, Edward Young & Co., 1858.

Matos, W. W., compiler. Philadelphia: Its Founding and Development. Philadelphia, Philadelphia Executive Committee, 1908.

Legal

Martin, John H. History of the Bench and Bar. Philadelphia, Welsh, 1883.

Libraries

Gray, Austin. The First American Library; A Short Account of the Library Company of Philadelphia, 1731—1931. Library Company, 1936.

Literature

Gibbs, George. Old Philadelphia. New York, Appleton, 1931.

Lippard, George. Quaker City. Philadelphia, G. Lippard, 1846.

Mitchell, S. Weir. Hugh Wynne. New York, Century Co., 1896.

Mitchell, S. Weir. Red City. New York, Century Co., 1908.

Taylor, Bayard. Story of Kennett. New York, Putnam's, 1894.

Medical

Anders, James M. History of the Outstanding Achievements of Philadelphia as a Medical Center. Philadelphia, World's Medical Center.

Keen, W. W. History of the Philadelphia School of Anatomy. Philadelphia, Lippincott, 1875.

Military

Clarke, Maj. William P. Official History of the Militia and the National Guard of the State of Pennsylvania. Philadelphia, C. J. Hendler, 1909. 3 vols.

Music

Lytle, Clyde F. Pennsylvania in Song and Story. Minneapolis, Burgess Publishing Co., 1932.

Wister, F. A. Twenty-Five Years of the Philadelphia Orchestra. Philadelphia, Women's Committee for the Philadelphia Orchestra, 1925.

Natural Resources

Gordon, Samuel G. Mineralogy of Pennsylvania. Philadelphia, Academy of Natural Sciences, 1922.

Iddings, Joseph P. Igneous Rocks. Philadelphia, American Philosophical Society, 1911.

Negro Progress

Turner, E. R. Negro in Pennsylvania. Washington, American Historical Association, 1911.

Wright, R. R. Negro in Pennsylvania. Philadelphia, A. M. E. Book Concern, 1912.

Points of Interest

Morley, Christopher. Travels in Philadelphia. Philadelphia, David McKay Co., 1920.

Social Service

Cloud, Esther. Social Service Directory of Philadelphia, 1935. Philadelphia, Council of Social Service Agencies, Welfare Federation of Philadelphia, 1935.

INDEX

Abbey, Edwin Austin, 251
Abbott Dairies, 506
Aberle, H. C., & Co., 520
Abington, 658
Abington Library, 658
Abington Memorial Hospital, 658
Abington Presbyterian Church, 658
Academy of Fine Arts, 82
Academy of Music, 64, 234, 235, 348
Academy of Natural Sciences, 60, 289, 583
Accommodations, XXIII
Acorn Club, 435
Act of Consolidation, 63, 64, 109
Actors, 213
Adams, John, 48, 328, 411; Samuel, 48; Weyman, 426
Adelphia Hotel, 399
African Methodist Episcopal Book Concern, 107
African Methodist Episcopal Church, 107
Agnew, D. Hayes, 199; James, 479
Agriculture, 124
Alcott, Louisa M., 192
Alden Park Players, 227
Alexander, Dr. Virginia M., 299
Allen, Richard, 200, 201; Rev. Thomas G., 305
Allibone, S. Austin, 198
All Saints Spiritual Church, 170
A'mhouses, 304, 305
Alpha Baptist Church, 163
American Baptist Publication Society, 432
American Entomological Society, 292, 585
American Federation of Hosiery Workers, 468, 526
American Federation of Labor, 157
American Fiction Guild, 201
American Institute of Architects, 277
American Magazine and Monthly Chronicle for the British Colonies, 188
American Medical Association, 62
American Museum Magazine, 190, 191
American Penal Labor Association, 308
American Philosophical Society, 286, 288, 334
American Red Cross, 310, 438
American Swedish Historical Museum, 449, 450
American Theatre Society, 224
American Weekly Mercury, 202, 203, 214
Amusements & Sports, 90, 91
Anderson, Marian, 242
Andre, Major, 479, 487
Andrews, Jedediah, 161
Andros, Sir Edmund, 645
Annals of Philadelphia, (Watson), 192
Annenberg, M. L., 208
Annual Celebrations, 91
Annual Events, XXVIII, XXIX
Anshutz, Thomas, 426
Anti-Catholic Riots, 62, 63, 408
Anvil Tavern, 641
Aquarium, 78, 580
Aquetong, 667
Arch Street Friends Meeting House, 392, 393
Arch Street Methodist Episcopal Church, 169
Architecture, 256; Colonial, 256; Greek revival, 265; Gothic, 268; Victorian, 270; French Renaissance, 270; Romanesque, 270, 271; Modern, 271, 272; Clubs, 277
Ardmore, 684
Area of Philadelphia, 11
Argall, Capt. Samuel, 25
Arliss, George, 416
Arm-in-Arm Convention, 72
Armistice, the, 81

Armory, 103rd Cavalry, 508; 108th Field Artillery, 467
Armstrong Association, 108
Armstrong, General John, 604
Army and Navy Pylons, 578
Arnold, Benedict, 56, 204, 403, 552
Art, 243
Art Alliance, 82, 436
Art Club of Philadelphia, 444
Art Museums, 360, 362, 363, 365
Arthur House, 547
Arthur, Timothy Shay, 547
Articles of Association, 48
Articles of Confederation, 58, 321
Artists Union, 426
Asbury, Bishop Francis, 389, 390
Ashurst Collection, 352
Ashurst, John, 310, 352
Assembly, 89
Association of Philadelphia Settlements, 310
Automotive Industry, 115
Awbury Arboretum and Park, 485

Bache, Dr. Franklin, 297
Bachelors Barge Club, 559
Baederwood Golf Course, 658
Bailly, Joseph A., 250
Bainbridge, William, 392
Ba'a-Cynwyd, 674
Baldwin Locomotive Works, 73, 117, 459, 646
Baldwin, Matthias, 117, 287
Ba'dwin School, 683
Ball bearings, manufacture of, 521
Baltimore and Ohio Railroad, 146; Station, 439, 440
Baltimore, Lord, 37
Bancroft, George, 233
Banking, 125
Banks, 125
North America, 57, 128, 129, 404; Pennsylvania, 57, 64, 127, 128; United States, 129, 132, 133, 406; Central Penn National, 431; Fidelity Philadelphia Trust Co., 443; First National of Philadelphia, 404; Girard National, 406; Girard Trust Co., 443, 382; National Bank of Germantown, 480; Pennsylvania Company for Insurance on Lives and Granting of Annuities, 60, 126, 133; Philadelphia Saving Fund Society, 61, 126, 132, 256, 385; Second Bank of the United States, 132, 133
Baptist Home, 471
Bar'elin, Father Felix Joseph, 407
Bardley, John, 488
Barnes, Albert, 199, 254, 685
Barnes Foundation, 685
Barralett, John James, 246, 247
Barry, Com. John, 254, 320, 411, 447
Barrymore, Ethel, 221, 416; John, 221; Lionel, 221; Maurice, 221
Bartol, Henry W., 290, 632
Barton, Dr. Benjamin Smith, 286, 289, 295; William P. C., 295
Bartram, John, 12, 190, 284, 495
Bartram's Gardens, 495
"Battle of the Kegs," (Hopkins), 55
Beaux, Cecilia, 250
Bell's Mill Road Bridge, 615
Bell Telephone Company, 141
Bel'evue-Stratford Hotel, 444
Belmont: Filtration Plant and Reservoir, 509; Mansion, 572
Rembridge, Henry, 244
Benezet, Anthony, 179, 190
Benjamin Franklin, Hotel 403; Parkway, 81, 574
Benjamin West House, 632

Benson, Dr. Francis Colgate, Jr., 299
Bergdoll, Grover C., 81
Berkowitz, Henry, 168
Beth Israel, 168
Betsy Ross House, 342, 393
Better Homes in America Association, 308
Beury, Dr. Charles E., 466
Biddle, Edward, 48; Francis, 197; Capt. James, 502, 503; Com. Nicholas, 133, 265, 396; Capt. Thomas, 61
Bigler, Governor, 64
Billikopf, Jacob, 156
Billmeyer House, 488
Binney, Constance, 232; Horace, 69, 292
Birch, Thomas, 246; William, 246; William Young, 513
Birds, 14
Birmingham Meetinghouse, 640
Bishop, Richard, 426
Bispham, David, 241
Black Horse Tavern, 637
Blai, Boris, 254
Blankenburg, Mrs. Lucretia, 79; Rudolph, 78
Bloch, Julius, 254
Blockey Almshouse, 305
Blue Anchor Inn, 22
Blue Bell Tavern, 500
Blue Laws, 4, 85
Board of Education, 230, 310; Building, 583; Board of Public Education, 177
Boardman, Eleanor, 233
Boathouse Row, 558
Boat Clubs, 558, 561
Bok Award, 82, 197
Bok, Edward William, 196, 197; Mrs. Edward W., 240; Mary Louise Curtis, 238, 432, 545
Boker, George Henry, 69, 195, 222
Bonaparte House, 416
Bonaparte, Joseph, 416
Bond, Dr. Phineas, 418; Dr. Thomas, 295, 418
Booth, Edwin, 416; Junius Brutus, 416
Borie, Adolphe, 253
Boston: Port Bill, 46; Tea Party, 46
Botanical Society, 289
Boulevard Airport, 471
Boundaries, 11
Bowman's Hill Observation Tower, 670
Boxall, Joseph, 142
Boy Scouts of America, 583
Boyle, John J., 250
Brackenridge, Hugh H., 190
Bradford, Andrew, 202, 203; William, 126, 202, 203, 204
Brandywine Baptist Church, 638
Brandywine, Battle of, 329
Breckenridge, Hugh, 251
Breda, Treaty of, 29
Brethren, 163, 164
Brethren, First Church of the, 489
Breyer Ice Cream Company, 494, 495
Brill Manufacturing Company, 115, 498, 500
Broad Street: Baptist Church, 446; Hospital, 445; Station, 383; Subway, 84, 145; Theatre, 444
Broadwood Hotel, 458
Brooks High License Law, 72
Brooks, Phillips, 199
Bromley and Sons, 518, 520
Brown, Charles Brockden, 190, 191; Maj. Gen. Jacob, 61
Brown Preparatory School, 182
Brown's Raid, 65
Brush Electric Company, 140
Bryn Athyn, 671; Cathedral, 653, 671
Bryn Mawr College, 684
Buckingham, 666; Meeting House, 666
Bucks County Historical Society Museum, 665
Budd Manufacturing Company, 115
Bulletin Building, 383

Bullitt Act, 75
Bureaus: for Colored Children, 314; of Legal Aid, 315; of Municipal Research, 307; of Recreation, 307
Bustleton Avenue Bridge, 621
Butler, Pierce, 473; Gen. Smedley D., 81
Butler Place, 473
Buttercup Cottage, 609
Buttonwood Inn, 666

Cadwalader, Gen. George, 62, 63, 68; John, 64; Dr. Thomas, 293; Gen. Thomas 61
Cadwalader, Grays, 68
Cahill, Thomas E., 180
Calder, Alexander Milne, 250, 379; Alexander Stirling, 250
Caledonian Club, 461
Calvary Methodist Episcopal Church, 169
Calvary Presbyterian Church, 412
Camac Street, 424, 425, 426
Camac, Turner, 425
Canadians, 103
Cardington, 625
Carey, Matthew, 190, 297
Carl Mackley Houses, 274, 525-527
Carpenter, Edward Child, 223
Carpenters' Company, 149, 262, 341, 342; Hall, 48, 262, 339; Society of, 339
Carriage building trade, 115
Cassatt, Mary, 249, 250
Catalpa Inn, 666
Cathedral of SS. Peter and Paul, 69
Catholic Apostolic Church, 172
Catholic Children's Bureau, 313
Catholic Y. M. A., 311
Catto, Octavius V., 73
Cedar Grove Mansion, 568
Centennial, The, 74, 75, 568-570, 571, 572
Center Square, 279, 379
Central High School, 77, 176, 177, 459
Central Labor Union, 157
Central-Penn National Bank, 431
Chadds Ford, 638, 639; battle of, 638-640; Inn, 638
Chadds House, 640
Chamber of Commerce, 60
Chambers-Wylie Memorial Presbyterian Church, 444
Chamounix Drive, 573; Lake, 573
Chapman, Nathaniel, 297
Charlotte Cushman Club, 219
Chase, Isaiah, 73
Chemicals, manufacture of, 118
Chester, 646
Chestnut Hill Players, 227
Chestnut Street Baptist Church, 163
Chestnut Street Bridge, 73
Cheves, Langdon, 133
Chew, Benjamin, 52, 486
Chew Mansion, 486, 487
Childs, Cephas Gier, 247; George W., 208, 501
Chinatown, 387
Chinese, 98
Chinese Burial Ground, 674
"Chinese Wall", 6, 282, 505
Christ Church, 161, 394
Churches:
    Baptist: Alpha, 163; Brandywine, 638; Broad Street, 446; Chestnut Street, 163; First, 431, 432; Grace, 162, 175, 467; Old Pennepek, 162, 621; Second, 163
    Christian Science: First Church, 170; Second Church, 170
    Friends: Arch St., 392, 393; Buckingham, 666; Germantown 480; Horsham 661; Race Street, 74
    Lutheran: St. Michael's, 159, 489; Zion, 387, 388
    Methodist Episcopal: Calvary, 169; First of Germantown, 169; St. George's, 169, 188; African, 107, Arch St., 169

Presbyterian: Calvary, 412; Chambers-Wylie Memorial, 444; Clinton Street, 424; First, 412; Northern Liberties, 162; Market Square, 480, 481; Over-brook, 512; Second, 162, 305; Third, 162; Abington, 658; of Neshaminy, 64; Old Newtown, 671

Protestant Episcopal: Christ Church, 161, 394; Gloria Dei (Old Swedes' Church), 159, 161, 234, 257, 542, 543; St. Mark's, 435; St. Paul's, 408; St. Peter's, 395, 406; Holy Trinity, 439; St. David's, 681

Reformed: Evangelical and Reformed, 162; First, 164

Roman Catholic: Holy Child, 471; Holy Trinity, 166, 412; Our Lady of Lourdes, 512; Our Lady of the Blessed Sacrament (Negro), 461; St. Augustine's, 62, 166, 390; St. Joseph's, 166, 179, St. Mary's, 179, 180, 411; SS. Peter and Paul, 576; St. Philip de Neri, 62

Spiritualist: All Saints, 170; First Association of, 170; St. John's Spiritual Alliance, 170; Third, 170; Universal Brotherhood, 170

Hebrew: Keneseth Israel, 168, 464; Mikveh Israel, 100, 167, 168, 417, 468; Rodeph Shalom, 168, 459; Beth Ismel, 168

Unitarian: First, 169; Germantown, 169, 491; United Brethren in Christ, 170

Universal: Church of the Messiah, 169, 464; First, 169

Miscellaneous: First Church of the Brethren, 489; Church of God in North America, 172; Church of the New Jerusalem, 172; Church of the Redeemer, 172; Conservative Dunkards, 163; Progressive Dunkards, 163; St. George's Greek Catholic, 417; Bryn Athyn Cathedral, 653, 671; Catholic Apostolic 172; Seamen's Church Institute, 170, 312; Germantown Mennonite, 483; Mennonite, 163

Church of the Redeemer, 172
Cigar, manufacture of, 114
Cinema, 232, 349; Stars, 232
City Hall, 73, 256, 279, 379; Annex, 381
City Planning, 279
City Tavern, 126
Civic Improvements of Early 1800, 60
Civil Works Administration, 85
Clarke, E. W. and Co., 73
Clarkson, Matthew, 333
Clarkson Park, 471
Clay, John Curtis, 543
Claypoole, James, 31, 244
Claypoole's Daily Advertiser, 205, 206
Clifton Heights, 629
Climate and Clothing, XXIV XXV
Clinton Street, 422-424; Presbyterian Church, 424
Clothier, Isaac, 79
Clothier Memorial, 631
Coates Collection, 251
Cobbett, William, 189, 190
Cobbs Creeks Falls, 627; Golf Club, 627; Guard House (New), 625; Guard House (Old), 625; Park, 625
Coins, manufacture of, 375
Coleman, William, 135, 554
Coles House, 424
Colleges:
Bryn Mawr, 683, 684; Drevel Institute of Art, Science, and Industry, 183, 500; Dropsie, 180, 468; Girard, 62, 132, 182, 313, 370, 374; Gratz, 180, 468; Hahnemann Medical, 183, 303; Haverford, 684; Jefferson Medical, 61, 183, 294, 302, 400; La Salle, 182; Philadelphia College of Osteopathy, 183; Philadelphia School of Occupational Therapy, 303, 439; Philadelphia College of Pharmacy and

Science, 61, 183, 494; Physicians and Surgeons, 303; Rosemont, 683; St Joseph's, 182, 183, 510; Villanova, 683; Log College, 664; Swarthmore, 631 Pennsylvania, 589-593; Temple, 464-467
Collin, Nicholas, 543
Columbus, Christopher, 570
Combs Conservatory of Music, 445
Commercial Museum, 76, 493, 494
Committee for Industrial Organization, 158
Compton, Bishop Henry, 395
Concordville, 637, 638
Concord Meeting House, 638; School House, 486
Congoleum-Nairn, 645, 646
Congress Hall, 79, 327, 337, 338
Consolidation of the City, 63
Constitution (Ship), 447
Constitutional Convention, 58, 59
Continental Congress, First, 48, 49, 339, 341; Second, 49, 51
Convention Hall, 493, 494
Conwell, Dr. Russell H., 162, 163, 175, 464
Cooke, Jay, 69, 134, 657; and Company, 69, 73, 134
Co-operative Center, 475
Cope, Edward D., 199
Cornell, Dr. Walter S., 299
Corporation for Relief of Distressed Presbyterian Ministers, 136
Corssen, Arent, 26
Costello, Paul, 559
Council Fair of the Sanitary Commissions, 71
Council at Upland, 36
Cournos, John, 198
Cowboy, The, (Remington), 550
Cram & Ferguson, 272
Cramp, William, 531
Cramp's Shipbuilding Company, 73, 117, 531, 532
Crawford, Earl Stetson, 250; Gen. Samuel Wylie, 71
Crescent Boat Club 559
Cresheim Creek, 608; Drive, 607; Valley, 607
Cret, Paul Philippe, 82, 277, 280, 402 578
Crime Prevention Association, 308
Crooked Billet, 538; Monument, 663; Tavern, 663
Crosby, Joshua, 418
Cummings, Alexander, 206, 208
Cuneo Eastern Press, 523
Curtin, Governor, 70
Curtis, Cyrus H. K., 79, 208, 392, 590
Curtis Institute of Music, 82, 234, 238, 241, 432
Curtis Publishing Company, 414, 415
Custom House, 404, 405
Customs and Folklore, 88, 89
Czecho-Slavs, 105

DaCosta, Dr. Jacob M., 199, 298
Dahlgren, Admiral, John A. 71
Daily News, 210
Dale, Richard, 392
Daly, Thomas A., 196
Danes, 104
Darrah, Lydia, 392
Darley, Felix, 247
D'Ascenzo, Nicola, 254, 426, 440; Glass Works, 440
Davenport Family, 220
Davis, Dunlap and Barney, 431
Davis, Grove, 661
Davis, Richard Harding, 194, 210, 224
Dawson, George Walter, 251
Deaver, Dr. John B., 298
de Casseres, Benjamin, 198
Declaration of Independence, 49, 321, 394
Declaratory Act, 45

Deeter, Jasper, 226, 636
De Forrest, William, 118
Delancey Street, 438
Delaware Avenue, 535
Delaware County: Court House, 636, 637;
War Memorial Bridge, 634
Delaware River, 12; Bridge, 7, 81, 145,
537
Delaware Valley Ornithological Club,
585
Delawares, The, 16
Democratic National Convention, 87
Dennie, Joseph, 190, 191
Denny, Governor, 215, 216
Deschamps, Edward, 142
de Schweinitz, Dr. George Edmund, 298
de Toussard, Col. Louis, 649
Devil's Pool, 612
Devon, 681
De Vries, David Pieterszen, 26
Diagnostic Hospital, 302
Dickens, Charles, 201, 403, 424; Rev.
John, 390
Dickens Fellowship, 201
Dickinson, John, 48, 189
Disston and Sons, Inc., 528
Disston, Henry, 528, 529
Dock, Christopher, 186
Dock Street, 405, 540
Donnelly, Ignatius, 198
Doolittle, Helen, 198
Dougherty, Dennis Cardinal, 167
Douglas Hospital, 302, 303
Doylestown, 664, 665
Dress, early habits of, 88
Drew, John, 220; John (the younger),
220; Mrs. John, 216, 220, 425
Drexel and Company, 134
Drexel, Anthony, 79, 134, 170, 183; Francis,
79
Drexel Institute of Technology, 183, 500
Drinker Family, the, 405
Dropsie College, 180, 468
Dropsie, Moses A., 468
Duche, Rev. Jacob, 186, 190, 191
Duffield, Rev. George, D. D., 410, 411
Duhring, Dr. Louis A., 298
Durham, Israel, 75
Dutch West India Company, 25, 26

Eagles, Fraternal Order of, 461
Eakins, Thomas, 248, 249
Early Settlement, 31
Eastern Baptist Theological Seminary,
181, 436
Eastern Penitentiary, 474
East Laurel Hill Cemetery, 557
East Park Reservoir, 551
Economic Philadelphia, 89, 112
Eddy, Nelson, 241
Eddystone Catastrophe, The, 80
Education, 173
Edwin Forrest Home for Actors, 219, 315,
509
Electricity, 75, 139, 140
Elfreth's Alley, 262, 393, 394; Association,
394
Elfreth family, 394
Elkins Park, 651
Elkins, William L., 79, 471;
Masonic Orphanage For Girls, 471
Elkins Collection (Pennsylvania Museum
of Art), 254
Ellmaker, Lee, 210
Elm Treaty of Shackamaxon, 38
Elverson Building, 458
Elverson, James, 208
English, 103; Village, 439
Epidemics, 68, 297
Episcopal Academy For Boys, 510
Ericsson, Capt. John, 450, 580
Ericsson Fountain, 580
Espy, James Pollard, 286
Ethical Culture Society, 172

Evangelical and Reformed Church, 164
Evangelical Home for the Aged, 471
Evans, Oliver, 286
Evelyn, Robert, 29
Evening Bulletin, 208, 383
Evening Public Ledger, 208, 404
Eyre, Mrs. Alice MacFadden, 435

Fabritius, Rev. Jacobus, 542
Fairmount Rowing Club, 558
Farley, R. Blossom, 426
Farmer's Letters (by John Dickinson), 45
Faulkner, Daniel, 186; Justus, 543
Fauna, 14, 15
Fauset, Arthur Huff, 201; Jessie, 201
Febiger, Admiral John C., 71
Federal: Art Project (W. P. A.) 255;
Building, 386, 402; Reserve Bank of
Philadelphia, 401, 402; Social Security
Board, 313
Federal Society of Journeymen Cord-
wainers, 149
Fels Planetarium, 290, 359, 360
Female Improvement Society, 151
Fidelity Mutual Life Insurance Company,
580
Fidelity-Philadelphia Trust Company, 443
Fields, W. C., 222
Fifth Ward Election Murder, 80
Finance, 125
Fincher's Trades' Review, 153
Fire Companies, 92, 93
Fire Customs, early, 92, 93
First: Almshouse, 304; Association of
Spiritualists, 170; Bank of United
States, 129, 132, 133; Building and
Loan Association in the United States,
527; City Troop, 68, 440; Continental
Congress, 48, 49, 339, 341; Inhabitants,
16; Mummer's Parade, 77, 91; Na-
tional Bank of Philadelphia, 404; Pub-
lic Demonstration of Telephone, 140,
Trade Association, 149; United States
Mint, 136, 375, 376, 474
Fitch, John, 286, 663, 664
Fitzgerald, Thomas, 210, 224
Flag House, 342, 393
Fleisher, Samuel S., 255, 546
Fleisher School, 181
Flora, 13
Flower, Enoch, 173
Foerderer, Robert H., 114
Fonthill (Doylestown), 666
Foods, 95
Forrest, Edwin, 216, 217, 222, 408, 415
Fort Mifflin, 263, 648
Fort Washington Redoubt, 679
Forten, James, 107
Fountain Hotel (Willow Grove), 660
Fountain House (Doylestown), 665, 666
Fox, Daniel, 72; Joseph, 135
Fraley, Frederick, 531
Frankford: 513; Arsenal, 530, 531; His-
torical Society, 528
Frankford Southwark Philadelphia City
Passenger Railroad Co., 143
Franklin, Benjamin, 41, 51, 135, 210, 353,
393; arrival, 41; delegate to Congress,
49; University of Pennsylvania, 173,
598; literary works, 184, 186, 188; Poor
Richard's Almanac, 184, 210, 592; prin-
ter, 202; Pennsylvania Gazette, 202;
Scientific achievements, 285, 286;
American Philosophical Society, 334;
statue of, (Boyle), 386; experiments
with lightning, 387; grave of, 390, 392;
Christ Church, 394; Pennsylvania Hos-
pital, 418; Library Company, 428; relations with John Bartram, 497, 498
Franklin Field Stadium, 594
Franklin Inn Club, 201, 426

Franklin Institute, 61, 289, 353, 403, 583;
description of, 353; Fels Planetarium,
359; Locomotive Room, 358; Medicine,

Surgery and Dentistry exhibits, 358;
Paper making and Graphic Arts exhibit, 357
  Halls: Aviation, 358; Astronomy, 359;
  Electrical Communication, 356;
  Electrical engineering and illumination, 357; Mechanism, 356; Pepper
  Hall, 359; Prime movers, 356
Franklin Medical College, 294
Franklin Square, 387
Free Library of Philadelphia, 82, 84, 310,
  341, 350, 516; books for blind, 350;
  Widener Memorial branch, 353
  Collections: Ashhurst, 352; Carson,
  351; Carvalho, 351; Edmunds, 351;
  Fleisher, 351; Lewis, 351; Norris, 352;
  Rawle, 351; Rosenwald, 352
  Departments: children's, 351; extension, 352; periodical, 352; public
  documents, 351
Free Society of Traders, 31
Friedlander, Julius R., 513
Friends—Hicksites and Orthodox, 34, 160
Friends' Central School, 160, 513
Friends' Hospital for Mental and Nervous
  diseases, 469
Friends' Meeting House (Fourth Street),
  390
Friends' Meeting House (Race Street),
  74
Friends' Public School, 173, 177, 181, 386,
  491
Friends' Select School, 575, 673
Fulton, Robert, 246
Furness, Dr. Horace Howard, 198, 426;
  Horace Howard, Jr., 198
Furniture-Making, 243

Galloway, Joseph, 48, 551
Garber, Daniel, 253
Garfield Memorial, 557
Gas Works, 138
Gaynor, Janet, 232
Geary, John W., 72
General Greene Inn (Buckingham), 666
General Steel Castings Co., 646
General Wayne Inn, 685
George, Henry, 194; Nancy, 215
Gerhard, Benjamin, 69; William Wood,
  297
Germans, 101, 102
Germantown, 34, 35, 475; Academy, 175,
  181, 481, 483; battle of, 475, 479, 481,
  485, 486, 604; branch of the Y. W. C.
  A., 482; Friends Library, 480; Friends
  Meeting House, 480; High School, 483;
  Historical Society, 478, 479; Mennonite
  Church, 483; Union School, 483; Unitarian Church, 169, 491; Town Hall,
  482, 483
Gettysburg, Battle of, 70
Giannini, Dusolina, 241
Gibbs, George, 426
Gibbons, Charles, 69
Gibson Collection, (Pennsylvania Academy of Fine Arts), 251
Gilbert Stuart House, 478
Gilbert's Alley, 394
Gilliams, Dr. Jacob, 289
Gilmore, W. E. Garrett, 559
Gimbel Brothers Store, 77, 403
Girard College, 63, 132, 182, 313, 370, 474
Girard House, 68, 77
Girard National Bank, 406
Girard, Stephen, 60, 121, 126, 265, 373,
  374, 538; begins career as merchant, 131;
  marriage of, 131; banker, 131; death of,
  132; will of, 132; College, 132; wills
  money for city improvement, 280, 281;
  wills money for college, 370; statue of,
  (Gevelot), 371; lodges in Elfreth's Alley,
  393; purchases original Bank of U. S.
  building, 406; grave of, 412
Girard Trust Company Building, 382, 443

Girls': Friendly Society, 312; High School,
  177; Normal School, 177
Glen Riddle, 637; Farm, 637
Gloria Dei Church, 159, 161, 234, 257, 542,
  543
Goddard, William, 205
Godey's Lady's Book, 192
Godfrey, Thomas, Jr., 222
Goodson, John, 293
Goodyear, Charles, 118
Gorgas, Joseph, 606; Capt. Josiah, 531
Gould, Dr. George Millbry, 199
Government, 109; Bureaus, 113
Grace Baptist Temple, 162, 175, 467
Graeme Park, 661-663
Graham's Magazine, 193, 194, 247
Grand Fountain, 552
Grant, U. S., 74, 75, 550
Grant's Cabin, 549
Graphic Sketch Club, 255, 546, 547
Gratz: College, 180, 468; Hyman, 180, 468;
  Rebecca, 167, 417, 418; Simon, 100
Gray's Ferry Bridge, 77
Greaton, Father Joseph, 166, 407
Greber, Jacques, 82, 277, 576
Greeks, 99, 106, 441
Green, Thomas, 403
Green Tree Inn, 483
Green's Hotel, 403
Greenwood, Charlotte, 222
Griffith, Dr. John P. Crozer, 299
Griffiths, William, 135
Gross, Dr. S. D. 199, 295
Grumblethorpe, (Wister Big House), 479,
  481
Gulph Mills, 676
Gustine Lake, 557

Hahnemann Hospital, 458; Medical College, 183, 303, 458
Hale, Sarah Josepha Buell, 192
Hall, David, 203; John Caskell, 19
Hallam, Lewis, 215
Hallowell, Mrs. S. C., 400
Hamilton, Alexander, 136; Col. Andrew,
  40, 256, 336; Charles K., 78; James, 126,
  247
Hammerstein, Oscar, 235, 236, 461
Hancock, John, 49, 323
Hannah Penn House, 435
Hanson, John, 449
Harding, Father, 166; Jesper, 207
Hare, Judge J. Clark, 69; Dr. Robert, 286
Harrison, Birge, 253; John, 118; Thomas
  Alexander, 253
Hatboro, 663; Union Library, 663
Hathaway Shakespeare Club, 201
Hat Manufacturing, 113, 114, 517, 518
Haupt, Herman, 287, 288
Haverford College, 684
Haviland, John, 265, 404, 412, 415, 417
Hayes, Dr. Isaac, 289
Haynes, Dr. Israel, 200
Health Legislation, 305
Hedgerow Theatre, 226, 634
Helton, Roy Addison, 197
Henry Avenue Bridge, 602, 604
Henri-Louis, Jean Pierre, 244
Henry, Mayor Alexander, 65, 70
Herbert, Victor, 239, 240
Hermit Lane Bridge, 602; Nursery, 603
Hermitage Estate, 602
Hesselius, Gustavus, 234
Hewes, Joseph, 392
Heyl, Henry R., 232
Hill Meeting House, 410
Hilton, Dr. George R., 299
Hillegas, Michael, 392
Hirsch, Dr. Samuel, 168, 305
Historical Society of Pennsylvania, 61, 78,
  427, 428; Tower Collection, 427; Cassel
  Collection, 427; Gratz Collection, 427;
  Gilpin Library, historical items in, 427,
  428

696

Hodge, Dr. Hugh L., 295
Hofmann, Josef, 241, 433
Hog Island, 80, 146
Holicong, 666
Holland, John Joseph, 246
Hollows Athletic Field, 625
Holmes Avenue Bridge, 623
Holmes, Capt. George, 29; Capt. Thomas, 21, 31, 279, 282
Holy Child R. Catholic Church, 471
Holy Trinity R. Catholic Church, 166, 412
Holy Trinity Protestant Episcopal, 439
Home for Aged Widows and Wives of Free Masons, 471
"Hominy Man," 95
Homeopathic Medical College of Pennsylvania, 294, 303
Hood's Cemetery, 477, 478
Hood, William, 478
Hope Fire Engine Company, 408
Hoover, Walter, 559
Hopkinson, Francis, 55, 189, 392
Horsham, 661; Friends Meeting House, 661
Horstmann, William, 287
Horter, Earl, 254
Horticultural Hall, 571, 572
Hosiery, manufacture of, 520
Howe and Lescaze, 132, 385; Sir William, 52, 479, 629
Howe's Campaign, 54
Hudson, Henry, 25
Humboldt Monument (Drake), 549
Humphries, Charles, 48
Huneker, James Gibbons, 196, 210, 242
Hungarians, 106
Hunting Park, 469
Hurrie, William, 411

Ice Cream, 97, 495
Imports and Exports, 119
Independence Hall, 256, 321, 336, 337; art items in, 325; architecture of, 336; events taking place in, 321; historical items in, 325, 326; Resolution, 49, 321, 394; Day Celebration, 53; Square Group, 319; Square, 319, 320; Congress Hall, 327; Old City Hall, 331
Independent, 108
Independent Grays, 68
Indian Medicine Man, 551; Names, 16
Indian Rock, 617
Indians, 16
Industry, 112
Information, General, xxi-xxvii
Ingersoll, Jared, 52
Ingham, Samuel D., 667
Ingles, Annie G., 509
Irish, 62, 63, 102, 103, 441
Irish-American Club, 464
Iron, manufacture of, 117, 118
Irvin, James H., 107
Italians, 100, 101
Ives, Frederick Eugene, 288

Jackson, Dr. Chevalier, 298; Joseph, 200, 342
Jamison, 664
Japanese Gardens and Pagoda, 570, 571
Jarvis, John Wesley, 244
Jeanne D'Arc (Fremiet), 549
Jefferson Medical Hospital, 400; Medical College, 61, 183, 294, 302, 400
Jefferson, Joseph, 217, 220; Thomas, 49, 51, 136, 169, 323, 329, 479
Jehovah's Witnesses, 172, 464
Jenkins, C. Francis, 232; Stephen, 658
Jenkintown, 658
Jennings, Samuel, 246
Jewish Charities, Federation of, 306, 307; Foster Home, 418; Hospital Association, 303; Hospital, 473

Jews, 99, 100, 167, 168, 441
John Brown's Raid, 65
Johnson: Daniel Claypoole, 247; Henry N., 488; John G., 363; House, 485
Jones, Absalom, 108, 200, 201; Henry B., 201; John Paul, 329
Journalism, 202
Junior Employment Service, 310, 311
Junker, Jules, 76
Junto Club, 428

Kahal Kadosh Mikveh Israel, 167
Kane, Elisha Kent, 200, 289, 297
Kearsley, Dr. John, 259, 395, 396
Keach, Rev. Elias, 162
Keating, Dr. William Hypolitus, 289, 290, 353
"Keely Motor Hoax", 119
Keen, Dr. William W., 298
Keimer, Samuel, 185, 202
Keith, George, 173; Governor William, 661; House, 661
Kelly, George, 223; John B. 559; Wallace, 254
Kelpius, Johann, 186, 602
Kendrick, W. Freeland, 81, 83
Keneseth Israel Reformed Congregation, 168, 464
Kenilworth Apartments, 557
Kennett Meetinghouse, 641
Kennett Square, 644; Township, 641
Kenrick, Bishop Francis P., 166
Kensington, 513
Kent, A. Atwater, 344
Keyser, Dirck, 485; House, 485
Keystone Quartet, 240; Telephone Company, 141
King of Prussia, 676; Inn, 676
Kirkbride, Dr. Thomas S., 420, 508, 509
"Kirkbride's", 300, 420, 508
Kitchen's Lane Bridge, 605
Knight, Daniel Ridgway, 250
Knights of Columbus, 464; of Labor, 154
Know-Nothing Movement, 62
Knox, General: Headquarters of, 681
Kolmer, Dr. John A., 298
Koster, Heinrich Bernard, 186
Krauskopf, Joseph, 168, 464
Krider Gun Shop, 405
Krimmel, John Lewis, 247
Krisheimers, 34
Kugler, Dr. Charles, 287
Kunders House, 478

Labor, 147
Labor Institute Dramatic Guild, 229
Lacey, General John, 663
Ladies Home Journal, 196
Laessle, Albert, 253
Lafayette Cemetery, 640
Lafayette, Marquis de, 61, 328, 388, 420, 483, 664, 676
La France Art Institute, 527
Lahaska, 666
Lake Surprise, 609
Lambdin, James R., 248
Lancaster, Joseph, 176
Lane, David, 75; Jonathan, 135; Louisa, 415; Peter, 75
Lankenau Hospital, 474
Lansdowne, 629
Lantern Lane, 440
La Salle College, 182
Latham Park, 657
Latrobe, Benjamin H., 137, 265, 266, 404
Latter Day Saints, 172
Lawrence, Mayor John, 551
Lazaretto, 646
Lea, Henry Charles, 199, 200
League Island Park, 447
Leary's Book Store, 402
Leather Industry, 114
Le Brun, Napoleon, 270, 349
Le Coin D'Or, 425

Lee, Gen. Charles, 396; Gen. Harry, 388; Richard Henry, 48, 321
Leeds, William R., 75
Legal Aid Society, 315
Legends and Superstitions, 93
Leidy, Joseph, 199, 254, 289, 298, 585
Leighton, David, 294
Leland, Charles Godfrey, 195
Lemon Hill, 64, 549; Concerts, 238, 549
L'Enfant, Maj. Pierre Charles, 129, 263, 649
Lenni-Lenapes, 16, 21
Lester, Elliot, 223
Letitia Street House, 564
Leutze, Emmanuel, 248
Levering Mill Lane, 617
Lewis, Judge William, 554
Levy, Rabbi Nathan, 417
"Liberties", 280
Liberty Bell, 324
Library Company of Philadelphia, 428; Library, Free, 82, 84, 310, 341, 350, 353
Lincoln, Abraham, 63, 66, 71, 443; Monument, 549
Lincoln-Liberty Building, 382
Lincoln Theatre, 225, 445
Lind, Jenny, 416, 424, 449, 450
Linnard, Col. William, 411
Lioness Carrying a Wild Boar to her Young, 549
Lippard, George, 192, 604
Lister, Thomas, 324
Lit Brothers Store, 77
Literary Clubs, 184, 201
Literature, 184-201
"Little Italy", 7, 441
Little, Nathaniel, 426
Little Theatres, 226; Alden Park Players, 227; Chestnut Hill Players, 227; Germantown Theatre Guild, 227; Hedgerow Theatre, 226, 634; Labor Institute Dramatic Guild, 229; Mask and Wig Club, 228; Neighborhood Center Players, 228; New Theatre, 229, 440, 441; Players Club of Swarthmore, 227; Plays and Players, 227; Quince Street Players, 227; Show Crafters, 227; Stagecrafters, 226; Theatre Crafts, 229; Theatre League, 227; Vanguard Group, 228; Workers Theatre Alliance, 228
Livezey House, 259, 612; Mill, 612; Thomas, III, 612
Lloyd Committee, 314
Lloyd, David, 392; wife of, 392; Horatio Gates, 314; Thomas, 35, 293
Locke, Alain Leroy, 201
Locust Street Theatre, 225
Log College, 664
Logan, James, 40, 185, 284, 392
London Coffee House, 125, 126, 204, 389
Long, Dr. Crawford Williamson, 298; John Luther, 223
Longacre, James Barton, 247
Longwood Gardens, 641; Meeting House, 644
Lorimer, George Horace, 195
Loudoun Mansion, 477
Lovelace, Col. Francis, 30
Lover's Leap, 604
Lovett Memorial Library, 489
Lower Burial Ground, 477
Lubin, Sigmund, 232
Lucy, Ernest, 223
Lu Lu Temple, 461
Lutheran Hospice, 311; Orphanage, 489; Theological Seminary, 489
Lutherans, 159
Lyle, Col. Peter, 72

McArthur, John, 379, 400
McCall, Archibald, 125; Gen. George A., 70
McClellan, Gen. George Brinton, 70

McClure, Alexander, 75
MacDonald, Harl, 241; Jeanette, 232
McDougald, Dr. J. Q., 299
McIntyre, John T., 197, 223
Mack, Connie, 557
McKean, William, 71
MacKenzie, Dr. George W., 299; R. Tait, 253, 426
Mackey, Harry A., 493
McKim, Mead & White, 272
McLean, William L., 208
McMaster, John Bach, 199, 200
McMichael, Morton, 69, 207, 549
McMullin's Independent Rangers, 68
MacPherson's Directory, 343
McPherson, John, 552
Maennerchor Society, 240
Magazine Printing, 118, 523
Magdalen Society, 305
Majestic Hotel, 463
Malbone, Edward Green, 246
Malta Boat Club, 559
"Manor of Frank," 31
Manufacturers and Bankers Club, 444
Marcus Hook, 645
Market Square, 481; Presbyterian Church, 480
Market Street Bridge, 60; National Bank Building, 381; Subway-elevated, 77, 81, 144
Markham, Capt. William, 21, 36, 37
Marriage Council, 306
Marshall, Charles, 118; Christopher, 118
Martin, John C., 208
Mask and Wig Club, 228
Mason, David H., 117; Jeremiah, 133; William, 247
Mason-Dixon Line, 37, 66
Masonic Home for the Aged, 459; Temple, 73, 383, 452, 453
Massey, Henry V., 592
Mastbaum, Jules E., 84, 578; Vocational School, 180
Maternal Health Centers, 306
Matthews, James, 481
Mayfair House, 557
Meade, Gen. George Gordon, 70, 71, 73
Mechanics Union of Trade Associations, 150
Media, 636
Medical School of the College of Philadelphia, 293
Megargee Paper Mill, 617
Medicine, 293; early doctors, 293, 294; colonial medical practice, 294; medicine in 19th century, 297; contemporary physician, 299; legislation and hygiene, 300; hospitals, 300
Medico-Chirurgical College, 302
Meigs House, 428
Melrose Academy, 657
Memorial Hall, 254, 568
Memorial Hall (G. A. R.), 459
Monuments and Memorials, 250, 251, 568, 572
Mendelssohn Club, 240
Meng, John, 244
Mennonite Church, 163
Mennonites, 163
Mercantile Library, 400
Mercer, Henry, 665; Gen. Hugh, 396
Merchants' Coffee House, 126, 401; Exchange Building, 127, 256, 264
Mercy Hospital, 303, 495
Meridian Club, 426
Merrick, Samuel Vaughan, 289, 353
Meschianza, 56, 89, 479
Methodist Episcopal Church, 168, 390; Episcopal Home for the Aged, 572; Episcopal Hospital, 446; Episcopal Orphanage, 572
Metropolitan Opera House, 240, 461
Mey, Capt. Cornelius Jacobson, 26
Meyers, Kenneth, 559

Mifflin, Governor, 649; John, 135; Thomas, 48
Mikveh Israel Congregation, 100, 167, 168, 417, 418, 468
Mineral Springs Hotel (Willow Grove), 660
Ministerium of Pennsylvania, 159, 160
Minstrels, 230, 231
Mint, 136, 375, 474
Minton, Dr. Henry M., 299
Minuit, Peter, 28
Mitchell, Langdon Elwyn, 223; Dr. John K., 297; Dr. Silas Weir, 199, 223, 298, 426, 510; Thomas, 494
Mitten Bank Building, 383; Thomas/E., 79
Model Farm, 648
Modjeski, Ralph, 277, 530, 537, 604
Molarsky, Morris, 253
Molyneaux, Father, 166
Mom Rinker's Rock, 606
Monastery, The, 606
Montressor, Capt. John, 649
Memorials and Monuments, 250, 251, 253, 254, 568, 572
Moore, Charles Leonard, 195; J. Hampton, 82, 83; Nicholas, 31
Moore Institute of Art, Science & Industry, 255, 464
Moose Hall, 463, 464
Morais, Rabbi Sabato, 168
Moran Brothers, 248
Moravians, 167
Mordell, Albert, 198
Morgan, Dr. John, 294, 295, 588
Morley, Christopher, 196, 210
Morris, Arboretum, 292, 490, 491; House, 259, 415, 480; I. P. Iron Co., 532; John and Lyda, 292, 490, 568; Mansion, 128, 129, 490, 491
Morris, Robert, 57, 125, 328, 331, 412; birth of, 125; founds America's first banks, 125; aids financing of Revolution, 127, 128; death of, 129; aids establishing first mint, 136; statue of, 259, 404; portrait of, (Hesselius), 244; family vault of, 396; president of Bank of North America, 404
Morton, John, Memorial Museum, 449, 450
Morton, Dr. Samuel George, 297
Mossel, Dr. Nathan F., 299
Mothers' Assistance Fund, 313
Motion Pictures in Philadelphia, 232, 233, 349
Mott, Lucretia, 657
Mount Joy, 676; Observatory, 677, 679; Society for Recovery of Stolen Horses and Detection of Thieves, 676
Mount Pleasant, 259, 552; Mansion, 552
Mud Fort, 648
Muhlenberg, Frederick Augustus Conrad, 186; Peter 575; Rev. Henry Melchior, 159, 186, 387, 489
Mummers' Parade, The, 91
Municipal Stadium, 447
Murdoch, James Edward, 220
Murray, Samuel, 253, 320
Murry, Rev. John, 169
Music, 234; early, 234; Academy of, 64, 234, 235, 348; Hermit's Concert, 234; Philadelphia Orchestra, 236, 237; Curtis Institute of, 238; musical groups, 238; celebrities, 240, 242; youth movement, 237
Musical Fund Hall, 64, 416, 417
Mustin: Airfield, 448; Capt. Henry C., 448
Myers, Albert Cook, 200, 342

Nasmith, David, 305
National: Bank of Germantown, 480; Guards, 68, 467; Industrial Recovery Act, 155; Trades Union, 152

Native-American ("Know-Nothing") Movement, 62
Naval Home, 502, Hospital, 446
Navigation Act, 42
Navy Yard, 60, 66, 67, 447
Neagle, John, 246
Negroes, 7, 73, 106, 441, 443; first public school opened for, 61; educatiin of, 178, 179; newspapers, 108, 214; doctors, 299
Neighborhood Center Players, 228
Nelson, Mrs. Mary, 411
Neumann, John Nepomucene, 167
New Century Club, 399
New Hope, 667; residence of the literati in, 668; old Canal of, 667
Newspapers; early, 202; foreign language, 210
New Theatre, 229, 440
Newton, A. Edward, 198,199
Newtown, 671
Nicolls, Col., Richard, 30
Nixon, John, 51, 319
Norris, Joseph, 135
North American, Bank of, 57, 128, 129, 404
North American, 206
North Philadelphia Station (Pennsylvania Railroad), 468
North Philadelphia Station (Reading Railroad), 84, 468
Northern Liberties Gas Company, 138
Northern Liberties Presbyterian Church, 162
Notman, John, 268
Nuttall, Thomas, 286

Oakland Cemetery, 469
Oakley, Violet, 251, 435
Oberholtzer, Ellis P., 199, 200, 342
Octagonal Schoolhouse, 640, 641
Odets, Clifford, 224, 229
Olcott, Chauncey, 416
Old; Buck Inn, 684; City Hall, 331, 338; Colony House, (Wanamaker Store), 382; Covered Bridge, 615; Custom House, 404; Forge Inn, 660; Green Tree Inn, 483; "Old Ironsides", 61, 117, 142, 287; London Coffee House, 125, 126, 204, 399; Merion Meeting House, 685; Newtown Presbyterian Church, 671; Pennepek Baptist Church, 162, 621; Pine Street Church, 410, 411; St. David's at Radnor, (Longfellow), 682; St. George's Methodist Episcopal Church, 169, 388; "Old Solitude", 564; Stone Fountain, 607; Swedes' Church, 159, 161, 234, 257, 542, 543; York Road Country Club, 658
Origin of Name of Philadelphia, 36
Ormiston Mansion, 551
Orphans Guardian, 305
Orphans' Society of Philadelphia, 305
Orpheus Club, 240
Orthodox Friends' Meeting House, 528
Orthopedic School, 181
Otis, Bass, 246
Ottey, Mrs. D. W., 393
Our Lady of the Blessed Sacrament Church, 461
Our Lady of Lourdes Church, 512
Overbrook Presbyterian Church, 512
Overhanging Rock, 676
Owen, Griffith, 293
Oxford Provident Beneficial Association, 136; Provident Building Association, 527

Paine, Thomas, 49, 184, 188, 210
Painting and Sculpture, 243, early painters, 243, 244; post-Revolutionary painters, 244; painters of early 1800's, 245, impressionism, 248, 249; painters in early 1900's, 251; contemporary painters, 253, 254; art schools, 255; art clubs, 254, 255
Pancoast, Dr. Joseph, 298

Paper, production of, 118
Paper Mill Run, 617
Parkway, The Benjamin Franklin, 81, 574
Parlin, Olavius, 542
Parochial School System, 179, 180
Parrish, Ann, 305; Maxfield, 251, 414
Pastorius, Francis Daniel, 34, 35, 102, 258; birth, 34, 480; trip to new land 35; literary works, 185; grave of, 480
Patriotic Order Sons of America, 464
Patterson, Gen. Robert, 63, 67, 68
Paxton Boys, The, 42, 481; Massacre, 42
Peale, Charles Willson, 229, 244, 245, 286, 453, 457, 478; James, 245; Titian Ramsey, 585
Pemberton, Isaac, Jr., 135
Pendergrast, Garret, 71
Penn: Athletic Club, 432; Club, 201; Mutual Life Insurance Company, 412; Treaty Park, 16
Penn, John, 19, 42, 52, 394, 564; Thomas, 19, 41
Penn, William, 4, 16, 21, 23, 605; statue atop City Hall, 3; description of Indians, 17, 18; marriage, 24; "Frame of Government," 24, 25; policy of good will, 35; treaty troubles, 37, 39; sails for Europe, 39; second marriage, 39; returns to Pennsylvania, 39; returns to England, 40; death, 40; literary works of, 184; Penn's City Plan, 279, 387; statue of, 420
Pennell, Joseph, 251, 426
Pennington, Miles, 389
Pennsylvania Academy of the Fine Arts, 60, 251, 253, 255, 453; history of, 453, 454; description of, 455; Temple Collection 455; Lambert Collection, 455, 456; Gibson Collection, 456; Contes Collection, 456; Gilpin Gallery, 456; Fields Collection, 456
Pennsylvania: Bank of, 57, 64, 127, 128; Barge Club, 559; Birth Control Federation, 306; Chronicle, 45, 205; Company for Insurances on Lives and Granting Annuities, 60, 126, 133; Evening Post 206; Gazette, 202, 203; Horticultural Society, 292; Hospital, 293, 300, 419; Hospital for Mental and Nervous Diseases, 302, 420, 508; Instructon of the Deaf, 444; Medical College, 294
Pennsylvania: Museum of Art, 254, 360, 580; Elkins Collection, 254; Johnson Collection, 363; Williams Collection, 366; Museum of the School of Industrial Arts, 181;
Pennsylvania: Prison Society, 305; Railroad, 146; Railroad Station (Thirtieth Street), 505, Railroad (Suburban Station), 585; Reserves, 70; School for the Instruction of the Blind, 182; Society for the Abolition of Slavery, 62; Society for the Encouragement of Manufactures and Useful Arts, 57; Sugar Company, 532; School for the Deaf, 490; Women, State Federation of, 400; Working Home for Blind Men, 508
Penn Valley, 676
Pennypack Bridge, 624; Park, 471, 620
Penrose, Boies, 75, 78; Dr. Charles B., 562; Research Laboratory, 292, 562
Pepper Pot, 96
Pepper, William, 199, 298
Pet Animal Cemetery, 676
Peters Island, 573
Peterson, Jan, 293
Philadelphia: Almshouse, 293, 304; American League Baseball Park, 78, 473; Area of, 11; and Delaware Railroad Company, 142, and Germantown Railroad Company, 142, 146; and Reading Railroad Company, 146; and West Chester Railroad, 146; Art Club of, 444; Board of Brokers, 127, Bourse, 404; Brigade, 70;

Bureau of Fire, 457; City Planning Commission, 282; Clearing House Association, 133, 134; College of Dental Surgery, 294; of Medicine, 293; of Osteopathy, 183; of Pharmacy and Science, 61, 183, 394; Physicians and Surgeons, 303; Conference on Social Work, 307; Contributionship for Insuring Houses from Loss by Fire, 126, 135, 412; Council of Older Boys' Clubs, 308; County Medical Society, 63; Relief Board, 314; Dental College, 294; Department of Public Health, 310; During Civil War, 66; Revolutionary War, 52; World War, 79; Electric Company, 139; First National Bank of, 404; Gas Works Company, 138; General Hospital, 302, 418, 494; Post Office, 507; Gold Challenge Cup, 561; Grand Opera Company, 239; Grays, 68; High School for Girls, 474; Home for Incurables, 509, 510; Hospital for Mental Diseases, 471; Housing Association, 308; Inquirer, 207, 208; League for the Hard of Hearing, 310; Mineralogical Society, 585; Mint, 136, 375, 376, 474; National League Baseball Park, 468; Normal School and School of Practice, 461; Opera House, 78; Orchestra, 82, 234, 236, 237, 555; Orphans' Society, 418; Polyclinic and College for Graduates in Medicine, 294; Port of, 119; Public School System, 173; Rapid Transit Company, 77, 78, 145, 146; Record, 73, 219, 458; Saving Fund Society, 61, 126, 132, 256, 385, 386; School of Anatomy, 294; of Design for Women, 181, 464; School of Occupational Therapy, 303, 439; the Theatre and Playhouse, 232; Shipping Business, 119; Society for Organizing Charity and Repressing Mendicancy, 305; the Preservation of Landmarks, 346, 393; Stock Exchange, 431; Textile School and School of Industrial Art, 444, 445; Traction Company, 144; Trades' Assembly, 153; Zoning Commission, 308
Philco Radio and Television Corporation, 520, 521
Physick, Dr. Philip Syng, 295, 551
Pieterson, Evert, 173
Pilmoor, Dr. Joseph, 168
Pine Road Loop, 621
Pine, Robert, 244
Pitcairn Autogiro Company, 661
Pitcairn, John, 653; Raymond, 653
Plants, 12
Players Club of Swarthmore, 227
Plays and Players Club, 227; Theatre, 439
Plumstead Estate, 572, 573
Poe, Edgar Allan, 184, 185, 192, 388, 685, House, 193, 388
Poinsett, George McKenzie, 471
Points of Special Interest, xxx
Pohlig, Carl, 236
Polish, 103
Polly, The (ship), 46, 481
Poor Richard Club, 78, 425; Richard's Almanac, 184, 210, 592
Porter, Admiral David D., 71
Port Richmond, 62
Post Office (new), 506
Postels, Wilbert D., 299
Potter, Dr. James, 299; Rev. Alonzo, 172
Pound, Ezra, 198
Powel House, 345, 346, 408; Samuel, 346
Pratt, Matthew, 244
Presbyterian Church, 161, 162; of Neshaminy, 664
Presidential Mansion, 588
Price, Eli Kirk, 199
Press, The, 202
Priestley, Dr. Joseph, 169, 286
Princeton Club, 426
Print Club, 435, 436
Printing Industry, 118, 523

700

Printz, Capt. John, 28
Provincial Assembly, 48, 339
Protestant Episcopal Church, 160, 161
Public Health, Department of, 306
Public Ledger, 73, 208
Public Utilities, 137
Puppet Shows and Marionettes, 229
230
Puritan, The (Statue), 561
Puritans, The, 29
Purvis, Robert, 107
Pyle, Howard, 251

Quaker City Barge Club, 558
Quay, Matthew S., 75, 76
Queen Lane Pumping Station, 557
Quince St. Players, 227

Racial Groups, 98
Radio, 211, 212
Raditz, Lazar, 253
Radnor Open Golf Course, 683
Rafinesque, Constantine Samuel, 286
Raguet, Col. Condy, 132
Railroad Strike of 1877, 75
Railroads, 145
Railroads, B. & O., 146
Randolph, Edmund, 480; Peyton, 48, 49,
396; Mansion, 551
Raul, Dr. Charles Sigmund, 299
Read, George Campbell, 71; Thomas
Buchanan, 195, 403
Reading Terminal, 386
Redman, John, 440
Reed, Admiral, 72
Reformed Church in the United States,
164
Relief Acts, 314
Religions, 159; Baptist, 162; Brethren, 163;
Christian Science, 170; Evangelical and
Reformed, 164; Friends—Hicksites and
Orthodox, 34, 160; Judaism, 167; Luth-
eran, 159; Mennonites, 163; Methodist
Episcopal, 168; Moravians, 167; Pres-
byterian, 161; Protestant Episcopal, 160;
Quakers, 160; Roman Catholic, 164;
Spiritualists, 170; United Brethren in
Christ, 170; Universalists, 169; Miscel-
laneous, 172
Repplier, Agnes, 195
Revolutionary Period, 45, 46
Rex Avenue Bridge, 617
Reyburn Plaza, 574
Rhawn Street Bridge, 624
Rhoads, Samuel, 48, 135, 421
Ricciardi, Cesare, 253
Richards, William Trost, 248
Richardson Henry Hobson, 271
Richboro, 671
Riddle Mills, 637
Riddle, Samuel, 637
Ridgway Library, 445
Rittenhouse, David, 284, 285, 605; Wil-
liam, 284, 285; Home, 605; Square, 432
Ritz-Carlton Hotel, 444
Robbins House (Hartsville), 664
Roberts, G. Brook, Estate, 674; Howard,
250; Hugh, 34, 135; Robert R., 390
Robin Hood Dell, 239, 555
Rockland Mansion, 551
Rodeph Shalom, 168, 459
Rodin, Augusta, 578; Museum, 84, 254, 578
Rodney, Caesar, 323
Roman Catholic Centennial Fountain,
570; High School for Boys, 180, 458
Roosevelt Boulevard, 469
Roosevelt, Franklin Delano, 85, 493
Root, Maj. Stanley W., 157
Rosemont College, 683
Rosenbach Galleries, 428, 429
Rosenthal, Albert, 253; Max, 253
Ross, Betsy, 342, 543; George, 48, 392,
Rothermel, Peter F., 248
"Rowbottoms", 597
Rudman, Rev. Andrew, 542, 543

Rugs, manufacture of, 518
Rumanians, 104, 105
Rush, Benjamin, 247, 295, 392; Col. Lewis,
61; James, 445; William, 252
Rush Hospital, 508
Russians, 104
Rydal Country Club, 671

St. Augustine, Church of, 62, 166, 390;
hermits of, 390
St. Charles Borromeo Seminary, 166, 512
St. David's Protestant Episcopal Church,
681, 682
St. George's Greek Catholic Church, 417
St. George's Methodist Episcopal Church,
169, 388
St. James Church, 395, 500
St. John's Spiritual Alliance Church, 170
St. Joseph's Church, 166, 179, 406; Col-
lege, 182, 510; Society for the Education
of Poor Orphan Children, 180
St. Mark's Protestant Episcopal Church,
435
St. Mary's Church, 179, 180, 411
St. Michael's Lutheran Church, 159, 489
St. Paul's Memorial Church, 512
St. Paul's Protestant Episcopal Church,
408
St. Peter's Protestant Episcopal Church,
395, 408
St. Philip de Neri, Church of, 62
St. Theresa's Roman Catholic Church,
445
SS. Peter and Paul, Cathedral of, 576
Saloons, rise of, 72
Salvation Army, 311, 461
Samaroff, Mme. Olga, 241
Sartain, John, 193, 247
Sartain's Magazine, 193
Saturday Evening Post, 193, 195, 196,
203, 207, 414
Sauer, Christopher, 163, 489; Bible 163,
489
Saul Medical Service, 316
Savoy Opera Company, 239
Saw Manufacture, 528
Say, Thomas, 286, 289
Scheel, Fritz, 236
School of Design for Women, 63, 181,
464
Schofield, W. Elmer, 253
Schumann-Heink, Mme., 416
Schuyler, Philip, 329
Schuylkill Arsenal, 60, 504; Canal, 61;
Navy, 64, 558; River, 12
Schwenkfelders, 540
Science, 284; pioneers, 284; industrial,
286; scientific institutions, 288
Science, Academy of, Natural, 60, 289, 583
Scots, 103
Scott, Bishop Levi, 390; Sir Walter, 417
Scottish Rite Temple, 456
Scrapple, 96
Sculpturing, 243
Seabury, Bishop Samuel, 190
Seaman, Eben C., 97
Seamen's Air Society, 312; Church Insti-
tute, 170, 312
Sears, Roebuck, Company, 469
Seaweed Fountain, 549
Sea Horse Fountain, 580
Second: Bank of the United States, 132;
Baptist Church, 163; Church of Christ,
Scientist, 170; Continental Congress, 49,
51; Presbyterian Church, 365; Street
Market, 408
Segal, Vivienne, 232
Seixas, David, 490; Rabbi Gershon Man-
des Israel, 167
Seldes, Gilbert, 198
Sellers, Coleman, 64, 287, 288
Seminaries; Eastern Baptist Theological

701

181; Lutheran Theological, 181; Protestant Episcopal Church Divinity School, 181; Reformed Episcopal Church Theological, 181; St. Charles Borromeo, 181; St. Vincent's Theological, 181; Westminster Theological, 181
Sesqui-Centennial Exposition, 82
Settlement Music School, 240, 545
Shakespeare Memorial 576; Society, 63
Shallcross School for Truants, 181
Sharples, James, 246
Sharswood, George, 199
Shenton, Edward, 197
Shibe Park, 78, 473
Shipbuilding, 117
"Ship Graveyard", 543
Shippen, Edward, 403, 408; Peggy, 403; Residence, 411; Dr. William, Jr., 294, 295, 411
Shipping, 121
Shoemaker, Samuel, 551
Shopping Information, xxiv
Showcrafters, 227
Shriner's Home for Crippled Children, 469
Shubert Theatre, 229, 444
Shut-In Society, 310
Sidebotham, Thomas, 527
Sidney, Algernon, 32
Silenus and the Infant Bacchus, 547
Simes, Snyder Binn, 543
Sketch Club, 425
SKF Plant, 521
Skinner, Mrs. Otis, 439
Sloane-Blabon Corporation, 523
Slums, 56, 87, 273, 443
Smith Memorial Arch, 568
Smith, Gen. Persifor, 63; Robert, 263, 408; Thomas B., 80; Dr. William, 588
Snellenburg Store, 386
Sobel, Alfred, 228
Social Service 304; early Almshouse, 304; charitable Church organizations 305; charity groups, 306; municipal health aid, 307; penal organizations, 308; better housing associations, 308; recreational services, 308; settlement houses, 310; relief acts, 314; Boys' Clubs, 308; residences for women and girls, 312; seamen's homes, 312
Society Hill Theatre, 215, 216
Society of Carpenters, 339; of Friends, 304, 305; of St. Vincent de Paul, 315
Solebury Baptist Church, 667
Solebury Copper Mine, 669
Solis-Cohen, Dr. Solomon, 298
Solomon, Haym, 100
Southampton Baptst Meetinghouse, 671
South Philadelphia High School, 446; Street Ferry, 60
Sparrowjack's House, 488
Speakman, John, 289, 583, 584
Spiritualists, 170
Sports, 90, 91
Springfield Avenue Bridge, 619
Spring Garden Institute, 180, 459
Spruance, Benton, 254
Stage and Screen, 213
Stagecrafters, 226
Stage Personalities, 219
Stamp Act, 42, 43
Stanford, Dr. Thomas, Jr., 299
State: Fencibles, 68, 440; House, 258; Houseyard, 319
Steele, Gen. John, 411
Stern, J. David, 209
Stetson, John B., 515; Plant 515
Stevens, Thaddeus, 176
Stevenson, Christine Wetherill, 437
Stewardson, Edmund Austin, 251
Stewart, Commodore Charles, 67, 71
Still, William, 107, 201
Stock Exchange Building, Old 406
Stockton, Frank R., 194
Stokeley, William, 74

Stokowski, Leopold, 82, 234, 236
Stone Age in America, 567
Stone Plaza, 557
Stotesbury, E. T., 79, 134
Stoves, manufacture of, 115
Strawberry Mansion, 554
Strawbridge, Justin, 79
Strawbridge & Clothier Company Chorus, 239
Street Numbering, xxiii, xxxiv
Strettel, Amos, 135
Strickland, William, 265, 290, 336, 406, 408
Strikes, 149, 406
Stringart Quartet, 239
Stuart, George H., 71; Gilbert, 244, 478, 676
Sugar, refining of, 114, 532
Sully, Thomas, 244, 246
Superstitions, 93
Susan, Robert, 253
Swarthmore, 631; College, 631
Swedes, 21, 26, 28, 29, 35, 103
Swedenborgians, 653
Swedish West India Company, 26
Sweetbriar Mansion 566
Syng, Philip, 135

Tacony-Palmyra Bridge, 84, 530
Talleyrand, 393
Tam O' Shanter Group (James Thom), 561
Tanner, Henry Ossawa, 250
Taylor, Bayard, 194, 644; Christopher, 173; Frederick Winslow, 287, 288; Dr. Joseph W., 684; Zachary, 63
Tea Tax disturbances, 46
Teeth, artificial, Manufacture of, 119
Telephone Companies, 140
Temple University, 19, 84, 162, 163, 175, 464; Dental School, 466; Medical College, 183, 467, 469; Stella Elkins Tyler School of Fine Arts, 255; Theological School, 466; Hospital, 466, 467, 469; Conwell Hall, 466, 467; Carnell Hall, 467; Mitten Memorial Hall, 467; Thomas D. Sullivan Memorial Library, 467; Professional Schools, 467
Tennent, Gilbert, 162, 186; Rev. William, 186, 664
Terminal Commerce Building, 459
Textile Industry, 115, 120, 155, 515
Thackeray, William Makepeace, 416
Thayer, Mary Dixon, 197
Theatre Crafts, 226
Theatre League, 227
Theatres, 213, 444; history of, 214; personalities of, 219; playwrights, 222; existing theatres, 224; little theatres, 226; workers' theatre, 228, 229; puppet shows and marionettes, 229, 230; minstrels, 230, 231; cinema, 232, 233; actors playing at Walnut, 415, 416; Arch Street Theatre, 217; Bijou Theatre, 225; Broad St. Theatre, 225; Chestnut Street Theatre, 78, 216, 217; Chestnut St. Opera House 224; Erlanger Theatre, 225; Forrest Theatre, 224; Garrick Theatre, 217; Keith's Theatre, 224, 225; Lincoln Theatre, Locust Street Theatre, 225; Shubert Theatre, 229, 444; Society Hill Theatre, 215, 216; Trocadero Theatre, 226; Walnut Street Theatre, 216, 225, 415
Third Presbyterian Church, 162
Third Spiritualist Church, 170
Thomas, Gabriel, 186; Walter, 555
Thompson-Neely House, 669
Thomson, Charles, 48, 51
Thorp's Lane, 617
Tiffany, Louis C., 414
Tily, Dr. Herbert J., 239
Tobacco Trade, 114
Toogood, Granville, 197

702

Topography, 11
Town Hall, 258
Towne, Benjamin, 204
Townsend Acts, 45
Trade, 119; Union Movement, 149, 406
Transportation, 142
Transportation Facilities xxi
Traubel, Horace, 194
Trees, 12
Triassic Lowland, 11, 12
Tribune, 108
Trocadero Theatre, 226
Troost, Gerard, 286
Trott, Benjamin, 246
Truxtun, Thomas, 392; William, 71
Tun Tavern, 540
Turner, Dr. John P., 299; Robert, 34
Tyson, Dr. James, 298

Unami, 16, 21
Underground Railroad, 62, 201
Undine Barge Club, 559
Union: Benevolent Association, 305, Co-
operative Association, 153; Fire Com-
pany, 286, League, 8, 69, 70, 443;
Library, 663; Paper Mills, 669
Unitarians, 169
United: Brethren in Christ, 170; Campaign,
305, 306; Gas Improvement Company,
139, 140; Service Club, 424
United States: Marine Corps, 540; Build-
ing 445; Mint, 136, 375, 474
United States, Bank of, 129, 132, 133, 406
United States, Second Bank of, 132, 133
Universal Spiritualist Brotherhood
Church, 170
Universalist Church of the Messiah, 169,
464
Universalist Church of Philadelphia, 169
University of Pennsylvania, 9, 82, 173, 175,
587; Bennett Hall, 592; Botanic Gar-
dens, 292; Botanical Gardens, 597; Col-
lege Hall, 589; early history of, 588; En-
gineering Building, 593; Fine Arts
Building, 593; Graduate Hospital, 302;
Graduate School of Medicine, 589; Hous-
ton Hall, 590; Hutchinson Gymnasium,
594; Hygiene Laboratory, 593; Irvine
Auditorium, 590; John Harrison Labora-
tory of Chemistry, 593; Law School, 599;
Library, 590; Logan Hall, 590; Mask and
Wig Club, 228; Medical School, 183, 302,
589; Men's Dormitories, 595; Moore
School of Electrical Engineering, 594;
Morris Arboretum, 292; Museum, 290;
594; Randal Morgan Laboratory of
Physics, 593; Robert Hare Chemical La-
boratory, 590; School of Fine Arts, 255;
School of Music, 239; Thomas W. Evans
Institute, 599; University Hospital, 596;
Vivarium, 599; Wharton School of Fi-
nance and Commerce, 589; Wistar In-
stitute of Anatomy and Biology, 596
Upland Settlement, The, 21
Upper Burial Ground, 486
Upsala House, 487, 488

Valley Creek Canoe Club, 612
Valley Green, 619
Valley Forge, 677; Dogwood Grove,
679; Grand Parade, 678; Memorial Arch,
679; Museum of American History, 678;
Old Camp School House 678, 679; Park,
673, 677; Pennsylvania Columns, 679
Vanguard Group, 228
Van Lennep, Dr. William B., 298
Vare Brothers, 78; William, 7, 78, 84, 210
Vaux, Richard, 64
Verree Road, 621
Vernon Park, 481
Victoria Plush Mills (Swarthmore), 634
Viking, 557
Villanova College, 683
Viscose Company, 645
Vivarium, The, 599
Voluntary Defender Association, 315, 316

Von Steuben, Baron, 678, 679
Vonnoh, Robert W., 253

Wade, Robert, 21
Wagner Free Institute of Science, 290-
473, 474
Wagner House, The, 477
Wagner, William, 473
"Walking Purchase", 18, 19
Waln, Robert, 401
Walnut Lane Bridge, 605
Walnut Street (1616,) 431; Theatre, 216,
225, 415
Walter, Thomas U., 265, 371, 379, 396, 412
Walton Hotel, 444
Wanamaker, John, 71, 76, 79; Store,, 381
Warminster, 663, 664
Warwick Hotel, 435
Washington Crossing: Inn, 670; State
Park, 670
Washington, George, 327, 331, 386, 457, 479,
480, 486, 670, 676; approves act for U. S.
Mint, 138; at Valley Forge, 678, 680;
battle of Brandywine, 629; Chadds Ford,
638; Germantown, 486; delegate to First
Continental Congress 48, 49; funeral
services for, 388; given title of "Father
of His Country," 407; mementos of, 328;
monument of, (Siemering,) 580; pew in
Christ Church, 394; portraits of, 245,
478; statue of (Siemering), 254
Washington Grays, 68
Washington: Inn, 679; Memorial Chapel,
678; Memorial National Carillon, 678;
Square, 414; Headquarters at Valley
Forge, 680
Water Works, 137
Water Front, 533
Water Street, 535
Watkins, Franklin C., 254, 578; Shirley,
197
Watson's Annals of Philadelphia, 192
Watson, John Fanning, 192, 480; House,
479
Wayne, Gen. Anthony, 679, 681
Wayne, 683
Wayside Shrine, 619
Weaver, Dr. Rufus B., 298
Webb, Capt. Thomas, 168, 389
Welcome, 20, 21, 25
Welfare Federation, 305, 306
Welsh, 33, 34, 103
Welsh Avenue Bridge, 625
Welsh Barony, 33, 94
Welsh, John, 570; Memorial Fountain,
570
Wertmuller, Adolph Ulric, 247
West, Benjamin, 38, 244, 407, 421
West Laurel Hill Cemetery, 673
Wetherill, Elisha Kent, 250; Samuel
Price, 118, 437; Samuel, Jr., 118
Wharton, George M., 64; Joseph, 408;
Thomas I., 427
Whatcoat, Richard, 390
White, Dr. A. E., 299; Samuel S., 119;
Bishop William, 129, 161, 305, 395, 399
399
Whitefield, George, 162, 186, 253, 410
Whitman, Walt, 184, 192, 194
Whittier Center, 308
Widener Home for Crippled Children, 79
Widener, H. Josephine, Memorial Library,
463
Widener, Peter A. B., 79
Wilbank, John, 324, 325
William Penn Charter School, 173, 177,
181, 386, 491
Williams, William, 244
Willing Charles, 125, 346; Thomas, 48,
125, 129
Willow Grove, 660; Park, 660
Wills Hospital, 474
Wilson, Alexander, 286, 543; Francis, 221,
222; James, 396, 589; S. Davis, 87
Wilstach Collection of Paintings, 254, 570

703

"Windows of Old Philadelphia," 424
Windrim, James H., 452; John T., 355
Wisconsin House, 673, 674
Wissahickon Hall, 602; Hermits of the, 602; Valley, 557
Wistar, Dr. Caspar, 295, 411; General Isaac, 596; Charles J., 479; John, 479, 481; Sally, 479; Owen, 195, 426, 473
Wistar Institute of Anatomy and Biology, 596
Wistar Museum, 60, 295
Witchcraft, 95
Witt, Dr. Christopher, 186, 603
Women's Medical College of Pennsylvania 294
Wood, Dr. George Bacon, 302; George B., 199, 297
Woodford Mansion, 554
Woodlands Cemetery, 494
Woodside Park, 572
Woodward Estate, 610
Woollcott, Alexander, 198
Woolman, John, 186
Workers', Theatre, 228, 229; Alliance, 228
Working Men's Party, 150, 151
Works Progress Administration, 85, 255, 315, 369, 550

Wrestlers, The, 549
Wright, Joseph, 244
Writers, 184; Colonial, 185; clubs, 201; historical, 199, 200; legal, 199; medical, 199; Post-Revolutionary, 188; present day, 201
"Wyck," 483
Wynn, Ed, 222
Wynnestay Mansion, 510
Wynne, Dr. Thomas, 293, 510, 685
Yachtsmen's Club, 425

Yeadon, 629
Yellin, Samuel, 254
Yellow Fever Epidemic, 297, 300
Y.M.C.A., 71, 78, 311. 475
Y.M.H.A. and Y.W.H.A. Building, 445
Y. W. C. A. 316, 482
Young, Thomas, 29
Yugoslavs, 105

Zachary, Lloyd, Dr., 418
Zinzendorf, Count, 167
Zion Lutheran Church, 387, 388
Zoological Gardens, 561; Society, 64

704